Contemporary Analytic and Linguistic Philosophies

Contemporary Analytic and Linguistic Philosophies

edited by E. D. Klemke

 Prometheus Books

700 East Amherst St. Buffalo, New York 14215

TO

Russell Compton
May Brodbeck
Paul Holmer
William Earle
Herbert Hochberg
and
Gustav Bergmann

Published 1983 by Prometheus Books
700 East Amherst Street, Buffalo, New York, 14215

Library of Congress Catalog Card Number: 82-48970
ISBN 0-87975-197-5

Printed in the United States of America

CONTENTS

PREFACE *9*

ACKNOWLEDGMENTS *11*

INTRODUCTION: The Rise of Analytic Philosophy *15*

PART 1. THE PRE-ANALYTIC TRADITION

Introduction *23*

IDEALISM

1. Reality and Idealism *31*
   Josiah Royce

Study Questions *53*

Selected Bibliography *53*

PRAGMATISM

2. How to Make Our Ideas Clear *55*
   C. S. Peirce

3. Pragmaticism *71*
   C. S. Peirce

Study Questions *78*

Selected Bibliography *78*

AMERICAN REALISM

4. The Program and Platform of Six Realists *79*
   E. B. Holt, et al.

5. The Approach to Critical Realism *87*

   Durant Drake

Study Questions *107*

Selected Bibliography *107*

PART 2. ANALYTIC AND LINGUISTIC PHILOSOPHIES

Introduction *111*

REALISM AND COMMON SENSE

6. The Refutation of Idealism *121*

   G. E. Moore

7. The Subject Matter of Ethics   *121*
    G. E. Moore

8. A Defense of Common Sense   *163*
    G. E. Moore

9. Proof of an External World   *184*
    G. E. Moore

Study Questions   *202*

Selected Bibliography   *203*

LOGICAL ATOMISM

10. Facts and Propositions   *205*
    Bertrand Russell

11. Particulars, Predicates, and Relations   *213*
    Bertrand Russell

12. Excursus Into Metaphysics: What There Is   *223*
    Bertrand Russell

Study Questions   *233*

Selected Bibliography   *233*

LOGICAL POSITIVISM

13. The Elimination of Metaphysics   *235*
    A. J. Ayer

14. The Function of Philosophy   *247*
    A. J. Ayer

15. The A Priori   *253*
    A. J. Ayer

16. Truth and Probability   *265*
    A. J. Ayer

17. Critique of Ethics and Theology   *271*
    A. J. Ayer

Study Questions   *285*

Selected Bibliography   *286*

CONCEPTUAL ANALYSIS

18. Systematically Misleading Expressions   *287*
    Gilbert Ryle

19. Wittgenstein's Lectures in 1930-33   *307*
     G. E. Moore

20. Philosophical Perplexity   *320*
     John Wisdom

21. Philosophy, Anxiety, and Novelty   *322*
     John Wisdom

22. Gods   *338*
     John Wisdom

23. Descartes' Myth   *353*
     Gilbert Ryle

Study Questions   *364*

Selected Bibliography   *365*

LOGICO-METAPHYSICAL ANALYSIS

24. Logical Positivism, Language and the Reconstruction of Metaphysics   *367*
     Gustav Bergmann

25. On What There Is   *378*
     W. V. Quine

26. Two Dogmas of Empiricism   *391*
     W. V. Quine

Study Questions   *410*

Selected Bibliography   *410*

LINGUISTIC ANALYSIS

27. Performative-Constative   *411*
     J. L. Austin

28. Intention and Convention in Speech Acts   *421*
     P. F. Strawson

29. What Is a Speech Act?   *437*
     J. R. Searle

Study Questions   *452*

Selected Bibliography   *452*

General Works on Analytic Philosophy   *453*

Sources of More Complete Bibliographies   *454*

Preface

Most of the major movements and figures of twentieth-century philosophy in England, the United States, and elsewhere all fall under the broad heading of *analytic philosophy*. In a way this is a misleading label, since there are many forms and varieties of analytic (and linguistic) philosophies. (These are discussed in detail in the Introduction to Part 2.)

This book is intended to be an *introduction* to the various philosophies that have been designated as analytic and/or linguistic philosophy. The editor tried to include selections that are both a) representative of the different forms of analytic philosophy; and b) accessible to and of interest to *undergraduate* students. Thus some highly technical works in the philosophy of language, etc., have been omitted.

For reasons stated in the Introduction, a few selections representative of pre-analytic philosophies were included in Part 1. The movements represented are idealism, pragmatism, and American realism.

I would like to express my gratitude to all those who made suggestions concerning the volume or contributed to the task of preparing the manuscript and performing other duties needed to bring the book into being. Among these are: Rowena Wright, Bernice Power, David Schejbal, William Robinson, Robert Hollinger, John Elrod, A. David Kline, Laura Kline, and Steven L. Mitchell.

E.D.K.

Acknowledgments

The editor gratefully acknowledges the kind permission of the authors, editors, and publishers that has enabled him to print the essays in this book.

PART ONE

Josiah Royce, "Reality and Idealism." From *The Spirit of Modern Philosophy*. Boston: Houghton-Mifflin Co., 1892, Ch. 11.

C. S. Peirce, "How to Make Our Ideas Clear." Reprinted from *Popular Science*, with permission © 1878, Times Mirror Magazines Inc. Vol. 12 (1878): pp. 286–302.

C. S. Peirce, "Pragmaticism." From "What Pragmatism Is." *The Monist* 15 (1905): pp. 161–181. (Excerpt.)

E. B. Holt, et al., "The Program and Platform of Six Realists." *The Journal of Philosophy* 7 (1910): pp. 393–401.

Durant Drake, "The Approach to Critical Realism." From D. Drake, et al., *Essays in Critical Realism*. New York: Macmillan Publishing Co., Inc., 1920.

PART TWO

G. E. Moore, "The Refutation of Idealism." *Mind* 12 (1903):433–453. Reprinted with the permission of Basil Blackwell, Publisher.

G. E. Moore, "The Subject Matter of Ethics." From *Principia Ethica*, Ch. 1, pp. 1–36. Cambridge: Cambridge University Press, 1903.

G. E. Moore, "A Defence of Common Sense." From J. H. Muirhead (ed.) *Contemporary British Philosophy*, Second Series. London: Macmillan Co., 1925; and London: George Allen and Unwin, 1925, pp. 193–223. Reprinted with the permission of George Allen and Unwin.

G. E. Moore, "Proof of an External World." From *Proceedings of the British Academy* 25 (1939):273–300.

Bertrand Russell, "Facts and Propositions." From "The Philosophy of Logical Atomism." *The Monist*, 1918. Reprinted with the permission of George Allen and Unwin.

Bertrand Russell, "Particulars, Predicates, and Relations." From "The Philosophy of Logical Atomism." *The Monist,* 1918. Reprinted with the permission of George Allen and Unwin.

Bertrand Russell, "Particulars, Predicates, and Relations." From "The Philosophy of Logical Atomism." *The Monist,* 1918. Reprinted with the permission of George Allen and Unwin.

Bertrand Russell, "Excursus Into Metaphysics: What There Is." From "The Philosophy of Logical Atomism." *The Monist,* 1918. Reprinted with the permission of George Allen and Unwin.

A. J. Ayer, "The Elimination of Metaphysics." From *Language, Truth and Logic,* by A. J. Ayer. London: Victor Gollancz Ltd., 1936. © 1936, by A. J. Ayer.

A. J. Ayer, "The Function of Philosophy." From *Language, Truth and Logic,* by A. J. Ayer. London: Victor Gollancz Ltd., 1936. © 1936, by A. J. Ayer.

A. J. Ayer, "The A Priori." From *Language, Truth and Logic,* by A. J. Ayer. London: Victor Gollancz Ltd., 1936. © 1936, by A. J. Ayer.

A. J. Ayer, "Truth and Probability." From *Language, Truth and Logic,* by A. J. Ayer. London: Victor Gollancz Ltd., 1936. © 1936, by A. J. Ayer.

A. J. Ayer, "Critique of Ethics and Theology." From *Language, Truth and Logic,* by A. J. Ayer. London: Victor Gollancz Ltd., 1936. © 1936, by A. J. Ayer.

Gilbert Ryle, "Systematically Misleading Expressions." *Proceedings of the Aristotelian Society, 1931-1932.* Reprinted by courtesy of the editor of The Aristotelian Society. © 1932 by The Aristotelian Society.

G. E. Moore, "Wittgenstein's Lectures in 1930-1933." *Mind* 53 (1954) and 54 (1955). Reprinted with the permission of Basil Blackwell, Publisher.

John Wisdom, "Philosophical Perplexity." *Proceedings of The Aristotelian Society, 1936-1937.* Reprinted by the courtesy of the editor of The Aristotelian Society. © 1937, by The Aristotelian Society.

John Wisdom, "Philosophy, Anxiety, and Novelty." *Mind* 43 (1944). Reprinted with the permission of Basil Blackwell, Publisher.

John Wisdom, "Gods." *Proceedings of The Aristotelian Society, 1944-1945.* Reprinted by the courtesy of the editor of The Aristotelian Society. © 1945 by The Aristotelian Society.

Gilbert Ryle, "Descartes' Myth." From *The Concept of Mind,* Ch. 1. London: Hutchinson Publishing Group Limited, 1949.

Gustav Bergmann, "Logical Positivism, Language, and the Reconstruction of Metaphysics." *Rivista Critica di Storia della Filosofia,* 1953.

W. V. Quine, "On What There Is." Originally published in the *Review of Metaphysics,* 2 (1948). Reprinted with permission.

W. V. Quine, "Two Dogmas of Empiricism." *The Philosophical Review,* 1951.

J. L. Austin, "Performative-Constative." From C. E. Caton (ed.).

Philosophy and Ordinary Language. Urbana: University of Illinois Press, 1963, pp. 22–33.

P. F. Strawson, "Intention and Convention in Speech Acts." *The Philosophical Review,* 63 (1964): 439–460.

J. R. Searle, "What Is a Speech Act?" From M. Black (ed.), *Philosophy in America.* London: George Allen and Unwin, 1965, pp. 221–239.

Introduction

The Rise of Analytic Philosophy

I

The twentieth century has been referred to as *the age of analysis*. Throughout this period, a number of philosophical positions have been put forth and defended, all of which are now commonly classified under the heading of *analytic philosophy* or philosophical analysis or, sometimes, linguistic philosophy. Some of these philosophies were the work of individual thinkers such as G. E. Moore. Others represent the combined efforts of numerous thinkers who formed various groups and came close to being representatives of certain schools: for example, logical positivism. What is analytic philosophy? As we shall see, there is no simple or universally agreed-upon answer to that question. Rather, we find that there are a number of very different philosophical positions that to some extent overlap or show similarities and affinities with one another. Hence, it would be best to speak of (contemporary) analytic *philosophies,* and to restate our question as: What are analytic philosophies?

Before attempting to answer that question, let us look at what was taking place on the philosophical scene prior to the development of analytic philosophies.

Toward the end of the nineteenth century, the dominant philosophy in England was absolute idealism. To a great extent this was true in the United States as well, although pragmatism had begun to have more influence here than it did in England.

What is (absolute) idealism? Brand Blanshard has given a nice characterization of what might be called its central methodology or procedure.

Put briefly, it was this: start anywhere in experience, develop what is implied in what is before you, and you will find yourself committed, on the principle of the flower in the crannied wall, or of the widening circles in the pool, to an all-comprehensive system in which everything is bound by necessity to everything else. To judge that this is a flower is to use a universal. But the universal, when you attend to it, burgeons. It is necessarily connected through genus and species with a hierarchy about it. Its appearance at this spot and moment is connected spatially,

15

temporally, and causally with every other event in the universe. And these relations, if we saw clearly enough, would turn out to be necessary also. We cannot
now prove this in detail, but as philosophers we must make it our working
assumption till nature flouts us, and there is no reason to expect that she will. The
business of philosophy is to understand; to understand is to explain; and to explain is to place things in a context that reveals them as necessary. Such explanation is genuine discovery; the necessities thought discerns in things are not made by
us, and neither are such values as beauty, or the goodness of justice or happiness.
What from our point of view is increasing understanding of the world is thus
from another point of view an increasing self-revelation of the Absolute in finite
minds.[1]

That was the prevailing philosophical outlook in England and to a large extent
in the United States. As Blanshard has said: "now it has all but vanished."
What has taken its place? For a time, pragmatism and realism were dominant
in the United States, and a number of British philosophers advocated realism
also. But after a time it became apparent that what took the place of idealism
in large measure, in both England and the United States, was analytic
philosophy or the philosophy of analysis.

What is analytic philosophy? As we will see (Introduction to Part 2), it is
difficult to provide a definition or neat summary of analytic philosophy, since
there are at least six forms of it, each of which differs from the others in important respects. Blanshard has stated what he takes to be the five principal
theses of the philosophy of analysis. For now, let us take his list as a starting
point.[2]

The five theses are:

(1) As against the rationalist view that the building bricks of the universe are
concepts or universals, the philosophy of analysis has offered a doctrine of
meaning which would in effect abolish such things. This doctrine is that
the meaning of any statement of fact lies in what would verify it in sense
perception.

(2) As against the conviction held unanimously by rationalists from Plato to
McTaggart that reason can supply us with knowledge of the world, and
also extend it by inference, analysts have commonly held that no necessary
insights give knowledge of the world at all; they only explicate meanings
already in mind.

(3) As against the view that both concepts and things are so linked together
that each depends for its very nature on its relations to others, stands the
theory of 'logical atomism', namely, that none of the ultimate bricks of
which the universe is built is necessarily related to any other.

(4) As against the view that values such as good and evil, beauty and ugliness,
were in some sense out there in the frame of things, that nature itself, for
example, 'means intensely and means good', arose the conviction that
judgments of value were not really judgements at all, but exclamations expressing or reporting nothing but our own feelings.

(5) As against the view of the absolute idealists that philosophy, through
criticizing the assumptions and systematizing the conclusions of science,

was an important means to truth, comes the contention that the philosopher's office is the far humbler one of clarifying the meaning of statements whose truth or falsity is otherwise known. One particularly interesting form of this contention is that the business of philosophy is to clear up the vagueness and ambiguity of ordinary language.

As Blanshard himself notes, these theses do not form a system of philosophy. They are independent of each other. And most analytic philosophies advocate some but not all of the theses. For example, logical positivism generally held (1), (2), and (4), but not (3), and (5) only with restrictions. G E. Moore, on the other hand, rejected (1), (2), and (3). Many analytic philosophies reject (3). Nevertheless, Blanshard is right in maintaining that these theses are among the most central doctrines advocated by some of the various philosophical outlooks that have come to be placed under the heading of analytic philosophy in its earlier years. Later (Introduction to Part 2) we will examine six forms of analytic philosophy via the works of some of their chief practitioners.

But if there is nothing by way of a common set of doctrines uniting all contemporary analytic philosophies might there be something in the way of an approach or methodology that unites them—and thereby provides a basis for a single definition or characterization? Not really. The best that one could do is to come up with some broad and unilluminating slogans like "Analytic philosophy is concerned—obviously—with analysis." Analysis of what? Since 'analytic (philosophy)' and 'linguistic (philosophy)' are often used as synonyms, one might think that the answer to that question is: The analysis of language. But that would not be a correct answer. For example, in one form of analytic philosophy (logical atomism) it was claimed that the object of analysis is the *world* and its metaphysical constituents. And at times G. E. Moore claimed to not be interested in mere words. However (as is often the case) this erroneous answer—that analytic philosophy analyzes language—has a kernel of truth. It is this: Contemporary analytic philosophies have all stressed, in varying degree, the importance of language—and in some cases, of logic—in philosophical inquiry.

Robert R. Ammerman has expressed the relation between analysis and language in this way:

The word 'analysis' when used in philosophy bears obvious affinities to the word's use in a science such as chemistry. To analyze, we may say roughly, is to take apart in order to gain a better understanding of what is being analyzed. The chemist is concerned with the analysis of complex physical substances into their constituent parts. The philosopher, on the other hand, is interested in analyzing linguistic or conceptual units. He is concerned, in general, with coming to understand the structure of language by a careful study of its elements and their interrelations.[3]

But this is misleading. Ammerman suggests that philosophical analysis is the study of language. But then, how does it differ from lexicography, grammer, philology, etc., all of which are involved in the study of language? Furthermore, Ammerman's characterization does not apply to various forms of analytic philosophy—for example, the realism and common sense philosophy of G. E. Moore, the logical atomism of Bertrand Russell and Ludwig Wittgenstein, and the logico-metaphysical analysis of Gustav Bergmann. It doesn't fit some of the other forms very well either. It perhaps applies to a large degree to the philosophers whom I have placed under the heading of "linguistic analysis."

A more accurate way of characterizing philosophical analysis is in terms of its function and goal. Most philosophical analysts have held, explicitly or implicitly, that analysis is essential in order to solve—some would say dissolve—certain deep philosophical problems. Before we can hope to provide an answer to a philosophical question, or even to ascertain whether or not it is a genuine question, we must engage in analysis. We must make necessary distinctions and discriminations among terms and concepts, clarify that which is obscure or opaque, and try to eliminate ambiguity and overabstractness. Then we can attempt to solve (or dissolve) our problem, or to look for arguments on behalf of answers to that problem, and so on.

An excellent example of philosophical analysis occurs in G. E. Moore's "Proof of an External World." As the title suggests, Moore was concerned to prove that there exists an external world of material objects. In Moore's *Philosophical Papers,* this essay is 24 pages long. Moore's proof occupies about a page, followed by a couple pages of comment on the proof. So what was Moore doing in the first 20 pages? He was engaged in analysis, in getting at all the possible meanings of the concepts involved and in making clear which are relevant to his proof and why. Without those preceding pages of analysis, Moore's proof is meaningless—or perhaps trivial. His complete proof of an external world consists of both the analysis and the shorter "proof" that follows it.[4]

I am not suggesting that every analytic philosopher followed Moore's procedure. But many of them have indicated that something like it is appropriate for philosophy.

Some have suggested that if what I have said is true, then there seems to be nothing new about analytic philosophy, since most philosophers throughout history have been concerned with clarification, meanings of terms, etc. I believe that to some extent that is indeed true. But what distinguishes the practitioners of twentieth-century analytic philosophy from their predecessors is the high degree of, and emphasis upon the role and importance of analysis and language, along with—in some cases—the importance of modern logic. In some cases it seems that, in philosophical inquiry, it is language itself that is the object of study. But in many (perhaps most) cases, it is apparent that language and logic are important only in their relations to the world.

By striving for clarity in language we also achieve (or seek) insight into what the world or reality is like. Isn't that what most philosophy has always sought?

II

Many students, upon first encountering analytic philosophy or the writings of contemporary analytic philosophers, ask themselves (or their instructors): "What's the value of all this stuff? It seems like a lot of nit-picking and logic-chopping. Words! Words! Words! What's this got to do with anything important? How will it help me with regard to my life?" I doubt if I can provide answers to these questions that will apply universally to all persons. But I think I can provide an answer that applies to many.

Some of us (perhaps most of us) have a reflective bent to our personalities. We want to understand things. We seek answers to certain vexing and difficult problems. And we hope to find true answers and good arguments or reasons on behalf of those answers. I have constantly found that the likelihood of getting good (or any) answers to those questions is increased if we become very clear as to just what the problem is or what its various facets are. The same words may be used to express different concepts and hence different questions, or the same words may seem to indicate a single question when in fact there are several. And so on. In order to be able to make any progress in our pursuit of true answers, we must engage in analysis.

Many people are very suspicious and even hostile when they hear talk of analysis. They think that one who analyzes breaks up things or analyzes them away, or they think that anyone who analyzes performs *idle* hair-splitting and logic-chopping. And perhaps some practitioners of analysis do such things at times. But surely not all of them do. Speaking for myself, I prefer wholes to scattered bits, for the most part. And I have no wish to remove good and important things from the world. (I would be foolish if I did.) As for hair-splitting, etc., well, if there is a distinction to be made, and making it illuminates something about the world or our experience of it, then I say: Hurray for hair-splitting!

Let me give an example: There are some people on this earth who hold what I think is the silliest of all philosophical beliefs, namely: "Acts of consciousness, mental awarenesses, thoughts, sensations, etc., are nothing but electro-chemical impulses in the brain and/or nervous system. In short, mental states are nothing but brain states. They are *the same as* brain states. Thus, sentences using the terms 'mental states' and 'brain states' express the same fact." I have shown elsewhere that this philosophical thesis rests and trades on the ambiguity of the word 'same' when used (misleadingly) in expressions like 'the same as' or 'the same fact'. I have distinguished five different senses of 'same'. Only one of these is identity. In the rest, 'same' means something different. And whereas it may be the case that the above claim holds for a loose sense of 'same', such as the case where a correlation holds between two things, it does not hold for identity. And that of course is what the proponent of the above claim holds: that "mental" states are identical with brain states. And that — as I have tried to show — is false. But the claim cannot be shown to be false without going through a lot of analysis.[5]

This, I believe, is the value of analysis — and of analytic philosophy. By engaging in analysis we can hope to provide answers to the many difficult questions — philosophical and otherwise — we encounter as we reflect about the world, ourselves, and our place in the world. We can show that certain answers are false — and why. We can show that certain answers are true — or at least are very likely true — and why. In short, by engaging in analysis we increase the probability of finding good answers to questions and good reasons for those answers. And not just in philosophy, but in any discipline. That is surely something of great value, both in our theoretical and philosophical pursuits and in everyday life.

NOTES

1. Brand Blanshard, "The Philosophy of Analysis," *Proceedings of British Academy*, XXXVIII, p. 40.

2. Ibid., p. 41.

3. R. R. Ammerman, *Classics of Analytic Philosophy* (New York: McGraw-Hill, Inc., 1965), p. 2.

4. See E. D. Klemke, "G. E. Moore's Proof of an External World" in Klemke (ed.), *Studies in the Philosophy of G. E. Moore* (New York: Quadrangle, 1969), pp. 276–287.

5. See E. D. Klemke, *Reflections and Perspectives: Essays in Philosophy* (West Berlin: Mouton-de Gruyter, 1974), pp. 1–13.

Part One

The Pre-analytic Tradition

Part 1: The Pre-analytic Tradition

Introduction

Our chief task in this volume is to examine the various forms of twentieth-century analytic and linguistic philosophy. But before we do that, it would be best for us to look briefly at some of the pre-analytic traditions that appeared in the nineteenth century and in the earlier part of the twentieth century (in the Western world). Why begin with these pre-analytic philosophies? For three main reasons: First, virtually every movement in twentieth-century philosophy can best be understood as being in opposition to one or more of the central tenets of one of those pre-analytic philosophies—namely, absolute idealism. Second, with regard to both themes and methodology, there are various affinities between some pragmatists (especially Peirce) and certain analytic philosophers. (And some of the latter have a definite pragmatic slant in their views.) Third, some analytic philosophies maintain positions that are realistic in nature. Hence, in this part of the book, we will briefly examine (absolute) idealism (as represented by Josiah Royce), pragmatism (as represented by Charles Sanders Peirce), and realism [as represented by E. B. Holt, et al. (the new realism) and Durant Drake (critical realism)].

IDEALISM

In nineteenth-century Germany there occurred a great flowering of metaphysical philosophies. A number of systems were put forth that claimed to reveal what reality is in its innermost essence. The philosophers of this era stressed the significance of human reason and had great confidence in its power. In fact, they saw reality as the manifestation of an Infinite Reason, and thought that by philosophical reflection, the whole development of this manifestation could be plotted and grasped. This movement was known as absolute idealism (or objective idealism) in order to distinguish it from the subjective idealism of Bishop Berkeley. Its major figures were Johann Gottlieb Fichte (1763–1814), Friedrich Wilhelm Joseph von Schelling (1775–1854), and George Wilhelm Friedrich Hegel (1770–1831).

23

It is difficult to present a concise summary or characterization of idealism that is at all accurate. It is even difficult to formulate a description that suggests (rather than states) what idealism is all about. However, Brand Blanshard has managed to come close to doing the impossible in a passage quoted at the beginning of the Introduction to this volume. I urge the reader to reread that description before going on.

Blanshard's account provides a nice characterization of the methodology of idealism and somewhat of its content as well. It would be desirable to go a little more deeply into the latter. Perhaps this can best be done by listing the main theses or tenets common to most (if not all) idealistic philosophies. These are:

1. Reality is unitary. From the standpoint of ordinary experiences, to be sure, there is a plurality. But this is merely apparent. In its essence, reality is a single unified *whole*. (This claim is known as monism, as opposed to pluralism, and/or holism, as opposed to atomism.)

2. In the whole that constitutes reality, everything is *logically* connected with everything else. Thus everything that happens is the result of some causal necessity.

3. What is known is, at least in some ways, dependent on its being known. To be is to be capable of being known, or to be known, by some mind. Hence, there cannot be any unknown things.

4. Reality is mental (or spiritual). To be is to be known or capable of being known. What is known is mental. Thus reality is mental.

5. Reality is organic. The whole (reality) is not static. It is a process, something like the life process of an organism or the reasoning of a mind.

6. Value is objective. Goodness, beauty, etc., are not subjective or relative. Rather, they are objective structures or attributes in the objective universe.

7. The world (or reality) is known only through (philosophical) reason. One cannot apprehend the innermost essence of reality through sensation, science, etc. What is needed is philosophical reason.

Josiah Royce (1855-1916) was an American idealist who studied in Germany and then taught at the University of California and at Harvard. He was a contemporary (and for years, a colleague) of William James. Although his form of idealism differs in certain respects from that of Hegel (by incorporating voluntaristic elements in his theory of the will), nevertheless Royce is perhaps the best representative of idealism for the student who is not familiar with the Hegelian tradition. The selection included in this volume is one chapter from Royce's *The Spirit of Modern Philosophy*. In this chapter Royce undertakes to establish that : (1) The *world of our experience* is "such stuff as ideas are made of." It is a system of ideas. (2) The *real world* is the world of a single infinite self, or the total system of ideas of this self. Both (1) and (2) are thus extended to establish the main claim of idealism: (3) All reality is ideal or mental (or spiritual).

Idealism dominated the philosophical scene in England for decades. Its major advocates were T. H. Green (1836-1882), F. H. Bradley (1846-1924),

Bernard Bosanquet (1848–1923), and J. M. E. McTaggart (1866–1925).

PRAGMATISM

Pragmatism was the most widespread and influential philosophical movement in the United States during the first 20 or 25 years of this century. It is also one of the few philosophies largely indigenous to this country. However, it has influenced a number of European thinkers as well.

The word 'pragmatic' has of course become part of our common, everyday vocabulary. This ordinary use of the term 'pragmatic' comes pretty close to meaning the same as 'practical' – or perhaps 'practical and realistic'. To judge a belief or theory or idea as pragmatic is to suggest that it serves as a sort of plan for acting based upon consequences rather than set principles, or whatever. Likewise, to judge a person as being pragmatic is to say that he/she acts (and thinks) in terms of practical consequences, results, or implications, rather than in terms of first principles, unrealistic theories, or "idealistic" norms.

Although the ordinary use of a term does not always reflect its technical (philosophical or scientific) use, in this case, there is some connection. Pragmatism is a form of empiricism. But rather than focusing backward to the origins of our ideas and beliefs (in the manner of the eighteenth-century British empiricists – John Locke, Bishop Berkeley, and David Hume), pragmatism looks at consequences. It judges beliefs and concepts in terms of fruitful consequences. It is concerned with practical plans for action rather than with first principles or absolute truths. In fact, pragmatism abandoned the notion of absolute truths.

As we have seen, idealism was concerned to find out what reality is "in its innermost essence." The pragmatist has no hope of finding out what the world or reality *really* is. He is concerned with what it is given to be in our experience when approached via our goals and plans. To be sure, we can have a metaphysical viewpoint. But it is not a static, holistic one. Rather, it is fluid and pluralistic.

The chief American pragmatists were Charles Sanders Peirce (1839–1914), William James (1843–1910), and John Dewey (1859–1952).

C. S. Peirce was the originator of pragmatism, and indeed he coined the word 'pragmatism'. Peirce thought of pragmatism as being primarily a method of determining and clarifying the meanings of terms and concepts. He held that a concept could be defined only in terms of its bearing on actual behavior or results, i.e., in terms of consequences. In "How to Make Our Ideas Clear" (included in this volume), Peirce writes: "Consider what effects, which might conceivably have practical bearings, we conceive the object of our conception to have. Then our conception of these effects is the whole of our conception of the object." Elsewhere he maintained that "in order to ascertain the meaning of an intellectual conception one should consider what practical consequences might conceivably result by necessity from the truth of that conception; and the sum of these consequences will constitute the entire meaning of the conception" *(Collected Papers,* Volume 5, paragraph 9, Peirce also attempted to work out, but never fully completed, a general theory of signs concerning various types of words and their relations and ways of signifying. After James and others made use of the term 'pragmatism', Peirce was dissatisfied with their use, so in 1905 he coined the word 'pragmaticism' to refer to his position and said that it was "ugly enough to be safe from kidnappers."

As a result of the efforts of William James, pragmatism became a famous philosophy. The works in which he articulated and defended it were widely read. James conceived of pragmatism as a method and a theory of truth. As a method pragmatism consists in "looking away from first things, principles, 'categories', supposed necessities; and of looking towards last things, fruits, consequences, facts." Thus the pragmatic method (said James) can serve as a way of settling metaphysical disputes—e.g., is the world one or many? "The pragmatic method . . . is to interpret each notion by tracing its respective practical consequences. What difference would it practically make to anyone if this notion rather than that notion were true? If no practical difference whatever can be traced, then the alternatives mean practically the same thing, and all dispute is idle." And echoing Peirce, James maintained that the meaning of an idea consists solely of the particular consequences to which it leads. "Test every concept by the question, 'What sensible difference to anyone will its truth make'? If. . . you can think of absolutely nothing that would practically differ in two cases you may assume that the alternative is meaningless, and that your concept is no distinct idea."

The pragmatic theory of truth claims that "ideas . . . become true just in so far as they help us to get into satisfactory relation with other parts of our experience." "Any idea . . . that will carry us prosperously from any one part of our experience to any other part, linking things satisfactorily, working securely, simplifying, saving labor, is true for just so much . . ., true instrumentally." Again: Any idea "makes itself true, gets itself classified as true, by the way it works." The notion of any purely objective truth is discarded by James. Rather, "the reasons why we call things true is the reason why they *are* true." The "true," says James, is only "the expedient in the way of our thinking," just as the "right" is merely "the expedient in the way of our behaving."

It should be mentioned that James, who was also a psychologist, wrote a number of works in the areas of ethics and the philosophy of religion. He wrote many essays and gave numerous lectures, some of which have been published in various volumes.

In his later years, James developed a very different philosophical position, which he called radical empiricism. Although it includes elements of pragmatism, it differs in this respect: his pragmatism, as we have seen, laid great stress on actions, consequences, practicality; but his radical empiricism is much more rooted in a strict empirical tradition. There are four main aspects of James's radical empiricism. These are: (1) Anti-elementarism. This is the view that the relations between the objects of our experience are themselves part of our given experience. They are not a contribution of the self, as Kant thought. (2) The distinction between knowledge of and knowledge about. (3) Pluralism. This is the view that there are many different kinds of things in the universe. (4) Neutral monism. This is a view on the relation of mind and matter. According to it, there is no uniquely mental "stuff" and no matter as an ultimate substance either. There is just one single ontological stuff. What we call mind and matter are just different organizations of this one stuff. James's radical empiricism is presented and defended in a number of essays contained in his *Essays in Radical Empiricism* (1912). Perhaps the best are his "Does Consciousness Exist?" and "A World of Pure Experience."

John Dewey was born in 1859, the year in which Darwin's *Origin of Species* was published. It is clear that Dewey owed a lot to Darwin, for Dewey's writings are filled with biological concepts such as process, development, and change. And Dewey made frequent use of a kind of genetic method of explaining things in terms of their origin and function.

Dewey's concept of truth is related to his concept of mind. According to Dewey, mind arose in the process of man's adjustment to his environment. It was brought about to solve practical problems. We find ourselves faced with conflicts requiring resolution. Inquiry, then, results as the need to solve some practical problem. Hence real knowledge, too, is practical and not contemplative or absolute. Thus, according to Dewey, we have no use for a notion of absolute truth. To say that an idea is true is simply to say that it has warranted assertability. It is true in so far as it is a tool or instrument for some purpose. Therefore, truths are not statements describing reality. Rather, they are—echoing Peirce—plans of action and therefore must be judged in terms of how successful they are in serving our ends and purposes.

Dewey admired science a great deal, for it made contributions to man's control of his environment. It has opened the way to social engineering. Dewey suggests that philosophy should follow suit. Instead of being concerned with pure knowledge and thus unproductive, a "reconstructed" philosophy must face the great social, political, and moral problems facing us and deal successfully with them. It must be practical and accomplish practical ends.

It should be mentioned that Dewey wrote widely in the fields of logic, theory of knowledge, ethics, esthetics, political philosophy, and education. For years his was the dominant influence on public education in the United States.

AMERICAN REALISM

The term 'realism' is used in several senses, even when the context of philosophy is considered seperately. In its broadest philosophical sense, realism is primarily a theory concerning the relation between the knower and the known or the relation between the knowing mind and the objects known.

Its main theses are: the world is real in the sense that it is independent of our knowing or experiencing it, and thus knowledge makes no difference to the things known. In the first two or three decades of the twentieth century, two different groups of philosophers defended two forms of realism. Their positions can be best understood by placing them in a historical context.

Throughout the history of what is often known as modern philosophy, beginning with the seventeenth century, three different views were held with regard to the relation between the knower and the known and with regard to the nature of that which is known. These were:

1. Naive realism. This position (held by some Scottish philosophers) is the view that the object known is directly present to consciousness and is exactly what it appears to be. Nothing intervenes between the knower and the external world. Objects are not represented in consciousness via ideas or images; rather objects themselves are directly perceived.

2. Representative realism. According to this view (held by Rene Descartes and John Locke), the mind never perceives anything external to itself. It can only perceive its own ideas, images, or representations. Why, then, maintain that there are any external objects? Because ideas occur in an orderly way. I look at my desk. A color, shape, etc., all go together in a coherent manner. So we must infer that a world of external objects exists and causes our ideas, which, to some extent, resemble those objects. What we perceive, thus, is a kind of image or picture representing the external object.

3. Subjective idealism. This view (held by Bishop Berkeley) leaves out the world of extra-mental objects. It says: the world consists only of minds and their ideas. In this view, there can be no object without a subject, no existent thing without consciousness of it. As Berkeley said: to be *is* to be perceived or to perceive. There is no world of objects existing independently of the knower.

Let us turn now to the two schools of American realism. Whereas the pragmatists attacked mainly the holistic and absolutistic aspects of absolute idealism, the realists attacked mainly the idealistic, subjective aspects of it. There are two main versions of realism.

1. The new realism (E. B. Holt, R. B. Perry, W. T. Marvin, E. G. Spaulding, W. B. Pitkin, W. P. Montague). Actually, there was nothing new about the new realism. It was largely a return to the position of naive realism — the view that the world is as it appears to be, and that we perceive things as they really are and perceive them directly, without any intervening image or idea.

According to the new realists, the basic fallacy of idealism consisted in arguing from the truism that 'Anything known or thought is known or thought by someone' to the different claim that 'Nothing can exist independently of being known or thought'. The new realists maintained that, on the contrary, knowledge makes no difference to the object known; the object exists antecedently to being known. Knowing and the object known are two different things.

It didn't take too long to find some difficulties with this view. For example, take optical illusions—such as the bent look of a straight oar when partially submerged in water. Surely here we don't see things as they really are. Or take the case of color blindness. I see a plant as red, whereas someone else sees it as gray. Is it both red and gray all over?

In 1912, the new realists published a book entitled *The New Realism*. It contained a "program and platform," which appears in this volume.

2. Critical realism. (G. Santayana, C. A. Strong, A. K. Rogers, A. O. Lovejoy, R. W. Sellars, J. B. Pratt, D. Drake) The critical realists were in agreement with the new realists regarding the independence of the knower and the known. But they opposed the claim that we have *direct* knowledge or awareness of external things. According to critical realism, we do not see external physical objects directly. We believe them to exist, and our beliefs about them are mediated by an inference to their existence. What we directly apprehend are ideas or images that represent external objects.

The main theses of critical realism were: (a) The world is composed of both material objects and mental states or ideas. (b) The ideas alone are "given," or presented, as objects of consciousness and directly known. Material objects are inferred to exist as the causes of our ideas. (c) The inferred objects are distinct from the ideas, both numerically and qualitatively.

But critical realism had its problems too. For example, it was asked: If only ideas or images are (directly) given, how do we know that they correspond to any objects? In fact, how do we know that there are any objects at all? At least one critical realist (Santayana) replied: We don't. It's all animal faith.

In 1920, the critical realists published a book called *Essays in Critical Realism*. A selection from that book by one of the critical realists, Durant Drake (1878–1933), appears in this volume.

These, then, are some of the main pre-analytic traditions of twentieth-century philosophy. The few selections that follow are meant to represent only some of what went on in those traditions.

Idealism

1. Reality and Idealism

Josiah Royce

The business of the present lecture is to tell you in what sense and for what reasons I am an idealist. . . .

I

I am very sorry that I cannot state my idealism in a simple and unproblematic form; but the nature of the doctrine forbids. I must first of all puzzle you with a paradox, by saying that my idealism has nothing in it which contradicts the principal propositions of what is nowadays called scientific Agnosticism, in so far, namely, as this agnosticism relates to that world of facts of experience which man sees and feels and which science studies. Of such agnosticism we learned something in our last lecture. But I must go on to say that the fault of our modern so-called scientific agnosticism is only that it has failed to see how the world in space and time, the world of causes and effects, the world of matter and of finite mind, whereof we know so little and long to know so much, is a very subordinate part of reality. It will be my effort to explain how we do know something very deep and vital about what reality is in its innermost essence. My explanation will indeed be very poor and fragmentary, but the outcome of it will be the very highly paradoxical assertion that while the whole finite world is full of dark problems for us, there is absolutely nothing, not even the immediate facts of our sense at this moment, so clear, so certain, as the existence and the unity of that infinite conscious Self of whom we have now heard so much. About the finite world, as I shall assert, we know in general only what experience teaches us and science records. There is nothing in the universe absolutely sure except the Infinite. That will be the curious sort of agnosticism that I shall try in a measure to expound. Of the infinite we know that it is one and conscious. Of the finite things, that is, of the particular fashions of behavior in terms of which the infinite Consciousness

31

gives himself form and plays the world-game, we know only what we experience. Yet doubtless it will at once seem to you that in *one* important respect my announced doctrine is in obvious conflict with a wise agnosticism. For is it not confessedly anthromorphic in its character? And is not anthropomorphism precisely the defect that modern thinkers have especially taught us to avoid?

Anthropomorphism was the savage view, which led primitive man to interpret extraordinary natural events as expressions of the will of beings like himself. However he came by his fancy, whether by first believing in the survival of the ghosts of his ancestors, and then conceiving them as the agents who produced lightning, and who moved the sun, or by a simple and irreducible instinct of his childish soul, leading him to see himself in nature, and to regard it all as animate; in any case he made the bad induction, created the gods in his own image, and then constituted them as the causes of all natural events. His ignorant self-multiplication we must avoid. Shall our limited inner experience be the only test of what sorts of causation may exist in the world? What we know is that events happen to us, and happen in a certain fixed order. We do not know the ultimate causes of these events. If we lived on some other planet, doubtless causes of a very novel sort would become manifest to us, and our whole view of nature would change. It is self contradictory, it is absurd, to make our knowledge the measure of all that is! The real world that causes our experience is a great *x*, wholly unknown to us except in a few select phenomena, which happen to fall within our ken. How wild to guess about the mysteries of the infinite!

But now *this* agnosticism, too, as I assure you, I ardently and frankly agree with, so far as it concerns itself with precisely *that* world in which it pretends to move, and to which it undertakes to apply itself. I have no desire to refute it. Touching all the world in space and time beyond experience, in the scientific sense of the term experience, I repeat that I know nothing positive. I know, for instance, nothing about the stratification of Saturn, or the height of the mountains on the other side of the moon. For the same reason, also, I know nothing of any anthropomorphic daemons or gods here or there in nature, acting as causes of noteworthy events. Of these I know nothing, because science has at present no need for such hypotheses. There may be such beings; there doubtless are in nature many curious phenomena; but what curiosities further experience might show us, we must wait for experience to point out ere we shall know. I repeat, in its own world, agnosticism is in all these respects in the right. For reasons that you will later see, I object indeed to the unhappy word *unknowable*. In the world of experience, as in the world of abstracter problems, there are infinitely numerous things unknown to us. But there is no rational question that could not somehow be answered by a sufficiently wise person. There are things relatively unknowable for us, not things absolutely so. There are numberless experiences that I shall never have, in my individual capacity; and there are numberless problems that I shall never solve. But the only absolute insoluble mysteries, as I shall hereafter point out to you, would be the questions that it is essentially absurd to ask. Still, not to quarrel over words, what many agnostics mean by unknowable is simply the stubbornly unknown, and, in that sense, I fully agree and indeed insist that human knowledge is an island in the vast ocean of mystery, and that numberless questions, which it deeply concerns humanity to answer, will never be answered so long as we are in our present limited state, bound to one planet, and left for our experience to our senses, our emotions, and our moral activities.

But, if I thus accept this agnostic view of the world of experience, what chance is left, you will say, for anything like an absolute system of philosophy? In what sense can I pretend to talk of idealism, as giving any final view of the whole nature of things? In what sense, above all, can I pretend to be a theist, and to speak of the absolute Self as the very essence and life of the whole world? For is this not mere anthropomorphism? Isn't it making our private human experience the measure of all reality? Isn't it making hypotheses in terms of our experience, about things beyond our experience? Isn't it making our petty notions of causation a basis for judging of the nature of the unknown first cause? Isn't it another case of what the savage did when he saw his gods in the thunder-clouds, because he conceived that causes just like his own angry moods must be here at work? Surely, at best, this is sentiment, faith, mystical dreaming. It can't be philosophy.

I answer, just to change our whole view of the deeper reality of things, just to turn away our attention from any illusive search for first causes in the world of experience, just to get rid of fanciful faith about the gods in outer nature, and just to complete the spiritual task of agnosticism by sending us elsewhere than to phenomena for the true and inner nature of things, — for just this end was the whole agony of modern philosophy endured by those who have wrestled with its problems. Is any one agnostic about the finite world? Then I more. I know nothing of any first cause in the world of appearances yonder. I see no gods in the thunder clouds, no Keplerian angels carrying the planets in conic sections around the sun; I imagine no world-maker far back in the ages, beginning the course of evolution. Following Laplace, I need, once more, no such hypothesis. I await the verdict of science about all facts and events in physical nature. And yet that is just *why* I am an idealist. It is my agnosticism about the causes of my experience that makes me search elsewhere than amongst causes for the meaning of experience. The outer world which the agnostic sees and despairs of knowing is not the region where I look for light. The living God, whom idealism knows, is not the first cause in any physical sense at all. No possible experience could find him as a thing amongst things or show any outer facts that would prove his existence. He isn't anywhere in space or in time. He makes from without no worlds. He is no hypothesis of empirical science. But he is all the more real for that, and his existence is all the surer. For causes are, after all, very petty and subordinate truths in the world, and facts, phenomena, as such, could never demonstrate any important spiritual truth. The absolute Self simply doesn't *cause* the world. The very idea of causation belongs to things of finite experience, and is only a mythological term when applied to the real truth of things. Not because I interpret the causes of my experience in terms of my limited ideas of causation is the universe of God a live thing to me, but for a far deeper reason; for a reason which deprives this world of agnosticism of all substantiality and converts it once for all into mere show. I am ignorant of this world just because it is a show-world.

And this deeper reason of the idealist I may as well first suggest in a form which may perhaps seem just now even more mysterious than the problem which I solve by means of it. My reason for believing that there is one absolute World-Self, who embraces and is all reality, whose consciousness includes and infinitely transcends our own, in whose unity all the laws of nature and all the mysteries of experience must have their solution and their very being, — is simply that the profoundest agnosticism which you can possibly state in any coherent fashion, the deepest doubt which you can any way formulate about the world or the things that are therein, already presupposes, implies, demands, asserts, the existence of such a World-Self. The agnostic, I say, already asserts this existence — unconsciously, of course, as a rule, but none the less inevitably. For, as we shall find, there is no escape from the infinite Self except by self-contradiction. Ignorant as I am about first causes, I am at least clear, therefore, about the Self. If you deny him, you already in denying affirm him. You reckon ill when you leave him out. Him when you fly, he is the wings. He is the doubter and the doubt. You in vain flee from his presence. The wings of the morning will not aid you. Nor do I mean all this now as any longer a sort of mysticism. This truth is, I assure you, simply a product of dry logic. When I try to tell you about it in detail, I shall weary you by my wholly unmystical analysis of commonplaces. Here is, in fact, as we shall soon find, the very presupposition of presuppositions. You cannot stir, nay, you cannot even stand still in thought without it. Nor is it an unfamiliar idea. On the contrary, philosophy finds trouble in bringing it to your consciousness merely *because* it is so familiar. When they told us in childhood that we could not see God just *because* he was everywhere, just because his omnipresence gave us no chance to discern him and to fix our eyes upon him, they told us a deep truth in allegorical fashion. The infinite Self, as we shall learn, is actually asserted by you in every proposition you utter, is there at the heart, so to speak, of the very multiplication table. The Self is so little a thing merely guessed at as the unknowable source of experience, that already, *in* the very least of daily experiences you unconsciously know him as something present. This, as we shall find, is the deepest tragedy of our finitude, that continually he comes to his own, and his own receive him not, that he becomes flesh in every least incident of our lives; whilst we, gazing with wonder upon his world, search here and there for first causes, look for miracles, and beg him to show us the Father, since that alone will suffice us. No wonder that thus we have to remain agnostics. "Hast thou been so long time with me, and yet hast thou not *known* me?" Such is the eternal answer of the Logos to every doubting question. Seek him not as an outer hypothesis to explain experience. Seek him not anywhere yonder in the clouds. He is no "thing in itself." But for all that, experience contains him. He is the reality, the soul of it. "Did not our heart burn within us while he talked with us by the way?" And, as we shall see, he does not talk merely to our hearts. He reveals himself to our coolest scrutiny.

II

But enough of speculative boasting. Coming to closer quarters with my topic, I must remind you that idealism has two aspects. It is, for the first, a kind of analysis of the world, an analysis which so far has no absolute character about it, but which undertakes, in a fashion that might be acceptable to any skeptic, to examine what you mean by all the things, whatever they are, that you believe in or experience. This idealistic analysis consists merely in a pointing out, by various devices, that the world of your knowledge, whatever it contains, is through and through such stuff as ideas are made of, that you never in your life believed in anything definable *but* ideas, that, as Berkeley put it, "this whole choir of heaven and furniture of earth" is nothing for any of us but a system of ideas which govern our belief and our conduct. Such idealism has numerous statements, interpretations, embodiments: forms part of the most various systems and experiences, is consistent with Berkeley's theism, with Fichte's ethical absolutism, with Professor Huxley's agnostic empiricism, with Clifford's mind-stuff theory, with countless other theories that have used such idealism as a part of their scheme. In this aspect idealism is already a little puzzling to our natural consciousness, but it becomes quickly familiar, in fact almost commonplace, and seems after all to alter our practical faith or to solve our deeper problems very little.

The other aspect of idealism is the one which gives us our notion of the absolute Self. To it the first is only preparatory. This second aspect is the one which from Kant until the present time has formed the deeper problem of thought. Whenever the world has become more conscious of its significance, the work of human philosophy will be, not nearly ended (Heaven forbid an end!), but for the first time fairly begun. For then, in critically estimating our passions, we shall have some truer sense of whose passions they are.

I begin with the first and the less significant aspect of idealism. Our world, I say, whatever it may contain, is such stuff as ideas are made of. This preparatory sort of idealism is the one that, as I just suggested, Berkeley made prominent, and, after a fashion familiar. I must state it in my own way, although one in vain seeks to attain novelty in illustrating so frequently described a view.

Here, then, is our so real world of the senses, full of light and warmth and sound. If anything could be solid and external, surely, one at first will say, it is this world. Hard facts, not mere ideas, meet us on every hand. Ideas any one can mould as he wishes. Not so facts. In idea socialists can dream out Utopias, disappointed lovers can imagine themselves successful, beggars can ride horses, wanderers can enjoy the fireside at home. In the realm of facts, society organizes itself as it must, rejected lovers stand for the time defeated, beggars are alone with their wishes, oceans roll drearily between home and the wanderer. Yet this world of fact is, after all, not entirely stubborn, not merely hard. The strenuous will can mould facts. We can form our world, in part, according to our ideas. Statesmen influence the social order, lovers woo afresh, wanderers find the way home. But thus to alter the world we must work, and just because the laborer is worthy of his hire, it is well that the real world should thus have such fixity of things as enables us to anticipate what facts will prove lasting, and to see of the travail of our souls when it is once done. This, then, is the presupposition of life, that we work in a real world, where house-walls do not melt away as in dreams, but stand firm against the winds of many winters, and can be felt as real. We do not wish to find facts wholly plastic; we want them to be stubborn, if only the stubbornness be not altogether unmerciful. Our will makes constantly a sort of agreement with the world, whereby, if the world will continually show some respect to the will, the will shall consent to be strenuous in its industry. Interfere with the reality of my world, and you therefore take the very life and heart out of my will.

The reality of the world, however, when thus defined in terms of its stubbornness, its firmness as against the will that has not conformed to its laws, its kindly rigidity in preserving for us the fruits of our labors, — such reality, I say, is still something wholly unanalyzed. In what does this stubbornness consist? Surely, many different sorts of reality, as it would seem, may be stubborn. Matter is stubborn when it stands in hard walls against us, or rises in vast mountain ranges before the path-finding explorer. But minds can be stubborn also. The lonely wanderer, who watches by the seashore the waves that roll between him and his home, talks of cruel facts, material barriers that, just because they *are* material, and not ideal, shall be the irresistible foes of his longing heart. "In wish," he says, "I am with my dear ones, but alas, wishes cannot cross oceans! Oceans are material facts, in the cold outer world. Would that the world of the heart were all!" But alas! to the rejected lover the world of the heart *is* all, and that is just his woe. Were the barrier between him and his beloved only made of those stubborn material facts, only of walls or of oceans, how lightly might his will erelong transcend them all! Matter stubborn! Outer nature cruelly the foe of ideas! Nay, it is just an idea that now opposes him, — just an idea, and that, too, in the mind of the maiden he loves. But in vain does he call this stubborn bit of disdain a merely ideal fact. No flint was ever more definite in preserving its identity and its edge than this disdain may be. Place me for a moment, then, in an external world that shall consist wholly of ideas, — the ideas, namely, of other people about me, a world of maidens who shall scorn me, of old friends who shall have learned to hate me, of angels who shall condemn me, of God who shall judge me. In what piercing north winds, amidst what fields of ice, in the labyrinths of what tangled forests, in the depths of what thick-walled dungeons, on the edges of what tremendous precipices, should I be more genuinely in the presence of stubborn and unyielding facts than in that conceived world of ideas! So, as one sees, I by no means deprive my world of stubborn reality, if I merely call it a world of ideas. On the contrary, as every teacher knows, the ideas of the people are often the most difficult of facts to influence. We were wrong, then, when we said that whilst matter was stubborn, ideas could be moulded at pleasure. Ideas are often the most implacable of facts. Even my own ideas, the facts of my own inner life, may cruelly decline to be plastic to my wish. The wicked will that refuses to be destroyed, — what rock has often more consistency for our senses than this will has for our inner consciousness! The king, in his soliloquy in "Hamlet," — in what an unyielding world of hard facts does he not move! and yet they are now only inner facts. The fault is past; he is alone with his conscience.

> "What rests?
> Try what repentance can. What can it not?
> Yet what can it, when one cannot repent?
> O wretched state! O bosom black as death!
> O limëd soul, that, struggling to be free,
> Art more engaged!"

No, here are barriers worse than any material chains. The world of ideas has its own horrible dungeons and chasms. Let those who have refuted Bishop Berkeley's idealism by the wonder why he did not walk over every precipice or into every fire if these things existed only in his idea, let such, I say, first try some of the fires and the precipices of the inner life, ere they decide that dangers cease to be dangers as soon as they are called ideal, or even subjectively ideal in me.

Many sorts of reality, then, may be existent at the heart of any world of facts. But this bright and beautiful sense-world of ours, — what, amongst these many possible sorts of reality, does that embody? Are the stars and the oceans, the walls and the pictures, real as the maiden's heart is real, — embodying the ideas of somebody, but none the less stubbornly real for that? Or can we make something else of their reality? For, of course, that the stars and the oceans, the walls and the pictures have *some* sort of stubborn reality, just as the minds of our fellows have, our analysis so far does not for an instant think of denying. Our present question is, what sort of reality? Consider, then, in detail, certain aspects of the reality that seems to be exemplified in our sense-world. The sublimity of the sky, the life and majesty of the ocean, the interest of a picture, — to what sort of real facts do these belong? Evidently here we shall have no question. So far as the sense-world is beautiful, is majestic, is sublime, this beauty and dignity exist only for the appreciative observer. If they exist beyond him, they exist only for some other mind, or as the thought and embodied purpose of some universal soul of nature. A man who sees the same world, but who has no eye for the fairness of it, will find all the visible facts, but will catch nothing of their value. At once, then, the sublimity and beauty of the world are thus truths that one who pretends to insight ought to see, and they are truths which have no meaning except for such a beholder's mind, or except as embodying the thought of the mind of the world. So here, at least, is so much of the outer world that is ideal, just as the coin or the jewel or the bank-note or the bond has its value not alone in its physical presence, but in the idea that it symbolizes to a beholder's mind, or to the relatively universal thought of the commercial world. But let us look a little deeper. Surely, if the objects yonder are unideal and outer, odors and tastes and temperatures do not exist in these objects in just the way in which they exist in us. Part of the being of these properties, at least, if not all of it, is ideal and exists for us, or at best is once more the embodiment of the thought or purpose of some world-mind. About tastes you cannot dispute, because they are not only ideal but personal. For the benumbed tongue and palate of diseased bodily conditions, all things are tasteless. As for temperatures, a well known experiment will show how the same water may seem cold to one hand and warm to the other. But even so, colors and sounds are at least in part ideal. Their causes may have some other sort of reality; but colors themselves are not in the things, since they change with the light that falls on the things, vanish in the dark (whilst the things remained unchanged), and differ for different eyes. And as for sounds, both the pitch and the quality of tones depend for us upon certain interesting peculiarities of our hearing organs, and exist in nature only as voiceless sound-waves trembling through the air. All such sense qualities, then, are ideal. The world yonder may—yes, must—have attributes that give reasons why these qualities are thus felt by us; for so we assume. The world yonder may even be a mind that thus expresses its will to us. But these qualities need not, nay, cannot resemble the ideas that are produced in us, unless, indeed, that is because these qualities have place as ideas in some world-mind. Sound-waves in the air are not like our musical sensations; nor is the symphony as we hear it and feel it any physical property of the strings and the wind instruments; nor are the ether-vibrations that the sun sends us like our ideas when we see the sun; nor yet is the flashing of moonlight on the water as we watch the waves a direct expression of the actual truths of fluid motion as the water embodies them.

Unless, then, the real physical world yonder is itself the embodiment of some world-spirit's ideas, which he conveys to us, unless it is real only as the maiden's heart is real, namely, as itself a conscious thought, then we have so far but one result: that real world (to repeat one of the commonplaces of modern popular science) is in itself, apart from somebody's eyes and tongue and ears and touch, neither colored nor tasteful, neither cool nor warm, neither light nor dark, neither musical nor silent. All these qualities belong to our ideas, being indeed none the less genuine facts for that, but being in so far ideal facts. We must see colors when we look, we must hear music when there is playing in our presence; but this *must* is a must that consists in a certain irrestible presence of an idea in us under certain conditions. *That* this idea must come is, indeed, a truth as unalterable, once more, as the king's settled remorse in "Hamlet." But like this remorse, again, it exists as an ideal truth, objective, but through and through objective *for* somebody, and not *apart from* anybody.

What this truth implies we have yet to see. So far it is only an ideal truth for the beholder, with just the bare possibility that behind it all there is the thought of a world-spirit. And, in fact, *so* far we must all go together if we reflect.

But now, at this point, the Berkeleyan idealist goes one step further. The real outside world that is still left unexplained and unanalyzed after its beauty, its warmth, its odors, its tastes, its colors, and its tones, have been relegated to the realm of ideal truths, what do you now *mean* by calling it real? No doubt it *is* known as somehow real, but *what* is this reality *known as* being? If you know that this world is still there and outer, as by hypothesis you know, you are bound to say *what* this outer character implies for your thought. And here you have trouble. Is the outer world, as it exists outside of your ideas, or of anybody's ideas, something having shape, filling space, possessing solidity, full of moving things? That would in the first place seem evident. The sound isn't outside of me, but the sound-waves, you say, are. The colors are ideal facts; but the ether-waves don't need a mind to know them. Warmth is ideal, but the physical fact called heat, this playing to and fro of molecules, is real, and is there apart from any mind. But once more, *is* this so evident? What do I *mean* by the shape of anything, or by the size of anything? Don't I mean just the idea of shape or of size that I am obliged to get under certain circumstances? What is the meaning of any property that I give to the real outer world? How can I express that property except in case I think it in terms of my ideas? As for the sound-waves and the ether-waves, what are they but things ideally conceived to explain the facts of nature? The conceptions have doubtless their truth, but it is an ideal truth. What I mean by saying that the things yonder have shape and size and trembling molecules, and that there is air with sound-waves, and ether with light-waves in it, — what I *mean* by all this is that experience forces upon me, directly or indirectly, a vast system of ideas, which may indeed be founded in truth beyond me, which in fact *must* be founded in such truth if my experience has any sense, but which, like my ideas of color and of warmth, are simply expressions of how the world's order must appear to me, and to anybody constituted like me. Above all, is this plain about space. The real things, I say, outside of me, fill space, and move about in it. But what do I mean by space? Only a vast system of ideas which experience and my own mind force upon me. Doubtless these ideas have a validity. They have *this* validity, that I, at all events, when I look upon the world, am bound to see it in space, as much bound as the king in "Hamlet" was, when he looked within, to see himself as guilty and unrepentant. But just as his guilt was an idea, — a crushing, an irresistible, an overwhelming idea, — but still just an idea, so, too, the space in which I place my world is one great formal idea of mine. That is just why I can describe it to other people. "It has three dimensions," I say, "length, breadth, depth." I describe each. I form, I convey, I construct, an idea of it through them. I know space, as an idea, very well. I can compute all sorts of unseen truths about the relations of its parts. I am sure that you, too, share this idea. But, then, for all of us alike it is just an idea; and when we put our world into space, and call it real there, we simply think one idea into another idea, not voluntarily, to be sure, but inevitably, and yet without leaving the realm of ideas.

Thus, all the reality that *we* attribute to our world, in so far as *we* know and can tell what we mean thereby, becomes ideal. There is, in fact, a certain system of ideas, forced upon us by experience, which we have to use as the guide of our conduct. This system of ideas we can't change by our wish; it is for us as overwhelming a fact as guilt, or as the bearing of our fellows towards us, but we know it only *as* such a system of ideas. And we call it the world of matter. John Stuart Mill very well expressed the puzzle of the whole thing, as we have now reached the statement of this puzzle, when he called matter a mass of "permanent possibilities of experience" for each of us. Mill's definition has its faults, but it is a very fair beginning. You know matter as something that either now gives you this idea or experience, or that would give you some other idea or experience under other circumstances. A fire, while it burns, is for you a permanent possibility of either getting the idea of an agreeable warmth, or of getting the idea of a bad burn, and you treat it accordingly. A precipice amongst mountains is a permanent possibility of your experiencing a fall, or of your getting a feeling of the exciting or of the sublime in mountain scenery. You have no experience just now of the tropics or of the poles, but both tropical and polar climates exist in your world as permanent possibilities of experience. When you call the sun 92,000,000 miles away, you mean that between you and the sun (that is, between your present experience and the possible experience of the sun's surface) there would inevitably lie the actually inaccessible, but still numerically conceivable series of experiences of distance expressed by the number of miles in question. In short, your whole attitude towards the real world may be summed up by saying: "I have experiences now which I seem bound to have, experiences of color, sound, and all the rest of my present ideas; and I am also bound by experience to believe that in case I did certain things (for instance, touched the wall, traveled to the tropics, visited Europe, studied physics), I then should get, in a determinate order, dependent wholly upon *what* I had done, certain other experiences (for instance, experiences of the wall's solidity, or of a tropical climate, or of the scenes of an European tour, or of the facts of physics)." And this acceptance of actual experience, this belief in possible experience, constitutes all that you mean by your faith in the outer world.

But, you say, Is not, then, all this faith of ours after all well founded? Isn't there really something yonder that corresponds in fact to this series of experiences in us? Yes, indeed, there no doubt is. But what if this, which so shall correspond without us to the ideas within us, what if this hard and fast reality should itself be a system of ideas, outside of our minds but not outside of every mind? As the maiden's disdain is outside the rejected lover's mind, unchangeable so far for him, but not on that account the less ideal, not the less a fact in a mind, as, to take afresh a former fashion of illustration, the price of a security or the objective existence of this lecture is an ideal fact, but real and external for the individual person, — even so why might not this world beyond us, this "permanent possibility of experience," be in essence itself a system of ideal experiences of some standard thought of which ours is only the copy? Nay, must it not be such a system in case it has any reality at all? For, after all, isn't this precisely what our analysis brings us to? Nothing whatever can I say about my world yonder that I do not express in terms of mind. *What* things are, extended, moving, colored, tuneful, majestic, beautiful, holy, *what* they are in any aspect of their nature, mathematical, logical, physical, sensuously pleasing, spiritually valuable, all this must mean for me only something that I have to express in the fashion of ideas. The more I am to know my world, the more of a mind I must have for the purpose. The closer I come to the truth about the things, the more ideas I get. Isn't it plain, then, that *if* my world yonder is anything knowable at all, it must be in and for itself essentially a mental world? Are my ideas to *resemble* in any way the world? Is the truth of my thought to consist in its *agreement* with reality? And am I thus capable, as common sense supposes, of *conforming* my ideas to things? Then reflect. What can, after all, so well agree with an idea as another idea? To what can things that go on in my mind conform unless it be to another mind? If the more my mind grows in mental clearness, the nearer it gets to the nature of reality, then surely the reality that my mind thus resembles must be in itself mental.

After all, then, would it deprive the world here about me of reality, nay, would it not rather save and assure the reality and the knowableness of my world of experience, if I said that this world, as it exists outside of my mind, and of any other human minds, exists in and for a standard, an universal mind, whose system of ideas simply constitutes the world? Even if I fail to prove that there is such a mind, do I not at least thus make plausible that, as I said, our world of common sense has no fact in it which we cannot interpret in terms of ideas, so that this world is throughout such stuff as ideas are made of? To say this, as you see, in no wise deprives our world of its due share of reality. If the standard mind knows now that its ideal fire has the quality of burning those who touch it, and if I in my finitude am bound to conform in my experiences to the thoughts of this standard mind, then in case I touch that fire I shall surely get the idea of a burn. The standard mind will be at least as hard and fast and real in its ideal consistency as is the maiden in her disdain for the rejected lover; and I, in presence of the ideal stars and the oceans, will see the genuine realities of fate as certainly as the lover hears his fate in the voice that expresses her will.

I need not now proceed further with an analysis that will be more or less familiar to many of you, especially after our foregoing historical lectures. What I have desired thus far is merely to give each of you, as it were, the sensation of being an idealist in this first and purely analytical sense of the word idealism. The sum and substance of it all is, you see, this: you know your world in fact as a system of ideas about things, such that from moment to moment you find this system forced upon you by experience. Even matter you know just as a mass of coherent ideas that you cannot help having. Space and time, as you think them, are surely ideas of yours. Now, what is more natural than to say that *if* this be so, the real world beyond you must in itself be a system of somebody's ideas? If it is, then you can comprehend what its existence means. If it isn't, then since all you can know of it is ideal, the real world must be utterly unknowable, a bare *x*. Minds I can understand, because I myself am a mind. An existence that has no mental attribute is wholly opaque to me. So far, however, from such a world of ideas, existent beyond me in another mind, seeming to coherent thought essentially *un*real, ideas and minds and their ways, are, on the contrary, the hardest and stubbornest facts that we can name. *If* the external world is in itself mental, then, be this reality a standard and universal thought, or a mass of little atomic minds constituting the various particles of matter, in any case one can comprehend what it is, and will have at the same time to submit to its stubborn authority as the lover accepts the reality of the maiden's moods. If the world *isn't* such an ideal thing, then indeed all our science, which is through and through concerned with our mental interpretations of things, can neither have objective validity, nor make satisfactory progress towards truth. For as science is concerned with ideas, the world beyond all ideas is a bare *x*.

III

But with this bare *x* you will say, this analytical idealism after all leaves me, as with something that, spite of all my analyses and interpretations, may after all be there beyond me as the real world, which my ideas are vainly striving to reach, but which eternally flees before me. So far, you will say, what idealism teaches is that the real world can only be interpreted by treating it as if it were somebody's thought. So regarded, the idealism of Berkeley and of other such thinkers is very suggestive; yet it doesn't tell us what the true world is, but only that *so much* of the true world as we ever get into our comprehension has to be conceived in ideal terms. Perhaps, however, whilst neither beauty, nor majesty, nor odor, nor warmth, nor fame, nor color, nor form, nor motion, nor space, nor time (all these being but ideas of ours), can be said to belong to the extra-mental world, — perhaps, after all, there does exist there yonder an extra-mental world, which has nothing to do, except by accident, with *any* mind, and which is through and through just extra-mental, something unknowable, inscrutable, the basis of experience, the source of ideas, but itself never experienced as it is in itself, never adequately represented by any idea in us. Perhaps it is there. Yes, you will say, *must* it not be there? Must not one accept our limitations once for all, and say, "What reality is, we can never hope to make clear to ourselves. That which has been made clear becomes an idea in us. But always there is the beyond, the mystery, the inscrutable, the real, the *x*. To be sure, perhaps we can't even know so much as that this *x* after all does exist. But then we feel bound to regard it as existent; or even if we doubt or deny it, may it not be there all the same?" In such doubt and darkness, then, this first form of idealism closes. If that were all there were to say, I should indeed have led you a long road in vain. Analyzing what the known world is for you, in case there is haply any world known to you at all, — this surely isn't proving that there is any real world, or that the real world can be known. Are we not just where we started?

No; there lies now just ahead of us the goal of a synthetic idealistic conception, which will not be content with this mere analysis of the colors and forms of things, and with the mere discovery that all these are for us nothing but ideas. In this second aspect, idealism grows bolder, and fears not the profoundest doubt that may have entered your mind as to whether there is any world at all, or as to whether it is in any fashion knowable. State in full the deepest problem, the hardest question about the world that your thought ever conceived. In this new form idealism offers you a suggestion that indeed will not wholly answer nor do away with every such problem, but that certainly will set the meaning of it in a new light. What this new light is, I must in conclusion seek to illustrate.

Note the point we have reached. *Either,* as you see, your real world yonder is through and through a world of ideas, an outer mind that you are more or less comprehending through your experience, *or else,* in so far as it is real and outer it is unknowable, an inscrutable x, an absolute mystery. The dilemma is perfect. There is no third alternative. Either a mind yonder, or else the unknowable; that is your choice. Philosophy loves such dilemmas, wherein all the mightiest interests of the spirit, all the deepest longings of human passion, are at stake, waiting as for the fall of a die. Philosophy loves such situations, I say, and loves, too, to keep its scrutiny as cool in the midst of them as if it were watching a game of chess, instead of the great world-game. Well, try the darker choice that the dilemma gives you. The world yonder shall be an x, an unknowable something, outer, problematic, foreign, opaque. And you, — you shall look upon it and believe in it. Yes, you shall for argument's sake first put on an air of resigned confidence, and say, "I do not only fancy it to be an extra-mental and unknowable something there, an impenetrable x, but I know it to be such. I can't help it. I didn't make it unknowable. I regret the fact. But there it is. I have to admit its existence. But I know that I shall never solve the problem of its nature." Ah, its nature is a *problem,* then. But what do you mean by this *"problem"*? Problems are, after a fashion, rather familiar things, — that is, in the world of ideas. There are problems soluble and problems insoluble in that world of ideas. It is a soluble problem if one asks what whole number is the square root of 64. The answer is 8. It is an insoluble problem if one asks me to find what whole number is the square root of 65. There is, namely, no such whole number. If one asks me to name the length of a straight line that shall be equal to the circumference of a circle of a known radius, that again, in the world of ideas, is an insoluble problem, because, as can be proved, the circumference of a circle is a length that cannot possibly be exactly expressed in terms of any statable number when the radius is of a stated length. So in the world of ideas, problems are definite questions which can be asked in knowable terms. Fair questions of this sort either may be fairly answered in our present state of knowledge, or else they could be answered if we knew a little or a good deal more, or finally they could not possibly be answered. But in the latter case, if they could not possibly be answered, they always must resemble the problem how to square the circle. They then always turn out, namely, to be absurdly stated questions, and it is their absurdity that makes these problems absolutely insoluble. Any fair question could be answered by one who knew enough. No fair question has an unknowable answer. But now, *if* your unknowable world out there is a thing of wholly, of absolutely problematic and inscrutable nature, is it so because you don't *yet* know enough about it, or because in its very nature and essence it is an absurd thing, an *x* that *would* answer a question, which actually it is nonsense to ask? Surely one must choose the former alternative. The real world may be unknown; it can't be essentially unknowable.

This subtlety is wearisome enough, I know, just here, but I shall not dwell long upon it. Plainly *if* the unknowable world out there is through and through in its nature a really inscrutable problem, this must mean that in nature it resembles such problems as, What is the whole number that is the square root of 65? Or, What two adjacent hills are there that have no valley between them? For in the world of thought such are the *only* insoluble problems. All others either may now be solved, or would be solved if we knew more than we now do. But, once more, *if* this unknowable is only just the real world as now unknown to us, but capable some time of becoming known, then remember that, as we have just seen, only a mind can ever become an object known to a mind. If I know you as external to me, it is only because you are minds. If I can come to know *any* truth, it is only in so far as this truth is essentially mental, is an idea, is a thought, that I can ever come to know it. Hence, if that so-called unknowable, that unknown outer world there, ever could, by any device, come within our ken, then it is already an ideal world. For just that is what our whole idealistic analysis has been proving. Only ideas are knowable. And nothing absolutely unknowable can exist. For the absolutely unknowable, the *x* pure and simple, the Kantian thing in itself, simply cannot be admitted. The notion of it is nonsense. The assertion of it is a contradiction. Round-squares, and sugar salt-lumps, and Snarks, and Boojums, and Jabberwocks, and Abracadabras; such, I insist, are the only unknowables there are. The unknown, that which our human and finite selfhood hasn't grasped, exists spread out before us in a boundless world of truth; but the unknowable is essentially, confessedly, *ipso facto* a fiction.

The nerve of our whole argument in the foregoing is now pretty fairly exposed. We have seen that the outer truth must be, if anything, a "possibility of experience." But we may now see that a *bare* "possibility" as such, is, like the unknowable, something meaningless. That which, whenever I come to know it, turns out to be through and through an idea, an experience, must be in itself, before I know it, either somebody's idea, somebody's experience, or it must be nothing. What is a "possibility" of experience that is outside of me, and that is still nothing *for* any one else than myself? Isn't it a bare *x*, a nonsense phrase? Isn't it like an unseen color, an untasted taste, an unfelt feeling? In proving that the world is one of "possible" experience, we have proved that in so far as it is real it is one of actual experience.

Once more, then, to sum up here, *if,* however vast the world of the unknown, only the essentially knowable can exist, and *if* everything knowable is an idea, a mental somewhat, the content of some mind, then once for all we are the world of ideas. Your deepest doubt proves this. Only the nonsense of that inscrutable *x*, of that Abracadabra, of that Snark, the Unknowable of whose essence you make your real world, prevents you from seeing this.

To return, however, to our dilemma. *Either* idealism, we said, *or* the unknowable. What we have now said is that the absolutely unknowable is essentially an absurdity, a non-existent. For any fair and statable problem admits of an answer. *If* the world exists yonder, its essence is then already capable of being known by some mind. If capable of being known by a mind, this essence is then already essentially ideal and mental. A mind that knew the real world would, for instance, find it a something possessing qualities. But qualities are ideal existences, just as much as are the particular qualities called odors or tones or colors. A mind knowing the real world would again find in it relations, such as equality and inequality, attraction and repulsion, likeness and unlikeness. But such relations have no meaning except as objects of a mind. In brief, then, the world as known would be found to be a world that had all the while been ideal and mental, even before it became known to the particular mind that we are to conceive as coming into connection with it. Thus, then, we are driven to the second alternative. The real world must be a mind, or else a group of minds.

IV

But with this result we come in presence of a final problem. All this, you say, depends upon my assurance that there is after all a real and therefore an essentially knowable and rational world yonder. Such a world would have to be in essence a mind, or a world of minds. But after all, how does one ever escape from the prison of the inner life? Am I not in all this merely wandering amidst the realm of my own ideas? *My* world, of course, isn't and can't be a mere *x*, an essentially unknowable thing, just because it *is my* world, and I have an idea of it. But then does not this mean that *my* world is, after all, forever just *my* world, so that I never get to any truth beyond myself? Isn't this result very disheartening? My world is thus a world of ideas, but alas! how do I then ever reach those ideas of the minds beyond me?

The answer is a simple, but in one sense a very problematic one. You, in one sense, namely, never *do* or can get beyond your own ideas, nor ought you to wish to do so, because in truth all those other minds that constitute your outer and real world are in essence one with your own self. This whole world of ideas is essentially *one* world, and so it is essentially the world of one self and *That art Thou.*

The truth and meaning of this deepest proposition of all idealism is now not at all remote from us. The considerations, however, upon which it depends are of the dryest possible sort, as commonplace as they are deep.

Whatever objects you may think about, whether they are objects directly known to you, or objects infinitely far removed, objects in the distant stars, or objects remote in time, or objects near and present, — such objects, then, as a number with fifty places of digits in it, or the mountains on the other side of the moon, or the day of your death, or the character of Cromwell, or the law of gravitation, or a name that you are just now trying to think of and have forgotten, or the meaning of some mood or feeling or idea now in your mind, — all such objects, I insist, stand in a certain constant and curious relation to your mind whenever you are thinking about them, — a relation that we often miss because it is so familiar. What is this relation? Such an object, while you think about it, needn't be, as popular thought often supposes it to be, the *cause* of your thoughts concerning it. Thus, when you think about Cromwell's character, Cromwell's character isn't just now *causing* any ideas in you, — isn't, so to speak, doing anything to you. Cromwell is dead, and after life's fitful fever his character is a very inactive thing. Not as the *cause,* but as the *object* of your thought is Cromwell present to you. Even so, if you choose now to think of the moment of your death, that moment is somewhere off there in the future, and you can make it your object, but it isn't now an active cause of your ideas. The moment of your death has no present physical existence at all, and just now causes nothing. So, too, with the mountains on the other side of the moon. When you make them the object of your thought, they remain indifferent to you. They do not affect you. You never saw them. But all the same you can think about them.

Yet this thinking *about* things is, after all, a very curious relation in which to stand to things. In order to think *about* a thing, it is *not* enough that I should have an idea in me that merely resembles that thing. This last is a very important observation. I repeat, it is *not* enough that I should merely have an idea in me that resembles the thing whereof I think. I have, for instance, in me the idea of a pain. Another man has a pain just like mine. Say we both have toothache; or have both burned our finger-tips in the same way. Now my idea of pain is just like the pain in him, but I am not on that account necessarily thinking about *his* pain, merely because what I am thinking about, namely my own pain, resembles his pain. No; to think about an object you must not merely have an idea that resembles the object, but you must *mean* to have your idea resemble that object. Stated in other form, to think of an object you must consciously aim at that object, you must pick out that object, you must already in some measure possess that object enough, namely, to identify it as what you mean. But how can you *mean,* how can you *aim at,* how can you *possess,* how can you *pick out,* how can you *identify* what is not already present in essence to your own hidden self? Here is surely a deep question. When you aim at yonder object, be it the mountains in the moon or the day of your death, you really say, "I, as my real self, as my larger self, as my complete consciousness, already in deepest truth possess that object, have it, own it, identify it. And that, and that alone, makes it possible for me in my transient, my individual, my momentary personality, to mean yonder object, to inquire about it, to be partly aware of it and partly ignorant of it." You can't mean what is utterly foreign to you. You mean an object, you assert about it, you talk about it, yes, you doubt or wonder about it, you admit your private and individual ignorance about it, only in so far as your larger self, your deeper personality, your total of normal consciousness already *has* that object. Your momentary and private wonder, ignorance, inquiry, or assertion, about the object, implies, asserts, presupposes, that your total self is in full and immediate possession of the object. This, in fact, is the very nature of that curious relation of a thought to an object which we are not considering. The self that is doubting or asserting, or that is even feeling its private ignorance about an object, and that still, even in consequence of all this, is *meaning,* is *aiming at* such object, is in essence identical with the self for which this object exists in its complete and consciously known truth.

So paradoxical seems this final assertion of idealism that I cannot hope in one moment to make it very plain to you. It is a difficult topic, about which I have elsewhere printed a very lengthy research, wherewith I cannot here trouble you. But what I intend by thus saying that the self which thinks about an object, which really, even in the midst of the blindest ignorance and doubt concerning its object still means the object, — that this self is identical with the deeper self which possesses and truly knows the object, — what I intend hereby I can best illustrate by simple cases taken from your own experience. You are in doubt, say, about a name that you have forgotten, or about a thought that you just had, but that has now escaped you. As you hunt for the name or the lost idea, you are all the while sure that you mean just one particular name or idea and no other. But you don't yet know what name or idea this is. You try, and reject name after name. You query, "Was this what I was thinking of, or this?" But after searching you erelong find the name or the idea, and now at once you *recognize* it. "Oh, that," you say, "was what I meant all along, only—I didn't know what I meant." Did not know? Yes, in one sense you knew all the while, —that is, your deeper self, your true consciousness knew. It was your momentary self that did not know. But when you found the long-sought name, recalled the lost idea, you recognized it at once, because it was all the while your own, because you, the true and larger self, who owned the name or the idea and were aware of what it was, now were seen to include the smaller and momentary self that sought the name or tried to recall the thought. Your deeper consciousness of the lost idea was all the while there. In fact, did you not presuppose this when you sought the lost idea? How can I mean a name, or an idea, unless I in truth am the self who knows the name, who possesses the idea? In hunting for the name or the lost idea, I am hunting for my own thought. Well, just so I know nothing about the far-off stars in detail, but in so far as I mean the far-off stars at all, as I speak of them, I am identical with that remote and deep thought of my own that already knows the stars. When I study the stars, I am trying to find out what I really mean by them. To be sure, only experience can tell me, but that is because only experience can bring me into relation with my larger self. The escape from the prison of the inner self is simply the fact that the inner self is through and through an appeal to a larger self. The self that inquires, either inquires without meaning, or if it has a meaning, this meaning exists in and for the larger self that knows.

Here is a suggestion of what I mean by Synthetic Idealism. No truth, I repeat, is more familiar. That I am always meaning to inquire into objects beyond me, what clearer fact could be mentioned? That only in case it is already I who, in deeper truth, in my real and hidden thought, *know* the lost object yonder, the object whose nature I seek to comprehend, that only in this case I can truly *mean* the thing yonder, – this, as we must assert, is involved in the very idea of *meaning*. That is the logical analysis of it. You can mean what your deeper self knows; you cannot mean what your deeper self doesn't know. To be sure, the complete illustration of this most critical insight of idealism belongs elsewhere. Few see the familiar. Nothing is more common than for people to think that they mean objects that have nothing to do with themselves. Kant it was, who, despite his things in themselves, first showed us that nobody really means an object, really knows it, or doubts it, or aims at it, unless he does so by aiming at a truth that is present to his own larger self. Except for the unity of my true self, taught Kant, I have no objects. And so it makes no difference whether I know a thing or am in doubt about it. So long as I really *mean* it, that is enough. The self that *means* the object is identical with the larger self that possesses the object, just as when you seek the lost idea you are already in essence with the self that possesses the lost idea.

In this way I suggest to you the proof which a rigid analysis of the logic of our most commonplace thought would give for the doctrine that in the world there is but *one* Self, and that it is *his* world which we all alike are truly meaning, whether we talk of one another or of Cromwell's character or of the fixed stars or of the far-off aeons of the future. The relation of my thought to its object has, I insist, this curious character, that *unless* the thought and its object are parts of one larger thought, I can't even be *meaning* that object yonder, can't even be in error about it, can't even doubt its existence. You, for instance, are part of one larger self with me, or else I can't even be meaning to address you as outer beings. You are part of one larger self along with the most mysterious or most remote fact of nature, along with the moon, and all the hosts of heaven, along with all truth and all beauty. Else could you not even intend to speak of such objects beyond you. For whatever you speak of you will find that your world is meant by you as just your world. Talk of the unknowable, and it forthwith becomes your unknowable, your problem, whose solution, unless the problem be a mere nonsense question, your larger self must own and be aware of. The deepest problem of life, "What is this deeper self?" And the only answer is, *It is the self that knows in unity all truth.*

This, I insist, is no hypothesis. It is actually the presupposition of your deepest doubt. And that is why I say: Everything finite is more or less obscure, dark, doubtful. Only the Infinite Self, the problem-solver, the complete thinker, the one who knows what we mean even when we are most confused and ignorant, the one who includes us, who has the world present to himself in unity, before whom all past and future truth, all distant and dark truth is clear in one eternal moment, to whom far and forgot is near, who thinks the whole of nature, and in whom are all things, the Logos, the world-possessor, — only his existence, I say, is perfectly sure.

V

Yet I must not state the outcome thus confidently without a little more analysis and exemplification. Let me put the whole matter in a slightly different way. When a man believes that he knows any truth about a fact beyond his present and momentary thought, what is the position, with reference to that fact, which he gives himself? We must first answer, He believes that one who really knew his, the thinker's, thought, and compared it with the fact yonder, would perceive the agreement between the two. Is this *all*, however, that the believer holds to be true of his own thought? No, not so, for he holds not only that his thought, as it is, agrees with *some* fact outside his present self (as my thought, for instance, of my toothache may agree with the fact yonder called my neighbor's toothache), but also that his thought agrees with the fact with which it *meant* to agree. To *mean* to agree, however, with a specific fact beyond my present self, involves such a relation to that fact that if I could somehow come directly into the presence of the fact itself, could somehow absorb it into my present consciousness, I should become immediately aware of it as the fact that I all along had meant. Our previous examples have been intended to bring clearly before us this curious and in fact unique character of the relation called *meaning* an object of our thought. To return, then, to our supposed believer: he believes that he *knows* some fact beyond his present consciousness. This involves, as we have now seen, the assertion that he believes himself to stand in such an actual relation to the fact yonder that were it in, instead of out of his present consciousness, he would recognize it both as the object *meant* by his present thought, and also as in agreement therewith; and it is all this which, as he believes, an immediate observer of his own thought and of the object — that is, an observer who should include our believer's present self, and the fact yonder, and who should reflect on their relations — would find as the real relation. Observe, however, that only by *reflection* would this higher observer find out that real relation. Nothing but Reflective Self-consciousness could discover it. To believe that you know anything beyond your present and momentary self, is, therefore, to believe that you do stand in such a relation to truth as only a larger and reflectively observant self, that included you and your object, could render intelligible. Or once more, so to believe is essentially to appeal confidently to a possible larger self for approval. But now to say, I know a truth, and yet to say, This larger self to whom I appeal is appealed to only as to a possible self, that needn't be real, — all this involves just the absurdity against which our whole idealistic analysis has been directed in case of all the sorts of fact and truth in the world. To believe, is to say, I stand in a *real* relation to truth, a relation which transcends wholly my present momentary self; and this real relation is of such a curious nature that only a larger inclusive self which consciously reflected upon my meaning and consciously possessed the object that I mean, could know or grasp the reality of the relation. If, however, this *relation* is a real one, it must, like the colors, the sounds, and all the other things of which we spoke before be real *for* somebody. Bare possibilities are nothing. Really possible things are already in some sense real. If, then, my relation to the truth, this complex relation of meaning an object and conforming to it, when the object, although at this moment meant by me, is not now present to my momentary thought, — if this relation is genuine, and yet is such as only a possible larger self could render intelligible, then my possible larger self must be real in order that my momentary self should in fact possess the truth in question. Or, in briefest form, The relation of conforming one's thought to an outer object meant by this thought is a relation which only a Reflective Larger Self could grasp or find real. If the relation is real, the larger self is real, too.

So much, then, for the case when one *believes* that one has grasped a truth beyond the moment. But now for the case when one is actually in *error* about some object of his momentary and finite thought. Error is the actual failure to agree, not with any fact taken at random, but with just the fact that one had meant to agree with. Under what circumstances, then, is error possible? Only in case one's real thought, by virtue of its meaning, does transcend his own momentary and in so far ignorant self. As the true believer, meaning the truth that he believes, must be in real relation thereto, even so the blunderer, really meaning, as he does, the fact yonder, in order that he should be able even to blunder about it, must be, in so far, in the same real relation to truth as the true believer. His error lies in missing that conformity with the meant object at which he aimed. None the less, however, did he really mean and really aim; and, therefore, he is in error, because his real and larger self finds him to be so. True thinking and false thinking alike involve, then, the same fundamental conditions, in so far as both are carried on in moments; and in so far as, in both cases, the false moment and the true are such by virtue of being organic parts of a larger, critical, reflective, and so conscious self.

To sum up so far: Of no object do I speak either falsely or truly, unless I mean that object. Never do I mean an object, unless I stand in such relation thereto that were the object in this conscious moment, and immediately present to me, I should myself recognize it as completing and fulfilling my present and momentary meaning. The relation of meaning an object is thus one that only conscious Reflection can define, or observe, or constitute. No merely *foreign* observer, no external test, could decide upon what is meant at any moment. Therefore, when what is meant is outside of the moment which means, only a Self inclusive of the moment and its object could complete, and so confirm or refute, the opinion that the moment contains. Really to mean an object, then, whether in case of true opinion or in case of false opinion, involves the real possibility of such a reflective test of one's meaning from the point of view of a larger self. But to say, My relation to the object is such that a reflective self, and *only* such a reflective and inclusive self, could see that I meant the object, is to assert a fact, a relation, an existent truth in the world, that either is a truth for nobody, or is a truth for an actual reflective self, inclusive of the moment, and critical of its meaning. Our whole idealistic analysis, however, from the beginning of this discussion, has been to the effect that facts must be facts for somebody, and can't be facts for nobody, and that *bare* possibilities are really impossible. Hence whoever believes, whether truly or falsely, about objects beyond the moment of his belief, is an organic part of a reflective and conscious larger self that has those objects immediately present to itself, and has them in organic relation with the erring or truthful momentary self that believes.

Belief, true and false, having been examined, the case of doubt follows at once. To doubt about objects beyond my momentary self is to admit the "possibility of error" as to such objects. Error would involve my inclusion in a larger self that has directly present to it the object meant by me as I doubt. Truth would involve the same inclusion. The inclusion itself, then, is, so far, no object of rational doubt. To doubt the inclusion would be merely to doubt whether I meant anything at all beyond the moment, and not to doubt as to my particular knowledge about the *nature* of some object beyond, when once the object had been supposed to be meant. Doubt presupposes then, whenever it is a definite doubt, the real possibility, and so, in the last analysis, the reality of the normal self-consciousness that possesses the object concerning which one doubts.

But if, passing to the extreme of skepticism, and stating one's most despairing and most uncompromising doubt, one so far confines himself to the prison of the inner life as to doubt whether one ever does mean any object beyond the moment at all, there comes the final consideration that in doubting one's power to transcend the moment, one has already transcended the moment, just as we found in following Hegel's analysis. To say, It is impossible to mean any object beyond this moment of my thought, and the moment is for itself "the measure of all things," is at all events to give a meaning to the words *this moment*. And *this moment* means something only in opposition to *other* moments. Yes, even in saying *this moment,* I have already left this moment, and am meaning and speaking of a past moment. Moreover, to deny that one can mean an object "beyond the moment" is already to give a meaning to the phrase *beyond the moment,* and then to deny that anything is meant to fall within the scope of this meaning. In every case, then, one must transcend by one's meaning the moment to which one is confined by one's finitude.

Flee where we will, then, the net of the larger Self ensnares us. We are lost and imprisoned in the thickets of its tangled labyrinth. The moments are not at all in themselves, for as moments they have no meaning; they exist only in relation to the beyond. The larger Self alone is, and they are by reason of it, organic parts of it. They perish, but it remains; they have truth or error only in its overshadowing presence.

And now, as to the unity of this Self. Can there be many such organic selves, mutually separate unities of moments and of the objects that these moments mean? Nay, were there *many* such, would not their manifoldness be a truth? Their relations, would not these be real? Their distinct places in the world-order, would not these things be objects of possible true or false thoughts? If so, must not there be once more the inclusive real Self for whom these truths were true, these separate selves interrelated, and their variety absorbed in the organism of its rational meaning?

There is, then, at last, but one Self, organically, reflectively, consciously inclusive of all the selves, and so of all truth. I have called this self, Logos, problem-solver, all-knower. Consider, then, last of all, his relation to problems. In the previous lecture we doubted many things; we questioned the whole seeming world of the outer order; we wondered as to space and time, as to nature and evolution, as to the beginning and the end of things. Now he who wonders is like him who doubts. Has his wonder any rationality about it? Does he *mean* anything by his doubt? Then the truth that he means, and about which he wonders, has its real constitution. As wonderer, he in the moment possesses not this solving truth; he appeals to the self who can solve. That self must possess the solution just as surely as the problem has a meaning. The real nature of space and time, the real beginning of things, where matter was at any point of time in the past, what is to become of the world's energy: these are matters of truth, and truth is necessarily present to the Self as in one all-comprehending self-completed moment, beyond which is naught, within which is the world.

The world, then, is such stuff as ideas are made of. Thought possesses all things. But the world isn't unreal. It extends infinitely beyond our private consciousness, because it is the world of an universal mind. What facts it is to contain only experience can inform us. There is no magic that can anticipate the work of science. Absolutely the *only* thing sure from the first about this world, however, is that it is intelligent, rational, orderly, essentially comprehensible, so that all its problems are somewhere solved, all its darkest mysteries are known to the supreme Self. This Self infinitely and reflectively transcends our consciousness, and therefore, since it includes us, it is at the very least a person, and more definitely conscious than we are; for what it possesses is self-reflecting knowledge, and what is knowledge aware of itself, but consciousness? Beyond the seeming wreck and chaos of our finite problems, its eternal insight dwells, therefore, in absolute and supreme majesty. Yet it is not far from every one of us. There is no least or most transient thought that flits through a child's mind, or that troubles with the faintest line of care a maiden's face, and that still does not contain and embody something of this divine Logos.

Study Questions

1. What is scientific agnosticism? How, according to Royce, is idealism compatible with it?
2. What are the two aspects of idealism?
3. How does Royce go about arguing for the first aspect? State his argument(s).
4. What leads Royce to bring up the "real world yonder"?
5. He says that that real world can be only one of two things. What are they?
6. He rejects one of these. Why?
7. In the final sections, Royce argues for the existence of an Infinite Self. He claims that (a) thinking requires the existence of such a self, and (b) that knowledge does. State his arguments.
8. What are the main theses of Royce's idealism?

Selected Bibliography

Bradley, F. H. *Appearance and Reality*. Oxford: Oxford University Press, 1893. [Difficult, but an important work. Chapter 26 could be read as a somewhat self-contained work].

Ewing, A. C. *The Idealist Tradition*. Glencoe: Free Press, 1957. [Good selections by idealists from the eighteenth to the twentieth centuries.]

Muelder, W. G. and Sears, Laurence. *The Development of American Philosophy*. Boston: Houghton-Mifflin, 1940. Part Five. [Selections by a number of American idealists; suitable for a beginning student.]

Royce, Josiah. *The Spirit of Modern Philosophy*. New York: W. W. Norton, 1967. [Originally published in 1892. The selection in this volume is one chapter of Royce's book.]

Pragmatism

2. How to Make Our Ideas Clear

C. S. Peirce

Whoever has looked into a modern treatise on logic of the common sort, will doubtless remember the two distinctions between *clear* and *obscure* conceptions, and between *distinct* and *confused* conceptions. They have lain in the books now for nigh two centuries, unimproved and unmodified, and are generally reckoned by logicians as among the gems of their doctrine.

A clear idea is defined as one which is so apprehended that it will be recognized wherever it is met with, and so that no other will be mistaken for it. If it fails of this clearness, it is said to be obscure.

This is rather a neat bit of philosophical terminology; yet, since it is clearness that they were defining, I wish the logicians had made their definition a little more plain. Never to fail to recognize an idea, and under no circumstances to mistake another for it, let it come in how recondite a form it may, would indeed imply such prodigious force and clearness of intellect as is seldom met with in this world. On the other hand, merely to have such an acquaintance with the idea as to have become familiar with it, and to have lost all hesitancy in recognizing it in ordinary cases, hardly seems to deserve the name of clearness of apprehension, since after all it only amounts to a subjective feeling of mastery which may be entirely mistaken. I take it, however, that when the logicians speak of "clearness," they mean nothing more than such a familiarity with an idea, since they regard the quality as but a small merit, which needs to be supplemented by another, which they call *distinctness*.

A distinct idea is defined as one which contains nothing which is not clear. This is technical language; by the *contents* of an idea logicians understand whatever is contained in its definition. So that an idea is *distinctly* apprehended, according to them, when we can give a precise definition of it, in abstract terms. Here the professional logicians leave the subject; and I would not have troubled the reader with what they have to say if it were not such a striking example of how they have been slumbering through ages of intellectual activity, listlessly disregarding the enginery of modern thought, and never dreaming of applying its lessons to the improvement of logic. It is easy to show that the doctrine that familiar use and abstract distinctness make the perfection of apprehension, has its only true place in philosophies which have long been extinct; and it is now time to formulate the method of attaining to a more perfect clearness of thought, such as we see and admire in the thinkers of our own time.

When Descartes set about the reconstruction of philosophy, his first step was to (theoretically) permit skepticism and to discard the practice of the schoolmen of looking to authority as the ultimate source of truth. That done, he sought a more natural fountain of true principles, and professed to find it in the human mind; thus passing, in the directest way, from the method of authority to that of apriority, as described in my first paper *(The Fixation of Belief)*. Self-consciousness was to furnish us with our fundamental truths, and to decide what was agreeable to reason. But since, evidently, not all ideas are true, he was led to note, as the first condition of infallibility, that they must be clear. The distinction between an idea *seeming* clear and really being so, never occurred to him. Trusting to introspection, as he did, even for a knowledge of external things, why should he question its testimony in respect to the contents of our own minds? But then, I suppose, seeing men, who seemed to be quite clear and positive, holding opposite opinions upon fundamental principles, he was further led to say that clearness of ideas is not sufficient, but that they need also to be distinct, i.e., to have nothing unclear about them. What he probably meant by this (for he did not explain himself with precision) was that they must sustain the test of dialectical examination; that they must not only seem clear at the outset, but that discussion must never be able to bring to light points of obscurity connected with them.

Such was the distinction of Descartes, and one sees that it was precisely on the level of his philosophy. It was somewhat developed by Leibniz. This great and singular genius was as remarkable for what he failed to see as for what he saw. That a piece of mechanism could not do work perpetually without being fed with power in some form, was a thing perfectly apparent to him; yet he did not understand that the machinery of the mind can only transform knowledge, but never originate it, unless it be fed with facts of observatin. He thus missed the most essential point of the Cartesian philosophy, which is, that to accept proposition which seem perfectly evident to us is a thing which, whether it be logical or illogical, we cannot help doing. Instead of regarding the matter in this way, he sought to reduce the first principles of science to formulas which cannot be denied without self-contradiction, and was apparently unaware of the great difference between his position and that of Descartes.[4] So he reverted to the old formalities of logic, and, above all, abstract definitions played a great part in his philosophy. It was quite natural, therefore, that on observing that the method of Descartes labored under the difficulty that we may seem to ourselves to have clear apprehensions of ideas which in truth are very hazy, no better remedy occurred to him than to require an abstract definition of every important term. Accordingly, in adopting the distinction of *clear* and *distinct* notions, he described the latter quality as the clear apprehension of everything contained in the definition; and the books have ever since copies his words. There is no danger that his chimerical scheme will ever again be overvalued. Nothing new can ever be learned by analyzing definitions. Nevertheless, our existing beliefs can be set in order by this process, and order is an essential element of intellectual economy, as of every other. It may be acknowledged, therefore, that the books are right in making familiarity with a notion the first step toward clearness of apprehension, and the defining of it the second. But in omitting all mention of any higher perspicuity of thought, they simply mirror a philosophy which was exploded a hundred years ago. That much-admired "ornament of logic" — the doctrine of clearness and distinctness — may be pretty enough, but it is high time to relegate to our cabinet of curiosities the antique *bijou,* and to wear about us something better adapted to modern uses.

The very first lesson that we have a right to demand that logic shall teach us is how to make our ideas clear; and a most important one it is, depreciated only by minds who stand in need of it. To know what we think, to be masters of our own meaning, will make a solid foundation for great and weighty thought. It is most easily learned by those whose ideas are meagre and restricted; and far happier they than such as wallow helplessly in a rich mud of conceptions. A nation, it is true, may, in the course of generations, overcome the disadvantage of an excessive wealth of language and its natural concomitant, a vast, unfathomable deep of ideas. We may see it in history, slowly perfecting its literary forms, sloughing at length its metaphysics, and, by virtue of the untirable patience which is often a compensation, attaining great excellence in every branch of mental acquirement. The page of history is not yet unrolled which is to tell us whether such a people will or will not in the long run prevail over one whose ideas (like the words of their language) are few, but which possesses a wonderful mastery over those which it has. For an individual, however, there can be no question that a few clear ideas are worth more than many confused ones. A young man would hardly be persuaded to sacrifice the greater part of his thoughts to save the rest; and the muddled head is the least apt to see the necessity of such a sacrifice. Him we can usually only commiserate, as a person with a congenital defect. Time will help him, but intellectual maturity with regard to clearness comes rather late, an unfortunate arrangement of nature, inasmuch as clearness is of less use to a man settled in life, whose errors have in great measure had their effect, than it would be to one whose path lies before him. It is terrible to see how a single unclear idea, a single formula without meaning, lurking in a young man's head, will sometimes act like an obstruction of inert matter in an artery, hindering the nutrition of the brain, and condemning its victim to pine away in the fullness of his intellectual vigor and in the midst of intellectual plenty. Many a man has cherished for years as his hobby some vague shadow of an idea, too meaningless to be positively false; he has, nevertheless, passionately loved it, has made it his companion by day and by night, and has given to it his strength and his life, leaving all other occupations for its sake, and in short has lived with it and for it, until it has become, as it were, flesh of his flesh and bone of his bone; and then he has waked up some bright morning to find it gone, clean vanished away like the beautiful Melusina of the fable, and the essence of his life gone with it. I have myself known such a man; and who can tell how many histories of circle-squarers, metaphysicians, astrologers, and what not, may not be told in the old German story?

II

The principles set forth in the first of these papers lead, at once, to a method of reaching a clearness of thought of a far higher grade than the "distinctness" of the logicians. We have there found that the action of thought is excited by the irritation of doubt, and ceases when belief is attained; so that the production of belief is the sole function of thought. All these words, however, are too strong for my purpose. It is as if I had described the phenomena as they appear under a mental microscope. Doubt and Belief, as the words are commonly employed, relate to religious or other grave discussions. But here I use them to designate the starting of any question, no matter how small or how great, and the resolution of it. If, for instance, in a horsecar, I pull out my purse and find a five-cent nickel and five coppers, I decide, while my hand is going to the purse, in which way I will pay my fare. To call such a question Doubt, and my decision Belief, is certainly to use words very disproportionate to the occasion. To speak of such a doubt as causing an irritation which needs to be appeased, suggests a temper which is uncomfortable to the verge of insanity. Yet, looking at the matter minutely, it must be admitted that, if there is the least hesitation as to whether I shall pay the five coppers or the nickel (as there will be sure to be, unless I act from some previously contracted habit in the matter), though irritation is too strong a word, yet I am excited to such small mental activity as may be necessary to deciding how I shall act. Most frequently doubts arise from some indecision, however momentary, in our action. Sometimes it is not so. I have, for example, to wait in a railway station, and to pass the time I read the advertisements on the walls, I compare the advantages of different trains and different routes which I never expect to take, merely fancying myself to be in a state of hesitancy, because I am bored with having nothing to trouble me. Feigned hesitancy, whether feigned for mere amusement or with a lofty purpose, plays a great part in the production of scientific inquiry. However the doubt may originate, it stimulates the mind to an activity which may be slight or energetic, calm or turbulent. Images pass rapidly through consciousness, one incessantly melting into another, until at last, when all is over—it may be a fraction of a second, in an hour, or after long years—we find ourselves decided as to how we should act under such circumstances as those which occasioned our hesitation. In other words, we have attained belief.

In this process we observe two sorts of elements of consciousness, the distinction between which may best be made clear by means of an illustration. In a piece of music there are the separate notes, and there is the air. A single tone may be prolonged for an hour or a day, and it exists as perfectly in each second of that time as in the whole taken together; so that, as long as it is sounding, it might be present to a sense from which everything in the past was as completely absent as the future itself. But it is different with the air, the performance of which occupies a certain time, during the portions of which only portions of it are played. It consists in an orderliness in the succession of sounds which strike the ear at different times; and to perceive it there must be some continuity of consciousness which makes the events of a lapse of time present to us. We certainly only perceive the air by hearing the separate notes; yet we cannot be said to directly hear it, for we hear only what is present at the instant, and an orderliness of succession cannot exist in an instant. These two sorts of objects, what we are *immediately* conscious of and what we are *mediately* conscious of, are found in all consciousness. Some elements (the sensations) are completely present at every instant so long as they last, while others (like thought) are actions having beginnning, middle, and end, and consist in a congruence in the succession of sensations which flow through the mind. They cannot be immediately present to us, but must cover some portion of the past or future. Thought is a thread of melody running through the succession of our sensations.

We may add that just as a piece of music may be written in parts, each part having its own air, so various systems of relationship of succession subsist together between the same sensations. These different systems are distinguished by having different motives, ideas, or functions. Thought is only one such system; for its sole motive, idea, and function is to produce belief, and whatever does not concern that purpose belongs to some other system of relations. The action of thinking may incidentally have other results. It may serve to amuse us for example, and among *dilettanti* it is not rare to find those who have so perverted thought to the purposes of pleasure that it seems to vex them to think that the questions upon which they delight to exercise it may ever get finally settled; and a positive discovery which takes a favorite subject out of the arena of literary debate is met with ill-concealed dislike. This disposition is the very debauchery of thought. But the soul and meaning of thought, abstracted from the other elements which accompany it, though it may be voluntarily thwarted, can never be made to direct itself toward anything but the production of belief. Thought in action has for its only possible motive the attainment of thought at rest; and whatever does not refer to belief is no part of the thought itself.

And what, then, is belief? It is the demi-cadence which closes a musical phrase in the symphony of our intellectual life. We have seen that it has just three properties: first, it is something that we are aware of; second, it appeases the irritation of doubt; and, third, it involves the establishment in our nature of a rule of action, or, say for short, a *habit*. As it appeases the irritation of doubt, which is the motive for thinking, thought relaxes, and comes to rest for a moment when belief is reached. But, since belief is a rule for action, the application of which involves further doubt and further thought, at the same time that it is a stopping-place, it is also a new starting-place for thought. That is why I have permitted myself to call it thought at rest, although thought is essentially an action. The *final* upshot of thinking is the exercise of volition, and of this thought no longer forms a part; but belief is only a stadium of mental action, an effect upon our nature due to thought, which will influence future thinking.

The essence of belief is the establishment of a habit, and different modes of action to which they give rise. If beliefs do not differ in this respect, if they appease the same doubt by producing the same rule of action, then no mere differences in the manner of consciousness of them can make them different beliefs, any more than playing a tune in different keys is playing different tunes. Imaginary distinctions are often drawn between beliefs which differ only in their mode of expression – the wrangling which ensues is real enough, however. To believe that any objects are arranged among themselves as in Fig. 1, and to believe that they are arranged as in Fig. 2, are one and the same belief; yet it is conceivable that a man should assert one proposition and deny

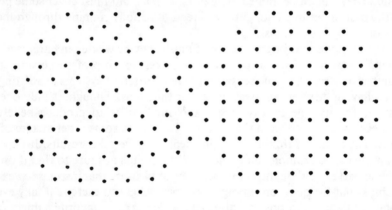

the other. Such false distinctions do as much harm as the confusion of beliefs really different, and are among the pitfalls of which we ought constantly to beware, especially when we are upon metaphysical ground. One singular deception of this sort, which often occurs, is to mistake the sensation produced by our own unclearness of thought for a character of the object we are thinking. Instead of perceiving that the obscurity is purely subjective, we fancy that we contemplate a quality of the object which is essentially mysterious; and if our conception be afterward presented to us in a clear form we do not recognize it as the same, owing to the absence of the feeling of unintelligibility. So long as this deception lasts, it obviously puts an impassable barrier in the way of perspicuous thinking; so that it equally interests the opponents of rational thought to perpetuate it, and its adherents to guard against it.

Another such deception is to mistake a mere difference in the grammatical construction of two words for a distinction between the ideas they express. In this pedantic age, when the general mob of writers attend so much more to words than to things, this error is common enough. When I just said that thought is an *action,* and that it consists in a *relation,* although a person performs an action but not a relation, which can only be the result of an action, yet there was no inconsistency in what I said, but only a grammatical vagueness.

From all these sophisms we shall be perfectly safe so long as we reflect that the whole function of thought is to produce habits of action; and that whatever there is connected with a thought, but irrelevant to its purpose, is an accretion to it, but no part of it. If there be a unity among our sensations which has no reference to how we shall act on a given occasion, as when we listen to a piece of music, why we do not call that thinking. To develop its meaning, we have, therefore, simply to determine what habits it produces, for what a thing means is simply what habits it involves. Now, the identity of a habit depends on how it might lead us to act, not merely under such circumstances as are likely to arise, but under such as might possibly occur, no matter how improbable they may be. What the habit is depends on *when* and *how* is causes us to act. As for the *when,* every stimulus to action is derived from perception; as for the *how,* every purpose of action is to produce some sensible result. Thus, we come to what is tangible and practical as the root of every real distinction of thought, no matter how subtle it may be; and there is no distinction of meaning so fine as to consist in anything but a possible difference of practice.

To see what this principle leads to, consider in the light of it such a doctrine as that of transubstantiation. The Protestant churches generally hold that the elements of the sacrament are flesh and blood only in a tropical sense; they nourish our souls as meat and the juice of it would our bodies. But the Catholics maintain that they are literally just that, meat and blood; although they possess all the sensible qualities of wafer-cakes and diluted wine. But we can have no conception of wine except what may enter into a belief, either—

1. That this, that, or the other, is wine; or,
2. That wine possesses certain properties.

Such beliefs are nothing but self-notifications that we should, upon occasion, act in regard to such things as we believe wine to possess. The occasion of such action would be some sensible perception, the motive of it to produce some sensible result. Thus our action has exclusive reference to what affects the senses, our habit has the same bearing as our action, our belief the same as our habit, our conception the same as our belief; and we can consequently mean nothing by wine but what has certain effects, direct or indirect, upon our senses; and to talk of something as having all the sensible characters of wine, yet being in reality blood, is senseless jargon. Now, it is not my object to pursue the theological question; and having used it as a logical example I drop it, without caring to anticipate the theologian's reply. I only desire to point out how impossible it is that we should have an idea in our minds which relates to anything but conceived sensible effects of things. Our idea of anything *is* our idea of its sensible effects; and if we fancy that we have any other we deceive ourselves, and mistake a mere sensation accompanying the thought for a part of the thought itself. It is absurd to say that thought has any meaning unrelated to its only function. It is foolish for Catholics and Protestants to fancy themselves in disagreement about the elements of the sacrament, if they agree in regard to all their sensible effects, here or hereafter.

It appears, then, that the rule for attaining the third grade of clearness of apprehension is as follows: consider what effects, which might conceivably have practical bearings, we conceive the object of our conception to have. Then, our conception of these effects is the whole of our conception of the object.

III

Let us illustrate this rule by some examples; and, to begin with the simplest one possible, let us ask what we mean by calling a thing *hard*. Evidently that it will not be scratched by many other substances. The whole conception of this quality, as of every other, lies in its conceived effects. There is absolutely no difference between a hard thing and a soft thing so long as they are not brought to the test. Suppose, then, that a diamond could be crystallized in the midst of a cushion of soft cotton, and should remain there until it was finally burned up. Would it be false to say that that diamond was soft? This seems a foolish question, and would be so, in fact, except in the realm of logic. There such questions are often of the greatest utility as serving to bring logical principles into sharper relief than real discussions ever could. In studying logic we must not put them aside with hasty answers, but must consider them with attentive care, in order to make out the principles involved. We may, in the present case, modify our question, and ask what prevents us from saying that all hard bodies remain perfectly soft until they are touched, when their hardness increases with the pressure until they are scratched. Reflection will show that the reply is this: there would be no *falsity* in such modes of speech. They would involve a modification of our present usage of speech with regard to the words "hard" and "soft," but not of their meanings. For they represent no fact to be different from what it is; only they involve arrangements of facts which would be exceedingly maladroit. This leads us to remark that the question of what would occur under circumstances which do not actually arise is not a question of fact, but only of the most perspicuous arrangement of them. For example, the question of free-will and fate in its simplest form, stripped of verbiage, is something like this: I have done something of which I am ashamed; could I, by an effort of the will, have resisted the temptation, and done otherwise? The philosophical reply is that this is not a question of fact, but only of the (possible) arrangement of facts. Arranging them so as to exhibit what is particularly pertinent to my question—namely, that I ought to blame myself for having done wrong—it is perfectly true to say that, if I had willed to do otherwise than I did, I should have done otherwise. On the other hand, arranging the facts so as to exhibit another important consideration, it is equally true that when a

temptation has once been allowed to work, it will, if it has a certain force, produce its effect, let me struggle how I may. There is no objection to a contradiction in what would result from a false supposition. The *reductio ad absurdum*
consists in showing that contradictory results would follow from a hypothesis
which is consequently judged to be false. Many questions are involved in the
free-will discussion, and I am far from desiring to say that both sides are
equally right. On the contrary, I am of opinion that one side (determinism)
denies important facts, and that the other does not. But what I do say is that
the above single question was the origin of the whole doubt; that, had it not
been for this question, the controversy would never have arisen; and that this
question is perfectly solved in the manner which I have indicated.

Let us next seek a clear idea of Weight. This is another very easy case. To
say that a body is heavy means simply that, in the absence of opposing force, it
will fall. This (neglecting certain specifications of how it will fall, etc., which
exist in the mind of the physicist who uses the word) is evidently the whole conception of weight. It is a fair question whether some particular facts may not
account for gravity; but what we mean by the force itself is completely involved in its effects.

This leads us to undertake an account of the idea of Force in general. This
is the great conception which, developed in the early part of the seventeenth
century from the rude idea of a cause, and, constantly improved upon since,
has shown us how to explain all the changes of motion which bodies experience, and how to think about all physical phenomena; which has given
birth to modern science, and changed the face of the globe; and which, aside
from its more special uses, has played a principal part in directing the course of
modern thought, and in furthering modern social development. It is,
therefore, worth some pains to comprehend it. According to our rule, we must
begin by asking what is the immediate use of thinking about force; and the
answer is that we thus account for changes of motion. If bodies were left to
themselves, without the intervention of forces, every motion would continue
unchanged both in velocity and in direction. Furthermore, change of motion
never takes place abruptly; if its direction is changed, it is always through a
curve without angles; if its velocity alters, it is by degrees. The gradual changes
which are constantly taking place are conceived by geometers to be compounded together according to the rules of the parallelogram of forces. If the reader
does not already know what this is, he will find it, I hope, to his advantage to
endeavor to follow the following explanation; but if mathematics are insup-
portable to him, pray let him skip three paragraphs rather than that we should
part company here.

A *path* is a line whose beginning and end are distinguished. Two paths are
considered to be equivalent, which, beginning at the same point, lead to the
same point. Thus the two paths, *A B C D E* and *A F G H E* (Fig. 3), are
equivalent. Paths which do *not* begin at the same point are considered to be
equivalent, provided that, on moving either of them without turning it, but
keeping it always parallel to its original position, (so that) when its beginning

coincides with that of the other path, the ends also coincide. Paths are considered as geometrically added together, when one begins where the other ends; thus the path $A E$ is conceived to be a sum of $A B, B C, C D,$ and $D E.$ In the parallelogram of Fig. 4 the diagonal $A C$ is the sum of $A B$ and $B C;$ or, since $A D$ is geometrically equivalent to $B C, A C$ is the geometrical sum of $A B$ and $A D.$

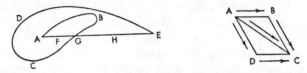

All this is purely conventional. It simply amounts to this: that we choose to call paths having the relations I have described equal or added. But, though it is a convention, it is a convention with a good reason. The rule for geometrical addition may be applied not only to paths, but to any other things which can be represented by paths. Now, as a path is determined by the varying direction and distance of the point which moves over it from the starting-point, it follows that anything which from its beginning to its end is determined by a varying direction and a varying magnitude is capable of being represented by a line. Accordingly, *velocities* may be represented by lines, for they have only directions and rates. The same thing is true of *accelerations,* or changes of velocities. This is evident enough in the case of velocities; and it becomes evident for accelerations if we consider that precisely what velocities are to positions—namely, states of change of them—that accelerations are to velocities.

The so-called "parallelogram of forces" is simply a rule for compounding accelerations. The rule is, to represent the accelerations by paths, and then to geometrically add the paths. The geometers, however, not only use the "parallelogram of forces" to compound different accelerations, but also to resolve one acceleration into a sum of several. Let $A B$ (Fig. 5) be the path which represents a certain acceleration—say, such a change in the motion of a body that at the end of one second the body will, under the influence of that change, be in a position different from what it would have had if its motion had continued unchanged, such that a path equivalent to $A B$ would lead from the latter position to the former. This acceleration may be considered as the sum of the accelerations represented by $A C$ and $C B.$ It may also be considered as the sum of the very different accelerations represented by $A D$ and $D B,$ where $A D$ is almost the opposite of $A C.$ And it is clear that there is an immense variety of ways in which $A B$ might be resolved into the sum of two accelerations.

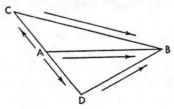

After this tedious explanation, which I hope, in view of the extraordinary interest of the conception of force, may not have exhausted the reader's patience, we are prepared at last to state the grand fact which this conception embodies. This fact is that if the actual changes of motion which the different particles of bodies experience are each resolved in its appropriate way, each component acceleration is precisely such as is prescribed by a certain law of Nature, according to which bodies in the relative positions which the bodies in question actually have at the moment[2] always receive certain accelerations, which, being compounded by geometrical addition, give the acceleration which the body actually experiences.

This is the only fact which the idea of force represents, and whoever will take the trouble clearly to apprehend what this fact is perfectly comprehends what force is. Whether we ought to say that a force *is* an acceleration, or that it *causes* an acceleration, is a mere question of propriety of language, which has no more to do with our real meaning than the difference between the French idiom *"Il fait froid"* and its English equivalent *"It is cold."* Yet it is surprising to see how this simple affair has muddled men's minds. In how many profound treatises is not force spoken of as a "mysterious entity," which seems to be only a way of confessing that the author despairs of ever getting a clear notion of what the word means! In a recent, admired work on *Analytic Mechanics* [by Kirchhoff] it is stated that we understand precisely the effect of force, but what force itself is we do not understand! This is simply a self-contradiction. The idea which the word "force" excites in our minds has no other function than to affect our actions, and these actions can have no reference to force otherwise than through its effects. Consequently, if we know what the effects of force are, we are acquainted with every fact which is implied in saying that a force exists, and there is nothing more to know. The truth is, there is some vague notion afloat that a question may mean something which the mind cannot conceive; and when some hair-splitting philosophers have been confronted with the absurdity of such a view, they have invented an empty distinction between positive and negative conceptions, in the attempt to give their non-idea a form not obviously nonsensical. The nullity of it is sufficiently plain from the considerations given a few pages back; and, apart from those considerations, the quibbling character of the distinction must have struck every mind accustomed to real thinking.

IV

Let us now approach the subject of logic, and consider a conception which particularly concerns it, that of *reality*. Taking clearness in the sense of familiarity, no idea could be clearer than this. Every child uses it with perfect confidence, never dreaming that he does not understand it. As for clearness in its second grade, however, it would probably puzzle most men, even among those of a reflective turn of mind, to give an abstract definition of the real. Yet such a definition may perhaps be reached by considering the points of difference between reality and its opposite, fiction. A figment is a product of somebody's imagination; it has such characters as his thought impresses upon it. That those characters are independent of how you or I think is an external reality. There are, however, phenomena within our own minds, dependent upon our thought, which are at the same time real in the sense that we really think them. But though their characters depend on how we think, they do not depend on what we think those characters to be. Thus, a dream has a real existence as a mental phenomenon, if somebody has really dreamt it; that he dreamt so and so, does not depend on what anybody thinks was dreamt, but is completely independent of all opinion on the subject. On the other hand, considering, not the fact of dreaming, but the thing dreamt, it retains its peculiarities by virtue of no other fact than that it was dreamt to possess them. Thus we may define the real as that whose characters are independent of what anybody may think them to be.

But, however satisfactory such a definition may be found, it would be a great mistake to suppose that it makes the idea of reality perfectly clear. Here, then, let us apply our rules. According to them, reality, like every other quality, consists in the peculiar, sensible effects which things partaking of it produce. The only effect which real things have is to cause belief, for all the sensations which they excite emerge into consciousness in the form of beliefs. The question, therefore, is, how is true belief (or belief in the real) distinguished from false belief (or belief in fiction). Now, as we have seen in the former paper, the ideas of truth and falsehood, in their full development, appertain exclusively to the scientific method of settling opinion. A person who arbitrarily chooses the propositions which he will adopt can use the word truth only to emphasize the expression of his determination to hold on to his choice. Of course, the method of tenacity never prevailed exclusively; reason is too natural to men for that. But in the literature of the Dark Ages we find some fine examples of it. When Scotus Erigena is commenting upon a poetical passage in which hellebore is spoken of as having caused the death of Socrates, he does not hesitate to inform the inquiring reader that Helleborus and Socrates were two eminent Greek philosophers, and that the latter having been overcome in argument by the former took the matter to heart and died of it! What sort of an idea of truth could a man have who could adopt and teach, without the qualification of a "perhaps," an opinion taken so entirely at random? The real spirit of Socrates, who I hope would have been delighted to have been "overcome in argument," because he would have learned something by it, is in curious contrast with the naïve idea of the glossist, for whom (as for the "born missionary" of today) discussion would seem to have been simply a struggle. When philosophy began to awake from its long slumber, and before theology completely dominated it, the practice seems to have been for each professor to seize upon any philosophical position he found unoccupied and which seemed a strong one, to intrench himself in it, and to sally forth from time to time to give battle to the others. Thus, even the scanty records we possess of those disputes enable us to make out a dozen or more opinions held by different teachers at one time concerning the question of nominalism and realism. Read the opening part of the *Historia Calamitatum* of Abélard, who was certainly as philosophical as any of his contemporaries, and see the spirit of combat which it breathes. For him, the truth is simply his particular stronghold. When the method of authority prevailed, the truth meant little more than the Catholic faith. All the efforts of the scholastic doctors are directed toward harmonizing their faith in Aristotle and their faith in the Church, and one may search their ponderous folios through without finding an argument which goes any further. It is noticeable that where different faiths flourish side by side, renegades are looked upon with contempt even by the party whose belief they adopt; so completely has the idea of loyalty replaced that of truth-seeking. Since the time of Descartes, the defect in the conception of truth has been less apparent. Still, it will sometimes strike a scientific man that the philosophers have been less intent on finding out what the facts are than on inquiring what belief is most in harmony with their system. It is hard to convince a follower of the *a priori* method by adducing facts; but show him that an opinion he is defending is inconsistent with what he has laid down elsewhere, and he will be very apt to retract it. These minds do not seem to believe that disputation is ever to cease; they seem to think that the opinion which is natural for one man is not so for another, and that belief will, consequently, never be settled. In contenting themselves with fixing their own opinions by a method which would lead another man to a different result, they betray their feeble hold of the conception of what truth is.

On the other hand, all the followers of science are fully persuaded that the processes of investigation, if only pushed far enough, will give one certain solution to each question to which they can be applied. One man may investigate the velocity of light by studying the transits of Venus and the aberration of the stars; another by the oppositions of Mars and the eclipses of Jupiter's satellites; a third by the method of Fizeau; a fourth by that of Foucault; a fifth by the motions of the curves of Lissajoux; a sixth, a seventh, an eighth, and a ninth, may follow the different methods of comparing the measures of statical and dynamical electricity. They may at first obtain different results, but, as each perfects his method and his processes, the results will move steadily together toward a destined center. So with all scientific research. Different minds may set out with the most antagonistic views, but the progress of investigation carries them by a force outside of themselves to one and the same conclusion. This activity of thought by which we are carried, not where we wish, but to a foreordained goal, is like the operation of destiny. No modification of the point of view taken, no selection of other facts for study, no natural bent of mind even, can enable a man to escape the predestinate opinion. This great law is embodied in the conception of truth and reality. The opinion which is fated [3] to be ultimately agreed to by all who investigate is what we mean by the truth, and the object represented in this opinion is real. That is the way I would explain reality.

But it may be said that this view is directly opposed to the abstract definition which we have given of reality, inasmuch as it makes the characters of the real depend on what is ultimately thought about them. But the answer to this is that, on the one hand, reality is independent, not necessarily of thought in general, but only of what you or I or any finite number of men may think about it; and that, on the other hand, though the object of the final opinion depends on what that opinion is, yet what that opinion is does not depend on what you or I or any man thinks. Our perversity and that of others may indefinitely postpone the settlement of opinion; it might even conceivably cause an arbitrary proposition to be universally accepted as long as the human race should last. Yet even that would not change the nature of the belief, which alone could be the result of investigation carried sufficiently far; and if, after the extinction of our race, another should arise with faculties and disposition for investigation, that true opinion must be the one which they would ultimately come to. "Truth crushed to earth shall rise again," and the opinion which would finally result from investigation does not depend on how anybody may actually think. But the reality of that which is real does depend on the real fact that investigation is destined to lead, at last, if continued long enough, to a belief in it.

But I may be asked what I have to say to all the minute facts of history, forgotten never to be recovered, to the lost books of the ancients, to the buried secrets.

> Full many a gem of purest ray serene
> The dark, unfathomed caves of ocean bear;
> Full many a flower is born to blush unseen,
> And waste its sweetness on the desert air.

Do these things not really exist because they are hopelessly beyond the reach of our knowledge? And then, after the universe is dead (according to the prediction of some scientists), and all life has ceased forever, will not the shock of atoms continue though there will be no mind to know it? To this I reply that, though in no possible state of knowledge can any number be great enough to express the relation between the amount of what rests unknown to the amount of the known, yet it is unphilosophical to suppose that, with regard to any given question (which has any clear meaning), investigation would not bring forth a solution of it, if it were carried far enough. Who would have said, a few years ago, that we could ever know of what substances stars are made whose light may have been longer in reaching us than the human race has existed? Who can be sure of what we shall not know in a few hundred years? Who can guess what would be the result of continuing the pursuit of science for ten thousand years, with the activity of the last hundred? And if it were to go on for a million, or a billion, or any number of years you please, how is it possible to say that there is any question which might not ultimately be solved?

But it may be objected, "Why make so much of these remote considerations, especially when it is your principle that only practical distinctions have a meaning?" Well, I must confess that it makes very little difference whether we say that a stone on the bottom of the ocean, in complete darkness, is brilliant or not—that is to say, that it *probably* makes no difference, remembering always that that stone *may* be fished up tomorrow. But that there are gems at the bottom of the sea, flowers in the untraveled desert, etc., are propositions which, like that about a diamond being hard when it is not pressed, concern much more the arrangement of our language than they do the meaning of our ideas.

It seems to me, however, that we have, by the application of our rule, reached so clear an apprehension of what we mean by reality, and of the fact which the idea rests on, that we should not, perhaps, be making a pretension so presumptuous as it would be singular, if we were to offer a metaphysical theory of existence for universal acceptance among those who employ the scientific method of fixing belief. However, as metaphysics is a subject much more curious than useful, the knowledge of which, like that of a sunken reef, serves chiefly to enable us to keep clear of it, I will not trouble the reader with any more Ontology at this moment. I have already been led much further into that path than I should have desired; and I have given the reader such a dose of mathematics, psychology, and all that is most abstruse, that I fear he may already have left me, and that what I am now writing is for the compositor and proofreader exclusively. I trusted to the importance of the subject. There is no royal road to logic, and really valuable ideas can only be had at the price of close attention. But I know that in the matter of ideas the public prefer the cheap and nasty; and in my next paper I am going to return to the easily intelligible, and not wander from it again. The reader who has been at the pains of wading through this paper shall be rewarded in the next one by seeing how beautifully what has been developed in this tedious way can be applied to the ascertainment of the rules of scientific reasoning.

We have, hitherto, not crossed the threshold of scientific logic. It is certainly important to know how to make our ideas clear, but they may be ever so clear without being true. How to make them so, we have next to study. How to give birth to those vital and procreative ideas which multiply into a thousand forms and diffuse themselves everywhere, advancing civilization and making the dignity of man, is an art not yet reduced to rules, but of the secret of which the history of science affords some hints.

NOTES

1. He was, however, above all, one of the minds that grow; while at first he was an extreme nominalist, like Hobbes, and dabbled in the nonsensical and impotent *Ars Magna* of Raymond Lully, he subsequently embraced the law of continuity and other doctrines opposed to nominalism. I speak here of his early views. [1903].

2. Possibly the velocities also have to be taken into account.

3. Fate means merely that which is sure to come true, and can nohow be avoided. It is a superstition to suppose that a certain sort of events are ever fated, and it is another to suppose that the word "fate" can never be freed from its superstitious taint. We are all fated to die.

3. Pragmaticism

C. S. Peirce

After awaiting in vain, for a good many years, some particularly opportune conjuncture of circumstances that might serve to recommend his notions of the ethics of terminology, the writer has now, at last, dragged them in over head and shoulders, on an occasion when he has no specific proposal to offer nor any feeling but satisfaction at the course usage has run without any canons or resolutions of a congress. His word "pragmatism" has gained general recognition in a generalized sense that seems to argue power of growth and vitality. The famed psychologist, James, first took it up, seeing that his "radical empiricism" substantially answered to the writer's definition of pragmatism, albeit with a certain difference in the point of view. Next, the admirably clear and brilliant thinker, Mr. Ferdinand C. S. Schiller, casting about for a more attractive name for the "anthropomorphism" of his *Riddle of the Sphinx,* lit, in that most remarkable paper of his on *Axioms as Postulates,* upon the same designation "pragmatism," which in its original sense was in generic agreement with his own doctrine, for which he has since found the more appropriate specification "humanism," while he still retains "pragmatism" in a somewhat wider sense. So far all went happily. But at present, the word begins to be met with occasionally in the literary journals, where it gets abused in the merciless way that words have to expect when they fall into literary clutches. Sometimes the manners of the British have effloresced in scolding at the word as ill-chosen— ill-chosen, that is, to express some meaning that it was rather designed to exclude. So then, the writer, finding his bantling "pragmatism" so promoted, feels that it is time to kiss his child good-by and relinquish it to its higher destiny; while to serve the precise purpose of expressing the original definition, he begs to announce the birth of the word "pragmaticism," which is ugly enough to be safe from kidnappers. . . .

Let us now hasten to the exposition of pragmaticism itself. Here it will be convenient to imagine that somebody to whom the doctrine is new, but of rather preternatural perspicacity, asks questions of a pragmaticist. Everything that might give a dramatic illusion must be stripped off, so that the result will be a sort of cross between a dialogue and a catechism, but a good deal liker the latter — something rather painfully reminiscent of Mangnall's *Historical Questions.*

Questioner: I am astounded at your definition of your pragmatism, because only last year I was assured by a person above all suspicion of warping the truth — himself a pragmatist — that your doctrine precisely was "that a conception is to be tested by its practical effects." You must surely, then, have entirely changed your definition very recently.

Pragmaticist: If you will turn to Vols. VI and VII of the *Revue Philosophique,* or to the *Popular Science Monthly* for November 1877 and January 1878, you will be able to judge for yourself whether the interpretation you mention was not then clearly excluded. The exact wording of the English enunciation (changing only the first person into the second) was: "Consider what effects that might conceivably have practical bearing you conceive the object of your conception to have. Then your conception of those effects is the WHOLE of your conception of the object."

Questioner: Well, what reason have you for asserting that this is so?

Pragmaticist: That is what I specially desire to tell you. But the question had better be postponed until you clearly understand what those reasons profess to prove.

Questioner: What, then, is the *raison d'être* of the doctrine? What advantage is expected from it?

Pragmaticist: It will serve to show that almost every proposition of ontological metaphysics is either meaningless gibberish — one word being defined by other words, and they by still others, without any real conception ever being reached — or else is downright absurd; so that all such rubbish being swept away, what will remain of philosophy will be a series of problems capable of investigation by the observational methods of the true sciences — the truth about which can be reached without those interminable misunderstandings and disputes which have made the highest of the positive sciences a mere amusement for idle intellects, a sort of chess — idle pleasure its purpose, and reading out of a book its method. In this regard, pragmaticism is a species of prope-positivism. But what distinguishes it from other species is, first, its retention of a purified philosophy; secondly, its full acceptance of the main body of our instinctive beliefs; and thirdly, its strenuous insistence upon the truth of scholastic realism (or a close approximation to that, well-stated by the late Dr. Francis Ellingwood Abbot in the Introduction to his *Scientific Theism*). So instead of merely jeering at metaphysics, like other prope-positivists, whether by long-drawn-out parodies or otherwise, the pragmaticist extracts from it a precious essence, which will serve to give life and light to cosmology and physics. At the same time, the moral applications of the doctrine are positive and potent; and there are many other uses of it not easily classed. On another occasion, instances may be given to show that it really has these effects.

Questioner: I hardly need to be convinced that your doctrine would wipe out metaphysics. Is it not as obvious that it must wipe out every proposition of science and everything that bears on the conduct of life? For you say that the only meaning that, for you, any assertion bears is that a certain experiment has resulted in a certain way: Nothing else but an experiment enters into the meaning. Tell me, then, how can an experiment, in itself, reveal anything more than that something once happened to an individual object and that subsequently some other individual event occurred?

Pragmaticist: That question is, indeed, to the purpose—the purpose being to correct any misapprehensions of pragmaticism. You speak of an experiment in itself, emphasizing *"in itself."* You evidently think of each experiment as isolated from every other. It has not, for example, occurred to you, one might venture to surmise, that every connected series of experiments constitutes a single collective experiment. What are the essential ingredients of an experiment? First, of course, an experimenter of flesh and blood. Secondly, a verifiable hypothesis. This is a proposition relating to the universe environing the experimenter, or to some well-known part of it and affirming or denying of this only some experimental possibility or impossibility. The third indispensable ingredient is a sincere doubt in the experimenter's mind as to the truth of that hypothesis.

Passing over several ingredients on which we need not dwell, the purpose, the plan, and the resolve, we come to the act of choice by which the experimenter singles out certain indentifiable objects to be operated upon. The next is the external (or quasi-external) ACT by which he modifies those objects. Next, comes the subsequent *reaction* of the world upon the experimenter in a perception; and finally, his recognition of the teaching of the experiment. While the two chief parts of the event itself are the action and the reaction, yet the unity of essence of the experiment lies in its purpose and plan, the ingredients passed over in the enumeration.

Another thing: in representing the pragmaticist as making rational meaning to consist in an experiment (which you speak of as an event in the past), you strikingly fail to catch his attitude of mind. Indeed, it is not in an experiment, but in *experimental phenomena,* that rational meaning is said to consist. When an experimentalist speaks of a *phenomenon,* such as "Hall's phenomenon," Zeemann's phenomenon" and its modification, "Michelson's phenomenon," or "the chessboard phenomenon," he does not mean any particular event that did happen to somebody in the dead past, but what *surely will* happen to everybody in the living future who shall fulfill certain conditions. The phenomenon consists in the fact that when an experimentalist shall come to *act* according to a certain scheme that he has in mind, then will something else happen, and shatter the doubts of sceptics, like the celestial fire upon the altar of Elijah.

And do not overlook the fact that the pragmaticist maxim says nothing of single experiments or of single experimental phenomena (for what is conditionally true *in futuro* can hardly be singular), but only speaks of *general* kinds of experimental phenomena. Its adherent does not shrink from speaking of general objects as real, since whatever is true represents a real. Now the laws of nature are true.

The rational meaning of every proposition lies in the future. How so? The meaning of a proposition is itself a proposition. Indeed, it is no other than the very proposition of which it is the meaning: it is a translation of it. But of the myriads of forms into which a proposition may be translated, what is that one which is to be called its very meaning? It is, according to the pragmaticist, that form in which the proposition becomes applicable to human conduct, not in these or those special circumstances, nor when one entertains this or that special design, but that form which is most directly applicable to self-control under every situation, and to every purpose. This is why he locates the meaning in future time; for future conduct is the only conduct that is subject to self-control. But in order that that form of the proposition which is to be taken as its meaning should be applicable to every situation and to every purpose upon which the proposition has any bearing, it must be simply the general description of all the experimental phenomena which the assertion of the proposition virtually predicts. For an experimental phenomenon is the fact asserted by the proposition that action of a certain description will have a certain kind of experimental result; and experimental results are the only results that can affect human conduct. No doubt, some unchanging idea may come to influence a man more than it had done; but only because some experience equivalent to an experiment has brought its truth home to him more intimately than before. Whenever a man acts purposively, he acts under a belief in some experimental phenomenon. Consequently, the sum of the experimental phenomena that a proposition implies makes up its entire bearing upon human conduct. Your question, then, of how a pragmaticist can attribute any meaning to any assertion other than that of a single occurrence is substantially answered.

Questioner: I see that pragmaticism is a thorough-going phenomenalism. Only why should you limit yourself to the phenomena of experimental science rather than embrace all observational science? Experiment, after all, is an uncommunicative informant. It never expatiates: it only answers "yes" or "no"; or rather it usually snaps out "No!", or at best only utters an inarticulate grunt for the negation of its "no." The typical experimentalist is not much of an observer. It is the student of natural history to whom nature opens the treasury of her confidence, while she treats the cross-examining experimentalist with the reserve he merits. Why should your phenomenalism sound the meagre jew's-harp of experiment rather than the glorious organ of observation?

Pragmaticist: Because pragmaticism is not definable as "thorough-going phenomenalism," although the latter doctrine may be a kind of pragmatism. The *richness* of phenomena lies in their sensuous quality. Pragmaticism does not intend to define the phenomenal equivalents of words and general ideas, but, on the contrary, eliminates their sential element, and endeavours to define the rational purport, and this it finds in the purposive bearing of the word or proposition in question.

Questioner: Well, if you choose so to make Doing the Be-all and the End-all of human life, why do you not make meaning to consist simply in doing? Doing has to be done at a certain time upon a certain object. Individual objects and single events cover all reality, as everybody knows, and as a practicalist ought to be the first to insist. Yet, your meaning, as you have described it, is *general*. Thus, it is of the nature of a mere word and not a reality. You say yourself that your meaning of a proposition is only the same proposition in another dress. But a practical man's meaning is the very thing he means. What do you make to be the meaning of "George Washington"?

Pragmaticist: Forcibly put! A good half dozen of your points must certainly be admitted. It must be admitted, in the first place, that if pragmaticism really made Doing to be the Be-all and the End-all of life, that would be its death. For to say that we live for the mere sake of action, as action, regardless of the thought it carries out, would be to say that there is no such thing as rational purport. Secondly, it must be admitted that every proposition professes to be true of a certain real individual object, often the environing universe. Thirdly, it must be admitted that pragmaticism fails to furnish any translation or meaning of a proper name, or other designation of an individual object. Fourthly, the pragmaticistic meaning is undoubtedly general; and it is equally indisputable that the general is of the nature of a word or sign. Fifthly, it must be admitted that individuals alone exist; and sixthly, it may be admitted that the very meaning of a word or significant object ought to be the very essence of reality of what it signifies. But when those admissions have been unreservedly made, you find the pragmaticist still constrained most earnestly to deny the force of your objection, you ought to infer that there is some consideration that has escaped you. Putting the admissions together you will perceive that the pragmaticist grants that a proper name (although it is not customary to say that it has a *meaning*) has a certain denotative function peculiar, in each case, to that name and its equivalents; and that he grants that every assertion contains such a denotative or pointing-out function. In its peculiar individuality, the pragmaticist excludes this from the rational purport of the assertion, although *the like* of it, being common to all assertions, and so, being general and not individual, may enter into the pragmaticistic purport. Whatever exists, *ex-sists,* that is, really acts upon other existents, so obtains a self-identity, and is definitely individual. As to the general, it will be a help to thought to notice that there are two ways of being general. A statue of a soldier on some village monument, in his overcoat and with his musket, is for each of a hundred families the image of its uncle, its sacrifice to the Union. That statue, then, though it is itself single, represents any one man of whom a certain predicate may be true. It is *objectively* general. The word "soldier," whether spoken or written, is general in the same way; while the name, "George Washington," is not so. But each of these two terms remains one and the same noun, whether it be spoken or written, and whenever and wherever it be spoken or written. This noun is not an existent thing: it is a *type,* or *form,* to which objects, both those that are externally existent and those which are imagined, may conform, but which none of them can exactly be. This is subjective generality. The pragmaticistic purport is general in both ways.

As to reality, one finds it defined in various ways; but if that principle of terminological ethics that was proposed to be accepted, the equivocal language will soon disappear. For *realis* and *realitas* are not ancient words. They were invented to be terms of philosophy in the thirteenth century, and the meaning they were intended to express is perfectly clear. That is *real* which has such and such characters, whether anybody thinks it to have those characters or not. At any rate, that is the sense in which the pragmaticist uses the word. Now, just as conduct controlled by ethical reason tends toward fixing certain habits of conduct, the nature of which (as to illustrate the meaning, peaceable habits and not quarrelsome habits) does not depend upon any accidental circumstances, and *in that sense* may be said to be *destined;* so, thought, controlled by a rational experimental logic, tends to the fixation of certain opinions, equally destined, the nature of which will be the same in the end, however the perversity of thought of whole generations may cause the postponement of the ultimate fixation. If this be so, as every man of us virtually assumes that it is, in regard to each matter the truth of which he seriously discusses, then, according to the adopted definition of "real," the state of things which will be believed in that ultimate opinion is real. But, for the most part, such opinions will be general. Consequently, *some* general objects are real. (Of course, nobody ever thought that *all* generals were real; but the scholastics used to assume that generals were real when they had hardly any, or quite no, experiential evidence to support their assumption; and their fault lay just there, and not in holding that generals could be real.) One is struck with the inexactitude of thought even of analysts of power, when they touch upon modes of being. One will meet, for example, the virtual assumption that what is relative to thought cannot be real. But why not, exactly? *Red* is relative to sight, but the fact that this or that is in that relation to vision that we call being red is not *itself* relative to sight; it is a real fact.

Not only may generals be real, but they may also be *physically efficient,* not in every metaphysical sense, but in the common-sense acception in which human purposes are physically efficient. Aside from metaphysical nonsense, no sane man doubts that if I feel the air in my study to be stuffy, that thought may cause the window to be opened. My thought, be it granted, was an individual event. But what determined it to take the particular determination it did, was in part the general fact that stuffy air is unwholesome and in part other *Forms,* concerning which Dr. Carus has caused so many men to reflect to advantage — or rather, *by* which, and the general truth concerning which Dr. Carus's mind was determined to the forcible enunciation of so much truth. For truths, on the average, have a greater tendency to get believed than falsities have. Were it otherwise, considering that there are myriads of false hypotheses to account for any given phenomenon, against one sole true one (or if you will have it so, against every true one), the first step toward genuine knowledge must have been next door to a miracle. So, then, when my window was opened, because of the truth that stuffy aid is *malsain,* a physical effort was brought into existence by the efficiency of a general and non-existent truth. This has a droll sound because it is unfamiliar; but exact analysis is with it and not against it; and it has besides, the immense advantage of not blinding us to great facts—such as that the ideas "justice" and "truth" are, notwithstanding the inquity of the world, the mightiest of the forces that move it. Generality is, indeed, an indispensable ingredient of reality; for mere individual existence or actuality without any regularity whatever is a nullity. Chaos is pure nothing.

That which any true proposition asserts is *real,* in the sense of being as it is regardless of what you or I may think about it. Let this proposition be a general conditional proposition as to the future, and it is a real general such as is calculated really to influence human conduct; and such the pragmaticist holds to be the rational purport of every concept.

Accordingly, the pragmaticist does not make the *summum bonum* to consist in action, but makes it to consist in that process of evolution whereby the existent comes more and more to embody those generals which were just now said to be *destined,* which is what we strive to express in calling them *reasonable.* In its higher stages, evolution takes place more and more largely through self-control, and this gives the pragmaticist a sort of justification for making the rational purport to be general.

There is much more in elucidation of pragmaticism that might be said to advantage, were it not for the dread of fatiguing the reader. It might, for example, have been well to show clearly that the pragmaticist does not attribute any different essential mode of being to an event in the future from that which he would attribute to a similar event in the past, but only that the practical attitude of the thinker toward the two is different. It would also have been well to show that the pragmaticist does not make Forms to be the *only* realities in the world, any more than he makes the reasonable purport of a word to be the only kind of meaning there is. These things are, however, implicitly involved in what has been said. . . .

Study Questions

C. S. Peirce: "How to Make Our Ideas Clear"

1. Peirce distinguishes three "levels" of clarity of ideas. What are they? Why does he reject the first two?
2. What is the relation of doubt, belief and thought? Of thought and habit?
3. What is the meaning of a thought (or concept)?
4. Illustrate this via the doctrine of transubstantiation.
5. State Peirce's rule for the third grade of clarity. Now state it in your own words.
6. Illustrate with the concepts of *hard, weight,* and *force.*
7. Illustrate with the concept of *reality.*

C. S. Peirce: "Pragmaticism"

1. Why does Peirce re-label his position as "pragmaticism"?
2. What are the central tenets of pragmaticism?
3. Which of the main theses of absolute idealism does Peirce reject? Why?

Selected Bibliography

Dewey, John. *Reconstruction in Philosophy.* New York: Mentor, 1950. [Perhaps the best book to begin with by Dewey.]

James, William. *Essays in Pragmatism.* New York: Hafner, 1948. [Contains several of James's most famous essays. Suitable for a beginning student.]

Konvitz, M. R. and Kennedy, G., eds. *The American Pragmatists.* New York: Meridian Books, 1960. [A fine anthology with selections by many pragmatists.]

Peirce, C. S. *Philosophical Writings of Peirce.* New York: Dover, 1955. [A varied collection of a number of essays on different topics. Suitable for the intermediate student.]

American Realism

4. The Program and First Platform of Six Realists

E. B. Holt, et al.

Philosophy is famous for its disagreements, which have contributed not a little towards bringing it into disrepute as being unscientific, subjective, or temperamental. These disagreements are due in part, no doubt, to the subject-matter of philosophy, but chiefly to the lack of precision and uniformity in the use of words and to the lack of deliberate cooperation in research. In having these failings philosophy still differs widely from such sciences as physics and chemistry. They tend to make it seem mere opinion; for through the appearance of many figurative or loose expressions in the writings of isolated theorists, the impression is given that philosophical problems and their solutions are essentially personal. This impression is strengthened by the fact that philosophy concerns itself with emotions, temperaments and taste. A conspicuous result of this lack of cooperation, common terminology, and a working agreement as to fundamental presuppositions is that genuine philosophical problems have been obscured, and real philosophical progress has been seriously hindered.

It is therefore with the hope that by cooperation genuine problems will be revealed, philosophical thought will be clarified, and a way opened for real progress, that the undersigned have come together, deliberated, and endeavored to reach an agreement. Such cooperation has three fairly distinct, though not necessarily successive stages: first, it seeks a statement of fundamental principles and doctrines; secondly, it aims at a program of constructive work following a method founded on these principles and doctrines; finally, it endeavors to obtain a system of axioms, methods, hypotheses, and facts, which have been so arrived at and formulated that at least those investigators who have cooperated can accept them as a whole.

After several conferences the undersigned have found that they hold certain doctrines in common. Some of these doctrines, which constitute a realistic

79

platform, they herewith publish in the hope of carrying out further the program stated above. Each list has a different author, but has been discussed at length, revised, and agreed to by the other conferees. The six lists, therefore, though differently formulated, are held to represent the same doctrines.

By conferring on other topics, by interchange of ideas, and by systematic criticism of one another's phraseology, methods, and hypotheses, we hope to develop a common technique, a common terminology, and so finally a common doctrine which will enjoy some measure of that authority which the natural sciences possess. We shall have accomplished one of our purposes if our publications tempt other philosophers to form small cooperative groups with similar aims.

EDWIN B. HOLT, *Harvard University.*

WALTER T. MARVIN, *Rutgers College.*

W. P. MONTAGUE, *Columbia University.*

RALPH BARTON PERRY, *Harvard University.*

WALTER B. PITKIN, *Columbia University.*

E. G. SPAULDING, *Princeton University.*

I

1. The entities (objects, facts, *et caet.)* under study in logic, mathematics, and the physical sciences are not mental in any usual or proper meaning of the word "mental."

2. The being and nature of these entities are in no sense conditioned by their being known.

3. The degree of unity, consistency, or connection subsisting among entities is a matter to be empirically ascertained.

4. In the present stage of our knowledge there is a presumption in favor of pluralism.

5. An entity subsisting in certain relations to other entities enters into new relations without necessarily negating or altering its already subsisting relations.

6. No self-consistent or satisfactory logic (or system of logic) so far invented countenances the "organic" theory of knowledge or the "internal" view of relations.

7. Those who assert this (anti-realistic) view, use in their exposition a logic which is inconsistent with their doctrine.

EDWIN B. HOLT

II

1. Epistemology is not logically fundamental.[1]

2. There are many existential, as well as non-existential, propositions which are logically prior to epistemology.[2]

3. There are certain principles of logic which are logically prior to all scientific and metaphysical systems.

One of these is that which is usually called the external view of relations.

4. This view may be stated thus: In the proposition, "the term a is in the relation R to the term b," aR in no degree constitutes b, nor does Rb constitute a, nor does R constitute either a or b.

5. It is possible to add new propositions to some bodies of information without thereby requiring any modification of those bodies of information.

6. There are no propositions which are (accurately speaking) partly true and partly false, for all such instances can be logically analyzed into at least two propositions one of which is true and the other false. Thus as knowledge advances only two modifications of any proposition of the older knowledge are logically possible; it can be rejected as false or it can be analyzed into at least two propositions one of which is rejected.

As corollaries of the foregoing:

7. The nature of reality can not be inferred merely from the nature of knowledge.

8. The entities under study in logic, mathematics, physics, and many other sciences are not mental in any proper or usual meaning of the word mental.

9. The proposition, "This or that object is known," does not imply that such object is conditioned by the knowing. In other words, it does not force us to infer that such object is spiritual, that it exists only as the experiential content of some mind, or that it may not be ultimately real just as known.

WALTER T. MARVIN

III

The Meaning of Realism

1. Realism holds that things known may continue to exist unaltered when they are not known, or that things may pass in and out of the cognitive relation without prejudice to their reality, or that the existence of a thing is not correlated with or dependent upon the fact that anybody experiences it, perceives it, conceives it, or is in any way aware of it.

2. Realism is opposed to subjectivism or epistemological idealism which denies that things can exist apart from an experience of them, or independently of the cognitive relation.

3. The point at issue between realism and idealism should not be confused with the points at issue between materialism and spiritualism, automatism and interactionism, empiricism and rationalism, or pluralism and absolutism.

The Opposition to Realism.

Among the various classic refutations of realism the following fallacious assumptions and inferences are prominent.

1, THE PHYSIOLOGICAL ARGUMENT: The mind can have for its direct object only its own ideas or states, and external objects, if they exist at all, can only be known indirectly by a process of inference, of questionable validity and doubtful utility. This principle is fallacious because a knowing process is never its own object, but is rather the means by which some other object is known. The object thus known or referred to may be another mental state, a physical thing, or a merely logical entity.

2. THE INTUITIONAL ARGUMENT: This argument stands out most prominently in the philosophy of Berkeley. It has two forms. The first consists of a confused identification of a truism and an absurdity. The truism: *We can only know that objects exist, when they are known.* The absurdity: *We know that objects can only exist when they are known.* The second form of the arguments derives its force from a play upon the word idea, as follows: *Every "idea" (meaning a mental process or state) is incapable of existing apart from a mind; every known entity is an "idea" (meaning an object of thought):* therefore, *every known entity is incapable of existing apart from a mind.* It is to the failure to perceive these fallacies that idealism owes its supposedly axiomatic character.

3. THE PHYSIOLOGICAL ARGUMENT: Because the sensations we receive determine what objects we shall know, therefore the objects known are constructs or products of our perceptual experience. The fallacy here consists in arguing from the true premise that sensations are the *ratio cognoscendi* of the external world, to the false conclusion that they are therefore its *ratio fiendi* or *essendi.*

The Implications of Realism:

1. Cognition is a peculiar type of relation which may subsist between a living being and any entity.

2. Cognition belongs to the same world as that of its objects. It has its place in the order of nature. There is nothing transcendental or supernatural about it.

3. The extent to which consciousness pervades nature, and the conditions under which it may arise and persist, are questions which can be solved, if at all, only by the methods of empiricism and naturalism.

W. P. MONTAGUE

IV

1. The object or content of consciousness is any entity in so far as it is responded to by another entity in a specific manner exhibited by the reflex nervous system. Thus physical nature, for example, is, under certain circumstances, directly present in consciousness.

In its historical application, this means that Cartesian dualism and the representative theory are false; and that attempts to overcome these by reducing mind and nature to one another or to some third substance, are gratuitous.

2. The specific response which determines an entity to be content of consciousness, does not directly modify such entities otherwise than to endow them with this content status. In other words, consciousness selects from a field of entities which it does not create.

In its historical application, this implies the falsity of Berkeleyan and post-Berkeleyan idealism in so far as this asserts that consciousness is a general *ratio essendi*.

3. The response which determines an entity to be content, may itself be responded to and made content in like manner. In other words, the difference between subject and object of consciousness is not a difference of quality or substance, but a difference of office or place in a configuration.

In its historical application, this implies the falsity not only of the Cartesian dualism, but of all idealistic dualisms that, because they regard subject and object as non-interchangeable, conclude that the subject is either unknowable, or knowable only in some unique way such as intuitively or reflexively.

4. The same entity possesses both immanence, by virtue of its membership in one class, and also transcendence, by virtue of the fact that it may belong also to indefinitely many other classes. In other words, immanence and transcendence are compatible and not contradictory predicates.

In its historical application, this implies the falsity of the subjectivistic argument from the ego-centric predicament, *i.e.,* the argument that because entities are content of consciousness they can not also transcend consciousness; it also implies that, so far as based on such subjectivistic premises, the idealistic theory of a transcendent subjectivity is gratuitous.

5. An entity possesses some relations independently of one another; and the ignorance or discovery of further relations does not invalidate a limited knowledge of relations.

In its historical applications, this implies the falsity of the contention of absolute idealism that it is necessary to know all of an entity's relations in order to know any of its relations, or that only the whole truth is wholly true.

6. The logical categories of unity, such as homogeneity, consistency, coherence, interrelation, etc., do not in any case imply a determinate degree of unity. Hence the degree of unity which the world possesses can not be determined logically, but only by assembling the results of the special branches of knowledge. On the basis of such evidence, there is a present presumption in favor of the hypothesis that the world as a whole is less unified than are certain of its parts.

In its historical application, this implies that the great speculative monisms, such as those of Plato, Spinoza, and certain modern idealists, are both dogmatic and contrary to the evidence.

RALPH BARTON PERRY

V

The realist holds that things known are not products of the knowing relation nor essentially dependent for their existence or behavior upon that relation. This doctrine has three claims upon your acceptance: first, it is the natural, instinctive belief of all men, and for this, if for no other reason, puts the burden of proof upon those who would discredit it; secondly, all refutations of it known to the present writer presuppose or even actually employ some of its exclusive implications; and, thirdly, it is logically demanded by all the observations and hypotheses of the natural sciences, including psychology.

Involved more or less intimately in a realistic view are the following:

1. One identical term may stand in many relations.

2. A term may change some of its relations to some other terms without thereby changing all its other relations to those same or to other terms.

3. What relations are changed by a given change of relation can not always be deduced merely from the nature of either the terms involved or their relation.

4. The hypothesis that "there can be no object without a subject" is pure tautology. It is confessedly a description of the cognitive situation only; and it says, in effect, that everything experienced is experienced. It becomes significant only by virtue of the wholly unwarranted assumption that doctrines 1, 2, and 3, above given, are false. This assumption, however, is fatal to the idealist's supposed discovery, inasmuch as it means that there can be no true propositions. In conceding this, the idealist refutes himself.

5. In no body of knowledge, not even in evidences about the nature of the knowledge relation, can we discover that possible knowledge is limited or what its limits may be.

6. Entities are transcendent to the so-called "knowing mind" or "consciousness" only as a term is to the relations in which it may stand, viz., in two radically different manners: first, as the term is not identical with a particular relation in which it stands, so too a thing in the knowledge relation is not the relation itself; secondly, as the term may enter into or go out of a particular relation, without thereby being changed essentially or destroyed, so too can an object of knowledge exist prior to and after its entrance into or removed from the knowledge relation. Transcendence thus means, in the first place, distinctness and, in the second place, functional independence.

7. There may be axiomatic truths or intuitive truths. But the fact that a truth belongs to either of these classes does not make it fundamental or important for a theory of knowledge, much less for a theory of reality. Like all other truths, it too must be interpreted in the light of other relevant truths.

8. Though terms are not modified by being brought into new contexts, this does not imply that an existent can not be changed by another existent.

WALTER B. PITKIN

VI

1. Realism, while admitting the tautology that every entity which is known is in relation to knowing or experience or consciousness, holds that this knowing, etc., is eliminable, so that the entity is known as it would be if the knowing were not taking place. Briefly, the entity is, in its being, behavior, and character, independent of the knowing. This position agrees with common sense and with science in holding (1) that not all entities are mental, conscious, or spiritual, and (2) that entities are knowable without being known.

2. The fact that terms are in the cognitive relation does not imply that the terms are mutually dependent on, or capable of modifying, either each other or the relation, any more than this dependence, etc., is implied for any two terms in any other relation. The proposition that there is this dependence, etc., constitutes the "internal view" of relations.[3] Most of those systems which are opposed to realism can be shown to presuppose this "internal view," but this view can be shown to be self-contradictory and to presuppose the "external view."

3. That position which is based in part on the acceptance and the consistent use and development of the implications of those logical doctrines which are presupposed as a condition for any position being stated, argued, and held to be true has, thereby, a strong presumption created in favor of its truth.[4]

4. There is at least one logical doctrine and one principle which are ultimately presupposed by any system which is held to be true. That doctrine is the "external view" of relations, and the principle is that truth is independent of proof, although proof is not independent of truth. The first of these means, briefly:

5. (1) That both a term and a relation are (unchangeable) elements or entities; (2) that a term may stand in one or in many relations to one or many other terms; and (3) that any of these terms and that some of these relations could be absent or that other terms and relations could be present without there being any resulting modification, etc., of the remaining or already present terms or relations.

6. By this "external view" it is made logically possible that the knowing process and its object should be qualitatively dissimilar. (Cf.$_1$)

7. The principle (see 4) means, that, while on the one hand no proposition is so certain that it can be regarded as exempt from examination, criticism, and the demand for proof, on the other hand, any proposition, if free from self-contradiction, may be true (in some system). In this sense every proposition is tentative, even those of this platform.

CorOLLARY. — It is impossible to get a criterion, definition, theory, or content for the concept "absolute" by which it can be absolutely known or proved that any criterion, definition, theory, or content is absolutely true, *i.e.,* is more than tentative. The most that can be claimed for such a criterion, etc., is that it may be absolutely true, although not proved to be.

8. Any entity may be known as it really is in some respects without its being known in all respects and without the other entities to which it is related being known, so that knowledge can increase by *accretion*.

9. Knowing, consciousness, etc., are facts to be investigated only in the same way as are other facts, and are not necessarily more important than are other facts.

10. The position stated in this platform, which is a position concerning knowing as well as other things, can apply to itself, as a special instance of knowledge, all its own propositions about knowledge.

EDWARD GLEASON SPAULDING

NOTES

[1] Some of the principles of logic are logically prior to any proposition that is deduced from other propositions. The theories of the nature of knowledge and of the relation of knowledge to its object are for this reason logically subsequent to the principles of logic. In short, logic is logically prior to any epistemological theory. Again, as theories of reality are deduced and are made to conform to the laws of logic they too are logically subsequent to logic; and in so far as logic is logically present in them it is itself a theory or part of a theory of reality.

[2] The terms knowledge, consciousness, and experience found in common sense and in psychology are not logically fundamental, but are logically subsequent to parts at least of a theory of reality that asserts the existence of terms and relations which are not consciousness or experience. *E.g.,* the psychical is distinguished from the physical and the physiological.

Now idealism has not shown that the terms knowledge, consciousness, and experience of its epistemology or of its theory of reality are logically fundamental or indefinable, nor has it succeeded in defining them without logically prior terms that are elsewhere explicitly excluded from its theory of reality. In short, idealistic epistemologists have borrowed the terms knowledge, consciousness, and experience from psychology, but have ignored or denied the propositions in psychology that are logically prior. In other words, epistemology has not thus far made itself logically independent of psychology nor has it freed itself logically from the commonsense dualism of psychology. On the contrary, epistemology from Locke until to-day has been and has remained, in part at least, a branch of psychology.

[3] To hold the "internal view" means, in my opinion, to hold that, in order that a relation may relate, the relation must either (1) penetrate its terms, or (2) be mediated by an underlying (transcendent) reality. From the penetration there is deduced (*a*) modification, or (*b*) similarity, or (*c*) the generation of a contradiction. Cf. my paper, "The Logical Structure of Self-refuting Systems," *Phil. Review,* XIX., 3, pp. 277-282.

[4] Such a system *I hold* to be realism, its chief feature being the interpretation of the cognitive relation in accordance with the "external view." This "external view" can be held to be true quite consistently with itself, and is in this sense, I hold, self-consistent, as is also, in my opinion, realism. Accordingly I hold further that realism is not a merely dogmatic system, and that, as self-consistent, it refutes and does not merely contradict certain opposed systems which, as based on the "internal view," are self-refuting.

5. The Approach to Critical Realism

Durant Drake

I. The Justification of Realism

There are two familiar starting-points for knowledge, the objective and the subjective. The objectively-minded philosophers suppose that the data of perception are the very physical existents which we all practically believe to be surrounding and threatening our bodies. These physical objects themselves somehow get within experience, are directly apprehended; their surfaces constitute our visual and tactile data. The subjectively-minded philosophers suppose, on the contrary, that the data of perception are psychological existents, so many pulses or throbs of a stream of psychic life. At best they are merely copies or representatives of the outer objects. In so far, both approaches are realistic; but the subjectively minded realist is, in a sense, shut in, according to his theory, to "ideas," *i.e.* to mental substitutes for outer objects, whereas the objectively-minded, or naîve, realist (for this seems to be the view of the plain man) believes that his experience extends beyond his body, and includes, in some of their aspects, those outer subjects. Whatever arguments are then adduced for "realistic epistemological monism" and "realistic epistemological dualism" respectively do little to shake the faith thus based upon an initial definition. An *impasse* exists here, and will exist until it is seen that *neither* starting-point, objective nor subjective, correctly describes what we have to start with, what is "given" (= what appears, what is apprehended) in immediate experience. It is the object of this paper, then, to expose the error in each of these views, and to point out a third view—we call it Critical Realism—which combines the insights of both these historic positions while free from the objections which can properly be raised to each.[1]

Before proceeding, however, to consider these two historic types of realism, it will be well to deal with the spectre of pure subjectivism, which is a likely, though not a logically necessary, deduction from the psychological starting-point. If we are shut in to our mental states, we can never know positively that anything exists beyond them. Perhaps, then, our experience (psychologically taken) = existence. It is doubtful, indeed, if any one practically believes this; for the content of our experience is very narrow, and we all really believe that many things exist, have existed, and will exist, that we, individually, and, for that matter, collectively, have never so much as thought of, and never will think of or know anything about. Moreover, those objects which we do think of, or perceive, are irresistibly believed to have an existence of their own, far more extensive, both as to nature and in time, than that of our evanescent and shallow experience. All who thus believe that existence is far wider than experience – that objects exist in or for themselves, apart from our experiencing them – are properly to be called realists. And we are now first to consider whether realism – any sort of realism – is philosophically indicated (as physicians say) as well as practically inevitable.

Now, as has been said above, it is the conviction of the authors of this volume* that the psychological starting-point is as erroneous as the objective or physical. Our data – the character-complexes "given" in conscious experience – are simply character-complexes, essences, logical entities, which are irresistibly taken to be the characters of the existents perceived, or otherwise known. If this is true, it becomes necessary to ask what reason we have for believing in the existence of our mental states, as well as to ask what reason we have for believing in the existence of physical objects. For the present, however, we will postpone the former question, and confine ourselves to asking what right we have to believe in the existence of physical objects. The answer, in a word, is that our instinctive (and practically inevitable) belief in the existence of the physical world about us is pragmatically justifiable. We cannot, indeed, *deduce* from the character-complexes that follow one another in that stream that is the little private "movie" of each of us any proof of existence. This little realm of Appearance (*i.e.* what appears, what is "given") might conceivably be merely the visions of a mind in an empty world. But we instinctively feel these appearances to be the characters of real objects. We react to them as if they had an existence of their own even when we are asleep or forgetting them. We find that this belief, those reactions, *work* – in the strictest scientific sense. Realism works just as the Copernican theory works, but with overwhelmingly greater evidence. The alternative possibilities are far less plausible. We can, indeed, refuse to make any hypothesis, and content ourselves with a world consisting merely of appearance. A philosopher who refuses to consider anything beyond appearance can fully *describe* what appears to him. But he cannot *explain* its peculiarities. Why should our sense-data appear and disappear and change just as they do in this abrupt fashion? The particular nature and sequence of our data remain unintelligible to the subjectivist, surds in his doctrine. Whereas, if there is a whole world of existents, the characteristics and relations of our data become marvelously intelligible. The argument could be strengthened in many ways, some of which

* I.e., *Essays in Critical Realism,* containing essays by all of the critical realists, – Ed.

Professor Santayana's essay suggests; but this is surely enough for most of us. Everything is *as if* realism were true; and the *as if* is so strong that we may consider our instinctive and actually unescapable belief justified.

As a matter of fact, the so-called subjectivist is really a mental pluralist. He believes in existents that transcend *his* experience — namely, in many minds. And the justification of that belief is no whit easier than that of the belief in physical existents. Indeed, the common argument, from analogy, rests upon a belief in physical existents outside of experience. The subjectivist, in short, is a realist as regards minds; and it should be enough to show him that there is no reason for stopping at this quantity of realism. Consistency demands either universal scepticism or a fearless and full-fledged realism.

It is a realization of the inadequacy of mental pluralism that constituted the chief urge toward the various forms of epistemological idealism. But instead of moving on into these unnatural doctrines, why should not even the psychologically-minded philosopher accept the realistic universe, and thereby avoid the necessity of moving on? Primarily (though other motives enter in) because of his initial description of his data as mental states; and the presumption that all existence is of like sort. Even on his own ground, two sufficient objections can be raised to this assumption. In the first place, the fact that we are shut up to mental existence does not constitute a presumption that there is no other kind of existence — as the discussion of the "egocentric predicament" has made clear. In the second place, the rest of existence might be conceived as more or less like our experience in its intrinsic characters, and yet not *be* experience or experienced. For the differentia of experience from the rest of existence might be not its describable character, but an existential status, or an external relation, which does not apply to all of existence. It is not necessary, then, to expose the inaccuracy of the supposition that what is "given" — what we are conscious of — is a mental existent, in order to put in a demurrer to the movement from subjectivism toward epistemological idealism. There never was any necessity of an Absolute, or any such other far-fetched expedient to patch together the tattered world of the subjectivist. The belief in the existence of independent physical objects is not only the view of common sense and practical life — which, in lack of strong argument to the contrary, gives it an immense presumption — but is, from a standpoint unbiased by practical considerations, far the simplest and most sensible hypothesis to account for the peculiarities of what appears.

II. The Mechanism of Perception

Granting, then, our right to be realists, however objectively or subjectively we may describe our data, let us proceed to examine naïve realism. We must admit at once that it is *a priori* conceivable that our perceptual data are actually portions of external existence, slices or surfaces of the physical objects about us. But a very little reflection shows us difficulties in the way of this simple solution of the problem of perception. For our data, the characters which appear, are not only inadequate aspects of outer objects, but are often *different* from any aspect of them which we can believe to be a part of their independent, physical existence. There is what Professor Montague has called "the epistemological triangle," the outer object, the conscious organism, and the datum of perception, the character-complex apprehended, which, in the case of perception, always includes character-traits not belonging to the actual character of the object itself.

It is necessary to go into detail upon this matter, since the point of view of naïve realism has been adopted, more or less clearly, by various contemporary philosophers who, plagued by the difficulties of the traditional dualistic realism, and weary of the intellectual excesses of idealism, have sought to take refuge in a simpler and more natural outlook. All the qualities which we seem to see in objects are really there, we are told, aspects of the spatially extended object; and our fields of consciousness overlap spatially when two or more of us look at the same object. Thus Professor Holt declares that his view "implies that the soul, so called, is extended in space."[2]

Elsewhere Mr. Holt and his confrères tell us that the sense-datum is a spatial *projection* of the outer object, so that the data of different perceivers of the same object are not in quite the same "perspectives." But all the sense-data are between the source of radiation and the several perceivers, and are, together with that core, a real part of the object sensed. The term "object" here refers to a definite portion of space, but includes this aura of sense-qualities that surrounds the core—the spot where we commonly take the object to be. Thus objects interpenetrate, as well as fields of consciousness. This view may, however, be classed, for our purposes, with what Professor Holt calls the "crude, brickbat" view of matter of some other naïve realists. According to both views, our fields of consciousness extend out into physical space and overlap. We may then group them as varieties of naïve realism, which in any form requires us to accept either one or the other horn of a trying dilemma. Either we must assert that our infinitely various sense-qualities all exist with relative permanence in the object, independently of whether or no it is perceived, or else we must explain how the qualities sensed by the various perceivers *get* there at the moment of perception.

Let us first suppose the naïve realist to take the latter alternative and to say that sense-data are *produced* by the organism, and spatially *projected* into the object at the moment of perception. Perception is thus a boomerang, projecting the qualities produced (by the co-operation of organic factors with the message coming in from the outer existent) out into the outer source of perception. The perceiver literally clothes that outer physical existent with his sense-data, which thereupon, for the time, really exist in the object. This is quite conceivable; but it is quite contrary to the evidence. There is no evidence of the existence of any such spatially projective mechanism. Perception is a one-way process, proceeding from the outer source of radiation to the organism. There is a sense, indeed, in which it is true to say that we project our sense-data into the objects we perceive: we *imagine them there.* But this "projection" is not an existential proceeding; the characters we conjure up in the world about us are not really *there,* except in so far as they really *were* there before perception took place. And so far as secondary and tertiary qualities go, and most of the primary qualities of pure sensations, they are never there at all.

Suppose, then, the naïve realist to take the other horn of the dilemma, and to declare that all sense-data are really aspects of the object prior to perception, although only selected qualities enter into any one conscious field. Every change in sense-organ or brain-event enables a perceiver to become aware of some new one of the myriad qualities of the spatial object, and requires it to exclude all the other qualities that are there, some of which other fields of consciousness may be simultaneously including. To say that the tree is green or beautiful "for me" means simply that the green quality really exists all the time out there in the tree, within my field of consciousness, but not within my colour-blind neighbour's field, which instead includes the grey quality, equally existing out there, which keeps out of my field. Our respective mechanisms of perception are differently selective. . . . But are they? Actually the same sort of ether-wave travels, from the identical physical event, to both you and me. We do not select different bits of existence to affect our several organisms; we are simply affected differently by the same bits of existence. This is not true of observers who look at different sides of objects, but it is true of observers on the same side of an object, though one may be near and the other far, one normal-sighted, clear-headed, and filled with the beauty of the object, the other colour-blind, drugged with alcohol, and seeing the object blurred or double. Can I truly be said to "select" the grey out of a grey-red total, while you select the red? That would be true only if the ether-wave contained both the "red" and the "grey" vibrations simultaneously, your eyes for some reason making no response to the latter, while mine make no response to the former. The fact is, of course, that only the "red" vibrations come to our eyes—*i.e.* vibrations of the rate which produce the perception of red via ordinary human eyes; my eyes, being of an uncommon type, set up a different sort of reaction, which causes my different sense-datum to appear.

In this case, chosen for the sharp colour-contrast it offers, my eyes are "abnormal." But it is not the case that perception even then is "selective"; it is simply, if you please, pervertive. And in the case of the infinitely different shades of colour seen by "normal" eyes in an object, there is no ground for saying that all the sense-data but one pervert the "real" colour of the object. Each datum has equal claims to validity. Neither at the origin-end of the ether-wave nor in our organisms is there so much selection as a passive causal process. The differences are differences produced primarily *in our organisms* by the same outward causes. But if this is true, our differing sense-data do not exist out there in the physical objects.

It is further clear to the student of psychology that the issue as to what perceptual data shall appear is largely determined by the past history of the particular organism involved. A baby has very different data from an adult when perceiving the same objects, and a Hottentot from a European. We are accustomed to note this fact by speaking of the "subjective" elements in perception. In the cases of memory and thought, the "subjective" factors (the organism's past history and brain-organization) are proportionately still more important. Do these "subjective" elements, then, exist also in the object independently of perception? That seems a flagrant case of the pathetic fallacy. Some naïve realists do indeed, for consistency's sake, declare that "affectional" qualities really belong to the life of the object. Storm clouds are really in themselves sullen, and sunshine gay. The same physical existents are really familiar and strange at the same time, sublime and ridiculous, alluring and repellent; all these qualities really exist out there in space.

To state this position seems enough to discredit it. It is indeed the *reductio ad absurdum* of naïve realism. And yet the case is really no different for secondary and many sensational primary qualities than for tertiary qualities. All sense-data report the nature of the perceiver quite as much as the nature of the object perceived; and these "subjective" elements the organism has no way of ejecting into the outer existent. To say that primary and secondary qualities pre-exist in the object, while tertiary qualities are put there momentarily by the perceiver, would be to have *both* difficulties on our hands at once; perception would have to be shown to be *both* a selective and a projective mechanism (in the sense explained), whereas it is neither! Finally, to consider some aspects of our sense-data as bits of outer objects, and other aspects as "mental," or "in our minds," would be to have the difficulties both of naïve realism and of dualistic realism to cope with. In short, naïve realism, whether partial or thorough-going, falsifies the nature of the mechanism of perception.

III. The Existential Incompatibility of Diverse Sense-data

An even more obvious difficulty of naïve realism lies in its implicit implication that contradictory qualities coexist at the same point in space. Illustrations familiar to controversialists have clearly shown how lavish the endowment of objects must be if every quality we seem to perceive in them is existentially present in them. So lavish that they would cease to have any definite nature, and become mere blurs of contradictory qualities. If we reject the "brickbat notion of physical objects," and call many of their perceived qualities "projective properties,"[3] the situation becomes still more chaotic. The red that is now at a given distance from the disc occupies the identical position of the blue that some other observer sees in another object. Pushing the qualities of physical existents into near-by spaces outside of them makes a vast interlacing of auras, and confusion worse confounded.

In short, consistently objectivistic realists have to give up what Professor Montague calls the "axiom of uniplicity," and declare that contradictory qualities can exist together at one and the same point of space, although, owing to the limitation of our organisms, we can perceive only one at a time. Thus Mr. G. E. Moore calls it "an assumption"

. . . that if a certain kind of thing exists at a certain time and in a certain place, certain other kinds of things cannot exist at the same time in the same place.[4]

Mr. Percy Nunn calls the idea of the "true" colour of a thing a "pragmatically simplified concept."

A hot body owns at the same time all the hotnesses that can be experienced around it. The buttercup actually owns — 'as co-ordinate substantive features' — all the colours that may be presented under different conditions.[5]

Few of the upholders of this contention attempt any proof that it is true. They try to make themselves content (albeit one can discern uneasiness) with the fact that it cannot be disproved, and accept it as the unpalatable but logically necessary corollary of the doctrine which they have espoused. Professor Holt, however, boldly glories in it, defending it by a sort of *tu quoque* argument. The whole world is chock-full of contradictions:

Every case of collision, interference, acceleration and retardation, youth and decay, equilibrium, etc., etc., is an instance. The entire universe is brimming full of just such mutually contradictory propositions.[6]

But this opposition of forces or laws is not really a case of contradiction; these laws or forces are really but *tendencies*, which are not *actualized* simultaneously. This is a very different matter from the compresence at one point, at the same moment, of contradictory variations of one generic quality (such as colour) which he seems to think becomes thereby more plausible. It may indeed be true that there are conflicting tendencies, each of which, unchecked, would produce its particular shade of colour in an object. But the actual result of these conflicting tendencies would be, not to produce compresent colours, but to produce a compromise; the resultant colour, while physically a blend or mean, would be none the less a single definite colour, just as the movement of a body is not a superposition of various contradictory simultaneous motions, but a single compromise motion.

Professor Holt hints at another solution, however, viz. that some of these superfluous and troublesome qualities exist not in "real space," but in other spaces "equally objective"; yet they are not "unreal, still less existent merely for consciousness."[7] Mr. Bertrand Russell more explicitly adopts this view in his lectures on the Scientific Method in Philosophy; the physical universe consists of an infinite number of private worlds, or "perspectives."

Each mind sees at each moment an immensely complex three-dimensioned world; but there is absolutely nothing which is seen by two minds simultaneously. . . . The three-dimensioned world seen by one mind contains no place in common with that seen by another. Yet each exists entire exactly as it is perceived, and might be exactly as it is even if it were not perceived. There are as many private spaces as there are perspectives; there are, therefore, at least as many as there are percipients, and there may be any number of others which may have a merely material existence and are not seen by any one.[8]

But is this not jumping from the frying-pan into the fire? Such a multiplication of existing spatial orders is even less credible than the multiplication of existent qualities in one spatial order, and open to the same objections.[9]

A variation of this view is that developed by Professor McGilvary. According to him, one definite set of qualities makes up the "material world," and is studied in science, while all the other qualities are equally existent and "out there," but not a part of "the executive order of the world," and not found there by science. Qualities are to be divided into those which are "space-monopolizing," and those which are "space-occupying." The former sort he calls "material qualities"; only one of each genus of these can exist at a given point. But an infinite number of the latter, which he calls "immaterial qualities," may exist there.[10] But it is not clear how the difficulty of conceiving the presence at the same point in space of synthetically incompatible qualities is lessened by calling some of them "immaterial," if they are thought of nevertheless as really existing there.

What, then, are our objections to such a telescoping together of qualities as objectivistic realism involves? In the first place, it goes sharply against both common sense and science, which view physical existents as having a definite shape, size, colour, etc., and not as consisting of a chaos of mutually exclusive qualities simultaneously occupying the same points. These qualities (as all the shades of colour seen at a given point by different observers, and by the same observers at different times) are synthetically incompatible; they will not fuse together into a single existent. Hence, the view we are criticizing is a thorough-going relativism, repudiating definiteness of character in existence, and giving us, instead of a single, coherent world, an infinite welter of qualities.

In the second place, it apparently makes error impossible. If all the qualities we see in objects really exist "out there" in space, how can any one's verdict as to the nature of the physical existent be any truer than any one else's? The naïve realists have never answered this question in a manner satisfactory to their critics. But this theme is sufficiently developed by Professor Rogers.

In short, neo-realism multiplies the qualities of the outer existent *praeter necessitatem*; we cannot really believe it to be so rainbow-tinted. Objective idealism, it may be noted in passing, lies open, at least in its simplest formulations, to the same objection. An absolute Mind, being a synthesis of all finite minds, must therefore be an indescribable and inconceivable blend of myriads of mutually contradictory items. In opposition to both of these theories, we affirm that the existent at a given point of space at a given time never has more than one set of compatible qualities.[11]

A further cause of complications for the naïve realists results from the temporal-spatial dislocation of Appearance from Reality. The star Vega appears within my field of consciousness now, directly overhead; whereas the astronomical star Vega may, for aught we know, have been dissipated into vapour years ago, and, if not, is certainly not now in the direction from me in which this twinkling point of light appears. What is strikingly true in the case of stars is true, in some measure, of all perception. Physical events send off their messages to us; our perceptual data appear at a later moment, and seem to be in the direction from us in which the object existed at the time when the message started. If, then, our perceptual data are existents, they cannot be the same existents as those from which the message came, because they have a different temporal-spatial locus. For the very meaning of "existence" involves a definite locus. If a particular somewhat has no particular describable locus, we do not call it an existent. If it exists at one place and also at another place at the same time, we call the second case of existence another object. Naïve realism gives us, thus, a world reduplicated not only by the infinite differences in quality which different observers see in objects, but also by the temporal-spatial dislocation that occurs in a single act of perception. Even if qualitatively identical data appeared to all of us when we perceived an object, the data of the different perceivers, standing at different distances from the object, would have a different temporal locus from one another, and from the locus of the event in the object that bears the same name. In the case of sounds a stopwatch will reveal the temporal differences. In the case of sight, the ether-waves travel so fast that the temporal difference of the appearances in different fields of consciousness is inappreciable. But it is clear that if human observers could stand upon different planets, the difference in temporal locus would amount to minutes. And the principle is always the same, however slight the difference.

It might, of course, be held that the star sense-datum, while existentially another fact from the astronomer's star, nevertheless exists up there in the physical sky above my organism, a sort of lingering after-effect of the physical star, a temporal-spatial shadow. Similarly, physical existence may always have its series of shadows, which, instead of the original events, constitute our sense-data. But this again multiplies physical existence *praeter necessitatem,* is repugnant to common sense, and raises the question why these existent shadows are physically inefficacious, and never discovered by physical science.

One or two contemporary thinkers seek to avoid the problem by asserting that our data are not qualities at all, but merely *relations* which physical objects have to conscious organisms. If a given tree looks green to you and grey to me, then green is a relation which it has to your organism and grey a relation which it has to mine. Thus Professor Cohen writes:

All qualities are essentially relational, *i.e.,* characteristics or processes which a thing can exercise only in relation to other things or within a system. . . . Physical qualities are surely not the private possession of things in themselves, but determinate relations which terms have in a physical system. This view, of course, does not deny the existence of terms, literally termini of relations, but it denies that terms have any nature apart from relations. The world of existence is thus a network of relations whose intersections are called terms.[12]

Now it is true that "physical qualities"—the qualities which physical science talks about—are apparently reducible to relations. *E.g.* hardness, in the scientific sense, is nothing but the fact of the relative impenetrability of the body in question by other bodies; colour, heat, and light are but rates of electronic vibration and ether pulsation. But this merely shows that science uses these terms in another sense from that of common sense and psychology. The experienced-quality "hardness" is not the fact of impenetrability, nor is the "whiteness" seen on this paper merely a vibration. Qualities in the psychological sense are— just what they appear to be. There is no use in language at all, if it cannot make clear so simple a fact as that when we speak of such a quality we mean something different from what we mean when we speak of a relation. In other words, the distinction between "quality" (in the ordinary sense of the word) and "relation" is one of those primary distinctions which, though difficult to explain in other words, is irreducible. To say that qualities are really relations is like saying that what we call bad is really good; it is to blur an indispensable distinction in meaning. An outer existent may be supposed to have any relation you please to an organism. That relation will not be what we mean by the term "green." We know what we mean by the term, we mean a certain quality that appears, a somewhat that (being a simple, and not a complex object) is definable and describable only by its relations—as by showing its place in a colour series, or by telling what mixture of pigments or what whirling segments of designated cardboards will produce it. That there appears, on occasion, such a quality, we know.

A relation, on the other hand, has a totally different kind of being. It is not a quality, but a truth *about* qualities. It could not *be* unless there were qualities to be related. So that to do away with qualities would be, *ipso facto,* to do away with relations. A relation may have a relation to another relation; perhaps this new relation may have a relation to a fourth relation; but reversing this series, we get back somewhere to qualities. For the *very meaning of the term* "relation" includes reference to something related; the very first relation could not come into existence until there were two entities to be related. The distinction comes out sharply in the world of existence; no existent can have (or *be*) contradictory qualities, it must be one particular somewhat and nothing else, just as it must occupy one position in space and time and no other. But it can have contradictory relations to its heart's content. The motive behind the attempt to reduce qualities to relations is precisely the hope of thereby escaping the principle of contradiction. But the escape can be made only by breaking down an indispensable and valid distinction. We must insist that the data of consciousness are *qualia,* which must not be ignored in describing the perceptual situation. These three factors are always present in veridical perception: the outer physical event, the mental event, and the Appearance or datum. When two observers are perceiving the same object, there are five items to be discriminated: the outer physical event, the two minds concerned, the two sets of data. These two sets of data are, in veridical perception, to some extent identical. But to a large extent they are dissimilar, and incompatible as aspects of a single object.

IV. The Status of Sense-Data

The preceding arguments suffice to discredit the view which we have called naïve realism. Our data of perception are not actual portions, or selected aspects, of the objects perceived. They are character-complexes (= essences), irresistibly *taken,* in the moment of perception, to be the characters of existing outer objects. That is, the sense of the outer existence of these essences is indistinguishably fused with their appearance. But these two aspects of perception, the appearance of the character-complex and the (implicit) affirmation of its outer existence, must, in reflection, be distinguished. For the belief in its existence may be mistaken, while the character that appears does really appear. In so far as perception is veridical, the characters that appear are the characters of physical objects. But there is never a guaranty, in the moment of perception, that they really are the characters of any outer existent; there is always the theoretic possibility that they are merely imaginary or hallucinatory data. The reason for holding that our instinctive attribution of outer existence is usually warranted, in veridical perception, was given in the opening section of this essay. But after all, even "veridical" perception is only partially veridical; our perceptual data are at best only in part genuine aspects of outer reality. So that what appears, *as a whole,* is never quite what exists.

But neither, now, are the essences that appear in perception my mental states.[13] To anticipate the view defended in the concluding section of this essay, mental states always do exist when data appear. But the datum, what is "given," present to my mind, in perception is the essence "such and such a physical object," not the essence "such and such a mental state." And the two essences are necessarily quite different. When I dream, for example, of a bear chasing me, my datum at the moment is the character-complex or essence "a bear chasing me." The dream-states, as we shall see, exist; but the *bear,* what I am dreaming of, is not a mental state. It is a character-complex taken to have existence at the moment, but in reality having no actual existence at all. So if I think of a centaur, or imagine I see a ghost, or get drunk and seem to see a snake under the table, in each case my mental states exist, but their data, the appearances they yield me, are to be distinguished from the mental states themselves. Exactly so is it in veridical perception. There appears to me the character-complex "a black, oblong desk over there." *That* is not a mental state; we do not *mean* by those words the mental state (whose existence is implied, as we shall see, in the appearance of that datum), but the character-complex apprehended. No; our data are, *qua data,* simply character-complexes which we *take* to exist (except in cases of recognized illusion, imagination, etc.), but which have no existence, except as some of the traits of the complex are actual traits of the physical object perceived, and some are traits of the perceiving state. In other words, "givenness" simply means concretion for discourse, and for action, and does not imply a similar concretion in existence.

Of course this peculiar status — givenness, or appearance — which essences have when they float before consciousness might be called "mental existence," since, like Humpty-Dumpty, we are, after all, masters of our own terms. But there are two objections. In the first place, we need the name "mental states" for what *does* exist — the mental existents which make possible the appearance of the essences. In the second place, if we say that the datum exists, even "mentally," we shall be tempted to locate it, and naturally, to locate it where it appears to be. But as soon as we do this, the troubles that we have noted in the two preceding sections of this essay are again on our hands. Merely calling these supposed existents "mental" solves no problem. If they are really existent, then, even when they are hallucinatory data, they have a definite locus. The ghost that I see in my doorway is really there, the snake seen by the drunken man is really under the table. But if so, how do they *get* there? Why are they not discoverable there by any one else? Why are they so inefficacious, finding no place in the constructions of science? Do they pop in and out of existence out there when I open and close my eyes?

No, *qua* data they are only imagined or dreamed to exist — if the words "imagine" and "dream" may be taken in a sense broader than the usual. We may imagine *truly,* we may dream *truly;* but whether we do or no, the status of the imagined (or "given") essence is the same, apart from the further question whether or not it be the essence of an actually existing object. Perception is, in a sense, imagining character-complexes out there in the world, together with an implicit attribution of existence which may conceivably be, and is occasionally, entirely mistaken. These imagined character-complexes are our data. Usually some of the traits of the character-complex are real, some are *merely* imaginary. But whether really there, or not there, they are never *found* there, but a sort of telepathic vision, but are *imagined* there by a mind. They become data only when the organism, affected by the outer object, imagines them as characters of the object, in those vivid ways we call "seeing," "feeling" (with our fingers), etc. The organism does not actually project the qualities there, so as to change or add to the character of the object, which is quite unaffected by the perceptual process; if the character-traits apprehended were not there before the organism was affected, they never get there. Perception, unlike what in the narrower sense we call imagination, occurs whether we wish or no; the nature of what we shall imagine is partly determined by the messages reaching our brains from the objects; and the imagined character-complexes have a vividness and tang of reality which our centrally excited states of imagination seldom have. But with these qualifications, we may call perception a sort of imagination—vivid, controlled, involuntary imagination, which is to some extent veridical. The appearance, or givenness, of character-complexes, which makes them *data,* is nothing but the fact that they are, in this broad sense, imagined.

To what *extent* perception is veridical is not our present problem. We may accept the general verdict here, which holds that only the primary perceptual qualities are literal characteristics of objects. That is, in the case of the black-oblong-desk-over-there, there really is a "desk" in existence, it really is "over there" (*i.e.* at a certain distance from the perceiver), it really is "oblong," and of such and such a size. But it is not, in itself, "black," except in the sense that it has certain definite characteristics which cause the character-trait "black" to appear to us. But however this may be, the thesis of this volume is that *in so far as* perception gives us accurate knowledge, it does so by causing the actual characteristics of objects to appear to us. The objects themselves, *i.e.* those bits of *existence,* do not get within our consciousness. Their existence is their own affair, private, incommunicable. One existent (my organism, or mind) cannot go out beyond itself literally, and include another existent; between us all, existentially speaking, is "the unplumb'd, salt, estranging sea." But the mechanism of consciousness is such that I can conjure up, imagine, "perceive" the location and characteristics of the objects about me, to a certain extent correctly. We thus directly "perceive" what is *there*—the character of the objects. This is not naïve realism, but it is nearer to it than the traditional dualistic realism realized that it could get, and enough, one would suppose, to satisfy the plain man. At any rate, it is all we have got, and we might as well be content!

Though we have been speaking hitherto only of perception, the same analysis applies to conception, memory, and introspection. But the case of perception is the stronghold of naïve realism; and if we can expose the inadequacy of that doctrine, then there should be no difficulty in applying our revised terms to the other cases. Indeed, naïve realism has always had a hard time in making its position with regard to these cases even clear, much less plausible. When we perceive an object, it is (initially) plausible to suppose that our consciousness somehow is out there in space resting upon the object—or, to put the same view in other terms, that "consciousness" is but a group of, or relation between, certain aspects of outer objects, caught out there in their spatial existence. But when I remember a past event, how can the past event, now dead and gone, actually get within my consciousness? When I think of the other side of the earth, how can my consciousness actually include it? The difficulty is so apparent that the plain man ceases to be a "naïve realist" when he thinks of these very common cases. And indeed, no solution can be reached until we recognize that the datum that appears, the character-complex remembered or thought of, is not, *qua* datum, an existent, but is simply a character-complex, *now* "given" ("imagined"), but which (if memory or conception is accurate) was or is the actual character of the object remembered or thought of. The only *existents* concerned, in all cases of cognition (using this as a blanket term for all cases of recognized or implicit knowledge of reality), are the objects known (if they are, or were, existent objects), the mental states that are the ground of cognition, and the intermediary processes, such as ether-waves, sense-organs, and brain-processes. What *appear,* our *data* (sense-data, memory-data, thought-data, etc.), are merely character-complexes, logical entities, not another set of existents to find a locus for in the world of existence.

V. Mental States *Versus* Data

We have postponed consideration of the question which must have been recurrently arising in the mind of the reader: viz. how do we know that there *are* any "mental states," or any "minds," anything in addition to organisms and outer objects and the essences that appear? To approach the problem from another angle, what must the mechanism of cognition be, that these complexes of qualities get "imagined" as existing out there in the world? Could a mere brain do that? How? It is, certainly, only if they influence a brain that outer objects cause the appearance of their characteristics as our data. But is merely influencing a brain enough? What happens in the brain is, doubtless, that brain-states come into existence whose characteristics (so far as perception is accurate) have a one-one correspondence with the characteristics of the outer objects. But the characteristics of brain-states (as we ordinarily understand the nature of brain-states) are very different from the characteristics of our data. This is a commonplace of philosophy, and the obvious objection to materialism. These peculiar qualities that make up the data presented to consciousness — the sense-quality "red," for example — can a brain-state cause these to appear? To the writer it seems clear that either the brain is a good deal more than we commonly think it to be, or else there is a series of mental states, those existents which can be introspected, in addition to the brain. In the former case, the brain-states have really the qualities, in addition to their other characteristics, that we call "mental"; so that, in either case, there do exist, in or in intimate connection with the brain, a series of "mental states," which have the qualities that make our data appear. Unless this is so, no intelligible account can be given of how our data can appear at all; they would remain mere not-given, not-appearing essences — mere potentialities, not actual perceptual (or conceptual) data.

It is important to emphasize the fact of the *existence* of mental states, as well as of physical objects, since many passages in current writings of the neo-realistic school blur the very concept *existence.* Take, for example, the following passage from Professor Holt:

> The landscape that I experience is, if we take certain simple precautions, in all essentials identical with the landscape that you experience. . . . A certain shade of red can be the quality on a tulip and can be immediately within the experience of a hundred lookers-on at the same time.[14]

To this may we say, so far so good! The essence, or logical ("neutral") entity, which is my datum in a given case of perception or conception may be identically the same essence that is your datum, and even the very essence, or character, of the existing object perceived or conceived by us both. This essence may be said to have being or subsistence independently of my, or your, consciousness of it, and of its embodiment in the object. That is a convenient manner of speech, and need not imply a Platonic belief in the priority or ontological significance of this sort of being.

But these "logical realists" seem sometimes to be content with a world composed merely of essences. They fail to explain how a "given" essence differs from an essence that is not given. That is, having postulated the identity of the essence given to you and to me, and that embodied in the object, they call the knowledge-problem, in that case, solved, ignoring the fact that the essence could not be given to either of us unless we each had mental states which are existents and therefore different existents. What my experience and yours have in common is merely (on occasion) the essences that we are conscious of; our existing mental life is never identical, our minds never overlap. Each has its own locus. For that is the way with existence. An existent is something that occurs at some definite time and place (or, if the reader objects to the putting of mental states into space, he may substitute for "place" the clause "is somehow related to some definite place"). In order that your datum and mine may be the identical shade of red, you and I must have *similar* mental states; your mental state may even be an exact duplicate of mine, but it is a second case of existence, having a different locus. Two copies of a book are not existentially identical, however logically identical their character; nor are two mental states. Moreover, whereas logical essences have no causal efficacy, mental states have causal efficacy; your state has one set of causes and effects, mine quite another set of causal relations.

As a matter of fact, it is doubtful whether, however identical the data of my consciousness and yours, my mental states and yours are ever exactly similar. Identical essences can be "given" by means of very varying mental states. A vivid sensation, a faint sensation, a memory or conceptual state, can be the vehicles, at different times, by which one and the same essence can be given; so that, for all the fluidity of our mental life, and the disparity between my mental life and yours, we live in the presence of common and relatively stable objects. This is possible because the essence given is a mere intent, a focus for discourse and action; the fact that just this essence is given is the result not of the mental state alone, but of that plus the attitude of the organism, all the irradiations (including verbal associates) of that sensational or conceptual nucleus.

So when Professor Holt speaks of the "conceptual nature of the universe," and essays to deduce consciousness from simpler logical essences, he is attempting a fundamentally impossible enterprise. You cannot deduce existence from logical terms and propositions. The essence "existence" is not existence itself; a mere logical term cannot tell us whether anything corresponding to it has an actual locus in the flux of events that is the existential world. You can have the essence "consciousness" in a conceptual universe. But to have actual consciousness you have to have really existing minds.

The situation is, then, more complicated, contains more factors, than the logical realists suppose. We must make room in our picture of the universe for the separate mental states of all the conscious beings in it, each group of mental states forming a separate mind. We must also keep these existents sharply distinct from the existing physical objects of which these minds have knowledge. We do indeed, in a sense, immediately grasp or apprehend (are conscious, or aware, of) outer objects. But it is a logical, essential, virtual grasp of objects, not the existential identity of object and experience which the neo-realists assume. Our instinctive and irresistible feeling that what we have given, what we are aware of, is not a screen of "ideas," but the object known itself, is, in a very real and important sense, true. Knowledge *is* a beholding of outer and absent objects in a very real and important sense — a beholding, that is, of their *what,* their nature. But the physical existent itself does not get within experience, and we are left with a multiplicity of existents — my mental state, yours, and other peoples, and the several objects known.

Why, then, once more, if mental states do exist, can we not simply say that our data are the qualities of those mental states? This would be to rest in the traditional or "old" realism. The reason, we must repeat, for discarding the simple solution is that it is not an accurate statement of the facts. If it were, heaven knows we should all be saved much bother, and the epistemological problem would long ago have been happily solved. But the persistent dissatisfaction with the traditional dualism is based upon its inadequacy of analysis.

Suppose, *e.g.,* that my perceptual datum is the character-complex "a round-wheel-about-three-feet-in-diameter,-moving-away-from-me-and-now-between-this-house-and-the-next." My mental state is not round (on any theory), since the wheel is endwise towards me; nor is it three feet in diameter, or moving away from me, or between this house and the next; nor does it have many, if any, of the qualities connoted by the word "wheel," which more or less implicitly belong to the datum. The qualities of the mental state by means of which that essence was given (as revealed in introspection) are: an elongated oval shape of greyish colour changing position between other masses of colour, vaguely revived tactile sensations, sensations of eyeball movements, convergence and accommodation of eyes, together with all sorts of other slightly aroused mental elements. This "fringe" of mental stuff leads readily to discourse concerning a "wheel," or to bodily movements appropriate to dealing with a wheel. It is this *function* of the mental state which constitutes the "implicit affirmation" of physical existence. When a complex mental state of the sort just indicated exists, together with the readiness of the organism to act in a certain way, then we say and feel, that a certain datum has been "given," or has "appeared." This is all there is to "givenness." If the term "consciousness" be restricted to the cognitive relation, this is all there is to consciousness.

On another occasion my datum may be: a-round-blue-cushion-over-there.

My mental state consists then, according to introspection, of the qualities: blue, round, together with the eyeball and tactile sensations, possibly a lip-motor or auditory image of the words "blue," "cushion," etc., together with the incipient tendencies to believe, speak, and act. "Blueness" here belongs to both datum and mental state. But even this may not be true, as, *e.g.*, if I see the cushion in a faint light, when it is nearly black, or through tinted glasses, and yet perceive it as a blue cushion. So it is clear that the characters that make up the datum depend more upon the associations than upon the actual characters of the mental state.

The writer of this essay has his own ontological beliefs, the exposition of which would, in his judgment, clear up this whole situation and make the epis-temological theory here defended far more plausible than any mere epistemol-ogy, standing alone, can expect to be. But the limitations of this volume forbid its exposition here. All that can be said here, then, is that mental states exist with all the qualities which make our data "appear"—*i.e.* make us suppose cer-tain quality-groups to exist about us. The exigencies of life have made us inter-ested not primarily in mental states but in outer objects. When, therefore, those mental states exist which are directly caused by the messages coming from outer objects, we give our attention at once to the *objects,* adjust our bodies and beliefs to their presence, picturing them by means of our mental states and their mutual interaction, and so live and move in the presence of what are, in a sense, hybrid objects—existences really there, but clothed, in our mind's eye, with the qualities which are mental states put into them. Our data are charac-ters which may be said to be projected, taken to be the characteristics of outer objects. Not *actually* projected—for that would bring back the difficulties we have escaped—but simply supposed to be out there, "imagined" out there. It is not a conscious attribution, or supposing, or projection. It is simply that com-mon sense takes it for granted that they are out there, and has never grappled with the difficulty of how they are revealed if they are there, or what their status is when they aren't there—*i.e.* when perception is inaccurate.

Mental states are, of course, bits of sentiency. There are many times in our lives when we sink back into the mere throb of existence, without cognition. But such moments have no interest for the solution of the problem with which this volume is concerned. Whenever we are perceiving, remembering, thinking of, noticing anything, the situation becomes complicated to the degree above insisted upon. "Introspection" is such a cognitive state. Like outer perception, it gives us, strictly, merely a passing show of appearances, which may or may not be the actual character of the mental states introspected. The character-istics are taken as belonging to the mental state, *i.e.* are "introspected," by being "projected" as its qualities by the introspecting state. In so far, however, as we cease turning the opera-glass upon our own minds, and just sink into the momentary feeling, we cease *knowing* our own mental states, we just *are* our mental states.

Psychology deals with "subjective" data—*i.e.* with the characteristics of our mental states as we know them by introspection. Even in the midst of a perceptual experience, we may turn our attention to our mental state, and thereupon have a somewhat different datum. The character-complex "this outer object," and the character-complex "this mental state," are not, however, apprehended simultaneously. For example, in looking at a coin, I may have as perceptual datum the character-complex "a-round-coin-turned-slantwise-toward-me." Or I may have a sensation-datum, the character-complex "an-elliptical-brownish-image." These two somewhat diverse essences may appear in rapid alternation, but they are not to be confused. The former is the character (more or less truly) of the outer object, which we may feel very certain is there, although there is always a bare possibility of illusion or hallucination. The latter is the character (more or less truly) of the mental state, which we may be perfectly certain is, or has just been, existent. Our knowledge of our own introspected mental states is surely much more accurate than that of outer objects, though there is a bare possibility that even the first reverberations of memory may distort them, and a greater likelihood that they may preserve only a partial record. All cognitive experiences have this tantalizing peculiarity, that they are "knowledge" of, not possession of, the existent known (if it is an existent); their validity must be tested by other means than the intuition of the moment.

Naïve realism, which wants more than this, can never have want it wants. The disappointment, the lack of absolute certainty (*practical* certitude we have, in many cases) lies not with our theory, it lies in the actual situation. The motive behind "epistemological monism" has been largely the desire for certainty, for getting right hold of the object known, rather than depending upon a fallible mind to know it. But since our knowledge is obviously fallible, any theory that seeks to accredit it as intuitive, actual *possession* of the object known is at variance with the facts. From all such theories we must return to a sober satisfaction in the situation as it is, and a marvel that our mechanism of consciousness is so admirably adapted to body forth to us the actual nature of the world in which we live.

NOTES

1. In the above paragraph I have, for convenience, given the names *epistemological monism* and *epistemological dualism* to the two historic positions which we believe to be transcended by our analysis. There is, I should add, some doubt among us as to whether our position should be called a *dualism*.

On the one hand, in certain contexts it is desirable to emphasize the duality which we believe to exist between the cognitive state which is the vehicle of knowledge and the object known. By contrast with neo-realists, idealists, and believers in "pure experience," we are dualists.

On the other hand, the term "dualism" implies to most readers, probably, the notion that what we *know* is a mental state (or "idea"), an existent from which we have to infer the existence and character of the physical object. This notion, however, we repudiate. What we perceive, conceive, remember, think of, is the outer object itself (or, on occasion, the mental state introspected, remembered, or conceived), which is independent of the knowledge-process, and beyond which there is nothing else.

Further, if the analysis is accepted (made in this essay, and, at greater length, in the concluding essay) which discriminates the "datum" in cases of knowledge from the mental state which is the vehicle of its givenness, we cannot say that the datum (what is "given" to the knower, what we start with in our epistemological inquiry) is an existent, representing the object. On the contrary, it is (in so far as knowledge is accurate) simply the essence or character (the *what*) of the object known. Professors Sellars, Lovejoy, and Pratt, however, maintain that although what is *given* is a mere character-complex, it is in reality *in toto* the character of the mental state of the moment, and so *is* an existent, in spite of the fact that its existence is not given (see on this point the footnote on p. 20); they may perhaps therefore be called dualistic by somewhat better right than the rest of us, although we all agree as to what the existential situation in knowledge is, and as to the fact that what we *know* is the independent object itself. Critics of our view are asked, therefore, not to label us simply as "dualists," but to recognize precisely what sort of duality we do and do not admit.

2. *The Concept of Consciousness,* pp. 150 ff. See also his essay in *The New Relation.*

3. Holt, in *The New Realism,* pp. 371–372.

4. *Proc. of Aristotelian Soc.* (N.S.), vol. vi, p. 122.

5. *Ibid.,* vol. x, pp. 197, 203. See similarly S. Alexander, *ibid.,* vol. x, p. xi.

6. *The New Realism,* pp. 364, 370. Cf. also his *The Concept of Consciousness,* ch. xiii.

7. *Ibid.,* pp. 354, 367.

8. Pp. 87, 89.

9. It is to be noted that Mr. Russell's "perspectives" are real physical existents, out there in real space, and not mere appearances. As appearances we must all recognize them. And if we are content to give their incompatible aspects no existential status no difficulty will arise.

10. *Philosophical Review,* vol. xxi, p. 152.

11. The present writer would go further, and say that only *one quale* exists at any one point at a given instant. But that is a further doctrine not here defended.

12. *Journal of Philosophy, Psychology, and Scientific Methods,* vol. xi, pp. 622–662.

13. The question whether we should or should not make this distinction between what is "given" (the "datum") and the character of the mental existent which is the vehicle of the givenness, is the one question in our inquiry upon which we have not been able fully to agree. This appears, however, to be a question as to terms, not a disagreement as to the existential situation in knowledge. Our uncertainty as to the pertinence to our doctrine of the term "dualism," discussed in the footnote on p. 4, hinges mainly upon this question.

We agree that what is "given" is what is grasped in knowledge, what is contemplated, the starting-point for discourse; and that what we thus contemplate (are aware of) is, in the case of perception, something outward, *apparently* the very physical object itself. This outer existent, however, is not literally grasped, as the neo-realists suppose; only its *what,* its essence or character, is grasped, as explained in this essay and throughout the volume.

The point of difference is this: Professors Lovejoy, Pratt, and Sellars hold that what is "given" is, in all cases, and *in toto* in each case, the character of the mental existent of the moment, although its existence is not given. The other four of us hold that what is "given" results not merely from this cognitive use of the character of the mental state of the moment, but also, in part, in most cases, from the attitude of the organism, which may not be represented in the character of that mental state. In other words, the *function* of the mental state, as well as its actual content, or character, helps to determine what is "given." If this is so, the datum as a whole (the total character given) is not the character of any existent; the separate traits that make up its complex nature may be traits of the mental existent, traits of the object known, or both, or neither.

This *situation* is recognized by us all; hence the propriety of calling our difference a terminological one. Our difference of opinion consists in a divergent use of the terms "given," "datum," etc. Some of us speak of as "given" only those traits that are traits of the mental existent of the moment—traits, that is, that have actual, literal, psychological existence. The rest of us include in the term the traits apprehended as belonging to the object through the attitude, or reaction, of the organism. According to the latter usage, adopted in this essay, the datum is, *qua* datum, a mere essence, an imputed but not necessarily actual existent. It may or it may not have existence. It exists just to the extent in which it is, in fact, the nature either of the object known or of the cognitive state (mental existent) of the moment—an extent which varies from case to case. Meanwhile, according to the former usage, the datum has *in toto* a psychological existence, and may be spoken of as "mental content."

14. *The Concept of Consciousness,* pp. 152-153.

Study Questions

1. Distinguish the various types of realism advocated by the new realists.
2. Which of the main theses of absolute idealism are rejected by the new realism?
3. What are the main criticisms that Drake levels against "new" realism?
4. What are the most significant differences between new realism and critical realism?
5. Which of the main theses of idealism are attacked by critical realism?

Selected Bibligraphy

Chisholm, R. M. *Realism and the Background of Phenomenology.* Glencoe: Free Press, 1960. pp. 283–304. [Covers *all* forms of realism.]

Drake, Durant, et al. *Essays in Critical Realism.* New York: Macmillan, 1920. [Essays by each of the critical realists.]

Holt, E. B., et al. *The New Realism.* New York: Macmillan, 1912. [Essays by each of the new realists.]

Muelder, W. G., and Sears, Laurence, eds. *The Development of American Philosophy.* Boston: Houghton-Mifflin, 1940. Part Seven. [Interesting selections by several American realists: suitable for a beginning student.]

Part Two

Analytic and Linguistic

Philosophies

Part 2: Analytic and Linguistic Philosophies

Introduction

We have made a brief survey of some of the main philosophical movements of the pre-analytic tradition of the late nineteenth and early twentieth centuries. What, then, is analytic philosophy? It would be nice if some neat definition or characterization were available. But, again, none is — or at least none that goes beyond making some rather broad and vague remarks, such as: Analytic philosophy is concerned with analysis, with meaning, clarification, making distinctions, etc. Rather than chasing after an elusive formula (for analytic philosophy), it would be more fruitful to examine the main tenets and activities of some of the major philosophers who have been influential — all of whom are generally recognized as being within the analytic tradition in philosophy. Following this approach, it is necessary to distinguish at least six types of analytic philosophy. The labels given to some of these have become famous. Others have not been officially named; and in those cases I have, for convenience, chosen some labels that seem appropriate.

REALISM AND COMMON SENSE

The main figures and the most influential philosophers who represent this form of analytic philosophy were G. E. Moore (1873–1958) and Bertrand Russell (1872–1970). As we have seen, the most widespread philosophical movement of the nineteenth century was (Hegelian) idealism. To some extent, Hegelianism had begun to collapse in Germany by the latter part of the nineteenth century, as neo-Kantianism became predominant. But in England there was a new interest in Hegel and a resurgence of idealism. So pervasive was this philosophy that even Moore and Russell started out as idealists of a sort. But neither could take it for long. Both revolted and leveled devastating blows at idealism. As Russell put it:

G. E. Moore took the lead in the rebellion, and I followed, with a sense of emancipation. Bradley [one of the British idealists] argued that everything common sense believes in is mere appearance. We reverted to the opposite extreme, and thought

111

that *everything* is real that common sense, uninfluenced by philosophy or theology, supposes real. With a sense of escaping from prison, we allowed ourselves to think that grass is green, and that the sun and stars would exist if no one was aware of them; and also that there is a pluralistic, timeless world of Platonic ideas. The world, which had been thin and logical, suddenly become rich and varied and solid.[1]

Let us look at some of Moore's contributions. (I shall focus mainly on Moore, since Russell will be discussed in connection with another form of analytic philosophy.)

In his important essay, "The Refutation of Idealism," Moore undertook to prove that the main conclusion of idealism — that reality is spiritual or mental — can never be proven true by any idealistic argument. Why not? Because every such argument must contain an essential premise that is false under every non-tautological interpretation of it — namely, the premise: to be is to be perceived (i.e., the object of sensation *or* thought). Moore demonstrates that, under certain interpretations, this premise is self-contradictory. In all others it is false (but not self-contradictory). Hence the idealist conclusion can never be shown to be true. And Moore presents arguments to show that it is in fact false.

Moore's positive views on behalf of realism were presented in a number of other essays. One of the most important of these is his "A Defense of Common Sense." In this essay he claims that the common sense view of the world is wholly true and can be known with certainty. He also argues for what he takes to be the chief tenet of realism, namely, that there is no good reason to hold either (a) that every physical fact is logically dependent on some mental fact or (b) that every physical fact is causally dependent on some mental fact. What does all this have to do with analysis? Moore claims that philosophers must begin by accepting as true certain common sense statements — statements that everyone would admit as being true when not engaged in philosophy. It is not the business of philosophy to deny the truth of these statements. It is the task of philosophy to analyze these true statements. Moore maintains: (1) We know many such propositions to be true. (2) We can understand them in their ordinary sense. (3) But such understanding is not equivalent to being able to give a correct analysis of their meaning. Hence the task of philosophy is to provide such an analysis. In section IV of "A Defense of Common Sense," Moore illustrates this with regard to the proposition 'Material things exist'. He goes through four stages of analysis. In many other works Moore manifested that philosophy is concerned with analysis. And he distinguishes several forms of analysis. One form of it is clearly revealed in "Proof of an External World," which is reprinted in this volume.

It should be mentioned that Moore wrote many works in the theory of perception, theory of knowledge in general, and in the area of ethics. He is noted for his claim that the notion of *good* is indefinable and unanalyzable. His case for that claim appears in the first chapter of his *Principia Ethica,* which is reprinted in this volume.

In many of his papers and books, Bertrand Russell also defended realism, although he did not lay quite as much stress on common sense. But he soon became an advocate of another form of analytic philosophy: logical atomism. A very readable defense of realism may be found in Russell's *The Problems of Philosophy*.

LOGICAL ATOMISM

According to Bertrand Russell, the themes that make up what he called logical atomism were first put forth by Ludwig Wittgenstein (1889–1951), who was at one time a student of Russell's.

Wittgenstein was perhaps one of the most original and influential philosophers of the first half of the twentieth century. Although he was a native of Austria, he did much of his philosophical work, primarily via lectures, at Cambridge University in England. He has the distinction of having put forth a philosophical position—articulated in his *Tractatus Logico-Philosophicus* (1922)—in which he claimed to have definitively solved a number of problems, and then rejecting these views some years later. This later position is developed most fully in *Philosophical Investigations* (1953), *Remarks on the Foundations of Mathematics* (1956), and also in various compilations, by former students, of his lecture notes. Although there are some strands running from the earlier views to the later ones, the two positions, and the approaches to philosophy that they manifest, are sufficiently different to require that we distinguish them. Here I shall take up only the earlier views.

In the *Tractatus*, Wittgenstein deals with three major questions: (1) What is the nature of logic? (2) How is logic related to language? (3) How are both logic and language related to the world? He is concerned to defend, or at least articulate, the view that logic has ontological implications. Roughly, his line of argument is this: In order for us to think or talk about the world, there must be something in common between thought or language and the world. This common element is the *structure* of both. Thus, our knowledge of the structure of one will lead to our knowledge of the structure of the other. Logic is concerned with and reveals the structure of language. And since the structure of language is the structure of the world, it follows that logic is concerned with and reveals the structure of the world. Consequently, the tasks in which Wittgenstein engages are: to inquire into the nature of logic, then to move to examine the nature of language, and most importantly to attain knowledge of the nature of the world.

Although some emphasis on the activity of analysis occurs in the *Tractatus*, this was developed in greater detail in Russell's version of logical atomism (which differs significantly from Wittgenstein's in some respects).

The Problems of Philosophy (1912), one of Russell's most accessible books for the ordinary reader, deals with a number of metaphysical problems. In it he is concerned to refute the main thesis of idealism and to establish that of realism.

But in "The Philosophy of Logical Atomism" (1918), he advocates a very different metaphysics. He characterizes logical atomism as the view that there are many separate things, or that *the world can be analyzed* into a number of separate things. These are known as logical atoms (in contrast to physical atoms) and consist of particulars, predicates (or properties) and relations. All of these are momentary entities—such things as patches of color, sounds, etc. Russell therefore defends a phenomenalist metaphysics in this work. Indeed, such things as tables, chairs, streets (physical objects) are said to be series of classes of sense-data and hence "logical fictions."

Parts of "The Philosophy of Logical Atomism" are somewhat technical. But most of the eight lectures that comprise it are quite readable, and together they serve as a good introduction to logical atomism.

Due to the impact of Russell and Wittgenstein, philosophers in England were for years concerned with analysis in the sense of getting at the form of the facts in the world. But in Vienna, a group of philosophers were articulating a very different form of analytic philosophy.

LOGICAL POSITIVISM

In the early 1920s a number of scientists, mathematicians, and philosophers formed a group that was later dubbed "The Vienna Circle." Among its most prominent members were: R. Carnap, H. Feigl, K. Godel, H. Hahn, O. Neurath, M. Schlick, and F. Waismann. The philosophical movement resulting from their discussions and publications was later called "logical positivism," or as some preferred, "logical empiricism." The members of this movement shared a distaste for metaphysics, which they interpreted as the effort to establish that there are entities beyond the scope or grasp of any possible experience. More specifically, they were concerned to attack the main doctrines of absolute idealism and of certain philosophies, such as that of Heidegger. But their attack did not consist of an effort to show that those doctrines were false. Rather, it was the far stronger claim that all such doctrines are meaningless. Hence, the adherents of this philosophy engaged, not in the task of arguing against metaphysics or metaphysical statements, but rather in the task of *outlawing* metaphysics, of repudiating metaphysical assertions on the grounds that they are cognitively meaningless. In their view, if a metaphysician makes such claims as "Reality is the Absolute," etc., it is a waste of effort to argue against him. For no possible experience is relevant to ascertaining whether or not such claims are true. Thus it would be equally senseless (in their view) to advocate that "Reality is not the Absolute," etc. Neither of these claims can be verified. Hence, all such assertions and all disputes about them are meaningless.

The main theses of logical positivism were presented in many articles and books. They were given prominence through what became the classic text on the subject, A. J. Ayer's *Language, Truth, and Logic,* first published in 1936. (A long Introduction, modifying some of these views appeared in the second edition published ten years later.) These tenets may be briefly stated as follows:

(1) A proposition (a statement) is factually meaningful if and only if it is verifiable – in the sense that it is possible for experience to render it probable, not in the sense that its truth can be conclusively established by experience.

(2) A proposition is verifiable if and only if it is either an experiential proposition or one such that some experiential proposition can be deduced from it in conjunction with other premises. (This criterion was modified and refined many times.)

(3) A proposition is formally meaningful if and only if it is true by virtue of the definitions of its terms – i.e., tautologous. Such propositions and only such are a priori.

(4) The laws of logic and mathematics are all tautologous.

(5) A proposition is literally meaningful if and only if it is either verifiable or tautologous.

(6) Since metaphysical statements meet neither of the conditions in (5), they are literally meaningless.

(7) Since ethical, aesthetical, and theological statements also fail to meet either of the conditions in (5), they too are cognitively meaningless – although they may possess "emotive" meaning.

(8) Since metaphysics, ethics, philosophy of religion, etc., are all "eliminated," the only tasks of philosophy are clarification and analysis. Thus the propositions of philosophy are linguistic, not factual, and philosophy is a "department" of logic.

A vigorous and readable exposition and defense of logical positivism was put forth by A. J. Ayer (b. 1910) in his *Language, Truth, and Logic* and in various essays by Schlick and Carnap. Selections from Ayer appear in this volume.

CONCEPTUAL ANALYSIS

As was already mentioned, Wittgenstein (after abandoning philosophy for a time) put forth a later position that differs significantly from his earlier view and in many ways is a direct critique of his previous position. This form of analytic philosophy is often referred to as conceptual analysis or ordinary language philosophy. It is developed in Wittgenstein's *Philosophical Investigations*.

Upon first reading, the *Philosophical Investigations* seems to be a study of language, and much of it is concerned with language. Whereas in his earlier works, Wittgenstein suggests that language has primarily one function, that of discoursing about the world, he now sees language as an instrument of many human purposes and needs. It can be used not only by scientists or to impart information, but language can also be used by poets, joke-tellers, persons giving orders, etc. And all of these use language in their own ways and for different ends. As long as language is used in these ways, no great problems arise.

But there are points at which language has got "out of order." These are the strange questions posed by traditional philosophies and the paradoxical, conflicting, and misleading doctrines that they have given in answer to these questions. Wittgenstein is greatly interested in the roots of philosophical perplexity and finds that they are located in language.

In order to understand this, he claims, we must look at language in its ordinary functioning. He describes various simple languages, such as one used by a builder to give orders to his assistant, or one used by a person who is shopping for apples. It is maintained that our natural language is partially like these but also different and, of course, far more complex. His point is that natural language did not come to us ready-made. It is a part of our social behavior and has evolved for certain purposes that are determined by human needs—whether to assert, command, amuse, or whatever. Again, in these contexts, language normally works fairly well. But in others it breaks down, "goes on a holiday," doesn't do the job it was intended to do. These pertain to the philosophical use of language.

Wittgenstein noted that great minds have tackled philosophical problems but haven't given accepted solutions. Why have philosophers nevertheless been so persistent in raising these problems? Because they have been involved in linguistic difficulties of which they were not aware. Philosophical problems are generated as a result of the misuse and overextension of certain terms that we know how to use quite well in ordinary life, but we work "too hard," thus giving rise to philosophical problems. Among these are: 'cause', 'perceive', 'understand', etc. We must find the linguistic root that got us into these problems and thereby find a "way out" of our difficulties. We do this, in large part, by examining our normal uses of the problematic terms. (This is only a rough sketch of Wittgenstein's views. The details are complex and often dense.)

Wittgenstein maintained that philosophical statements are misleading and are symptoms of linguistic confusion. John Wisdom (b. 1904), a sort of disciple of Wittgenstein, held that philosophical statements are also illuminating and are symptoms of linguistic penetration. This conception of philosophy is brought out clearly in Wisdom's essay, "Philosophical Perplexity." In many respects, the beginning student will find it best to approach conceptual analysis via the writings of Wisdom rather than Wittgenstein. For this reason, several of his essays have been included in this volume.

LOGICO-METAPHYSICAL ANALYSIS

As we have seen, at least one form of analytic philosophy, logical atomism, involved a highly elaborate metaphysics. And we have noted that another form, logical positivism, rejected metaphysics and attempted to eliminate it, thereby purifying philosophy. Conceptual analysis (or ordinary language philosophy) for the most part continued to reject metaphysical problems— although some have argued that it merely put forth another metaphysics of its own. Starting about 1950, it became apparent that some philosophers were returning to metaphysical problems, although via the "linguistic turn" in philosophy. Ontologies were put forth, and criteria for ontological commitment as well. No single figure was totally responsible for this turn in philosophy. But among those who made significant contributions, several stand out: Gustav Bergmann (b. 1906), Wilfrid Sellars (b. 1912), and W. V. Quine (b. 1908). Since these philosophers have placed great importance upon logic as well as metaphysical concerns, I have referred to their form of analytic philosophy as logico-metaphysical analysis.

Gustav Bergmann began his philosophical career as a logical positivist. For some time after he advocated the primacy of metaphysics, he still kept the label "logical positivism" to designate his philosophy. But it hardly fitted, since Bergmann had rejected many of the main theses of positivism. (More recently he has rejected even more.) Historically, Bergmann's return to metaphysical concerns, via the rigors and techniques of logic, is best expressed in his "Logical Positivism, Language and the Reconstruction of Metaphysics," a portion of which is reprinted in this volume. In this essay Bergmann holds that the old metaphysics — or the traditional problems of metaphysics — are to be reconstructed, using a new method, in which these questions and their answers are re-interpreted. In what way? According to Bergmann, philosophical inquiry is linguistic. It starts from common sense. It is descriptive and it seeks the logical form of statements. Hence, it is concerned with an ideal language. Indeed, philosophical inquiry is commonsensical discourse about an ideal or logically perfect (or perspicuous) language.

Some years after the publication of this essay, the role of an ideal language was minimized (if not dropped) by Bergmann. For at least two decades, most of his work has been much more explicitly metaphysical in defense of ontological realism.

Among those who, to some extent, share Bergmann's conception of philosophy but differ vigorously with regard to many claims and even with regard to methodology are Wilfrid Sellars and W. V. Quine. Most of Sellars's works are extremely difficult to read. But two essays of Quine have been included in this volume. In his famous essay "On What There Is," Quine is concerned with the answers to two questions: (1) What is it that involves us in and indicates ontological commitment? (2) What is (are) the criterion (criteria) for the acceptance of an ontology? His answers are: (1) The range and use of bound variables (in any logic-system) are what involve us in and indicate ontological commitment. To be assumed as an entity is to be taken as the value of a variable in a logical system. (2) We adjudicate between rival ontologies with the help of criteria that are similar to those used for accepting scientific theories — criteria such as simplicity and comprehensiveness.

The two "dogmas" Quine attacks in "Two Dogmas of Empiricism" are: (1) All statements are either analytic or synthetic, and there is a sharp boundary between them. (2) All meaningful synthetic statements are either translatable into statements about our immediate experience (i.e., into a sense-data language) or at least they are confirmable or disconfirmable by some range of possible sensory events.

LINGUISTIC ANALYSIS

To some extent, every form of analytic philosophy has been linguistic in character (as well as analytical). But there is one form of analytic philosophy in which the linguistic emphasis has been stressed as primary — some would say to an extreme. There is no commonly accepted name for this form of analytic philosophy. For convenience, I have chosen the name "linguistic analysis" to designate this form of analytic philosophy.

The chief practitioner of this form of philosophy has been J. L. Austin (1911–1960). His position has been characterized as follows:

> For Austin, as for others, the central task of philosophy — the 'begin-all' if not the 'end-all' — is the careful elucidation of some of the concepts of ordinary language. But unlike Wittgenstein (and others), this elucidation is regarded as valuable for its own sake, not simply for the alleviation of philosophical puzzlement. Clarification of the subtle distinctions embodied in ordinary language illuminates equally subtle discriminata in the world.[2]

At one time, Austin made a distinction between utterances that are sayings (actual statements) and those that are performances or speech acts (e.g., promises). In "Performative-Constative," he argues that both of these are speech acts. If we make an assertion or give a description, we are performing a speech act just as much as in the case where we make a promise or issue a command. So constatives are also performatives. In a later essay, Austin made a distinction between illocutionary (speech) acts, such as statements, promises, and so on; and perlocutionary acts: persuading, amusing, frightening, and the like.

P. F. Strawson (b. 1919) and J. R. Searle (b. 1932), among others, have responded to and raised various criticisms of Austin. Essays by both of these philosophers appear in this volume.

The main forms of twentieth-century analytic and linguistic philosophy have now been examined. Now perhaps the reader can see why I said earlier (in the beginning of this introduction) that it is difficult to come up with a single definition or characterization of analytic philosophy that fits all of its various forms. Obviously, all of these forms have been very much concerned with the analysis of language. But that is perhaps about as far as one can go in giving a characterization applicable to all of them.

Of course, there is much more that I have not gone into. For example, I have not said anything about the development of modern logic or the philosophy of mathematics and the philosophy of science. (This is why I have not included any works in this book by the great philosopher-logician-mathematician Gottlob Frege.) Also I have not gone into recent work in semantics and linguistic studies. Most of the works in these areas are far too technical and difficult for inclusion in this volume.

NOTES

1. "My Mental Development," in P. Schilpp, ed., *The Philosophy of Bertrand Russell.*
2. Morris Weitz, *20th Century Philosophy: The Analytic Tradition* (New York: Macmillan, 1966), p. 327.

Realism and Common Sense

6. The Refutation of Idealism

G. E. Moore

I

Modern Idealism, if it asserts any general conclusion about the universe at all, asserts that it is *spiritual*. There are two points about this assertion to which I wish to call attention. These points are that, whatever be its exact meaning, it is certainly meant to assert (1) that the universe is very different indeed from what it seems, and (2) that it has quite a large number of properties which it does not seem to have. Chairs and tables and mountains *seem* to be very different from us; but, when the whole universe is declared to be spiritual, it is certainly meant to assert that they are far more like us than we think. The idealist means to assert that they are *in some sense* neither lifeless nor unconscious, as they certainly seem to be; and I do not think his language is so grossly deceptive, but that we may assume him to believe that they really are very different indeed from what they seem. And secondly when he declares that they are *spiritual,* he means to include in that term quite a large number of different properties. When the whole universe is declared to be spiritual, it is meant not only that it is in some sense *conscious,* but that it has what we recognise in ourselves as the *higher* forms of consciousness. That it is intelligent; that it is purposeful; that it is not mechanical; all these different things are commonly asserted of it. In general, it may be said, this phrase 'reality is spiritual' excites and expresses the belief that the *whole* universe possesses *all the qualities* the possession of which is held to make us so superior to things which seem to be inanimate: at least, if it does not possess exactly those which we possess, it possesses not one only, but several others, which, by the same ethical standard, would be judged equal to or better than our own. When we say it is *spiritual* we mean to say that it has quite a number of excellent qualities, different from any which we commonly attribute either to stars or planets or to cups and saucers.

Now why I mention these two points is that when engaged in the intricacies of philosophic discussion, we are apt to overlook the vastness of the difference between this idealistic view and the ordinary view of the world, and to overlook

121

the number of *different* propositions which the idealist must prove. It is, I think, owing to the vastness of this difference and owing to the number of different excellences which Idealists attribute to the universe, that it seems such an interesting and important question whether Idealism be true or not. But, when we begin to argue about it, I think we are apt to forget what a vast number of arguments this interesting question must involve: we are apt to assume, that if one or two points be made on either side, the whole case is won. I say this lest it should be thought that any of the arguments which will be advanced in this paper would be sufficient to disprove, or any refutation of them sufficient to prove, the truly interesting and important proposition that reality is spiritual. For my own part I wish it to be clearly understood that I do not suppose that anything I shall say has the smallest tendency to prove that reality is not spiritual: I do not believe it possible to refute a single one of the many important propositions contained in the assertion that it is so. Reality may be spiritual, for all I know; and I devoutly hope it is. But I take "Idealism" to be a wide term and to include not only this interesting conclusion but a number of arguments which are supposed to be, if not sufficient, at least *necessary,* to prove it. Indeed I take it that modern Idealists are chiefly distinguished by certain arguments which they have in common. That reality is spiritual has, I believe, been the tenet of many theologians; and yet, for believing that alone, they should hardly be called Idealists. There are besides, I believe, many persons, not improperly called Idealists, who hold certain characteristic propositions, without venturing to think them quite sufficient to prove so grand a conclusion. It is, therefore, only with Idealistic *arguments* that I am concerned; and if any Idealist holds that *no* argument is necessary to prove that reality is spiritual, I shall certainly not have refuted him. I shall, however, attack at least one argument, which, to the best of my belief, is considered necessary to their position by *all* Idealists. And I wish to point out a certain advantage which this procedure gives me—an advantage which justifies the assertion that, if my arguments are sound, they will have refuted Idealism. If I can refute a single proposition which is a necessary and essential step in all Idealistic arguments, then, no matter how good the rest of these arguments may be, I shall have proved that Idealists have *no reason whatever* for their conclusion.

Suppose we have a chain of argument which takes the form: Since A is B, and B is C, and C is D, it follows A is D. In such an argument though 'B is C' and 'C is D' may both be perfectly true, yet if 'A is B' be false, we have no more reason for asserting A is D than if all three were false. It does not, indeed, follow that A is D is false; nor does it follow that no other arguments would prove it to be true. But it does follow that, so far as this argument goes, it is the barest supposition, without the least bit of evidence. I propose to attach a proposition which seems to me to stand in this relation to the conclusion 'Reality is spiritual.' I do not propose to dispute that 'Reality is spiritual'; I do not deny that there may be reasons for thinking that it is: but I do propose to show that one reason upon which, to the best of my judgment, all other arguments ever used by Idealists depend is *false*. These other arguments may, for all I shall say, be eminently ingenious and true; and they are very many and various, and different Idealists use the most different arguments to prove the same most important conclusions. Some of these *may* be sufficient to prove that B is C and C is D; but if, as I shall try to show, their 'A is B' is false the conclusion A is D remains a pleasant supposition. I do not deny that to suggest pleasant and plausible suppositions may be the proper function of philosophy: but I am assuming that the name Idealism can only be properly applied where there is a certain amount of argument, intended to be cogent.

The subject of this paper is, therefore, quite uninteresting. Even if I prove my point, I shall have proved nothing about the Universe in general. Upon the important question whether Reality is or is not spiritual my argument will not have the remotest bearing. I shall only attempt to arrive at the truth about a matter, which is in itself quite trivial and insignificant, and from which, so far as I can see and certainly so far as I shall say, no conclusions can be drawn about any of the subjects about which we most want to know. The only importance I can claim for the subject I shall investigage is that it seems to me to be a matter upon which not Idealists only, but all philosophers and psychologists also, have been in error, and from their erroneous view of which they have inferred (validly or invalidly) their most striking and interesting conclusions. And that it has even this importance I cannot hope to prove. If it has this importance, it will indeed follow that all the most striking results of philosophy—Sensationalism, Agnosticism and Idealism alike—have, for all that has hitherto been urged in their favour, no more foundation than the supposition that a chimera lives in the moon. It will follow that, unless new reasons never urged hitherto can be found, all the most important philosophic doctrines have as little claim to assent as the most superstitious beliefs of the lowest savages. Upon the question what we have *reason* to believe in the most interesting matters, I do therefore think that my results will have an important bearing; but I cannot too clearly insist that upon the question whether these beliefs are true they will have none whatever.

The trivial proposition which I propose to dispute is this: that *esse* is *percipi*. This is a very ambiguous proposition, but, in some sense or other, it has been very widely held. That it is, in some sense, essential to Idealism, I must for the present merely assume. What I propose to show is that, in all the senses ever given to it, it is false.

But, first of all, it may be useful to point out briefly in what relation I conceive it to stand to Idealistic arguments. That wherever you can truly predicate *esse* you can truly predicate *percipi*, in some sense or other, is, I take it, a necessary step in all arguments, properly to be called Idealistic, and, what is more, in all arguments hitherto offered for the Idealistic conclusion. If *esse* is *percipi*, this is at once equivalent to saying that whatever is, is experienced; and this, again, is equivalent, in a sense, to saying that whatever is, is something mental. But this is not the sense in which the Idealist *conclusion* must maintain that Reality is *mental*. The Idealist *conclusion* is that *esse* is *percipere;* and hence, whether *esse* be *percipi* or not, a further and different discussion is needed to show whether or not it is also *percipere*. And again, even if *esse* be *percipere*, we need a vast quantity of further argument to show that what has *esse* has also those higher mental qualities which are denoted by spiritual. This is why I said that *the* question I should discuss, namely, whether or not *esse* is *percipi*, must be utterly insufficient either to prove or to disprove that reality is spiritual. But, on the other hand, I believe that every argument ever used to show that reality is spiritual has inferred this (validly or invalidly) from '*esse* is *percipere*' as one of its premises; and that this again has never been pretended to be proved except by use of the premiss that *esse* is *percipi*. The type of argument used for the latter purpose is familiar enough. It is said that since whatever is, is experienced, and since some things are which are not experienced by the individual, these must at least form part of some experience. Or again that, since an object necessarily implies a subject, and since the whole world must be an object, we must conceive it to belong to some subject or subjects, in the same sense in which whatever is the object of our experience belongs to us. Or again, that, since thought enters into the essence of all reality, we must conceive behind it, in it, or as its essence, a spirit akin to ours, who think: that 'spirit greets spirit' in its object. Into the validity of these inferences I do not propose to enter: they obviously require a great deal of discussion. I only desire to point out that, however correct they may be, yet if *esse* is not *percipi*, they leave us as far from a proof that reality is spiritual, as if they were all false too.

But now: Is *esse percipi?* There are three very ambiguous terms in this proposition, and I must begin by distinguishing the different things that may be meant by some of them.

And first with regard to *percipi*. This term need not trouble us long at present. It was, perhaps, originally used to mean 'sensation' only; but I am not going to be so unfair to modern Idealists—the only Idealists to whom the term should now be applied without qualification—as to hold that, if they say *esse* is *percipi*, they mean by *percipi* sensation only. On the contrary I quite agree with them that, if *esse* be *percipi* at all, *percipi* must be understood to include not sensation only, but that other type of mental fact, which is called 'thought'; and, whether *esse* be *percipi* or not, I consider it to be the main service of the philosophic school, to which modern Idealists belong, that they have insisted on distinguishing 'sensation' and 'thought' and on emphasising the importance of the latter. Against Sensationalism and Empiricism they have maintained the true view. But the distinction between sensation and thought need not detain us here. For, in whatever respects they differ, they have at least this in common, that they are both forms of consciousness or, to use a term that seems to be more in fashion just now, they are both ways of experiencing. Accordingly, whatever *esse* is *percipi* may mean, it does *at least* assert that whatever is, is *experienced*. And since what I wish to maintain is, that even this is untrue, the question whether it be experienced by way of sensation or thought or both is for my purpose quite irrelevant. If it be not experienced at all, it cannot be either an object of thought or an object of sense. It is only if being involves 'experience' that the question, whether it involves sensation or thought or both, becomes important. I beg, therefore, that *percipi* may be understood, in what follows, to refer merely to what is *common* to sensation and thought. A very recent article states the meaning of *esse* is *percipi* with all desirable clearness in so far as *percipi* is concerned. 'I will undertake to show,' says Mr. Taylor,[1] 'that what makes [any piece of fact] real can be nothing but its presence as an inseparable aspect of *a sentient experience,*' I am glad to think that Mr. Taylor has been in time to supply me with so definite a statement that this is the ultimate premiss of Idealism. My paper will at least refute Mr. Taylor's Idealism, if it refutes anything at all: for I *shall* undertake to show that what makes a thing real cannot possibly be its presence as an inseparable aspect of a sentient experience.

But Mr. Taylor's statement though clear, I think, with regard to the meaning of *percipi* is highly ambiguous in other respects. I will leave it for the present to consider the next ambiguity in the statement: *Esse* is *percipi*. What does the copula mean? What can be meant by saying that Esse *is* percipi? There are just three meanings, one or other of which such a statement *must* have, if it is to be true; and of these there is only one which it can have, if it is to be important. (1) The statement may be meant to assert that the word 'esse' is used to signify nothing either more or less than the word 'percipi': that the two words are precise synonyms: that they are merely different names for one and the same thing: that what is meant by *esse* is absolutely identical with what is meant by *percipi*. I think I need not prove that the principle *esse* is *percipi* is *not* thus intended merely to define a word; nor yet that, if it were, it would be extremely bad definition. But if it does *not* mean this, only two alternatives remain. The second is (2) that what is meant by *esse,* though not absolutely identical with what is meant by *percipi,* yet *includes* the latter as a *part* of its meaning. If this were the meaning of 'esse is percipi,' then to say that a thing was real would not be the same thing as to say that it was experienced. That it was *real* would mean that it was experienced and *something else besides:* 'being experienced' would be *analytically essential* to reality, but would not be the whole meaning of the term. From the fact that a thing was real we should be able to infer, by the law of contradiction, that it was experienced; since the latter would be *part* of what is meant by the former. But, on the other hand, from the fact a thing was experienced we should *not* be able to infer that it was real; since it would not follow from the fact that it had one of the attributes essential to reality, that it *also* had the other or others. Now, if we understand *esse* is *percipi* in this second sense, we must distinguish *three* different things which it asserts. First of all, it gives a definition of the word 'reality,' asserting that word stands for a complex whole, of which what is meant by 'percipi' forms a part. And secondly it asserts that 'being experienced' forms a part of a certain whole. Both these propositions may be true, and at all events I do not wish to dispute them. I do not, indeed, think that the word 'reality' is commonly used to include 'percipi': but I do not wish to argue about the meaning of words. And that many things which are experienced are also something else—that to be experienced forms part of certain wholes, is, of course, indisputable. But what I wish to point out is, that neither of these propositions is of any importance, unless we add to them a *third*. That 'real' is a convenient name for a union of attributes which *sometimes* occurs, it could not be worth any one's while to assert: no inferences of any importance could be drawn from such an assertion. Our principle could only mean that when a thing happens to have *percipi* as well as the other qualities included under *esse*, it has *percipi*: and we should never be able to *infer* that it was experienced, except from a proposition which already asserted that it was both experienced and something else. Accordingly, if the assertion that *percipi* forms part of the whole meant by reality is to have any importance, it must mean that the whole is organic, at least in this sense, that the other constituent or constituents of it *cannot* occur without percipi, even if percipi can occur without them. Let us call these other constituents *x*. The proposition that *esse* includes *percipi*, and that therefore from *esse percipi* can be inferred, can only be important if it is meant to assert that *percipi* can be inferred from *x*. The only importance of the question whether the whole *esse* includes the part *percipi* rests therefore on the question whether the part *x* is necssarily connected with the part *percipi*. And this is (3) the third possible meaning of the assertion *esse is percipi*: and, as we now see, the only important one. *Esse* is *percipi* asserts that wherever you have *x* you also have *percipi* that whatever has the property *x* also has the property that it is *experienced*. And this being so, it will be convenient if, for the future, I may be allowed to use the term '*esse*' to denote *x alone*. I do not wish thereby to beg the question whether what we commonly mean by the word 'real' does or does not include *percipi* as well as *x*. I am quite content that my definition of '*esse*' to denote *x*, should be regarded merely as an arbitrary verbal definition. Whether it is so or not, the only question of interest is whether from *x percipi* can be inferred, and I should prefer to be able to express this in the form: can *percipi* be inferred from *esse*? Only let it be understood that when I say *esse*, that term will not for the future *include percipi*: it denotes only that *x*, which Idealists, perhaps rightly include *along with percipi* under *their* term *esse*. That there is such an *x* they admit on pain of making the proposition an *absolute* tautology; and that from this *x percipi* can be inferred they must admit, on pain of making it a perfectly barren analytic proposition. Whether *x* along should or should not be called *esse* is not worth a dispute: what is worth dispute is whether *percipi* is necessarily connected with *x*.

We have therefore discovered the ambiguity of the copula in *esse is percipi*, so far as to see that this principle asserts two distinct terms to be so related, that whatever has the *one*, which I call *esse*, has *also* the property that it is experienced. It asserts a necessary connexion between *esse* on the one hand and *percipi* on the other; these two words denoting each a distinct term, and *esse* denoting a term in which that denoted by *percipi* is not included. We have, then in *esse is percipi*, a *necessary synthetic* proposition which I have undertaken to refute. And I may say at once that, understood as such, it cannot be refuted. If the Idealist chooses to assert that it is merely a self-evident truth, I have only to say that it does not appear to me to be so. But I believe that no Idealist ever has maintained it to be so. Although this — that two distinct terms are necessarily related — is the only sense which 'esse is percipi' can have if it is to be true and important, it *can* have another sense, if it is to be an important falsehood. I believe that Idealists all hold this important falsehood. They do not perceive that *Esse* is *percipi* must, if true, be *merely* a self-evident synthetic truth; they either identify with it or give as a reason for it another proposition which must be false because it is self-contradictory. Unless they did so, they would have to admit that it was a perfectly unfounded assumption; and if they recognised that it was *unfounded,* I do not think they would maintain its truth to be evident. *Esse* is *percipi*, in the sense I have found for it, *may* indeed be true; I cannot refute it: but if this sense were clearly apprehended, no one, I think, would *believe* that it was true.

Idealists, we have seen, must assert that whatever is experienced, is *necessarily* so. And this doctrine they commonly express by saying that 'the object of experience is inconceivable apart from the subject.' I have hitherto been concerned with pointing out what meaning this assertion must have, if it is to be an important truth. I now propose to show that it may have an important meaning, which must be false, because it is self-contradictory.

It is a well-known fact in the history of philosophy that *necessary* truths in general, but especially those of which it is said that the opposite is inconceivable, have been commonly supposed to be *analytic*, in the sense that the proposition denying them was self-contradictory. It was in this way, commonly supposed, before Kant, that many truths could be proved by the law of contradiction alone. This is, therefore, a mistake which it is plainly easy for the best philosophers to make. Even since Kant many have continued to assert it; but I am aware that among those Idealists, who most properly deserve the name, it has become more fashionable to assert that truths are *both* analytic and synthetic. Now with many of their reasons for asserting this I am not concerned: it is possible that in some connexions the assertion may bear a useful and true sense. But if we understand 'analytic' in the sense just defined, namely, what is proved by the law of contradiction *alone,* it is plain that, if 'synthetic' means what is *not* proved by this alone, no truth can be both analytic and synthetic. Now it seems to me that those who do maintain truths to be both, do nevertheless maintain that they are so in this as well as in other senses. It is, indeed, extremely unlikely that so essential a part of the historical meaning of 'analytic' and 'synthetic' should have been entirely discarded, especially since we find no express recognition that it is discarded. In that case it is fair to suppose that modern Idealists have been influenced by the view that certain truths can be proved by the law of contradiction alone. I admit they also expressly declare that they can *not:* but this is by no means sufficient to prove that they do not also think they are; since it is very easy to hold two mutually contradictory opinions. What I suggest then is that Idealists hold the particular doctrine in question, concerning the relation of subject and object in experience, because they think it is an analytic truth in this restricted sense that it is proved by the law of contradiction alone.

I am suggesting that the Idealist maintains that object and subject are necessarily connected, mainly because he fails to see that they are *distinct,* that they are *two,* at all. When he thinks of 'yellow' and when he thinks of the 'sensation of yellow,' he fails to see that there is anything whatever in the latter which is not in the former. This being so, to deny that yellow can ever *be* apart from the sensation of yellow is merely to deny that yellow can ever be other than it is; since yellow and the sensation of yellow are absolutely identical. To assert that yellow is necessarily an object of experience is to assert that yellow is necessarily yellow — a purely identical proposition, and therefore proved by the law of contradiction alone. Of course, the proposition also implies that experience is, after all, something distinct from yellow — else there would be no reason for insisting that yellow is a sensation: and that the argument thus both affirms and denies that yellow and sensation of yellow are distinct, is what sufficiently refutes it. But this contradiction can easily be overlooked, because though we are convinced, in other connexions, that 'experience' does mean something and something most important, yet we are never distinctly aware *what* it means, and thus in every particular case we do not notice its presence. The facts present themselves as a kind of antinomy: (1) Experience *is* something unique and different from anything else: (2) Experience of green is entirely indistinguishable from green; two propositions which cannot both be true. Idealists, holding both, can only take refuge in arguing from the one in some connexions and from the other in others.

But I am well aware that there are many Idealists who would repel it as an utterly unfounded charge that they fail to distinguish between a sensation or idea and what I will call its object. And there are, I admit, many who not only imply, as we all do, that green is distinct from the sensation of green, but expressly insist upon the distinction as an important part of their system. They would perhaps only assert that the two form an inseparable unity. But I wish to point out that many, who use this phrase, and who do admit the distinction, are not thereby absolved from the charge that they deny it. For there is a certain doctrine, very prevalent among philosophers nowadays, which by a very simple reduction may be seen to assert that two distinct things both are and are not distinct. A distinction is asserted; but it is *also* asserted that the things distinguished form an 'organic unity.' But, forming such a unity, it is held, each would not be what it is *apart from its relation to the other.* Hence to consider either by itself is to make an *illegitimate abstraction.* The recognition that there are 'organic unities' and 'illegitimate abstractions' in this sense is regarded as one of the chief conquests of modern philosophy. But what is the sense attached to these terms? An abstraction is illegitimate, when and only when we attempt to assert of *a part* — of something abstracted — that which is true only of the *whole* to which it belongs: and it may perhaps be useful to point out that this should not be done. But the application actually made of this principle, and what perhaps would be expressly acknowledged as its meaning, is something much the reverse of useful. The principle is used to assert that certain abstractions are *in all cases* illegitimate; that whenever you try to assert *anything whatever* of that which is *part* of an organic whole, what you assert can only be true of the whole. And this principle, so far from being a useful truth, is necessarily false. For if the whole can, nay *must*, be substituted for the part in all propositions and for all purposes, this can only be because the whole is absolutely identical with the part. When, therefore, we are told that green and the sensation of green are certainly distinct but yet are not separable, or that it is an illegitimate abstraction to consider the one apart from the other, what these provisos are used to assert is, that though the two things are distinct yet you not only can but must treat them as if they were not. Many philosophers, therefore, when they admit a distinction, yet (following the lead of Hegel) boldly assert their right, in a slightly more obcure form of words, *also* to deny it. The principle of organic unities, like that of combined analysis and synthesis, is mainly used to defend the practice of holding *both* of two contradictory propositions, wherever this may seem convenient. In this, as in other matters, Hegel's main service to philosophy has consisted in giving a name to and erecting into a principle, a type of fallacy to which experience had shown philosophers, along with the rest of mankind, to be addicted. No wonder that he has followers and admirers.

I have shown then, so far, that when the Idealist asserts the important principle '*Esse* is *percipi*' he must, if it is to be true, mean by this that: Whatever is experienced also *must* be experienced. And I have also shown that he *may* identify with, or give as a reason for, this proposition, one which must be false, because it is self contradictory. But at this point I propose to make a complete break in my argument. '*Esse* is *percipi*,' we have seen, asserts of two terms, as distinct from one another as 'green' and 'sweet,' that whatever has the one has also the other: it asserts that 'being' and 'being experienced' are necessarily connected: that whatever *is* is *also* experienced. And this, I admit cannot be directly refuted. But I believe it to be false; and I have asserted that anybody who saw that '*esse* and *percipi* *were* as distinct as 'green' and 'sweet' would be no more ready to believe that whatever *is* is *also* experienced, than to believe that whatever is green is also sweet. I have asserted that no one would believe that '*esse* is *percipi*' if they saw how different *esse* is from *percipi*: but *this* I shall not try to prove. I have asserted that all who do believe that '*esse* is *percipi*' identify with it or take as a reason for it a self-contradictory proposition: but this I shall not try to prove. I shall only try to show that certain propositions which I assert to be believed, are false. That they are believed, and that without this belief '*esse* is *percipi*' would not be believed either, I must leave without a proof.

II

I pass, then, from the uninteresting question 'Is *esse percipi*?' to the still more uninteresting and apparently irrelevant question 'What is a sensation or idea?'

We all know that the sensation of blue differs from that of green. But it is plain that if both are *sensations* they also have some point in common. What is it that they have in common? And how is this common element related to the points in which they differ?

I will call the common element 'consciousness' without yet attempting to say what the thing I so call *is*. We have then in every sensation two distinct terms, (1) 'consciousness,' in respect of which all sensations are alike; and (2) something else, in respect of which one sensation differs from another. It will be convenient if I may be allowed to call this second term the 'object' of a sensation: this also without yet attempting to say what I mean by the word.

We have then in every sensation two distinct elements, one which I call consciousness, and another which I call the object of consciousness. This must be so if the sensation of blue and the sensation of green, though different in one respect, are alike in another: blue is one object of sensation and green is another, and consciousness, which both sensations have in common, is different from either.

But, further, sometimes the sensation of blue exists in my mind and sometimes it does not; and knowing, as we now do, that the sensation of blue includes two different elements, namely consciousness and blue, the question arises whether, when the sensation of blue exists, it is the consciousness which exists, or the blue which exists, or both. And one point at least is plain: namely that these three alternatives are all different from one another. So that, if any one tells us that to say 'Blue exists' is the *same* thing as to say that 'Both blue and consciousness exist,' he makes a mistake and a self-contradictory mistake.

But another point is also plain, namely, that when the sensation exists, the consciousness, at least, certainly does exist; for when I say that the sensations of blue and of green both exist, I certainly mean that what is common to both and in virtue of which both are called sensations, exists in each case. The only alternative left, then, is that *either* both exist or the consciousness exists alone. If, therefore, any one tell us that the existence of blue is the same thing as the existence of the sensation of blue he makes a mistake and a self-contradictory mistake, for he asserts *either* that blue is the same thing as blue together with consciousness, *or* that it is the same thing as consciousness alone.

Accordingly to identify either "blue" or any other of what I have called "*objects*" of sensation, with the corresponding sensation is in every case, a self-contradictory error. It is to identify a part either with the whole of which it is a part or else with the other part of the same whole. If we are told that the assertion "Blue exists" is *meaningless* unless we mean by it that "The sensation of blue exists," we are told what is certainly false and self-contradictory. If we are told that the existence of blue is inconceivable apart from the existence of the sensation, the speaker *probably* means to convey to us, by this ambiguous expression, what is a self-contradictory error. For we can and must conceive the existence of blue as something quite distinct from the existence of the sensation. We can and must conceive that blue might exist and yet the sensation of blue not exist. For my own part I not only conceive this, but conceive it to be true. Either therefore this terrific assertion of inconceivability means what is false and self-contradictory or else it means only that *as a matter of fact* blue never can exist unless the sensation of it exists also.

And at this point I need not conceal my opinion that no philosopher has ever yet succeeded in avoiding this self-contradictory error: that the most striking results both of Idealism and of Agnosticism are only obtained by identifying blue with the sensation of blue: that *esse* is held to be *percipi*, solely because *what is experienced* is held to be identical with *the experience of it*. That Berkeley and Mill committed this error will, perhaps, be granted: that modern Idealists make it will, I hope, appear more probable later. But that my opinion is plausible, I will now offer two pieces of evidence. The first is that language offers us no means of referring to such objects as "blue" and "green" and "sweet," except by calling them sensations: it is an obvious violation of language to call them "things" or "objects" or "terms." and similarly we have no natural means of referring to such objects as "causality" or "likeness" or "identity," except by calling them "ideas" or "notions" or "conceptions." But it is hardly likely that if philosophers had clearly distinguished in the past between a sensation or idea and what I have called its object, there should have been no separate name for the latter. They have always used the same name for these two different "things" (if I may call them so): and hence there is some probability that they have supposed these "things" *not* to be two and different, but one and the same. And, secondly, there is a very good reason why they should have supposed so, in the fact that when we refer to introspection and try to discover what the sensation of blue is, it is very easy to suppose that we have before us only a single term. The term "blue" is easy enough to distinguish, but the other element which I have called "consciousness"—that which sensation of blue has in common with sensation of green—is extremely difficult to fix. That many people fail to distinguish it at all is sufficiently shown by the fact that there are materialists. And, in general, that which makes the sensation of blue a mental fact seems to escape us: it seems, if I may use a metaphor, to be transparent—we look through it and see nothing but the blue; we may be convinced that there *is something* but *what* it is no philosopher, I think, has yet clearly recognised.

But this was a digression. The point I had established so far was that in every sensation or idea we must distinguish two elements, (1) the "object," or that in which one differs from another; and (2) "consciousness," or that which all have in common—that which makes them sensations or mental facts. This being so, it followed that when a sensation or idea exists, we have to choose between the alternatives that either object alone, or consciousness alone, or both, exist; and I showed that of these alternatives one, namely that the object only exists, is excluded by the fact that what we mean to assert is certainly the existence of a mental fact. There remains the question: Do both exist? Or does the consciousness alone? And to this question one answer has hitherto been given universally: That both exist.

This answer follows from the analysis hitherto accepted of the relation of what I have called "object " to "consciousness" in any sensation or idea. It is held that what I call the object is merely the "content" of a sensation or idea. It is held that in each case we can distinguish two elements and two only, (1) the fact that there is feeling or experience, and (2) *what* is felt or experienced; the sensation or idea, it is said, forms a whole, in which we must distinguish two "inseparable aspects," "content" and "existence." I shall try to show that this analysis is false; and for that purpose I must ask what may seem an extraordinary question: namely what is meant by saying that one thing is "content" of another? It is not usual to ask this question; the term is used as if everybody must understand it. But since I am going to maintain that "blue" is *not* the content of the sensation of blue, and what is more important, that, even if it were this analysis would leave out the most important element in the sensation of blue, it is necessary that I should try to explain precisely what it is that I shall deny.

What then is meant by saying that one thing is the "content" of another? First of all I wish to point out that "blue" is rightly and properly said to be part of the content of a blue flower. If, therefore, we also assert that it is part of the content of the sensation of blue, we assert that it has to the other parts (if any) of this whole the same relation which it has to the other parts of a blue flower—and we assert only this: we cannot mean to assert that it has to the sensation of blue any relation which it does not have to the blue flower. And we have seen that the sensation of blue contains at least one other element beside blue—namely, what I call "consciousness," which makes it a sensation. So far then as we assert that blue is the content of the sensation, we assert that it has to this "consciousness" the same relation which it has to the other parts of a blue flower: we do assert this, and we assert no more than this. Into the question what exactly the relation is between blue and a blue flower in virtue of which we call the former part of its "content" I do not propose to enter. It is sufficient for my purpose to point out that it is the general relation most commonly meant when we talk of a thing and its qualities; and that this relation is such that to say the thing exists implies that the qualities also exist. The *content* of the thing is *what* we assert to exist, when we assert *that* the thing exists.

When, therefore, blue is said to be part of the content of the "sensation of blue," the latter is treated as if it were a whole constituted in exactly the same way as any other "thing." The "sensation of blue," on this view, differs from a blue bead or a blue beard, in exactly the same way in which the two latter differ from one another: the blue bead differs from the blue beard, in that while the former contains glass, the latter contains hair; and the "sensation of blue" differs from both in that, instead of glass or hair, it contains consciousness. The relation of the blue to the consciousness is conceived to be exactly the same as that of the blue to the glass or hair: it is in all three cases the *quality* of a *thing*.

But I said just now that the sensation of blue was analysed into "content" and "existent," and that blue was said to be *the* content of the idea of blue. There is an ambiguity in this and a possible error, which I must note in passing. The term "content" may be used in two senses. If we use "content" as equivalent to what Mr. Bradley calls the "*what*"—if we mean by it the *whole* of what is said to exist, when the thing is said to exist, then blue is certainly not *the* content of the sensation of blue: part of the *content* of the sensation is, in this sense of the term, that other element which I have called consciousness. The analysis of this sensation into the "content" "blue," on the one hand, and mere existence on the other, is therefore certainly false; in it we have again the self-contradictory identification of "Blue exists" with "The sensation of blue exists." But there is another sense in which "blue" might properly be said to be *the* content of the sensation — namely, the sense in which "content," like eidos, is opposed to "substance" or "matter." For the element "consciousness," being common to all sensations, may be and certainly is regarded as in some sense their "substance," and by the "content" of each is only meant that in respect of which one differs from another. In this sense then "blue" might be said to be *the* content of the sensation; but, in that case, the analysis into "content" and "existence" is, at least, misleading, since under "existence" must be included "*what* exists" in the sensation other than blue.

We have it, then, as a universally received opinion that blue is related to the sensation or idea of blue, as its *content,* and that this view, if it is to be true, must mean that blue is part of *what* is said to exist when we say that the sensation exists. To say that the sensation exists is to say both that blue exists and that "consciousness," whether we call it the substance of which blue is *the* content or call it another part of the content, exists too. Any sensation or idea is a "*thing*," and what I have called its object is the quality of this thing. Such a "thing" is what we think of when we think of a *mental image.* A mental image is conceived as if it were related to that of which it is the image (if there be any such thing) in exactly the same way as the image in a looking-glass is related to that of which it is the reflection; in both cases there is identity of content, and the image in the looking-glass differs from that in the mind solely in respect of the fact that in the one case the other constituent of the image is "glass" and in the other case it is consciousness. If the image is of blue, it is not conceived that this "content" has any relation to the consciousness but what it has to the glass: it is conceived *merely* to be its *content.* And owing to the fact that sensations and ideas are all considered to be *wholes* of this description — things in the mind — the question: What do we know? is considered to be identical with the question: What reason have we for supposing that there are things outside the mind *corresponding* to these that are inside it?

What I wish to point out is (1) that we have no reason for supposing that there are such things as mental images at all — for supposing that blue *is* part of the content of the sensation of blue, and (2) that even if there are mental images, no mental image and no sensation or idea is *merely* a thing of this kind: that 'blue,' even if it is part of the content of the image or sensation or idea of blue, is always *also* related to it in quite another way, and that this other relation, omitted in the traditional analysis, is the *only* one which makes the sensation of a mental fact at all.

The true analysis of a sensation or idea is as follows. The element that is common to them all, and which I have called 'consciousness,' really *is* consciousness. A sensation is, in reality, a case of 'knowing' or 'being aware of' or 'experiencing' something. When we know that the sensation of blue exists, the fact we know is that there exists an awareness of blue. And this awareness is not merely, as we have hitherto seen it must be, itself something distinct and unique, utterly different from blue: it also has a perfectly distinct and unique relation to blue, a relation which is *not* that of thing or substance to content, nor of one part of content to another part of content. This relation is just that which we mean in every case by 'knowing.' To have in your mind 'knowledge' of blue, is *not* to have in your mind a 'thing' or 'image' of which blue is the content. To be aware of the sensation of blue is *not* to be aware of a mental image—of a 'thing,' of which 'blue' and some other element are constituent parts in the same sense in which blue and glass are constituents of a blue bead. It is to be aware of an awareness of blue; awareness being used, in both cases, in exactly the same sense. This element, we have seen, is certainly neglected by the 'content' theory: that theory entirely fails to express the fact that there is, in the sensation of blue, this unique relation between blue and the other constituent. And what I contend is that this omission is *not* mere negligence of expression, but is due to the fact that though philosophers have recognised that *something* distinct is meant by consciousness, they have never yet had a clear conception of *what* that something is. They have not been able to hold *it* and *blue* before their minds and to compare them, in the same way in which they can compare *blue* and *green*. And this for the reason I gave above: namely that the moment we try to fix our attention upon consciousness and to see *what,* distinctly, it is, it seems to vanish: it seems as if we had before us a mere emptiness. When we try to introspect the sensation of blue, all we can see is the blue: the other element is as if it were diaphanous. Yet it *can* be distinguished if we look attentively enough, and if we know that there is something to look for. My main object in this paragraph has been to try to make the reader *see* it; but I fear I shall have succeeded very ill.

It being the case, then, that the sensation of blue includes in its analysis, beside blue, *both* a unique element 'awareness' *and* a unique relation of this element to blue, I can make plain what I meant by asserting, as two distinct propositions, (1) that blue is probably not part of the content of the sensation at all, and (2) that, even if it were, the sensation would nevertheless not be the sensation *of* blue, if blue had only this relation to it. The first hypothesis may now be expressed by saying that, if it were true, then, when the sensation of blue exists, there exists a *blue awareness:* offence may be taken at the expression, but yet it expresses just what should be and is meant by saying that blue is, in this case, a *content* of consciousness or experience. Whether or not, when I have the sensation of blue, my consciousness or awareness is thus blue, my introspection does not enable me to decide with certainty: I only see no reason for thinking that it is. But whether it is or not, the point is unimportant, for introspection *does* enable me to decide that something else is also true: namely that I am aware *of* blue, and by this I mean, that my awareness has to blue a quite different and distinct relation. It is possible, I admit, that my awareness is blue *as well* as being *of* blue: but what I am quite sure of is that it is *of* blue; that it has to blue the simple and unique relation the existence of which alone justifies us in distinguishing knowledge of a thing from the thing known, indeed in distinguishing mind from matter. And this result I may express by saying that what is called the *content* of a sensation is in very truth what I originally called it—the sensation's *object*.

But, if all this be true, what follows?

Idealists admit that some things really exist of which they are not aware: there are some things, they hold, which are not inseparable aspects of *their* experience, even if they be inseparable aspects of some experience. They further hold that some of the things of which they are sometimes aware do really exist, even when they are not aware of them: they hold for instance that they are sometimes aware of other minds, which continue to exist even when they are not aware of them. They are, therefore, sometimes aware of something which is *not* an inseparable aspect of their own experience. They do *know some* things which are *not* a mere part or content of their experience. And what my analysis of sensation has been designed to show is, that whenever I have a mere sensation or idea, the fact is that I am then aware of something which is equally and in the same sense *not* an inseparable aspect of my experience. The awareness which I have maintained to be included in sensation is the very same unique fact which constitutes every kind of knowledge: "blue" is as much an object, and as little a mere content, of my experience, when I experience it, as the most exalted and independent real thing of which I am ever aware. There is, therefore, no question of how we are to "get outside the circle of our own ideas and sensations." Merely to have a sensation is already to *be* outside that circle. It is to know something which is as truly and really *not* a part of my experience, as anything which I can ever know.

Now I think I am not mistaken in asserting that the reason why Idealists suppose that everything which *is* must be an inseparable aspect of some experience, is that they suppose some things, at least, to be inseparable aspects of *their* experience. And there is certainly nothing which they are so firmly convinced to be an inseparable aspect of their experience as what they call the *content* of their ideas and sensations. If, therefore, *this* turns out in every case, whether it be also the content or not, to be at least *not* an inseparable aspect of the experience of it, it will be readily admitted that nothing else which *we* experience ever is such an inseparable aspect. But if we never experience anything but what is *not* an inseparable aspect of *that* experience, how can we infer that anything whatever, let alone *everything,* is an inseparable aspect of *any* experience? How utterly unfounded is the assumption that "*esse* is *percipi*" appears in the clearest light.

But further I think it may be seen that if the object of an Idealist's sensation were, as he supposes, *not* the object but merely the content of that sensation, if, that is to say, it really were an inseparable aspect of his experience, each Idealist could never be aware either of himself or of any other real thing. For the relation of a sensation to its object is certainly the same as that of any other instance of experience to its object; and this, I think, is generally admitted even by Idealists: they state as readily that *what is* judged or thought or perceived is the *content* of that judgment or thought or perception, as that blue is the content of the sensation of blue. But, if so, then when any Idealist thinks he is *aware* of himself or of any one else, this cannot really be the case. The fact is, on his own theory, that himself and that other person are in reality mere *contents* of an awareness, which is aware *of* nothing whatever. All that can be said is that there is an awareness in him, *with* a certain content: it can never be true that there is in him a consciousness *of* anything. And similarly he is never aware either of the fact that he exists or that reality is spiritual. The real fact which he describes in those terms, is that his existence and the spirituality of reality are *contents* of an awareness, which is aware of nothing—certainly not, then, of its own content.

And further if everything, of which he thinks he is aware, is in reality merely a content of his own experience he has certainly no *reason* for holding that anything does exist except himself: it will, of course, be possible that other persons do exist; solipsism will not be necessarily true; but he cannot possibly infer from anything he holds that it is not true. That he himself exists will of course follow from his premiss that many things are contents of *his* experience. But since everything, of which he thinks himself aware, is in reality merely an inseparable aspect of that awareness; this premiss allows no inference that any of these contents far less any other consciousness, exists at all except as an inseparable aspect of his awareness, that is, as part of himself.

Such, and not those which he takes to follow from it, are the consequences which *do* follow from the Idealist's supposition that the object of an experience is in reality merely a content or inseparable aspect of that experience. If, on the other hand, we clearly recognise the nature of that peculiar relation which I have called "awareness of anything"; if we see that *this* is involved equally in the analysis of *every* experience—from the merest sensation to the most developed perception or reflexion, and that *this* is in fact the only essential element in an experience—the only thing that is both common and peculiar to all experiences—the only thing which gives us reason to call any fact mental; if, further, we recognise that this awareness is and must be in all cases of such a nature that its object, when we are aware of it, is precisely what it would be, if we were not aware: then it becomes plain that the existence of a table in space is related to my experience of *it* in precisely the same way as the existence of my own experience is related to my experience of *that*. Of both we are merely aware: if we are aware that the one exists, we are aware in precisely the same sense that the other exists; and if it is true that my experience can exist, even when I do not happen to be aware of its existence, we have exactly the same reason for supposing that the table can do so also. When, therefore, Berkeley, supposed that the only thing of which I am directly aware is my own sensations and ideas, he supposed what was false; and when Kant supposed that the objectivity of things in space *consisted* in the fact that they were "Vorstellungen" having to one another different relations from those which the same

"Vorstellungen" have to one another in subjective experience, he supposed what was equally false. I am as directly aware of the existence of material things in space as of my own sensations; and *what* I am aware of with regard to each is exactly the same—namely that in one case the material thing, and in the other case my sensation does really exist. The question requiring to be asked about material things is thus not: What reason have we for supposing that anything exists *corresponding* to our sensations? but: What reason have we for supposing that material things do *not* exist, since *their* existence has precisely the same evidence as that of our sensations? That either exist *may* be false; but if it is a reason for doubting the existence of matter, that it is an inseparable aspect of our experience, the same reasoning will prove conclusively that our experience does not exist either, since that must also be an inseparable aspect of our experience of *it*. The only *reasonable* alternative to the admission that matter exists *as well* as spirit, is absolute Scepticism—that, as likely as not *nothing* exists at all. All other suppositions—the Agnostic's, that something, at all events, does exist, as much as the Idealist's, that spirit does—are, if we have no reason for believing in matter, as baseless as the grossest superstitions.

NOTE

1. *International Journal of Ethics,* October, 1902

7. The Subject-Matter of Ethics*

G. E. Moore

1. It is very easy to point out some among our every-day judgments, with the truth of which Ethics is undoubtedly concerned. Whenever we say, 'So and so is a good man,' or 'That fellow is a villain'; whenever we ask, 'What ought I to do?' or 'Is it wrong for me to do like this?'; whenever we hazard such remarks as 'Temperance is a virtue and drunkenness a vice' — it is undoubtedly the business of Ethics to discuss such questions and such statements; to argue what is the true answer when we ask what it is right to do, and to give reasons for thinking that our statements about the character of persons or the morality of actions are true or false. In the vast majority of cases, where we make statements involving any of the terms 'virtue,' 'vice,' 'duty,' 'right,' 'ought,' 'good,' 'bad,' we are making ethical judgments; and if we wish to discuss their truth, we shall be discussing a point of Ethics.

So much as this is not disputed; but it falls very far short of defining the province of Ethics. That province may indeed be defined as the whole truth about that which is at the same time common to all such judgments and peculiar to them. But we have still to ask the question: What is it that is thus common and peculiar? And this is a question to which the very different answers have been given by ethical philosophers of acknowledged reputation, and none of them, perhaps, completely satisfactory.

2. If we take such examples as those given above, we shall not be far wrong in saying that they are all of them concerned with the question of 'conduct' — with the question, what, in the conduct of us, human beings, is good, and what is bad, what is right, and what is wrong. For when we say that a man is good, we commonly mean that he acts rightly; when we say that drunkenness is a vice, we commonly mean that to get drunk is a wrong or wicked action. And this discussion of human conduct is, in fact, that with which the name 'Ethics' is most intimately associated. It is so associated by derivation; and conduct is undoubtedly by far the commonest and most generally interesting object of ethical judgments.

Accordingly, we find that many ethical philosophers are disposed to accept as an adequate definition of 'Ethics' the statement that it deals with the question what is good or bad in human conduct. They hold that its enquiries are properly confined to 'conduct' or to 'practice'; they hold that the name 'practical philosophy' covers all the matter with which it has to do. Now, without discussing the proper meaning of the word (for verbal questions are properly left to the writers of dictionaries and other persons interested in literature; philosophy, as we shall see, has no concern with them), I may say that I intend to use 'Ethics' to cover more than this—a usage, for which there is, I think, quite sufficient authority. I am using it to cover an enquiry for which, at all events, there is no other word: the general enquiry into what is good.

Ethics is undoubtedly concerned with the question what good conduct is; but, being concerned with this, it obviously does not start at the beginning, unless it is prepared to tell us what is good as well as what is conduct. For 'good conduct' is a complex notion: all conduct is not good; for some is certainly bad and some may be indifferent. And on the other hand, other things, beside conduct, may be good; and if they are so, then, 'good' denotes some property, that is common to them and conduct; and if we examine good conduct alone of all good things, then we shall be in danger of mistaking for this property, some property which is not shared by those other things: and thus we shall have made a mistake about Ethics even in this limited sense; for we shall not know what good conduct really is. This is a mistake which many writers have actually made, from limiting their enquiry to conduct. And hence I shall try to avoid it by considering first what is good in general; hoping, that if we can arrive at any certainty about this, it will be much easier to settle the question of good conduct: for we all know pretty well what 'conduct' is. This, then, is our first question: What is good? and What is bad? and to the discussion of this question (or these questions) I give the name of Ethics, since that science must, at all events, include it.

3. But this is a question which may have many meanings. If, for example, each of us were to say 'I am doing good now' or 'I had a good dinner yesterday,' these statements would each of them be some sort of answer to our question, although perhaps a false one. So, too, when A asks B what school he ought to send his son to, B's answer will certainly be an ethical judgment. And similarly all distribution of praise or blame to any personage or thing that has existed, now exists, or will exist, does give some answer to the question 'What is good?' In all such cases some particular thing is judged to be good or bad: the question 'What?' is answered by 'This.' But this is not the sense in which a scientific Ethics asks the question. Not one, of all the many million answers of this kind, which must be true, can form a part of an ethical system; although that science must contain reasons and principles sufficient for deciding on the truth of all of them. There are far too many persons, things and events in the world, past, present, or to come, for a discussion of their individual merits to be embraced in any science. Ethics, therefore, does not deal at all with facts of this nature, facts that are unique, individual, absolutely particular; facts with

which such studies as history, geography, astronomy, are compelled, in part at least, to deal. And, for this reason, it is not the business of the ethical philosopher to give personal advice or exhortation.

4. But there is another meaning which may be given to the question 'What is good?' 'Books are good' would be an answer to it, though an answer obviously false; for some books are very bad indeed. And ethical judgments of this kind do indeed belong to Ethics; though I shall not deal with many of them. Such is the judgment 'Pleasure is good' – a judgment, of which ethics should discuss the truth, although it is not nearly as important as that other judgment, with which we shall be much occupied presently – 'Pleasure *alone* is good.' It is judgments of this sort, which are made in such books on Ethics as contain a list of 'virtues' – in Aristotle's 'Ethics' for example. But it is judgments of precisely the same kind, which form the substance of what is commonly supposed to be a study different from Ethics, and one much less respectable – the study of Casuistry. We may be told that Casuistry differs from Ethics, in that it is much more detailed and particular, Ethics much more general. But it is more important to notice that Casuistry does not deal with anything that is absolutely particular – particular in the only sense in which a perfectly precise line can be drawn between it and what is general. It is not particular in the sense just noticed, the sense in which this book is a particular book, and A's friend's advice particular advice. Casuistry may indeed be *more* particular and Ethics *more* general; but that means that they differ only in degree and not in kind. And this is universally true of 'particular' and 'general,' when used in this common, but inaccurate, sense. So far as Ethics allows itself to give lists of virtues or even to name constituents of the Ideal, it is indistinguishable from Casuistry. Both alike deal with what is general, in the sense in which physics and chemistry deal with what is general. Just as chemistry aims at discovering what are the properties of oxygen, *wherever it occurs,* and not only of this or that particular specimen of oxygen; so Casuistry aims at discovering what actions are good, *wherever they occur.* In this respect Ethics and Casuistry alike are to be classed with such sciences as physics, chemistry and physiology, in their absolute distinction from those of which history and geography are instances. And it is to be noted that, owing to their detailed nature, casuistical investigations are actually nearer to physics and to chemistry than are the investigations usually assigned to Ethics. For just as physics cannot rest content with the discovery that light is propagated by waves of ether, but must go on to discover the particular nature of the ether-waves corresponding to each several colour; so Casuistry, not content with the general law that charity is a virtue must attempt to discover the relative merits of every different form of charity. Casuistry forms, therefore, part of the ideal of ethical science: Ethics cannot be complete without it. The defects of Casuistry are not defects of principle; no objection can be taken to its aim and object. It has failed only because it is far too difficult a subject to be treated adequately in our present state of knowledge. The casuist has been unable to distinguish, in the cases which he treats, those elements upon which their value depends. Hence he often thinks two

cases to be alike in respect of value, when in reality they are alike only in some other respect. It is to mistakes of this kind that the pernicious influence of such investigations has been due. For Casuistry is the goal of ethical investigation. It cannot be safely attempted at the beginning of our studies, but only at the end.

5. But our question 'What is good?' may have still another meaning. We may, in the third place, mean to ask, not what thing or things are good, but how 'good' is to be defined. This is an enquiry which belongs only to Ethics, not to Casuistry; and this is the enquiry which will occupy us first.

It is an enquiry to which most special attention should be directed; since this question, how 'good' is to be defined, is the most fundamental question in all Ethics. That which is meant by 'good' is, in fact, except its converse 'bad,' the *only* simple object of thought which is peculiar to Ethics. Its definition is, therefore, the most essential point in the definition of Ethics; and moreover a mistake with regard to it entails a far larger number of erroneous ethical judgments than any other. Unless this first question be fully understood, and its true answer clearly recognised, the rest of Ethics is as good as useless from the point of view of systematic knowledge. True ethical judgments, of the two kinds last dealt with, may indeed be made by those who do not know the answer to this question as well as by those who do; and it goes without saying that the two classes of people may lead equally good lives. But it is extremely unlikely that the *most general* ethical judgments will be equally valid, in the absence of a true answer to this question: I shall presently try to shew that the gravest errors have been largely due to beliefs in a false answer. And, in any case, it is impossible that, till the answer to this question be known, any one should know *what is the evidence* for any ethical judgment whatsoever. But the main object of Ethics, as a systematic science, is to give correct *reasons* for thinking that this or that is good; and, unless this question be answered, such reasons cannot be given. Even, therefore, apart from the fact that a false answer leads to false conclusions, the present enquiry is a most necessary and important part of the science of Ethics.

6. What, then, is good? How is good to be defined? Now, it may be thought that this is a verbal question. A definition does indeed often mean the expressing of one word's meaning in other words. But this is not the sort of definition I am asking for. Such a definition can never be of ultimate importance in any study except lexicography. If I wanted that kind of definition I should have to consider in the first place how people generally used the word 'good'; but my business is not with its proper usage, as established by custom. I should, indeed, be foolish, if I tried to use it for something which it did not usually denote: if, for instance, I were to announce that, whenever I used the word 'good,' I must be understood to be thinking of that object which is usually denoted by the word 'table.' I shall, therefore, use the word in the sense in which I think it is ordinarily used; but at the same time I am not anxious to discuss whether I am right in thinking that it is so used. My business is solely with that object or idea, which I hold, rightly or wrongly, that the word is generally

used to stand for. What I want to discover is the nature of that object or idea, and about this I am extremely anxious to arrive at an agreement.

But, if we understand the question in this sense, my answer to it may seem a very disappointing one. If I am asked 'What is good?' my answer is that good is good, and that is the end of the matter. Or if I am asked 'How is good to be defined?' my answer is that it cannot be defined, and that is all I have to say about it. But disappointing as these answers may appear, they are of the very last importance. To readers who are familiar with philosophic terminology, I can express their importance by saying that they amount to this: That propositions about the good are all of them synthetic and never analytic; and that is plainly no trivial matter. And the same thing may be expressed more popularly, by saying that, if I am right, then nobody can foist upon us such an axiom as that 'Pleasure is the only good' or that 'The good is the desired' on the pretence that this is 'the very meaning of the word.'

7. Let us, then, consider this position. My point is that 'good' is a simple notion, just as 'yellow' is a simple notion; that, just as you cannot, by any manner of means, explain to any one who does not already know it, what yellow is, so you cannot explain what good is. Definitions of the kind that I was asking for, definitions which describe the real nature of the object or notion denoted by a word, and which do not merely tell us what the word is used to mean, are only possible when the object or notion in question is something complex. You can give a definition of a horse, because a horse has many different properties and qualities, all of which you can enumerate. But when you have enumerated them all, when you have reduced a horse to his simplest terms, then you can no longer define those terms. They are simply something which you think of or perceive, and to any one who cannot think of or perceive them, you can never, by any definition, make their nature known. It may perhaps be objected to this that we are able to describe to others, objects which they have never seen or thought of. We can, for instance, make a man understand what a chimaera is, although he has never heard of one or seen one. You can tell him that it is an animal with a lioness's head and body, with a goat's head growing from the middle of its back, and with a snake in place of a tail. But here the object which you are describing is a complex object; it is entirely composed of parts, with which we are all perfectly familiar — a snake, a goat, a lioness; and we know, too, the manner in which those parts are to be put together, because we know what is meant by the middle of a lioness's back, and where her tail is wont to grow. And so it is with all objects, not previously known, which we are able to define: they are all complex; all composed of parts, which may themselves, in the first instance, be capable of similar definition, but which must in the end be reducible to simplest parts, which can no longer be defined. But yellow and good, we say, are not complex: they are notions of that simple kind, out of which definitions are composed and with which the power of further defining ceases.

8. When we say, as Webster says, 'The definition of horse is "A hoofed quadruped of the genus Equus,"' we may, in fact, mean three different things.

(1) We may mean merely: 'When I say "horse," you are to understand that I am talking about a hoofed quadruped of the genus Equus.' This might be called the arbitrary verbal definition: and I do not mean that good is indefinable in that sense. (2) We may mean, as Webster ought to mean: 'When most English people say "horse," they mean a hoofed quadruped of the genus Equus.' This may be called the verbal definition proper, and I do not say that good is indefinable in this sense either; for it is certainly possible to discover how people use a word: otherwise, we could never have known that 'good' may be translated by 'gut' in German and by 'bon' in French. But (3) we may, when we define horse, mean something much more important. We may mean that a certain object, which we all of us know, is composed in a certain manner: that it has four legs, a head, a heart, a liver, etc., etc., all of them arranged in definite relations to one another. It is in this sense that I deny good to be definable. I say that it is not composed of any parts, which we can substitute for it in our minds when we are thinking of it. We might think just as clearly and correctly about a horse, if we thought of all its parts and their arrangement instead of thinking of the whole: we could, I say, think how a horse differed from a donkey just as well, just as truly, in this way, as now we do, only not so easily; but there is nothing whatsoever which we could so substitute for good; and that is what I mean, when I say that good is indefinable.

9. But I am afraid I have still not removed the chief difficulty which may prevent acceptance of the proposition that good is indefinable. I do not mean to say that *the* good, that which is good, is thus indefinable; if I did think so, I should not be writing on Ethics, for my main object is to help towards discovering that definition. It is just because I think there will be less risk of error in our search for a definition of "the good," that I am now insisting that *good* is indefinable. I must try to explain the difference between these two. I suppose it may be granted that 'good' is an adjective. Well 'the good,' 'that which is good,' must therefore be the substantive to which the adjective 'good' will apply: it must be the whole of that to which the adjective will apply, and the adjective must *always* truly apply to it. But if it is that to which the adjective will apply, it must be something different from that adjective itself; and the whole of that something different, whatever it is, will be our definition of *the* good. Now it may be that this something will have other adjectives, besides 'good,' that will apply to it. It may be full of pleasure, for example; it may be intelligent: and if these two adjectives are really part of its definition, then it will certainly be true, that pleasure and intelligence are good. And many people appear to think that, if we say 'Pleasure and intelligence are good,' or if we say 'Only pleasure and intelligence are good,' we are defining 'good.' Well, I cannot deny that propositions of this nature may sometimes be called definitions; I do not know well enough how the word is generally used to decide upon this point. I only wish it to be understood that this is not what I mean when I say there is no possible definition of good, and that I shall not mean this if I use the word again. I do most fully believe that some true proposition of the form 'Intelligence is good and intelligence alone is good' can be found; if

none could be found, our definition of *the* good would be impossible. As it is, I believe *the* good to be definable; and yet I still say that good itself is indefinable.

10. 'Good,' then, if we mean by it that quality which we assert to belong to a thing, when we say that the thing is good, is incapable of any definition, in the most important sense of that word. The most important sense of 'definition' is that in which a definition states what are the parts which invariably compose a certain whole; and in this sense 'good' has no definition because it is simple and has no parts. It is one of those innumerable objects of thought which are themselves incapable of definition, because they are the ultimate terms by reference to which whatever *is* capable of definition must be defined. That there must be an indefinite number of such terms is obvious, on reflection; since we cannot define anything except by an analysis, which, when carried as far as it will go, refers us to something, which is simply different from anything else, and which by that ultimate difference explains the peculiarity of the whole which we are defining: for every whole contains some parts which are common to other wholes also. There is, therefore, no intrinsic difficulty in the contention that 'good' denotes a simple and indefinable quality. There are many other instances of such qualities.

Consider yellow, for example. We may try to define it, by describing its physical equivalent; we may state what kind of light-vibrations must stimulate the normal eye, in order that we may perceive it. But a moment's reflection is sufficient to shew that those light-vibrations are not themselves what we mean by yellow. *They* are not what we perceive. Indeed we should never have been able to discover their existence, unless we had first been struck by the patent difference of quality between the different colours. The most we can be entitled to say of those vibrations is that they are what corresponds in space to the yellow which we actually perceive.

Yet a mistake of this simple kind has commonly been made about 'good.' It may be true that all things which are good are *also* something else, just as it is true that all things which are yellow produce a certain kind of vibration in the light. And it is a fact, that Ethics aims at discovering what are those other properties belonging to all things which are good. But far too many philosophers have thought that when they named those other properties they were actually defining good; that these properties, in fact, were simply not 'other,' but absolutely and entirely the same with goodness. This view I propose to call the 'naturalistic fallacy' and of it I shall now endeavour to dispose.

11. Let us consider what it is such philosophers say. And first it is to be noticed that they do not agree among themselves. They not only say that they are right as to what good is, but they endeavour to prove that other people who say that it is something else, are wrong. One, for instance, will affirm that good is pleasure, another, perhaps, that good is that which is desired; and each of these will argue eagerly to prove that the other is wrong. But how is that possible? One of them says that good is nothing but the object of desire, and at the same time tries to prove that it is not pleasure. But from his first assertion, that good just means the object of desire, one of two things must follow as regards his proof:

(1) He may be trying to prove that the object of desire is not pleasure. But, if this be all, where is his Ethics? The position he is maintaining is merely a psychological one. Desire is something which occurs in our minds, and plea- sure is something else which so occurs; and our would-be ethical philosopher is merely holding that the latter is not the object of the former. But what has that to do with the question in dispute? His opponent held the ethical proposition that pleasure was the good, and although he should prove a million times over the psychological proposition that pleasure is not the object of desire, he is no nearer proving his opponent to be wrong. The position is like this. One man says a triangle is a circle: another replies 'A triangle is a straight line, and I will prove to you that I am right: *for*' (this is the only argument) 'a straight line is not a circle.' 'That is quite true,' the other may reply; 'but nevertheless a triangle is a circle, and you have said nothing whatever to prove the contrary. What is proved is that one of us is wrong, for we agree that a triangle cannot be both a straight line and a circle: but which is wrong, there can be no earthly means of proving, since you define triangle as straight line and I define it as circle.' — Well, that is one alternative which any naturalistic Ethics has to face; if good is *defined* as something else, it is then impossible either to prove that any other definition is wrong or even to deny such definition.

(2) The other alternative will scarcely be more welcome. It is that the discus- sion is after all a verbal one. When A says 'Good means pleasant' and B says 'Good means desired,' they may merely wish to assert that most people have used the word for what is pleasant and for what is desired respectively. And this is quite an interesting subject for discussion: only it is not a whit more an ethical discussion than the last was. Nor do I think that any exponent of naturalistic Ethics would be willing to allow that this was all he meant. They are all so anx- ious to persuade us that what they call the good is what we really ought to do. 'Do, pray, act so, because the word "good" is generally used to denote actions of this nature': such, on this view, would be the substance of their teaching. And in so far as they tell us how we ought to act, their teaching is truly ethical, as they mean it to be. But how perfectly absurd is the reason they would give for it! 'You are to do this, because most people use a certain word to denote conduct such as this.' 'You are to say the thing which is not, because most people call it lying.' That is an argument just as good! — My dear sirs, what we want to know from you as ethical teachers, is not how people use a word; it is not even, what kind of actions they approve, which the use of this word 'good' may certainly imply: what we want to know is simply what *is* good. We may indeed agree that what most people do think good, is actually so; we shall at all events be glad to know their opinions: but when we say their opinions about what *is* good, we do mean what we say; we do not care whether they call that thing which they mean 'horse' or 'table' or 'chair,' 'gut' or 'bon' or 'ἀγαθos': we want to know what it is that they so call. When they say 'Pleasure is good,' we cannot believe that they merely mean 'Pleasure is pleasure' and nothing more than that.

12. Suppose a man says 'I am pleased'; and suppose that is not a lie or a mistake but the truth. Well, if it is true, what does that mean? It means that his

mind, a certain definite mind, distinguished by certain definite marks from all others, has at this moment a certain definite feeling called pleasure. 'Pleased' *means* nothing but having pleasure, and though we may be more pleased or less pleased, and even, we may admit for the present, have one or another kind of pleasure; yet in so far as it is pleasure we have, whether there be more or less of it, and whether it be of one kind or another, what we have is one definite thing, absolutely indefinable, some one thing that is the same in all the various degrees and in all the various kinds of it that there may be. We may be able to say how it is related to other things: that, for example, it is in the mind, that it causes desire, that we are conscious of it, etc., etc. We can, I say, describe its relations to other things, but define it we can *not*. And if anybody tried to define pleasure for us as being any other natural object; if anybody were to say, for instance, that pleasure *means* the sensation of red, and were to proceed to deduce from that that pleasure is a colour, we should be entitled to laugh at him and to distrust his future statements about pleasure. Well, that would be the same fallacy which I have called the naturalistic fallacy. That 'pleased' does not mean 'having the sensation of red,' or anything else whatever, does not prevent us from understanding what it does mean. It is enough for us to know that 'pleased' does mean 'having the sensation of pleasure,' and though pleasure is absolutely indefinable, though pleasure is pleasure and nothing else whatever, yet we feel no difficulty in saying that we are pleased. The reason is, of course, that when I say 'I am pleased,' I do *not* mean that 'I' am the same thing as 'having pleasure.' And similarly no difficulty need be found in my saying that 'pleasure is good' and yet not meaning that 'pleasure' is the same thing as 'good,' that pleasure *means* good, and that good *means* pleasure. If I were to imagine that when I said 'I am pleased,' I mean that I was exactly the same thing as 'pleased,' I should not indeed call that a naturalistic fallacy, although it would be the same fallacy as I have called naturalistic with reference to Ethics. The reason of this is obvious enough. When a man confuses two natural objects with one another, defining the one by the other, if for instance, he confuses himself, who is one natural object, with 'pleased' or with 'pleasure' which are others, then there is no reason to call the fallacy naturalistic. But if he confuses 'good,' which is not in the same sense a natural object, with any natural object whatever, then there is a reason for calling that a naturalistic fallacy; its being made with regard to 'good' marks it as something quite specific, and this specific mistake deserves a name because it is so common. As for the reasons why good is not to be considered a natural object, they may be reserved for discussion in another place. But, for the present, it is sufficient to notice this: Even if it were a natural object, that would not alter the nature of the fallacy nor diminish its importance one whit. All that I have said about it would remain quite equally true: only the name which I have called it would not be so appropriate as I think it is. And I do not care about the name: what I do care about is the fallacy. It does not matter what we call it, provided we recognise it when we meet with it. It is to be met with in almost every book on Ethics; and yet it is not recognised: and that is why it is necessary to multiply illustrations of it, and convenient to give it a name. It is a very simple fallacy indeed. When we say that an orange is yellow, we do not think our statement binds us to hold that 'orange' means nothing else than 'yellow,' or that nothing can be yellow but an orange. Supposing the orange is also sweet! Does that bind us to say that 'sweet' is exactly the same thing as 'yellow,' that 'sweet' must be defined as 'yellow'? And supposing it be recognised that 'yellow' just means 'yellow' and nothing else whatever, does that make it any more difficult to hold that oranges are yellow? Most certainly it does not: on the contrary, it would be absolutely meaningless to say that oranges were yellow, unless yellow did in the end mean just 'yellow' and nothing else whatever — unless it was absolutely indefinable. We should not get any very clear notion about things, which are yellow — we should not get very far with our science, if we were bound to hold that everything which was yellow, *meant* exactly the same thing as yellow. We should find we had to hold that an orange was exactly the same thing as a stool, a piece of paper, a lemon, anything you like. We could prove any number of absurdities; but should we be the nearer to the truth? Why, then, should it be different with 'good'? Why, if good is good and indefinable, should I be held to deny that pleasure is good? Is there any difficulty in holding both to be true at once? On the contrary, there is no meaning in saying that pleasure is good, unless good is something different from pleasure. It is absolutely useless, so far as Ethics is concerned, to prove, as Mr. Spencer tried to do, that increase of pleasure coincides with increase of life, unless good *means* something different from either life or pleasure. He might just as well try to prove that an orange is yellow by shewing that it always is wrapped up in paper.

13. In fact, if it is not the case that 'good' denotes something simple and indefinable, only two alternatives are possible: either it is a complex, a given whole, about the correct analysis of which there may be disagreement; or else it means nothing at all, and there is no such subject as Ethics. In general, however, ethical philosophers have attempted to define good, without recognising what such an attempt must mean. They actually use arguments which involve one or both of the absurdities considered in §11. We are, therefore, justified in concluding that the attempt to define good is chiefly due to want of clearness as to the possible nature of definition. There are, in fact, only two serious alternatives to be considered, in order to establish the conclusion that 'good' does denote a simple and indefinable notion. It might possibly denote a complex, as 'horse' does; or it might have no meaning at all. Neither of these possibilities has, however, been clearly conceived and seriously maintained, as such, by those who presume to define good; and both may be dismissed by a simple appeal to facts.

(1) The hypothesis that disagreement about the meaning of good is disagreement with regard to the correct analysis of a given whole, may be most plainly seen to be incorrect by consideration of the fact that, whatever definition be offered, it may be always asked, with significance, of the complex so defined, whether it is itself good. To take, for instance, one of the more plausible, because one of the more complicated, of such proposed definitions, it

may easily be thought, at first sight, that to be good may mean to be that which we desire to desire. Thus if we apply this definition to a particular instance and say 'When we think that A is good, we are thinking that A is one of the things which we desire to desire,' our proposition may seem quite plausible. But, if we carry the investigation further, and ask ourselves 'Is it good to desire to desire A?' it is apparent, on a little reflection, that this question is itself as intelligible, as the original question 'Is A good?' – that we are, in fact, now asking for exactly the same information about the desire to desire A, for which formerly asked with regard to A itself. But it is also apparent that the meaning of this second question cannot be correctly analysed into 'Is the desire to desire A one of the things which we desire to desire?': we have not before our minds anything so complicated as the question 'Do we desire to desire to desire to desire A?' Moreover any one can easily convince himself by inspection that the predicate of this proposition – 'good' – is positively different from the notion of 'desiring to desire' which enters into its subject: 'That we should desire to desire A is good' is *not* merely equivalent to 'That A should be good is good.' It may indeed be true that what we desire to desire is always also good; perhaps, even the converse may be true: but it is very doubtful whether this is the case, and the mere fact that we understand very well what is meant by doubting it, shews clearly that we have two different notions before our minds.

(2) And the same consideration is sufficient to dismiss the hypothesis that 'good' has no meaning whatsoever. It is very natural to make the mistake of supposing that what is universally true is of such a nature that its negation would be self-contradictory: the importance which has been assigned to analytic propositions in the history of philosophy shews how easy such a mistake is. And thus it is very easy to conclude that what seems to be a universal ethical principle is in fact an identical proposition; that if, for example, whatever is called 'good' seems to be pleasant, the proposition 'Pleasure is the good' does not assert a connection between two different notions, but involves only one, that of pleasure, which is easily recognised as a distinct entity. But whoever will attentively consider with himself what is actually before his mind when he asks the question 'Is pleasure (or whatever it may be) after all good?' can easily satisfy himself that he is not merely wondering whether pleasure is pleasant. And if he will try this experiment with each suggested definition in succession, he may become expert enough to recognise that in every case he has before his mind a unique object, with regard to the connection of which with any other object, a distinct question may be asked. Every one does in fact understand the question 'Is this good?' When he thinks of it, his state of mind is different from what it would be, were he asked 'Is this pleasant, or desired, or approved?' It has a distinct meaning for him, even though he may not recognise in what respect it is distinct. Whenever he thinks of 'intrinsic value,' or 'intrinsic worth,' or says that a thing 'ought to exist,' he has before his mind the unique object – the unique property of things – which I mean by 'good.' Everybody is constantly aware of this notion, although he may never become aware at all that it is different from other notions of which he is also aware. But, for correct

ethical reasoning, it is extremely important that he should become aware of this fact; and, as soon as the nature of the problem is clearly understood, there should be little difficulty in advancing so far in analysis.

14. 'Good,' then, is indefinable; and yet, so far as I know, there is only one ethical writer, Prof. Henry Sidgwick, who has clearly recognised and stated this fact. We shall see, indeed, how far many of the most reputed ethical systems fall short of drawing the conclusions which follow from such recognition. At present I will only quote one instance, which will serve to illustrate the meaning and importance of this principle that 'good' is indefinable, or, as Prof. Sidgwick says, an 'unanalysable notion.' It is an instance to which Prof. Sidgwick himself refers in a note on the passage, in which he argues that 'ought' is unanalysable.[1]

'Bentham,' says Sidgwick, 'explains that his fundamental principle "states the greatest happiness of all those whose interest is in question as being the right and proper end of human action"'; and yet 'his language in other passages of the same chapter would seem to imply' that he *means* by the word "right" "conducive to the general happiness." Prof. Sidgwick sees that, if you take these two statements together, you get the absurd result that 'greatest happiness is the end of human action, which is conducive to the general happiness'; and so absurd does it seem to him to call this result, as Bentham calls it, 'the fundamental principle of a moral system,' that he suggests that Bentham cannot have meant it. Yet Prof. Sidgwick himself states elsewhere[2] that Psychological Hedonism is 'not seldom confounded with Egoistic Hedonism'; and that confusion, as we shall see, rests chiefly on that same fallacy, the naturalistic fallacy, which is implied in Bentham's statements. Prof. Sidgwick admits therefore that this fallacy is sometimes committed, absurd as it is; and I am inclined to think that Bentham may really have been one of those who committed it. Mill, as we shall see, certainly did commit it. In any case, whether Bentham committed it or not, his doctrine, as above quoted, will serve as a very good illustration of this fallacy, and of the importance of the contrary proposition that good is indefinable.

Let us consider this doctrine. Bentham seems to imply, so Prof. Sidgwick says, that the word 'right' *means* 'conducive to general happiness.' Now this, by itself, need not necessarily involve the naturalistic fallacy. For the word 'right' is very commonly appropriated to actions which lead to the attainment of what is good; which are regarded as *means* to the ideal and not as ends-in-themselves. This use of 'right,' as denoting what is good as a means, whether or not it be also good as an end, is indeed the use to which I shall confine the word. Had Bentham been using 'right' in this sense, it might be perfectly consistent for him to *define* right as 'conducive to the general happiness,' *provided only* (and notice this proviso) he had already proved, or laid down as an axiom, that general happiness was *the* good, or (what is equivalent to this) that general happiness alone was good. For in that case he would have already defined *the* good as general happiness (a position perfectly consistent, as we have seen, with the contention that 'good' is indefinable), and, since right was to be defined as 'conducive to *the* good,' it would actually *mean* 'conducive to general happiness.' But this method of escape from the charge of having committed the naturalistic fallacy has been closed by Bentham himself. For his fundamental principle is, we see, that the greatest happiness of all concerned is the *right* and proper *end* of human action. He applies the word 'right,' therefore, to the end, as such, not only to the means which are conducive to it; and, that being so, right can no longer be defined as 'conducive to the general happiness,' without involving the fallacy in question. For now it is obvious that the definition of right as conducive to general happiness can be used by him in support of the fundamental principle that general happiness is the right end; instead of being itself derived from that principle. If right, by definition, means conducive to general happiness, then it is obvious that general happiness is the right end. It is not necessary now first to prove or assert that general happiness is the right end, before right is defined as conducive to general happiness—a perfectly valid procedure; but on the contrary the definition of right as conducive to general happiness proves general happiness to be the right end—a perfectly invalid procedure, since in the case the statement that 'general happiness is the right end of human action' is not an ethical principle at all, but either, as we have seen, a proposition about the meaning of words, or else a proposition about the *nature* of general happiness, not about its righteousness or goodness.

Now, I do not wish the importance I assign to this fallacy to be misunderstood. The discovery of it does not at all refute Bentham's contention that greatest happiness is the proper end of human action, if that be understood as an ethical proposition, as he undoubtedly intended it. That principle may be true all the same; we shall consider whether it is so in succeeding chapters. Bentham might have maintained it, as Prof. Sidgwick does, even if the fallacy had been pointed out to him. What I am maintaining is that the *reasons* which he actually gives for his ethical proposition are fallacious ones so far as they consist in a definition of right. What I suggest is that he did not perceive them to be fallacious; that, if he had done so, he would have been led to seek for other reasons in support of his Utilitarianism; and that, had he sought for other reasons, he *might* have found none which he thought to be sufficient. In that case he would have changed his whole system—a most important consequence. It is undoubtedly also possible that he would have thought other reasons to be sufficient, and in that case his ethical system, in its main results, would still have stood. But, even in this latter case, his use of the fallacy would be a serious objection to him as an ethical philosopher. For it is the business of Ethics, I must insist, not only to obtain true results, but also to find valid reasons for them. The direct object of Ethics is knowledge and not practice; and any one who uses the naturalistic fallacy has certainly not fulfilled this first object, however correct his practical principles may be.

My objections to Naturalism are then, in the first place, that it offers no reason at all, far less any valid reason, for any ethical principle whatever; and in this it already fails to satisfy the requirements of Ethics, as a scientific study.

But in the second place I contend that, though it gives a reason for no ethical principle, it is a *cause* of the acceptance of false principles — it deludes the mind into accepting ethical principles, which are false; and in this it is contrary to every aim of Ethics. It is easy to see that if we start with a definition or right conduct as conduct conducive to general happiness; then, knowing that right conduct is universally conduct conducive to the good, we very easily arrive at the result that the good is general happiness. If, on the other hand, we once recognise that we must start our ethics without a definition, we shall be much more apt to look about us, before we adopt any ethical principle whatever; and the more we look about us, the less likely are we to adopt a false one. It may be replied to this: Yes, but we shall look about us just as much, before we settle on our definition, and are therefore just as likely to be right. But I will try to shew that this is not the case. If we start with the conviction that a definition of good can be found, we start with the conviction that good *can mean* nothing else than some one property of things; and our only business will then be to discover what that property is. But if we recognise that, so far as the meaning of good goes, anything whatever may be good, we start with a much more open mind. Moreover, apart from the fact that, when we think we have a definition, we cannot logically defend our ethical principles in any way whatever, we shall also be much less apt to defend them well, even if illogically. For we shall start with the conviction that good must mean so and so, and shall therefore be inclined either to misunderstand our opponent's arguments or to cut them short with the reply. 'This is not an open question: the very meaning of the word decides it; no one can think otherwise except through confusion.'

15. Our first conclusion as to the subject-matter of Ethics is, then, that there is a simple, indefinable, unanalysable object of thought by reference to which it must be defined. By what name we call this unique object is a matter of indifference, so long as we clearly recognise what it is and that it does differ from other objects. The words which are commonly taken as the signs of ethical judgments all do refer to it; and they are expressions of ethical judgments solely because they do so refer. But they may refer to it in two different ways, which it is very important to distinguish, if we are to have a complete definition of the range of ethical judgments. Before I proceeded to argue that there was such an indefinable notion involved in ethical notions, I stated (§4) that it was necessary for Ethics to enumerate all true universal judgments, asserting that such and such a thing was good, whenever it occurred. But, although all such judgments do refer to that unique notion which I have called 'good,' they do not all refer to it in the same way. They may either assert that this unique property does always attach to the thing in question, or else they may assert only that the thing in question is *a cause or necessary condition* for the existence of other things to which this unique property does attach. The nature of these two species of universal ethical judgments is extremely different; and a great part of the difficulties, which are met with in ordinary ethical speculation, are due to the failure to distinguish them clearly. Their difference has, indeed, received expression in ordinary language by the contrast between the

terms 'good as means' and 'good in itself,' 'value as a means' and 'intrinsic value.' But these terms are apt to be applied correctly only in the more obvious instances; and this seems to be due to the fact that the distinction between the conceptions which they denote has not been made a separate object of investigation. This distinction may be briefly pointed out as follows.

16. Whenever we judge that a thing is 'good as a means,' we are making a judgment with regard to its causal relations: we judge *both* that it will have a particular kind of effect, *and* that that effect will be good in itself. But to find causal judgments that are universally true is notoriously a matter of extreme difficulty. The late date at which most of the physical sciences became exact, and the comparative fewness of the laws which they have succeeded in establishing even now, are sufficient proofs of this difficulty. With regard, then, to what are the most frequent objects of ethical judgments, namely actions, it is obvious that we cannot be satisfied that any of our universal causal judgments are true, even in the sense in which scientific laws are so. We cannot even discover hypothetical laws of the form 'Exactly this action will always, under these conditions, produce exactly that effect.' But for a correct ethical judgment with regard to the effect of certain actions we require more than this in two respects. (1) We require to know that a given action will produce a certain effect, *under whatever circumstances it occurs.* But this is certainly impossible. It is certain that in different circumstances the same action may produce effects which are utterly different in all respects upon which the value of the effects depends. Hence we can never be entitled to more than a *generalisation* — to a proposition of the form 'This result *generally* follows this kind of action'; and even this generalisation will only be true, if the circumstances under which the action occurs are generally the same. This is in fact the case, to a great extent, within any one particular age and state of society. But, when we take other ages into account, in many most important cases the normal circumstances of a given kind of action will be so different, that the generalisation which is true for one will not be true for another. With regard then to ethical judgments which assert that a certain kind of action is good as a means to a certain kind of effect, none will be *universally* true; and many, though *generally* true at one period, will be generally false at others. But (2) we require to know not only that *one* good effect will be produced, but that, among all subsequent events affected by the action in question, the balance of good will be greater than if any other possible action had been performed. In other words, to judge that an action is generally a means to good is to judge not only that it generally does *some* good, but that it generally does the greatest good of which the circumstances admit. In this respect ethical judgments about the effects of action involve a difficulty and a complication far greater than that involved in the establishment of scientific laws. For the latter we need only consider a single effect; for the former it is essential to consider not only this, but the effects of that effect, and so on as far as our view into the future can reach. It is, indeed, obvious that our view can never reach far enough for us to be certain that any action will produce the best possible effects. We must be content,

if the greatest possible balance of good seems to be produced within a limited period. But it is important to notice that the whole series of effects within a period of considerable length is actually taken account of in our common judgments that an action is good as a means; and that hence this additional complication, which makes ethical generalisations so far more difficult to establish than scientific laws, is one which is involved in actual ethical discussions, and is of practical importance. The commonest rules of conduct involve such considerations as the balancing of future bad health against immediate gains; and even if we can never settle with any certainty how we shall secure the greatest possible total of good, we try at least to assure ourselves that probable future evils will not be greater than the immediate good.

17. There are, then, judgments which state that certain kinds of things have good effects; and such judgments, for the reasons just given, have the important characteristics (1) that they are unlikely to be true, if they state that the kind of thing in question *always* has good effects, and (2) that, even if they only state that it *generally* has good effects, many of them will only be true of certain periods in the world's history. On the other hand there are judgments which state that certain kinds of things are themselves good; and these differ from the last in that, if true at all, they are all of them universally true. It is, therefore, extremely important to distinguish these two kinds of possible judgments. Both may be expressed in the same language: in both cases we commonly say 'Such and such a thing is good.' But in the one case 'good' will mean 'good as means,' *i.e.* merely that the thing is a means to good—will have good effects: in the other case it will mean 'good as end'—we shall be judging that the thing itself has the property which, in the first case, was asserted only to belong to its effects. It is plain that these are very different assertions to make about a thing; it is plain that either or both of them may be made, both truly and falsely, about all manner of things; and it is certain that unless we are clear as to which of the two we mean to assert, we shall have a very poor chance of deciding rightly whether our assertion is true or false. It is precisely this clearness as to the meaning of the question asked which has hitherto been almost entirely lacking in ethical speculation. Ethics has always been predominantly concerned with the investigation of a limited class of actions. With regard to these we may ask *both* how far they are good in themselves *and* how far they have a general tendency to produce good results. And the arguments brought forward in ethical discussion have always been of both classes—both such as would prove the conduct in question to be good in itself and such as would prove it to be good as a means. But that these are the only questions which any ethical discussion can have to settle, and that to settle the one is *not* the same thing as to settle the other—these two fundamental facts have in general escaped the notice of ethical philosophers. Ethical questions are commonly asked in an ambiguous form. It is asked 'What is a man's duty under these circumstances?' or 'Is it right to act in this way?' or 'What ought we to aim at securing?' But all these questions are capable of further analysis; a correct answer to any of them involves both judgments of what is good in itself and causal judgments. This is

implied even by those who maintain that we have a direct and immediate judgment of absolute rights and duties. Such a judgment can only mean that the course of action in question is *the* best thing to do; that, by acting so, every good that *can* be secured will have been secured. Now we are not concerned with the question whether such a judgment will ever be true. The question is: What does it imply, if it is true? And the only possible answer is that, whether true or false, it implies both a proposition as to the degree of goodness of the action in question, as compared with other things, and a number of causal propositions. For it cannot be denied that the action will have consequences: and to deny that the consequences matter is to make a judgment of their intrinsic value, as compared with the action itself. In asserting that the action is *the* best thing to do, we assert that it together with its consequences presents a greater sum of intrinsic value than any possible alternative. And this condition may be realised by any of the three cases: – (*a*) If the action itself has greater intrinsic value than any alternative, whereas both its consequences and those of the alternatives are absolutely devoid either of intrinsic merit or intrinsic demerit; or (*b*) if, though, its consequences are intrinsically bad, the balance of intrinsic value is greater than would be produced by any alternative; or (*c*) if, its consequences being intrinsically good, the degree of value belonging to them and it conjointly is greater than that of any alternative series. In short, to assert that a certain line of conduct is, at a given time, absolutely right or obligatory, is obviously to assert that more good or less evil will exist in the world, if it be adopted than if anything else be done instead. But this implies a judgment as to the value both of its own consequences and of those of any possible alternative. And that an action will have such and such consequences involves a number of causal judgments.

Similarly, in answering the question 'What ought we to aim at securing?' causal judgments are again involved, but in a somewhat different way. We are liable to forget, because it is so obvious, that this question can never be answered correctly except by naming something which *can* be secured. Not everything can be secured; and, even if we judge that nothing which cannot be obtained would be of equal value with that which can, the possibility of the latter, as well as its value, is essential to its being a proper end of action. Accordingly neither our judgments as to what actions we ought to perform, nor even our judgments as to the ends which they ought to produce, are pure judgments of intrinsic value. With regard to the former, an action which is absolutely obligatory *may* have no intrinsic value whatsoever; that it is perfectly virtuous may mean merely that it causes the best possible effects. And with regard to the latter, these best possible results which justify our action can, in any case, have only so much of intrinsic value as the laws of nature allow us to secure and they in their turn *may* have no intrinsic value whatsoever, but may merely be a means to the attainment (in a still further future) of something that has such value. Whenever, therefore, we ask 'What ought we to do?' or 'What ought we to try to get?' we are asking questions which involve a correct answer to two others, completely different in kind from one another. We must know *both* what degree of intrinsic value different things have, *and* how these different things may be obtained. But the vast majority of questions which have actually been discussed in Ethics — all practical questions, indeed — involve this double knowledge; and they have been discussed without any clear separation of the two distinct questions involved. A great part of the vast disagreements prevalent in Ethics is to be attributed to this failure in analysis. By the use of conceptions which involve both that of intrinsic value and that of causal relation, as if they involved intrinsic value only, two different errors have been rendered almost universal. Either it is assumed that nothing has intrinsic value which is not possible, or else it is assumed that what is necessary must have intrinsic value. Hence the primary and peculiar business of Ethics, the determination what things have intrinsic value and in what degrees, has received no adequate treatment at all. And on the other hand a *thorough* discussion of means has been also largely neglected, owing to an obscure perception of the truth that it is perfectly irrelevant to the question of intrinsic values. But however this may be, and however strongly any particular reader may be convinced that some one of the mutually contradictory systems which hold the field has given a correct answer either to the question what has intrinsic value, or to the question what we ought to do, or to both, it must at least be admitted that the questions what is best in itself and what will bring about the best possible, are utterly distinct; that both belong to the actual subject-matter of Ethics; and that the more clearly distinct questions are distinguished, the better is our chance of answering both correctly.

18. There remains one point which must not be omitted in a complete description of the kind of questions which Ethics has to answer. The main division of those questions is, as I have said, into two; the question what things are good in themselves, and the question to what other things these are related as effects. The first of these, which is the primary ethical question and is presupposed by the other, includes a correct comparison of the various things which have intrinsic value (if there are many such) in respect of the degree of value which they have; and such comparison involves a difficulty of principle which has greatly aided the confusion of intrinsic value with mere 'goodness as a means.' It has been pointed out that one difference between a judgment which asserts that a thing is good in itself, and a judgment which asserts that it is a means to good, consists in the fact that the first, if true of one instance of the thing in question, is necessarily true of all; whereas a thing which has good effects under some circumstances may have bad ones under others. Now it is certainly true that all judgments of intrinsic value are in this sense universal; but the principle which I have now to enunciate may easily make it appear as if they were not so but resembled the judgment of means in being merely general. There is, as will presently be maintained, a vast number of different things, each of which has intrinsic value; there are also very many which are positively bad; and there is a still larger class of things, which appear to be indifferent. But a thing belonging to any of these three classes may occur as part of a whole, which includes among its other parts other things belonging both to the

same and to the other two classes; and these wholes, as such, may also have intrinsic value. The paradox, to which it is necessary to call attention, is that *the value of such a whole bears no regular proportion to the sum of the values of its parts*. It is certain that a good thing may exist in such a relation to another good thing that the value of the whole thus formed is immensely greater than the sum of the values of the two good things. It is certain that a whole formed of a good thing and an indifferent thing may have immensely greater value than that good thing itself possesses. It is certain that two bad things or a bad thing and an indifferent thing may form a whole much worse than the sum of badness of its parts. And it seems as if indifferent things may also be the sole constituents of a whole which has great value, either positive or negative. Whether the addition of a bad thing to a good whole may increase the positive value of the whole, or the addition of a bad thing to a bad may produce a whole having positive value, may seem more doubtful; but it is, at least possible, and this possibility must be taken into account in our ethical investigations. However we may decide particular questions, the principle is clear. *The value of a whole must not be assumed to be the same as the sum of the values of its parts.*

A single instance will suffice to illustrate the kind of relation in question. It seems to be true that to be conscious of a beautiful object is a thing of great intrinsic value; whereas the same object, if no one be conscious of it has certainly comparatively little value, and is commonly held to have none at all. But the consciousness of a beautiful object is certainly a whole of some sort in which we can distinguish as parts the object on the one hand and the being conscious on the other. Now this latter factor occurs as part of a different whole, whenever we are conscious of anything; and it would seem that some of these wholes have at all events very little value, and may even be indifferent or positively bad. Yet we cannot always attribute the slightness of their value to any positive demerit in the object which differentiates them from the consciousness of beauty; the object itself may approach as near as possible to absolute neutrality. Since, therefore, mere consciousness does not always confer great value upon the whole of which it forms a part, even though its object may have no great demerit, we cannot attribute the great superiority of the consciousness of a beautiful thing over the beautiful thing itself to the mere addition of the value of consciousness to that of the beautiful thing. Whatever the intrinsic value of consciousness may be, it does not give to the whole of which it forms a part a value proportioned to the sum of its value and that of its object. If this be so, we have here an instance of a whole possessing a different intrinsic value from the sum of that of its parts; and whether it be so or not, what is meant by such a difference is illustrated by this case.

19. There are, then, wholes which possess the property that their value is different from the sum of the values of their parts; and the relations which subsist between such parts and the whole of which they form a part have not hitherto been distinctly recognised or received a separate name. Two points are especially worthy of notice. (1) It is plain that the existence of any such part

is a necessary condition for the existence of that good which is constituted by the whole. And exactly the same language will also express the relation between a means and the good thing which is its effect. But yet there is a most important difference between the two cases, constituted by the fact that the part is, whereas the means is not, a part of the good thing for the existence of which its existence is a necessary condition. The necessity by which, if the good in question is to exist, the means to it must exist is merely a natural or causal necessity. If the laws of nature were different, exactly the same good might exist, although what is now a necessary condition of its existence did not exist. The existence of the means has no intrinsic value; and its utter annihilation would leave the value of that which it is now necessary to secure entirely unchanged. But in the case of a part of such a whole as we are now considering, it is otherwise. In this case the good in question cannot conceivably exist, unless the part exist also. The necessity which connects the two is quite independent of natural law. What is asserted to have intrinsic value is the existence of the whole; and the existence of the whole includes the existence of its part. Suppose the part removed, and what remains is *not* what was asserted to have intrinsic value; but if we suppose a means removed, what remains is just what *was* asserted to have intrinsic value. And yet (2) the existence of the part may *itself* have no more intrinsic value than that of the means. It is this fact which constitutes the paradox of the relation which we are discussing. It has just been said that what has intrinsic value is the existence of the whole, and that this includes the existence of the part; and from this it would seem a natural inference that the existence of the part has intrinsic value. But the inference would be as false as if we were to conclude that, because the number of two stones was two, each of the stones was also two. The part of a valuable whole retains exactly the same value when it is, as when it is not, a part of that whole. If it had value under other circumstances, its value is not any greater, when it is part of a far more valuable whole; and if it had no value by itself, it has none still, however great be that of the whole of which it now forms a part. We are not then justified in asserting that one and the same thing is under some circumstances intrinsically good, and under others not so; as we are justified in asserting of a means that it sometimes does and sometimes does not produce good results. And yet we are justified in asserting that it is far more desirable that a certain thing should exist under some circumstances than under others; namely when other things will exist in such relations to it as to form a more valuable whole. *It* will not have more intrinsic value under these circumstances than under others; *it* will not necessarily even be a means to the existence of things having more intrinsic value: but it will, like a means, be a necessary condition for the existence of that which *has* greater intrinsic value, although, unlike a means, it will itself form a part of this more valuable existent.

20. I have said that the peculiar relation between part and whole which I have just been trying to define is one which has received no separate name. It would, however, be useful that it should have one; and there is a name, which might well be appropriated to it, if only it could be divorced from its present

unfortunate usage. Philosophers, especially those who profess to have derived great benefit from the writings of Hegel, have latterly made much use of the terms 'organic whole', 'organic unity', 'organic relation.' The reason why these terms might well be appropriated to the use suggested is that the peculiar relation of parts to whole, just defined, is one of the properties which distinguishes the wholes to which they are actually applied with the greatest frequency. And the reason why it is desirable that they should be divorced from their present usage is that, as at present used, they have no distinct sense and, on the contrary, both imply and propagate errors of confusion.

To say that a thing is an 'organic whole' is generally understood to imply that its parts are related to one another and to itself as means to end; it is also understood to imply that they have a property described in some such phrase as that they have 'no meaning or significance apart from the whole'; and finally such a whole is also treated as if it had the property to which I am proposing that the name should be confined. But those who use the term give us, in general, no hint as to how they suppose these three properties to be related to one another. It seems generally to be assumed that they are identical; and always, at least, that they are necessarily connected with one another. That they are not identical I have already tried to shew; to suppose them so is to neglect the very distinctions pointed out in the last paragraph; and the usage might well be discontinued merely because it encourages such neglect. But a still more cogent reason for its discontinuance is that, so far from being necessarily connected, the second is a property which can attach to nothing, being a self-contradictory conception; whereas the first, if we insist on its most important sense, applies to many cases, to which we have no reason to think that the third applies also, and the third certainly applies to many to which the first does not apply.

21. These relations between the three properties just distinguished may be illustrated by reference to a whole of the kind from which the name 'organic' was derived — a whole which is an organism in the scientific sense — namely the human body.

(1) There exists between many parts of our body (though not between all) a relation which has been familiarised by the fable, attributed to Menenius Agrippa, concerning the belly and its members. We can find in it parts such that the continued existence of the one is a necessary condition for the continued existence of the other; while the continued existence of this latter is also a necessary condition for the continued existence of the former. This amounts to no more than saying that in the body we have instances of two things, both enduring for some time, which have a relation of mutual causal dependence on one another — a relation of 'reciprocity.' Frequently no more than this is meant by saying that the parts of the body form an 'organic unity', or that they are mutually means and ends to one another. And we certainly have here a striking characteristic of living things. But it would be extremely rash to assert that this relation of mutual causal dependence was only exhibited by living things and hence was sufficient to define their peculiarity. And it is obvious that of two things which have this relation of mutual dependence, neither may have intrinsic

value, or one may have it and other lack it. They are not necessarily 'ends' to one another in any sense except that in which 'end' means 'effect.' And moreover it is plain that in this sense the whole cannot be an end to any of its parts. We are apt to talk of 'the whole' in contrast to one of its parts, when in fact we mean only *the rest* of the parts. But strictly the whole must include all its parts and no part can be a cause of the whole, because it cannot be a cause of itself. It is plain, therefore, that this relation of mutual causal dependence implies nothing with regard to the value of either of the objects which have it; and that, even if both of them happen also to have value, this relation between them is one which cannot hold between part and whole.

But (2) it may also be the case that our body as a whole has a value greater than the sum of values of its parts; and this may be what is meant when it is said that the parts are means to the whole. It is obvious that if we ask the question 'Why *should* the parts be such as they are?' a proper answer may be 'Because the whole they form has so much value.' But it is equally obvious that the relation which we thus assert to exist between part and whole is quite different from that which we assert to exist between part and part when we say 'This part exists, because that one could not exist without it.' In the latter case we assert the two parts to be causally connected; but, in the former, part and whole cannot be causally connected, and the relation which we assert to exist between them may exist even though the parts are not causally connected either. All the parts of a picture do not have that relation of mutual causal dependence, which certain parts of the body have, and yet the existence of those which do not have it may be absolutely essential to the value of the whole. The two relations are quite distinct in kind, and we cannot infer the existence of the one from that of the other. It can, therefore, serve no useful purpose to include them both under the same name; and if we are to say that a whole is organic because its parts are (in this sense) 'means' to the whole, we must *not* say that it is organic because its parts are causally dependent on one another.

22. But finally (3) the sense which has been most prominent in recent uses of the term 'organic whole' is one whereby it asserts the parts of such a whole to have a property which the parts of no whole can possibly have. It is supposed that just as the whole would not be what it is but for the existence of the parts, so the parts would not be what they are but for the existence of the whole; and this is understood to mean not merely that any particular part could not exist unless the others existed too (which is the case where relation (1) exists between the parts), but actually that the part is no distinct object of thought—that the whole, of which it is a part, is in its turn a part of it. That this supposition is self-contradictory a very little reflection should be sufficient to shew. We may admit, indeed, that when a particular thing is a part of a whole, it does possess a predicate which it would not otherwise possess— namely that it is a part of that whole. But what cannot be admitted is that this predicate alters the nature or enters into the definition of the thing which has it. When we think of the part *itself*, we mean just *that which* we assert, in this

case, to *have* the predicate that it is part of the whole; and the mere assertion that *it* is a part of the whole involves that it should itself be distinct from that which we assert of it. Otherwise we contradict ourselves since we assert that, not *it,* but something else — namely it together with that which we assert of it — has the predicate which we assert of it. In short, it is obvious that no part contains analytically the whole to which it belongs, or any other parts of that whole. The relation of part to whole is *not* the same as that of whole to part; and the very definition of the latter is that it does contain analytically that which is said to be its part. And yet this very self-contradictory doctrine is the chief mark which shews the influence of Hegel upon modern philosophy — an influence which pervades almost the whole of orthodox philosophy. This is what is generally implied by the cry against falsification by abstraction: that a whole is always a part of its part! 'If you want to know the truth about a part,' we are told, 'you must consider *not* that part, but something else — namely the whole: *nothing* is true of the part, but only of the whole.' Yet plainly it must be true of the part at least that it is a part of the whole; and it is obvious that when we say it is, we do *not* mean merely that the whole is a part of itself. This doctrine, therefore that a part can have 'no meaning or significance apart from its whole' must be utterly rejected. It implies itself that the statement 'This is a part of that whole' has a meaning; and in order that this may have one, both subject and predicate must have a distinct meaning. And it is easy to see how this false doctrine has arisen by confusion with the two relations (1) and (2) which may really be properties of wholes.

(*a*) The *existence* of a part may be connected by a natural or causal necessity with the existence of the other parts of its whole; and further what is a part of a whole and what has ceased to be such a part, although differing intrinsically from one another, may be called by one and the same name. Thus, to take a typical example, if an arm be cut off from the human body, we still call it an arm. Yet an arm, when it is a part of the body, undoubtedly differs from a dead arm; and hence we may easily be led to say 'The arm which is a part of the body would not be what it is, if it were not such a part,' and to think that the contradiction thus expressed is in reality a characteristic of things. But, in fact, the dead arm never was a part of the body; it is only *partially* identical with the living arm. Those parts of it which are identical with parts of the living arm are exactly the same, whether they belong to the body or not; and in them we have an undeniable instance of one and the same thing at one time forming a part, and at another not forming a part of the presumed 'organic whole.' On the other hand those properties which *are* possessed by the living, and *not* by the dead arm, do not exist in a changed form in the latter: they simply do not exist there *at all.* By a causal necessity their existence depends on their having that relation to the other parts of the body which we express by saying that they form part of it. Yet, most certainly, *if* they ever did not form part of the body, they *would* be exactly what they are when they do. That they differ intrinsically from the properties of the dead arm and that they form part of the body are propositions not analytically related to one another. There is no contradiction in supposing them to retain such intrinsic differences and yet not to form part of the body.

But (*b*) when we are told that a living arm has no *meaning* or *significance* apart from the body to which it belongs, a different fallacy is also suggested. 'To have meaning or significance' is commonly used in the sense of 'to have importance'; and this again means 'to have value either as a means or as an end.' Now it is quite possible that even a living arm, apart from its body, would have no intrinsic value whatever; although the whole of which it is a part has great intrinsic value owing to its presence. Thus we may easily come to say that, *as* a part of the body, it has great value, whereas *by itself* it would have none; and thus that its whole 'meaning' lies in its relation to the body. But in fact the value in question obviously does not belong to *it* at all. To have value merely as a part is equivalent to having no value at all, but merely being a part of that which has it. Owing, however, to neglect of this distinction, the assertion that a part has value, *as a part,* which it would not otherwise have, easily leads to the assumption that it is also different, as a part, from what it would otherwise be; for it is, in fact, true that two things which have a different value must also differ in other respects. Hence the assumption that one and the same thing, because it is a part of a more valuable whole at one time than at another, therefore has more intrinsic value at one time than at another, has encouraged the self-contradictory belief that one and the same thing may be two different things, and that only in one of its forms is it truly what it is.

For these reasons, I shall, where it seems convenient, take the liberty to use the term 'organic' with a special sense. I shall use it to denote the fact that a whole has an intrinsic value different in amount from the sum of the values of its parts. I shall use it to denote this and only this. The term will not imply any causal relation whatever between the parts of the whole in question. And it will not imply either, that the parts are inconceivable except as parts of that whole, or that, when they form parts of such a whole, they have a value different from that which they would have if they did not. Understood in this special and perfectly definite sense the relation of an organic whole to its parts is one of the most important which Ethics has to recognise. A chief part of that science should be occupied in comparing the relative values of various goods; and the grossest errors will be committed in such comparison if it be assumed that wherever two things form a whole, the value of that whole is merely the sum of the values of those two things. With this question of 'organic wholes,' then, we complete the enumeration of the kind of problems, with which it is the business of Ethics to deal.

23. In this chapter I have endeavoured to enforce the following conclusions. (1) The peculiarity of Ethics is not that it investigates assertions about human conduct, but that it investigates assertions about that property of things which is denoted by the term 'good,' and the converse property denoted by the term 'bad.' It must, in order to establish its conclusions, investigate the truth of *all* such assertions, *except* those which assert the relation of this property only to a single existent (1–4). (2) This property, by reference to which the

subject-matter of Ethics must be defined, is itself simple and indefinable (5–14). And (3) all assertions about its relation to other things are of two, and only two, kinds: they either assert in what degree things themselves possess this property, or else they assert causal relations between other things and those which possess it (5–17). Finally, (4) in considering the different degrees in which things themselves possess this property, we have to take account of the fact that a whole may possess it in a degree different from that which is obtained by summing the degrees in which its parts possess it (18–22).

NOTES

*In *Principia Ethica* this chapter is divided into four major parts:

    A: subsections 1-4
    B: subsections 5-14
    C: subsections 15-17
    D: subsections 18-23

1. *Methods of Ethics,* Bk. I, Chap. iii, § 1 (6th edition).
2. *Methods of Ethics,* Bk. I, Chap. iv, § 1.

8. A Defence of Common Sense

G. E. Moore

In what follows I have merely tried to state, one by one, some of the most important points in which my philosophical position differs from positions which have been taken up by *some* other philosophers. It may be that the points which I have had room to mention are not really the most important, and possibly some of them may be points as to which no philosopher has ever really differed from me. But, to the best of my belief, each is a point as to which many have really differed; although (in most cases, at all events) each is also a point as to which many have agreed with me.

I

The first point is a point which embraces a great many other points. And it is one which I cannot state as clearly as I wish to state it, except at some length. The method I am going to use for stating it is this. I am going to begin by enunciating, under the heading (1), a whole long list of propositions, which may seem, at first sight, such obvious truisms as not to be worth stating: they are, in fact, a set of propositions, every one of which (in my own opinion) I *know,* with certainty, to be true. I shall, next, under the heading (2), state a single proposition which makes an assertion about a whole set of *classes* of propositions — each class being defined, as the class consisting of all propositions which resemble *one* of the propositions in (1) in a certain respect. (2), therefore, is a proposition which could not be stated, until the list of propositions in (1), or some similar list, had already been given. (2) is itself a proposition which may seem such an obvious truism as not to be worth stating; and it is also a proposition which (in my own opinion) I *know,* with certainty, to be true. But, nevertheless, it is, to the best of my belief, a proposition with regard to which many philosophers have, for different reasons, differed from me; even if they have not directly denied (2) itself, they have held views incompatible with it. My first

163

point, then, may be said to be that (2), together with all its implications, some of which I shall expressly mention, is true.

(1) I begin, then, with my list of truisms, every one of which (in my own opinion) I *know,* with certainty, to be true. The propositions to be included in this list are the following: —

There exists at present a living human body, which is *my* body. This body was born at a certain time in the past, and has existed continuously ever since, though not without undergoing changes; it was, for instance, much smaller when it was born, and for some time afterwards, than it is now. Ever since it was born, it has been either in contact with or not far from the surface of the earth; and, at every moment since it was born, there have also existed many other things, having shape and size in three dimensions (in the same familiar sense in which it has), from which it has been *at various distances* (in the familiar sense in which it is now at a distance both from that mantel-piece and from that book-case, and at a greater distance from the book-case than it is from the mantel-piece); also there have (very often, at all events) existed some other things of this kind with which it was *in contact* (in the familiar sense in which it is now in contact with the pen I am holding in my right hand and with some of the clothes I am wearing). Among the things which have, in this sense, formed part of its environment (i.e. have been either in contact with it, or at *some* distance from it, however *great*) there have, at every moment since its birth, been large numbers of other living human bodies, each of which has, like it, (*a*) at some time been born, (*b*) continued to exist for some time after birth, (*c*) been, at every moment of its life after birth, either in contact with or not far from the surface of the earth; and many of these bodies have already died and ceased to exist. But the earth had existed also for many years before my body was born; and for many of these years, also, large numbers of human bodies had, at every moment, been alive upon it; and many of these bodies had died and ceased to exist before it was born. Finally (to come to a different class of propositions), I am a human being, and I have, at different times since my body was born, had many different experiences, of each of many different kinds: e.g. I have often perceived both my own body and other things which formed part of its environment, including other human bodies; I have not only perceived things of this kind, but have also observed facts about them, such as, for instance, the fact which I am now observing, that that mantel-piece is at present nearer to my body than that book-case; I have been aware of other facts, which I was not at the time observing such as, for instance, the fact, of which I am now aware, that my body existed yesterday and was then also for some time nearer to that mantel-piece than to that book-case; I have had expectations with regard to the future, and many beliefs of other kinds, both true and false; I have thought of imaginary things, and persons and incidents, in the reality of which I did not believe; I have had dreams; and I have had feelings of many different kinds. And, just as my body has been the body of a human being, namely myself, who has, during its life-time, had many experiences of each of these (and other) different kinds; so, in the case of very many of the other human bodies which have lived upon the earth, each has been the body of a different human being, who has, during the life-time of that body, had many different experiences of each of these (and other) different kinds.

(2) I now come to the single truism which, as will be seen, could not be stated except by reference to the whole list of truisms, just given in (1). This truism also (in my own opinion) I *know,* with certainty, to be true; and it is as follows: —

In the case of *very many* (I do not say *all*) of the human beings belonging to the class (which includes myself) defined in the following way, i.e. as human beings who have had human bodies, that were born and lived for some time upon the earth, and who have, during the life-time of those bodies, had many different experiences of each of the kinds mentioned in (1), it is true that each has frequently, during the life of his body, known, with regard to *himself* or *his* body, and with regard to some time earlier than any of the times at which I wrote down the propositions in (1), a proposition *corresponding* to each of the propositions in (1), in the sense that it asserts with regard to *himself* or *his* body and the earlier time in question (namely, in each case, the time at which he knew it), just what the corresponding proposition in (1) asserts with regard to *me* or *my* body and the time at which I wrote that proposition down.

In other words what (2) asserts is only (what seems an obvious enough truism) that each of *us* (meaning by "us," very many human beings of the class defined) has frequently *known,* with regard to *himself* or *his* body and the time at which he knew it, everything which, in writing down my list of propositions in (1), I was claiming to know about *my*self or *my* body and the time at which I wrote that proposition down. I.e. just as *I* knew (when I wrote it down) "There exists at present a living human body which is my body," so each of us has frequently known with regard to himself and some other time the different but corresponding proposition, which *he* could *then* have properly expressed by, "There exists *at present* a human body which is *my* body"; just as *I* know "Many human bodies other than mine have before now lived on the earth," so each of us has frequently known the different but corresponding proposition "Many human bodies other than *mine* have before *now* lived on the earth"; just as *I* know "Many human human beings other than myself have before now perceived, and dreamed, and felt," so each of *us* has frequently known the different but corresponding proposition "Many human beings other than *myself* have before *now* perceived, and dreamed, and felt"; and so on, in the case of *each* of the propositions enumerated in (1).

I hope there is no difficulty in understanding, so far, what this proposition (2) asserts. I have tried to make clear by examples what I mean by "propositions *corresponding* to each of the propositions in (1)." And what (2) asserts is merely that each of us has frequently known to be true a proposition *corresponding* (in that sense) to each of the propositions in (1) — a *different* corresponding proposition, of course, at each of the times at which he knew such a proposition to be true.

But there remain two points, which, in view of the way in which some philosophers have used the English language, ought, I think, to be expressly mentioned, if I am to make quite clear exactly how much I am asserting in asserting (2).

The first point is this. Some philosophers seem to have thought it legitimate to use the word "true" in such a sense, that a proposition which is partially false may nevertheless also be true; and some of these, therefore, would perhaps *say* that propositions like those enumerated in (1) are, in their view, true, when all the time they believe that every such proposition is partially false. I wish, therefore, to make it quite plain that I am not using "true" in any such sense. I am using it in such a sense (and I think this is the ordinary usage) that if a proposition is partially false, it follows that it is *not* true, though, of course, it may be *partially* true. I am maintaining, in short, that all the propositions in (1), and also many propositions corresponding to each of these, are *wholly* true; I am asserting this in asserting (2). And hence any philosopher, who does in fact believe, with regard to any or all of these classes of propositions, that every proposition of the class in question is partially false, is, in fact, disagreeing with me and holding a view incompatible with (2), even though he may think himself justified in *saying* that he believes some propositions belonging to all of these classes to be "true."

And the second point is this. Some philosophers seem to have thought it legitimate to use such expressions as, e.g., "The earth has existed for many years past," as if they expressed something which they really believed, when in fact they believe that every proposition, which such an expression would *ordinarily* be understood to express, is, at least partially, false; and all they really believe is that there is some *other* set of propositions, related in a certain way to those which such expressions do actually express, which, unlike these, really are true. That is to say, they use the expression "The earth has existed for many years past" to express, not what it would ordinarily be understood to express, but the proposition that some proposition, related to this in a certain way, is true; when all the time they believe that the proposition, which this expression would ordinarily be understood to express is, at least partially, false. I wish, therefore, to make it quite plain that I was not using the expressions I used in (1) in any such subtle sense. I meant by each of them precisely what every reader, in reading them, will have understood me to mean. And any philosopher, therefore, who holds that any of these expressions, if understood in this popular manner, expresses a proposition which embodies some popular error, is disagreeing with me and holding a view incompatible with (2), even though he may hold that there is some *other,* true, proposition which the expression in question might be legitimately used to express.

In what I have just said, I have assumed that there is some meaning which is *the* ordinary or popular meaning of such expressions as "The earth has existed for many years past." And this, I am afraid, is an assumption which some philosophers are capable of disputing. They seem to think that the question "Do you believe that the earth has existed for many years past?" is not a plain question, such as should be met either by a plain "Yes" or "No," or by a plain "I can't make up my mind," but is the sort of question which can be properly met by:

"It all depends on what you mean by 'the earth' and 'exists' and 'years': if you mean so and so, and so and so, and so and so, then I do; but if you mean so and so, and so and so, and so and so, or so and so, and so and so, and so and so, or so and so, and so and so, and so and so, then I don't, or at least I think it is extremely doubtful." It seems to me that such a view is as profoundly mistaken as any view can be. Such an expression as "The earth has existed for many years past" is the very type of an unambiguous expression, the meaning of which we all understand. Any one who takes a contrary view must, I suppose, be confusing the question whether we understand its meaning (which we all certainly do) with the entirely different question whether we *know what it means,* in the sense that we are able to *give a correct analysis* of its meaning. The question what is the correct analysis of *the* proposition meant *on any occasion* (for, of course, as I insisted in defining (2), a different proposition is meant at every different time at which the expression is used) by "The earth has existed for many years past" is, it seems to me, a profoundly difficult question, and one to which, as I shall presently urge, no one knows the answer. But to hold that we do not know what, in certain respects, is the analysis of what we understand by such an expression, is an entirely different thing from holding that we do not understand the expression. It is obvious that we cannot even raise the question how what we do understand by it is to be analysed, unless we do understand it. So soon, therefore, as we know that a person who uses such an expression, is using it in its ordinary sense, we understand his meaning. So that in explaining that I was using the expressions used in (1) in their ordinary sense (those of them which have an ordinary sense, which is not the case with quite all of them), I have done all that is required to make my meaning clear.

But now, assuming that the expressions which I have used to express (2) are understood, I think, as I have said, that many philosophers have really held views incompatible with (2). And the philosophers who have done so may, I think, be divided into two main groups. A. What (2) asserts is, with regard to a whole set of *classes* of propositions, that we have, each of us, frequently *known* to be true propositions belonging to *each* of these classes. And one way of holding a view incompatible with this proposition is, of course, to hold, with regard to one or more of the classes in question, that *no* propositions of that class *are* true—that all of them are, at least partially, false; since if, in the case of any one of these classes, *no* propositions of that class *are* true, it is obvious that nobody can have *known* any propositions of that class to be true, and therefore that *we* cannot have known to be true propositions belonging to *each* of these classes. And my first group of philosophers consists of philosophers who have held views incompatible with (2) for this reason. They have held, with regard to one or more of the classes in question, simply that no propositions of that class *are* true. Some of them have held this with regard to *all* the classes in question; some only with regard to *some* of them. But, of course, whichever of these two views they have held, they have been holding a view inconsistent with (2). B. Some philosophers, on the other hand, have not ventured to assert, with regard to *any* of the classes in (2), that no propositions of that class *are* true, but what they have asserted is that, in the case of some of these classes, no human being has ever *known,* with certainty, that any propositions of the class in question are true. That is to say, they differ profoundly from philosophers of group A, in that they hold that propositions of *all* these classes *may* be true; but nevertheless they hold a view incompatible with (2) since they hold, with regard to some of these classes, that none of us has ever *known* a proposition of the class in question to be true.

A. I said that some philosophers, belonging to this group, have held that no propositions belonging to *any* of the classes in (2) are wholly true, while others have only held this with regard to *some* of the classes in (2). And I think the chief division of this kind has been the following. Some of the propositions in (1) (and, therefore, of course, all propositions belonging to the corresponding classes in (2)) are propositions which cannot be true, unless some *material things* have existed and have stood *in spatial relations* to one another: that is to say, they are propositions which, *in a certain sense,* imply *the reality of material things,* and *the reality of Space.* E.g. the proposition that my body has existed for many years past, and has, at every moment during that time been either in contact with or not far from the earth, is a proposition which implies both the *reality of material things* (provided you use "material things" in such a sense that to deny the reality of material things implies that no proposition which asserts that human bodies have existed, or that the earth has existed, is wholly true) and also the *reality of Space* (provided, again, that you use "Space" in such a sense that to deny the reality of Space implies that no proposition which asserts that anything has ever been in contact with or at a distance from another, in the familiar senses pointed out in (1), is wholly true). But others among the propositions in (1) (and, therefore, propositions belonging to the corresponding classes in (2)), do not (at least obviously) imply either the reality of material things or the reality of Space: e.g. the propositions that I have often had dreams, and have had many different feelings at different times. It is true that propositions of this second class do imply one thing which is also implied by all propositions of the first, namely that (*in a certain sense*) *Time is real,* and imply also one thing not implied by propositions of the first class, namely that (*in a certain sense*) *at least one Self is real.* But I think there are some philosophers, who, while denying that (in the senses in question) either material things or Space are real, have been willing to admit that Selves and Time are real, in the sense required. Other philosophers, on the other hand, have used the expression "Time is not real," to express some view that they held; and some, at least, of these have, I think, meant by this expression something which is incompatible with the truth of *any* of the propositions in (1)—they have meant, namely, that *every* proposition of the sort that is expressed by the use of "now" or "at present," e.g. "I am now both seeing and hearing" or "There exists at present a living human body," or by the use of a *past* tense, e.g. "I *have* had many experiences in the past," or "The earth *has* existed for many years," are, at least partially, false.

All the four expressions I have just introduced, namely "Material things are not real," "Space is not real," "Time is not real," "The Self is not real," are, I think, unlike the expressions I used in (1), really ambiguous. And it may be that, in the case of each of them, some philosopher has used the expression in question to express some view he held which was not incompatible with (2). With such philosophers, if there are any, I am not, of course, at present concerned. But it seems to me that the most natural and proper usage of each of these expressions is a usage in which it *does* express a view incompatible with (2); and, in the case of each of them, some philosophers have, I think, really used the expression in question to express such a view. All such philosophers have, therefore, been holding a view incompatible with (2).

All such views, whether incompatible with *all* of the propositions in (1), or only with *some* of them, seem to me to be quite certainly false; and I think the following points are specially deserving of notice with regard to them: —

(*a*) If *any* of the classes of propositions in (2) is such that no proposition of that class is true, then no philosopher has ever existed, and therefore none can ever have held with regard to any such class, that no proposition belonging to it is true. In other words, the proposition that some propositions belonging to each of these classes are true is a proposition which has the peculiarity, that, if any philosopher has ever denied it, it follows from the fact that he has denied it, that he must have been wrong in denying it. For when I speak of "philosophers" I mean, of course (as we all do), exclusively philosophers who have been human beings, with human bodies that have lived upon the earth, and who have at different times had many different experiences. If, therefore, there have been any philosophers, there have been human beings of this class; and if there have been human beings of this class, all the rest of what is asserted in (1) is certainly true too. Any view, therefore, incompatible with the proposition that many propositions corresponding to each of the propositions in (1) are true, can only be true, on the hypothesis that no philosopher has ever held any such view. It follows, therefore, that, in considering whether this proposition is true, I cannot consistently regard the fact that many philosophers, whom I respect, have, to the best of my belief, held views incompatible with it, as having any weight at all against it. Since, if I know that they have held such views, I am, *ipso facto,* knowing that they were mistaken; and, if I have no reason to believe that the proposition in question is true, I have still less reason to believe that they held views incompatible with it; since I am more certain that they have existed and held *some* views, i.e. that the proposition in question is true, than that they have held any views incompatible with it.

(*b*) It is, of course, the case that all philosophers who have held such views have repeatedly, even in their philosophical works, expressed other views inconsistent with them: i.e. no philosopher has ever been able to hold such views consistently. One way in which they have betrayed this inconsistency, is by alluding to the existence of other philosophers. Another way is by alluding to the existence of the human race, and in particular by using "we" in the sense in which I have already constantly used it, in which any philosopher who asserts that "we" do so and so, e.g. that "*we* sometimes believe propositions that are not true," is asserting not only that he himself has done the thing in question, but that *very many other human beings, who have had bodies and lived upon the earth,* have done the same. The fact is, of course, that all philosophers have belonged to the class of human beings, which exists only if (2) be true: that is to say, to the class of human beings, who have frequently *known* propositions corresponding to each of the propositions in (1). In holding views incompatible with the proposition that propositions of all these classes are true, they have, therefore, been holding views inconsistent with propositions which they themselves *knew* to be true; and it was, therefore, only to be expected that they should sometimes betray their knowledge of such propositions. The strange thing is that philosophers should have been able to hold sincerely, as part of their philosophical creed, propositions inconsistent with what they themselves *knew* to be true; and yet, so far as I can make out, this has really frequently happened. My position, therefore, on the first point, differs from that of philosophers belonging to this group A, not in that I hold anything which they don't hold, but only in that I don't hold, as part of my philosophical creed, things which they do hold as part of theirs—that is to say propositions inconsistent with some which they and I both hold in common. But this difference seems to me to be an important one.

(c) Some of these philosophers have brought forward, in favour of their position, arguments designed to show, in the case of some or all of the propositions in (1), that no proposition of that type can possibly be wholly true, because every such proposition entails both of two incompatible propositions. And I admit, of course, that if any of the propositions in (1) did entail both of two incompatible propositions it could not be true. But it seems to me I have an absolutely conclusive argument to show that none of them does entail both of two incompatible propositions. Namely this: All of the propositions in (1) are true; no true proposition entails both of two incompatible propositions; therefore, none of the propositions in (1) entails both of two incompatible propositions.

(d) Although, as I have urged, no philosopher who has held with regard to any of these types of proposition, that no propositions of that type are true, has failed to hold also other views inconsistent with his view in this respect, yet I do not think that the view, with regard to any or all of these types, that no proposition belonging to them is true, is *in itself* a self-contradictory view, i.e. entails both of two incompatible propositions. On the contrary, it seems to me quite clear that it *might* have been the case that Time was not real, material things not real, Space not real, selves not real. And in favour of my view that none of these things, which might have been the case, *is* in fact the case, I have, I think, no better argument than simply this—namely, that all the propositions in (1) are, in fact, true.

B. This view, which is usually considered a much more modest view than A, has, I think, the defect that, unlike A, it really is self-contradictory, i.e. entails both of two mutually incompatible propositions.

Most philosophers who have held this view, have held, I think, that though each of us knows propositions corresponding to *some* of the propositions in

(1), namely to those which merely assert that *I* myself have had in the past experiences of certain kinds at many different times, yet none of us knows *for certain* any propositions either of the type (*a*) which assert the existence of material things or of the type (*b*) which assert the existence of *other* selves, beside myself, and that *they* also have had experiences. They admit that we do in fact *believe* propositions of both these types, and that they *may* be true; some would even say that we know them to be highly probable; but they deny that we ever know them, *for certain, to be true.* Some of them have spoken of such beliefs as "beliefs of Common Sense," expressing thereby their conviction that beliefs of this kind are very commonly entertained by mankind: but they are convinced that these things are, in all cases, only *believed,* not known for certain; and some have expressed this by saying that they are matters of Faith, not of Knowledge.

Now the remarkable thing, which those who take this view have not, I think, in general duly appreciated, is that, in each case, the philosopher who takes it is making an assertion about "us"—that is to say, not merely about himself, but about *many other human beings as well.* When he says "No human being has ever *known* of the existence of other human beings," he is saying: "There have been many other human beings beside myself, and none of them (including myself) has ever known of the existence of other human beings." If he says: "These beliefs are beliefs of Common Sense, but they are not matters of *knowledge,*" he is saying: "There have been many other human beings, besides myself, who have shared these beliefs, but neither I nor any of the rest has ever known them to be true." In other words, he asserts with confidence that these beliefs *are* beliefs of Common Sense, and seems often to fail to notice that, *if* they are, they must be true; since the proposition that they are beliefs of Common Sense, is one which logically entails propositions both of type (*a*) and of type (*b*); it logically entails the proposition that many human beings, beside the philosopher himself, have had human bodies, which lived upon the earth, and have had various experiences, including beliefs of this kind. This is why this position, as contrasted with positions of group A, seems to me to be self-contradictory. Its difference from A consists in the fact that it is making a proposition about *human knowledge* in general, and therefore is actually asserting the existence of many human beings, whereas philosophers of group A in stating their position are not doing this: they are only contradicting *other* things which they hold. It is true that a philosopher who says "There have existed many human beings beside myself and none of us has ever known of the existence of any human beings beside himself," is only contradicting himself, if what he holds is "There have *certainly* existed many human beings beside myself" or, in other words, "*I* know that there have existed other human beings beside myself." But this, it seems to me, is what such philosophers have in fact been generally doing. They seem to me constantly to betray the fact that they regard the proposition that those beliefs *are* beliefs of Common Sense, or the proposition that they themselves are not the only members of the human race, as not merely true, but *certainly* true; and *certainly* true it cannot be, unless one member, at least, of the human race, namely themselves, has *known* the very things which that member is declaring that no human being has ever known.

Nevertheless, my position that I *know,* with certainty, to be true all of the propositions in (1), is certainly not a position, the denial of which entails both of two incompatible propositions. If I do *know* all these propositions to be true, then, I think, it is quite certain that other human beings also have known corresponding propositions: that is to say (2) also *is* true, and *I* know it to be true. But do I really *know* all the propositions in (1) to be true? Isn't it possible that I merely believe them? Or I know them to be highly probable? In answer to this question, I think I have nothing better to say than that it seems to me that I *do* know them, with certainty. It is, indeed, obvious that, in the case of most of them, I do not know them *directly*: that is to say, I only know them because, in the past, I have known to be true *other* propositions which were evidence for them. If, for instance, I do know that the earth had existed for many years before I was born, I certainly only know this because I have known other things in the past which were evidence for it. And I certainly do not know exactly what the evidence was. Yet all this seems to me to be no good reason for doubting that I do know it. We are all, I think, in this strange position that we do *know* many things, with regard to which we *know* further that we must have had evidence for them, and yet we do not know *how* we know them, i.e. we do not know what the evidence was. If there is any "we," and if we know that there is, this must be so: for, that there is a "we," is one of the things in question. And that I do know that there is a "we," that is to say, that many other human beings, with human bodies, have lived upon the earth, it seems to me that I do know, for certain.

If this first point in my philosophical position, namely my belief in (2), is to be given any name, which has actually been used by philosophers in classifying the positions of other philosophers, it would have, I think, to be expressed by saying that I am one of those philosophers who have held that the "Common Sense view of the world" is, in certain fundamental features, *wholly* true. But it must be remembered that, according to me, *all* philosophers, without exception, have agreed with me in holding this: and that the real difference, which is commonly expressed in this way, is only a difference between those philosophers, who have *also* held views inconsistent with these features in "the Common Sense view of the world," and those who have not.

The features in question (namely, propositions of any of the classes defined in defining (2)) are all of them features, which have this peculiar property— namely, that *if we know that they are features in the "Common Sense view of the world," it follows that they are true:* it is self-contradictory to maintain that *we* know them to be features in the Common Sense view, and that yet they are not true; since to say that *we* know this, is to say that they are true. And many of them also have the further peculiar property that, *if they are features in the Common Sense view of the world (whether "we" know this or not), it follows that they are true,* since to say that there is a "Common Sense view of the world," is to say that they are true. The phrases "Common Sense view of the world" or "Common Sense beliefs" (as used by philosophers) are, of course, extraordinarily vague; and, for all I know, there may be many propositions which may be properly called features in "the Common Sense view of the world" or "Common Sense beliefs," which are not true, and which deserve to be mentioned with the contempt with which some philosophers speak of "Common Sense beliefs." But to speak with contempt of those "Common Sense beliefs" which I have mentioned is quite certainly the height of absurdity. And there are, of course, enormous numbers of other features in "the Common Sense view of the world" which, if these are true, are quite certainly true too: e.g. that there have lived upon the surface of the earth not only human beings, but also many different species of plants and animals, etc., etc.

II

What seems to me the next in importance of the points in which my philosophical position differs from positions held by *some* other philosophers, is one which I will express in the following way. I hold, namely, that there is no good reason to suppose either (A) that *every* physical fact is *logically* dependent upon some mental fact or (B) that *every* physical fact is *causally* dependent upon some mental fact. In saying this, I am not, of course, saying that there *are* any physical facts which are wholly independent (i.e. both logically and causally) of mental facts: I do, in fact, believe that there are; but that is not what I am asserting. I am only asserting that there is *no good reason* to suppose the contrary; by which I mean, of course, that none of the human beings, who have had human bodies that lived upon the earth, have, during the life-time of their bodies, had any good reason to suppose the contrary. Many philosophers have, I think, not only believed either that *every* physical fact is *logically* dependent upon some mental fact ("physical fact" and "mental fact" being understood in the sense in which I am using these terms) or that *every* physical fact is *causally* dependent upon some mental fact, or both, but also that they themselves had good reason for these beliefs. In this respect, therefore, I differ from them.

In the case of the term "physical fact," I can only explain how I am using it *spatial* by giving examples. I mean by "physical facts," facts *like* the following: "That mantel-piece it at present nearer to this body than that book-case is," "The earth has existed for many years past," "The moon has at every moment for many years past been nearer to the earth than to the sun," "That mantel-piece is of a light colour." But, when I say "facts *like* these," I mean, of course, facts like them *in a certain respect;* and what this respect is, I cannot define. The term "physical fact" is, however, in common use; and I think that I am using it in its ordinary sense. Moreover, there is no need for a definition to make my point clear; since among the examples I have given, there are some with regard to which I hold that there is no reason to suppose *them* (i.e. these particular physical facts) either logically or causally dependent upon any mental fact.

"Mental fact," on the other hand, is a much more unusual expression, and I am using it in a specially limited sense, which, though I think it is a natural one, does need to be explained. There may be many other senses in which the term can be properly used. But I am only concerned with this one; and hence it is essential that I should explain what it is.

There may, possibly, I hold, be "mental facts" of three different kinds. It is only with regard to the first kind that I am sure that there are facts of that kind; but if there were any facts of either of the other two kinds, they would be "mental facts" in my limited sense, and therefore I must explain what is meant by the hypothesis that there are facts of those two kinds.

(a) My first kind is this. I am conscious now; and also I am seeing something now. These two facts are both of them mental facts of my first kind; and my first kind consists exclusively of facts which resemble one or another of the two in a certain respect.

(α) The fact that I am conscious now is obviously, in a certain sense, a fact, with regard to a particular individual and a particular time, to the effect that that individual is conscious at that time. And every fact which resembles this one in that respect is to be included in my first kind of mental fact. Thus the fact that I was also conscious at many different times yesterday is not itself a fact of this kind: but it entails that there *are* (or, as we should commonly say, because the times in question are past times, "were") many other facts of this kind, namely each of the facts, which, at each of the times in question, I could have properly expressed by "I am conscious *now*." *Any* fact which is, in this sense, a fact with regard to an individual and a time (whether the individual be myself or another, and whether the time be past or present), to the effect that that individual *is* conscious at that time, is to be included in my first kind of mental fact: and I call such facts, facts of class (α).

(β) The second example I gave, namely the fact that I am seeing something now, is obviously related to the fact that I am conscious now in a peculiar manner. It not only *entails* the fact that I am conscious now (for from the fact that I am seeing something it *follows* that I am conscious: I *could* not have been seeing anything, unless I had been conscious, though I might quite well have been conscious without seeing anything) but it also is a fact, with regard to a *specific way* (or mode) of being conscious, to the effect that I am conscious in that way: in the same sense in which the proposition (with regard to any particular thing) "This is red" both entails the proposition (with regard to the same thing) "This is coloured," and is also a proposition, with regard to a *specific way* of being coloured, to the effect that that thing is coloured in that way. And any fact which is related in this peculiar manner to any fact of class (α), is also to be included in my first kind of mental fact, and is to be called a fact of class (β). Thus the fact that I am hearing now, is, like the fact that I am seeing now, a fact of class (β); and so is any fact, with regard to myself and a past time, which could at that time have been properly expressed by "I am dreaming now," "I am imagining now," "I am at present aware of the fact that . . ." etc., etc. In short, any fact, which is a fact with regard to a particular individual (myself or another), a particular time (past or present), and *any particular kind of experience,* to the effect that that individual is having at that time an experience of that particular kind, is a fact of class (β): and only such facts are facts of class (β).

My first kind of mental facts consists exclusively of facts of classes (α) and (β), and consists of *all* facts of either of these kinds.

(b) That there are many facts of classes (α) and (β) seems to me perfectly certain. But many philosophers seem to me to have held a certain view with regard to the *analysis* of facts of class (α), which is such that, if it were true, there would be facts of another kind, which I should wish also to call "mental facts." I don't feel at all sure that this analysis is true; but it seems to me that it *may* be true; and since we can understand what is meant by the supposition that it is true, we can also understand what is meant by the supposition that there are "mental facts" of this second kind.

Many philosophers have, I think, held the following view as to the analysis of what each of us knows, when he knows (at any time) "I am conscious now." They have held, namely, that there is a certain intrinsic property (with which we are all of us familiar and which might be called that of "being an experience") which is such that, at any time at which any man knows "I am conscious now," he is knowing, with regard to that property and himself and the time in question, "There is occurring now an event which has this property (i.e. "is an experience") and which is an experience of *mine,"* and such that this fact is what he expresses by "I am conscious now." And if this view is true, there must be many facts of each of three kinds, each of which I should wish to call "mental facts"; viz. (1) facts with regard to some event, which has this supposed intrinsic property, and to some time, to the effect that that event is occurring at that time, (2) facts with regard to this supposed intrinsic property and some time, to the effect that *some* event which has that property is occurring at that time, and (3) facts with regard to some property, which is a *specific way* of having the supposed intrinsic property (in the sense above explained in which "being red" is a specific way of "being coloured") and some time, to the effect that some event which has that specific property is occurring at that time. Of course, there not only are not, but *cannot* be, facts of any of these kinds, unless there is an intrinsic property related to what each of us (on any occasion) expresses by "I am conscious now," in the manner defined above; and I feel very doubtful whether there is any such property; in other words, although I know for certain both that I have had many experiences, and that I have had experiences of many different kinds, I feel very doubtful whether to say the first is the same thing as to say that there have been many events, each of which was an experience and an experience of mine, and whether to say the second is the same thing as to say that there have been many events, each of which was an experience of mine, and each of which also had a different property, which was a specific way of being an experience. The proposition that I have had experiences does not necessarily entail the proposition that there have been any events which were experiences; and I cannot satisfy myself that I am acquainted with any events of the supposed kind. But yet it seems to me possible that the proposed analysis of "I am conscious now" is correct: that I am really acquainted with events of the supposed kind, though I cannot see that I am. And *if* I am, then I should wish to call the three kinds of facts defined above, "mental facts." Of course, if there are "experiences" in the sense defined, it would be possible (as many have held) that there *can* be no experiences which are not *some individual's experiences;* and in that case any fact of any of these three kinds would be logically dependent on, though not necessarily identical with, some fact of class (α) or class (β). But it seems to me also a possibility that, if there are "experiences," there might be experiences which did not belong to any individual; and, in that case, there would be "mental facts" which were neither identical with nor logically dependent on any fact of class (α) or class (β).

(c) Finally some philosophers have, so far as I can make out, held that there are or may be facts, which are facts with regard to some individual, to the effect that he is conscious, or is conscious in some specific way, which differ from facts of classes (α) and (β), in the important respect that they are not facts *with regard to any time:* they have conceived the possibility that there may be one or more individuals, who are *timelessly* conscious, and timelessly conscious in specific modes. And others, again, have, I think, conceived the hypothesis that the intrinsic property defined in (*b*) may be one which does not belong only to *events,* but may also belong to one or more wholes, which do *not* occur at any time: in other words, that there may be one or more *timeless* experiences, which might or might not be the experiences of some individual. It seems to me very doubtful whether any of these hypotheses are even possibly true; but I cannot see for certain that they are not possible: and, if they are possible, then I should wish to give the name "mental fact" to any fact (if there were any) of any of the five following kinds, viz. (1) to any fact which is the fact, with regard to any individual, that he is *timelessly* conscious, (2) to any fact which is the fact, with regard to any individual, that he is *timelessly* conscious in any specific way, (3) to any fact which is the fact with regard to a *timeless* experience that it exists, (4) to any fact which is the fact with regard to the supposed intrinsic property "being an experience," which is the fact that something timelessly exists which has that property, and (5) to any fact which is the fact, with regard to any property, which is a specific mode of this supposed intrinsic property, that something timelessly exists which has that property.

I have then defined three different kinds of facts, each of which is such that, if there *were* any facts of that kind (as there certainly *are,* in the case of the first kind), the facts in question *would* be "mental facts" in my sense; and to complete the definition of the limited sense in which I am using "mental facts," I have only to add that I wish also to apply the name to one *fourth* class of facts: namely to any fact, which is the fact, with regard to any of these three kinds of facts, or any kinds included in them, *that there are facts of the kind in question;* i.e. not only will each individual fact of class (α) be, in my sense, a "mental fact," but also the general fact "that there are facts of class (α)," will itself be a "mental fact"; and similarly in all other cases: e.g. not only will the fact that I am now perceiving (which is a fact of class (β)) be a "mental fact," but also the general fact that *there are* facts, with regard to individuals and times, to the effect that the individual in question is perceiving at the time in question, will be a "mental fact."

A. Understanding "physical fact" and "mental fact" in the senses *just* explained, I hold, then, that there is no good reason to suppose that *every* physical fact is *logically* dependent upon some mental fact. And I use the phrase, with regard to two facts, F_1 and F_2, "F_1 is *logically dependent* on F_2," wherever and only where F_1 *entails* F_2, either in the sense in which the proposition "I am seeing now" *entails* the proposition "I am conscious now," or the proposition (with regard to any particular thing) "This is red" entails the proposition (with regard to the same thing) "This is coloured," or else in the more strictly logical sense in which (for instance) the conjunctive proposition "All men are mortal, and Mr. Baldwin is a man" entails the proposition "Mr. Baldwin is mortal." To say, then, of two facts, F_1 and F_2 is *not* logically dependent upon F_2, is only to say that F_1 *might* have been a fact, even if there had been no such fact as F_2; or that the conjunctive proposition "F_1 is a fact, but there is no such fact as F_2" is a proposition which is not self-contradictory, i.e. does not entail both of two mutually incompatible propositions.

I hold, then, that, in the case of *some* physical facts, there is no good reason to suppose that there is some mental fact, such that the physical fact in question could not have been a fact unless the mental fact in question had also been one. And my position is perfectly definite, since I hold that this is the case with all the four physical facts, which I have given as examples of physical facts. E.g. there is no good reason to suppose that there is any mental fact whatever, such that the fact that that mantel-piece is at present nearer to my body than that book-case could not have been a fact, unless the mental fact in question had also been a fact; and, similarly, in all the other three cases.

In holding this I am certainly differing from some philosophers. I am, for instance, differing from Berkeley, who held that that mantel-piece, that book-case, and my body are, all of them, either "ideas" or "constituted by ideas," and that no "idea" can possibly exist without being perceived. He held, that is, that this physical fact is logically dependent upon a mental fact of my fourth class: namely a fact which is the fact that there is at least one fact, which is a fact with regard to an individual and the present time, to the effect that that individual is now perceiving something. He does not say that this physical fact is logically dependent upon any fact which is a fact of any of my first three classes, e.g. on any fact which is the fact, with regard to a particular individual and the present time, that *that* individual is now perceiving something: what he does say is that the physical fact couldn't have been a fact, unless it had been a fact that there was *some* mental fact of this sort. And it seems to me that many philosophers, who would perhaps disagree either with Berkeley's assumption that my body is an "idea" or "constituted by ideas," or with his assumption that "ideas" cannot exist without being perceived, or with both, nevertheless would agree with him in thinking that this physical fact is logically dependent upon *some* "mental fact": e.g. they might say, that it could not have been a fact, unless there had been, at some time or other, or, were timelessly, *some* "experience." Many, indeed, so far as I can make out, have held that *every* fact is logically dependent on every other fact. And, of course, they have held in the case of their opinions, as Berkeley did in the case of his, that they had good reasons for them.

B. I also hold that there is no good reason to suppose that *every* physical fact is *causally* dependent upon some mental fact. By saying that F_1 is *causally* dependent on F_2, I mean only that F_1 *wouldn't* have been a fact unless F_2 had been; *not* (which is what "logically dependent" asserts) that F_1 *couldn't conceivably* have been a fact, unless F_2 had been. And I can illustrate my meaning by reference to the example which I have just given. The fact that that mantel-piece is at present nearer to my body than that book-case, is (as I have just explained) so far as I can see, not *logically* dependent upon any mental fact; it *might* have been a fact, even if there had been no mental facts. But it certainly is *causally* dependent on many mental facts: my body *would* not have been here unless I had been conscious in various ways in the past; and the mantel-piece and the book-case certainly *would* not have existed, unless other men had been conscious too.

But with regard to two of the facts, which I gave as instances of physical facts, namely the fact that the earth has existed for many years past, and the fact that the moon has for many years past been nearer to the earth than to the sun, I hold that there is no good reason to suppose that these are *causally* dependent upon any mental fact. So far as I can see, there is no reason to suppose that there is any mental fact of which it could be truly said: unless this fact had been a fact, the earth would not have existed for many years past. And in holding this, again, I think I differ from some philosophers. I differ, for instance, from those who have held that all material things were created by God, and that they had good reasons for supposing this.

III

I have just explained that I differ from those philosophers who have held that there is good reason to suppose that all material things were created by God. And it is, I think, an important point in my position, which should be mentioned, that I differ also from all philosophers who have held that there is good reason to suppose that there is a God at all, whether or not they have held it likely that he created all material things.

And similarly, where as some philosophers have held that there is good reason to suppose that we, human beings, shall continue to exist and to be conscious after the death of our bodies, I hold that there is no good reason to suppose this.

IV

I now come to a point of a very different order.

As I have explained under I, I am not at all sceptical as to the *truth* of such propositions as "The earth has existed for many years past," "Many human bodies have each lived for many years upon it," i.e. propositions which assert the existence of material things: on the contrary, I hold that we all know, with certainty, many such propositions to be true. But I am very sceptical as to what, in certain respects, the correct *analysis* of such propositions is. And this is a matter as to which I think I differ from many philosophers. Many seem to hold that there is no doubt at all as to their *analysis,* nor, therefore, as to the analysis of the proposition "Material things have existed," in certain respects in which I hold that the analysis of the propositions in question is extremely doubtful; and some of them, as we have seen, while holding that there is no doubt as to their *analysis,* seem to have doubted whether any such propositions are *true*. I, on the other hand, while holding that there is no doubt whatever that many such propositions are wholly true, hold also that no philosopher, hitherto, has succeeded in suggesting an analysis of them, as regards certain important points, which comes anywhere near to being certainly true.

It seems to me quite evident that the question how propositions of the type I have just given are to be analysed, depends on the question how propositions of another and simpler type are to be analysed. I know, at present, that I am perceiving a human hand, a pen, a sheet of paper, etc.; and it seems to me that I cannot know how the proposition "Material things exist" is to be analysed, until I know how, in certain respects, these simpler propositions are to be analysed. But even these are not simple enough. It seems to me quite evident that my knowledge that I am now perceiving a human hand is a deduction from a pair of propositions simpler still — propositions which I can only express in the form "I am perceiving *this*" and "*This* is a human hand." It is the analysis of propositions of the latter kind, which seems to me to present such great difficulties; while nevertheless the whole question as to the *nature* of material things obviously depends upon their analysis. It seems to me a surprising thing that so few philosophers, while saying a great deal as to what material things *are* and as to what it is to perceive them, have attempted to give a clear account as to what precisely they suppose themselves to *know* (or to *judge,* in case they have held that we don't *know* any such propositions to be true, or even that no such propositions *are* true) when they know or judge such things as "This is a hand," "That is the sun," "This is a dog," etc. etc. etc.

Two things only seem to me to be quite certain about the analysis of such propositions (and even with regard to these I am afraid some philosophers would differ from me) namely that whenever I know, or judge, such a proposition to be true, (1) there is always some *sense-datum* about which the proposition in question is a proposition — some sense-datum which is *a* subject (and, in a certain sense, the principal or ultimate subject) of the proposition in question, and (2) that, nevertheless, *what* I am knowing or judging to be true about this sense-datum is not (in general) that it is *itself* a hand, or a dog, or the sun, etc. etc., as the case may be.

Some philosophers have I think doubted whether there are any such things as other philosophers have meant by "sense-data" or "sensa." And I think it is quite possible that some philosophers (including myself, in the past) have used these terms in senses, such that it is really doubtful whether there are any such things. But there is no doubt at all that there are sense-data, in the sense in which I am now using that term. I am at present seeing a great number of them, and feeling others. And, in order to point out to the reader what sort of things I mean by sense-data, I need only ask him to look at his own right hand. If he does this he will be able to pick out something (and, unless he is seeing double, *only* one thing) with regard to which he will see that it is, at first sight, a natural view to take that that thing is identical, not, indeed, with his whole right hand, but with that part of its surface which he is actually seeing, but will also (on a little reflection) be able to see that it is doubtful whether it can be identical with the part of the surface of his hand in question. Things of *the sort* (in a certain respect) of which this thing is, which he sees in looking at his hand, and with regard to which he can understand how some philosophers should have supposed it to *be* the part of the surface of his hand which he is seeing, while others have supposed that it can't be, are what I mean by "sense-data." I therefore define the term in such a way that it is an open question whether the sense-datum which I now see in looking at my hand and which is a sense-datum of my hand is or is not identical with that part of its surface which I am now actually seeing.

That what I know, with regard to this sense-datum, when I know "This is a human hand," is not that it is *itself* a human hand, seems to me certain because I know that my hand has many parts (e.g. its other side, and the bones inside it), which are quite certainly *not* parts of this sense-datum.

I think it certain, therefore, that the analysis of the proposition "This a human hand" is, roughly at least, of the form "There is a thing, and only one thing, of which it is true both that it is a human hand and that *this surface* is a part of its surface." In other words, to put my view in terms of the phrase "theory of representative perception," I hold it to be quite certain that I do not *directly* perceive *my hand;* and that when I am said (as I may be correctly said) to "perceive" it, that I "perceive" it means that I perceive (in a different and more fundamental sense) something which is (in a suitable sense) *representative* of it, namely, a certain part of its surface.

This is all that I hold to be *certain* about the analysis of the proposition "This is a human hand." we have seen that it includes in its analysis a proposition of the form "This is part of the surface of a human hand" (where "This," of course, has a different meaning from that which it has in the original proposition which has now been analysed). But this proposition also is undoubtedly a proposition about the sense-datum, which I am seeing, which is a sense-datum *of* my hand. And hence the further question arises: *What,* when I know *"This is part of the surface of* a human hand," am I knowing about the sense-datum in question? Am I, in this case, really knowing, about the sense-datum in question that it *itself* is part of the surface of a human hand? Or, just as we found in the case of "This is a human hand," that what I was knowing about the sense-datum was certainly not that it *itself* was a human hand, so, is it perhaps the case, with this new proposition, that even here I am not knowing, with regard to the sense-datum, that it is *itself* part of the surface of a hand? and, if so, what is it that I am knowing about the sense-datum itself?

This is the question to which, as it seems to me, no philosopher has hitherto suggested an answer which comes anywhere near to being *certainly* true.

There seem to me to be three, and only three, alternative types of answer possible; and to any answer yet suggested, of any of these types, there seem to me to be very grave objections.

(1) Of the first type, there is but one answer: namely, that in this case what I am knowing really is that the sense-datum *itself* is part of the surface of a human hand. In other words that, though I don't perceive *my hand* directly, I do *directly* perceive part of its surface; that the sense-datum itself *is* this part of its surface and not merely something which (in a sense yet to be determined) "represents" this part of its surface; and that hence the sense in which I "perceive" this part of the surface of my hand, is not in its turn a sense which needs to be defined by reference to yet a third more ultimate sense of "perceive," which is the only one in which perception is direct, namely that in which I perceive the sense-datum.

If this view is true (as I think it may just possibly be), it seems to me certain that we must abandon a view which has been held to be certainly true by most philosophers, namely the view that our sense-data always really have the qualities which they sensibly appear to us to have. For I know that if another man were looking through a microscope at the same surface which I am seeing with the naked eye, the sense-datum which he saw would sensibly appear to him to have qualities very different from and incompatible with those which my sense-datum sensibly appears to me to have: and yet, if my sense-datum is identical with the surface we are both of us seeing, his must be identical with it also. My sense-datum can, therefore, be identical with this surface only on condition that it is identical with his sense-datum; and, since his sense-datum sensibly appears to him to have qualities incompatible with those which mine sensibly appears to me to have, his sense-datum can be identical with mine, only on condition that the sense-datum in question either has not got the qualities which it sensibly appears to me to have, or has not got those which it sensibly appears to him to have.

I do not, however, think that this is a fatal objection to this first type of view. A far more serious objection seems to me to be that, when we see a thing double (have what is called "a double image" of it), we certainly have *two* sense-data each of which is *of* the surface seen, and which cannot therefore both be identical with it; and that yet it seems as if, if any sense-datum is ever identical with the surface *of* which it is a sense-datum, each of these so-called "images" must be so. It looks, therefore, as if every sense-datum is, after all, only "representative" of the surface, *of* which it is a sense-datum.

(2) But, if so, what relation has it to the surface in question?

This second type of view is one which holds that when I know "This is part of the surface of a human hand," what I am knowing with regard to the sense-datum which is *of* that surface, is, *not* that it is *itself* part of the surface of a human hand, but something of the following kind. There is, it says, *some* relation, R, such that what I am knowing with regard to the sense-datum is either "There is one thing and only one thing, of which it is true both that it is a part of the surface of a human hand, and that it has R to this sense-datum," or else "There are a set of things, of which it is true both that that set, taken collectively, *are* part of the surface of a human hand, and also that each member of the set has R to this sense-datum, and that nothing which is not a member of the set has R to it."

Obviously, in the case of this second type, many different views are possible, differing according to the view they take as to what the relation R is. But there is only one of them, which seems to me to have any plausibility; namely that which holds that R is an ultimate and unanalysable relation, which might be expressed by saying that "xRy" means the same as "y is an appearance or manifestation of X." I.e. the analysis which this answer would give of "This is part of the surface of a human hand" would be "There is one and only one thing of which it is true both that it is part of the surface of a human hand, and that this sense-datum is an appearance or manifestation of it."

To this view also there seem to me to be very grave objections, chiefly drawn from a consideration of the questions how we can possibly *know* with regard to any of our sense-data that there is one thing and one thing only which has to them such a supposed ultimate relation; and how, if we do, we can possibly *know* anything further about such things, e.g. of what size or shape they are.

(3) The third type of answer, which seems to me to be the only possible alternative if (1) and (2) are rejected, is the type of answer which J. S. Mill seems to have been implying to be the true one when he said that material things are "permanent possibilities of sensation." He seems to have thought that when I know such a fact as "This is part of the surface of a human hand," what I am knowing with regard to the sense-datum which is the principal subject of that fact, is not that it is itself part of the surface of a human hand, nor yet, with regard to any relation, that *the* thing which has to it that relation is part of the surface of a human hand, but a whole set of hypothetical facts each of which is a fact of the form "If *these* conditions had been fulfilled, I should have been perceiving a sense-datum intrinsically related to *this* sense-datum in *this* way," "If *these* (other) conditions had been fulfilled, I should have been perceiving a sense-datum intrinsically related to *this* sense-datum in *this* (other) way," etc. etc.

With regard to this third type of view as to the analysis of propositions of the kind we are considering, it seems to me, again, just *possible* that it is a true one; but to hold (as Mill himself and others seem to have held) that it is *certainly,* or nearly certainly, true, seems to me as great a mistake, as to hold with regard either to (1) or to (2), that they are *certainly,* or nearly certainly, true. There seem to me to be very grave objections to it; in particular the three, (*a*) that though, in general, when I know such a fact as "This is a hand," I certainly do

know some hypothetical facts of the form "If *these* conditions had been fulfilled, I should have been perceiving a sense-datum of *this* kind, which would
have been a sense-datum of the same surface of which *this* is a sense-datum," it
seems doubtful whether any conditions with regard to which I know this are
not themselves conditions of the form "If this and that *material thing* had been
in those positions and conditions . . ." (*b*) that it seems again very doubtful
whether there is any intrinsic relation, such that my knowledge that (under
these conditions) I should have been perceiving a sense-datum of *this* kind,
which would have been a sense-datum of the same surface of which *this* is a
sense-datum is equivalent to a knowledge, with regard to that relation, that I
should, under those conditions, have been perceiving a sense-datum related by
it to *this* sense-datum and (*c*) that, if it were true, the sense in which a material
surface is "round" or "square," would necessarily be utterly different from that
in which our sense-data sensibly appear to us to be "round" or "square."

V

Just as I hold that the proposition "There are and have been material
things" is quite certainly true, but that the question how this proposition is to
be analysed is one to which no answer that has been hitherto given is anywhere
near certainly true; so I hold that the proposition "There are and have been
many Selves" is quite certainly true, but that here again all the analyses of this
proposition that have been suggested by philosophers are highly doubtful.

That I am now perceiving many different sense-data, and that I have at
many times in the past perceived many different sense-data, I know for certain—
that is to say, I know that there are mental facts of class (β), connected in a
way which it is proper to express by saying that they are all of them facts about
me; but how this kind of connection is to be analysed, I do not know for certain, nor do I think that any other philosopher knows with any approach to
certainty. Just as in the case of the proposition "This is part of the surface of a
human hand," there are several extremely different views as to its analysis,
each of which seems to me *possible,* but none nearly certain, so also in the case
of the proposition "This, that and that sense-datum are all at present being
perceived by *me,*" and still more so in the case of the proposition "*I* am now
perceiving this sense-datum, and *I* have in the past perceived sense-data of
these other kinds." Of the *truth* of these propositions there seems to me to be
no doubt, but as to what is the correct analysis of them there seems to me to be
the gravest doubt—the true analysis may, for instance, *possibly* be quite as
paradoxical as is the third view given above under IV as to the analysis of "This
is part of the surface of a human hand"; but whether it *is* as paradoxical as this
seems to me to be quite as doubtful as in that case. Many philosophers, on the
other hand, seem to me to have assumed that there is little or no doubt as to
the correct analysis of such propositions; and many of these, just reversing my
position, have also held that the propositions themselves are not true.

9. Proof of an External World

G. E. Moore

In the preface to the second edition of Kant's *Critique of Pure Reason* some words occur, which, in Professor Kemp Smith's translation, are rendered as follows:

> It still remains a scandal to philosophy . . . that the existence of things outside of us . . . must be accepted merely on *faith,* and that, if anyone thinks good to doubt their existence, we are unable to counter his doubts by any satisfactory proof.[1]

It seems clear from these words that Kant thought it a matter of some importance to give a proof of 'the existence of things outside of us' or perhaps rather (for it seems to me possible that the force of the German words is better rendered in this way) of 'the existence of *the* things outside of us'; for had he not thought it important that a proof should be given, he would scarcely have called it a 'scandal' that no proof had been given. And it seems clear also that he thought that the giving of such a proof was a task which fell properly within the province of philosophy; for, if it did not, the fact that no proof had been given could not possibly be a scandal to *philosophy*.

Now, even if Kant was mistaken in both of these two opinions, there seems to me to be no doubt whatever that it is a matter of some importance and also a matter which falls properly within the province of philosophy, to discuss the question what sort of proof, if any, can be given of 'the existence of things outside of us.' And to discuss this question was my object when I began to write the present lecture. But I may say at once that, as you will find, I have only, at most, succeeded in saying a very small part of what ought to be said about it.

The words 'it . . . remains a scandal to philosophy . . . that we are unable . . .' would, taken strictly, imply that, at the moment at which he wrote

184

them, Kant himself was unable to produce a satisfactory proof of the point in question. But I think it is unquestionable that Kant himself did not think that he personally was at the time unable to produce such a proof. On the contrary, in the immediately preceding sentence, he has declared that he has, in the second edition of his *Critique,* to which he is now writing the Preface, given a 'rigorous proof' of this very thing; and has added that he believes this proof of his to be 'the only possible proof.' It is true that in this preceding sentence he does not describe the proof which he has given as a proof of 'the objective reality of outer intuition.' But the context leaves no doubt that he is using these two phrases, 'the objective reality of outer intuition' and 'the existence of things (*or* 'the things') outside of us,' in such a way that whatever is a proof of the first is also necessarily a proof of the second. We must, therefore, suppose that when he speaks as if *we* are unable to give a satisfactory proof, he does not mean to say that he himself, as well as others, is *at the moment* unable; but rather that, until he discovered the proof which he has given, both he himself and everybody else *were* unable. Of course, if he is right in thinking that he has given a satisfactory proof, the state of things which he describes came to an end as soon as his proof was published. As soon as that happened, any one who read it was able to give a satisfactory proof by simply repeating that which Kant had given, and the 'scandal' to philosophy had been removed once for all.

If, therefore, it were certain that the proof of the point in question given by Kant in the second edition, is a satisfactory proof, it would be certain that at least one satisfactory proof can be given; and all that would remain of the question which I said I proposed to discuss, would be, firstly, the question as to what *sort* of a proof this of Kant's is, and secondly the question whether (contrary to Kant's own opinion) there may not perhaps be other proofs, of the same or of a different sort, which are also satisfactory. But I think it is by no means certain that Kant's proof is satisfactory. I think it is by no means certain that he did succeed in removing once for all the state of affairs which he considered to be a scandal to philosophy. And I think, therefore, that the question whether it is possible to give *any* satisfactory proof of the point in question still deserves discussion.

But what is the point in question? I think it must be owned that the expression 'things outside of us' is rather an odd expression, and an expression the meaning of which is certainly not perfectly clear. It would have sounded less odd if, instead of 'things outside of us' I had said 'external things,' and perhaps also the meaning of this expression would have seemed to be clearer; and I think we make the meaning of 'external things' clearer still, if we explain that this phrase has been regularly used by philosophers as short for 'things external to *our minds.*' The fact is that there has been a long philosophical tradition, in accordance with which the three expressions 'external things,' 'things external to *us,*' and 'things external to *our minds*' have been used as equivalent to one another and have, each of them, been used as if they needed no explanation. The origin of this usage I do not know. It occurs already in Descartes; and since he uses the expressions as if they needed no explanation, they had presumably been used with the same meaning before. Of the three, it seems to me that the expression 'external to *our minds*' is the clearest, since it at least makes clear that what is meant is not 'external to *our bodies*'; whereas both the other expressions might be taken to mean this: and indeed there has been a good deal of confusion, even among philosophers, as to the relation of the two conceptions 'external things' and 'things external to *our bodies*'. But even the expression 'things external to our minds' seems to me to be far from perfectly clear; and if I am to make really clear what I mean by 'proof of the existence of things outside of us', I cannot do it by merely saying that by 'outside of us' I mean 'external to our minds'.

There is a passage (*K.d.r.V.*, A 373) in which Kant himself says that the expression 'outside of us' 'carries with it an unavoidable ambiguity'. He says that 'sometimes it means something which exists *as a thing in itself* distinct from us, and sometimes something which merely belongs to external *appearance*'; he calls things which are 'outside of us' in the first of these two senses 'objects which might be called external in the transcendental sense', and things which are so in the second *'empirically external* objects'; and he says finally that, in order to remove all uncertainty as to the latter conception, he will distinguish empirically external objects from objects which might be called 'external' in the transcendental sense, 'by calling them outright things which are *to be met with in space*'.

I think that this last phrase of Kant's, 'things which are to be met with in space', does indicate fairly clearly what sort of things it is with regard to which I wish to inquire what sort of proof, if any, can be given that there are any things of that sort. My body, the bodies of other men, the bodies of animals, plants of all sorts, stones, mountains, the sun, the moon, stars and planets, houses and other buildings, manufactured articles of all sorts — chairs, tables, pieces of paper, &c., are all of them 'things which are to be met with in space'. In short all things of the sort that philosophers have been used to call 'physical objects', 'material things', or 'bodies' obviously come under this head. But the phrase 'things that are to be met with in space' can be naturally understood as applying also in cases where the names 'physical object', 'material thing', or 'body' can hardly be applied. For instance, shadows are sometimes to be met with in space, although they could hardly be properly called 'physical objects', 'material things', or 'bodies'; and although in one usage of the term 'thing', it would not be proper to call a shadow a 'thing', yet the phrase 'things which are to be met with in space' can be naturally understood as synonymous with 'whatever can be met with in space', and this is an expression which can quite properly be understood to include shadows. I wish the phrase 'things which are to be met with in space' to be understood in this wide sense; so that if a proof can be found that there ever have been as many as two different shadows it will follow at once that there have been at least two 'things which were to be met with in space', and this proof will be as good a proof of the point in question, as would be a proof that there have been at least two 'physical objects' of no matter what sort.

The phrase 'things which are to be met with in space' can, therefore, be naturally understood as having a very wide meaning—a meaning even wider than that of 'physical object' or 'body', wide as is the meaning of these latter expressions. But wide as is its meaning, it is not, in one respect, so wide as that of another phrase which Kant uses as if it were equivalent to this one; and a comparison between the two will, I think, serve to make still clearer what sort of things it is with regard to which I wish to ask what proof, if any, can be given that there are such things.

The other phrase which Kant uses as if it were equivalent to 'things which are to be met with in space' is used by him in the sentence immediately preceding that previously quoted in which he declares that the expression 'things outside of us' 'carries with it an unavoidable ambiguity' (A 373). In this preceding sentence he says that an 'empirical object' 'is called *external,* if it is presented (*vorgestellt*) *in space*'. He treats, therefore, the phrase 'presented in space' as if it were equivalent to 'to be met with in space'. But it is easy to find examples of 'things,' of which it can hardly be denied that they are 'presented in space,' but of which it could, quite naturally, be emphatically denied that they are 'to be met with in space.' Consider, for instance, the following description of one set of circumstances under which what some psychologists have called a 'negative after-image' and others a 'negative after-sensation' can be obtained. 'If, after looking steadfastly at a white patch on a black ground, the eye be turned to a white ground a grey patch is seen for some little time.' (Foster's *Text-book of Physiology,* iv. iii. 3, p. 1266; quoted in Stout's *Manual of Psychology,* 3rd edition, p. 280.) Upon reading these words recently, I took the trouble to cut out of a piece of white paper a four-pointed star, to place it on a black ground, to 'look steadfastly' at it, and then to turn my eyes to a white sheet of paper: and I did find that I saw a grey patch for some little time—I not only saw a grey patch, but I saw it *on* the white ground, and also this grey patch was of roughly the same shape as the white four-pointed star at which I had 'looked steadfastly' just before—it also was a four-pointed star. I repeated this simple experiment successfully several times. Now each of those grey four-pointed stars, one of which I saw in each experiment, was what is called an 'after-image' or 'after-sensation'; and can anybody deny that each of these after-images can be quite properly said to have been presented in space? I saw each of them on a real white background, and, if so, each of them was 'presented' on a real white background. But though they were 'presented in space' everybody, I think, would feel that it was gravely misleading to say that they were 'to be met with in space.' The white star at which I 'looked steadfastly,' the black ground on which I saw it, and the white ground on which I saw the after-images, were, of course, 'to be met with in space': they were, in fact, 'physical objects' or surfaces of physical objects. But one important difference between them, on the one hand, and the grey after-images, on the other, can be quite naturally expressed by saying that the latter were *not* 'to be met with in space.' And one reason why this is so is, I think, plain. To say that so and so was at a given time 'to be met with in space' naturally suggests that there are conditions such that *any one* who fulfilled them might, conceivably, have 'perceived' the 'thing' in question—might have seen it, if it was a visible object, have felt it, if it was a tangible one, have heard it, if it was a sound, have smelt it, if it was a smell. When I say that the white four-pointed paper star, at which I looked steadfastly, was a 'physical object' and was 'to be met with in space,' I am implying that *any one,* who had been in the room at the time, and who had normal eyesight and a normal sense of touch, might have seen and felt it. But, in the case of those grey after-images which I saw, it is not conceivable that any one besides myself should have seen any one of them. It is, of course, quite conceivable that other people, if they had been in the room with me at the time, and had carried out the same experiment which I carried out, would have seen grey after-images *very like* one of those which I saw: there is no absurdity in supposing even that they might have seen after-images *exactly* like one of those which I saw. But there is an absurdity in supposing that any one of the after-images which I saw could also have been seen by any one else: in supposing that two different people can ever see the *very same* after-image. One reason, then, why we should say that none of those grey after-images which I saw was 'to be met with in space,' although each of them was certainly 'presented in space' to me, is simply that none of them could conceivably have been seen by any one else. It is natural so to understand the phrase 'to be met with in space', that is to say of anything which a man perceived that it was to be met with in space is to say that it might have been perceived by *others* as well as by the man in question.

Negative after-images of the kind described are, therefore, one example of 'things' which, though they must be allowed to be 'presented in space', are nevertheless *not* 'to be met with in space', and are *not* 'external to our minds' in the sense with which we shall be concerned. And two other important examples may be given.

The first is this. It is well known that people sometimes see things double, an occurrence which has also been described by psychologists by saying that they have a 'double image', or two 'images', of some object at which they are looking. In such cases it would certainly be quite natural to say that each of the two 'images' is 'presented in space': they are seen, one in one place, and the other in another, in just the same sense in which each of those grey after-images which I saw was seen at a particular place on the white background at which I was looking. But it would be utterly unnatural to say that, when I have a double image, each of the two images is 'to be met with in space'. On the contrary it is quite certain that *both* of them are not 'to be met with in space'. If both were, it would follow that somebody else might see the *very same* two images which I see; and, though there is no absurdity in supposing that another person might see a pair of images exactly similar to a pair which I see, there is an absurdity in supposing that any one else might see the *same identical pair*. In every case, then, in which any one sees anything double, we have an example of at least one 'thing' which, though 'presented in space' is certainly not 'to be met with in space'.

And the second important example is this. Bodily pains can, in general, be quite properly said to be 'presented in space'. When I have a toothache, I feel it *in* a particular region of my jaw or *in* a particular tooth; when I make a cut on my finger smart by putting iodine on it, I feel the pain in a particular place in my finger; and a man whose leg has been amputated may feel a pain *in* a place where his foot might have been if he had not lost it. It is certainly perfectly natural to understand the phrase 'presented in space' in such a way that if, in the sense illustrated, a pain is felt *in* a particular place, that pain is 'presented in space'. And yet of pains it would be quite unnatural to say that they are 'to be met with in space', for the same reason as in the case of after-images or double images. It is quite conceivable that another person should feel a pain exactly like one which I feel, but there is an absurdity in supposing that he could feel *numerically the same* pain which I feel. And pains are in fact a typical example of the sort of 'things' of which philosophers say that they are *not* 'external' to our minds, but 'within' them. Of any pain which *I* feel they would say that it is necessarily *not* external to my mind but *in* it.

And finally it is, I think, worth while to mention one other class of 'things', which are certainly not 'external' objects and certainly not 'to be met with in space', in the sense with which I am concerned, but which yet some philosophers would be inclined to say are 'presented in space', though they are not 'presented in space' in quite the same sense in which pains, double images, and negative after-images of the sort I described are so. If you look at an electric light and then close your eyes, it sometimes happens that you see, for some little time, against the dark background which you usually see when your eyes are shut, a bright path similar in shape to the light at which you have just been looking. Such a bright patch, if you see one, is another example of what some psychologists have called 'after-images' and others 'after-sensations'; but, unlike the negative after-images of which I spoke before, it is seen when your eyes are shut. Of such an after-image, seen with closed eyes, some philosophers might be inclined to say that this image too was 'presented in space', although it is certainly not 'to be met with in space'. They would be inclined to say that it is 'presented in space', because it certainly is presented as at some little distance from the person who is seeing it: and how can a thing be presented as at some little distance from me, without being 'presented in space'? Yet there is an important difference between such after-images, seen with closed eyes, and after-images of the sort I previously described — a difference which might lead other philosophers to deny that these after-images, seen with closed eyes, are 'presented in space' at all. It is a difference which can be expressed by saying that when your eyes are shut, you are not seeing any part of *physical* space at all — of the space which is referred to when we talk of 'things which are to be met with in *space*'. An after-image seen with closed eyes certainly is presented in *a* space, but it may be questioned whether it is proper to say that it is presented in *space*.

It is clear, then, I think, that by no means everything which can naturally be said to be 'presented in space' can also be naturally said to be 'a thing which is to be met with in space'. Some of the 'things', which are presented in space, are very emphatically *not* to be met with in space: or, to use another phrase, which may be used to convey the same notion, they are emphatically *not* 'physical realities' at all. The conception 'presented in space' is therefore, in one respect, much wider than the conception 'to be met with in space': many 'things' fall under the first conception which do not fall under the second — many after-images, one at least of the pair of 'images' seen whenever any one sees double, and most bodily pains, are 'presented in space', though none of them are to be met with in space. From the fact that a 'thing' is presented in space, it by no means follows that it is to be met with in space. But just as the first conception is, in one respect, wider than the second, so, in another, the second is wider than the first. For there are many 'things' to be met with in space, of which it is not true that they are presented in space. From the fact that a 'thing' is to be met with in space, it by no means follows that it is presented in space. I have taken 'to be met with in space' to imply, as I think it naturally may, that a 'thing' *might be* perceived; but from the fact that a thing *might be* perceived, it does not follow that it *is* perceived; and if it is not actually perceived, then it will not be presented in space. It is characteristic of the sorts of 'things', including shadows, which I have described as 'to be met with in space', that there is no absurdity in supposing with regard to any one of them which *is,* at a given time, perceived, both (1) that it might have existed at that very time, without being perceived; (2) that it might have existed at another time, without being perceived at that other time; and (3) that during the whole period of its existence, it need not have been perceived at any time at all. There is, therefore, no absurdity in supposing that many things, which were at one time to be met with in space, never were 'presented' at any time at all, and that many things which *are* to be met with in space now, are not now 'presented' and also never were and never will be. To use a Kantian phrase, the conception of 'things which are to be met with in space' embraces not only objects of actual experience, but also objects of *possible* experience; and from the fact that a thing is or was an object of *possible* experience, it by no means follows that it either was or is or will be 'presented' at all.

I hope that what I have now said may have served to make clear enough what sorts of 'things' I was originally referring to as 'things outside us' or 'things external to our minds'. I said that I thought that Kant's phrase 'things that are to be met with in space' indicated fairly clearly the sorts of 'things' in question; and I have tried to make the range clearer still, by pointing out that this phrase only serves the purpose, if (*a*) you understand it in a sense, in which many 'things', e.g. after-images, double images, bodily pains, which might be said to be 'presented in space', are nevertheless *not* to be reckoned as 'things that are to be met with in space', and (*b*) you realize clearly that there is no contradiction in supposing that there have been and are 'to be met with in space' things which never have been, are not now, and never will be perceived, nor in supposing that among those of them which have at some time been perceived many existed at times at which they were not being perceived. I think it will now be clear to every one that, since I do not reckon as 'external things' after-images, double images, and bodily pains, I also should not reckon as 'external things', any of the 'images' which we often 'see with the mind's eye' when we are awake, nor any of those which we see when we are asleep and dreaming; and also that I was so using the expression 'external' that from the fact that a man was at a given time having a visual hallucination, it will follow that he was seeing at that time something which was *not* 'external' to his mind, and from the fact that he was at a given time having an auditory hallucination, it will follow that he was at the time hearing a sound which was *not* 'external' to his mind. But I certainly have not made my use of these phrases, 'external to our minds' and 'to be met with in space', so clear that in the case of every kind of 'thing' which might be suggested, you would be able to tell at once whether I should or should not reckon it as 'external to our minds' and 'to be met with in space'. For instance, I have said nothing which makes it quite clear whether a reflection which I see in a looking-glass is or is not to be regarded as 'a thing that is to be met with in space' and 'external to our minds', nor have I said anything which makes it quite clear whether the sky is or is not to be so regarded. In the case of the sky, everyone, I think, would feel that it was quite inappropriate to talk of it as 'a thing that is to be met with in space'; and most people, I think, would feel a strong reluctance to affirm, without qualification, that reflections which people see in looking-glasses are 'to be met with in space'. And yet neither the sky nor reflections seen in mirrors are in the same position as bodily pains or after-images in the respect which I have emphasized as a reason for saying of these latter that they are *not* to be met with in space—namely that there is an absurdity in supposing that *the very same* pain which I feel could be felt by some one else or that *the very same* after-image which I see could be seen by some one else. In the case of reflections in mirrors we should quite naturally, in certain circumstances, use language which implies that another person may see the same reflection which we see. We might quite naturally say to a friend: 'Do you see that reddish reflection in the water there? I can't make out what it's a reflection of', just as we might say, pointing to a distant hill-side: 'Do you see that white speck on the hill over there? I can't make out what it is.' And in the case of the sky, it is quite obviously *not* absurd to say that other people see it as well as I.

It must, therefore, be admitted that I have not made my use of the phrase 'things to be met with in space', nor therefore that of 'external to our minds', which the former was used to explain, so clear that in the case of every kind of 'thing' which may be mentioned, there will be no doubt whatever as to whether things of that kind are or are not 'to be met with in space' or 'external to our minds'. But this lack of a clear-cut definition of the expression 'things that are to be met with in space', does not, so far as I can see, matter for my present purpose. For my present purpose it is, I think, sufficient if I make clear, in the case of many kinds of things, that I am so using the phrase 'things that are to be met with in space', that, in the case of each of these kinds, from the proposition that there are things of that kind it *follows* that there are things to be met with in space. And I have, in fact, given a list (though by no means an exhaustive one) of kinds of things which are related to my use of the expression 'things that are to be met with in space' in this way. I mentioned among others the bodies of men and of animals, plants, stars, houses, chairs, and shadows; and I want now to emphasize that I am so using 'things to be met with in space' that, in the case of each of these kinds of 'things', from the proposition that there are 'things' of that kind it *follows* that there are things to be met with in space: e.g. from the proposition that there are plants or that plants exist it *follows* that there are things to be met with in space, from the proposition that shadows exist, it *follows* that there are things to be met with in space, and so on, in the case of all kinds of 'things' which I mentioned in my first list. That this should be clear is sufficient for my purpose, because, if it is clear, then it will also be clear that, as I implied before, if you have proved that two plants exist, or that a plant and a dog exist, or that a dog and a shadow exist, &c., &c., you will *ipso facto* have proved that there are things to be met with in space: you will not require *also* to give a separate proof that from the proposition that there are plants it *does* follow that there are things to be met with in space.

Now with regard to the expression 'things that are to be met with in space' I think it will readily be believed that I may be using it in a sense such that no proof is required that from 'plants exist' there follows 'there are things to be met with in space'; but with regard to the phrase 'things external to our minds' I think the case is different. People may be inclined to say: 'I can see quite clearly that from the proposition "At least two dogs exist at the present moment" there *follows* the proposition "At least two things are to be met with in space at the present moment", so that if you can prove that there are two dogs in existence at the present moment you will *ipso facto* have proved that two things at least are to be met with in space at the present moment. I can see that you do not also require a separate proof that from "Two dogs exist" "Two things are to be met with in space" *does* follow; it is quite obvious that there couldn't be a dog which wasn't to be met with in space. But it is not by any means so clear to me that if you can prove that there are two dogs or two shadows, you will *ipso facto* have proved that there are two things *external to our minds*. Isn't it possible that a dog, though it certainly must be "to be met with in space", might *not* be an external object — an object external to our minds? Isn't a separate proof required that anything that is to be met with in space must be external to our minds? Of course, if you are using "external" as a mere synonym for "to be met with in space", no proof will be required that dogs are external objects: in that case, if you can prove that two dogs exist, you will *ipso facto* have proved that there are some external things. But I find it difficult to believe that you, or anybody else, do really use "external" as a mere synonym for "to be met with in space"; and if you don't, isn't some proof required that whatever is to be met with in space must be external to our minds?'

Now Kant, as we saw, asserts that the phrases 'outside of us' or 'external' are in fact used in two very different senses; and with regard to one of these two senses, that which he calls the 'transcendental' sense, and which he tries to explain by saying that it is a sense in which 'external' means 'existing *as a thing in itself* distinct from us', it is notorious that he himself held that things which are to be met with in space are *not* 'external' in that sense. There is, therefore, according to him, *a* sense of 'external', a sense in which the word has been commonly used by philosophers — such that, if 'external' be used in that sense, then from the proposition 'Two dogs exist' it will *not* follow that there are some external things. What this supposed sense is I do not think that Kant himself ever succeeded in explaining clearly; nor do I know of any reason for supposing that philosophers ever have used 'external' in a sense, such that in *that* sense things that are to be met with in space are *not* external. But how about the other sense, in which, according to Kant, the word 'external' has been commonly used — that which he calls 'empirically external'? How is this conception related to the conception 'to be met with in space? It may be noticed that in the passages which I quoted (A 373), Kant himself does not tell us at all clearly what he takes to be the proper answer to this question. He only makes the rather odd statement that, in order to remove all uncertainty as to the conception 'empirically external', he will distinguish objects to which it applies from those which might be called 'external' in the transcendental sense, by 'calling them outright things which are *to be met with in space*'. These odd words certainly suggest, as one possible interpretation of them, that in Kant's opinion the conception 'empirically external' is *identical* with the conception 'to be met with in space' — that he does think that 'external', when used in this second sense, is a mere synonym for 'to be met with in space'. But, if this is his meaning, I do find it very difficult to believe that he is right. Have philosophers, in fact, ever used 'external' as a mere synonym for 'to be met with in space'? Does he himself do so?

I do not think they have, nor that he does himself; and, in order to explain how they have used it, and how the two conceptions 'external to our minds' and 'to be met with in space' are related to one another, I think it is important expressly to call attention to a fact which hitherto I have only referred to incidentally: namely the fact that those who talk of certain things as 'external to' our minds, do, in general, as we should naturally expect, talk of other 'things', with which they wish to contrast the first, as 'in' our minds. It has, of course, been often pointed out that when 'in' is thus used, followed by 'my mind', 'your mind', 'his mind', &c., 'in' is being used metaphorically. And there are some metaphorical uses of 'in', followed by such expressions, which occur in common speech, and which we all understand quite well. For instance, we all understand such expressions as 'I had you in mind, when I made that arrangement' or 'I had you in mind, when I said that there are some people who can't bear to touch a spider'. In these cases 'I was thinking of you' can be used to mean the same as 'I had you in mind'. But it is quite certain that this particular metaphorical use of 'in' is not the one in which philosophers are using it when they contrast what is 'in' my mind with what is 'external' to it. On the contrary, in their use of 'external', you will be external to my mind even at a moment when I have you in mind. If we want to discover what this peculiar metaphorical use of '*in* my mind' is, which is such that nothing, which is, in the sense we are now concerned with, 'external' to my mind, can ever be 'in' it, we need, I think, to consider instances of the sort of 'things' which they would say are 'in' my mind in this special sense. I have already mentioned three such instances, which are, I think, sufficient for my present purpose: any bodily pain which I feel, any after-image which I see with my eyes shut, and any image which I 'see' when I am asleep and dreaming, are typical examples of the sort of 'thing' of which philosophers have spoken as '*in* my mind'. And there is no doubt, I think, that when they have spoken of such things as my body, a sheet of paper, a star — in short 'physical objects' generally — as 'external', they have meant to emphasize some important difference which they feel to exist between such things as these and such 'things' as a pain, an after-image seen with closed eyes, and a dream-image. But *what* difference? What difference do they feel to exist between a bodily pain which I feel or an after-image which I see with closed eyes, on the one hand, and my body itself, on the other — what difference which leads them to say that whereas the bodily pain and the after-image are '*in*' my mind, my body itself is *not* 'in' my mind — not even when I am feeling it and seeing it or thinking of it? I have already said that one difference which there is between the two, is that my body is to be met with in space, whereas the bodily pain and the after-image are not. But I think it would be quite wrong to say that this is *the* difference which has led philosophers to speak of the two latter as 'in' my mind, and of my body as *not* 'in' my mind.

The question what the difference is which has led them to speak in this way, is not, I think, at all an easy question to answer; but I am going to try to give, in brief outline, what I *think* is a right answer.

It should, I think, be noted, first of all, that the use of the word 'mind', which is being adopted when it is said that any bodily pains which I feel are 'in my mind', is one which is not quite in accordance with any usage common in ordinary speech, although we are very familiar with it in philosophy. Nobody, I think, would say that bodily pains which I feel are 'in my mind', unless he was also prepared to say that it is *with* my mind that I feel bodily pains; and to say this latter is, I think, not quite in accordance with common non-philosophic usage. It is natural enough to say that it is with my mind that I remember, and think, and imagine, and feel *mental* pains — e.g. disappointment, but not, I think, quite so natural to say that it is with my mind that I feel *bodily* pains, e.g. a severe headache; and perhaps even less natural to say that it is with my mind that I see and hear and smell and taste. There is, however, a well-established usage according to which seeing, hearing, smelling, tasting, and having a bodily pain are just as much *mental* occurrences or processes as are remembering, or thinking, or imagining. This usage was, I think, adopted by philosophers, because they saw a real resemblance between such statements as 'I saw a cat', 'I heard a clap of thunder', 'I smelt a strong smell of onions', 'My finger smarted horribly', on the one hand, and such statements as 'I remembered having seen him', 'I was thinking out a plan of action', 'I pictured the scene to myself', 'I felt bitterly disappointed', on the other — a resemblance which puts all these statements in one class together, as contrasted with other statements in which 'I' or 'my' is used, such as, e.g., 'I was less than four feet high', 'I was lying on my back', 'My hair was very long'. What is the resemblance in question? It is a resemblance which might be expressed by saying that all the first eight statements are the sort of statements which furnish data for psychology, while the three latter are not. It is also a resemblance which may be expressed, in a way now common among philosophers, by saying that in the case of all the first eight statements, if we make the statement more specific by adding a date, we get a statement such that, if it is true, then it *follows* that I was 'having an experience' at the date in question, whereas this does not hold for the three last statements. For instance, if it is true that I saw a cat between 12 noon and 5 minutes past, to-day, it *follows* that I was 'having some experience' between 12 noon and 5 minutes past, to-day; whereas from the proposition that I was less than four feet high in December 1877, it does not *follow* that I had any experiences in December 1877. But this philosophic use of 'having an experience' is one which itself needs explanation, since it is not identical with any use of the expression that is established in common speech. An explanation, however, which is, I think, adequate for the purpose, can be given by saying that a philosopher, who was following this usage, would say that I was at a given time 'having an experience' if and only if either (1) I was conscious at the time or (2) I was dreaming at the time or (3) something else was true of me at the time, which resembled what is true of me when I am conscious and when I am dreaming, in a certain very obvious respect in which what is true of me when I am dreaming resembles what is true of me when I am conscious, and in which what would be true of me, if at any time, for instance, I had a vision, would resemble both. This explanation is, of course, in some degree vague; but I think it is clear enough for our purpose. It amounts to saying that, in this philosophic usage of 'having an experience', it would be said of me that I was, at a given time, having *no* experience, if I was at the time neither conscious nor dreaming nor having a vision nor *anything else of the sort;* and, of course, this is vague in so far as it has not been specified what else would be *of the sort:* this is left to be gathered from the instances given. But I think this is sufficient: often at night when I am asleep, I am neither conscious nor dreaming nor having a vision nor *anything else of the sort* — that is to say, I am having no experiences. If this explanation of this philosophic usage of 'having an experience' is clear enough, then I think that what has been meant by saying that any pain which I feel or any after-image which I see with my eyes closed is '*in* my mind', can be explained by saying that what is meant is neither more nor less than that there would be a contradiction in supposing *that very same pain* or *that very same after-image* to have existed at a time at which I was having no experience; or, in other words, that from the proposition, with regard to any time, that *that* pain or *that* after-image existed at that time, it *follows* that I was having some experience at the time in question. And if so, then we can say that the felt difference between bodily pains which I feel and after-images which I see, on the one hand, and my body on the other, which has led philosophers to say that any such pain or after-image is '*in* my mind', whereas my body *never* is but is always 'outside of' or 'external to' my mind, is just this, that whereas there is a contradiction in supposing a pain which I feel or an after-image which I see to exist at a time when I am having no experience, there is no contradiction in supposing my body to exist at a time when I am having no experience; and we can even say, I think, that just this and nothing more is what they have meant by these puzzling and misleading phrases 'in my mind' and 'external to my mind'.

But now, if to say of anything, e.g. my body, that it is external to *my* mind, merely means that from a proposition to the effect that it existed at a specified time, there in no case follows the further proposition that *I* was having an experience at the time in question, then to say of anything that it is external to *our* minds, will mean similarly that from a proposition to the effect that it existed at a specified time, it in no case follows that any of *us* were having experiences at the time in question. And if by *our* minds be meant, as is, I think, usually meant, the minds of human beings living on the earth, then it will follow that any pains which animals may feel, any after-images they may see, any experiences they may have, though not external to *their* minds, yet are external to *ours*. And this at once makes plain how different is the conception 'external to our minds' from the conception 'to be met with in space'; for, of course, pains which animals feel or after-images which they see are no more to be met with in space than are pains which *we* feel or after-images which *we* see. From the proposition that there are external objects — objects that are not in any of *our* minds, it does *not* follow that there are things to be met with in space; and hence 'external to our minds' is not a mere synonym for 'to be met with in space': that is to say, 'external to our minds' and 'to be met with in space' are two different conceptions. And the true relation between these conceptions seems to me to be this. We have already seen that there are ever so many kinds of 'things', such that, in the case of each of these kinds, from the proposition that there is at least one thing of that kind there *follows* the proposition that there is at least one thing to be met with in space: e.g. this follows from 'There is at least one star', from 'There is at least one human body', from 'There is at least one shadow', &c. And I think we can say that of every kind of thing of which this is true, it is also true that from the proposition that there is at least one 'thing' of that kind there *follows* the proposition that there is at least one thing external to our minds: e.g. from 'There is at least one star' there follows not only 'There is at least one thing to be met with in space' but also 'There is at least one external thing', and similarly in all other cases. My reason for saying this is as follows. Consider any kind of thing, such that anything of that kind, if there is anything of it, must be 'to be met with in space': e.g. consider the kind 'soap-bubble'. If I say of anything which I am perceiving, 'That is a soap-bubble', I am, it seems to me, certainly implying that there would be no contradiction in asserting that it existed before I perceived it and that it will continue to exist, even if I cease to perceive it. This seems to me to be part of what is meant by saying that it is a real soap-bubble, as distinguished, for instance, from an hallucination of a soap-bubble. Of course, it by no means follows, that if it really is a soap-bubble, it did in fact exist before I perceived it or will continue to exist after I cease to perceive it: soap-bubbles are an example of a kind of 'physical object' and 'thing to be met with in space', in the case of which it is notorious that particular specimens of the kind often do exist only so long as they are perceived by a particular person. But a thing which I perceive would not be a soap-bubble unless its existence at any given time were *logically independent* of my perception of it at that time; unless that is to say, from the proposition, with regard to a particular time, that it existed at that time, it *never* follows that I perceived it at that time. But, if it is true that it would not be a soap-bubble, unless it *could* have existed at any given time without being perceived by me at that time, it is certainly also true that it would not be a soap-bubble, unless it *could* have existed at any given time, without its being true that I was having any experience of any kind at the time in question: it would not be a soap-bubble, unless, whatever time you take, from the proposition that it existed at that time it does *not* follow that I was having any experience at that time. That is to say, from the proposition with regard to anything which I am perceiving that it is a soap-bubble, there *follows* the proposition that it is external to *my* mind. But if, when I say that anything which I perceive is a soap-bubble, I am implying that it is external to *my* mind, I am, I think, certainly also implying that it is also external to all other minds: I am implying that it is not a thing of a sort such that things of that sort *can* only exist at a time when somebody is having an experience. I think, therefore, that from any proposition of the form 'There's a soap-bubble!' there does really *follow* the proposition 'There's an external object!' 'There's an object external to *all* our minds!' And, if this is true of the kind 'soap-bubble', it is certainly also true of any other kind (including the kind 'unicorn') which is such that, if there are any things of that kind, it follows that there are *some* things to be met with in space.

I think, therefore, that in the case of all kinds of 'things', which are such that if there is a pair of things, both of which are of one of these kinds, or a pair of things one of which is of one of them and one of them of another, then it will follow at once that there are some things to be met with in space, it is true also that if I can prove that there are a pair of things, one of which is of one of these kinds and another of another, or a pair both of which are of one of them, then I shall have proved *ipso facto* that there are at least two 'things outside of us'. That is to say, if I can prove that there exist now both a sheet of paper and a human hand, I shall have proved that there are now 'things outside of us'; if I can prove that there exist now both a shoe and sock, I shall have proved that there are now 'things outside of us'; &c.; and similarly I shall have proved it, if I can prove that there exist now two sheets of paper, or two human hands, or two shoes, or two socks, &c. Obviously, then, there are thousands of different things such that, if, at any time, I can prove any one of them, I shall have proved the existence of things outside of us. Cannot I prove any of these things?

It seems to me that, so far from its being true, as Kant declares to be his opinion, that there is only one possible proof of the existence of things outside of us, namely the one which he has given, I can now give a large number of different proofs, each of which is a perfectly rigorous proof; and that at many other times I have been in a position to give many others. I can prove now, for instance, that two human hands exist. How? By holding up my two hands, and saying, as I make a certain gesture with the right hand, 'Here is one hand', and adding, as I make a certain gesture with the left, 'and here is another'. And if, by doing this, I have proved *ipso facto* the existence of external things, you will all see that I can also do it now in numbers of other ways: there is no need to multiply examples.

But did I prove just now that two human hands were then in existence? I do want to insist that I did; that the proof which I gave was a perfectly rigorous one; and that it is perhaps impossible to give a better or more rigorous proof of anything whatever. Of course, it would not have been a proof unless three conditions were satisfied; namely (1) unless the premiss which I adduced as proof of the conclusion was different from the conclusion I adduced it to prove; (2) unless the premiss which I adduced was something which I *knew* to be the case, and not merely something which I believed but which was by no means certain, or something which, though in fact true, I did not know to be so; and (3) unless the conclusion did really follow from the premiss. But all these three conditions were in fact satisfied by my proof. (1) The premiss which I adduced in proof was quite certainly different from the conclusion, for the conclusion was merely 'Two human hands exist at this moment'; but the premiss was something far more specific than this — something which I expressed by showing you my hands, making certain gestures, and saying the words 'Here is one hand, and here is another'. It is quite obvious that the two were different, because it is quite obvious that the conclusion might have been true, even if the premiss had been false. In asserting the premiss I was asserting much more than I was asserting in asserting the conclusion. (2) I certainly did at the moment *know* that which I expressed by the combination of certain gestures with saying the words 'There is one hand and here is another'. I *knew* that there was one hand in the place indicated by combining a certain gesture with my first utterance of 'here' and that there was another in the different place indicated by combining a certain gesture with my second utterance of 'here'. How absurd it would be to suggest that I did not know it, but only believed it, and that perhaps it was not the case! You might as well suggest that I do not know that I am now standing up and talking — that perhaps after all I'm not, and that it's not quite certain that I am! And finally (3) it is quite certain that the conclusion did follow from the premiss. This is as certain, as it is that if there is one hand here and another here *now*, then it follows that there are two hands in existence *now*.

My proof, then, of the existence of things outside of us did satisfy three of the conditions necessary for a rigorous proof. Are there any other conditions necessary for a rigorous proof, such that perhaps it did not satisfy one of them?

Perhaps there may be; I do not know; but I do want to emphasize that, so far as I can see, we all of us do constantly take proofs of this sort as absolutely conclusive proofs of certain conclusions—as finally settling certain questions, as to which we were previously in doubt. Suppose, for instance, it were a question whether there were as many as three misprints on a certain page in a certain book. A says there are, B is inclined to doubt it. How could A prove that he is right? Surely he *could* prove it by taking the book, turning to the page, and pointing to three separate places on it, saying 'There's one misprint here, another here, and another here': surely that is a method by which it *might* be proved! Of course, A would not have proved, by doing this, that there were at least three misprints on the page in question, unless it was certain that there was a misprint in each of the places to which he pointed. But to say that he *might* prove it in this way, is to say that it *might* be certain that there was. And if such a thing as that could ever be certain, then assuredly it was certain just now that there was one hand in one of the two places I indicated and another in the other.

I did, then, just now, give a proof that there were *then* external objects; and obviously, if I did, I could *then* have given many other proofs of the same sort that there were external objects *then,* and could now give many proofs of the same sort that there are external objects *now.*

But if what I am asked to do is to prove that external objects have existed *in the past,* then I can give many different proofs of this also, but proofs which are in important respects of a different *sort* from those just given. And I want to emphasize that, when Kant says it is a scandal not to be able to give a proof of the existence of external objects, a proof of their existence in the past would certainly *help* to remove the scandal of which he is speaking. He says that, if it occurs to any one to question their existence, we ought to be able to confront him with a satisfactory proof. But by a person who questions their existence, he certainly means not merely a person who questions whether any exist at the moment of speaking, but a person who questions whether any have *ever* existed; and a proof that some have existed in the past would certainly therefore be relevant to *part* of what such a person is questioning. How then can I prove that there have been external objects in the past? Here is one proof. I can say: 'I held up two hands above this desk not very long ago; therefore two hands existed not very long ago; therefore at least two external objects have existed at some time in the past, Q.E.D.' This is a perfectly good proof, provided I *know* what is asserted in the premiss. But I *do* know that I held up two hands above this desk not very long ago. As a matter of fact, in this case you all know it too. There's no doubt whatever that I did. Therefore I have given a perfectly conclusive proof that external objects have existed in the past; and you will all see at once that, if this is a conclusive proof, I could have given many others of the same sort, and could now give many others. But it is also quite obvious that this sort of proof differs in important respects from the sort of proof I gave just now that there were two hands existing *then.*

I have, then, given two conclusive proofs of the existence of external objects. The first was a proof that two human hands existed at the time when I gave the proof; the second was a proof that two human hands had existed at a time previous to that at which I gave the proof. These proofs were of a different sort in important respects. And I pointed out that I could have given, then, many other conclusive proofs of both sorts. It is also obvious that I could give many others of both sorts now. So that, if these are the sort of proof that is wanted, nothing is easier than to prove the existence of external objects.

But now I am perfectly well aware that, in spite of all that I have said, many philosophers will still feel that I have not given any satisfactory proof of the point in question. And I want briefly, in conclusion, to say something as to why this dissatisfaction with my proofs should be felt.

One reason why, is, I think, this. Some people understand 'proof of an external world' as including a proof of things which I haven't attempted to prove and haven't proved. It is not quite easy to say *what* it is that they want proved — *what* it is that is such that unless they got a proof of it, they would not say that they had a proof of the existence of external things; but I can make an approach to explaining what they want by saying that if I had proved the propositions which I used as *premisses* in my two proofs, then they would perhaps admit that I had proved the existence of external things, but, in the absence of such a proof (which, of course, I have neither given, nor attempted to give), they will say that I have not given what they mean by a proof of the existence of external things. In other words they want a proof of what I assert *now* when I hold up my hands and say 'Here's one hand and here's another'; and, in the other case, they want a proof of what I assert *now* when I say 'I did hold up two hands above this desk just now'. Of course what they really want is not merely a proof of these two propositions, but something like a general statement as to how *any* propositions of this sort may be proved. This, of course, I haven't given; and I do not believe it can be given: if this is what is meant by proof of the existence of external things, I do not believe that any proof of the existence of external things is possible. Of course, in some cases what might be called a proof of propositions which seem like these can be got. If one of you suspected that one of my hands was artificial he might be said to get a proof of my proposition 'Here's one hand, and here's another', by coming up and examining the suspected hand close up, perhaps touching and pressing it, and so establishing that it really was a human hand. But I do not believe that any proof is possible in nearly all cases. How am I to prove now that 'Here's one hand, and here's another'? I do not believe I can do it. In order to do it, I should need to prove for one thing, as Descartes pointed out, that I am not now dreaming. But how can I prove that I am not? I have, no doubt, conclusive reasons for asserting that I am not now dreaming; I have conclusive evidence that I am awake: but that is a very different thing from being able to prove it. I could not tell you what all my evidence is; and I should require to do this at least, in order to give you a proof.

But another reason, why some people would feel dissatisfied with my proofs is, I think, not merely that they want a proof of something which I haven't proved, but that they think that, if I cannot give such extra proofs, then the proofs that I have given are not conclusive proofs at all. And this, I think, is a definite mistake. They would say: 'If you cannot prove your premiss that here is one hand and here is another, then you do not know it. But you yourself have admitted that, if you did not know it, then your proof was not conclusive. Therefore your proof was not, as you say it was, a conclusive proof.' This view that, if I cannot prove such things as these, I do not know them, is, I think, the view that Kant was expressing in the sentence which I quoted at the beginning of this lecture, when he implies that so long as we have no proof of the existence of external things, their existence must be accepted merely on *faith*. He means to say, I think, that if I cannot prove that there is a hand here, I must accept it merely as a matter of faith — I cannot know it. Such a view, though it has been very common among philosophers, can, I think, be shown to be wrong — though shown only by the use of premisses which are not known to be true, unless we do know of the existence of external things. I can know things, which I cannot prove; and among things which I certainly did know, even if (as I think) I could not prove them, were the premisses of my two proofs. I should say, therefore, that those, if any, who are dissatisfied with these proofs merely on the ground that I did not know their premisses, have no good reason for their dissatisfaction.

NOTE

1. B xxxix, note: Kemp Smith, p. 34. The German words are 'so bleibt es immer ein Skandal der Philosophie . . . , das Dasein der Dinge ausser uns . . . bloss auf *Glauben* annehmen zu müssen, und wenn es jemand einfällt es zu bezweifeln, ihm keinen genugtuenden Beweis entgegenstellen zu können'.

Study Questions

G. E. Moore: "The Refutation of Idealism"

1. In what sense does Moore propose to refute idealism?
2. What is the crucial premiss in idealistic arguments?
3. Show how that premiss could be taken to be an analytic statement. Why can't it be so interpreted?
4. Moore goes through various interpretations which make the premiss a synthetic proposition. He then says he has caught the idealist maintaining a contradiction. What is it?
5. After making a break in the argument, Moore tries to show that certain propositions are false. What are they, and why are they false?

G. E. Moore: "The Subject of Ethics"

1. What is the main question of ethics (according to Moore)? Why is this the main question?
2. How does Moore answer it? What is his argument on behalf of that answer?
3. What are the two senses of *good*? How do they differ and how are they related?

G. E. Moore: "A Defence of Common Sense"

1. State the main thesis of each section of "A Defence of Common Sense."
2. How have philosophers held views inconsistent with Moore's (section I)?
3. What are his criticisms of them?
4. State Moore's argument on behalf of his main thesis in section II.
5. Show how Moore, in stages, analyzes the proposition, "Material things exist." (section IV)

G. E. Moore: "Proof of an External World"

1. Trace through Moore's analysis of 'things outside of us' in "Proof of an External World." Why is this essential to his proof?
2. Has Moore defended his claim that his proof is a rigorous one?
3. Does Moore's "Proof" added anything to his refutation of idealism? Explain your answer.

Selected Bibliography

Klemke, E. D. *The Epistemology of G. E. Moore.* Evanston: Northwestern University Press, 1969. [Exposition and criticism of main components of Moore's theory of knowledge.]

Moore, G. E. *Philosophical Papers.* London: G. Allen & Unwin, 1959. [Somewhat difficult.]

Moore, G. E. *Philosophical Studies.* London: Routledge & Kegan Paul, Ltd., 1922. [More difficult than the Russell book.]

Moore, G. E. *Principia Ethica.* Cambridge: Cambridge University Press, 1903. [Difficult in spots, but worth reading.]

Passmore, John. *A Hundred Years of Philosophy.* London: Duckworth, 1957. Chapter 9. [Nice account of Moore and Russell and of other realists.]

Russell, Bertrand. *The Problems of Philosophy.* Oxford: Oxford University Press, 1912, 1959. [An excellent elementary introduction to realism and to philosophy in general.]

Logical Atomism

10. Facts and Propositions[1]

Bertrand Russell

This course of lectures which I am now beginning I have called the Philosophy of Logical Atomism. Perhaps I had better begin by saying a word or two as to what I understand by that title. The kind of philosophy that I wish to advocate, which I call Logical Atomism, is one which has forced itself upon me in the course of thinking about the philosophy of mathematics, although I should find it hard to say exactly how far there is a definite logical connection between the two. The things I am going to say in these lectures are mainly my own personal opinions and I do not claim that they are more than that.

As I have attempted to prove in *The Principles of Mathematics,* when we analyze mathematics we bring it all back to logic. It all comes back to logic in the strictest and most formal sense. In the present lectures, I shall try to set forth in a sort of outline, rather briefly and rather unsatisfactorily, a kind of logical doctrine which seems to me to result from the philosophy of mathematics — not exactly logically, but as what emerges as one reflects: a certain kind of logical doctrine, and on the basis of this a certain kind of metaphysic. The logic which I shall advocate is atomistic, as opposed to the monistic logic of the people who more or less follow Hegel. When I say that my logic is atomistic, I mean that I share the common-sense belief that there are many separate things; I do not regard the apparent multiplicity of the world as consisting merely in phases and unreal divisions of a single indivisible Reality. It results from that, that a considerable part of what one would have to do to justify the sort of philosophy I wish to advocate would consist in justifying the process of analysis. One is often told that the process of analysis is falsification, that when you analyze any given concrete whole you falsify it and that the results of analysis are not true. I do not think that is a right view. I do not mean to say, of course, and nobody would maintain, that when you have analyzed you keep everything that you had before you analyzed. If you did, you would never attain anything in analyzing. I do not propose to meet the views that I disagree with by controversy, by arguing against those views, but rather by positively setting forth what I believe to be the truth about the matter, and endeavoring all the way through to make the views that I advocate result inevitably from absolutely undeniable data. When I talk of "undeniable data" that is not to be regarded as synonymous with "true data," because "undeniable" is a psychological term and "true" is not. When I say that something is "undeniable," I mean that it is not the sort of thing that anybody is going to deny; it does not follow from that it is true though it does follow that we shall all think it true — and that is as near to truth as we seem able to get. When you are considering any sort of theory of knowledge, you are more or less tied to a certain unavoidable subjectivity, because you are not concerned simply with the question what is true of the world, but "What can I know of the world?" You always have to start any kind of argument from something which appears to you to be true; if it appears to you to be true, there is no more to be done. You cannot go outside yourself and consider abstractly whether the things that appear to you to be true are true; you may do this in a particular case, where one of your beliefs is changed in consequence of others among your beliefs.

The reason that I call my doctrine *logical* atomism is because the atoms that I wish to arrive at as the sort of last residue in analysis are logical atoms and not physical atoms. Some of them will be what I call "particulars" — such things as little patches of color or sounds, momentary things — and some of them will be predicates or relations and so on. The point is that the atom I wish to arrive at is the atom of logical analysis, not the atom of physical analysis.

It is a rather curious fact in philosophy that the data which are undeniable to start with are always rather vague and ambiguous. You can, for instance, say: "There are a number of people in this room at this moment." That is obviously in some sense undeniable. But when you come to try and define what this room is, and what it is for a person to be in a room, and how you are going to distinguish one person from another, and so forth, you find that what you have said is most fearfully vague and that you really do not know what you meant. That is a rather singular fact, that everything you are really sure of, right off is something that you do not know the meaning of, and the moment you get a precise statement you will not be sure whether it is true or false, at least right off. The process of sound philosophizing, to my mind, consists mainly in passing from those obvious, vague, ambiguous things, that we feel quite sure of, to something precise, clear, definite, which by reflection and analysis we find is involved in the vague thing that we started from, and is, so to speak, the real truth of which that vague thing is a sort of shadow. I should like, if time were longer and if I knew more than I do, to spend a whole lecture on the conception of vagueness. I think vagueness is very much more important in the theory of knowledge than you would judge it to be from the writings of most people. Everything is vague to a degree you do not realize till you have tried to make it precise, and everything precise is so remote from everything that we normally think, that you cannot for a moment suppose that is what we really mean when we say what we think.

When you pass from the vague to the precise by the method of analysis and reflection that I am speaking of, you always run a certain risk of error. If I start with the statement that there are so and so many people in this room, and then set to work to make that statement precise, I shall run a great many risks and it will be extremely likely that any precise statement I make will be something not true at all. So you cannot very easily or simply get from these vague undeniable things to precise things which are going to retain the undeniability of the starting-point. The precise propositions that you arrive at may be *logically* premises to the system that you build up upon the basis of them, but they are not premises for the theory of knowledge. It is important to realize the difference between that from which your knowledge is, in fact, derived, and that from which, if you already had complete knowledge, you would deduce it. Those are quite different things. The sort of premise that a logician will take for a science will not be the sort of thing which is first known or easiest known: it will be a proposition having great deductive power, great cogency and exactitude, quite a different thing from the actual premise that your knowledge started from. When you are talking of the premise for theory of knowledge, you are not talking of anything objective, but of something that will vary from man to man, because the premises of one man's theory of knowledge will not be the same as those of another man's. There is a great tendency among a very large school to suppose that when you are trying to philosophize about what you know, you ought to carry back your premises further and further into the region of the inexact and vague, beyond the point when you yourself are, right back to the child or monkey, and that anything whatsoever that *you* seem to know—but that the psychologist recognizes as being the product of previous thought and analysis and reflection on your part—cannot really be taken as a premise in your own knowledge. That, I say, is a theory which is very widely held and which is used against that kind of analytic outlook which I wish to urge. It seems to me that when your object is, not simply to study the history or development of mind; but to ascertain the nature of the world, you do not want to go any further back than you are already yourself. You do not want to go back to the vagueness of the child or monkey, because you will find that quite sufficient difficulty is raised by your own vagueness. But there one is confronted by one of those difficulties that occur constantly in philosophy, where you have two ultimate prejudices conflicting and where argument ceases. There is the type of mind which considers that what is called primitive experience must be a better guide to wisdom than the experience of reflective persons, and there is the type of mind which takes exactly the opposite view. On that point I cannot see any argument whatsoever. It is quite clear that a highly educated person sees, hears, feels, does everything in a very different way from a young child or animal, and that this whole manner of experiencing the world and of thinking about the world is very much more analytic than that of a more primitive experience. The things we have got to take as premises in any kind of work of analysis are the things which appear to *us* undeniable— to us here and now, as we are—and I think on the whole that the sort of method adopted by Descartes is right: that you should set to work to doubt things and retain only what you cannot doubt because of its clearness and distinctness, not because you are sure not to be induced into error, for there does not exist a method which will safeguard you against the possibility of error. The wish for perfect security is one of those snares we are always falling into, and is just as untenable in the realm of knowledge as in everything else. Nevertheless, granting all this, I think that Descartes's method is on the whole a sound one for the starting-point.

I propose, therefore, always to begin any argument that I have to make by appealing to data which will be quite ludicrously obvious. Any philosophical skill that is required will consist in the selection of those which are capable of yielding a good deal of reflection and analysis, and in the reflection and analysis themselves.

What I have said so far is by way of introduction.

The first truism to which I wish to draw your attention — and I hope you will agree with me that these things that I call truisms are so obvious that it is almost laughable to mention them — is that the world contains facts, which are what they are whatever we may choose to think about them and that there are also beliefs, which have reference to facts, and by reference to facts are either true or false. I will try first of all to give you a preliminary explanation of what I mean by a "fact." When I speak of a fact — I do not propose to attempt an exact definition, but an explanation, so that you will know what I am talking about — I mean the kind of thing that makes a proposition true or false. If I say "It is raining," what I say is true in a certain condition of weather and is false in other conditions of weather. The condition of weather that makes my statement true (or false as the case may be), is what I should call a "fact." If I say "Socrates is dead," my statement will be true owing to a certain physiological occurrence which happened in Athens long ago. If I say, "Gravitation varies inversely as the square of the distance," my statement is rendered true by astronomical fact. If I say, "Two and two are four," it is arithmetical fact that makes my statement true. On the other hand, if I say "Socrates is alive" or "Gravitation varies directly as the distance," or "Two and two are five," the very same facts which made my previous statements true show that these new statements are false.

I want you to realize that when I speak of a fact I do not mean a particular existing thing, such as Socrates or the rain or the sun. Socrates himself does not render any statement true or false. You might be inclined to suppose that all by himself he would give truth to the statement "Socrates existed," but as a matter of fact that is a mistake. It is due to a confusion which I shall try to explain in the sixth lecture of this course, when I come to deal with the notion of existence. Socrates[1] himself, or any particular thing just by itself, does not make any proposition true or false. "Socrates is dead" and "Socrates is alive" are both of them statements about Socrates. One is true and the other false. What I call a fact is the sort of thing that is expressed by a whole sentence, not by a single name like "Socrates." When a single word does come to express a fact, like "fire" or "wolf," it is always due to an unexpressed context, and the full expression of a fact will always involve a sentence. We express a fact, for example, when we say that a certain thing has a certain property, or that it has a certain relation to another thing; but the thing which has the property or the relation is not what I call a "fact."

It is important to observe that facts belong to the objective world. They are not created by our thoughts or beliefs except in special cases. That is one of the sort of things which I should set up as an obvious truism, but, of course, one is aware, the moment one has read any philosophy at all, how very much there is to be said before such a statement as that can become the kind of position that you want. The first thing I want to emphasize is that the outer world – the world, so to speak, which knowledge is aiming at knowing – is not completely described by a lot of "particulars," but that you must also take account of these things that I call facts, which are the sort of things that you express by a sentence, and that these, just as much as particular chairs and tables, are part of the real world. Except in psychology, most of our statements are not intended merely to express our condition of mind, though that is often all that they succeed in doing. They are intended to express facts, which (except when they are psychological facts) will be about the outer world. There are such facts involved, equally when we speak truly and when we speak falsely. When we speak falsely it is an objective fact that makes what we say false, and it is an objective fact which makes what we say true when we speak truly.

There are a great many different kinds of facts, and we shall be concerned in later lectures with a certain amount of classification of facts. I will just point out a few kinds of facts to begin with, so that you may not imagine that facts are all very much alike. There are particular facts, such as "This is white"; then there are general facts, such as "All men are mortal." Of course, the distinction between particular and general facts is one of the most important. There again it would be a very great mistake to suppose that you could describe the world completely by means of particular facts alone. Suppose that you had succeeded in chronicling every single particular fact throughout the universe, and that there did not exist a single particular fact of any sort anywhere that you had not chronicled, you still would not have got a complete description of the universe unless you also added: "These that I have chronicled are all the particular facts there are." So you cannot hope to describe the world completely without having general facts as well as particular facts. Another distinction, which is perhaps a little more difficult to make, is between positive facts and negative facts, such as "Socrates was alive" – a positive fact, and "Socrates is not alive" – you might say a negative fact. But the distinction is difficult to make precise. Then there are facts concerning particular things or particular qualities or relations, and, apart from them, the completely general facts of the sort that you have in logic, where there is no mention of any constituent whatever of the actual world, no mention of any particular thing or particular quality or particular relation, indeed strictly you may say no mention of anything. That is one of the characteristics of logical propositions, that they mention nothing. Such a proposition is: "If one class is part of another, a term which is a member of the one is also a member of the other." All those words that come in the statement of a pure logical proposition are words really belonging to syntax. They are words merely expressing form or connection, not mentioning any particular constituent of the proposition in which they occur. This is, of course, a thing that wants to be proved; I am not laying it down as self-evident. Then there are facts about the properties of single things; and facts about the relations between two things, three things, and so on; any number of different classifications of some of the facts in the world, which are important for different purposes.

It is obvious that there is not a dualism of true and false facts; there are only just facts. It would be a mistake, of course, to say that all facts are true. That would be a mistake because true and false are correlatives, and you would only say of a thing that it was true if it was the sort of thing that *might* be false. A fact cannot be either true or false. That brings us on to the question of statements or propositions or judgements, all those things that do have the duality of truth and falsehood. For the purposes of logic, though not, I think, for the purposes of theory of knowledge, it is natural to concentrate upon the proposition as the thing which is going to be our typical vehicle on the duality of truth and falsehood. A proposition, one may say, is a sentence in the indicative, a sentence asserting something, not questioning or commanding or wishing. It may also be a sentence of that sort preceded by the word "that." For example, "That Socrates is alive," "That two and two are four," "That two and two are five," anything of that sort will be a proposition.

A proposition is just a symbol. It is a complex symbol in the sense that it has parts which are also symbols: a symbol may be defined as complex when it has parts that are symbols. In a sentence containing several words, the several words are each symbols, and the sentence composing them is therefore a complex symbol in that sense. There is a good deal of importance to philosophy in the theory of symbolism, a good deal more than at one time I thought. I think the importance is almost entirely negative, i.e., the importance lies in the fact that unless you are fairly self-conscious about symbols, unless you are fairly aware of the relation of the symbol to what it symbolizes, you will find yourself attributing to the thing properties which only belong to the symbol. That, of course, is especially likely in very abstract studies such as philosophical logic, because the subject-matter that you are supposed to be thinking of is so exceedingly difficult and elusive that any person who has ever tried to think about it knows you do not think about it except perhaps once in six months for half a minute. The rest of the time you think about the symbols, because they are tangible but the thing you are supposed to be thinking about is fearfully difficult and one does not often manage to think about it. The really good philosopher is the one who does once in six months think about it for a minute. Bad philosophers never do. That is why the theory of symbolism has a certain importance, because otherwise you are so certain to mistake the properties of the symbolism for the properties of the thing. It has other interesting sides to it too. There are different kinds of symbols, different kinds of relations between symbol and what is symbolized, and very important fallacies arise from not realizing this. The sort of contradictions about which I shall be speaking in connection with types in a later lecture all arise from mistakes in symbolism, from putting one sort of symbol in the place where another sort of symbol ought to be. Some of the notions that have been thought absolutely fundamental in philosophy have arisen, I believe, entirely through mistakes as to symbolism—e.g., the notion of existence, or, if you like, reality. Those two words stand for a great deal that has been discussed in philosophy. There has been the theory about every proposition being really a description of reality as a whole and so on, and altogether these notions of reality and existence have played a very prominent part in philosophy. Now my own belief is that as they have occurred in philosophy, they have been entirely the outcome of a muddle about symbolism, and that when you have cleared up that muddle, you find that practically everything that has been said about existence is sheer and simple mistake, and that is all you can say about it. I shall go into that in a later lecture, but it is an example of the way in which symbolism is important.

Perhaps I ought to say a word or two about what I am understanding by symbolism, because I think some people think you only mean mathematical symbols when you talk about symbolism. I am using it in a sense to include all language of every sort and kind, so that every word is a symbol, and every sentence, and so forth. When I speak of a symbol I simply mean something that "means" something else, and as to what I mean by "meaning" I am not prepared to tell you. I will in the course of time enumerate a strictly infinite number of different things that "meaning" may mean, but I shall not consider that I have exhausted the discussion by doing that. I think that the notion of meaning is always more or less psychological, and it is not possible to get a pure logical theory of meaning, nor therefore of symbolism. I think that it is of the very essence of the explanation of what you mean by a symbol to take account of such things as knowing, of cognitive relations, and probably also of association. At any rate I am pretty clear that the theory of symbolism and the use of symbolism is not a thing that can be explained in pure logic without taking account of the various cognitive relations that you may have to things.

As to what one means by "meaning," I will give a few illustrations. For instance, the word "Socrates," you will say, means a certain man; the word "mortal" means a certain quality; and the sentence "Socrates is mortal" means a certain fact. But these three sorts of meanings are entirely distinct, and you will get into the most hopeless contradictions if you think the word "meaning" has the same meaning in each of these three cases. It is very important not to suppose that there is just one thing which is meant by "meaning," and that therefore there is just one sort of relation of the symbol to what is symbolized. A name would be a proper symbol to use for a person: a sentence (or a proposition) is the proper symbol for a fact.

A belief or a statement has duality of truth and falsehood, which the fact does not have. A belief or a statement always involves a proposition. You say that a man believes that so and so is the case. A man believes that Socrates is dead. What he believes is a proposition on the face of it, and for formal purposes it is convenient to take the proposition as the essential thing having the duality of truth and falsehood. It is very important to realize such things, for instance, as that propositions are not names for facts. It is quite obvious as soon as it is pointed out to you, but as a matter of fact I never had realized it until it was pointed out to me by a former pupil of mine, Wittgenstein. It is perfectly evident as soon as you think of it, that a proposition is not a name for a fact, from the mere circumstance that there are *two* propositions corresponding to each fact. Suppose it is a fact that Socrates is dead. You have two propositions: "Socrates is dead" and "Socrates is not dead." And those two propositions corresponding to the same fact, there is one fact in the world which makes one true and one false. That is not accidental, and illustrates how the relation of proposition to fact is a totally different one from the relation of name to the thing named. For each fact there are two propositions, one true and one false, and there is nothing in the nature of the symbol to show us which is the true one and which is the false one. If there were, you could ascertain the truth about the world by examining propositions without looking around you.

There are two different relations, as you see, that a proposition may have to a fact: the one the relation that you may call being true to the fact, and the other being false to the fact. Both are equally essentially logical relations which may subsist between the two, whereas in the case of a name, there is only one relation that it can have to what it names. A name can just name a particular, or, if it does not, it is not a name at all, it is a noise. It cannot be a name without having just that one particular relation of naming a certain thing, whereas a proposition does not cease to be a proposition if it is false. It has these two ways, of being true and being false, which together correspond to the property of being a name. Just as a word may be a name or be not a name but just a meaningless noise, so a phrase which is apparently a proposition may be either true or false, or may be meaningless, but the true and false belong together as against the meaningless. That shows, of course, that the formal logical characteristics of propositions are quite different from those of names, and that the relations they have to facts are quite different, and therefore propositions are not names for facts. You must not run away with the idea that you can name facts in any other way; you cannot. You cannot name them at all. You cannot properly name a fact. The only thing you can do is to assert it, or deny it, or desire it, or will it, or wish it, or question it, but all those are things involving the whole proposition. You can never put the sort of thing that makes a proposition to be true or false in the position of a logical subject. You can only have it there as something to be asserted or denied or something of that sort, but not something to be named.

NOTE

1. Lecture I of "The Philosophy of Logical Atomism."
2. I am here for the moment treating Socrates as a "particular." But we shall see shortly that this view requires modification.

11. Particulars, Predicates, and Relations[1]

Bertrand Russell

I propose to begin to-day the analysis of facts and propositions, for in a way the chief thesis that I have to maintain is the legitimacy of analysis, because if one goes into what I call Logical Atomism that means that one does believe the world can be analyzed into a number of separate things with relations and so forth, and that the sort of arguments that many philosophers use against analysis are not justifiable.

In a philosophy of logical atomism one might suppose that the first thing to do would be to discover the kinds of atoms out of which logical structures are composed. But I do not think that is quite the first thing; it is one of the early things, but not quite the first. There are two other questions that one has to consider, and one of these at least is prior. You have to consider:

1. Are the things that look like logically complex entities really complex?
2. Are they really entities?

The second question we can put off; in fact, I shall not deal with it fully until my last lecture. The first question, whether they are really complex, is one that you have to consider at the start. Neither of these questions is, as it stands, a very precise question. I do not pretend to start with precise questions. I do not think you can start with anything precise. You have to achieve such precision as you can, as you go along. Each of these two questions, however, is *capable* of a precise meaning, and each is really important.

There is another question which comes still earlier, namely: what shall we take as *prima facie* examples of logically complex entities? That really is the first question of all to start with. What sort of things shall we regard as *prima facie* complex?

Of course, all the ordinary objects of daily life are apparently complex entities: such things as tables and chairs, loaves and fishes, persons and principalities and powers—they are all on the face of it complex entities: Socrates, Piccadilly, Rumania, Twelfth Night or anything you like to think of, to which you give a proper name, they are all apparently complex entities. They seem to be complex systems bound together into some kind of a unity, that sort of a unity that leads to the bestowal of a single appellation. I think it is the contemplation of this sort of apparent unity which has very largely led to the philosophy of monism, and to the suggestion that the universe as a whole is a single complex entity more or less in the sense in which these things are that I have been talking about.

For my part, I do not believe in complex entities of this kind, and it is not such things as these that I am going to take as the *prima facie* examples of complex entities. My reasons will appear more and more plainly as I go on. I cannot give them all to-day, but I can more or less explain what I mean in a preliminary way. Suppose, for example, that you were to analyze what appears to be a fact about Piccadilly. Suppose you made any statement about Piccadilly, such as: "Piccadilly is a pleasant street." If you analyze a statement of that sort correctly, I believe you will find that the fact corresponding to your statement does not contain any constituent corresponding to the word "Piccadilly." The word "Piccadilly" will form a part of many significant propositions, but the facts corresponding to these propositions do not contain any single constituent, whether simple or complex, corresponding to the word "Piccadilly." That is to say, if you take language as a guide in your analysis of the fact expressed, you will be led astray in a statement of that sort. The reasons for that I shall give at length in Lecture VI, and partly also in Lecture VII, but I could say in a preliminary way certain things that would make you understand what I mean. "Piccadilly," on the face of it, is the name for a certain portion of the earth's surface, and I suppose, if you wanted to define it, you would have to define it as a series of classes of material entities, namely those which, at varying times, occupy that portion of the earth's surface. So that you would find that the logical status of Piccadilly is bound up with the logical status of series and classes, and if you are going to hold Piccadilly as real, you must hold that series of classes are real, and whatever sort of metaphysical status you assign to them you must assign to it. As you know, I believe that series and classes are of the nature of logical fictions: therefore that thesis, if it can be maintained, will dissolve Piccadilly into a fiction. Exactly similar remarks will apply to other instances: Rumania, Twelfth Night, and Socrates. Socrates, perhaps, raises some special questions, because the question what constitutes a person has special difficulties in it. But, for the sake of argument, one might identify Socrates with the series of his experiences. He would be really a series of classes, because one has many experiences simultaneously. Therefore he comes to be very like Piccadilly.

Considerations of that sort seem to take us away from such *prima facie* complex entities as we started with to others as being more stubborn and more deserving of analytic attention, namely facts. I explained last time what I meant by a fact, namely, that sort of thing that makes a proposition true or false, the sort of thing which is the case when your statement is true and is not the case when your statement is false. Facts are, as I said last time, plainly something you have to take account of if you are going to give a complete account of the world. You cannot do that by merely enumerating the particular things that are in it: you must also mention the relations of these things, and their properties, and so forth, all of which are facts, so that facts certainly belong to an account of the objective world, and facts do seem much more complex and much more not capable of being explained away than things like Socrates and Rumania. However you may explain away the meaning of the word "Socrates," you will still be left with the truth that the proposition "Socrates is mortal" expresses a fact. You may not know exactly what Socrates means, but it is quite clear that "Socrates is mortal" does express a fact. There is clearly some valid meaning in saying that the fact expressed by "Socrates is mortal" is *complex.* The things in the world have various properties, and stand in various relations to each other. That they have these properties and relations are *facts,* and the things and their qualities or relations are quite clearly in some sense or other components of the facts that have those qualities or relations. The analysis of apparently complex *things* such as we started with can be reduced by various means, to the analysis of facts which are apparently about those things. Therefore it is with the analysis of *facts* that one's consideration of the problem of complexity must begin, not by the analysis of apparently complex things.

The complexity of a fact is evidenced, to begin with, by the circumstance that the proposition which asserts a fact consists of several words, each of which may occur in other contexts. Of course, sometimes you get a proposition expressed by a single word, but if it is expressed fully it is bound to contain several words. The proposition "Socrates is mortal" may be replaced by "Plato is mortal" or by "Socrates is human"; in the first case we alter the subject, in the second the predicate. It is clear that all the propositions in which the word "Socrates" occurs have something in common, and again all the propositions in which the word "mortal" occurs have something in common, something which they do not have in common with all propositions, but only with those which are about Socrates or mortality. It is clear, I think, that the facts corresponding to propositions in which the word "Socrates" occurs have something in common corresponding to the common word "Socrates" which occurs in the propositions, so that you have that sense of complexity to begin with, that in a fact you can get something which it may have in common with other facts, just as you may have "Socrates is human" and "Socrates is mortal," both of them facts, and both having to do with Socrates, although Socrates does not constitute the whole of either of these facts. It is quite clear that in that sense there is a possibility of cutting up a fact into component parts, of which one component may be altered without altering the others, and one component may occur in certain other facts though not in all other facts. I want to make it clear, to begin with, that there is a sense in which facts can be analyzed. I am not concerned with all the difficulties of any analysis, but only with meeting the *prima facie* objections of philosophers who think you really cannot analyze at all.

I am trying as far as possible again this time, as I did last time, to start with perfectly plain truisms. My desire and wish is that the things I start with should be so obvious that you wonder why I spend my time stating them. That is what I am at, because the point of philosophy is to start with something so simple as not to seem worth stating, and to end with something so paradoxical that no one will believe it.

One *prima facie* mark of complexity in propositions is the fact that they are expressed by several words. I come now to another point, which applies primarily to propositions and thence derivatively to facts. You can understand a proposition when you understand the words of which it is composed even though you never heard the proposition before. That seems a very humble property, but it is a property which marks it as complex and distinguishes it from words whose meaning is simple. When you know the vocabulary, grammar, and syntax of a language, you can understand a proposition in that language even though you never saw it before. In reading a newspaper for example, you become aware of a number of statements which are new to you, and they are intelligible to you immediately, in spite of the fact that they are new, because you understand the words of which they are composed. This characteristic, that you can understand a proposition through the understanding of its component words, is absent from the component words when those words express something simple. Take the word "red," for example, and suppose — as one always has to do — that "red" stands for a particular shade of color. You will pardon that assumption, but one never can get on otherwise. You cannot understand the meaning of the word "red" except through seeing red things. There is no other way in which it can be done. It is no use to learn languages, or to look up dictionaries. None of these things will help you to understand the meaning of the word "red." In that way it is quite different from the meaning of a proposition. Of course, you can give a definition of the word "red," and here it is very important to distinguish between a definition and an analysis. All analysis is only possible in regard to what is complex, and it always depends, in the last analysis, upon direct acquaintance with the objects which are the meanings of certain simple symbols. It is hardly necessary to observe that one does not define a thing but a symbol. (A "simple" symbol is a symbol whose parts are not symbols.) A simple symbol is quite a different thing from a simple thing. Those objects which it is impossible to symbolize otherwise than by simple symbols may be called "simple," while those which can be symbolized by a combination of symbols may be called "complex." This is, of course, a preliminary definition, and perhaps somewhat circular, but that doesn't much matter at this stage.

I have said that "red" could not be understood except by seeing red things. You might object to that on the ground that you can define red, for example, as "The color with the greatest wave-length." That, you might say, is a definition of "red" and a person could understand that definition even if he had seen nothing red, provided he understood the physical theory of color. But that does not really constitute the meaning of the word "red" in the very slightest.

If you take such a proposition as "This is red" and substitute for it "This has the color with the greatest wave-length," you have a different proposition altogether. You can see that at once, because a person who knows nothing of the physical theory of color can understand the proposition "This is red," and can know that it is true, but cannot know that "This has the color which has the greatest wave-length." Conversely, you might have a hypothetical person who could not see red, but who understood the physical theory of color and could apprehend the proposition "This has the color with the greatest wave-length," but who would not be able to understand the proposition "This is red" as understood by the normal uneducated person. Therefore it is clear that if you define "red" as "The color with the greatest wave-length," you are not giving the actual meaning of the word at all; you are simply giving a true description, which is quite a different thing, and the propositions which result are different propositions from those in which the word "red" occurs. In that sense the word "red" cannot be defined, though in the sense in which a correct description constitutes a definition it can be defined. In the sense of analysis you cannot define "red." That is how it is that dictionaries are able to get on, because a dictionary professes to define all words in the language by means of words in the language, and therefore it is clear that a dictionary must be guilty of a vicious circle somewhere, but it manages it by means of correct descriptions.

I have made it clear, then, in what sense I should say that the word "red" is a simple symbol and the phrase "This is red" a complex symbol. The word "red" can only be understood through acquaintance with the object, whereas the phrase "Roses are red" can be understood if you know what "red" is and what "roses" are, without ever having heard the phrase before. That is a clear mark of what is complex. It is the mark of a complex symbol, and also the mark of the object symbolized by the complex symbol. That is to say, propositions are complex symbols, and the facts they stand for are complex.

The whole question of the meaning of words is very full of complexities and ambiguities in ordinary language. When one person uses a word, he does not mean by it the same thing as another person means by it. I have often heard it said that that is a misfortune. That is a mistake. It would be absolutely fatal if people meant the same things by their words. It would make all intercourse impossible, and language the most hopeless and useless thing imaginable, because the meaning you attach to your words must depend on the nature of the objects you are acquainted with, and since different people are acquainted with different objects, they would not be able to talk to each other unless they attached quite different meanings to their words. We should have to talk only about logic—a not wholly undesirable result. Take, for example, the word "Piccadilly." We, who are acquainted with Piccadilly, attach quite a different meaning to that word from any which could be attached to it by a person who had never been in London: and, supposing that you travel in foreign parts and expatiate on Piccadilly, you will convey to your hearers entirely different propositions from those in your mind. They will know Piccadilly as an important street in London; they may know a lot about it, but they will not know just the things one knows when one is walking along it. If you were to insist on language which was unambiguous, you would be unable to tell people at home what you had seen in foreign parts. It would be altogether incredibly inconvenient to have an unambiguous language, and therefore mercifully we have not got one.

Analysis not the same thing as definition. You can define a term by means of a correct description, but that does not constitute an analysis. It is analysis, not definition, that we are concerned with at the present moment, so I will come back to the question of analysis.

We may lay down the following provisional definitions:

That the components of a proposition are the symbols we must understand in order to understand the proposition;

That the components of the fact which makes a proposition true or false, as the case may be, are the *meanings* of the symbols which we must understand in order to understand the proposition.

That is not absolutely correct, but it will enable you to understand my meaning. One reason why it fails of correctness is that it does not apply to words which, like "or" and "not," are parts of propositions without corresponding to any part of the corresponding facts. This is a topic for Lecture III.

I call these definitions *preliminary* because they start from the complexity of the proposition, which they define psychologically, and proceed to the complexity of the fact, whereas it is quite clear that in an orderly, proper procedure it is the complexity of the fact that you would start from. It is also clear that the complexity of the fact cannot be something merely psychological. If in astronomical fact the earth moves round the sun, that is genuinely complex. It is not that you think it complex, it is a sort of genuine objective complexity, and therefore one ought in a proper, orderly procedure to start from the complexity of the world and arrive at the complexity of the proposition. The only reason for going the other way round is that in all abstract matters symbols are easier to grasp. I doubt, however, whether complexity, in that fundamental objective sense in which one starts from complexity of a fact, is definable at all. You cannot analyze what you mean by complexity in that sense. You must just apprehend it — at least so I am inclined to think. There is nothing one could say about it, beyond giving criteria such as I have been giving. Therefore, when you cannot get a real proper analysis of a thing, it is generally best to talk round it without professing that you have given an exact definition.

It might be suggested that complexity is essentially to do with symbols, or that it is essentially psychological. I do not think it would be possible seriously to maintain either of these views, but they are the sort of views that will occur to one, the sort of thing that one would try, to see whether it would work. I do not think they will do at all. When we come to the principles of symbolism which I shall deal with in Lecture VII, I shall try to persuade you that in a logically correct symbolism there will always be a certain fundamental identity of structure between a fact and the symbol for it; and that the complexity of the symbol corresponds very closely with the complexity of the facts symbolized by it. Also, as I said before, it is quite directly evident to inspection that the fact, for example, that two things stand in a certain relation to one another — e.g., that this is to the left of that — is itself objectively complex, and not merely that the apprehension of it is complex. The fact that two things stand in a certain relation to each other, or any statement of that sort, has a complexity all of its own. I shall therefore in future assume that there is an objective complexity in the world, and that it is mirrored by the complexity of propositions.

A moment ago I was speaking about the great advantages that we derive from the logical imperfections of language, from the fact that our words are all ambiguous. I propose now to consider what sort of language a logically perfect language would be. In a logically perfect language the words in a proposition would correspond one by one with the components of the corresponding fact, with the exception of such words as "or," "not," "if," "then," which have a different function. In a logically perfect language, there will be one word and no more for every simple object, and everything that is not simple will be expressed by a combination of words, by a combination derived, of course, from the words for the simple things that enter in, one word for each simple component. A language of that sort will be completely analytic, and will show at a glance the logical structure of the facts asserted or denied. The language which is set forth in *Principia Mathematica* is intended to be a language of that sort. It is a language which has only syntax and no vocabulary whatsoever. Barring the omission of a vocabulary I maintain that it is quite a nice language. It aims at being that sort of a language that, if you add a vocabulary, would be a logically perfect language. Actual languages are not logically perfect in this sense, and they cannot possibly be, if they are to serve the purposes of daily life. A logically perfect language, if it could be constructed, would not only be intolerably prolix, but, as regards its vocabulary, would be very largely private to one speaker. That is to say, all names that it would use would be private to that speaker and could not enter into the language of another speaker. It could not use proper names for Socrates or Piccadilly or Rumania for the reasons which I went into earlier in the lecture. Altogether you would find that it would be a very inconvenient language indeed. That is one reason why logic is so very backward as a science, because the needs of logic are so extraordinarily different from the needs of daily life. One wants a language in both, and unfortunately it is logic that has to give way, not daily life. I shall, however, assume that we have constructed a logically perfect language, and that we are going on state occasions to use it, and I will now come back to the question which I intended to start with, namely, the analysis of facts.

The simplest imaginable facts are those which consist in the possession of a quality by some particular thing. Such facts, say, as "This is white." They have to be taken in a very sophisticated sense. I do not want you to think about the piece of chalk I am holding, but of what you see when you look at the chalk. If one says, "This is white" it will do for about as simple a fact as you can get hold of. The next simplest would be those in which you have a relation between two facts, such as: "This is to the left of that." Next you come to those where you have a triadic relation between three particulars. (An instance which Royce gives is "A gives B to C.") So you get relations which require as their minimum three terms, those we call triadic relations; and those which require four terms, which we call tetradic, and so on. There you have a whole infinite hierarchy of facts — facts in which you have a thing and a quality, two things and a relation, three things and a relation, four things and a relation, and so on. That whole hierarchy constitutes what I call *atomic* facts, and they are the simplest sort of fact. You can distinguish among them some simpler than others, because the ones containing a quality are simpler than those in which you have, say, a pentadic relation, and so on. The whole lot of them, taken together, are as facts go very simple, and are what I call atomic facts. The propositions expressing them are what I call atomic propositions.

In every atomic fact there is one component which is naturally expressed by a verb (or, in the case of quality, it may be expressed by a predicate, by an adjective). This one component is a quality of dyadic or triadic or tetradic . . . relation. It would be very convenient, for purposes of talking about these matters, to call a quality a "monadic relation" and I shall do so; it saves a great deal of circumlocution.

In that case you can say that all atomic propositions assert relations of varying orders. Atomic facts contain, besides the relation, the terms of the relation — one term if it is a monadic relation, two if it is dyadic, and so on. These "terms" which come into atomic facts I define as "particulars."

Particulars = terms of relations in atomic facts. *Definition.*

That is the definition of particulars, and I want to emphasize it because the definition of a particular is something purely logical. The question whether this or that is a particular, is a question to be decided in terms of that logical definition. In order to understand the definition it is not necessary to know beforehand "This is a particular" or "That is a particular." It remains to be investigated what particulars you can find in the world, if any. The whole question of what particulars you actually find in the real world is a pure empirical one which does not interest the logician as such. The logician as such never gives instances, because it is one of the tests of a logical proposition that you need not know anything whatsoever about the real world in order to understand it.

Passing from atomic facts to atomic propositions, the word expressing a monadic relation or quality is called a "predicate," and the word expressing a relation of any higher order would generally be a verb, sometimes a single verb, sometimes a whole phrase. At any rate the verb gives the essential nerve, as it were, of the relation. The other words that occur in the atomic propositions, the words that are not the predicate or verb, may be called the subjects of the proposition. There will be one subject in a monadic proposition, two in a dyadic one, and so on. The subjects in a proposition will be the words expressing the terms of the relation which is expressed by the proposition.

The only kind of word that is theoretically capable of standing for a particular is a *proper name,* and the whole matter of proper names is rather curious.

Proper Name = words for particulars. *Definition.*

I have put that down although, as far as common language goes, it is obviously false. It is true that if you try to think how far you are to talk about particulars, you will see that you cannot ever talk about a particular particular except by means of a proper name. You cannot use general words except by way of description. How are we to express in words an atomic proposition? An atomic proposition is one which does mention actual particulars, not merely describe them but actually name them, and you can only name them by means of names. You can see at once for yourself, therefore, that every other part of speech except proper names is obviously quite incapable of standing for a particular. Yet it does seem a little odd if, having made a dot on the blackboard, I call it "John." You would be surprised, and yet how are you to know otherwise what it is that I am speaking of. If I say, "The dot that is on the right-hand side is white" that is a proposition. If I say "This is white" that is quite a different proposition. "This" will do very well while we are all here and can see it, but if I wanted to talk about it to-morrow it would be convenient to have christened it and called it "John." There is no other way in which you can mention it. You cannot really mention *it* itself except by means of a name.

What pass for names in language, like "Socrates," "Plato," and so forth, were originally intended to fulfill this function of standing for particulars, and we do accept, in ordinary daily life, as particulars all sorts of things that really are not so. The names that we commonly use, like "Socrates," are really abbreviations for descriptions; not only that, but what they describe are not particulars but complicated systems of classes or series. A name, in the narrow logical sense of a word whose meaning is a particular, can only be applied to a particular with which the speaker is acquainted, because you cannot name anything you are not acquainted with. You remember, when Adam named the beasts, they came before him one by one, and he became acquainted with them and named them. We are not acquainted with Socrates, and therefore cannot name him. When we use the word "Socrates," we are really using a description. Our thought may be rendered by some such phrase as, "The Master of Plato," or "The philosopher who drank the hemlock," or "The person whom logicians assert to be mortal," but we certainly do not use the name as a name in the proper sense of the word.

That makes it very difficult to get any instance of a name at all in the proper strict logical sense of the word. The only words one does use as names in the logical sense are words like "this" or "that." One can use "this" as a name to stand for a particular with which one is acquainted at the moment. We say "This is white." If you agree that "This is white," meaning the "this" that you see, you are using "this" as a proper name. But if you try to apprehend the proposition that I am expressing when I say "This is white," you cannot do it. If you mean this piece of chalk as a physical object, then you are not using a proper name. It is only when you use "this" quite strictly, to stand for an actual object of sense, that it is really a proper name. And in that it has a very odd property for a proper name, namely that it seldom means the same thing two moments running and does not mean the same thing to the speaker and to the hearer. It is an *ambiguous* proper name, but it is really a proper name all the same, and it is almost the only thing I can think of that is used properly and logically in the sense that I was talking of for a proper name. The importance of proper names, in the sense of which I am talking, is in the sense of logic, not of daily life. You can see why it is that in the logical language set forth in *Principia Mathematica* there are not any names, because there we are not interested in particular particulars but only in general particulars, if I may be allowed such a phrase.

Particulars have this peculiarity, among the sort of objects that you have to take account of in an inventory of the world, that each of them stands entirely alone and is completely self-subsistent. It has that sort of self-subsistence that used to belong to substance, except that it usually only persists through a very short time, so far as our experience goes. That is to say, each particular that there is in the world does not in any way logically depend upon any other particular. Each one might happen to be the whole universe; it is a merely empirical fact that this is not the case. There is no reason why you should not have a universe consisting of one particular and nothing else. That is a peculiarity of particulars. In the same way, in order to understand a name for a particular, the only thing necessary is to be acquainted with that particular. When you are acquainted with that particular, you have a full, adequate, and complete understanding of the name, and no further information is required. No further information as to the facts that are true of that particular would enable you to have a fuller understanding of the meaning of the name.

NOTE

1. Lecture II of "The Philosophy of Logical Atomism."

12. Excursus Into Metaphysics What There Is[1]

Bertrand Russell

I come now to the last lecture of this course, and I propose briefly to point to a few of the morals that are to be gathered from what has gone before, in the way of suggesting the bearing of the doctrines that I have been advocating upon various problems of metaphysics. I have dwelt hitherto upon what one may call philosophical grammar, and I am afraid I have had to take you through a good many very dry and dusty regions in the course of that investigation, but I think the importance of philosophical grammar is very much greater than it is generally thought to be. I think that practically all traditional metaphysics is filled with mistakes due to bad grammar, and that almost all the traditional problems of metaphysics and traditional results — supposed results — of metaphysics are due to a failure to make the kind of distinctions in what we may call philosophical grammar with which we have been concerned in these previous lectures.

Take, as a very simple example, the philosophy of arithmetic. If you think that 1, 2, 3, and 4, and the rest of the numbers, are in any sense entities, if you think that there are objects, having those names, in the realm of being, you have at once a very considerable apparatus for your metaphysics to deal with, and you have offered to you a certain kind of analysis of arithmetical propositions. When you say, e.g., that 2 and 2 are 4, you suppose in that case that you are making a proposition of which the number 2 and the number 4 are constituents, and that has all sorts of consequences, all sorts of bearings upon your general metaphysical outlook. If there has been any truth in the doctrines that we have been considering, all numbers are what I call logical fictions. Numbers are classes of classes, and classes are logical fictions, so that numbers are, as it were, fictions at two removes, fictions of fictions. Therefore you do not have, as part of the ultimate constituents of your world, these queer entities that you are inclined to call numbers. The same applies in many other directions.

One purpose that has run through all that I have said, has been the justification of analysis, i.e., the justification of logical atomism, of the view that you can get down in theory, if not in practice, to ultimate simples, out of which the world is built, and that those simples have a kind of reality not belonging to anything else. Simples, as I tried to explain, are of an infinite number of sorts. There are particulars and qualities and relations of various orders, a whole hierarchy of different sorts of simples, but all of them, if we were right, have in their various ways some kind of reality that does not belong to anything else. The only other sort of object you come across in the world is what we call *facts,* and facts are the sort of things that are asserted or denied by propositions, and are not properly entities at all in the same sense in which their constituents are. That is shown in the fact that you cannot name them. You can only deny, or assert, or consider them, but you cannot name them because they are not there to be named, although in another sense it is true that you cannot know the world unless you know the facts that make up the truths of the world; but the knowing of facts is a different sort of thing from the knowing of simples.

Another purpose which runs through all that I have been saying is the purpose embodied in the maxim called Occam's Razor. That maxim comes in, in practice, in this way: take some science, say physics. You have there a given body of doctrine, a set of propositions expressed in symbols—I am including words among symbols—and you think that you have reason to believe that on the whole those propositions, rightly interpreted, are fairly true, but you do not know what is the actual meaning of the symbols that you are using. The meaning they have *in use* would have to be explained in some pragmatic way: they have a certain kind of practical or emotional significance to you which is a datum, but the logical significance is not a datum, but a thing to be sought, and you go through, if you are analyzing a science like physics, these propositions with a view to finding out what is the smallest empirical apparatus—or the smallest apparatus, not necessarily wholly empirical—out of which you can build up these propositions. What is the smallest number of simple undefined things at the start, and the smallest number of undemonstrated premises, out of which you can define the things that need to be defined and prove the things that need to be proved? That problem, in any case that you like to take, is by no means a simple one, but on the contrary an extremely difficult one. It is one which requires a very great amount of logical technique; and the sort of thing that I have been talking about in these lectures is the preliminaries and first steps in that logical technique. You cannot possibly get at the solution of such a problem as I am talking about if you go at it in a straightforward fashion with just the ordinary acumen that one accumulates in the course of reading or in the study of traditional philosophy. You do need this apparatus of symbolical logic that I have been talking about. (The description of the subject as symbolical logic is an inadequate one. I should like to describe it simply as logic, on the ground that nothing else really is logic, but that would sound so arrogant that I hesitate to do so.)

Let us consider further the example of physics for a moment. You find, if you read the works of physicists, that they reduce matter down to certain elements—atoms, ions, corpuscles, or what not. But in any case the sort of thing that you are aiming at in the physical analysis of matter is to get down to very little bits of matter that still are just like matter in the fact that they persist through time, and that they travel about in space. They have in fact all the ordinary every-day properties of physical matter, not the matter that one has in ordinary life—they do not taste or smell or appear to the naked eye—but they have the properties that you very soon get to when you travel toward physics from ordinary life. Things of that sort, I say, are not the ultimate constituents of matter in any metaphysical sense. Those things are all of them, as I think a very little reflection shows, logical fictions in the sense that I was speaking of. At least, when I say they are, I speak somewhat too dogmatically. It is possible that there may be all these things that the physicist talks about in actual reality, but it is impossible that we should ever have any reason whatsoever for supposing that there are. That is the situation that you arrive at generally in such analyses. You find that a certain thing which has been set up as a metaphysical entity can either be assumed dogmatically to be real, and then you will have no possible argument either for its reality or against its reality; or, instead of doing that, you can construct a logical fiction having the same formal properties, or rather having formally analogous formal properties to those of the supposed metaphysical entity and itself composed of empirically given things, and that logical fiction can be substituted for your supposed metaphysical entity and will fulfill all the scientific purposes that anybody can desire. With atoms and the rest it is so, with all the metaphysical entities whether of science or of metaphysics. By metaphysical entities I mean those things which are supposed to be part of the ultimate constituents of the world, but not to be the kind of thing that is ever empirically given—I do not say merely not being itself empirically given, but not being the *kind* of thing that is empirically given. In the case of matter, you start from what is empirically given, what one sees and hears and smells and so forth, all the ordinary data, of sense, or you can start with some definite ordinary object, say this desk, and you can ask yourselves, "What do I mean by saying that this desk that I am looking at now is the same as the one I was looking at a week ago?" The first simple ordinary answer would be that it *is* the same desk, it is actually identical, there is a perfect identity of substance, or whatever you like to call it. But when that apparently simple answer is suggested, it is important to observe that you cannot have an empirical reason for such a view as that, and if you hold it, you hold it simply because you like it and for no other reason whatever. All that you really know is such facts as that what you see now, when you look at the desk, bears a very close similarity to what you saw a week ago when you looked at it. Rather more than that one fact of similarity I admit you know, or you may know. You might have paid some one to watch the desk continuously throughout the week, and might then have discovered that it was presenting appearances of the same sort all through that period, assuming that the light was kept on all through the night. In that way you could have established continuity. You have not in fact done so. You do not in fact know that

that desk has gone on looking the same all the time, but we will assume that. Now the essential point is this: What is the empirical reason that makes you call a numer of appearances, appearances of the same desk? What makes you say on successive occasions, I am seeing the same desk? The first thing to notice is this, that it does not matter what is the answer, so long as you have realized that the answer consists in something empirical and not in a recognized metaphysical identity of substance. There is something given in experience which makes you call it the same desk, and having once grasped that fact, you can go on and say, it is that something (whatever it is) that makes you call it the same desk which shall be *defined* as *constituting* it the same desk, and there shall be no assumption of a metaphysical substance which is identical throughout. It is little easier to the untrained mind to conceive of an identity than it is to conceive of a system of correlated particulars, hung one to another by relations of similarity and continuous change and so on. That idea is apparently more complicated, but that is what is empirically given in the real world, and substance, in the sense of something which is continuously identical in the same desk, is not given to you. Therefore in all cases where you seem to have a continous entity persisting through changes, what you have to do is to ask yourself what makes you consider the successive appearances as belonging to one thing. When you have found out what makes you take the view that they belong to the same thing, you will then see that that which has made you say so, is all that is *certainly* there in the way of unity. Anything that there may be over and above that, I shall recognize as something I cannot know. What I can know is that there are a certain series of appearances linked together, and the series of those appearances I shall define as being a desk. In that way the desk is reduced to being a logical fiction, because a series is a logical fiction. In that way all the ordinary objects of daily life are extruded from the world of what there is, and in their place as what there is you find a number of passing particulars of the kind that one is immediately conscious of in sense. I want to make clear that I am not *denying* the existence of anything; I am only refusing to affirm it. I refuse to affirm the existence of anything for which there is no evidence, but I equally refuse to deny the existence of anything against which there is no evidence. Therefore I neither affirm nor deny it, but merely say, that is not in the realm of the knowable and is certainly not a part of physics; and physics, if it is to be interpreted, must be interpreted in terms of the sort of thing that can be empirical. If your atom is going to serve purposes in physics, as it undoubtedly does, your atom has got to turn out to be a construction, and your atom will in fact turn out to be a series of classes of particulars. The same process which one applies to physics, one will also apply elsewhere. The application to physics I explained briefly in my book on the *External World,* Chapters III and IV (Open Court Publishing Co., 1914).

I have talked so far about the unreality of the things we think real. I want to speak with equal emphasis about the reality of things we think unreal, such as phantoms and hallucinations. Phantoms and hallucinations, considered in themselves, are, as I explained in the preceding lectures, on exactly the same level as ordinary sense-data. They differ from ordinary sense-data only in the fact that they do not have the usual correlations with other things. In themselves they have the same reality as ordinary sense-data. They have the most complete and absolute and perfect reality that anything can have. They are part of the ultimate constituents of the world, just as the fleeting sense-data are. Speaking of the fleeting sense-data, I think it is very important to remove out of one's instincts any disposition to believe that the real is the permanent. There has been a metaphysical prejudice always that if a thing is really real, it has to last either forever or for a fairly decent length of time. That is to my mind an entire mistake. The things that are really real last a very short time. Again I am not denying that there *may* be things that last forever, or for thousands of years; I only say that those are not within our experience, and that the real things that we know by experience last for a very short time, one tenth or half a second, or whatever it may be. Phantoms and hallucinations are among those, among the ultimate constituents of the world. The things that we call real, like tables and chairs, are systems, series of classes of particulars, and the particulars are the real things, the particulars being sense-data when they happen to be given to you. A table or chair will be a series of classes of particulars, and therefore a logical fiction. Those particulars will be on the same level of reality as a hallucination or a phantom. I ought to explain in what sense a chair is a series of classes. A chair presents at each moment a number of different appearances. All the appearances that it is presenting at a given moment make up a certain class. All those sets of appearances vary from time to time. If I take a chair and smash it, it will present a whole set of different appearances from what it did before, and without going as far as that, it will always be changing as the light changes, and so on. So you get a series in time of different sets of appearances, and that is what I mean by saying that a chair is a series of classes. That explanation is too crude, but I leave out the niceties, as that is not the actual topic I am dealing with. Now each single particular which is part of this whole system is linked up with the others in the system. Supposing, e.g., I take as my particular the appearance which that chair is presenting to me at this moment. That is linked up first of all with the appearance which the same chair is presenting to any one of you at the same moment, and with the appearance which it is going to present to me at later moments. There you get at once two journeys that you can take away from that particular, and that particular will be correlated in certain definite ways with the other particulars which also belong to that chair. That is what you mean by saying—or what you ought to mean by saying—that what I see before me is a real thing as opposed to a phantom. It means that it has a whole set of correlations of different kinds. It means that that particular, which is the appearance of the chair to me at this moment, is not isolated but is connected in a certain well-known familiar fashion with others, in the sort of way that makes it answer one's expectations. And so, when you go and buy a chair, you buy not only the appearance which it presents to you at that moment, but also those other appearances that it is going to present when it gets home. If it were a phantom chair, it would not present any appearances when it got home, and would not be the sort of thing you would want to buy. The sort one calls real is one of a whole correlated system, whereas the sort you call hallucinations are not. The respectable particulars in the world are all of them linked up with other particulars in respectable, conventional ways. Then sometimes you get a wild particular, like a merely visual chair that you cannot sit on, and say it is a phantom, a hallucination, you exhaust all the vocabulary of abuse upon it. That is what one means by calling it unreal, because "unreal" applied in that way is a term of abuse and never would be applied to a thing that *was* unreal because you would not be so angry with it.

I will pass on to some other illustrations. Take a person. What is it that makes you say, when you meet your friend Jones, "Why, this is Jones"? It is clearly not the persistence of a metaphysical entity inside Jones somewhere, because even if there be such an entity, it certainly is not what you see when you see Jones coming along the street; it certainly is something that you are not acquainted with, not an empirical datum. Therefore plainly there is something in the empirical appearances which he presents to you, something in their relations one to another, which enables you to collect all these together and say, "These are what I call the appearances of one person," and that something that makes you collect them together is not the persistence of a metaphysical subject, because that, whether there be such a persistent subject or not, is certainly not a datum, and that which makes you say "Why, it is Jones" is a datum. Therefore Jones is not constituted as he is known by a sort of pin-point ego that is underlying his appearances, and you have got to find some correlations among the appearances which are of the sort that makes you put all those appearances together and say, they are the appearances of one person. Those are different when it is other people and when it is yourself. When it is yourself, you have more to go by. You have not only what you look like, you have also your thoughts and memories and all your organic sensations, so that you have a much richer material and are therefore much less likely to be mistaken as to your own identity than as to some one else's. It happens, of course, that there are mistakes even as to one's own identity, in cases of multiple personality and so forth, but as a rule you will know that it is you because you have more to go by than other people have, and you would know it is you, not by a consciousness of the ego at all but by all sorts of things, by memory, by the way you feel and the way you look and a host of things. But all those are empirical data, and those enable you to say that the person to whom something happened yesterday was yourself. So you can collect a whole set of experiences into one string as all belonging to you, and similarly other people's experiences can be collected together as all belonging to them by relations that actually are observable and without assuming the existence of the persistent ego. It does not matter in the least to what we are concerned with, what exactly is the given empirical relation between two experiences that makes us say, "These are two experiences of the same person." It does not matter precisely what that relation is, because the logical formula for the construction of the person is the same whatever that relation may be, and because the mere fact that you can know that two experiences belong to the same person proves that there is such an empirical relation to be ascertained by analysis. Let us call the relation R. We shall say that when two experiences have to each other the relation R, then they are said to be experiences of the same person. That is a definition of what I mean by "experiences of the same person." We proceed here just in the same way as when we are defining numbers. We first define what is meant by saying that two classes "have the same number," and then define what a number is. The person who has a given experience x will be the class of all those experiences which are "experiences of the same person" as the one who experiences x. You can say that two events are co-personal when there is between them a certain relation R, namely that relation which makes us say that they are experiences of the same person. You can define the person who has a certain experience as being those experiences that are co-personal with that experience, and it will be better perhaps to take them as a series than as a class, because you want to know which is the beginning of a man's life and which is the end. Therefore we shall say that a person is a certain series of experiences. We shall not deny that there may be a metaphysical ego. We shall merely say that it is a question that does not concern us in any way, because it is a matter about which we know nothing and can know nothing, and therefore it obviously cannot be a thing that comes into science in any way. What we know is this string of experiences that makes up a person, and that is put together by means of certain empirically given relations, such, e.g., as memory.

I will take another illustration, a kind of problem that our method is useful in helping to deal with. You all know the American theory of neutral monism, which derives really from William James and is also suggested in the work of Mach, but in a rather less developed form. The theory of neutral monism maintains that the distinction between the mental and the physical is entirely an affair of arrangement, that the actual material arranged is exactly the same in the case of the mental as it is the case of the physical, but they differ merely in the fact that when you take a thing as belonging in the same context with certain other things, it will belong to psychology, while when you take it in a certain other context with other things, it will belong to physics, and the difference is as to what you consider to be its context, just the same sort of difference as there is between arranging the people in London alphabetically or geographically. So, according to William James, the actual material of the world can be arranged in two different ways, one of which gives you physics and the other psychology. It is just like rows or columns: in an arrangement of rows and columns, you can take an item as either a member of a certain row or a member of a certain column; the item is the same in the two cases, but its context is different.

If you will allow me a little undue simplicity I can go on to say rather more about neutral monism, but you must understand that I am talking more simply than I ought to do because there is not time to put in all the shadings and qualifications. I was talking a moment ago about the appearances that a chair presents.

If we take any one of these chairs, we can all look at it, and it presents a different appearance to each of us. Taken all together, taking all the different appearances that that chair is presenting to all of us at this moment, you get something that belongs to physics. So that, if one takes sense-data and arranges together all those sense-data that appear to different people at a given moment and are such as we should ordinarily say are appearances of the same physical object, then that class of sense-data will give you something that belongs to physics, namely, the chair at this moment. On the other hand, if instead of taking all the appearances that that chair presents to all of us at this moment, I take all the appearances that the different chairs in this room present to me at this moment, I get quite another group of particulars. All the different appearances that different chairs present to me now will give you something belonging to psychology, because that will give you my experiences at the present moment. Broadly speaking, according to what one may take as an expansion of William James, that should be the definition of the difference between physics and psychology.

We commonly assume that there is a phenomenon which we call seeing the chair, but what I call my seeing the chair according to neutral monism is merely the existence of a certain particular, namely the particular which is the sense-datum of that chair at that moment. And I and the chair are both logical fictions, both being in fact a series of classes of particulars, of which one will be that particular which we call my seeing the chair. That actual appearance that the chair is presenting to me now is a member of me and a member of the chair, I and the chair being logical fictions. That will be at any rate a view that you can consider if you are engaged in vindicating neutral monism. There is no simple entity that you can point to and say: this entity is physical and not mental. According to William James and neutral monists that will not be the case with any simple entity that you may take. Any such entity will be a member of physical series and a member of mental series. Now I want to say that if you wish to test such a theory as that of neutral monism, if you wish to discover whether it is true or false, you cannot hope to get any distance with your problem unless you have at your fingers' end the theory of logic that I have been talking of. You never can tell otherwise what can be done with a given material, whether you can concoct out of a given material the sort of logical fictions that will have the properties you want in psychology and in physics. That sort of thing is by no means easy to decide. You can only decide it if you really have a very considerable technical facility in these matters. Having said that, I ought to proceed to tell you that I have discovered whether neutral monism is true or not, because otherwise you may not believe that logic is any use in the matter. But I do not profess to know whether it is true or not. I feel more and more inclined to think that it may be true. I feel more and more that the difficulties that occur in regard to it are all of the sort that may be solved be ingenuity. But nevertheless there *are* a number of difficulties; there are a number of problems, some of which I have spoken about in the course of these lectures. One is the question of belief and the other sorts of facts involving two verbs.

If there are such facts as this, that, I think, may make neutral monism rather difficult, but as I was pointing out, there is the theory that one calls behaviorism, which belongs logically with neutral monism, and that theory would altogether dispense with those facts containing two verbs, and would therefore dispose of that argument against neutral monism. There is, on the other hand, the argument from emphatic particulars, such as "this" and "now" and "here" and such words as that, which are not very easy to reconcile, to my mind, with the view which does not distinguish between a particular and experiencing that particular. But the argument about emphatic particulars is so delicate and so subtle that I cannot feel quite sure whether it is a valid one or not, and I think the longer one pursues philosophy, the more conscious one becomes how extremely often one has been taken in by fallacies, and the less willing one is to be quite sure that an argument is valid if there is anything about it that is at all subtle or elusive, at all difficult to grasp. That makes me a little cautious and doubtful about all these arguments, and therefore although I am quite sure that the question of the truth or falsehood of neutral monism is not to be solved except by these means, yet I do not profess to know whether neutral monism is true or is not. I am not without hopes of finding out in the course of time, but I do not profess to know yet.

As I said earlier in this lecture, one thing that our technique does, is to give us a means of constructing a given body of symbolic propositions with the minimum of apparatus, and every diminution in apparatus diminishes the risk of error. Suppose, e.g., that you have constructed your physics with a certain number of entities and a certain number of premises; suppose you discover that by a little ingenuity you can dispense with half of those entities and half of those premises, you clearly have diminished the risk of error, because if you had before 10 entities and 10 premises, then the 5 you have now would be all right, but it is not true conversely that if the 5 you have now are all right, the 10 must have been. Therefore you diminish the risk of error with every diminution of entities and premises. When I spoke about the desk and said I was not going to assume the existence of a persistent substance underlying its appearances, it is an example of the case in point. You have anyhow the successive appearances, and if you can get on without assuming the metaphysical and constant desk, you have a smaller risk of error than you had before. You would not necessarily have a smaller risk of error if you were tied down to *denying* the metaphysical desk. That is the advantage of Occam's Razor, that it diminishes your risk of error. Considered in that way you may say that the whole of our problem belongs rather to science than to philosophy. I think perhaps that is true, but I believe the only difference between science and philosophy is that science is what you more or less know and philosophy is what you do not know. Philosophy is that part of science which at present people choose to have opinions about, but which they have no knowledge about. Therefore every advance in knowledge robs philosophy of some problems which formerly it had, and if there is any truth, if there is any value in the kind of procedure of mathematical logic, it will follow that a number of problems which had belonged to philosophy will have ceased to belong to philosophy and will belong to science. And of course the moment they become soluble, they become to a large class of philosophical minds uninteresting, because to many of the people who like philosophy, the charm of it consists in the speculative freedom, in the fact that you can play with hypotheses. You can think out this or that which *may* be true, which is a very valuable exercise until you discover what *is* true; but when you discover what is true the whole fruitful play of fancy in that region is curtailed, and you will abandon that region and pass on. Just as there are families in America who from the time of the Pilgrim Fathers onward had always migrated westward, toward the backwoods, because they did not like civilized life, so the philosopher has an adventurous disposition and likes to dwell in the region where there are still uncertainties. It is true that transferring of a region from philosophy into science will make it distasteful to a very important and useful type of mind. I think that is true of a good deal of the applications of mathematical logic in the directions that I have been indicating. It makes it dry, precise, methodical, and in that way robs it of a certain quality that it had when you could play with it more freely. I do not feel that it is my place to apologize for that, because if it is true, it is true. If it is not true, of course, I do owe you an apology; but if it is, it is not my fault, and therefore I do not feel I owe any apology for any sort of dryness or dullness in the world. I would say this, too, that for those who have any taste for mathematics, for those who like symbolic constructions, that sort of world is a very delightful one, and if you do not find it otherwise attractive, all that is necessary to do is to acquire a taste for mathematics, and then you will have a very agreeable world, and with that conclusion I will bring this course of lectures to an end.

NOTE

1. Lecture VIII of "The Philosophy of Logical Atomism."

Study Questions

Bertrand Russell: "Facts and Propositions"

1. Selections 10–12 are chapters from "The Philosophy of Logical Atomism." What is Russell's intent in this work?
2. What is logical atomism?
3. What do we begin with, what do we do with it, and where are we trying to go?
4. What does the world contain?
5. What are the various kinds of facts?
6. What is a proposition?

Bertrand Russell: "Particulars, Predicates, and Relations"

1. Why are facts needed?
2. Why are the propositions to be analyzed?
3. What is a logically perfect language?
4. What is an example of a logically perfect language?
5. What are logically proper names?

Bertrand Russell: "Excursus Into Metaphysics: What There Is"

1. What is the importance of philosophical grammar?
2. What is Russell's purpose in "The Philosophy of Logical Atomism?"
3. In the metaphysics of logical atomism (Russell says), the things we think are real are unreal, and the things we think are unreal are real. How so? Illustrate.
4. Are chairs real? Are persons? Explain your answers.

Selected Bibliography

Fann, K. T. *Wittgenstein's Conception of Philosophy.* Berkeley: University of California Press, 1971. Part I. [A good book for the beginner.]

Russell, Bertrand. "Logical Atomism." In *Logic and Knowledge* (ed. by R. C. Marsh). New York: Macmillan, 1956. pp. 323–343. [This book also contains the complete "Philosophy of Logical Atomism."]

Urmson, J. O. *Philosophical Analysis.* Oxford: Oxford University Press, 1956. Part I. [An excellent secondary discussion and perhaps one of the best books to read first, before turning to the works of Russell and Wittgenstein.]

Wittgenstein, Ludwig. *Notebooks 1914–1916*. Trans. G. E. M. Anscombe. Oxford: Basil Blackwell, 1961. Second edition, 1979. [Contains the first draft of many problems also discussed in the *Tractatus*.]

Wittgenstein, Ludwig. *Tractatus Logico-Philosophicus*. Trans. D. F. Pears & B. F. McGuinness. London: Routledge & Kegan Paul, 1961. [Difficult but worth struggling with.]

Logical Positivism

13. The Elimination of Metaphysics

A. J. Ayer

The traditional disputes of philosophers are, for the most part, as unwarranted as they are unfruitful. The surest way to end them is to establish beyond question what should be the purpose and method of a philosophical enquiry. And this is by no means so difficult a task as the history of philosophy would lead one to suppose. For if there are any questions which science leaves it to philosophy to answer, a straightforward process of elimination must lead to their discovery.

We may begin by criticising the metaphysical thesis that philosophy affords us knowledge of a reality transcending the world of science and common sense. Later on, when we come to define metaphysics and account for its existence, we shall find that it is possible to be a metaphysician without believing in a transcendent reality; for we shall see that many metaphysical utterances are due to the commission of logical errors, rather than to a conscious desire on the part of their authors to go beyond the limits of experience. But it is convenient for us to take the case of those who believe that it is possible to have knowledge of a transcendent reality as a starting-point for our discussion. The arguments which we use to refute them will subsequently be found to apply to the whole of metaphysics.

One way of attacking a metaphysician who claimed to have knowledge of a reality which transcended the phenomenal world would be to enquire from what premises his propositions were deduced. Must he not begin, as other men do, with the evidence of his senses? And if so, what valid process of reasoning can possibly lead him to the conception of a transcendent reality? Surely from empirical premises nothing whatsoever concerning the properties, or even the existence, of anything super-empirical can legitimately be inferred. But this objection would be met by a denial on the part of the metaphysician that his assertions were ultimately based on the evidence of his senses. He would say that he was endowed with a faculty of intellectual intuition which enabled him to know facts that could not be known through sense-experience. And even if it could be shown that he was relying on empirical premises, and that his venture into a nonempirical world was therefore logically unjustified, it would not follow that the assertions which he made concerning this nonempirical world could not be true. For the fact that a conclusion does not follow from its putative premise is not sufficient to show that it is false. Consequently one cannot overthrow a system of transcendent metaphysics merely by criticising the way in which it comes into being. What is required is rather a criticism of the nature of the actual statements which comprise it. And this is the line of argument which we shall, in fact, pursue. For we shall maintain that no statement which refers to a "reality" transcending the limits of all possible sense-experience can possibly have any literal significance; from which it must follow that the labours of those who have striven to describe such a reality have all been devoted to the production of nonsense.

It may be suggested that this is a proposition which has already been proved by Kant. But although Kant also condemned transcendent metaphysics, he did so on different grounds. For he said that the human understanding was so constituted that it lost itself in contradictions when it ventured out beyond the limits of possible experience and attempted to deal with things in themselves. And thus he made the impossibility of a transcendent metaphysic not, as we do, a matter of logic, but a matter of fact. He asserted, not that our minds could not conceivably have had the power of penetrating beyond the phenomenal world, but merely that they were in fact devoid of it. And this leads the critic to ask how, if it is possible to know only what lies within the bounds of sense-experience, the author can be justified in asserting that real things do exist beyond, and how he can tell what are the boundaries beyond which the human understanding may not venture, unless he succeeds in passing them himself. As Wittgenstein says, "in order to draw a limit to thinking, we should have to think both sides of this limit,"[1] a truth to which Bradley gives a special twist in maintaining that the man who is ready to prove that metaphysics is impossible is a brother metaphysician with a rival theory of his own.[2]

Whatever force these objections may have against the Kantian doctrine, they have none whatsoever against the thesis that I am about to set forth. It cannot here be said that the author is himself overstepping the barrier he maintains to be impassable. For the fruitlessness of attempting to transcend the limits of possible sense-experience will be deduced, not from a psychological hypothesis concerning the actual constitution of the human mind, but from the rule which determines the literal significance of language. Our charge against the metaphysician is not that he attempts to employ the understanding in a field where it cannot profitably venture, but that he produces sentences which fail to conform to the conditions under which alone a sentence can be literally significant. Nor are we ourselves obliged to talk nonsense in order to show that all sentences of a certain type are necessarily devoid of literal significance. We need only formulate the criterion which enables us to test whether a sentence expresses a genuine proposition about a matter of fact, and then point out that the sentences under consideration fail to satisfy it. And this we shall now proceed to do. We shall first of all formulate the criterion in somewhat vague terms, and then give the explanations which are necessary to render it precise.

The criterion which we use to test the genuineness of apparent statements of fact is the criterion of verifiability. We say that a sentence is factually significant to any given person, if, and only if, he knows how to verify the proposition which it purports to express—that is, if he knows what observations would lead him, under certain conditions, to accept the proposition as being true, or reject it as being false. If, on the other hand, the putative proposition is of such a character that the assumption of its truth, or falsehood, is consistent with any assumption whatsoever concerning the nature of his future experience, then, as far as he is concerned, it is, if not a tautology, a mere pseudo-proposition. The sentence expressing it may be emotionally significant to him; but it is not literally significant. And with regard to questions the procedure is the same. We enquire in every case what observations would lead us to answer the question, one way or the other; and, if none can be discovered, we must conclude that the sentence under consideration does not, as far as we are concerned, express a genuine question, however strongly its grammatical appearance may suggest that it does.

As the adoption of this procedure is an essential factor in the argument of this book, it needs to be examined in detail.

In the first place, it is necessary to draw a distinction between practical verifiability, and verifiability in principle. Plainly we all understand, in many cases believe, propositions which we have not in fact taken steps to verify. Many of these are propositions which we could verify if we took enough trouble. But there remain a number of significant propositions, concerning matters of fact, which we could not verify even if we chose; simply because we lack the practical means of placing ourselves in the situation where the relevant observations could be made. A simple and familiar example of such a proposition is the proposition that there are mountains on the farther side of the moon.[3] No rocket has yet been invented which would enable me to go and look at the farther side of the moon, so that I am unable to decide the matter by actual observation. But I do know what observations would decide it for me, if, as is theoretically conceivable, I were once in a position to make them. And therefore I say that the proposition is verifiable in principle, if not in practice, and is accordingly significant. On the other hand, such a metaphysical pseudo-proposition as "the Absolute enters into, but is itself incapable of, evolution and progress,"[4] is not even in principle verifiable. For one cannot conceive of an observation which would enable one to determine whether the Absolute did, or did not, enter into evolution and progress. Of course it is possible that the author of such a remark is using English words in a way in which they are not commonly used by English-speaking people, and that he does, in fact, intend to assert something which could be empirically verified. But until he makes us understand how the proposition that he wishes to express would be verified, he fails to communicate anything to us. And if he admits, as I think the author of the remark in question would have admitted, that his words were not intended to express either a tautology or a proposition which was capable, at least in principle, of being verified, then it follows that he has made an utterance which has no literal significance even for himself.

A further distinction which we must make is the distinction between the "strong" and the "weak" sense of the term "verifiable." A proposition is said to be verifiable, in the strong sense of the term, if, and only if, its truth could be conclusively established in experience. But it is verifiable, in the weak sense, if it is possible for experience to render it probable. In which sense are we using the term when we say that a putative proposition is genuine only if it is verifiable?

It seems to me that if we adopt conclusive verifiability as our criterion of significance, as some positivists have proposed,[5] our argument will prove too much. Consider, for example, the case of general propositions of law — such propositions, namely, as "arsenic is poisonous"; "all men are mortal"; a body tends to expand when it is heated." It is of the very nature of these propositions that their truth cannot be established with certainty by any finite series of observations. But if it is recognised that such general propositions of law are designed to cover an infinite number of cases, then it must be admitted that they cannot, even in principle, be verified conclusively. And then, if we adopt conclusive verifiability as our criterion of significance, we are logically obliged to treat these general propositions of law in the same fashion as we treat the statements of the metaphysician.

In face of this difficulty, some positivists[6] have adopted the heroic course of saying that these general propositions are indeed pieces of nonsense, albeit an essentially important type of nonsense. But here the introduction of the term "important" is simply an attempt to hedge. It serves only to mark the authors' recognition that their view is somewhat too paradoxical, without in any way removing the paradox. Besides, the difficulty is not confined to the case of general propositions of law, though it is there revealed most plainly. It is hardly less obvious in the case of propositions about the remote past. For it must surely be admitted that, however strong the evidence in favour of historical statements may be, their truth can never become more than highly probable. And to maintain that they also constituted an important, or unimportant, type of nonsense would be unplausible, to say the very least. Indeed, it will be our contention that no proposition, other than a tautology, can possibly be anything more than a probable hypothesis. And if this is correct, the principle that a sentence can be factually significant only if it expresses what is conclusively verifiable is self-stultifying as a criterion of significance. For it leads to the conclusion that it is impossible to make a significant statement of fact at all.

Nor can we accept the suggestion that a sentence should be allowed to be factually significant if, and only if, it expresses something which is definitely confutable by experience.[7] Those who adopt this course assume that, although no finite series of observations is ever sufficient to establish the truth of a hypothesis beyond all possibility of doubt, there are crucial cases in which a single observation, or series of observations, can definitely confute it. But, as we shall show later on, this assumption is false. A hypothesis cannot be conclusively confuted any more than it can be conclusively verified. For when we take the occurrence of certain observations as proof that a given hypothesis is false, we presuppose the existence of certain conditions. And though, in any given case, it may be extremely improbable that this assumption is false, it is not logically impossible. We shall see that there need be no self-contradiction in holding that some of the relevant circumstances are other than we have taken them to be, and consequently that the hypothesis has not really broken down. And if it is not the case that any hypothesis can be definitely confuted, we cannot hold that the genuineness of a proposition depends on the possibility of its definite confutation.

Accordingly, we fall back on the weaker sense of verification. We say that the question that must be asked about any putative statement of fact is not, Would any observations make its truth or falsehood logically certain? but simply, Would any observations be relevant to the determination of its truth or falsehood? And it is only if a negative answer is given to this second question that we conclude that the statement under consideration is nonsensical.

To make our position clearer, we may formulate it in another way. Let us call a proposition which records an actual or possible observation an experiential proposition. Then we may say that it is the mark of a genuine factual proposition, not that it should be equivalent to an experiential proposition, or any finite number of experiential propositions, but simply that some experiential propositions can be deduced from it in conjunction with certain other premises without being deducible from those other premises alone.[8]

This criterion seems liberal enough. In contrast to the principle of conclusive verifiability, it clearly does not deny significance to general propositions or to propositions about the past. Let us see what kinds of assertion it rules out.

A good example of the kind of utterance that is condemned by our criterion as being not even false but nonsensical would be the assertion that the world of sense-experience was altogether unreal. It must, of course, be admitted that our senses do sometimes deceive us. We may, as the result of having certain sensations, expect certain other sensations to be obtainable which are, in fact, not obtainable. But, in all such cases, it is further sense-experience that informs us of the mistakes that arise out of sense-experience. We say that the senses sometimes deceive us, just because the expectations to which our sense-experiences give rise do not always accord with what we subsequently experience. That is, we rely on our senses to substantiate or confute the judgements which are based on our sensations. And therefore the fact that our perceptual judgements are sometimes found to be erroneous has not the slightest tendency to show that the world of sense-experience is unreal. And, indeed, it is plain that no conceivable observation, or series of observations, could have any tendency to show that the world revealed to us by sense-experience was unreal. Consequently, anyone who condemns the sensible world as a world of mere appearance, as opposed to reality, is saying something which, according to our criterion of significance, is literally nonsensical.

An example of a controversy which the application of our criterion obliges us to condemn as fictitious is provided by those who dispute concerning the number of substances that there are in the world. For it is admitted both by monists, who maintain that reality is one substance, and by pluralists, who maintain that reality is many, that it is impossible to imagine any empirical situation which would be relevant to the solution of their dispute. But if we are told that no possible observation could give any probability either to the assertion that reality was one substance or to the assertion that it was many, then we must conclude that neither assertion is significant. We shall see later on[9] that there are genuine logical and empirical questions involved in the dispute between monists and pluralists. But the metaphysical question concerning "substance" is ruled out by our criterion as spurious.

A similar treatment must be accorded to the controversy between realists and idealists, in its metaphysical aspect. A simple illustration, which I have made use of in a similar argument elsewhere,[10] will help to demonstrate this. Let us suppose that a picture is discovered and the suggestion made that it was painted by Goya. There is a definite procedure for dealing with such a question. The experts examine the picture to see in what way it resembles the accredited works of Goya, and to see if it bears any marks which are characteristic of a forgery; they look up contemporary records for evidence of the existence of such a picture, and so on. In the end, they may still disagree, but each one knows what empirical evidence would go to confirm or discredit his opinion. Suppose, now, that these men have studied philosophy, and some of them proceed to maintain that this picture is a set of ideas in the perceiver's mind, or in God's mind, others that it is objectively real. What possible experience could any of them have which would be relevant to the solution of this dispute one way or the other? In the ordinary sense of the term "real," in which it is opposed to "illusory," the reality of the picture is not in doubt. The disputants have satisfied themselves that the picture is real, in this sense, by obtaining a correlated series of sensations of sight and sensations of touch. Is there any similar process by which they could discover whether the picture was real, in the sense in which the term "real" is opposed to "ideal"? Clearly there is none. But, if that is so, the problem is fictitious according to our criterion. This does not mean that the realist-idealist controversy may be dismissed without further ado. For it can legitimately be regarded as a dispute concerning the analysis of existential propositions, and so as involving a logical problem which, as we shall see, can be definitively solved.[11] What we have just shown is that the question at issue between idealists and realists becomes fictitious when, as is often the case, it is given a metaphysical interpretation.

There is no need for us to give further examples of the operation of our criterion of significance. For our object is merely to show that philosophy, as a genuine branch of knowledge, must be distinguished from metaphysics. We are not now concerned with the historical question how much of what has traditionally passed for philosophy is actually metaphysical. We shall, however, point out later on that the majority of the "great philosophers" of the past were not essentially metaphysicians, and thus reassure those who would otherwise be prevented from adopting our criterion by considerations of piety.

As to the validity of the verification principle, in the form in which we have stated it, a demonstration will be given in the course of this book. For it will be shown that all propositions which have factual content are empirical hypotheses; and that the function of an empirical hypothesis is to provide a rule for the anticipation of experience.[12] And this means that every empirical hypothesis must be relevant to some actual, or possible, experience, so that a statement which is not relevant to any experience is not an empirical hypothesis, and accordingly has no factual content. But this is precisely what the principle of verifiability asserts.

It should be mentioned here that the fact that the utterances of the metaphysician are nonsensical does not follow simply from the fact that they are devoid of factual content. It follows from that fact, together with the fact that they are not *a priori* propositions. And in assuming that they are not *a priori* propositions, we are once again anticipating the conclusions of a later chapter in this book.[13] For it will be shown there that *a priori* propositions, which have always been attractive to philosophers on account of their certainty, owe this certainty to the fact that they are tautologies. We may accordingly define a metaphysical sentence as a sentence which purports to express a genuine proposition, but does, in fact, express neither a tautology nor an empirical hypothesis. And as tautologies and empirical hypotheses form the entire class of significant propositions, we are justified in concluding that all metaphysical assertions are nonsensical. Our next task is to show how they come to be made.

The use of the term "substance," to which we have already referred, provides us with a good example of the way in which metaphysics mostly comes to be written. It happens to be the case that we cannot, in our language, refer to the sensible properties of a thing without introducing a word or phrase which appears to stand for the thing itself as opposed to anything which may be said about it. And, as a result of this, those who are infected by the primitive superstition that to every name a single real entity must correspond assume that it is necessary to distinguish logically between the thing itself and any, or all, of its sensible properties. And so they employ the term "substance" to refer to the thing itself. But from the fact that we happen to employ a single word to refer to a thing, and make that word the grammatical subject of the sentences in which we refer to the sensible appearances of the thing, it does not by any means follow that the thing itself is a "simple entity," or that it cannot be defined in terms of the totality of its appearances. It is true that in talking of "its" appearances we appear to distinguish the thing from the appearances, but that is simply an accident of linguistic usage. Logical analysis shows that what makes these "appearances" the "appearances of" the same thing is not their relationship to an entity other than themselves, but their relationship to one another. The metaphysician fails to see this because he is misled by a superficial grammatical feature of his language.

A simpler and clearer instance of the way in which a consideration of grammar leads to metaphysics is the case of the metaphysical concept of Being. The origin of our temptation to raise questions about Being, which no conceivable experience would enable us to answer, lies in the fact that, in our language, sentences which express existential propositions and sentences which express attributive propositions may be of the same grammatical form. For instance, the sentences "Martyrs exist" and "Martyrs suffer" both consist of a noun followed by an intransitive verb, and the fact that they have gramatically the same appearance leads one to assume that they are of the same logical type. It is seen that in the proposition "Martyrs suffer," the members of a certain species are credited with a certain attribute, and it is sometimes assumed that the same thing is true of such a proposition as "Martyrs exist." If this were actually the case, it would, indeed, be as legitimate to speculate about the Being of martyrs as it is to speculate about their suffering. But, as Kant pointed out,[14] existence is not an attribute. For, when we ascribe an attribute to a thing, we covertly assert that it exists: so that if existence were itself an attribute, it would follow that all positive existential propositions were tautologies, and all negative existential propositions self-contradictory; and this is not the case.[15] So that those who raise questions about Being which are based on the assumption that existence is an attribute are guilty of following grammar beyond the boundaries of sense.

A similar mistake has been made in connection with such propositions as "Unicorns are fictitious." Here again the fact that there is a superficial grammatical resemblance between the English sentences "Dogs are faithful" and "Unicorns are fictitious," and between the corresponding sentences in other languages, creates the assumption that they are of the same logical type. Dogs must exist in order to have the property of being faithful, and so it is held that unless unicorns in some way existed they could not have the property of being fictitious. But, as it is plainly self-contradictory to say that fictitious objects exist, the device is adopted of saying that they are real in some non-empirical sense — that they have a mode of real being which is different from the mode of being of existent things. But since there is no way of testing whether an object is real in the this sense, as there is for testing whether it is real in the ordinary sense, the assertion that fictitious objects have a special non-empirical mode of real being is devoid of all literal significance. It comes to be made as a result of the assumption that being fictitious is an attribute. And this is a fallacy of the same order as the fallacy of supposing that existence is an attribute, and it can be exposed in the same way.

In general, the postulation of real non-existent entities results from the superstition, just now referred to, that, to every word or phrase that can be the grammatical subject of a sentence, there must somewhere be a real entity corresponding. For as there is no place in the empirical world for many of these "entities," a special non-empirical world is invoked to house them. To this error must be attributed, not only the utterances of a Heidegger, who bases his metaphysics on the assumption that "Nothing" is a name which is used to denote something peculiarly mysterious,[16] but also the prevalence of such problems as those concerning the reality of propositions and universals whose senselessness, though less obvious, is no less complete.

These few examples afford a sufficient indication of the way in which most metaphysical assertions come to be formulated. They show how easy it is to write sentences which are literally nonsensical without seeing that they are nonsensical. And thus we see that the view that a number of the traditional "problems of philosophy" are metaphysical, and consequently fictitious, does not involve any incredible assumptions about the psychology of philosophers.

Among those who recognise that if philosophy is to be accounted a genuine branch of knowledge it must be defined in such a way as to distinguish it from metaphysics, it is fashionable to speak of the metaphysician as a kind of misplaced poet. As his statements have no literal meaning, they are not subject to any criteria of truth or falsehood: but they may still serve to express, or arouse, emotion, and thus be subject to ethical or aesthetic standards. And it is suggested that they may have considerable value, as means of moral inspiration, or even as works of art. In this way, an attempt is made to compensate the metaphysician for his extrusion from philosophy.[17]

I am afraid that this compensation is hardly in accordance with his deserts. The view that the metaphysician is to be reckoned among the poets appear to rest on the assumption that both talk nonsense. But this assumption is false. In the vast majority of cases the sentences which are produced by poets do have literal meaning. The difference between the man who uses language scientifically and the man who uses it emotively is not that the one produces sentences which are incapable of arousing emotion, and the other sentences which have no sense, but that the one is primarily concerned with the expression of true propositions, the other with the creation of a work of art. Thus, if a work of science contains true and important propositions, its value as a work of science will hardly be diminished by the fact that they are inelegantly expressed. And similarly, a work of art is not necessarily the worse for the fact that all the propositions comprising it are literally false. But to say that many literary works are largely composed of falsehoods, is not to say that they are composed of pseudo-propositions. It is, in fact, very rare for a literary artist to produce sentences which have no literal meaning. And where this does occur, the sentences are carefully chosen for their rhythm and balance. If the author writes nonsense, it is because he considers it most suitable for bringing about the effects for which his writing is designed.

The metaphysician, on the other hand, does not intend to write nonsense. He lapses into it through being deceived by grammar, or through committing errors of reasoning, such as that which leads to the view that the sensible world is unreal. But it is not the mark of a poet simply to make mistakes of this sort. There are some, indeed, who would see in the fact that the metaphysician's utterances are senseless a reason against the view that they have aesthetic value.

And, without going so far as this, we may safely say that it does not constitute a reason for it.

It is true, however, that although the greater part of metaphysics is merely the embodiment of humdrum errors, there remain a number of metaphysical passages which are the work of genuine mystical feeling; and they may more plausibly be held to have moral or aesthetic value. But, as far as we are concerned, the distinction between the kind of metaphysics that is produced by a philosopher who has been duped by grammar, and the kind that is produced by a mystic who is trying to express the inexpressible, is of no great importance: what is important to us is to realise that even the utterances of the metaphysician who is attempting to expound a vision are literally senseless; so that henceforth we may pursue our philosophical researches with as little regard for them as for the more inglorious kind of metaphysics which comes from a failure to understand the workings of our language.

ADDENDUM

(From Introduction to Second Edition)

It will be seen that, in this book, I begin by suggesting that a statement is "weakly" verifiable, and therefore meaningful, according to my criterion, if "some possible sense-experience would be relevant to the determination of its truth or falsehood." But, as I recognize, this itself requires interpretation; for the word "relevant" is uncomfortably vague. Accordingly, I put forward a second version of my principle, which I shall restate here in slightly different terms, using the phrase "observation-statement," in place of "experiential proposition," to designate a statement "which records an actual or possible observation." In this version, then, the principle is that a statement is verifiable, and consequently meaningful, if some observation-statement can be deduced from it in conjunction with certain other premises, without being deducible from those other premises alone.

I say of this criterion that it "seems liberal enough," but in fact it is far too liberal, since it allows meaning to any statement whatsoever. For, given any statement "S" and an observation-statement "O," "O" follows from "S" and "if S then O" without following from "if S then O" alone. Thus, the statements "the Absolute is lazy" and "if the Absolute is lazy, this is white" jointly entail the observation-statement "this is white," and since "this is white" does not follow from either of these premises, taken by itself, both of them satisfy my criterion of meaning. Furthermore, this would hold good for any other piece of nonsense that one cared to put, as an example, in place of "the Absolute is lazy," provided only that it had the grammatical form of an indicative sentence. But a criterion of meaning that allows such latitude as this is evidently unacceptable.[18]

It may be remarked that the same objection applies to the proposal that we should take the possibility of falsification as our criterion. For, given any statement "*S*" and any observation-statement "*O*", "*O*" will be incompatible with the conjunction of "*S*" and "if *S* then not *O*." We could indeed avoid the difficulty, in either case, by leaving out the stipulation about the other premises. But as this would involve the exclusion of all hypotheticals from the class of empirical propositions, we should escape from making our criteria too liberal only at the cost of making them too stringent.

Another difficulty which I overlooked in my original attempt to formulate the principle of verification is that most empirical propositions are in some degree vague. Thus, as I have remarked elsewhere,[19] what is required to verify a statement about a material thing is never the occurrence of precisely this or precisely that sense-content, but only the occurrence of one or other of the sense-contents that fall within a fairly indefinite range. We do indeed test any such statement by making observations which consist in the occurrence of particular sense-contents; but, for any test that we actually carry out, there is always an indefinite number of other tests, differing to some extent in respect either of their conditions or their results, that would have served the same purpose. And this means that there is never any set of observation-statements of which it can truly be said that precisely they are entailed by any given statement about a material thing.

Nevertheless, it is only by the occurrence of some sense-content, and consequently by the truth of some observation-statement, that any statement about a material thing is actually verified; and from this it follows that every significant statement about a material thing can be represented as entailing a disjunction of observation-statements, although the terms of this disjunction, being indefinite, can not be enumerated in detail. Consequently, I do not think that we need be troubled by the difficulty about vagueness, so long as it is understood that when we speak of the "entailment" of observation-statements, what we are considering to be deducible from the premises in question is not any particular observation-statement, but only one or other of a set of such statements, where the defining characteristic of the set is that all its members refer to sense-contents that fall within a certain specifiable range.

There remains the more serious objection that my criterion, as it stands, allows meaning to any indicative statement whatsoever. To meet this, I shall emend it as follows. I propose to say that a statement is directly verifiable if it is either itself an observation-statement, or is such that in conjunction with one or more observation-statements it entails at least one observation-statement which is not deducible from these other premises alone; and I propose to say that a statement is indirectly verifiable if it satisfies the following conditions: first, that in conjunction with certain other premises it entails one or more directly verifiable statements which are not deducible from these other premises alone; and secondly, that these other premises do not include any statement that is not either analytic, or directly verifiable, or capable of being independently established as indirectly verifiable. And I can now reformulate the principle of verification as requiring of a literally meaningful statement, which is not analytic, that it should be either directly or indirectly verifiable, in the foregoing sense. . . .[20]

NOTES

1. *Tractatus Logico-Philosophicus,* Preface.
2. Bradley, *Appearance and Reality,* 2nd ed., p. 1.
3. This example has been used by Professor Schlick to illustrate the same point.
4. A remark taken at random from *Appearance and Reality,* by F. H. Bradley.
5. e.g. M. Schlick, "Positivismus und Realismus," *Erkenntnis,* Vol. I, 1930. F. Waismann, "Logische Analyse des Warscheinlichkeitsbegriffs," *Erkenntnis,* Vol. I, 1930.
6. e.g. M. Schlick, "Die Kausalität in der gegenwärtigen Physik," *Naturwissenschaft,* Vol. 19, 1931.
7. This has been proposed by Karl Popper in his *Logik der Forschung.*
8. This is an over-simplified statement, which is not literally correct. I give what I believe to be the correct formulation in the Introduction, p. 13.
9. In Chapter VIII.
10. Vide "Demonstration of the Impossibility of Metaphysics," *Mind,* 1934, p. 339.
11. Vide Chapter VIII.
12. Vide Chapter V.
13. Chapter IV.
14. Vide *The Critique of Pure Reason,* "Transcendental Dialectic," Book II, Chapter iii, section 4.
15. This argument is well stated by John Wisdom, *Interpretation and Analysis,* pp. 62, 63.
16. Vide *Was ist Metaphysik,* by Heidegger: criticised by Rudolf Carnap in his "Überwindung der Metaphysik durch logische Analyse der Sprache," *Erkenntnis,* Vol. II, 1934.
17. For a discussion of this point, see also C. A. Mace, "Representation and Expression," *Analysis,* Vol. I, No. 3; and "Metaphysics and Emotive Language," *Analysis,* Vol. II, Nos. 1 and 2.
18. Vide I. Berlin, "Verifiability in Principle," *Proceedings of the Aristotelian Society,* Vol. XXXIX.
19. *The Foundations of Empirical Knowledge, pp. 240-1.*
20. This selection and the next four are all taken from Ayer, *Language, Truth, and Logic.* (Ed.)

14. The Function of Philosophy

A. J. Ayer

Among the superstitions from which we are freed by the abandonment of metaphysics is the view that it is the business of the philosopher to construct a deductive system. In rejecting this view we are not, of course, suggesting that the philosopher can dispense with deductive reasoning. We are simply contesting his right to posit certain first principles, and then offer them with their consequences as a complete picture of reality. To discredit this procedure, one has only to show that there can be no first principles of the kind it requires.

As it is the function of these first principles to provide a certain basis for our knowledge, it is clear that they are not to be found among the so-called laws of nature. For we shall see that the "laws of nature," if they are not mere definitions, are simply hypotheses which may be confuted by experience. And, indeed, it has never been the practice of the system-builders in philosophy to choose inductive generalizations for their premises. Rightly regarding such generalizations as being merely probable, they subordinate them to principles which they believe to be logically certain.

This is illustrated most clearly in the system of Descartes. It is commonly said that Descartes attempted to derive all human knowledge from premises whose truth was intuitively certain: but this interpretation puts an undue stress on the element of psychology in his system. I think he realised well enough that a mere appeal to intuition was insufficient for his purpose, since men are not all equally credulous, and that what he was really trying to do was to base all our knowledge on propositions which it would be self-contradictory to deny. He thought he had found such a proposition in "*cogito,*" which must not here be understood in its ordinary sense of "I think," but rather as meaning "there is a thought now." In fact he was wrong, because "*non cogito*" would be self-contradictory only if it negated itself: and this no significant proposition can do. But even if it were true that such a proposition as "there is a thought now" was logically certain, it still would not serve Descartes' purpose. For if "*cogito*" is taken in this sense, his initial principle, "*cogito ergo sum,*" is false. "I exist" does not follow from "there is a thought now." The fact that a thought occurs at a given moment does not entail that any other thought has occurred at any other moment, still less that there has occurred a series of thoughts sufficient to constitute a single self. As Hume conclusively showed, no one event intrinsically points to any other. We infer the existence of events which we are not actually observing, with the help of general principles. But these principles must be obtained inductively. By mere deduction from what is immediately given we cannot advance a single step beyond. And, consequently, any attempt to base a deductive system on propositions which describe what is immediately given is bound to be a failure.

The only other course open to one who wished to deduce all our knowledge from "first principles," without indulging in metaphysics, would be to take for his premises a set of *a priori* truths. But, as we have already mentioned, and shall later show, an *a priori* truth is a tautology. And from a set of tautologies, taken by themselves, only further tautologies can be validly deduced. But it would be absurd to put forward a system of tautologies as constituting the whole truth about the universe. And thus we may conclude that it is not possible to deduce all our knowledge from "first principles"; so that those who hold that it is the function of philosophy to carry out such a deduction are denying its claim to be a genuine branch of knowledge.

The belief that it is the business of the philosopher to search for first principles is bound up with the familiar conception of philosophy as the study of reality as a whole. And this conception is one which it is difficult to criticize, because it is so vague. If it is taken to imply, as it sometimes is, that the philosopher somehow projects himself outside the world, and takes a bird's-eye view of it, then it is plainly a metaphysical conception. And it is also metaphysical to assert, as some do, that "reality as a whole" is somehow generically different from the reality which is investigated piecemeal by the special sciences. But if the assertion that philosophy studies reality as a whole is understood to imply merely that the philosopher is equally concerned with the content of every science, then we may accept it, not indeed as an adequate definition of philosophy, but as a truth about it. For we shall find, when we come to discuss the relationship of philosophy to science, that it is not, in principle, related to any one science more closely than to any other.

In saying that philosophy is concerned with each of the sciences, in a manner which we shall indicate, we mean also to rule out the supposition that philosophy can be ranged alongside the existing sciences, as a special department of speculative knowledge. Those who make this supposition cherish the belief that there are some things in the world which are possible objects of speculative knowledge and yet lie beyond the scope of empirical science. But this belief is a delusion. There is no field of experience which cannot, in principle, be brought under some form of scientific law, and no type of speculative knowledge about the world which it is, in principle, beyond the power of science to give. We have already gone some way to substantiate this proposition by demolishing metaphysics; and we shall justify it to the full in the course of this book.

With this we complete the overthrow of speculative philosophy. We are now in a position to see that the function of philosophy is wholly critical. In what exactly does its critical activity consist?

One way of answering this question is to say that it is the philosopher's business to test the validity of our scientific hypotheses and everyday assumptions. But this view, though very widely held, is mistaken. If a man chooses to doubt the truth of all the propositions he ordinarily believes, it is not in the power of philosophy to reassure him. The most that philosophy can do, apart from seeing whether his beliefs are self-consistent, is to show what are the criteria which are used to determine the truth or falsehood or any given proposition: and then, when the sceptic realises that certain observations would verify his propositions, he may also realize that he could make those observations, and so consider his original beliefs to be justified. But in such a case one cannot say that it is philosophy which justifies his beliefs. Philosophy merely shows him that experience can justify them. We may look to the philosopher to show us what we accept as constituting sufficient evidence for the truth of any given empirical proposition. But whether the evidence is forthcoming or not is in every case a purely empirical question.

If anyone thinks that we are here taking too much for granted, let him refer to the chapter on "Truth and Probability," in which we discuss how the validity of synthetic propositions is determined. He will see there that the only sort of justification that is necessary or possible for self-consistent empirical propositions is empirical verification. And this applies just as much to the laws of science as to the maxims of common sense. Indeed there is no difference in kind between them. The superiority of the scientific hypothesis consists merely in its being more abstract, more precise, and more fruitful. And although scientific objects such as atoms and electrons seem to be fictitious in a way that chairs and tables are not, here, too, the distinction is only a distinction of degree. For both these kinds of objects are known only by their sensible manifestations and are definable in terms of them.

*   *   *

It should now be sufficiently clear that if the philosopher is to uphold his claim to make a special contribution to the stock of our knowledge, he must not attempt to formulate speculative truths, or to look for first principles, or to make *a priori* judgements about the validity of our empirical beliefs. He must, in fact, confine himself to works of clarification and analysis of a sort which we shall presently describe.

In saying that the activity of philosophising is essentially analytic, we are not, of course, maintaining that all those who are commonly called philosophers have actually been engaged in carrying out analyses. On the contrary, we have been at pains to show that a great deal of what is commonly called philosophy is metaphysical in character. What we have been in search of, in enquiring into the function of philosophy, is a definition of philosophy which should accord to some extent with the practice of those who are commonly called philosophers, and at the same time be consistent with the common assumption that philosophy is a special branch of knowledge. It is because metaphysics fails to satisfy this second condition that we distinguish it from philosophy, in spite of the fact that it is commonly referred to as philosophy. And our justification for making this distinction is that it is necessitated by our original postulate that philosophy is a special branch of knowledge, and our demonstration that metaphysics is not.

*   *   *

It is advisable to stress the point that philosophy, as we understand it, is wholly independent of metaphysics, inasmuch as the analytic method is commonly supposed by its critics to have a metaphysical basis. Being misled by the associations of the word "analysis," they assume that philosophical analysis is an activity of dissection; that it consists in "breaking up" objects into their constituent parts, until the whole universe is ultimately exhibited as an aggregate of "bare particulars," united by external relations. If this were really so, the most effective way of attacking the method would be to show that its basic presupposition was nonsensical. For to say that the universe was an aggregate of bare particulars would be as senseless as to say that it was Fire or Water or Experience. It is plain that no possible observation would enable one to verify such an assertion. But, so far as I know, this line of criticism is in fact never adopted. The critics content themselves with pointing out that few, if any, of the complex objects in the world are simply the sum of their parts. They have a structure, an organic unity, which distinguishes them, as genuine wholes, from mere aggregates. But the analyst, so it is said, is obliged by his atomistic metaphysics to regard an object consisting of parts $a, b, c,$ and d in a distinctive configuration as being simply $a + b + c + d,$ and thus gives an entirely false account of its nature.

If we follow the Gestalt psychologists, who of all men talk most constantly about genuine wholes, in defining such a whole as one in which the properties of every part depend to some extent on its position in the whole, then we may accept it as an empirical fact that there exist genuine, or organic, wholes. And if the analytic method involved a denial of this fact, it would indeed be a faulty method. But, actually, the validity of the analytic method is not dependent on any empirical, much less any metaphysical, presupposition about the nature of things. For the philosopher, as an analyst, is not directly concerned with the physical properties of things. He is concerned only with the way in which we speak about them.

In other words, the propositions of philosophy are not factual, but linguistic in character — that is, they do not describe the behaviour of physical, or even mental, objects; they express definitions, or the formal consequences of definitions. Accordingly, we may say that philosophy is a department of logic. For we shall see that the characteristic mark of a purely logical enquiry is that it is concerned with the formal consequences of our definitions and not with questions of empirical fact.

It follows that philosophy does not in any way compete with science. The difference in type between philosophical and scientific propositions is such that they cannot conceivably contradict one another. And this makes it clear that the possibility of philosophical analysis is independent of any empirical assumptions. That it is independent of any metaphysical assumptions should be even more obvious still. For it is absurd to suppose that the provision of definitions, and the study of their formal consequences, involves the nonsensical assertion that the world is composed of bare particulars, or any other metaphysical dogma.

What has contributed as much as anything to the prevalent misunderstanding of the nature of philosophical analysis is the fact that propositions and questions which are really linguistic are often expressed in such a way that they appear to be factual.[1] A striking instance of this is provided by the proposition that a material thing cannot be in two places at once. This looks like an empirical proposition, and is constantly invoked by those who desire to prove that it is possible for an empirical proposition to be logically certain. But a more critical inspection shows that it is not empirical at all, but linguistic. It simply records the fact that, as the result of certain verbal conventions, the proposition that two sense-contents occur in the same visual or tactual sense-field is incompatible, with the proposition that they belong to the same material thing.[2] And this is indeed a necessary fact. But it has not the least tendency to show that we have certain knowledge about the empirical properties of objects. For it is necessary only because we happen to use the relevant words in a particular way. There is no logical reason why we should not so alter our definitions that the sentence "A thing cannot be in two places at once" comes to express a self-contradiction instead of a necessary truth.

Another good example of linguistically necessary proposition which appears to be a record of empirical fact is the proposition, "Relations are not particulars, but universals." One might suppose that this was a proposition of the same order as, "Armenians are not Mohammedans, but Christians": but one would be mistaken. For, whereas the latter proposition is an empirical hypothesis relating to the religious practices of a certain group of people, the former is not a proposition about "things" at all, but simply about words. It records the fact that relation-symbols belong by definition to the class of symbols for characters, and not to the class of symbols for things.

The assertion that relations are universals provokes the question, "What is a universal?"; and this question is not, as it has traditionally been regarded, a question about the character of certain real objects, but a request for a definition of a certain term. Philosophy, as it is written, is full of questions like this, which seem to be factual but are not. Thus, to ask what is the nature of a material object is to ask for a definition of "material object," and this, as we shall shortly see, is to ask how propositions about material objects are to be translated into propositions about sense-contents. Similarly, to ask what is a number is to ask some such question as whether it is possible to translate propositions about the natural numbers into propositions about classes.[3] And the same thing applies to all the other philosophical questions of the form, "What is an x?" or, "What is the nature of x?" They are all requests for definitions, and, as we shall see, for definitions of a peculiar sort.

Although it is misleading to write about linguistic questions in "factual" language, it is often convenient for the sake of brevity. And we shall not always avoid doing it ourselves. But it is important that no one should be deceived by this practice into supposing that the philosopher is engaged on an empirical or a metaphysical enquiry. We may speak loosely of him as analysing facts, or notions, or even things. But we must make it clear that these are simply ways of saying that he is concerned with the definition of the corresponding words.

NOTES

1. Carnap has stressed this point. Where we speak of "linguistic" propositions expressed in "factual" or "pseudo-factual" language he speaks of "Pseudo-Objektsätze" or "quasi-syntaktische Sätze" as being expressed in the "Inhaltliche," as opposed to the "Formale Redeweise." Vide *Logische Syntax der Sprache,* Part V.

2. cf. my article "On Particulars and Universals," *Proceedings of the Aristotelian Society, 1933-4,* pp. 54, 55.

3. Rudolf Carnap, *Logische Syntax der Sprache,* Part V, 79B, and 84.

15. The A Priori

A. J. Ayer

The view of philosophy which we have adopted may, I think, fairly be described as a form of empiricism. For it is characteristic of an empiricist to eschew metaphysics, on the ground that every factual proposition must refer to sense-experience. And even if the conception of philosophizing as an activity of analysis is not to be discovered in the traditional theories of empiricists, we have seen that it is implicit in their practice. At the same time, it must be made clear that, in calling ourselves empiricists, we are not avowing a belief in any of the psychological doctrines which are commonly associated with empiricism. For, even if these doctrines were valid, their validity would be independent of the validity of any philosophical thesis. It could be established only by observation, and not by the purely logical considerations upon which our empiricism rests.

Having admitted that we are empiricists, we must now deal with the objection that is commonly brought against all forms of empiricism; the objection, namely, that it is impossible on empiricist principles to account for our knowledge of necessary truths. For, as Hume conclusively showed, no general proposition whose validity is subject to the test of actual experience can ever be logically certain. No matter how often it is verified in practice, there still remains the possibility that it will be confuted on some future occasion. The fact that a law has been substantiated in $n-1$ cases affords no logical guarantee that it will be substantiated in the nth case also, no matter how large we take n to be. And this means that no general proposition referring to a matter of fact can ever be shown to be necessarily and universally true. It can at best be a probable hypothesis. And this, we shall find, applies not only to general propositions, but to all propositions which have a factual content. They can none of them ever become logically certain. This conclusion, which we shall elaborate later on, is one which must be accepted by every consistent empiricist. It is often thought to involve him in complete scepticism; but this is not the case. For the fact that the validity of a proposition cannot be logically

253

guaranteed in no way entails that it is irrational for us to believe it. On the contrary, what is irrational is to look for a guarantee where none can be forthcoming; to demand certainty where probability is all that is obtainable. We have already remarked upon this, in referring to the work of Hume. And we shall make the point clearer when we come to treat of probability, in explaining the use which we make of empirical propositions. We shall discover that there is nothing perverse or paradoxical about the view that all the "truths" of science and common sense are hypotheses; and consequently that the fact that it involves this view constitutes no objection to the empiricist thesis.

Where the empiricist does encounter difficulty is in connection with the truths of formal logic and mathematics. For whereas a scientific generalisation is readily admitted to be fallible, the truths of mathematics and logic appear to everyone to be necessary and certain. But if empiricism is correct no proposition which has a factual content can be necessary or certain. Accordingly the empiricist must deal with the truths of logic and mathematics in one of the two following ways: he must say either that they are not necessary truths, in which case he must account for the universal conviction that they are; or he must say that they have no factual content, and then he must explain how a proposition which is empty of all factual content can be true and useful and surprising.

If neither of these courses proves satisfactory, we shall be obliged to give way to rationalism. We shall be obliged to admit that there are some truths about the world which we can know independently of experience; that there are some properties which we can ascribe to all objects, even though we cannot conceivably observe that all objects have them. And we shall have to accept it as a mysterious inexplicable fact that our thought has this power to reveal to us authoritatively the nature of objects which we have never observed. Or else we must accept the Kantian explanation which, apart from the epistemological difficulties which we have already touched on, only pushes the mystery a stage further back.

It is clear that any such concession to rationalism would upset the main argument of this book. For the admission that there were some facts about the world which could be known independently of experience would be incompatible with our fundamental contention that a sentence says nothing unless it is empirically verifiable. And thus the whole force of our attack on metaphysics would be destroyed. It is vital, therefore, for us to be able to show that one or other of the empiricist accounts of the propositions of logic and mathematics is correct. If we are successful in this, we shall have destroyed the foundations of rationalism. For the fundamental tenet of rationalism is that thought is an independent source of knowledge, and is moreover a more trustworthy source of knowledge than experience; indeed some rationalists have gone so far as to say that thought is the only source of knowledge. And the ground for this view is simply that the only necessary truths about the world which are known to us are known through thought and not through experience. So that if we can show either that the truths in question are not necessary or that they are not "truths about the world," we shall be taking away the support on which rationalism rests. We shall be making good the empiricist contention that there are no "truths of reason" which refer to matters of fact.

The course of maintaining that the truths of logic and mathematics are not necessary or certain was adopted by Mill. He maintained that these propositions were inductive generalizations based on an extremely large number of instances. The fact that the number of supporting instances was so very large accounted, in his view, for our believing these generalizations to be necessarily and universally true. The evidence in their favour was so strong that it seemed incredible to us that a contrary instance should ever arise. Nevertheless it was in principle possible for such generalizations to be confuted. They were highly probable, but, being inductive generalizations, they were not certain. The difference between them and the hypotheses of natural science was a difference in degree and not in kind. Experience gave us very good reason to suppose that a "truth" of mathematics or logic was true universally; but we were not possessed of a guarantee. For these "truths" were only empirical hypotheses which had worked particularly well in the past; and, like all empirical hypotheses, they were theoretically fallible.

I do not think that this solution of the empiricist's difficulty with regard to the propositions of logic and mathematics is acceptable. In discussing it, it is necessary to make a distinction which is perhaps already enshrined in Kant's famous dictum that, although there can be no doubt that all our knowledge begins with experience, it does not follow that it all arises out of experience.[1] When we say that the truths of logic are known independently of experience, we are not of course saying that they are innate, in the sense that we are born knowing them. It is obvious that mathematics and logic have to be learned in the same way as chemistry and history have to be learned. Nor are we denying that the first person to discover a given logical or mathematical truth was led to it by an inductive procedure. It is very probable, for example, that the principle of the syllogism was formulated not before but after the validity of syllogistic reasoning had been observed in a number of particular cases. What we are discussing, however, when we say that logical and mathematical truths are known independently of experience, is not a historical question concerning the way in which these truths were originally discovered, not a psychological question concerning the way in which each of us comes to learn them, but an epistemological question. The contention of Mill's which we reject is that the propositions of logic and mathematics have the same status as empirical hypotheses; that their validity is determined in the same way. We maintain that they are independent of experience in the sense that they do not owe their validity to empirical verification. We may come to discover them through an inductive process; but once we have apprehended them we see that they are necessarily true, that they hold good for every conceivable instance. And this serves to distinguish them from empirical generalizations. For we know that a proposition whose validity depends upon experience cannot be seen to be necessarily and universally true.

In rejecting Mill's theory, we are obliged to be somewhat dogmatic. We can do no more than state the issue clearly and then trust that his contention will be seen to be discrepant with the relevant logical facts. The following considerations may serve to show that of the two ways of dealing with logic and mathematics which are open to the empiricist, the one which Mill adopted is not the one which is correct.

The best way to substantiate our assertion that the truths of formal logic and pure mathematics are necessarily true is to examine cases in which they might seem to be confuted. It might easily happen, for example, that when I came to count what I had taken to be five pairs of objects, I found that they amounted only to nine. And if I wished to mislead people I might say that on this occasion twice five was not ten. But in that case I should not be using the complex sign "$2 \times 5 = 10$" in the way in which it is ordinarily used. I should be taking it not as the expression of a purely mathematical proposition, but as the expression of an empirical generalization, to the effect that whenever I counted what appeared to me to be five pairs of objects I discovered that they were ten in number. This generalization may very well be false. But if it proved false in a given case, one would not say that the mathematical proposition "$2 \times 5 = 10$" had been confuted. One would say that I was wrong in supposing that there were five pairs of objects to start with, or that one of the objects had been taken away while I was counting, or that two of them had coalesced, or that I had counted wrongly. One would adopt as an explanation whatever empirical hypothesis fitted in best with the accredited facts. The one explanation which would in no circumstances be adopted is that ten is not always the product of two and five.

To take another example: if what appears to be a Euclidean triangle is found by measurement not to have angles totalling 180 degrees, we do not say that we have met with an instance which invalidates the mathematical proposition that the sum of the three angles of a Euclidean triangle is 180 degrees. We say that we have measured wrongly, or, more probably, that the triangle we have been measuring is not Euclidean. And this is our procedure in every case in which a mathematical truth might appear to be confuted. We always preserve its validity by adopting some other explanation of the occurrence.

The same thing applies to the principles of formal logic. We may take an example relating to the so-called law of excluded middle, which states that a proposition must be either true or false, or, in other words, that it is impossible that a proposition and its contradictory should neither of them be true. One might suppose that a proposition of the form "x has stopped doing y" would in certain cases constitute an exception to this law. For instance, if my friend has never yet written to me, it seems fair to say that it is neither true nor false that he has stopped writing to me. But in fact one would refuse to accept such an instance as an invalidation of the law of excluded middle. One would point out that the proposition "My friend has stopped writing to me" is not a simple proposition, but the conjunction of the two propositions "My friend wrote to me in the past" and "My friend does not write to me now": and, furthermore, that the proposition "My friend has not stopped writing to me" is not, as it appears to be, contradictory to "My friend has stopped writing to me," but only contrary to it. For it means "My friend wrote to me in the past, and he still writes to me." When, therefore, we say that such a proposition as "My friend has stopped writing to me" is sometimes neither true nor false, we are speaking inaccurately. For we seem to be saying that neither it nor its contradictory is true. Whereas what we mean, or anyhow should mean, is that neither it nor its apparent contradictory is true. And its apparent contradictory is really only its contrary. Thus we preserve the law of excluded middle by showing that the negating of a sentence does not always yield the contradictory of the proposition originally expressed.

There is no need to give further examples. Whatever instance we care to take, we shall always find that the situations in which a logical or mathematical principle might appear to be confuted are accounted for in such a way as to leave the principle unassailed. And this indicates that Mill was wrong in supposing that a situation could arise which would overthrow a mathematical truth. The principles of logic and mathematics are true universally simply because we never allow them to be anything else. And the reason for this is that we cannot abandon them without contradicting ourselves, without sinning against the rules which govern the use of language, and so making our utterances self-stultifying. In other words, the truths of logic and mathematics are analytic propositions or tautologies. In saying this we are making what will be held to be an extremely controversial statement, and we must now proceed to make its implications clear.

The most familiar definition of an analytic proposition, or judgement, as he called it, is that given by Kant. He said[2] that an analytic judgement was one in which the predicate B belonged to the subject A as something which was covertly contained in the concept of A. He contrasted analytic with synthetic judgements, in which the predicate B lay outside the subject A, although it did stand in connection with it. Analytic judgements, he explains, "add nothing through the predicate to the concept of the subject, but merely break it up into those constituent concepts that have all along been thought in it, although confusedly." Synthetic judgements, on the other hand, "add to the concept of the subject a predicate which has not been in any wise thought in it, and which no analysis could possibly extract from it." Kant gives "all bodies are extended" as an example of an analytic judgement, on the ground that the required predicate can be extracted from the concept of "body," "in accordance with the principle of contradiction"; as an example of a synthetic judgement, he gives "all bodies are heavy." He refers also to "$7 + 5 = 12$" as a synthetic judgement, on the ground that the concept of twelve is by no means already thought in merely thinking the union of seven and five. And he appears to regard this as tantamount to saying that the judgement does not rest on the principle of contradiction alone. He holds, also, that through analytic judgements our knowledge is not extended as it is through synthetic judgements. For in analytic judgements "the concept which I already have is merely set forth and made intelligible to me."

I think that this is a fair summary of Kant's account of the distinction between analytic and synthetic propositions, but I do not think that it succeeds in making the distinction clear. For even if we pass over the difficulties which arise out of the use of the vague term "concept," and the unwarranted assumption that every judgement, as well as every German or English sentence, can be said to have a subject and a predicate, there remains still this crucial defect. Kant does not give one straightforward criterion for distinguishing between analytic and synthetic propositions; he gives two distinct criteria, which are by no means equivalent. Thus his ground for holding that the proposition "$7 + 5 = 12$" is synthetic is, as we have seen, that the subjective intension of "$7 + 5$" does not comprise the subjective intension of "12"; whereas his ground for holding that "all bodies are extended" is an analytic proposition is that it rests on the principle of contradiction alone. That is, he employs a psychological criterion in the first of these examples, and a logical criterion in the second, and takes their equivalence for granted. But, in fact, a proposition which is synthetic according to the former criterion may very well be analytic according to the latter. For, as we have already pointed out, it is possible for symbols to be synonymous without having the same intensional meaning for anyone: and accordingly from the fact that one can think of the sum of seven and five without necessarily thinking of twelve, it by no means follows that the proposition "$7 + 5 = 12$" can be denied without self-contradiction. From the rest of his argument, it is clear that it is this logical proposition, and not any psychological proposition, that Kant is really anxious to establish. His use of the psychological criterion leads him to think that he has established it, when he has not.

I think that we can preserve the logical import of Kant's distinction between analytic and synthetic propositions, while avoiding the confusions which mar his actual account of it, if we say that a proposition is analytic when its validity depends solely on the definitions of the symbols it contains, and synthetic when its validity is determined by the facts of experience. Thus, the proposition "There are ants which have established a system of slavery" is a synthetic proposition. For we cannot tell whether it is true or false merely by considering the definitions of the symbols which constitute it. We have to resort to actual observation of the behaviour of ants. On the other hand, the proposition "Either some ants are parasitic or none are" is an analytic proposition. For one need not resort to observation to discover that there either are or are not ants which are parasitic. If one knows what is the function of the words "either," "or," and "not," then one can see that any proposition of the form "Either p is true or p is not true" is valid independently of experience. Accordingly, all such propositions are analytic.

It is to be noticed that the proposition "Either some ants are parasitic or none are" provides no information whatsoever about the behaviour of ants, or, indeed, about any matter of fact. And this applies to all analytic propositions. They none of them provide any information about any matter of fact. In other words, they are entirely devoid of factual content. And it is for this reason that no experience can confute them.

When we say that analytic propositions are devoid of factual content, and consequently that they say nothing, we are not suggesting that they are senseless in the way that metaphysical utterances are senseless. For, although they give us no information about any empirical situation, they do enlighten us by illustrating the way in which we use certain symbols. Thus if I say, "Nothing can be coloured in different ways at the same time with respect to the same part of itself," I am not saying anything about the properties of any actual thing; but I am not talking nonsense. I am expressing an analytic proposition, which records our determination to call a colour expanse which differs in quality from a neighboring colour expanse a different part of a given thing. In other words, I am simply calling attention to the implications of a certain linguistic usage. Similarly, in saying that if all Bretons are Frenchmen, and all Frenchmen Europeans, then all Bretons are Europeans, I am not describing any matter of fact. But I am showing that in the statement that all Bretons are Frenchmen, and all Frenchmen Europeans, the further statement that all Bretons are Europeans is implicitly contained. And I am thereby indicating the convention which governs our usage of the words "if" and "all."

We see, then, that there is a sense in which analytic propositions do give us new knowledge. They call attention to linguistic usages, of which we might otherwise not be conscious, and they reveal unsuspected implications in our assertions and beliefs. But we can see also that there is a sense in which they may be said to add nothing to our knowledge. For they tell us only what we may be said to know already. Thus, if I know that the existence of May Queens is a relic of tree-worship, and I discover that May Queens still exist in England, I can employ the tautology "If p implies q and p is true, q is true" to show that there still exists a relic of tree-worship in England. But in saying that there are still May Queens in England, and that the existence of May Queens is a relic of tree-worship, I have already asserted the existence in England of a relic of tree-worship. The use of the tautology does, indeed, enable me to make this concealed assertion explicit. But it does not provide me with any new knowledge, in the sense in which empirical evidence that the election of May Queens had been forbidden by law would provide me with new knowledge. If one had to set forth all the information one possessed, with regard to matters of fact, one would not write down any analytic propositions. But one would make use of analytic propositions in compiling one's encyclopaedia, and would thus come to include propositions which one would otherwise have overlooked. And, besides enabling one to make one's list of information complete, the formulation of analytic propositions would enable one to make sure that the synthetic propositions of which the list was composed formed a self-consistent system. By showing which ways of combining propositions resulted in contradictions, they would prevent one from including incompatible propositions and so making the list self-stultifying. But in so far as we had actually used such words as "all" and "or" and "not" without falling into self-contradiction, we might be said already to know what was revealed in the formulation of analytic propositions illustrating the rules which govern our usage of these logical particles. So that here again we are justified in saying that analytic propositions do not increase our knowledge.

The analytic character of the truths of formal logic was obscured in the traditional logic through its being insufficiently formalized. For in speaking always of judgements, instead of propositions, and introducing irrelevant psychological questions, the traditional logic gave the impression of being concerned in some specially intimate way with the workings of thought. What it was actually concerned with was the formal relationship of classes, as is shown by the fact that all its principles of inference are subsumed in the Boolean class-calculus, which is subsumed in its turn in the propositional calculus of Russell and Whitehead.[3] Their system, expounded in *Principia Mathematica,* makes it clear that formal logic is not concerned with the properties of men's minds, much less with the properties of material objects, but simply with the possibility of combining propositions by means of logical particles into analytic propositions, and with studying the formal relationship of these analytic propositions, in virtue of which one is deducible from another. Their procedure is to exhibit the propositions of formal logic as a deductive system, based on five primitive propositions, subsequently reduced in number to one. Hereby the distinction between logical truths and principles of inference, which was maintained in the Aristotelian logic, very properly disappears. Every principle of inference is put forward as a logical truth and every logical truth can serve as a principle of inference. The three Aristotelian "laws of thought," the law of identity, the law of excluded middle, and the law of non-contradiction are incorporated in the system, but they are not considered more important than the other analytic propositions. They are not reckoned among the premises of the system. And the system of Russell and Whitehead itself is probably only one among many possible logics, each of which is composed of tautologies as interesting to the logician as the arbitrarily selected Aristotelian "laws of thought."[4]

A point which is not sufficiently brought out by Russell, if indeed it is recognised by him at all, is that every logical proposition is valid in its own right. Its validity does not depend on its being incorporated in a system, and deduced from certain propositions which are taken as self-evident. The construction of systems of logic is useful as a means of discovering and certifying analytic propositions, but it is not in principle essential even for this purpose. For it is possible to conceive of a symbolism in which every analytic proposition could be seen to be analytic in virtue of its form alone.

The fact that the validity of an analytic proposition in no way depends on its being deducible from other analytic propositions is our justification for disregarding the question whether the propositions of mathematics are reducible to propositions of formal logic, in the way that Russell supposed.[5] For even if it is the case that the definition of a cardinal number as a class of classes similar to a given class is circular, and it is not possible to reduce mathematical notions to purely logical notions, it will still remain true that the propositions of mathematics are analytic propositions. They will form a special class of analytic propositions, containing special terms, but they will be none the less analytic for that. For the criterion of an analytic proposition is that its validity should follow simply from the definition of the terms contained in it, and this condition is fulfilled by the propositions of pure mathematics.

The mathematical propositions which one might most pardonably suppose to be synthetic are the propositions of geometry. For it is natural for us to think, as Kant thought, that geometry is the study of the properties of physical space, and consequently that its propositions have factual content. And if we believe this, and also recognise that the truths of geometry are necessary and certain, then we may be inclined to accept Kant's hypothesis that space is the form of intuition of our outer sense, a form imposed by us on the matter of sensation, as the only possible explanation of our *a priori* knowledge of these synthetic propositions. But while the view that pure geometry is concerned with physical space was plausible enough in Kant's day, when the geometry of Euclid was the only geometry known, the subsequent invention of non-Euclidean geometries has shown it to be mistaken. We see now that the axioms of a geometry are simply definitions, and that the theorems of a geometry are simply the logical consequences of these definitions.[6] A geometry is not in itself about physical space; in itself it cannot be said to be "about" anything. But we can use a geometry to reason about physical space. That is to say, once we have given the axioms a physical interpretation, we can proceed to apply the theorems to the objects which satisfy the axioms. Whether a geometry can be applied to the actual physical world or not, is an empirical question which falls outside the scope of the geometry itself. There is no sense, therefore, in asking which of the various geometries known to us are false and which are true. In so far as they are all free from contradiction, they are all true. What one can ask is which of them is the most useful on any given occasion, which of them can be applied most easily and most fruitfully to an actual empirical situation. But the proposition which states that a certain application of a geometry is possible is not itself a proposition of that geometry. All that the geometry itself tells us is that if anything can be brought under the definitions, it will also satisfy the theorems. It is therefore a purely logical system, and its propositions are purely analytic propositions.

It might be objected that the use made of diagrams in geometrical treatises shows that geometrical reasoning is not purely abstract and logical, but depends on our intuition of the properties of figures. In fact, however, the use of diagrams is not essential to completely rigorous geometry. The diagrams are introduced as an aid to our reason. They provide us with a particular application of the geometry, and so assist us to perceive the more general truth that the axioms of the geometry involve certain consequences. But the fact that most of us need the help of an example to make us aware of those consequences does not show that the relation between them and the axioms is not a purely logical relation. It shows merely that our intellects are unequal to the task of carrying out very abstract processes of reasoning without the assistance of intuition. In other words, it has no bearing on the nature of geometrical propositions, but is simply an empirical fact about ourselves. Moreover, the appeal to intuition, though generally of psychological value, is also a source of danger to the geometer. He is tempted to make assumptions which are accidentally true of the particular figure he is taking as an illustration, but do not follow from his axioms. It has, indeed, been shown that Euclid himself was guilty of this, and consequently that the presence of the figure is essential to some of his proofs.[7] This shows that his system is not, as he presents it, completely rigorous, although of course it can be made so. It does not show that the presence of the figure is essential to a truly rigorous geometrical proof. To suppose that it did would be to take as a necessary feature of all geometries what is really only an incidental defect in one particular geometrical system.

We conclude, then, that the propositions of pure geometry are analytic. And this leads us to reject Kant's hypothesis that geometry deals with the form of intuition of our outer sense. For the ground for this hypothesis was that it alone explained how the propositions of geometry could be both true *a priori* and synthetic: and we have seen that they are not synthetic. Similarly our view that the propositions of arithmetic are not synthetic but analytic leads us to reject the Kantian hypothesis[8] that arithmetic is concerned with our pure intuition of time, the form of our inner sense. And thus we are able to dismiss Kant's transcendental aesthetic without having to bring forward the epistemological difficulties which it is commonly said to involve. For the only argument which can be brought in favour of Kant's theory is that it alone explains certain "facts." And now we have found that the "facts" which it purports to explain are not facts at all. For while it is true that we have *a priori* knowledge of necessary propositions, it is not true, as Kant supposed, that any of these necessary propositions are synthetic. They are without exception analytic propositions, or, in other words, tautologies.

We have already explained how it is that these analytic propositions are necessary and certain. We saw that the reason why they cannot be confuted in experience is that they do not make any assertion about the empirical world. They simply record our determination to use words in a certain fashion. We cannot deny them without infringing the conventions which are presupposed by our very denial, and so falling into self-contradiction. And this is the sole ground of their necessity. As Wittgenstein puts it, our justification for holding that the world could not conceivably disobey the laws of logic is simply that we could not say of an unlogical world how it would look.[9] And just as the validity of an analytic proposition is independent of the nature of the external world; so is it independent of the nature of our minds. It is perfectly conceivable that we should have employed different linguistic conventions from those which we actually do employ. But whatever these conventions might be, the tautologies in which we recorded them would always be necessary. For any denial of them would be self-stultifying.

We see, then, that there is nothing mysterious about the apodeictic certainty of logic and mathematics. Our knowledge that no observation can ever confute the proposition "$7 + 5 = 12$" depends simply on the fact that the symbolic expression "7 + 5" is synonymous with "12," just as our knowledge that every oculist is an eye-doctor depends on the fact that the symbol "eye-doctor" is synonymous with "oculist." And the same explanation holds good for every other *a priori* truth.

What is mysterious at first sight is that these tautologies should on occasion be so surprising, that there should be in mathematics and logic the possibility of invention and discovery. As Poincaré says: "If all the assertions which mathematics puts forward can be derived from one another by formal logic, mathematics cannot amount to anything more than an immense tautology. Logical inference can teach us nothing essentially new, and if everything is to proceed from the principle of identity, everything must be reducible to it. But can we really allow that these theorems which fill so many books serve no other purpose than to say in a round-about fashion 'A = A'?"[10] Poincaré finds this incredible. His own theory is that the sense of invention and discovery in mathematics belongs to it in virtue of mathematical induction, the principle that what is true for the number 1, and true for $n + 1$ when it is true for n,[11] is true for all numbers. And he claims that this is a synthetic *a priori* principle. It is, in fact, *a priori,* but it is not synthetic. It is a defining principle of the natural numbers, serving to distinguish them from such numbers as the infinite cardinal numbers, to which it cannot be applied.[12] Moreover, we must remember that discoveries can be made, not only in arithmetic, but also in geometry and formal logic, where no use is made of mathematical induction. So that even if Poincaré were right about mathematical induction, he would not have provided a satisfactory explanation of the paradox that a mere body of tautologies can be so interesting and so surprising.

The true explanation is very simple. The power of logic and mathematics to surprise us depends, like their usefulness, on the limitations of our reason. A being whose intellect was infinitely powerful would take no interest in logic and mathematics.[13] For he would be able to see at a glance everything that his definitions implied, and, accordingly, could never learn anything from logical inference which he was not fully conscious of already. But our intellects are not of this order. It is only a minute proportion of the consequences of our definitions that we are able to detect at a glance. Even so simple a tautology as "91 × 79 = 7189" is beyond the scope of our immediate apprehension. To assure ourselves that "7189" is synonymous with "91 × 79" we have to resort to calculation, which is simply a process of tautological transformation — that is, a process by which we change the form of expressions without altering their significance. The multiplication tables are rules for carrying out this process in arithmetic, just as the laws of logic are rules for the tautological transformation of sentences expressed in logical symbolism or in ordinary language. As the process of calculation is carried out more or less mechanically, it is easy for us to make a slip and so unwittingly contradict ourselves. And this accounts for the existence of logical and mathematical "falsehoods," which otherwise might appear paradoxical. Clearly the risk of error in logical reasoning is proportionate to the length and the complexity of the process of calculation. And in the same way, the more complex an analytic proposition is, the more chance it has of interesting and surprising us.

It is easy to see that the danger of error in logical reasoning can be minimized by the introduction of symbolic devices, which enable us to express highly complex tautologies in a conveniently simple form. And this gives us an opportunity for the exercise of invention in the pursuit of logical enquiries. For a well-chosen definition will call our attention to analytic truths, which would otherwise have escaped us. And the framing of definitions which are useful and fruitful may well be regarded as a creative act.

Having thus shown that there is no inexplicable paradox involved in the view that the truths of logic and mathematics are all of them analytic, we may safely adopt it as the only satisfactory explanation of their *a priori* necessity. And in adopting it we vindicate the empiricist claim that there can be no *a priori* knowledge of reality. For we show that the truths of pure reason, the propositions which we know to be valid independently of all experience, are so only in virtue of their lack of factual content. To say that a proposition is true *a priori* is to say that it is a tautology. And tautologies, though they may serve to guide us in our empirical search for knowledge, do not in themselves contain any information about any matter of fact.

NOTES

1. *Critique of Pure Reason,* 2nd ed., Introduction, section i.
2. *Critique of Pure Reason,* 2nd ed., Introduction, sections iv and v.
3. Vide Karl Menger, "Die Neue Logik," *Krise und Neuaufbau in den Exakten Wissenschaften,* pp. 94-6; and Lewis and Langford, *Symbolic Logic,* Chapter v.
4. Vide Lewis and Langford, *Symbolic Logic,* Chapter vii, for an elaboration of this point.
5. Vide *Introduction to Mathematical Philosophy,* Chapter ii.
6. cf.H. Poincaré, *La Science et l'Hypothèse,* Part II, Chapter iii.
7. cf.M. Black, *The Nature of Mathematics,* p. 154.
8. This hypothesis is not mentioned in the *Critique of Pure Reason,* but was maintained by Kant at an earlier date.
9. *Tractatus Logico-Philosophicus,* 3.031.
10. *La Science et l'hypothèse,* Part I, Chapter i.
11. This was wrongly stated in previous editions as "true for n when it is true for $n + 1$."
12. cf. B. Russell's *Introduction to Mathematical Philosophy,* Chapter iii, p. 27.
13. cf. Hans Hahn, "Logik, Mathematik und Naturerkennen," *Einheitswissenschaft,* Heft II, p. 18. "Ein allwissendes Wesen braucht keine Logik und keine Mathematik."

16. Truth and Probability

A. J. Ayer

Having shown how the validity of *a priori* propositions is determined, we shall now put forward the criterion which is used to determine the validity of empirical propositions. In this way we shall complete our theory of truth. For it is easy to see that the purpose of a "theory of truth" is simply to describe the criteria by which the validity of the various kinds of propositions is determined. And as all propositions are either empirical or *a priori*, and we have already dealt with the *a priori*, all that is now required to complete our theory of truth is an indication of the way in which we determine the validity of empirical propositions. And this we shall shortly proceed to give.

* * *

In saying that we propose to show "how propositions are validated," we do not of course mean to suggest that all propositions are validated in the same way. On the contrary we lay stress on the fact that the criterion by which we determine the validity of an *a priori* or analytic proposition is not sufficient to determine the validity of an empirical or synthetic proposition. For it is characteristic of empirical propositions that their validity is not purely formal. To say that a geometrical proposition, or a system of geometrical propositions, is false is to say that it is self-contradictory. But an empirical proposition, or a system of empirical propositions, may be free from contradiction, and still be false. It is said to be false, not because it is formally defective, but because it fails to satisfy some material criterion. And it is our business to discover what this criterion is.

We have been assuming so far that empirical propositions, though they differ from *a priori* propositions in their method of validation, do not differ in this respect among themselves. Having found that all *a priori* propositions are validated in the same way, we have taken it for granted that this holds good of empirical propositions also. But this assumption would be challenged by a great many philosophers who agree with us in most other respects.[1] They would say that among empirical propositions, there was a special class of propositions whose validity consisted in the fact that they directly recorded an immediate experience. They maintain that these propositions, which we may call "ostensive" propositions, are not mere hypotheses but are absolutely certain. For they are supposed to be purely demonstrative in character, and so incapable of being refuted by any subsequent experience. And they are, on this view, the only empirical propositions which are certain. The rest are hypotheses which derive what validity they have from their relationship to the ostensive propositions. For their probability is held to be determined by the number and variety of the ostensive propositions which can be deduced from them.

That no synthetic proposition which is not purely ostensive can be logically indubitable, may be granted without further ado. What we cannot admit is that any synthetic proposition can be purely ostensive.[2] For the notion of an ostensive proposition appears to involve a contradiction in terms. It implies that there could be a sentence which consisted of purely demonstrative symbols and was at the same time intelligible. And this is not even a logical possibility. A sentence which consisted of demonstrative symbols would not express a genuine proposition. It would be a mere ejaculation, in no way characterizing that to which it was supposed to refer.[3]

The fact is that one cannot in language point to an object without describing it. If a sentence is to express a proposition, it cannot merely name a situation; it must say something about it. And in describing a situation, one is not merely "registering" a sense-content; one is classifying it in some way or other, and this means going beyond what is immediately given. But a proposition would be ostensive only if it recorded what was immediately experienced, without referring in any way beyond. And as this is not possible, it follows that no genuine synthetic proposition can be ostensive, and consequently that none can be absolutely certain.

*   *   *

However, we shall not waste time speculating about the origins of this false philosophical doctrine. Such questions may be left to the historian. Our business is to show that the doctrine is false, and this we may fairly claim to have done. It should now be clear that there are no absolutely certain empirical propositions. It is only tautologies that are certain. Empirical propositions are one and all hypotheses, which may be confirmed or discredited in actual sense-experience. And the propositions in which we record the observations that verify these hypotheses are themselves hypotheses which are subject to the test of further sense-experience. Thus there are no final propositions. When we set about verifying a hypothesis we may make an observation which satisfies us at the time. But the very next moment we may doubt whether the observation really did take place, and require a fresh process of verification in order to be reassured. And, logically, there is no reason why this procedure should not continue indefinitely, each act of verification supplying us with a new hypothesis, which in turn leads to a further series of acts of verification. In practice we assume that certain types of observation are trustworthy, and admit the hypothesis that they have occurred without bothering to embark on a process of verification. But we do this, not from obedience to any logical necessity, but from a purely pragmatic motive, the nature of which will shortly be explained.

When one speaks of hypotheses being verified in experience, it is important to bear in mind that it is never just a single hypothesis which an observation confirms or discredits, but always a system of hypotheses. Suppose that we have devised an experiment to test the validity of a scientific "law." The law states that in certain conditions a certain type of observation will always be forthcoming. It may happen in this particular instance that we make the observation as our law predicts. Then it is not only the law itself that is substantiated, but also the hypotheses which assert the existence of the requisite conditions. For it is only by assuming the existence of these conditions that we can hold that our observation is relevant to the law. Alternatively, we may fail to make the expected observation. And in that case we may conclude that the law is invalidated by our experiment. But we are not obliged to adopt this conclusion. If we wish to preserve our law, we may do so by abandoning one or more of the other relevant hypotheses. We may say that the conditions were really not what they seemed to be, and construct a theory to explain how we came to be mistaken about them; or we may say that some factor which we had dismissed as irrelevant was really relevant, and support this view with supplementary hypotheses. We may even assume that the experiment was really not unfavourable, and that our negative observation was hallucinatory. And in that case we must bring the hypotheses which record the conditions that are deemed necessary for the occurrence of a hallucination into line with the hypotheses which describe the conditions in which this observation is supposed to have taken place. Otherwise we shall be maintaining incompatible hypotheses. And this is the one thing that we may not do. But, so long as we take suitable steps to keep our system of hypotheses free from self-contradiction, we may adopt any explanation of our observations that we choose. In practice our choice of an explanation is guided by certain considerations, which we shall presently describe. And these considerations have the effect of limiting our freedom in the matter of preserving and rejecting hypotheses. But logically our freedom is unlimited. Any procedure which is self-consistent will satisfy the requirements of logic.

It appears, then, that the "facts of experience" can never compel us to abandon a hypothesis. A man can always sustain his convictions in the face of apparently hostile evidence if he is prepared to make the necessary *ad hoc* assumptions. But although any particular instance in which a cherished hypotheses appears to be refuted can always be explained away, there must still remain the possibility that the hypothesis will ultimately be abandoned. Otherwise it is not a genuine hypothesis. For a proposition whose validity we are resolved to maintain in the face of any experience is not a hypothesis at all, but a definition. In other words, it is not a synthetic but an analytic proposition.

*   *   *

What we must do to solve this problem is to ask ourselves, What is the purpose of formulating hypotheses? Why do we construct these systems in the first place? The answer is that they are designed to enable us to anticipate the course of our sensations. The function of a system of hypotheses is to warn us beforehand what will be our experience in a certain field — to enable us to make accurate predictions. The hypotheses may therefore be described as rules which govern our expectation of future experience. There is no need to say why we require such rules. It is plain that on our ability to make successful predictions depends the satisfaction of even our simplest desires, including the desire to survive.

Now the essential feature of our procedure with regard to the formulation of these rules is the use of past experience as a guide to the future. We have already remarked upon this, when discussing the so-called problem of induction, and we have seen that there is no sense in asking for a theoretical justification of this policy. The philosopher must be content to record the facts of scientific procedure. If he seeks to justify it, beyond showing that it is self-consistent, he will find himself involved in spurious problems. This is a point which we stressed earlier on, and we shall not trouble to argue it over again.

We remark, then, as a fact that our forecasts of future experience are in some way determined by what we have experienced in the past. And this fact explains why science, which is essentially predictive, is also to some extent a description of our experience.[4] But it is noticeable that we tend to ignore those features of our experience which cannot be made the basis of fruitful generalizations. And furthermore, that which we do describe, we describe with some latitude. As Poincaré puts it: "One does not limit oneself to generalizing experience, one corrects it; and the physicist who consented to abstain from these corrections and really be satisfied with bare experience would be obliged to promulgate the most extraordinary laws."[5]

But even if we do not follow past experience slavishly in making our predictions, we are guided by it to a very large extent. And this explains why we do not simply disregard the conclusion of an unfavourable experiment. We assume that a system of hypotheses which has broken down once is likely to break down again. We could, of course, assume that it had not broken down at all, but we believe that this assumption would not pay us so well as the recognition that the system had really failed us, and therefore required some alteration if it was not to fail us again. We alter our system because we think that by altering it we shall make it a more efficient instrument for the anticipation of experience. And this belief is derived from our guiding principle that, broadly speaking, the future course of our sensations will be in accordance with the past.

This desire of ours to have an efficient set of rules for our predictions, which causes us to take notice of unfavourable observations, is also the factor which primarily determines how we adjust our system to cover the new data. It is true that we are infected with a spirit of conservatism and would rather make small alterations than large ones. It is disagreeable and troublesome for us to admit that our existing system is radically defective. And it is true that, other things being equal, we prefer simple to complex hypotheses, again from the desire to save ourselves trouble. But if experience leads us to suppose that radical changes are necessary, then we are prepared to make them, even though they do complicate our system, as the recent history of physics shows. When an observation runs counter to our most confident expectations, the easiest course is to ignore it, or at any rate to explain it away. If we do not do this, it is because we think that, if we leave our system as it is, we shall suffer further disappointments. We think it will increase the efficiency of our system as an instrument of prediction if we make it compatible with the hypothesis that the unexpected observation occurred. Whether we are right in thinking this is a question which cannot be settled by argument. We can only wait and see if our new system is successful in practice. If it is not, we alter it once again.

We have now obtained the information we required in order to answer our original question, "What is the criterion by which we test the validity of an empirical proposition?" The answer is that we test the validity of an empirical hypothesis by seeing whether it actually fulfills the function which it is designed to fulfill. And we have seen that the function of an empirical hypothesis is to enable us to anticipate experience. Accordingly, if an observation to which a given proposition is relevant conforms to our expectations, the truth of that proposition is confirmed. One cannot say that the proposition has been proved absolutely valid, because it is still possible that a future observation will discredit it. But one can say that its probability has been increased. If the observation is contrary to our expectations, then the status of the proposition is jeopardised. We may preserve it by adopting or abandoning other hypotheses: or we may consider it to have been confuted. But even if it is rejected in consequence of an unfavourable observation, one cannot say that it has been invalidated absolutely. For it is still possible that future observations will lead us to reinstate it. One can say only that its probability has been diminished.

*   *   *

NOTES

1. e.g. M. Schlick, "Über das fundament der Erkenntnis," *Erkenntnis,* Band IV, Heft II; and "Facts and Propositions," *Analysis,* Vol. II, No. 5; and B. von Juhos, "Empiricism and Physicalism," *Analysis,* Vol. II, No. 6.
2. See also Rudolf Carnap, "Über Protokolsätze," *Erkenntnis,* Band III; Otto Neurath, "Protokolsätze," *Erkenntnis,* Band III; and "Radikaler Physikalismus und 'Wirkliche Welt,'" *Erkenntnis,* Band IV, Heft V; and Carl Hempel, "On the Logical Positivists' Theory of Truth," *Analysis,* Vol. II, No. 4.
3. This question is reviewed in the Introduction, pp. 10-11 [of *Language, Truth, and Logic.* —Ed.]
4. It will be seen that even "descriptions of past experience" are in a sense predictive since they function as "rules for the anticipation of future experience." See the end of this chapter for an elaboration of this point.
5. *La Science et l'Hypothèse,* Part IV, Chapter ix, p. 170.

17. Critique of Ethics and Theology

A. J. Ayer

There is still one objection to be met before we can claim to have justified our view that all synthetic propositions are empirical hypotheses. This objection is based on the common supposition that our speculative knowledge is of two distinct kinds—that which relates to questions of empirical fact, and that which relates to questions of value. It will be said that "statements of value" are genuine synthetic propositions, but that they cannot with any show of justice be represented as hypotheses, which are used to predict the course of our sensations; and, accordingly, that the existence of ethics and aesthetics as branches of speculative knowledge presents an insuperable objection to our radical empiricist thesis.

In face of this objection, it is our business to give an account of "judgments of value" which is both satisfactory in itself and consistent with our general empiricist principles. We shall set ourselves to show that in so far as statements of value are significant, they are ordinary "scientific" statements; and that in so far as they are not scientific, they are not in the literal sense significant, but are simply expressions of emotion which can be neither true nor false. In maintaining this view, we may confine ourselves for the present to the case of ethical statements. What is said about them will be found to apply, *mutatis mutandis,* to the case of aesthetic statements also.[1]

The ordinary system of ethics, as elaborated in the works of ethical philosophers, is very far from being a homogeneous whole. Not only is it apt to contain pieces of metaphysics, and analyses of non-ethical concepts: its actual ethical contents are themselves of very different kinds. We may divide them, indeed, into four main classes. There are, first of all, propositions which express definitions of ethical terms, or judgements about the legitimacy or possibility of certain definitions. Secondly, there are propositions describing the phenomena of moral experience, and their causes. Thirdly, there are exhortations to moral virtue. And, lastly, there are actual ethical judgements. It is unfortunately the case that the distinction between these four classes, plain as it is, is commonly ignored by ethical philosophers; with the result that it is often very difficult to tell from their works what it is that they are seeking to discover or prove.

In fact, it is easy to see that only the first of our four classes, namely that which comprises the propositions relating to the definitions of ethical terms, can be said to constitute ethical philosophy. The propositions which describe the phenomena of moral experience, and their causes, must be assigned to the science of psychology, or sociology. The exhortations to moral virtue are not propositions at all, but ejaculations or commands which are designed to provoke the reader to action of a certain sort. Accordingly, they do not belong to any branch of philosophy or science. As for the expressions of ethical judgements, we have not yet determined how they should be classified. But inasmuch as they are certainly neither definitions nor comments upon definitions, nor quotations, we may say decisively that they do not belong to ethical philosophy. A strictly philosophical treatise on ethics should therefore make no ethical pronouncements. But it should, by giving an analysis of ethical terms, show what is the category to which all such pronouncements belong. And this is what we are now about to do.

A question which is often discussed by ethical philosophers is whether it is possible to find definitions which would reduce all ethical terms to one or two fundamental terms. But this question, though it undeniably belongs to ethical philosophy, is not relevant to our present enquiry. We are not now concerned to discover which term, within the sphere of ethical terms, is to be taken as fundamental; whether, for example, "good" can be defined in terms of "right" or "right" in terms of "good," or both in terms of "value." What we are interested in is the possibility of reducing the whole sphere of ethical terms to non-ethical terms. We are enquiring whether statements of ethical value can be translated into statements of empirical fact.

That they can be so translated is the contention of those ethical philosophers who are commonly called subjectivists, and of those who are known as utilitarians. For the utilitarian defines the rightness of actions, and the goodness of ends, in terms of the pleasure, or happiness, or satisfaction, to which they give rise; the subjectivist, in terms of the feelings of approval which a certain person, or group of people, has towards them. Each of these types of definition makes moral judgements into a sub-class of psychological or sociological judgements; and for this reason they are very attractive to us. For, if either was correct, it would follow that ethical assertions were not generically different from the factual assertions which are ordinarily contrasted with them; and the account which we have already given of empirical hypotheses would apply to them also.

Nevertheless we shall not adopt either a subjectivist or a utilitarian analysis of ethical terms. We reject the subjectivist view that to call an action right, or a thing good, is to say that it is generally approved of, because it is not self-contradictory to assert that some actions which are generally approved of are not right, or that some things which are generally approved of are not good.

And we reject the alternative subjectivist view that a man who asserts that a certain action is right, or that a certain thing is good, is saying that he himself approves of it, on the ground that a man who confessed that he sometimes approved of what was bad or wrong would not be contradicting himself. And a similar argument is fatal to utilitarianism. We cannot agree that to call an action right is to say that of all the actions possible in the circumstances it would cause, or be likely to cause, the greatest happiness, or the greatest balance of pleasure over pain, or the greatest balance of satisfied over unsatisfied desire, because we find that it is not self-contradictory to say that it is sometimes wrong to perform the action which would actually or probably cause the greatest happiness, or the greatest balance of pleasure over pain, or of satisfied over unsatisfied desire. And since it is not self-contradictory to say that some pleasant things are not good, or that some bad things are desired, it cannot be the case that the sentence "*x* is good" is equivalent to "*x* is pleasant," or to "*x* is desired." And to every other variant of utilitarianism with which I am acquainted the same objection can be made. And therefore we should, I think, conclude that the validity of ethical judgements is not determined by the felicific tendencies of actions, any more than by the nature of people's feelings; but that it must be regarded as "absolute" or "intrinsic," and not empirically calculable.

If we say this, we are not, of course, denying that it is possible to invent a language in which all ethical symbols are definable in non-ethical terms, or even that it is desirable to invent such a language and adopt it in place of our own; what we are denying is that the suggested reduction of ethical to non-ethical statements is consistent with the conventions of our actual language. That is, we reject utilitarianism and subjectivism, not as proposals to replace our existing ethical notions by new ones, but as analyses of our existing ethical notions. Our contention is simply that, in our language, sentences which contain normative ethical symbols are not equivalent to sentences which express psychological propositions, or indeed empirical propositions of any kind.

It is advisable here to make it plain that it is only normative ethical symbols, and not descriptive ethical symbols, that are held by us to be indefinable in factual terms. There is a danger of confusing these two types of symbols, because they are commonly constituted by signs of the same sensible form. Thus a complex sign of the form "*x* is wrong" may constitute a sentence which expresses a moral judgement concerning a certain type of conduct, or it may constitute a sentence which states that a certain type of conduct is repugnant to the moral sense of a particular society. In the latter case, the symbol "wrong" is a descriptive ethical symbol, and the sentence in which it occurs expresses an ordinary sociological proposition; in the former case, the symbol "wrong" is a normative ethical symbol, and the sentence in which it occurs does not, we maintain, express an empirical proposition at all. It is only with normative ethics that we are at present concerned; so that whenever ethical symbols are used in the course of this argument without qualification, they are always to be interpreted as symbols of the normative type.

In admitting that normative ethical concepts are irreducible to empirical concepts, we seem to be leaving the way clear for the "absolutist" view of ethics — that is, the view that statements of value are not controlled by observation, as ordinary empirical propositions are, but only by a mysterious "intellectual intuition." A feature of this theory, which is seldom recognized by its advocates, is that it makes statements of value unverifiable. For it is notorious that what seems intuitively certain to one person may seem doubtful, or even false, to another. So that unless it is possible to provide some criterion by which one may decide between conflicting intuitions, a mere appeal to intuition is worthless as a test of a proposition's validity. But in the case of moral judgements, no such criterion can be given. Some moralists claim to settle the matter by saying that they "know" that their own moral judgements are correct. But such an assertion is of purely psychological interest, and has not the slightest tendency to prove the validity of any moral judgement. For dissentient moralists may equally well "know" that their ethical views are correct. And, as far as subjective certainty goes, there will be nothing to choose between them. When such differences of opinion arise in connection with an ordinary empirical proposition, one may attempt to resolve them by referring to, or actually carrying out, some relevant empirical test. But with regard to ethical statements, there is, on the "absolutist" or "intuitionist" theory, no relevant empirical test. We are therefore justified in saying that on this theory ethical statements are held to be unverifiable. They are, of course, also held to be genuine synthetic propositions.

Considering the use which we have made of the principle that a synthetic proposition is significant only if it is empirically verifiable, it is clear that the acceptance of an "absolutist" theory of ethics would undermine the whole of our main argument. And as we have already rejected the "naturalistic" theories which are commonly supposed to provide the only alternative to "absolutism" in ethics, we seem to have reached a difficult position. We shall meet the difficulty by showing that the correct treatment of ethical statements is afforded by a third theory, which is wholly compatible with our radical empiricism.

We begin by admitting that the fundamental ethical concepts are unanalysable, inasmuch as there is no criterion by which one can test the validity of the judgements in which they occur. So far we are in agreement with the absolutists. But, unlike the absolutists, we are able to give an explanation of this fact about ethical concepts. We say that the reason why they are unanalysable is that they are mere pseudo-concepts. The presence of an ethical symbol in a proposition adds nothing to its factual content. Thus if I say to someone, "You acted wrongly in stealing that money," I am not stating anything more than if I had simply said, "You stole that money." In adding that this action is wrong I am not making any further statement about it. I am simply evincing my moral disapproval of it. It is as if I had said, "You stole that money," in a peculiar tone of horror, or written it with the addition of some special exclamation marks. The tone, or the exclamation marks, adds nothing to the literal meaning of the sentence. It merely serves to show that the expression of it is attended by certain feelings in the speaker.

If now I generalise my previous statement and say, "Stealing money is wrong," I produce a sentence which has no factual meaning — that is, expresses no proposition which can be either true or false. It is as if I had written "Stealing money!!" — where the shape and thickness of the exclamation marks show, by a suitable convention, that a special sort of moral disapproval is the feeling which is being expressed. It is clear that there is nothing said here which can be true or false. Another man may disagree with me about the wrongness of stealing, in the sense that he may not have the same feelings about stealing as I have, and he may quarrel with me on account of my moral sentiments. But he cannot, strictly speaking, contradict me. For in saying that a certain type of action is right or wrong, I am not making any factual statement, not even a statement about my own state of mind. I am merely expressing certain moral sentiments. And the man who is ostensibly contradicting me is merely expressing his moral sentiments. So that there is plainly no sense in asking which of us is in the right. For neither of us is asserting a genuine proposition.

What we have just been saying about the symbol "wrong" applies to all normative ethical symbols. Sometimes they occur in sentences which record ordinary empirical facts besides expressing ethical feeling about those facts; sometimes they occur in sentences which simply express ethical feeling about a certain type of action, or situation, without making any statement of fact. But in every case in which one would commonly be said to be making an ethical judgement, the function of the relevant ethical word is purely "emotive." It is used to express feeling about certain objects, but not to make any assertion about them.

It is worth mentioning that ethical terms do not serve only to express feeling. They are calculated also to arouse feeling, and so to stimulate action. Indeed some of them are used in such a way as to give the sentences in which they occur the effect of commands. Thus the sentence "It is your duty to tell the truth" may be regarded both as the expression of a certain sort of ethical feeling about truthfulness and as the expression of the command "Tell the truth." The sentence "You ought to tell the truth" also involves the command "Tell the truth," but here the tone of the command is less emphatic. In the sentence "It is good to tell the truth" the command has become little more than a suggestion. And thus the "meaning" of the word "good," in its ethical usage, is differentiated from that of the word "duty" or the word "ought." In fact we may define the meaning of the various ethical words in terms both of the different feelings they are ordinarily taken to express, and also the different responses which they are calculated to provoke.

We can now see why it is impossible to find a criterion for determining the validity of ethical judgements. It is not because they have an "absolute" validity which is mysteriously independent of ordinary sense-experience, but because they have no objective validity whatsoever. If a sentence makes no statement at all, there is obviously no sense in asking whether what it says is true or false. And we have seen that sentences which simply express moral judgements do not say anything. They are pure expressions of feeling and as such do not come under the category of truth and falsehood. They are unverifiable for the same reason as a cry of pain or a word of command is unverifiable—because they do not express genuine propositions.

Thus, although our theory of ethics might fairly be said to be radically subjectivist, it differs in a very important respect from the orthodox subjectivist theory. For the orthodox subjectivist does not deny, as we do, that the sentences of a moralizer express genuine propositions. All he denies is that they express propositions of a unique non-empirical character. His own view is that they express propositions about the speaker's feelings. If this were so, ethical judgements clearly would be capable of being true or false. They would be true if the speaker had the relevant feelings, and false if he had not. And this is a matter which is, in principle, empirically verifiable. Furthermore they could be significantly contradicted. For if I say, "Tolerance is a virtue," and someone answers. "You don't approve of it," he would, on the ordinary subjectivist theory, be contradicting me. On our theory, he would not be contradicting me, because, in saying that tolerance was a virtue, I should not be making any statement about my own feelings or about anything else. I should simply be evincing my feelings, which is not at all the same thing as saying that I have them.

The distinction between the expression of feeling and the assertion of feeling is complicated by the fact that the assertion that one has a certain feeling often accompanies the expression of that feeling, and is then, indeed, a factor in the expression of that feeling. Thus I may simultaneously express boredom and say that I am bored, and in that case my utterance of the words, "I am bored," is one of the circumstances which make it true to say that I am expressing or evincing boredom. But I can express boredom without actually saying that I am bored. I can express it by my tone and gestures, while making a statement about something wholly unconnected with it, or by an ejaculation, or without uttering any words at all. So that even if the assertion that one has a certain feeling always involves the expression of that feeling, the expression of a feeling assuredly does not always involve the assertion that one has it. And this is the important point to grasp in considering the distinction between our theory and the ordinary subjectivist theory. For whereas the subjectivist holds that ethical statements actually assert the existence of certain feelings, we hold that ethical statements are expressions and excitants of feeling which do not necessarily involve any assertions.

We have already remarked that the main objection to the ordinary subjectivist theory is that the validity of ethical judgements is not determined by the nature of their author's feelings. And this is an objection which our theory escapes. For it does not imply that the existence of any feelings is a necessary and sufficient condition of the validity of an ethical judgement. It implies, on the contrary, that ethical judgements have no validity.

There is, however, a celebrated argument against subjectivist theories which our theory does not escape. It has been pointed out by Moore that if ethical statements were simply statements about the speaker's feelings, it would be impossible to argue about questions of value.[2] To take a typical example: if a man said that thrift was a virtue, and another replied that it was a vice, they would not, on this theory, be disputing with one another. One would be saying that he approved of thrift, and the other that *he* didn't; and there is no reason why both these statements should not be true. Now Moore held it to be obvious that we do dispute about questions of value, and accordingly concluded that the particular form of subjectivism which he was discussing was false.

It is plain that the conclusion that it is impossible to dispute about questions of value follows from our theory also. For as we hold that such sentences as "Thrift is a virtue" and "Thrift is a vice" do not express propositions at all, we clearly cannot hold that they express incompatible propositions. We must therefore admit that if Moore's argument really refutes the ordinary subjectivist theory, it also refutes ours. But, in fact, we deny that it does refute even the ordinary subjectivist theory. For we hold that one really never does dispute about questions of value.

This may seem, at first sight, to be a very paradoxical assertion. For we certainly do engage in disputes which are ordinarily regarded as disputes about questions of value. But, in all such cases, we find, if we consider the matter closely, that the dispute is not really about a question of value, but about a question of fact. When someone disagrees with us about the moral value of a certain action or type of action, we do admittedly resort to argument in order to win him over to our way of thinking. But we do not attempt to show by our arguments that he has the "wrong" ethical feeling towards a situation whose nature he has correctly apprehended. What we attempt to show is that he is mistaken about the facts of the case. We argue that he has misconceived the agent's motive: or that he has misjudged the effects of the action, or its probable effects in view of the agent's knowledge; or that he has failed to take into account the special circumstances in which the agent was placed. Or else we employ more general arguments about the effects which actions of a certain type tend to produce, or the qualities which are usually manifested in their performance. We do this in the hope that we have only to get our opponent to agree with us about the nature of the empirical facts for him to adopt the same moral attitude towards them as we do. And as the people with whom we argue have generally received the same moral education as ourselves, and live in the same social order, our expectation is usually justified. But if our opponent happens to have undergone a different process of moral "conditioning" from ourselves, so that, even when he acknowledges all the facts, he still disagrees with us about the moral value of the actions under discussion, then we abandon the attempt to convince him by argument. We say that it is impossible to argue with him because he has a distorted or undeveloped moral sense; which signifies merely that he employs a different set of values from our own. We feel that our own system of values is superior, and therefore speak in such derogatory terms of his. But we cannot bring forward any arguments to show that our system is superior. For our judgement that it is so is itself a judgement of value, and accordingly outside the scope of argument. It is because argument fails us when we come to deal with pure questions of value, as distinct from questions of fact, that we finally resort to mere abuse.

In short, we find that argument is possible on moral questions only if some system of values is presupposed. If our opponent concurs with us in expressing moral disapproval of all actions of a given type *t*, then we may get him to condemn a particular action A, by bringing forward arguments to show that A is of type *t*. For the question whether A does or does not belong to that type is a plain question of fact. Given that a man has certain moral principles, we argue that he must, in order to be consistent, react morally to certain things in a certain way. What we do not and cannot argue about is the validity of these moral principles. We merely praise or condemn them in the light of our own feelings.

If anyone doubts the accuracy of this account of moral disputes, let him try to construct even an imaginary argument on a question of value which does not reduce itself to an argument about a question of logic or about an empirical matter of fact. I am confident that he will not succeed in producing a single example. And if that is the case, he must allow that its involving the impossibility of purely ethical arguments is not, as Moore thought, a ground of objection to our theory, but rather a point in favour of it.

Having upheld our theory against the only criticism which appeared to threaten it, we may now use it to define the nature of all ethical enquiries. We find that ethical philosophy consists simply in saying that ethical concepts are pseudo-concepts and therefore unanalysable. The further task of describing the different feelings that the different ethical terms are used to express, and the different reactions that they customarily provoke, is a task for the psychologist. There cannot be such a thing as ethical science, if by ethical science one means the elaboration of a "true" system of morals. For we have seen that, as ethical judgements are mere expressions of feeling, there can be no way of determining the validity of any ethical system, and, indeed, no sense in asking whether any such system is true. All that one may legitimately enquire in this connection is, What are the moral habits of a given person or group of people, and what causes them to have precisely those habits and feelings? And this enquiry falls wholly within the scope of the existing social sciences.

It appears, then, that ethics, as a branch of knowledge, is nothing more than a department of psychology and sociology. And in case anyone thinks that we are overlooking the existence of casuistry, we may remark that casuistry is not a science, but is a purely analytical investigation of the structure of a given moral system. In other words, it is an exercise in formal logic.

When one comes to pursue the psychological enquiries which constitute ethical science, one is immediately enabled to account for the Kantian and hedonistic theories of morals. For one finds that one of the chief causes of moral behaviour is fear, both conscious and unconscious, of a god's displeasure, and fear of the enmity of society. And this, indeed, is the reason why moral precepts present themselves to some people as "categorical" commands. And one finds, also, that the moral code of a society is partly determined by the beliefs of that society concerning the conditions of its own happiness — or, in other words, that a society tends to encourage or discourage a given type of conduct by the use of moral sanctions according as it appears to promote or detract from the contentment of the society as a whole. And this is the reason why altruism is recommended in most moral codes and egotism condemned. It is from the observation of this connection between morality and happiness that hedonistic or eudaemonistic theories of morals ultimately spring, just as the moral theory of Kant is based on the fact, previously explained, that moral precepts have for some people the force of inexorable commands. As each of these theories ignores the fact which lies at the root of the other, both may be criticized as being one-sided; but this is not the main objection to either of them. Their essential defect is that they treat propositions which refer to the causes and attributes of our ethical feelings as if they were definitions of ethical concepts. And thus they fail to recognise that ethical concepts are pseudo-concepts and consequently indefinable.

As we have already said, our conclusions about the nature of ethics aply to aesthetics also. Aesthetic terms are used in exactly the same way as ethical terms. Such aesthetic words as "beautiful" and "hideous" are employed, as ethical words are employed, not to make statements of fact, but simply to express certain feelings and evoke a certain response. It follows, as in ethics, that there is no sense in attributing objective validity to aesthetic judgements, and no possibility of arguing about questions of value in aesthetics, but only about questions of fact. A scientific treatment of aesthetics would show us what in general were the causes of aesthetic feeling, why various societies produced and admired the works of art they did, why taste varies as it does within a given society, and so forth. And these are ordinary psychological or sociological questions. They have, of course, little or nothing to do with aesthetic crticism as we understand it. But that is because the purpose of aesthetic criticism is not so much to give knowledge as to communicate emotion. The critic, by calling attention to certain features of the work under review, and expressing his own feelings about them, endeavours to make us share his attitude towards the work as a whole. The only relevant propositions that he formulates are propositions describing the nature of the work. And these are plain records of fact. We conclude, therefore, that there is nothing in aesthetics, any more than there is in ethics, to justify the view that it embodies a unique type of knowledge.

It should now be clear that the only information which we can legitimately derive from the study of our aesthetic and moral experiences is information about our own mental and physical make-up. We take note of these experiences as providing data for our psychological and sociological generalisations. And this is the only way in which they serve to increase our knowledge. It follows that any attempt to make our use of ethical and aesthetic concepts the basis of a metaphysical theory concerning the existence of a world of values, as distinct from the world of facts, involves a false analysis of these concepts. Our own analysis has shown that the phenomena of moral experience cannot fairly be used to support any rationalist or metaphysical doctrine whatsoever. In particular, they cannot, as Kant hoped, be used to establish the existence of a transcendent god.

This mention of God brings us to the question of the possibility of religious knowledge. We shall see that this possibility has already been ruled out by our treatment of metaphysics. But, as this is a point of considerable interest, we may be permitted to discuss it at some length.

It is now generally admitted, at any rate by philosophers, that the existence of a being having the attributes which define the god of any non-animistic religion cannot be demonstratively proved. To see that this is so, we have only to ask ourselves what are the premises from which the existence of such a god could be deduced. If the conclusion that a god exists is to be demonstratively certain, then these premises must be certain; for, as the conclusion of a deductive argument is already contained in the premises, any uncertainty there may be about the truth of the premises is necessarily shared by it. But we know that no empirical proposition can ever be anything more than probable. It is only *a priori* propositions that are logically certain. But we cannot deduce the existence of a god from an *a priori* proposition. For we know that the reason why *a priori* propositions are certain is that they are tautologies. And from a set of tautologies nothing but a further tautology can be validly deduced. It follows that there is no possibility of demonstrating the existence of a god.

What is not so generally recognised is that there can be no way of proving that the existence of a god, such as the God of Christianity, is even probable. Yet this also is easily shown. For if the existence of such a god were probable, then the proposition that he existed would be an empirical hypothesis. And in that case it would be possible to deduce from it, and other empirical hypotheses, certain experiential propositions which were not deducible from those other hypotheses alone. But in fact this is not possible. It is sometimes claimed, indeed, that the existence of a certain sort of regularity in nature constitutes sufficient evidence for the existence of a god. But if the sentence "God exists" entails no more than that certain types of phenomena occur in certain sequences, then to assert the existence of a god will be simply equivalent to asserting that there is the requisite regularity in nature; and no religious man would admit that this was all he intended to assert in asserting the existence of a god. He would say that in talking about God, he was talking about a transcendent being who might be known through certain empirical manifestations, but certainly could not be defined in terms of those manifestations. But in that case the term "god" is a metaphysical term. And if "god" is a metaphysical term, then it cannot be even probable that a god exists. For to say that "God exists" is to make a metaphysical utterance which cannot be either true or false. And by the same criterion, no sentence which purports to describe the nature of a transcendent god can possess any literal significance.

It is important not to confuse this view of religious assertions with the view that is adopted by atheists, or agnostics.[3] For it is characteristic of an agnostic to hold that the existence of a god is a possibility in which there is no good reason either to believe or disbelieve; and it is characteristic of an atheist to hold that it is at least probable that no god exists. And our view that all utterances about the nature of God are nonsensical, so far from being identical with, or even lending any support to, either of these familiar contentions, is actually incompatible with them. For if the assertion that there is a god is nonsensical, then the atheist's assertion that there is no god is equally nonsensical, since it is only a significant proposition that can be significantly contradicted. As for the agnostic, although he refrains from saying either that there is or that there is not a god, he does not deny that the question whether a transcendent god exists is a genuine question. He does not deny that the two sentences "There is a transcendent god" and "There is no transcendent god" express propositions one of which is actually true and the other false. All he says is that we have no means of telling which of them is true, and therefore ought not to commit ourselves to either. But we have seen that the sentences in question do not express propositions at all. And this means that agnosticism also is ruled out.

Thus we offer the theist the same comfort as we gave to the moralist. His assertions cannot possibly be valid, but they cannot be invalid either. As he says nothing at all about the world, he cannot justly be accused of saying anything false, or anything for which he has insufficient grounds. It is only when the theist claims that in asserting the existence of a transcendent god he is expressing a genuine proposition that we are entitled to disagree with him.

It is to be remarked that in cases where deities are identified with natural objects, assertions concerning them may be allowed to be significant. If, for example, a man tells me that the occurrence of thunder is alone both necessary and sufficient to establish the truth of the proposition that Jehovah is angry, I may conclude that, in his usage of words, the sentence "Jehovah is angry, is equivalent to "It is thundering" But in sophisticated religions, though they may be to some extent based on men's awe of natural process which they cannot sufficiently understand, the "person" who is supposed to control the empirical world is not himself located in it; he is held to be superior to the empirical world, and so outside it; and he is endowed with super-empirical attributes. But the notion of a person whose essential attributes are non-empirical is not an intelligible notion at all. We may have a word which is used as if it named this "person," but, unless the sentences in which it occurs express propositions which are empirically verifiable, it cannot be said to symbolize anything. And this is the case with regard to the word "god," in the usage in which it is intended to refer to a transcendent object. The mere existence of the noun is enough to foster the illusion that there is a real, or at any rate a possible entity corresponding to it. It is only when we enquire what God's attributes are that we discover that "God," in this usage, is not a genuine name.

It is common to find belief in a transcendent god conjoined with belief in an after-life. But, in the form which it usually takes, the content of this belief is not a genuine hypothesis. To say that men do not ever die, or that the state of death is merely a state of prolonged insensibility, is indeed to express a significant proposition, though all the available evidence goes to show that it is false. But to say that there is something imperceptible inside a man, which is his soul or his real self, and that it goes on living after he is dead, is to make a metaphysical assertion which has no more factual content than the assertion that there is a transcendent god.

It is worth mentioning that, according to the account which we have given of religious assertions, there is no logical ground for antagonism between religion and natural science. As far as the question of truth or falsehood is concerned, there is no opposition between the natural scientist and the theist who believes in a transcendent god. For since the religious utterances of the theist are not genuine propositions at all, they cannot stand in any logical relation to the propositions of science. Such antagonism as there is between religion and science appears to consist in the fact that science takes away one of the motives which make men religious. For it is acknowledged that one of the ultimate sources of religious feeling lies in the inability of men to determine their own destiny; and science tends to destroy the feeling of awe with which men regard an alien world, by making them believe that they can understand and anticipate the course of natural phenomena, and even to some extent control it. The fact that it has recently become fashionable for physicists themselves to be sympathetic towards religion is a point in favour of this hypothesis. For this sympathy towards religion marks the physicists' own lack of confidence in the validity of their hypotheses, which is a reaction on their part from the anti-religious dogmatism of nineteenth-century scientists, and a natural outcome of the crisis through which physics has just passed.

It is not within the scope of this enquiry to enter more deeply into the causes of religious feeling, or to discuss the probability of the continuance of religious belief. We are concerned only to answer those questions which arise out of our discussion of the possibility of religious knowledge. The point which we wish to establish is that there cannot be any transcendent truths of religion. For the sentences which the theist uses to express such "truths" are not literally significant.

An interesting feature of this conclusion is that it accords with what many theists are accustomed to say themselves. For we are often told that the nature of God is a mystery which transcends the human understanding. But to say that something transcends the human understanding is to say that it is unintelligible. And what is unintelligible cannot significantly be described. Again, we are told that God is not an object of reason but an object of faith. This may be nothing more than an admission that the existence of God must be taken on trust, since it cannot be proved. But it may also be an assertion that God is the object of a purely mystical intuition, and cannot therefore be defined in terms which are intelligible to the reason. And I think there are many theists who would assert this. But if one allows that it is impossible to define God in intelligible terms, then one is allowing that it is impossible for a sentence both to be significant and to be about God. If a mystic admits that the object of his vision is something which cannot be described, then he must also admit that he is bound to talk nonsense when he describes it.

For his part, the mystic may protest that his intuition does reveal truths to him, even though he cannot explain to others what these truths are; and that we who do not possess this faculty of intuition can have no ground for denying that it is a cognitive faculty. For we can hardly maintain *a priori* that there are no ways of discovering true propositions except those which we ourselves employ. The answer is that we set no limit to the number of ways in which one may come to formulate a true proposition. We do not in any way deny that a synthetic truth may be discovered by purely intuitive methods as well as by the rational method of induction. But we do say that every synthetic proposition, however it may have been arrived at, must be subject to the test of actual experience. We do not deny *a priori* that the mystic is able to discover truths by his own special methods. We wait to hear what are the propositions which embody his discoveries, in order to see whether they are verified or confuted by our empirical observations. But the mystic, so far from producing propositions which are empirically verified, is unable to produce any intelligible propositions at all. And therefore we say that his intuition has not revealed to him any facts. It is no use his saying that he has apprehended facts but is unable to express them. For we know that if he really had acquired any information, he would be able to express it. He would be able to indicate in some way or other how the genuineness of his discovery might be empirically determined. The fact that he cannot reveal what he "knows," or even himself devise an empirical test to validate his "knowledge," shows that his state of mystical intuition is not a genuinely cognitive state. So that in describing his vision the mystic does not give us any information about the external world; he merely gives us indirect information about the condition of his own mind.

These considerations dispose of the argument from religious experience, which many philosophers still regard as a valid argument in favour of the existence of a god. They say that it is logically possible for men to be immediately acquainted with God, as they are immediately acquainted with a sense-content, and that there is no reason why one should be prepared to believe a man when he says that he is seeing a yellow patch, and refuse to believe him when he says that he is seeing God. The answer to this is that if the man who asserts that he is seeing God is merely asserting that he is experiencing a peculiar kind of sense-content, then we do not for a moment deny that his assertion may be true. But, ordinarily, the man who says that he is seeing God is saying not merely that he is experiencing a religious emotion, but also that there exists a transcendent being who is the object of this emotion; just as the man who says that he sees a yellow patch is ordinarily saying not merely that his visual sense-field contains a yellow sense-content, but also that there exists a yellow object to which the sense-content belongs. And it is not irrational to be prepared to believe a man when he asserts the existence of a yellow object, and to refuse to believe him when he asserts the existence of a transcendent god. For whereas the sentence "There exists here a yellow-coloured material thing" expresses a genuine synthetic proposition which could be empirically verified, the sentence "There exists a transcendent god" has, as we have seen, no literal significance.

We conclude, therefore, that the argument from religious experience is altogether fallacious. The fact that people have religious experiences is interesting from the psychological point of view, but it does not in any way imply that there is such a thing as religious knowledge, any more than our having moral experiences implies that there is such a thing as moral knowledge. The theist, like the moralist, may believe that his experiences are cognitive experiences, but, unless he can formulate his "knowledge" in propositions that are empirically verifiable, we may be sure that he is deceiving himself. It follows that those philosophers who fill their books with assertions that they intuitively "know" this or that moral or religious "truth" are merely providing material for the psychoanalyst. For no act of intuition can be said to reveal a truth about any matter of fact unless it issues in verifiable propositions. And all such propositions are to be incorporated in the system of empirical propositions which constitutes science.

NOTES

1. The argument that follows should be read in conjunction with the Introduction, pp. 20-2 [of *Language, Truth, and Logic.* – Ed.]
2. cf. *Philosophical Studies,* "The Nature of Moral Philosophy."
3. This point was suggested to me by Professor H. H. Price.

Study Questions

Ayer: "The Elimination of Metaphysics"

1. How does Ayer propose to end philosophical disputes?
2. What are the two ways to attack metaphysics? Which is Ayer's?
3. How does Ayer first formulate a criterion for meaningfulness?
4. Distinguish: (1) practical verifiability and verifiability in principle; (2) strong and weak verifiability.
5. After making these distinctions, Ayer reformulates his criterion. State it and illustrate.
6. If metaphysical assertions are meaningless, how do they come to be made?
7. How does Ayer reformulate his criterion in the addendum?

Ayer: "The Function of Philosophy"

1. What is the function of philosophy?
2. What is the nature of philosophical questions?

Ayer: "The A Priori"

1. What is a common objection to empiricism?
2. How did Mill deal with it? What is wrong with Mill's view?
3. What are the characteristics of the propositions of (pure) logic and mathamatics?

Ayer: "Truth and Probability"

1. What is the nature of empirical propositions?
2. Can any such propositions be known with certainty?

Ayer: Critique of Ethics and Theology

1. What are the knids of assertions found in ethical writings? Which are *ethical* and which are not? Why?
2. What is wrong with ethical naturalism?
3. What is wrong with ethical intuitionism?
4. What *is* the nature of ethical sentences and terms?
5. What is the nature of theological propositions?

Selected Bibliography

Ayer, A. J. *Language, Truth and Logic.* Second Edition. New York: Dover Books, 1946. [The most readable defense of logical positivism — now a "classic."]

Ayer, A. J., ed. *Logical Positivism.* Glencoe: Free Press, 1959. [Contains a large number of the most important essays by various logical positivists such as Schlick, Carnap, Hahn, and Neurath.]

Feigl, Herbert. "Logical Empiricism." In H. Feigl and W. Sellars, eds., *Readings in Philosophical Analysis.* New York: Appleton-Century Crafts, 1949. [An excellent secondary account of the main thesis of logical positivism by a (then) positivist.]

Passmore, John. *A Hundred Years of Philosophy.* London: Duckworth, 1957. Ch. 16. [A good secondary discussion.]

Urmson, J. O. *Philosophical Analysis.* Oxford: Oxford University Press, 1956. Part 2 [An excellent secondary discussion — perhaps one of the best things to read first.]

Conceptual Analysis

18. Systematically Misleading Expressions

Gilbert Ryle

Philosophical arguments have always largely, if not entirely, consisted in attempts to thrash out 'what it means to say so and so.' It is observed that men in their ordinary discourse, the discourse, that is, that they employ when they are not philosophizing, use certain expressions, and philosophers fasten on to certain more or less radical types or classes of such expressions and raise their questions about all expressions of a certain type and ask what they really mean.

Sometimes philosophers say that they are analysing or clarifying the 'concepts' which are embodied in the 'judgements' of the plain man or of the scientist, historian, artist, or who-not. But this seems to be only a gaseous way of saying that they are trying to discover what is meant by the general terms contained in the sentences which they pronounce or write. For, as we shall see, 'x is a concept' and 'y is a judgement' are themselves systematically misleading expressions.

But the whole procedure is very odd. For, if the expressions under consideration are intelligently used, their employers must already know what they mean and do not need the aid or admonition of philosophers before they can understand what they are saying. And if their hearers understand what they are being told, they too are in no such perplexity that they need to have this meaning philosophically 'analysed' or 'clarified' for them. And, at least, the philosopher himself must know what the expressions mean, since otherwise he could not know what it was that he was analysing.

Certainly it is often the case that expressions are not being intelligently used and to that extent their authors are just gabbling parrot-wise. But then it is obviously fruitless to ask what the expressions really mean. For there is no reason

287

to suppose that they mean anything. It would not be mere gabbling if there was any such reason. And if the philosopher cares to ask what these expressions *would* mean *if* a rational man were using them, the only answer would be that they would mean what they would then mean. Understanding them would be enough, and that could be done by any reasonable listener. Philosophizing could not help him, and, in fact, the philosopher himself would not be able to begin unless he simply understood them in the ordinary way.

It seems, then, that if an expression can be understood, then it is already known in that understanding what the expression means. So there is no darkness present and no illumination required or possible.

And if it is suggested that the non-philosophical author of an expression (be he plain man, scientist, preacher, or artist) does know but only knows dimly or foggily or confusedly what his expression means, but that the philosopher at the end of his exploration knows clearly, distinctly, and definitely what it means, a two-fold answer seems inevitable. First, that if a speaker only knows confusedly what his expression means, then he is in that respect and to that extent just gabbling. And it is not the rôle—nor the achievement—of the philosopher to provide a medicine against that form of flux. And next, the philosopher is not *ex officio* concerned with ravings and ramblings: he studies expressions for what they mean when intelligently and intelligibly employed, and not as noises emitted by this idiot or that parrot.

Certainly expressions do occur for which better substitutes could be found and should be or should have been employed. (1) An expression may be a breach of, e.g., English or Latin grammar. (2) A word may be a foreign word, or a rare word or a technical or trade term for which there exists a familiar synonym. (3) A phrase or sentence may be clumsy or unfamiliar in its structure. (4) A word or phrase may be equivocal and so be an instrument of possible puns. (5) A word or phrase may be ill-chosen as being general where it should be specific, or allusive where the allusion is not known or not obvious. (6) Or a word may be a malapropism or a misnomer. But the search for paraphrases which shall be more swiftly intelligible to a given audience or more idiomatic or stylish or more grammatically or etymologically correct is merely applied lexicography or philology—it is not philosophy.

We ought then to face the question: Is there such a thing as analysing or clarifying the meaning of the expressions which people use, except in the sense of substituting philologically better expressions for philologically worse ones? (We might have put the problem in the more misleading terminology of 'concepts' and asked: How can philosophizing so operate by analysis and clarification, upon the concepts used by the plain man, the scientist, or the artist, that after this operation the concepts are illumined where before they were dark? The same difficulties arise. For there can be no such thing as a confused concept, since either a man is conceiving, i.e. knowing the nature of his subject-matter, or he is failing to do so. If he is succeeding, no clarification is required or possible; and if he is failing, he must find out more or think more about the subject-matter, the apprehension of the nature of which we call his 'concept.'

But this will not be philosophizing about the concept, but exploring further the nature of the thing, and so will be economics, perhaps, or astronomy or history. But as I think that it can be shown that it is not true in any natural sense that 'there are concepts,' I shall adhere to the other method of stating the problem.)

The object of this paper is not to show what philosophy in general is investigating, but to show that there remains an important sense in which philosophers can and must discover and state what is really meant by expressions of this or that radical type, and none the less that these discoveries do not in the least imply that the naïve users of such expressions are in any doubt or confusion about what their expressions mean or in any way need the results of the philosophical analysis for them to continue to use intelligently their ordinary modes of expression or to use them so that they are intelligible to others.

The gist of what I want to establish is this. There are many expressions which occur in non-philosophical discourse which, though they are perfectly clearly understood by those who use them and those who hear or read them, are nevertheless couched in grammatical or syntactical forms which are in a demonstrable way *improper* to the states of affairs which they record (or the alleged states of affairs which they profess to record). Such expressions can be reformulated and for philosophy but *not* for non-philosophical discourse must be reformulated into expressions of which the syntactical form is proper to the facts recorded (or the alleged facts alleged to be recorded).

I use 'expression' to cover single words, phrases, and sentences. By 'statement' I mean a sentence in the indicative. When a statement is true, I say it 'records' a fact or state of affairs. False statements do not record. To know that a statement is true is to know that something is the case and that the statement records it. When I barely understand a statement I do not know that it records a fact, nor need I know the fact that it records, if it records one. But I know what state of affairs *would* obtain, if the statement recorded a state of affairs.

Every significant statement is a quasi-record, for it has both the requisite structure and constituents to be a record. But knowing these, we don't yet know that it is a record of a fact. False statements are pseudo-records and are no more records than pseudo-antiquities are antiquities. So the question, What do false statements state? is meaningless if 'state' means 'record.' If it means, What *would* they record if they recorded something being the case? the question contains its own answer.

When an expression is of such a syntactical form that it is improper to the fact recorded, it is systematically misleading in that it naturally suggests to some people—though not to 'ordinary' people—that the state of affairs recorded is quite a different sort of state of affairs from that which it in fact is.

I shall try to show what I am driving at by examples. I shall begin by considering a whole class of expressions of one type which occur and occur perfectly satisfactorily in ordinary discourse, but which are, I argue, *systematically misleading*, that is to say, that they are couched in a syntactical form improper to the facts recorded and proper to facts of quite another logical form than the facts recorded. (For simplicity's sake, I shall speak as if all the statements adduced as examples are true. For false statements are not formally different from true ones. Otherwise grammarians could become omniscient. And when I call a statement 'systematically misleading' I shall not mean that it is false, and certainly not that it is senseless. By 'systematically' I mean that all expressions of that grammatical form would be misleading in the same way and for the same reason.)

I. Quasi-ontological Statements

Since Kant, we have, most of us, paid lip service to the doctrine that 'existence is not a quality' and so we have rejected the pseudo-implication of the ontological argument; 'God is perfect, being perfect entails being existent, ... God exists.' For if existence is not a quality, it is not the sort of thing that can be entailed by a quality.

But until fairly recently it was not noticed that if in 'God exists' 'exists' is not a predicate (save in grammar), then in the same statement 'God' cannot be (save in grammar) the subject of predication. The realization of this came from examining negative existential propositions like 'Satan does not exist' or 'unicorns are non-existent.' If there is no Satan, then the statement 'Satan does not exist' cannot be about Satan in the way in which 'I am sleepy' is about me. Despite appearances the word 'Satan' cannot be signifying a subject of attributes.

Philosophers have toyed with theories which would enable them to continue to say that 'Satan does not exist' is none the less still somehow about Satan, and that 'exists' still signifies some sort of attribute or character, although not a quality.

So some argued that the statement was about something described as 'the idea of Satan,' others that it was about a subsistent but nonactual entity called 'Satan.' Both theories in effect try to show that something may *be* (whether as being 'merely mental' or as being in 'the realm of subsistents'), but not be in existence. But as we can say 'round squares do not exist,' and 'real nonentities do not exist,' this sort of interpretation of negative existentials is bound to fill either the realm of subsistents or the realm of ideas with walking self-contradictions. So the theories had to be dropped and a new analysis of existential propositions had to begin.

Suppose I assert of (apparently) the general subject 'carnivorous cows' that they 'do not exist,' and my assertion is true, I cannot really be talking about carnivorous cows, for there are none. So it follows that the expression 'carnivorous cows' is not really being used, though the grammatical appearances are to the contrary, to denote the thing or things of which the predicate is being asserted. And in the same way as the verb 'exists' is not signifying the character asserted, although grammatically it looks as if it was, the real predicate must be looked for elsewhere.

So the clue of the grammar has to be rejected and the analysis has been suggested that 'carnivorous cows do not exist' means what is meant by 'no cows are carnivorous' or 'no carnivorous beasts are cows.' But a further improvement seems to be required.

'Unicorns do not exist' seems to mean what is meant by 'nothing is *both* a quadruped *and* herbivorous *and* the wearer of one horn' (or whatever the marks of being an unicorn are). And this does not seem to imply that there are some quadrupeds or herbivorous animals.

So 'carnivorous cows do not exist' ought to be rendered 'nothing is both a cow and carnivorous,' which does not as it stands imply that anything is either.

Take now an apparently singular subject as in 'God exists' or 'Satan does not exist.' If the former analysis was right, then here too 'God' and 'Satan' are in fact, despite grammatical appearance, predicative expressions. That is to say, they are that element in the assertion that something has a specified character, which signifies the character by which the subject is being asserted to be characterized. 'God exists' must mean what is meant by 'Something, and one thing only, is omniscient, omnipotent, and infinitely good' (or whatever else are the characters summed in the compound character of being a god and the only god). And 'Satan does not exist' must mean what is meant by 'nothing is both devilish and alone in being devilish,' or perhaps 'nothing is both devilish and called "Satan,"' or even '"Satan" is not the proper name of anything.' To put it roughly, 'x exists' and 'x does not exist' do not assert or deny that a given subject of attributes x has the attribute of existing, but assert or deny the attribute of being x-ish or being an x of something not named in the statement.

Now I can show my hand. I say that expressions such as 'carnivorous cows do not exist' are systematically misleading and that the expressions by which we paraphrased them are not or are not in the same way or to the same extent systematically misleading. But they are not false, nor are they senseless. They are true, and they really do mean what their less systematically misleading paraphrases mean. Nor (save in a special class of cases) is the non-philosophical author of such expressions ignorant or doubtful of the nature of the state of affairs which his expression records. He is not a whit misled. There is a trap, however, in the form of his expression, but a trap which only threatens the man who has begun to generalize about sorts or types of states of affairs and assumes that every statement gives in its syntax a clue to the logical form of the fact that it records. I refer here not merely nor even primarily to the philosopher, but to any man who embarks on abstraction.

But before developing this theme I want to generalize the results of our examination of what we must now ascribe as 'so-called existential statements.' It is the more necessary in that, while most philosophers are now forewarned by Kant against the systematic misleadingness of 'God exists,' few of them have observed that the same taint infects a whole host of other expressions.

If 'God exists' means what we have said it means, then patently 'God is an existent,' 'God is an entity,' 'God has being,' or 'existence' require the same analysis. So '. . . is an existent,' '. . . is an entity' are only bogus predicates, and that of which (in grammar) they are asserted is only a bogus subject.

And the same will be true of all the items in the following pair of lists.

Mr. Baldwin—	Mr. Pickwick—
is a being.	is a nonentity.
is real, or a reality.	is unreal or an unreality, or an appearance.
is a genuine entity.	is a bogus or sham entity.
is a substance.	is not a substance.
is an actual object or entity.	is an unreal object or entity.
is objective.	is not objective or is subjective.
is a concrete reality.	is a fiction or figment.
is an object.	is an imaginary object.
is.	is not.
	is a mere idea.
	is an abstraction.
	is a logical construction.

None of these statements is really about Mr. Pickwick. For if they are true, there is no such person for them to be about. Nor is any of them about Mr. Baldwin. For if they were false, there would be no one for them to be about. Nor in any of them is the grammatical predicate that element in the statement which signifies the character that is being asserted to be characterizing or not to be characterizing something.

I formulate the conclusion in this rather clumsy way. There is a class of statements of which the grammatical predicate *appears* to signify not the having of a specified character but the having (or not having) of a specified *status*. But in all such statements the appearance is a purely grammatical one, and what the statements really record can be stated in statements embodying no such quasi-ontological predicates.

And, again, in all such quasi-ontological statements the grammatical subject-word or phrase *appears* to denote or refer to something as that of which the quasi-ontological predicate is being predicated; but in fact the apparent subject term is a concealed predicative expression, and what is really recorded in such statements can be re-stated in statements no part of which even appears to refer to any such subject.

In a word, all quasi-ontological statements are systematically misleading. (If I am right in this, then the conclusion follows, which I accept, that those metaphysical philosophers are the greatest sinners, who, as if they were saying something of importance, make 'Reality' or 'Being' the subject of their propositions, or 'real' the predicate. For at best what they say is systematically misleading, which is the one thing which a philosopher's propositions have no right to be; and at worst it is meaningless.)

I must give warning again, that the naïve employer of such quasi-ontological expressions is not necessarily and not even probably misled. He has said what he wanted to say, and anyone who knew English would understand what he was saying. Moreover, I would add, in the cases that I have listed, the statements are not merely significant but true. Each of them records a real state of affairs. Nor *need* they mislead the philosopher. We, for instance, I hope are not misled. But the point is that anyone, the philosopher included, who abstracts and generalizes and so tries to consider what different facts of the same type (i.e. facts of the same type about different things) have in common, is compelled to use the common grammatical form of the statements of those facts as handles with which to grasp the common logical form of the facts themselves. For (what we shall see later) as the way in which a fact *ought* to be recorded in expressions *would* be a clue to the form of that fact, we jump to the assumption that the way in which a fact *is* recorded *is* such a clue. And very often the clue is misleading and suggests that the fact is of a different form from what really is its form. 'Satan is not a reality' from its grammatical form looks as if it recorded the same sort of fact as 'Capone is not a philosopher,' and so was just as much denying a character of a somebody called 'Satan' as the latter does deny a character of somebody called 'Capone.' But it turns out that the suggestion is a fraud; for the fact recorded would have been properly or less improperly recorded in the statement '"Satan" is not a proper name' or 'No one is called "Satan"' or 'No one is both called "Satan" and is infinitely malevolent, etc.', or perhaps 'Some people believe that someone is both called "Satan" and infinitely malevolent, but their belief is false.' And none of these statements even pretend to be 'about Satan.' Instead, they are and are patently about the noise 'Satan' or else about people who misuse it.

In the same way, while it is significant, true, and directly intelligible to say 'Mr. Pickwick is a fiction,' it is a systematically misleading expression (i.e. an expression misleading in virtue of a formal property which it does or might share with other expressions); for it does not really record, as it appears to record, a fact of the same sort as is recorded in 'Mr. Baldwin is a statesman.' The world does not contain fictions in the way in which it contains statesmen. There is no subject of attributes of which we can say '*there* is a fiction.' What we can do is to say of Dickens '*there* is a story-teller,' or of Pickwick Papers '*there* is a pack of lies'; or of a sentence in that novel, which contains the pseudo-name 'Mr. Pickwick' '*there* is a fable.' And when we say things of this sort we are recording just what we recorded when we said 'Mr. Pickwick is a fiction,' only our new expressions do not suggest what our old one did that some subject of attributes has the two attributes of being called 'Mr. Pickwick' and of being a fiction, but instead that some subject of attributes has the attributes of being called Dickens and being a coiner of false propositions and pseudo-proper names, or, on the other analysis, of being a book or a sentence which could only be true or false *if* someone was called 'Mr. Pickwick.' The proposition 'Mr. Pickwick is a fiction' is really, despite its *prima facies,* about Dickens or else about Pickwick Papers. But the fact that it is so is concealed and not exhibited by the form of the expression in which it is said.

It must be noted that the sense in which such quasi-ontological statements are misleading is not that they are false and not even that any word of them is equivocal or vague, but only that they are formally improper to facts of the logical form which they are employed to record and proper to facts of quite another logical form. What the implications are of these notions of formal propriety or formal impropriety we shall see later on.

II. Statements Seemingly about Universals, or Quasi-Platonic Statements

We often and with great convenience use expressions such as 'Unpunctuality is reprehensible' and 'Virtue is its own reward.' And at first sight these seem to be on all fours with 'Jones merits reproof' and 'Smith has given himself the prize.' So philosophers, taking it that what is meant by such statements as the former is precisely analogous to what is meant by such statements as the latter, have accepted the consequence that the world contains at least two sorts of objects, namely, particulars like Jones and Smith, and 'universals' like Unpunctuality and Virtue.

But absurdities soon crop up. It is obviously silly to speak of an universal meriting reproof. You can no more praise or blame an 'universal' than you can make holes in the Equator.

Nor when we say 'unpunctuality is reprehensible' do we really suppose that unpunctuality ought to be ashamed of itself.

What we do mean is what is also meant but better expressed by 'Whoever is unpunctual deserves that other people should reprove him for being unpunctual.' For it is unpunctual men and not unpunctuality who can and should be blamed, since they are, what it is not, moral agents. Now in the new expression 'whoever is unpunctual merits reproof' the word 'unpunctuality' has vanished in favour of the predicative expression '. . . is unpunctual.' So that while in the original expression 'unpunctuality' seemed to denote the subject of which an attribute was being asserted, it now turns out to signify the having of an attribute. And we are really saying that anyone who has that attribute, has the other.

Again, it is not literally true that Virtue is a recipient of rewards. What is true is that anyone who is virtuous is benefted thereby. Whoever is good, gains something by being good. So the original statement was not 'about Virtue' but about good men, and the grammatical subject word 'Virtue' meant what is meant by '. . . is virtuous' and so was, what it pretended not to be, a predicative expression.

I need not amplify this much. It is not literally true that 'honesty compels me to state so and so,' for 'honesty' is not the name of a coercive agency. What is true is more properly put 'because I am honest, or wish to be honest, I am bound to state so and so.' 'Colour involves extension' means what is meant by 'Whatever is coloured is extended'; 'hope deferred maketh the heart sick' means what is meant by 'whoever for a long time hopes for something without getting it becomes sick at heart.'

It is my own view that all statements which seem to be 'about universals' are analysable in the same way, and consequently that general terms are never really the names of subjects of attributes. So 'universals' are not objects in the way in which Mt. Everest is one, and therefore the age-old question what *sort* of objects they are is a bogus question. For general nouns, adjectives, etc., are not proper names, so we cannot speak of 'the objects called "equality," "justice" and "progress." '[1]

Platonic and anti-Platonic assertions, such as that 'equality is, or is not, a real entity,' are, accordingly, alike misleading, and misleading in two ways at once; for they are both quasi-ontological statements and quasi-Platonic ones.

However, I do not wish to defend this general position here, but only to show that in *some* cases statements which from their grammatical form seem to be saying that 'honesty does so and so' or 'equality is such and such,' are really saying in a formally improper way (though one which is readily understandable and idiomatically correct) 'anything which is equal to x is such and such' or 'whoever is honest, is so and so.' These statements state overtly, what the other stated covertly, that something's having one attribute necessitates its having the other.

Of course, the plain man who uses such quasi-Platonic expressions is not making a philosophical mistake. He is not philosophizing at all. He is not misled by and does not even notice the fraudulent pretence contained in such propositions that they are 'about Honesty' or 'about Progress.' He knows what he means and will, very likely, accept our more formally proper restatement of what he means as a fair paraphrase, but he will not have any motive for desiring the more proper form of expression, nor even any grounds for holding that it is more proper. For he is not attending to the form of the fact in abstraction from the special subject-matter that the fact is about. So for him the best way of expressing something is the way which is the most brief, the most elegant, or the most emphatic, whereas those who, like philosophers, must generalize about the *sorts* of statements that have to be made of *sorts* of facts about *sorts* of topics, cannot help treating as clues to the logical structures for which they are looking the grammatical forms of the common types of expressions in which these structures are recorded. And these clues are often misleading.

III. Descriptive Expressions and Quasi-descriptions

We all constantly use expressions of the form 'the so and so,' as 'the Vice-Chancellor of Oxford University.' Very often we refer by means of such expressions to some one uniquely described individual. The phrases 'the present Vice-Chancellor of Oxford University' and 'the highest mountain in the world' have such a reference in such propositions as 'the present Vice-Chancellor of Oxford University is a tall man' and 'I have not seen the highest mountain in the world.'

There is nothing intrinsically misleading in the use of 'the'-phrases as unique descriptions, though there is a sense in which they are highly condensed or abbreviated. And philosophers can and do make mistakes in the accounts they give of what such descriptive phrases mean. What are misleading are, as we shall see, 'the'-phrases which behave grammatically as if they were unique descriptions referring to individuals, when in fact they are not referential phrases at all. But this class of systematically misleading expressions cannot be examined until we have considered how genuine unique descriptions do refer.

A descriptive phrase is not a proper name, and the way in which the subject of attributes which it denotes is denoted by it is not in that subject's being *called* 'the so and so,' but in its possessing and being *ipso facto* the sole possessor of the idiosyncratic attribute which is what the descriptive phrase signifies. If Tommy is the eldest son of Jones, then 'the eldest son of Jones' denotes Tommy, not because someone or other *calls* him 'the eldest son of Jones,' but because he is and no one else can be both a son of Jones and older than all the other sons of Jones. The descriptive phrase, that is, is not a proper name but a predicative expression signifying the joint characters of being a son of Jones and older than the other sons of Jones. And it refers to Tommy only in the sense that Tommy and Tommy alone has those characters.

The phrase does not in any sense *mean* Tommy. Such a view would be, as we shall see, nonsensical. It means what is meant by the predicative expression, '. . . is both a son of Jones and older than his other sons,' and so it is itself only a predicative expression. By a 'predicative expression' I mean that fragment of a statement in virtue of which the having of a certain character or characters is expressed. And the having a certain character is not a subject of attributes but, so to speak, the tail end of the facts that some subject of attributes has it and some others lack it. By itself it neither names the subject which has the character nor records the fact that any subject has it. It cannot indeed occur by itself, but only as an element, namely, a predicative element in a full statement.

So the full statement 'the eldest son of Jones was married to-day' means what is meant by 'someone (namely, Tommy) (1) is a son of Jones, (2) is older than the other sons of Jones [this could be unpacked further] and (3) was married to-day.'

The whole statement could not be true unless the three or more component statements were true. But *that* there is someone of whom both (1) and (2) are true is not guaranteed by their being stated. (No statement can guarantee its own truth.) Consequently the characterizing expression '. . . is the eldest son of Jones' does not *mean* Tommy either in the sense of being his proper name or in the sense of being an expression the understanding of which involves the knowledge that Tommy has this idiosyncratic character. It only *refers* to Tommy in the sense that well-informed listeners will know already, that Tommy and Tommy only has in fact this idiosyncratic character. But this knowledge is not part of what must be known in order to understand the statement, 'Jones' eldest son was married to-day.' For we could know what it meant without knowing that Tommy was the eldest son or was married to-day. All we must know is that someone or other must be so characterized for the whole statement to be true.

For understanding a statement or apprehending what a statement means is not knowing that this statement records this fact, but knowing what *would* be the case if the statement *were* a record of fact.

There is no understanding or apprehending the meaning of an isolated proper name or of an isolated unique description. For *either* we know that someone in particular is called by that name by certain persons or else has the idiosyncratic characters signified by the descriptive phrase, which requires that we are acquainted both with the name or description and with the person named or described. *Or* we do not know these things, in which case we don't know that the quasi-name is a name at all or that the quasi-unique description describes anyone. But we can understand statements in which quasi-names or quasi-unique descriptions occur; for we can know what would be the case if someone were so called or so describable, and also had the other characters predicated in the predicates of the statements.

We see, then, that descriptive phrases are condensed predicative expressions, and so that their function is to be that element or (more often) one of those elements in statements (which as a whole record that something has a certain character or characters) in which the having of this or that character is expressed.

And this can easily be seen by another approach.

Take any 'the'-phrase which is naturally used referentially as the grammatical subject of a sentence, as 'The Vice-Chancellor of Oxford University' in 'The Vice-Chancellor of Oxford University is busy.' We can now take the descriptive phrase, lock, stock, and barrel, and use it non-referentially as the grammatical predicate in a series of statements and expressions, 'Who is the present Vice-Chancellor of Oxford University?' 'Mr. So-and-So is the present Vice-Chancellor of Oxford University,' 'Georges Carpentier is not the present Vice-Chancellor of Oxford University,' 'Mr. Such-and-Such is either the Vice-Chancellor of Oxford University or Senior Proctor,' 'Whoever is Vice-Chancellor of Oxford University is overworked,' etc. It is clear, anyhow, in the cases of the negative, hypothetical, and disjunctive statements containing this common predicative expression that it is not implied or even suggested that anyone does hold the office of Vice-Chancellor. So the 'the'-phrase is here quite non-referential, and does not even pretend to denote someone. It signifies an idiosyncratic character, but does not involve that anyone has it. This leads us back to our original conclusion that a descriptive phrase does not in any sense *mean* this person or that thing; or, to put it in another way, that we can understand a statement containing a descriptive phrase and still not know of this subject of attributes or of that one that the description fits it. (Indeed, we hardly need to argue the position. For no one with a respect for sense would dream of pointing to someone or something and saying 'that is the meaning of such and such an expression' or 'the meaning of yonder phrase is suffering from influenza.'

'Socrates is a meaning' is a nonsensical sentence. The whole pother about denoting seems to arise from the supposition that we could significantly describe an object as 'the meaning of the expression "*x*"' or 'what the expression "*x*" means.' Certainly a descriptive phrase can be said to *refer* to or *fit* this man or that mountain, and this man or that mountain can be described as that to which the expression '*x*' refers. But this is only to say that this man or that mountain has and is alone in having the characters the having of which is expressed in the predicative sentence-fragment '. . . is the so-and-so.')

All this is only leading up to another class of systematically misleading expressions. But the 'the'-phrases which we have been studying, whether occurring as grammatical subjects or as predicates in statements, were not formally fraudulent. There was nothing in the grammatical form of the sentences adduced to suggest that the facts recorded were of a different logical form from that which they really had.

The previous argument was intended to be critical of certain actual or possible philosophical errors, but they were errors about descriptive expressions and not errors *due* to a trickiness in descriptive expressions as such. Roughly, the errors that I have been trying to dispel are the views (1) that descriptive phrases are proper names and (2) that the thing which a description describes is what the description means. I want now to come to my long-delayed muttons and discuss a further class of systematically misleading expressions.

IV. Systematically Misleading Quasi-referential 'The'-Phrases

1. There frequently occur in ordinary discourse expressions which, though 'the'-phrases, are not unique descriptions at all, although from their grammatical form they look as if they are. The man who does not go in for abstraction and generalization uses them without peril or perplexity and knows quite well what he means by the sentences containing them. But the philosopher has to re-state them in a different and formally more proper arrangement of words if he is not to be trapped.

When a descriptive phrase is used as the grammatical subject of a sentence in a formally non-misleading way, as in 'the King went shooting to-day,' we know that if the statement as a whole is true (or even false) then there must be in the world someone in particular to whom the description 'the King' refers or applies. And we could significantly ask 'Who is the King?' and 'Are the father of the Prince of Wales and the King one and the same person?'

But we shall see that there are in common use quasi-descriptive phrases of the form 'the so-and-so,' in the cases of which there is in the world no one and nothing that could be described as that to which the phrase refers or applies, and thus that there is nothing and nobody about which or whom we could even ask 'Is it the so-and-so?' or 'Are he and the so-and-so one and the same person?'

It can happen in several ways. Take first the statement, which is true and clearly intelligible, 'Poincaré is not the King of France.' This at first sight looks formally analogous to 'Tommy Jones is not (i.e. is not identical with) the King of England.' But the difference soon shows itself. For whereas if the latter is true then its converse 'the King of England is not Tommy Jones' is true, it is neither true nor false to say 'The King of France is not Poincaré.' For there is no King of France and the phrase 'the King of France' does not fit anybody — nor did the plain man who said 'Poincaré is not the King of France' suppose the contrary. So 'the King of France' in this statement is not analogous to 'the King of England' in the others. It is not really being used referentially or as a unique description of somebody at all.

We can now redraft the contrasted propositions in forms of words which shall advertise the difference which the original propositions concealed between the forms of the facts recorded.

'Tommy Jones is not the same person as the King of England' means what is meant by '(1) Somebody and — of an unspecified circle — one person only is called Tommy Jones; (2) Somebody, and one person only has royal power in England; and (3) No one both is called Tommy Jones and is King of England.' The original statement could not be true unless (1) and (2) were true.

Take now 'Poincaré is not the King of France.' This means what is meant by '(1) Someone is called "Poincaré" and (2) Poincaré has not got the rank, being King of France.' And this does not imply that anyone has that rank.

Sometimes this twofold use, namely the referential and the non-referential use of 'the'-phrases, troubles us in the mere practice of ordinary discourse. 'Smith is not the only man who has ever climbed Mont Blanc' might easily be taken by some people to mean what is meant by 'One man and one man only has climbed Mont Blanc, but Smith is not he,' and by others, 'Smith has climbed Mont Blanc but at least one other man has done so too.' But I am not interested in the occasional ambiguity of such expressions, but in the fact that an expression of this sort which is really being used in the non-referential way is apt to be construed as if it *must* be referentially used, or as if any 'the'-phrase was referentially used. Philosophers and others who have to abstract and generalize tend to be misled by the verbal similarity of 'the'-phrases of the one sort with 'the'-phrases of the other into 'coining entities' in order to be able to show to what a given 'the'-phrase refers.

Let us first consider the phrase 'the top of that tree' or 'the centre of that bush' as they occur in such statements as 'an owl is perched on the top of that tree,' 'my arrow flew through the centre of the bush.' These statements are quite unambiguous, and convey clearly and correctly what they are intended to convey.

But as they are in syntax analogous to 'a man is sitting next to the Vice-Chancellor' and 'my arrow flew through the curtain,' and as further an indefinite list could be drawn up of different statements having in common the 'the'-phrases, 'the top of that tree' and 'the centre of that bush,' it is hard for people who generalize to escape the temptation of supposing or even believing that these 'the'-phrases refer to objects in the way in which 'the Vice-Chancellor' and 'the curtain' refer to objects. And this is to suppose or believe that the top of that tree is a genuine subject of attributes in just the same way as the Vice-Chancellor is.

But (save in the case where the expression is being misused for the expression 'the topmost branch' or 'the topmost leaf of the tree') 'the top of the tree' at once turns out not to be referring to any object. There is nothing in the world of which it is true (or even false) to say 'That is the top of such and such a tree.' It does not, for instance, refer to a bit of the tree, or it could be cut down and burned or put in a vase. 'The top of the tree' does not refer to anything, but it signifies an attribute, namely, the having of a relative position, when it occurs in statements of the form 'x is at or near or above or below the top of the tree.' To put it crudely, it does not refer to a thing but signifies a thing's being in a certain place, or else signifies not a thing but the site or locus of a thing such as of the bough or leaf which is higher than any of the other boughs or leaves on the tree. Accordingly it makes sense to say that now one bough and now another is at the top of the tree. But 'at the top of the tree' means no more than what is meant by 'higher than any other part of the tree,' which latter phrase no one could take for a referential phrase like 'the present Vice-Chancellor.'

The place of a thing, or the whereabouts of a thing is not a thing but the tail end of the fact that something is there. 'Where the bee sucks, there suck I,' but it is the clover flower that is there which holds the honey, and not the whereabouts of the flower. All that this amounts to is that though we can use quasi-descriptive phrases to enable us to state where something is, that the thing is there is a relational character of the thing and not itself a subject of characters.

I suspect that a lot of Cartesian and perhaps Newtonian blunders about Space and Time originate from the systematically misleading character of the 'the'-phrases which we use to date and locate things, such as 'the region occupied by x' 'the path followed by 'y', the moment or date at which z happened.' It was not seen that these are but hamstrung predicative expressions and are not and are not even ordinarily taken to be referentially used descriptive expressions, any more than 'the King of France' in 'Poincaré is not the King of France' is ordinarily treated as if it was a referentially used 'the'-phrase.

Take another case. 'Jones hates the thought of going to hospital,' 'the idea of having a holiday has just occurred to me.' These quasi-descriptive phrases suggest that there is one object in the world which is what is referred to by the phrase 'the thought of going to hospital' and another which is what is referred to by 'the idea of having a holiday.' And anyhow partly through accepting the grammatical *prima facies* of such expressions, philosophers have believed as devoutly in the existence of 'ideas,' 'conceptions' and 'thoughts' or 'judgements' as their predecessors did (from similar causes) in that of substantial forms or as children do (from similar causes) in that of the Equator, the sky, and the North Pole.

But if we re-state them, the expressions turn out to be no evidence whatsoever in favour of the Lockean demonology. For 'Jones hates the thought of going to hospital' only means what is meant by 'Jones feels distressed when he thinks of what he will undergo if he goes to hospital.' The phrase 'the thought of . . .' is transmuted into 'whenever he thinks of . . .', which does not even seem to contain a reference to any other entity than Jones and, perhaps, the hospital. For it to be true, the world must contain a Jones who is sometimes thinking and sometimes, say, sleeping; but it need no more contain both Jones and 'the thought or idea of so and so' than it need contain both someone called 'Jones' and something called 'Sleep.'

Similarly, the statement 'the idea of taking a holiday has just occurred to me' seems grammatically to be analogous to 'that dog has just bitten me.' And as, if the latter is true, the world must contain both me and the dog, so it would seem, if the former is true, the world must contain both me and the idea of taking a holiday. But the appearance is a delusion. For while I could not re-state my complaint against the dog in any sentence not containing a descriptive phrase referring to it, I can easily do so with the statement about 'the idea of taking a holiday,' e.g. in the statement 'I have just been thinking that I might take a holiday.'

A host of errors of the same sort has been generated in logic itself and epistemology by the omission to analyse the quasi-descriptive phrase 'the meaning of the expression "x."' I suspect that all the mistaken doctrines of concepts, ideas, terms, judgements, objective propositions, contents, objectives and the like derive from the same fallacy, namely, that there must be *something* referred to by such expressions as 'the meaning of the word (phrase or sentence) "x,"' on all fours with the policeman who really is referred to by the descriptive phrase in 'our village policeman is fond of football.' And the way out of the confusion is to see that some 'the'-phrases are only similar in grammar and not similar in function to referentially-used descriptive phrases, e.g. in the case in point, 'the meaning of "x"' is like 'the King of France' in 'Poincaré is not the King of France,' a predicative expression used non-referentially.

And, of course, the ordinary man does not pretend to himself or anyone else that when he makes statements containing such expressions as 'the meaning of "x"' he is referring to a queer new object: it does not cross his mind that his phrase might be misconstrued as a referentially used descriptive phrase. So he is not guilty of philosophical error or clumsiness. None the less, his form of words is systematically misleading. For an important difference of logical form is disguised by the complete similarity of grammatical form between 'the village policeman is reliable' and 'the meaning of "x" is doubtful' or again between 'I have just met the village policeman' and 'I have just grasped the meaning of "x"'

(Consequently, as there is no object describable as that which is referred to by the expression 'the meaning of "x,"' questions about the status of such objects are meaningless. It is as pointless to discuss whether word-meanings (i.e. 'concepts' or 'universals') are subjective or objective, or whether sentence-meanings (i.e. 'judgements' or 'objectives') are subjective or objective, as it would be to discuss whether the Equator or the sky is subjective or objective. For the questions themselves are not about anything.)

All this does not, of course, in the least prevent us from using intelligently and intelligibly sentences containing the expression 'the meaning of "x"' where this can be re-drafted as 'what "x" means'. For here the 'the'-phrase is being predicatively used and not as an unique description. 'The meaning of "x" is the same as the meaning of "y"' is equivalent to ' "x" means what "y" means', and that can be understood without any temptation to multiply entities.

But this argument is, after all, only about a very special case of the systematic misleadingness of quasi-descriptions.

2. There is another class of uses of 'the'-phrases which is also liable to engender philosophical misconstructions, though I am not sure that I can recall any good instances of actual mistakes which have occurred from this source.

Suppose I say, 'the defeat of the Labour Party has surprised me', What I say could be correctly paraphrased by 'the fact that the Labour Party was defeated, was a surprise to me' or 'the Labour Party has been defeated and I am surprised that it has been defeated'. Here the 'the'-phrase does not refer to a thing but is a condensed record of something's being the case. And this is a common and handy idiom. We can always say instead of 'because A is B, therefore C is D' 'the D-ness of C is due to the B-ness of A'. 'The severity of the winter is responsible for the high price of cabbages' means what is meant by 'Cabbages are expensive because the winter was severe'

But if I say 'the defeat of the Labour Party occurred in 1931', my 'the'-phrase is referentially used to describe an event and not as a condensed record of a fact. For events have dates, but facts do not. So the facts recorded in the grammatically similar statements 'the defeat of the Labour Party has surprised me' and 'the defeat of the Labour Party occurred in 1031' are in logical form quite different. And both sorts of facts are formally quite different from this third fact which is recorded in 'the victory of the Labour Party would have surprised me'. For this neither refers to an event, nor records the fact that the Labour Party was victorious, but says 'if the Labour Party had won, I should have been surprised'. So here the 'the'-phrase is a protasis. And, once more, all these three uses of 'the'-phrase is a protasis. And, once more, all these three uses of 'the'-phrases are different in their sort of significance from 'the defeat of the Conservative Party at the next election is probable', or 'possible', or 'impossible'. For these mean 'the available relevant data are in favour of' or 'not incompatible with' or 'incompatible with the Conservative Party being defeated at the next election'.

So there are at least these four different types of facts which can be and, in ordinary discourse, are conveniently and intelligibly recorded in statements containing grammatically indistinguishable 'the'-phrases. But they can be re-stated in forms of words which do exhibit in virtue of their special grammatical forms the several logical structures of the different sorts of facts recorded.

3. Lastly, I must just mention one further class of systematically misleading 'the'-phrase. 'The whale is not a fish but a mammal' and 'the true Englishman detests foul play' record facts, we may take it. But they are not

about this whale or that Englishman, and they might be true even if there were no whales or no true Englishmen. These are, probably, disguised hypothetical statements. But all I wish to point out is that they are obviously disguised.

I have chosen these three main types of systematically misleading expressions because all alike are misleading in a certain direction. They all suggest the existence of new sorts of objects, or, to put it in another way, they are all temptations to us to 'multiply entities'. In each of them, the quasi-ontological, the quasi-Platonic and the quasi-descriptive expressions, an expression is misconstrued as a denoting expression which in fact does not denote, but only looks grammatically like expressions which are used to denote. Occam's prescription was, therefore, in my view, 'Do not treat all expressions which are grammatically like proper names or referentially used "the"-phrases, as if they were therefore proper names or referentially used "the"-phrases'.

But there are other types of systematically misleading expressions, of which I shall just mention a few that occur to me.

'Jones is an alleged murderer', or 'a suspected murderer', 'Smith is a possible or probable Lord Mayor', 'Robinson is an ostensible, or seeming or mock or sham or bogus hero', 'Brown is a future or a past Member of Parliament', etc. These suggest what they do not mean, that the subjects named are of a special kind of murderer, or Lord Mayor, or hero, or Member of Parliament. But being an alleged murderer does not entail being a murderer, nor does being a likely Lord Mayor entail being a Lord Mayor.

'Jones is popular' suggests that being popular is like being wise, a quality; but in fact it is a relational character, and one which does not directly characterize Jones, but the people who are fond of Jones, and so 'Jones is popular' means what is meant by 'Many people like Jones, and many more like him than either dislike him or are indifferent to him', or something of the sort.

But I have, I think, given enough instances to show in what sense expressions may seem to mean something quite different from what they are in fact used to mean; and therefore I have shown in what sense some expressions are systematically misleading.

So I am taking it as established (1) that what is expressed in one expression can often be expressed in expressions of quite different grammatical forms, and (2) that of two expressions, each meaning what the other means, which are of different grammatical forms, one is often more systematically misleading than the other.

And this means that while a fact or state of affairs *can* be recorded in an indefinite number of statements of widely differing grammatical forms, it is stated better in some than in others. The ideal, which may never be realized, is that it should be stated in a completely non-misleading form of words.

Now, when we call one form of expression better than another, we do not mean that it is more elegant or brief or familiar or more swiftly intelligible to the ordinary listener, but that in virtue of its grammatical form it exhibits, in a way in which the others fail to exhibit, the logical form of the state of affairs or fact that is being recorded. But this interest in the best way of exhibiting the logical form of facts is not for every man, but only for the philosopher.

I wish now to raise, but not to solve, some consequential problems which arise.

1. Given that an expression of a certain grammatical form is proper (or anyhow approximates to being proper) to facts of a certain logical form and to those facts only, is this relation of propriety of grammatical to logical form *natural* or *conventional?*

I cannot myself credit what seems to be the doctrine of Wittgenstein and the school of logical grammarians who owe allegiance to him, that what makes an expression formally proper to a fact is some real and non-conventional one-one picturing relation between the composition of the expression and that of the fact. For I do not see how, save in a small class of specially-chosen cases, a fact or state of affairs can be deemed like or even unlike in structure a sentence, gesture or diagram. For a fact is not a collection — even an arranged collection — of bits in the way in which a sentence is an arranged collection of noises or a map an arranged collection of scratches. A fact is not a thing and so is not even an arranged thing. Certainly a map may be like a country or a railway system, and in a more general, or looser, sense a sentence, as an ordered series of noises, might be a similar sort of series to a series of vehicles in a stream of traffic or the series of days in the week.

But in Socrates being angry or in the fact that either Socrates was wise or Plato was dishonest, I can see no concatenation of bits such that a concatenation of parts of speech could be held to be of the same general architectural plan as it. But this difficulty may be just denseness on my part.

On the other hand, it is not easy to accept what seems to be the alternative that it is just by convention that a given grammatical form is specially dedicated to facts of a given logical form. For, in fact, customary usage is perfectly tolerant of systematically misleading expressions. And, moreover, it is hard to explain how in the genesis of languages our presumably non-philosophical forbears could have decided on or happened on the dedication of a given grammatical form to facts of a given logical form. For presumably the study of abstract logical form is later than the entry into common use of syntactical idioms.

It is, however, my present view that the propriety of grammatical to logical forms is more nearly conventional than natural: though I do not suppose it to be the effect of whim or of deliberate plan.

2. The next question is: How are we to discover in particular cases whether an expression is systematically misleading or not? I suspect that the answer to this will be of this sort. We meet with and understand and even believe a certain expression such as 'Mr. Pickwick is a fictitious person' and 'the Equator encircles the globe'. And we know that if these expressions are saying what they seem to be saying, certain other propositions will follow. But it turns out that the naturally consequential propositions 'Mr. Pickwick was born in such and such a year' and 'the Equator is of such and such a thickness' are not merely

false but, on analysis, in contradiction with something in that from which they seemed to be logical consequences. The only solution is to see that being a fictitious person is not to be a person of a certain sort, and that the sense in which the Equator girdles the earth is not that of being any sort of a ring or ribbon enveloping the earth. And this is to see that the original propositions were not saying what they seemed on first analysis to be saying. Paralogisms and antinomies are the evidence that an expression is systematically misleading.

None the less, the systematically misleading expressions as intended and as understood contain no contradictions. People do not really talk philosophical nonsense — unless they are philosophizing or, what is quite a different thing, unless they are being sententious. What they do is to use expressions which, from whatever cause — generally the desire for brevity and simplicity of discourse — disguise instead of exhibiting the forms of the facts recorded. And it is to reveal these forms that we abstract and generalize. These processes of abstraction and generalization occur before philosophical analysis begins. It seems indeed that their results are the subject matter of philosophy. Pre-philosophical abstract thinking is always misled by systematically misleading expressions, and even philosophical abstract thinking, the proper function of which is to cure this disease, is actually one of its worst victims.

3. I do not know any way of classifying or giving an exhaustive list of the possible types of systematically misleading expressions. I fancy that the number is in principle unlimited, but that the number of prevalent and obsessing types is fairly small.

4. I do not know any way of proving that an expression contains no systematic misleadingness at all. The fact that antinomies have not yet been shown to arise is no proof that they never will arise. We can know that of two expressions '*x*' and '*y*' which record the same fact, '*x*' is less misleading than '*y*'; but not that '*x*' cannot itself be improved upon.

5. Philosophy must then involve the exercise of systematic restatement. But this does not mean that it is a department of philology or literary criticism.

Its restatement is not the substitution of one noun for another or one verb for another. That is what lexicographers and translators excel in. Its restatements are transmutations of syntax, and transmutations of syntax controlled not by desire for elegance or stylistic correctness but by desire to exhibit the forms of the facts into which philosophy is the inquiry.

I conclude, then, that there is, after all, a sense in which we can properly inquire and even say 'what it really means to say so and so'. For we can ask what is the real form of the fact recorded when this is concealed or disguised and not duly exhibited by the expression in question. And we can often succeed in stating this fact in a new form of words which does exhibit what the other failed to exhibit. And I am for the present inclined to believe that this is what philosophical analysis is, and that this is the sole and whole function of philosophy. But I do not want to argue this point now.

But, as confession is good for the soul, I must admit that I do not very much relish the conclusions towards which these conclusions point. I would rather allot to philosophy a sublimer task than the detection of the sources in linguistic idioms of recurrent misconstructions and absurd theories. But that it is at least this I cannot feel any serious doubt.

19. Wittgenstein's Lectures in 1930-33

G. E. Moore

In January 1929, Wittgenstein returned to Cambridge after an absence of more than fifteen years. He came with the intention of residing in Cambridge and pursuing there his researches into philosophical problems. Why he chose Cambridge for this latter purpose I do not know: perhaps it was for the sake of having the opportunity of frequent discussion with F. P. Ramsey. At all events he did in fact reside in Cambridge during all three Full Terms of 1928, and was working hard all the time at his researches.[1] He must, however, at some time during that year, have made up his mind that, besides researching, he would like to do a certain amount of lecturing, since on October 16th, in accordance with his wishes, the Faculty Board of Moral Science resolved that he should be invited to give a course of lectures to be included in their Lecture List for the Lent Term of 1930.

During this year, 1928, when he was researching and had not begun to lecture, he took the Ph.D. degree at Cambridge. Having been entered as an "Advanced Student" during his previous period of residence in 1912 and 1913, he now found that he was entitled to submit a dissertation for the Ph.D. He submitted the *Tractatus* and Russell and I were appointed to examine him. We gave him an oral examination on June 6th, an occasion which I found both pleasant and amusing. We had, of course, no doubt whatever that his work deserved the degree: we so reported, and when our report had been approved by the necessary authorities, he received the degree in due course.

In the same month of June in which we examined him, the Council of Trinity College made him a grant to enable him to continue his researches. (They followed this up in December 1930, by electing him to a Research Fellowship, tenable for five years, which they afterwards prolonged for a time.)

In the following July of 1929 he attended the Joint Session of the Mind Association and Aristotelian Society at Nottingham, presenting a short paper entitled "Some Remarks on Logical Form." This paper was the only piece of philosophical writing by him, other than the *Tractatus,* published during his life-time. Of this paper he spoke in a letter to *Mind* (July 1933) as "weak"; and since 1945 he has spoken of it to me in a still more disparaging manner, saying something to the effect that, when he wrote it, he was getting new ideas about which he was still confused, and that he did not think it deserved any attention.

But what is most important about this year, 1929, is that in it he had frequent discussions with F. P. Ramsey—discussions which were, alas! brought to an end by Ramsey's premature death in January 1930.[2] Ramsey had written for *Mind* (October 1923, page 354) a long Critical Notice of the *Tractatus;* and subsequently, during the period when Wittgenstein was employed as a village schoolmaster in Austria, Ramsey had gone out to see him, in order to question him as to the meaning of certain statements in the *Tractatus.* He stayed in the village for a fortnight or more, having daily discussions with Wittgenstein. Of these discussions in Austria I only know that Ramsey told me that, in reply to his questions as to the meaning of certain statements, Wittgenstein answered more than once that he had forgotten what he had meant by the statement in question. But after the first half of the discussions at Cambridge in 1929, Ramsey wrote at my request the following letter in support of the proposal that Trinity should make Wittgenstein a grant in order to enable him to continue his researches.

"In my opinion Mr. Wittgenstein is a philosophic genius of a different order from anyone else I know. This is partly owing to his great gift for seeing what is essential in a problem and partly to his overwhelming intellectual vigour, to the intensity of thought with which he pursues a question to the bottom and never rests content with a mere possible hypothesis. From his work more than that of any other man I hope for a solution of the difficulties that perplex me both in philosophy generally and in the foundations of Mathematics in particular.

"It seems to me, therefore, peculiarly fortunate that he should have returned to research. During the last two terms I have been in close touch with his work and he seems to me to have made remarkable progress. He began with certain questions in the analysis of propositions which have now led him to problems about infinity which lie at the root of current controversies on the foundations of Mathematics. At first I was afraid that lack of mathematical knowledge and facility would prove a serious handicap to his working in this field. But the progress he has made has already convinced me that this is not so, and that here too he will probably do work of the first importance.

"He is now working very hard and, so far as I can judge, he is getting on well. For him to be interrupted by lack of money would, I think, be a great misfortune for philosophy."

The only other thing I know about these discussions with Ramsey at Cambridge in 1929 is that Wittgenstein once told me that Ramsey had said to him "I don't like your method of arguing."

Wittgenstein began to lecture in January 1930, and from the first he adopted a plan to which he adhered, I believe, throughout his lectures at

Cambridge.[3] His plan was only to lecture once a week in every week of Full Term, but on a later day in each week to hold a discussion class at which what he had said in that week's lecture could be discussed. At first both lecture and discussion class were held in an ordinary lecture-room in the University Arts School; but very early in the first term Mr. R. E. Priestley (now Sir Raymond Priestley), who was then Secretary General of the Faculties and who occupied a set of Fellows' rooms in the new building of Clare, invited Wittgenstein to hold his discussion classes in these rooms. Later on, I think, both lectures and discussion classes were held in Priestley's rooms, and this continued until, in October 1931, Wittgenstein, being then a Fellow of Trinity, was able to obtain a set of rooms of his own in Trinity which he really liked. These rooms were those which Wittgenstein had occupied in the academic year 1912-13, and which I had occupied the year before, and occupied again from October 1913, when Wittgenstein left Cambridge and went to Norway. Of the only two sets which are on the top floor of the gate-way from Whewell's Courts into Sidney Street, they were the set which looks westward over the larger Whewell's Court, and, being so high up, they had a large view of sky and also of Cambridge roofs, including the pinnacles of King's Chapel. Since the rooms were not a Fellow's set, their sitting room was not large, and for the purpose of his lectures and classes Wittgenstein used to fill it with some twenty plain cane-bottomed chairs, which at other times were stacked on the large landing outside. Nearly from the beginning the discussion classes were liable to last at least two hours, and from the time when the lectures ceased to be given in the Arts School they also commonly lasted at least as long. Wittgenstein always had a blackboard at both lectures and classes and made plenty of use of it.

I attended both lectures and discussion classes in all three terms of 1930 and in the first two terms of 1931. In the Michaelmas Term of 1931 and the Lent Term of 1932 I ceased, for some reason which I cannot now remember, to attend the lectures though I still went to the discussion classes; but in May 1932, I resumed the practice of attending the lectures as well, and throughout the academic year 1932-33 I attended both. At the lectures, though not at the discussion classes. I took what I think were very full notes, scribbled in notebooks of which I have six volumes nearly full. I remember Wittgenstein once saying to me that he was glad I was taking notes, since, if anything were to happen to him, they would contain some record of the results of his thinking.

My lecture-notes may be naturally divided into three groups, to which I will refer as (I), (II) and (III). (I) contains the notes of his lectures in the Lent and May Terms of 1930; (II) those of his lectures in the academic year 1930-31; and (III) those of lectures which he gave in the May Term of 1932, after I had resumed attending, as well as those of all the lectures he gave in the academic year 1932-33. The distinction between the three groups is of some importance, since, as will be seen, he sometimes in later lectures corrected what he had said in earlier ones.

The chief topics with which he dealt fall, I think, under the following heads. First of all, in all three periods he dealt (A) with some very general questions about language, (B) with some special questions in the philosophy of Logic, and (C) with some special questions in the philosophy of Mathematics. Next, in (III) and in (III) alone, he dealt at great length, (D) with the difference between the proposition which is expressed by the words "I have got toothache," and those which are expressed by the words "You have got toothache" or "He has got toothache," in which connection he said something about Behaviourism, Solipsism, Idealism and Realism, and (E) with what he called "the grammar of the word 'God' and of ethical and aesthetic statements." And he also dealt, more shortly, in (I) with (F) our use of the term "primary colour"; in (III) with (G) some questions about Time; and in both (II) and (III) with (H) the kind of investigation in which he was himself engaged, and its difference from and relation to what has traditionally been called "philosophy."

I will try to give some account of the chief things he said under all these heads; but I cannot possibly mention nearly everything, and it is possible that some of the things I omit were really more important than those I mention. Also, though I tried to get down in my notes the actual words he used, it is possible that I may sometimes have substituted words of my own which misrepresent his meaning: I certainly did not understand a good many of the things he said. Moreover, I cannot possibly do justice to the extreme richness of illustration and comparison which he used: he was really succeeding in giving what he called a "synoptic" view of things which we all know. Nor can I do justice to the intensity of conviction with which he said everything which he did say, nor to the extreme interest which he excited in his hearers. He, of course, never read his lectures: he had not, in fact, written them out, although he always spent a great deal of time in thinking out what he proposed to say.

(A) He did discuss at very great length, especially in (II), certain very general questions about language; but he said, more than once, that he did not discuss these questions because he thought that language was the subject-matter of philosophy. He did not think that it was. He discussed it only because he thought that particular philosophical errors or "troubles in our thought" were due to false analogies suggested by our actual use of expressions; and he emphasized that it was only necessary for him to discuss those points about language which, as he thought, led to these particular errors or "troubles."

The general things that he had to say about language fall naturally, I think, under two heads, namely (a) what he had to say about the meaning of single words, and (b) what he had to say about "propositions."

(a) About the meaning of single words, the positive points on which he seemed most anxious to insist were, I think, two, namely (α) something which he expressed by saying that the meaning of any single word in a language is "defined," "constituted," "determined" or "fixed" (he used all four expressions in different places) by the "grammatical rules" with which it is used in that language, and (β) something which he expressed by saying that every significant word or symbol must essentially belong to a "system," and (metaphorically) by saying that the meaning of a word is its "place" in a "grammatical system."

But he said in (III) that the sense of "meaning" of which he held these things to be true, and which was the only sense in which he intended to use the word, was only one of those in which we commonly use it: that there was another which he described as that in which it is used "as a name for a process accompanying our use of a word and our hearing of a word." By the latter he apparently meant that sense of "meaning" in which "to know the meaning" of a word means the same as to "understand" the word; and I think he was not quite clear as to the relation between this sense of "meaning" and that in which he intended to use it, since he seemed in two different places to suggest two different and incompatible views of this relation, saying in (II) that "the rules applying to negation actually describe my experience in using 'not,' i.e. describe my understanding of the word," and in one place in (III), on the other hand, saying, "perhaps there is a causal connection between the rules and the feeling we have when we hear 'not.'" On the former occasion he added that "a logical investigation doesn't teach us anything about the meaning of negation: we can't get any clearer about its meaning. What's difficult is to make the rules explicit."

Still later in (III) he made the rather queer statement that "the idea of meaning is in a way obsolete, except in such phrases as 'this means the same as that' or 'this has no meaning,'" having previously said in (III) that "the mere fact that we have the expression 'the meaning' of a word is bound to lead us wrong: we are led to think that the rules are responsible to something not a rule, whereas they are only responsible to rules."

As to (*a*) although he had said, at least once, that the meaning of a word was "constituted" by the grammatical rules which applied to it, he explained later that he did not mean that the meaning of a word *was* a list of rules; and he said that though a word "carried its meaning with it," it did not carry with it the grammatical rules which applied to it. He said that the student who had asked him whether he meant that the meaning of a word *was* a list of rules would not have been tempted to ask that question but for the false idea (which he held to be a common one) that in the case of a substantive like "the meaning" you have to look for something at which you can point and say "This is the meaning." He seemed to think that Frege and Russell had been misled by the same idea, when they thought they were bound to give an answer to the question. "What *is* the number 2?" As for what he meant by saying that the meaning of a word is "determined by" (this was the phrase which he seemed to prefer) the "grammatical rules" in accordance with which it is used, I do not think he explained further what he meant by this phrase.

(*β*) As to what he meant by saying that, in order that a word or other sign should have meaning, it must belong to a "system," I have not been able to arrive at any clear idea. One point on which he insisted several times in (II) was that if a word which I use is to have meaning, I must "commit myself" by its use. And he explained what he meant by this by saying "If I commit myself, that means that if I use, e.g., 'green' in this case, I have to use it in others," adding "If you commit yourself, there are consequences." Similarly he said a little later, "If a word is to have significance, we must commit ourselves," adding "There is no use in correlating noises to facts, unless we commit ourselves to using the noise in a particular way again—unless the correlation has consequences," and going on to say that it must be possible to be "led by a language." And when he expressly raised, a little later, the question "What is there in this talk of a 'system' to which a symbol must belong?" he answered that we are concerned with the phenomenon of "being guided by." It looked, therefore, as if one use which he was making of the word "system" was such that in order to say that a word or other sign "belonged to a system," it was not only necessary but *sufficient* that it should be used in the same way on several different occasions. And certainly it would be natural to say that a man who habitually used a word in the same way was using it "systematically."

But he certainly also frequently used "system" in such a sense that *different* words or other expressions could be said to belong to the *same* "system"; and where, later on, he gave, as an illustration of what he meant by "Every symbol must essentially belong to a system," the proposition "A crotchet can only give information on what note to play in a system of crotchets," he seemed to imply that for a sign to have significance it is *not* sufficient that we should "commit ourselves" by its use, but that it is also necessary that the sign in question should belong to the same "system" with other signs. Perhaps, however, he only meant, not that for a sign to have *some* meaning, but that for *some* signs to have the significance which they actually have in a given language, it is necessary that they should belong to the same "system" with other signs. This word "system" was one which he used very very frequently, and I do not know what conditions he would have held must be satisfied by two different signs in order that they may properly be said to belong to the same "system." He said in one place in (II) that the "system of projection" by which " 2 + 3 " can be projected into "5" is "in no way inferior" to the "system" by which "11 + 111" can be projected into "11111," and I think one can see, in this case, that "2 + 3 = 5" can be properly said to belong to the same "system" as, e.g., "2 + 2 = 4," and also can properly be said to belong to a different "system" from that to which "11 + 111 = 11111" and "11 + 11 = 1111" both belong, though I have no clear idea as to the sense in which these things can properly be said. Nor do I know whether Wittgenstein would have held, e.g., that in the case of *every* English word, it could not have the significance which it actually has in English unless it belonged to the same "system" as other English words, or whether he would have held that this is only true of *some* English words, e.g. of the words "five" and "four," and of the words "red" and "green."

But besides these two positive things, (α) and (β), which he seemed anxious to say about the meaning of words, he also insisted on three negative things, i.e. that three views which have sometimes been held are mistakes. The first of these mistakes was (γ) the view that the meaning of a word was some image which it calls up by association—a view to which he seemed to refer as the "causal" theory of meaning. He admitted that sometimes you cannot understand a word unless it calls up an image, but insisted that, even where this is the case, the image is just as much a "symbol" as the word is. The second mistake was (δ) the view that, where we can give an "ostensive" definition of a word, the object pointed at is the meaning of the word. Against this view, he said, for one thing, that, in such a case "the gesture of pointing together with the object pointed at can be used *instead* of the word," i.e. is itself something which has meaning and has the same meaning as the word has. In this connection he also pointed out that you may point at a red book, either to show the meaning of "book" or to show the meaning of "red," and that hence in "This is a book" and "This is the colour 'red,'" "this" has quite a different meaning; and he emphasized that, in order to understand the ostensive definition "This is 'red,'" the hearer must already understand what is meant by "colour." And the third mistake was (ε) that a word is related to its meaning in the same way in which a proper name is related to the "bearer" of that name. He gave as a reason for holding that this is false that the bearer of a name can be ill or dead, whereas we cannot possibly say that the meaning of the name is ill or dead. He said more than once that the bearer of a name can be "substituted" for the name, whereas the meaning of a word can never be substituted for that word. He sometimes spoke of this third mistake as the view that words are "representative" of their meanings, and he held that in no case is a word "representative" of its meaning, although a proper name is "representative" of its bearer (if it has one). He added in one place: "The meaning of a word is no longer for us an object corresponding to it."

On the statement, "Words, except in propositions, have no meaning" he said that this "is true or false, as you understand it"; and immediately went on to add that, in what he called "language games," single words "have meanings by themselves," and that they may have meaning by themselves even in our ordinary language "if we have provided one." In this connection he said, in (II), that he had made a mistake (I think he meant in the *Tractatus*) in supposing that a proposition must be complex. He said the truth was that we can replace a proposition by a simple sign, but that the simple sign must be "part of a system."

(*b*) About "propositions," he said a great deal in many places as to answers which might be given to the question "What is a proposition?"—a question which he said we do not understand clearly. But towards the end of (III) he had definitely reached the conclusion "It is more or less arbitrary what we call a 'proposition,'" adding that "therefore Logic plays a part different from what I and Russell and Frege supposed it to play"; and a little later he said that he could not give a general definition of "proposition" any more than of "game": that he could only give examples, and that any line he could draw would be "arbitrary, in the sense that nobody would have decided whether to call so-and-so a 'proposition' or not." But he added that we are quite right to use the word "game," so long as we don't pretend to have drawn a definite outline.

In (II), however, he had said that the word "proposition," "as generally understood," includes both "what I call propositions," also "hypotheses," and also mathematical propositions; that the distinction between these three "kinds" is a "logical distinction," and that therefore there must be some grammatical rules, in the case of each kind, which apply to that kind and not to the other two; but that the "truth-function" rules apply to all three, and that that is why they are all called "propositions."

He went on to illustrate the difference between the first two kinds by saying that "There seems to me to be a man here" is of the first kind, whereas "There is a man here" is a "hypothesis"; and said that one rule which applies to the first and not to the second is that I can't say "There seems to me to seem to me to be a man here" whereas I can say "There seems to me to be a man here." But, soon after, he said that the word "proposition" is used in *two* different ways, a wider and a narrower, meaning by the wider that in which it included all three of the kinds just distinguished, and by the narrower, apparently, that in which it included the first two kinds, but not the third. For propositions in this narrower sense he seemed later very often to use the expression "experiential propositions," and accordingly I will use this expression to include propositions of both the first two kinds. The things which he had to say about experiential propositions, thus understood, were extremely different from those which he had to say about the third kind; and I will therefore treat these two subjects separately.

(α) Of experiential propositions he said in (I) that they could be "compared with reality" and either "agreed or disagreed with it." He pointed out very early something whch he expressed by saying "Much of language needs outside help," giving as an example your use of a specimen of a colour in order to explain what colour you want a wall painted; but he immediately went on to say (using "language" in a different sense) that in such a case the specimen of a colour is "a part of your language." He also pointed out (as in the *Tractatus*) that you can assert a proposition or give an order without using any words or symbols (in the ordinary sense of "symbol"). One of the most striking things about his use of the term "proposition" was that he apparently so used it that in giving an order you are necessarily expressing a "proposition," although, of course, an order can be neither true nor false, and can be "compared with reality" only in the different sense that you can look to see whether it is carried out or not.

About propositions, understood in this sense, he made a distinction in (II) between what he called "the sign" and what he called "the symbol," saying that whatever was necessary to give a "sign" significance was a part of "the symbol," so that where, for instance, the "sign" is a sentence, the "symbol" is something which contains both the sign and also everything which is necessary to give that sentence sense. He said that a "symbol," thus understood, *is* a "proposition" and "cannot be nonsensical, though it can be either true or false." He illustrated this by saying that if a man says "I am tired" his mouth is part of the symbol; and said that any explanation of a sign "completes the symbol."

Here, therefore, he seemed to be making a distinction between a proposition and a sentence, such that no sentence can be identical with any proposition, and that no proposition can be without sense. But I do not think that in his actual use of the term "proposition" he adhered to this distinction. He seemed to me sometimes so to use "proposition" that every significant sentence *was* a proposition, although, of course, a significant sentence does not contain everything which is necessary to give it significance. He said, for instance, that signs with different meanings must *be* different "symbols." And very often he seemed to me to follow the example of Russell in the Introduction to *Principia Mathematica* in so using the word "proposition" that "propositions," and not merely sentences, could be without sense; as, for instance, when he said at the beginning of (II) that his object was to give us some "firm ground" such as "If a proposition has a meaning, its negation must have a meaning." And, towards the end of (III), in connection with the view at which he had then arrived that the words "proposition," "language" and "sentence" are all "vague," he expressly said that the answer to the question whether, when you say "A unicorn looks like this" and point at a picture of a unicorn, the picture is or is not a part of the proposition you are making, was "You can say which you please." He was, therefore, now rejecting his earlier view that a proposition must contain everything which is necessary to make a sentence significant, and seemed to be implying that the use of "proposition" to mean the same as "sentence" was a perfectly correct one.

In connection with the *Tractatus* statement that propositions, in the "narrower" sense with which we are now concerned are "pictures," he said he had not at that time noticed that the word "picture" was vague; but he still, even towards the end of (III), said that he thought it "useful to say 'A proposition is a picture *or something like one*'" although in (II) he had said he was willing to admit that to call a proposition a "picture" was misleading; that propositions are not pictures "in any ordinary sense"; and that to say that they are, "merely stresses a certain aspect of the grammar of the word 'proposition'—merely stresses that our uses of the words 'proposition' and 'picture' follow similar rules."

In connection with this question of the similarity between experiential "propositions" and pictures, he frequently used the words "project" and "projection." Having pointed out that it is paradoxical to say that the words "Leave the room" is a "picture" of what a boy does if he obeys the order, and having asserted that it is, in fact, *not* a "picture" of the boy's action "in any ordinary sense," he nevertheless went on to say that it is "as much" a picture of the boy's action as "2 + 3" is of "5," and that "2 + 3" really is a picture of "5" "*with reference to a particular system of projection,*" and that this system is "in no way inferior" to the system in which "11 + 111" is projected into "11111," only that "the method of projection is rather queer." He had said previously that the musical signs ' ♯ ' and ' ♭ ' are obviously not pictures of anything you do on the

keyboard of a piano; that they differ in this respect from what, e.g. " 𝄞 "

would be, if you had the rule that the second crotchet is to stand for the white key on the piano that is next to the right of that for which the first crotchet stands, and similarly for the third and second crotchet; but nevertheless, he said, '♯' and '♭' "work in exactly the same way" as these crotchets would work, and added that "almost all our words work as they do." He explained this by saying that a "picture" must have been given by an explanation of how '♯' and '♭' are used, and that an explanation is always of the same kind as a definition, viz. "replacing one symbol by another." He went on to say that when a man reads on a piano from a score, he is "led" or "guided" by the position of the crotchets, and that this means that he is "following a general rule," and that this rule, though not "contained" in the score, nor in the result, nor in both together, must be "contained" in his intention. But he said, that though the rule is "contained" in the intention, the intention obviously does not "contain" any *expression* of the rule, any more than, when I read aloud, I am conscious of the rules I follow in translating the printed signs into sounds. He said that what the piano player does is "to see the rule in the score," and that, even if he is playing automatically, he is still "guided by" the score, provided that he *would* use the general rule to judge whether he had made a mistake or not. He even said in one place that to say that a man is "guided" by the score "means" that he *would justify* what he played by reference to the score. He concluded by saying that, if he plays correctly, there is *a* "similarity" between what he does on the piano and the score, "though we usually confine "similarity" to projection according to certain rules only"; and that in the same sense there is *a* "similarity" between automatic traffic signals and the movements of traffic which are guided by them. Later on he said that for any sign whatever there *could* be a method of projection such that it made sense, but that when he said of any particular expression "That means nothing" or "is nonsense," what he meant was "*With the common method of projection* that means nothing," giving as an instance that when he called the sentence "It is due to human weakness that we can't write down all the cardinal numbers" "meaningless," he meant that it is meaningless if the person who says it is using "due to human weakness" as in "It's due to human weakness that we can't write down a billion cardinal numbers." Similarly, he said that surely Helmholtz must have been talking nonsense when he said that in happy moments he could imagine four-dimensional space, because *in the system he was using* those words make no sense, although "I threw the chalk into four-dimensional space" would make sense, if we were not using the words on the analogy of throwing from one room into another, but merely meant "It first disappeared and then appeared again." He insisted more than once that we are apt to think that we are using a new system of projection which would give sense to our words, when in fact we are not using a new system at all: "any expression" he said "*may* make sense, but you may think you are using it with sense, when in fact you are not."

One chief view about propositions to which he was opposed was a view which he expressed as the view that a proposition is a sort of "shadow" intermediate between the expression which we use in order to assert it and the fact (if any) which "verifies" it. He attributed this view to W. E. Johnson, and he said of it that it was an attempt to make a distinction between a proposition and a sentence. (We have seen that he himself had in (II) made a different attempt to do this.) He said that it regarded the supposed "shadow" as something "similar" to the fact which verifies it, and in that way different from the expression which expresses it, which is not "similar" to the fact in question; and he said that, even if there were such a "shadow" it would not "bring us any nearer to the fact," since "it would be susceptible of different interpretations just as the expression is." He said, "You can't give any picture which can't be misinterpreted" and "No interpolation between a sign and its fulfilment does away with a sign." He added that the only description of an expectation "which is relevant for us" is "the expression of it," and that "the expression of an expectation contains a description of the fact that would fulfil it," pointing out that if I expect to *see a red patch* my expectation is fulfilled if and only if I do *see a red patch,* and saying that the words "see a red patch" have the same meaning in both expressions.

Near the beginning of (I) he made the famous statement, "The sense of a proposition is the way in which it is verified"; but in (III) he said this only meant "You can determine the meaning of a proposition by asking how it is verified" and went on to say, "This is necessarily a mere rule of thumb, because 'verification' means different things, and because in some cases the question 'How is that verified?' makes no sense." He gave as an example of a case in which that question "makes no sense" the proposition "I've got toothache," of which he had already said that it makes no sense to ask for a verification of it—to ask "How do you know that you have?" I think that he here meant what he said of "I've got toothache" to apply to all those propositions which he had originally distinguished from "hypotheses" as "what I call propositions"; although in (II) he had distinguished the latter from "hypotheses" by saying that they had "a definite verification or falsification." It would seem, therefore, that in (III) he had arrived at the conclusion that what he had said in (II) was wrong, and that in the case of "what he called propositions," so far from their having "a definite verification," it was senseless to say that they had a verification at all. His "rule of thumb," therefore, could only apply, if at all, to what he called "hypotheses"; and he went on to say that, in many cases, it does not apply even to these, saying that statements in the newspapers could verify the "hypothesis" that Cambridge had won the boat-race, and that yet these statements "only go a very little way towards explaining the meaning of 'boat-race'"; and that similarly "The pavement is wet" may verify the proposition "It has been raining," and that yet "it gives very little of the grammar of 'It has been raining.'" He went on to say "Verification determines the meaning of a proposition only where it gives the grammar of the proposition in question"; and in answer to the question "How far is giving a verification of a proposition a grammatical statement about it?" he said that, whereas "When it rains the pavement gets wet" is not a grammatical statement at all, if we say "The fact that the pavement is wet is a *symptom* that it has been raining" this statement is "a matter of grammar."

*　　*　　*

(H) I was a good deal surprised by some of the things he said about the difference between "philosophy" in the sense in which what he was doing might be called "philosophy" (he called this "modern philosophy"), and what has traditionally been called "philosophy." He said that what he was doing was a "new subject," and not merely a stage in a "continuous development"; that there was now, in philosophy, a "kink" in the "development of human thought," comparable to that which occurred when Galileo and his contemporaries invented dynamics; that a "new method" had been discovered, as had happened when "chemistry was developed out of alchemy"; and that it was now possible for the first time that there should be "skilful" philosophers, though of course there had in the past been "great" philosophers.

He went on to say that, though philosophy had now been "reduced to a matter of skill," yet this skill, like other skills, is very difficult to acquire. One difficulty was that it required a "sort of thinking" to which we are not accustomed and to which we have not been trained—a sort of thinking very different from what is required in the sciences. And he said that the required skill could not be acquired merely by hearing lectures: discussion was essential. As regards his own work, he said it did not matter whether his results were true or not: what mattered was that "a method had been found."

In answer to the question why this "new subject" should be called "philosophy" he said in (III) that though what he was doing was certainly different from what, e.g., Plato or Berkeley had done, yet people might feel that it "takes the place of" what they had done—might be inclined to say "This is what I really wanted" and to identify it with what they had done, though it is really different, just as (as I said above) a person who had been trying to trisect an angle by rule and compasses might, when shown the proof that this is impossible, be inclined to say that this impossible thing was the very thing he had been trying to do, though what he had been trying to do was really different. But in (II) he had also said that the "new subject" did really resemble what had been traditionally called "philosophy" in the three respects that (1) it was very general, (2) it was fundamental both to ordinary life and to the sciences, and (3) it was independent of any special results of science; that therefore the application to it of the word "philosophy" was not purely arbitrary.

He did not expressly try to tell us exactly what the "new method" which had been found was. But he gave some hints as to its nature. He said, in (II), that the "new subject" consisted in "something like putting in order our notions as to what can be said about the world," and compared this to the tidying up of a room where you have to move the same object several times before you can get the room really tidy. He said also that we were "in a muddle about things," which we had to try to clear up; that we had to follow a certain instinct which leads us to ask certain questions, though we don't even understand what these questions mean; that our asking them results from "a vague mental uneasiness," like that which leads children to ask "Why?"; and that this uneasiness can only be cured "either by showing that a particular question is not permitted, or by answering it." He also said that he was not trying to teach us any new facts: that he would only tell us "trivial" things—"things which we all know already"; but that the difficult thing was to get a "synopsis" of these trivialities, and that our "intellectual discomfort" can only be removed by a synopsis of *many* trivialities—that "if we leave out any, we still have the feeling that something is wrong." In this connection he said it was misleading to say that what we wanted was an "analysis," since in science to "analyse" water means to discover some new fact about it, e.g. that it is composed of oxygen and hydrogen, whereas in philosophy "we know at the start all the facts we need to know." I imagine that it was in this respect of needing a "synopsis" of trivialities that he thought that philosophy was similar to Ethics and Aesthetics.

I ought, perhaps, finally to repeat what I said in the first part of this article namely, that he held that though the "new subject" must say a great deal about language, it was only necessary for it to deal with those points about language which have led, or are likely to lead, to definite philosophical puzzles or errors. I think he certainly thought that some philosophers nowadays have been misled into dealing with linguistic points which have no such bearing, and the discussion of which therefore, in his view, forms no part of the proper business of a philosopher.

NOTES

1. The statement in the Obituary notice in *The Times* for May 2, 1951, that he arrived in Cambridge in 1929 "for a short visit" is very far from the truth. Fortunately I kept a brief diary during the period in question and can therefore vouch for the truth of what I have stated above about his residence in 1929, though there is in fact other evidence.

2. In the Preface to his posthumously published *Philosophical Investigations,* where Wittgenstein acknowledges his obligations to Ramsey (p. x), Wittgenstein himself says that he had "innumerable" discussions with Ramsey "during the last two years of his life," which should mean both in 1928 and in 1929. But I think this must be a mistake. I imagine that Wittgenstein, trusting to memory alone, had magnified into a series of discussions continuing for two years, a series which in fact only continued for a single year. It will be noticed that in the letter from Ramsey himself which I am about to quote, and which is dated June 14, 1929, Ramsey states that he had been in close touch with Wittgenstein's work "during the last two terms," i.e. during the Lent and May Terms of 1929, implying that he had not been in close touch with it in 1928. And though I do not know where Wittgenstein was in 1928, he certainly was not resident in Cambridge where Ramsey was resident, so that it is hardly possible that they can have had in that year such frequent discussions as they certainly had in 1929.

3. Professor von Wright has subsequently informed me that I was mistaken in believing this: that in 1939, Wittgenstein lectured twice a week and held no discussion class; and that in the Easter Term of 1947, he both gave two lectures a week and also held a discussion class. I have also remembered that at one time (I do not know for how long) he gave, besides his ordinary lectures, a special set of lectures for mathematicians.

20. Philosophical Perplexity

John Wisdom

1. *Philosophical statements are really verbal.* — I have inquired elsewhere the real nature of philosophical requests such as 'Can we know what is going on in someone else's mind?' 'Can we really know the causes of our sensations?' 'What is a chair?' and of philosophical answers such as 'We can never really know the causes of our sensations', 'A chair is nothing but our sensations', or 'A chair is something over and above our sensations', 'The goodness of a man, of a picture, of an argument is something over and above our feelings of approval and over and above those features of the man, the picture or the argument, which "determine" its goodness'. There is no time to repeat the inquiry here and I have to say dogmatically:

A philosophical answer is really a verbal recommendation in response to a request which is really a request with regard to a sentence which lacks a conventional use whether there occur situations which could conventionally be described by it. The description, for example 'I know directly what is going on in Smith's mind', is not a jumble like 'Cat how is up', nor is it in conflict with conventional usage like 'There are two white pieces and three black so there are six pieces on the board'. It just lacks a conventional usage. To call both 'Can *2 + 3* = 6?' and 'Can I know what is going on in the minds of others?' nonsensical questions serves to bring out the likeness between them. But if one were to deny that there is a difference between them it would be an instance of that disrespect for other people which we may platitudinously say, so often damages philosophical work. A disrespect which blinds one to the puzzles they raise — in this instance the puzzle of the philosophical *can* which somehow seems between 'Can *2 + 3* make *6*?' and 'Can terriers catch hares?' Compare 'Can persons be in two places at once?' 'Do we have unconscious wishes?' 'Can you play chess without the queen?' (W).[1]

Even to say that 'I know directly what is going on in Smith's mind' is *meaningless,* is dangerous, especially if you have just said that 'There are two white pieces and three black so there are six' is meaningless.

It is not even safe to say that 'I know directly what is going on in Smith's mind' lacks a use or meaning and leave it at that. For though it has no meaning it tends to have a meaning, like 'All whifley was the tulgey wood', though of course it is unlike this last example in the important respect that it does not lack a meaning because its constituent words are unknown. Nor does it lack meaning because its syntax is unknown. This makes it puzzling and makes it resemble the logical case. It is clear that for these reasons it would be even more illuminating and more misleading to say that 'God exists' and 'Men are immortal' are meaningless—especially just after saying $2 + 3 = 6$ is meaningless.

2. *Philosophical statements are not verbal.* —I have said that philosophers' questions and theories are really verbal. But if you like we will not say this or we will say also the contradictory.[2] For of course (*a*) philosophic statements usually have not a verbal air. On the contrary they have a non-verbal air like 'A fox's brush is really a tail'. (W). And their non-verbal air is not an unimportant feature of them because on it very much depends their puzzlingness.

And (*b*) though really verbal a philosopher's statements have not a merely verbal point. Unlike many statements the primary point of uttering them is not to convey the information they convey but to do something else. Consequently all attempts to explain their peculiar status by explaining the peculiar nature of their subject-matter, fail. For their subject-matter is not peculiar; their truth or falsity, in so far as these are appropriate to them at all, is fixed by facts about words; e.g. Goodness is not approval by the majority, because 'The majority, sometimes approve what is bad' is not self-contradictory. But the point of philosophical statements is peculiar. It is the illumination of the ultimate structure of facts, i.e. the relations between different categories of being or (we must be in the mode) the relations between different sub-languages within a language.

The puzzles of philosophical propositions, of fictional propositions, general propositions, negative propositions, propositions about the future, propositions about the past, even the puzzle about psychological propositions, are not removed by explaining the peculiar nature of the subject-matter of the sentences in which they are expresssed but by reflecting upon the peculiar manner in which those sentences work. Mnemonic slogan: It's not the stuff, it's the style that stupefies.

3. *The divergence of point from content.* —The divergence of point from content which is found in necessary and near necessary propositions can be explained here only briefly.

Suppose a decoder, though still utterly ignorant of the meaning of both of two expressions 'monarchy' and 'set of persons ruled by the same king', has after prolonged investigation come to the conclusion that they mean the same in a certain code. He will say to his fellow-decoder ' "Monarchy" means the same as "set of persons ruled by the same king" '. The translator, and the philosopher also, may say the same. They all use the same form of words because what they say is the same. But the point of what they say is very different. The decoder's point can be got by anyone who knows the meaning of 'means the same as'; the translator does what he wants with the sentence only if his hearer knows the meaning either of 'monarchy' or of 'set of persons ruled by the same king'; the philosopher does what he wants with the sentence only if his hearer already uses, i.e. understands, i.e. knows the meaning of, *both* 'monarchy' and 'set of persons ruled by the same king'. This condition makes the case of the philosopher curious; for it states that he can do what he wants with the sentence only if his hearer already knows what he is telling him. But this is true in the required sense. The philosopher draws attention to what is already known with a view to giving insight into the structure of what 'monarchy', say, means, i.e. bringing into connection the sphere in which the one expression is used with that in which the other is. Compare the man who says 'I should have the change from a pound after spending five shillings on a book, one and sevenpence-halfpenny on stamps and two and twopence-halfpenny at the grocer's, so I should have eleven shillings and twopence'. This is Moore's example and I beg attention for it. It is tremendously illuminating in the *necessary synthetic* group of puzzles and in a far, far wider field that this, because it illuminates the use of 'means the same'—a phrase which stops so many. When on first going to France I learn the exchange rate for francs, do I know the meaning of 'worth 100 francs' or do I come to know this after staying three weeks?

The philosopher is apt to say 'A monarchy is a set of people under a king' rather than '"Monarchy" means the same as "a set of people under a king"'. By using the former sentence he intimates his point. Now shall we say 'A monarchy is a set of people under a king' means the same as '"Monarchy" means "a set of people under a king"' or not? My answer is 'Say which you like. But if you say "Yes" be careful, etc., and if you say "No" be careful, etc.'

If we decide to describe the difference between the two as a difference of meaning we must not say that the difference in meaning is a difference of subjective intension, nor that it is a difference of emotional significance merely. For these are not adequate accounts of the difference between the two—and not an adequate account of the difference between the use of '3 plus 5 plus 8' and the use of '16'.

4. *Philosophy, truth, misleadingness and illumination.* —Now that we have seen that the philosopher's intention is to bring out relations between categories of being, between spheres of language, we shall be more prepared to allow that false statements about the usage of words may be philosophically very useful and even adequate provided their falsity is realized and there is no confusion about what they are being used for.

The nature of the philosopher's intention explains how it is that one may call a philosophical theory such as *A proposition is a sentence,* certainly false, and yet feel that to leave one's criticism at that is to attend to the letter and not the spirit of the theory criticized.

The nature of the philosopher's intention explains also how it is that one cannot say of a philosopher's theory that it is false when he introduces it in his own terminology, while yet one often feels that such theories are somehow philosophically bad. Thus (W) suppose the word 'sense-datum' has never been used before and that someone says 'When Jones sees a rabbit, has an illusion of a rabbit, has an hallucination of a rabbit, dreams of a rabbit, he has a sense-datum of a rabbit'. One cannot protest that this is false, since no statement has been made, only a recommendation. But the recommendation purports to be enlightening and one may well protest if it is, on the contrary, misleading. This particular recommendation is liable to suggest that sense-data are a special sort of thing, *extremely* thin coloured pictures, and thus liable to raise puzzles, such as How are sense-data related to material things?' We can abuse a philosopher as much as we like if we use the right adjectives. *Good is an ultimate predicate* is useless, *A proposition is a subsistent entity* is useless and pretentious,[3] *We can never know the real cause of our sensations* is misleading. And we can praise him although he speaks falsely or even nonsensically. People have considered whether it is true that 'an event is a pattern of complete, particular, specific facts and a complete, particular, specific fact is an infinitely thin slice out of an event'.[4]

You may say 'How absurd of them since the statement is nonsense'. Certainly the statement is nonsense and so, if you like, it was absurd of them. But it was better than saying it was nonsense and ignoring it. Suppose I say 'The thoroughbred is a neurotic woman on four legs'. This is nonsense, but it is not negligible.[5]

5. *Provocation and Pacification.* — So far, however, little or nothing has been said to explain what sort of things make a philosophical statement misleading and what make it illuminating. Only a short answer is possible here.

In the first place there is the misleading feature which nearly all philosophical statements have — a non-verbal air. The philosopher *laments* that we can never really know what is going on in someone else's mind, that we can never really know the causes of our sensations, that inductive conclusions are never really justified. He laments these things as if he can dream of another world where we can see our friends and tables face to face, where scientists can justify their conclusions and terriers can catch hares. This enormous source of confusion we cannot study now.

Secondly philosophical statements mislead when by the use of like expressions for different cases, they suggest likenesses which do not exist, and by the use of different expressions for like cases, they conceal likenesses which do exist.

Philosophical theories are illuminating in a corresponding way, namely when they suggest or draw attention to a terminology which reveals likenesses and differences concealed by ordinary language.

I want to stress the philosophical usefulness of metaphysical surprises such as 'We can never really know the causes of our sensations', 'We can never know the real causes of our sensations', 'Inductive conclusions are never really justified', 'The laws of mathematics are really rules of grammar'. I believe that too much fun has been made of philosophers who say this king of thing.

Remember what Moore said about 1924—words to this effect: When a philosopher says that really something is so we are warned that what he says is really so is not so really. With horrible ingenuity Moore can rapidly reduce any metaphysical theory to a ridiculous story. For he is right, they are false—only there *is* good in them, poor things. This shall be explained.

Wittgenstein allows importance to these theories. They are for him expressions of deep-seated puzzlement. It is an important part of the treatment of a puzzle to develop it to the full.

But this is not enough. Wittgenstein allows that the theories are philosophically important not merely as specimens of the whoppers philosophers can tell. But he too much represents them as merely symptoms of linguistic confusion. I wish to represent them as also symptoms of linguistic penetration.

Wittgenstein gives the impression that philosophical remarks either express puzzlement or if not are remarks such as Wittgenstein himself makes with a view to curing puzzlement.

This naturally gives rise to the question 'If the proper business of philosophy is the removal of puzzlement, would it not be best done by giving a drug to the patient which made him entirely forget the statements puzzling him or at least lose his uneasy feelings?'

This of course will never do. And what we say about the philosopher's purposes must be changed so that it shall no longer seem to lead to such an absurd idea.

The philosopher's purpose is to gain a grasp of the relations between different categories of being, between expressions used in *different manners*.[6] He is confused about what he wants and he is confused by the relations between the expressions, so he is very often puzzled. But only such treatment of the puzzles as increases a grasp of the relations between different categories of being is philosophical. And not all the philosopher's statements are either complaints of puzzlement or pacificatory. Philosophers who say 'We never know the real causes of our sensations', 'Only my sensations are real', often bring out these 'theories' with an air of triumph (with a misleading air of empirical discovery indeed). True the things they say are symptoms of confusion even if they are not of puzzlement. But they are also symptoms of penetration, of noticing what is not usually noticed. Philosophical progress has two aspects, provocation and pacification.

6. *Example of the pointless doubts: (a) how misleading they are.*—Let us consider this with examples. Take first the philosopher who says to the plain man: 'We do not really know that there is cheese on the table; for might not all the sense evidence suggest this and yet there be no cheese—remember what happened at Madame Tussaud's'.

Our assertion with confidence that there is cheese on the table or our assertion that we know that there is cheese on the table raises at last these three puzzles: (1) *the category puzzle,* which finds expression in 'We ought not to speak of a cheese (of the soul) but of bundles of sense-data'; (2) *the knowledge* puzzle, which finds expression in 'We ought not to say "I know there is cheese on the table" but "Very, very probably there is cheese on the table"'; (3) *the justification puzzle,* which finds expression in 'Empirical conclusions are not really justified'.

We cannot here speak of all these. We are considering (2) the *knowledge* or *pointless doubt* puzzle. There are a group of pointless doubt puzzles including the following: 'We don't really know that there is cheese on the table'; 'We ought to say only "It is probable that there is cheese on the table"'; 'It is improper to say "I know that there is cheese on the table"'; 'It would be well if we prefixed every remark about material things with "probably"'.

All these suggestions are misleading—they all suggest that it has been discovered that we have been over-confident about material things. They should have slightly different treatment but I have only just *realized* this multiplicity. Let us take the puzzle in the crude form 'Couldn't there be no cheese here although all the sense-evidence suggests there is?'

Wittgenstein explains that this sentence though of the verbal form we associate with doubt and though it may be uttered with the intonation, expression and gestures we associate with doubt is not *used* as a sentence expressing doubt. To utter it is to raise a pseudo doubt. People say 'We ought not to say "There *is* cheese on the table" but "Probably there is cheese on the table" or "The sense-evidence suggests ever so strongly that there is cheese on the table". For whatever we do we never observe a cheese, we have to rely upon our senses. And we may be suffering from a joint hallucination of all the senses or a consistent dream. Remember how people are deceived at Madame Tussaud's. And we may see and touch cheesy patches, smell cheesy smells, obtain cheesy pictures from cameras and cheesy reactions from mice and yet the stuff to-morrow be soap in our mouth. And then to-morrow we shall say "Yesterday we were mistaken". So our "knowledge" to-day that there is cheese here is not real knowledge. Every one ought really to whisper "Possibly hallucinatory" after *every* sentence about material things however much he has made sure that he is right'.

What those who recommend this should notice is how not merely unusual but pointless a use of words they recommend. As language is at present used, I raise my hungry friends' hopes if I say 'There is cheese on the table', and I damp them if I add 'unless it is hallucinatory'. But this additional clause has its effect only because I do *not always* use it. If a parent adds 'be very careful' to everything he says to a child he will soon find his warnings ineffective. If I prefix every statement about material things with 'probably' this doubt-raiser will soon cease to frighten hungry friends, that is cease to function as it now does. Consequently in order to mark those differences which I now mark by saying in one case 'Probably that is cheese on the table' and in another case 'I know that is cheese on the table', I shall have to introduce a new notation, one to do the work the old did. 'To do the work the old did!' that is, to claim what I formerly claimed with 'know!'

It may now be said 'In the ordinary use of "know" we may know that that is cheese on the table, but this knowledge is not real knowledge'.

This gives the misleading idea that the philosopher has envisaged some kind of knowing which our failing faculties prevent us from attaining. Terriers cannot catch hares, men cannot really know the causes of their sensations. Nothing of the kind, however. For when we say to the philosopher 'Go on, describe this real knowledge, tell what stamp of man you want and we will see if we can buy or breed one' then he can never tell us.

It may now be said, 'No, no, the point is this: There is some inclination to use[7] "know" strictly so that we do not know that insulin cures diabetes, that the sun will rise to-morrow, because these propositions are only probable inferences from what we have observed. There is some inclination to use "know" only when what is known is observed or is entailed by something known for certain. Now you do not know in this sense that you will not have to correct yourself to-morrow and say "I was mistaken yesterday, that was not cheese", since nothing you know for certain to-day is incompatible with this. And if you do not know but what you may have to correct yourself to-morrow you do not know that you are right do-day'.

But what is meant by 'certain'? I should claim to know for certain that that is cheese on the table now. And as the objector rightly points out this entails that I shall not have to correct myself to-morrow. I therefore know in the strict sense that I shall not have to correct myself to-morrow.

It will be said that it is not *absolutely* certain that that is cheese on the table. But I should reply that it is.

It will be said that it is not *senseless to doubt* that that is cheese on the table, not even after the most exhaustive tests. I should reply that it is.

But, of course, by now I see what the sceptic is driving at. It is not senseless to doubt that that is cheese on the table, in the sense in which it is senseless to doubt 'I am in pain', 'I hear a buzzing'—not even after the most exhaustive tests—indeed the exhaustive tests make no difference to this. For, in this sense, it is not senseless to doubt that that is cheese on the table provided only that 'He says that that is cheese but perhaps he is mistaken' has a use in English. You see, 'He says he is in pain, but perhaps he is mistaken' has no use in English. Hence we may be 'absolutely certain' that he is not mistaken[8] about his pain, in the very special sense that 'He is mistaken' makes no sense in this connection.

Thus the sceptic's pretended doubts amount to pointing out that, unlike statements descriptive of sensations, statements about material things make sense with 'perhaps he is mistaken'. And the sceptic proposes to mark this by an extraordinary use of 'know' and 'probably'. He proposes that we should not say that we know that that is cheese on the table unless it is entailed by statements with regard to which a doubt is not merely out of the question but unintelligible, i.e. such that where S is P is one of them then 'S is P unless I am mistaken' raises a titter like 'I am in pain unless I am mistaken'. 'That is cheese on the table' is not such a statement and so of course it does not follow from such statements—otherwise a doubt with regard to it would be unintelligible, i.e. it would be absolutely certain in the strict, philosophic sense.

The sceptic's doubts become then a recommendation to use 'know' only with statements about sense-experience and mathematics and to prefix *all* other statements with 'probably'.[9]

This is very different talk and much less misleading. But still it is misleading unless accompanied by the explanation given above of the astounding certainty of statements about sense-experience. Even with the explanation the suggestion is highly dangerous, involving as it does a new and '*manner* — indicating' use of the familiar words 'know' and 'probable'. Without the explanation it suggests that there is a difference in degree of certainty between statements about material things and statements about sense-data, a difference in certainty dependent upon their subject-matter, in a sense analogous to that in which we say 'I am certain about what happened in Hyde Park — I was there — but I am not certain about what happened in Spain — I was not an eyewitness'. This suggests that I know what it would be like to be an eyewitness of cheese, but am in fact unfortunately obliged to *rely upon the testimony of* my senses.

Now the difference between statements about sense-experiences and statements about material things is not at all like this. The difference is not one of subject-matter (stuff) but of a different manner of use (style). And statements about sense-experiences are certain only because it makes no sense to say that they may be wrong.[10] Notice the connection between 'He says he is in pain but I think he is mistaken' and 'He cries "Ow!" but I think he is mistaken'. The difference between sense-statements and thing-statements cannot be adequately explained here. And consequently the full misleadingness of such a use of 'probably' as is recommended in what we may call the last form of the pseudo-doubt, cannot be adequately explained here.

But I hope I have said enough to bring out in good measure the misleadingness of saying such things as 'O dear, we can never know the causes of our sensations', and even 'It would be philosophically excellent to put "probably" before all statements about material things'.

7. *Example of the pointless doubts: (b) how importantly illuminating they are.* — But though the recommended use of 'probably' would be pointless as a cautionary clause and would thus be extremely misleading, the recommendation to use it so is not pointless, is not prompted wholly by confusion, but partly by penetration. The philosopher says to the plain man 'You do not really know that that is a cheese on the table'. We have pacified those who are opposed to this statement by bringing out the sources of their reluctance to agree with it. But the philosopher must pacify everyone and we must now pacify those philosophers who are pleased with it, and complete the pacification of those who are puzzled by it, being tempted to deny it and at the same time tempted to assert it. What *is* the point behind the misleading statement 'We can never know statements about material things'? The answer has been given already by the method of forcing reformulations. But we may now approach the answer by a different route. Under what circumstances are such things usually said?

It is when after considering hallucinations, illusions, etc., one wishes to emphasize (1) the likeness between such cases and cases in which there was 'something really there', and to emphasize the continuity between (*a*) cases in which one says 'I think that is cheese on the table', 'I believe that is a real dagger', 'Probably that is a snake, not a branch' and (*b*) cases in which one says 'That *is* cheese on the table', 'I found that it *was* a snake'; and to emphasize (2) the unlikeness between even so well assured a statement as 'This is my thumb' and such a statement as 'I see a pinkish patch', 'I feel a softish patch', 'I am in pain'.

It is not at all easy at first to see how in being revocable and correctable by others the most assured statement about a thing is more like the most precarious statement about another thing than it is to a statement descriptive of one's sensations. Ordinary language conceals these things because in ordinary language we speak both of some favourable material-thing-statements and of statements about our sensations, as certain, while we speak of other statements about material things as merely probable. This leads to pseudo-laments about the haunting uncertainty of even the best material-thing-statements and pseudo-congratulatons upon the astounding certainty of statements about our sensations.

We are all, when our attention is drawn to those cases so often described in which it looks for all the world as if our friend is standing in the room although he is dying two thousand miles away, or in which we think we see a banana and it turns out to be a reflection in a greengrocer's mirror, we are all, in such cases, inclined to say 'Strictly we ought always to add "unless it is a queer looking stick and not a banana, or a reflection or an hallucination or an illusion"'.[11] We do not stop to consider what would happen if we did always add this. Horrified at the deceptions our senses have practised upon us we feel we must abuse them somehow and so we say that they never *prove* anything, that we never *know* what is based on them.

The continuity and the difference which are concealed by ordinary language would be no longer concealed but marked if we used 'probably' in the way recommended. But what an unfortunate way of obtaining this result! And in what a misleading way was the recommendation made! I do not really know that this is a thumb. The huntsman's coat is not really pink. A fox's brush is really a tail. (W).

8. *Other Examples.* — Now many other examples should be given. 'What is a mathematical proposition?' 'Do inductive arguments give any probability to their conclusions?' These other puzzles should be re-created; the temptations to give the answers which have been given should be re-created. But this cannot be done in this paper. Without bringing up the puzzles and temptations the following accounts are half dead, but I offer them for what they are worth.

Take "The laws of mathematics and logic are really rules of grammar'. With this instructive incantation people puzzle themselves to death. Is it or isn't it true? And if false what amendment will give us the truth? If not rules then what? The answer is 'They are what they are, etc. Is a donkey a sort of horse but with *very* long ears?' People are puzzled because of course it isn't true that the laws of mathematics are rules of grammar (more obvious still that they are not commands). And yet they cannot bring themselves to lose the advantages of this falsehood. For this falsehood draws attention to (1) an unlikeness and (2) a likeness concealed by ordinary language; (1) an unlikeness to the laws of hydraulics and an unlikeness in this unlikeness to the unlikeness between the laws of hydraulics and those of aeronautics; for it is an unlikeness not of subject-matter but of manner of functioning — and (2) a likeness but not an exact likeness to the functioning of rules.

Again 'Inductive arguments do not really give any probability to their conclusions' gives the misleading idea that the scientists have been found out at last, that our confidence in our most careful research workers is entirely misplaced, their arguments being no better than those of the savage. Nothing of the kind of course. What is at the back of this lament is this: In ordinary language we speak of Dr. So and So's experiment with a group of 100 children whose teeth improved after six months extra calcium as having very much increased the probability of the proposition that bad teeth are due to calcium deficiency. We also say that my having drawn 90 white balls from a bag which we know to contain 100 balls, each either white or black, has very much increased the probability of the proposition that all the balls in that bag are white. We even speak numerically in connection with empirical probability — we not only argue *a priori* and say 'There were six runners, there are now only five, we still know nothing of any of them, so it is now 4-1 against the dog from trap 1' but we also argue empirically and say 'It was 5-1 against the dog from trap 1; but I hear a rumour that each of the others has been provided with a cup of tea, and I think we may now take 4-1 against him'.

The similarity in the way we speak of these cases leads us when asked how empirical arguments give probability to their conclusions to try to assimilate them to the formal cases, balls in bags, dice, etc. But when this attempt is made it begins to appear that the investigation of nature is much less like the investigation of balls in a bag than one is at first apt to think.

At the same time is revealed the shocking continuity between the scientist's arguments by the method of difference and the savage's *post hoc ergo propter hoc*,[12] between the method of agreement and the reflexes of rats, and struck by the difference and the continuity and how they are concealed by ordinary language we provoke attention to them with 'Even the best established scientific results are nothing but specially successful superstitions'. We say this although we have made no shocking discovery of scientsts faking figures, although the scientist's reasons for his belief in insulin still differ from my landlady's reasons for belief in Cure-all, in exactly the way which, in the ordinary use of language, makes us call the one belief scientifically grounded and the other a superstition. Similarly we may say, having seen a butterfly die or been told the age of an oak 'The strongest of us have really only a short time to live'. We say this although we have made no discovery of impending disaster, or we may say 'Man is nothing but a complicated parasite' when we watch the arrival of the 9.5 at the Metropolis.

Conclusion

The plain man has come to expect of philosophers paradoxical, provoking statements such as 'We can never really know the causes of our sensations', 'Causation is really nothing more than regular sequence', 'Inductive conclusions are really nothing but lucky superstitions', 'The laws of logic are ultimately rules of grammar'. Philosophers know that the statements are provocative; this is why they so often put in some apologetic word such as 'really' or 'ultimately'.

These untruths persist. This is not merely because they are symptoms of an intractable disorder but because they are philosophically useful. The curious thing is that their philosophical usefulness depends upon their paradoxicalness and thus upon their falsehood. They are false because they are needed where ordinary language fails, though it must not be supposed that they are or should be in some perfect language. They are in a language not free from the same sort of defects as those from the effects of which they are designed to free us.

To invent a special word to describe the status of, for example mathematical propositions would do no good. There is a phrase already, 'necessary yet synthetic'. It is, of course, perfectly true that mathematical propositions are 'necessary synthetics' — it should be true since the expression was made to measure. True but no good. We are as much inclined to ask 'What are necessary synthetic propositions?' as we were to ask 'What are mathematical propositions?' 'What is an instinct?' An innate disposition certainly. But philosophically that answer is useless. No — what is wanted is some device for bringing out the relations between the manner in which mathematical (or dispositional) sentences are used and the manners in which others are used — so as to give their place on the language map. This cannot be done with a plain answer, a single statement. We may try opposite falsehoods or we may say, 'Be careful that this expression "mathematical proposition" does not suggest certain analogies at the expense of others. Do not let it make you think that the difference between mathematical propositions and others is like that between the propositions of hydraulics and those of aeronautics. Do notice how like to rules, etc., and yet, etc.'

If you will excuse a suspicion of smartness: Philosophers should be continually trying to say what cannot be said.

NOTES

1. Wittgenstein has not read this over-compressed paper and I warn people against supposing it a closer imitation of Wittgenstein than it is. On the other hand I can hardly exaggerate the debt I owe to him and how much of the good in this work is his—not only in the treatment of this philosophical difficulty and that but in the matter of how to do philosophy. As far as possible I have put a W against examples I owe to him. It must not be assumed that they are used in a way he would approve.

2. I do not wish to suggest that Wittgenstein would approve of *this* sort of talk nor that he would disapprove of it.

3. Neither of these theories is entirely useless. They are for one thing good antitheses to the naturalistic error.

4. *Problems of Mind and Matter*, p. 32.

5. The matter can be put in terms of truth and falsehood. A philosophical theory involves an explicit claim, an equation, and an implicit claim that the equation is not misleading and is illuminating. The explicit claim may be false and the implicit true on one or both counts, or vice versa.

6. See 'different level' in *Proc. Aris. Soc.* Supp. Vol. XIII, p. 66.

7. Another form would be: 'It is proper' as opposed to 'usual' to use 'know' so that, etc.

8. Of course he may be *lying*.

9. Compare the tendency to use 'what ought to be done' irrevocably. People who do this lament thus: 'What one ought to do is always for the best, but unfortunately we never know what we really ought to do'. Others lament thus: 'We can know what we ought to do but unfortunately this does not always turn out for the best'.

10. This, I realize, stands very much in need of pacifying explanation.

11. Then every statement would be tautologous but *absolutely* certain!

12. See Keynes, *A Treatise on Probability*.

21. Philosophy, Anxiety, and Novelty

John Wisdom

Every philosophical question is really a request for a description of a class of animals — of a *very* familiar class of animals. That is my point, that the classes of animals are very familiar to us all. Consequently philosophical answers are descriptions of very familiar classes of animals — and because the animals are so familiar there is no question of the answers being wrong descriptions — but only of whether they are happy descriptions or not.

There are, of course, already descriptions of these animals, and when our minds are set in a certain way it may for a moment seem odd to us that anyone should want others. But then we may remember how, when our minds are set in a certain way, it may seem odd to us that anyone should wish to paint things at all, and then further seem still odder to us that he should want to paint them in some *queer* way when he has already painted them *beautifully,* with photographic faithfulness. And again, red roses are red roses and white ones white roses, and to say 'that the red rose is a falcon and white rose is a dove' is going out of one's way to say what isn't true. So it is to say that poverty is a crime, or that everyone who looks at a woman to lust after her has already committed adultery with her.

Of course there is here no question of making an untrue statement of fact. What such statements involve is logical or verbal impropriety, i.e. the introduction of a new logic. But these improprieties are not without a purpose: they reveal what is known but hidden. They wouldn't reveal if they weren't novel; in other words, they wouldn't reveal if they weren't wrong. I should like to expand all this a little.

I. *As to why every philosophical question is a request for a description of a familiar class of animals.* The proof for ontological questions is as follows: 'What is philosophy?' means 'What is a philosopher?' 'What is a necessary statement, a mathematical statement, an ethical statement, a statement of fact?' means 'What are mathematicians, etc.?' 'What is memory?' means 'What are those persons doing who remember?' and this means 'What are those

332

persons doing who say of someone that he is remembering?' One who asks philosophically 'What are mathematicians?' points to two people talking mathematically with one another, and asks 'What are they doing?' He doesn't ask this like one who, seeing two men creeping on their hands on wet ground, asks 'What are they doing?' when the proper answer is 'Wait and see' or 'Stalking deer'. For it isn't that the philosopher doesn't know what the mathematician is going to do next. That he knows just as well as he knows what people are going to do when they set out the chess pieces. [In knowing so well what people *do* do in chess he comes to know what they *should* do; he comes to know what they are really wanting to do. He knows this very well for mathematics too, and for statements about animals and things such as 'There's no cake left'. But he doesn't know it so well for philosophers nor for proposers of scientific theories. Here it is more a matter of knowing very well what they do do but not being able to extract very well from this what they really wish to do. This is a complication which I am ignoring for the present.]

2. To repeat: *It isn't that the philosopher doesn't know how one who makes, e.g. a mathematical statement, is going to proceed, so when he asks for a description of mathematicians he is not asking a question of fact.* One who asks 'What is a semaphorist?' may be asking for the translation of an unfamiliar word. Or he may be asking 'What is one who so moves his arms doing?' and be asking a question of fact about the purposes of such a person, which question is answered by explaining the understanding that exists between the semaphorist and the man on the opposite hill who then speaks on a telephone. It isn't a question like that which the philosopher is asking when he asks 'What is a mathematician?'

3. *The philosopher's question is like that asked by a person who, very well knowing all that there is in semaphoring, asks 'What is it to semaphore?'* The answer is, 'It is to semaphore'. This is much more accurate an answer than 'It's shouting with your arms'. In other words the philosopher is not like one who having seen part of a performance wishes to know its subsequent or hidden parts. He is more like someone who having seen a complete performance by kangaroo rats playing in the moonlight turns and asks 'What are they doing?' The answer is, 'Playing in the moonlight'. or 'Well, you have seen'.

Of course there are differences. First, as we have already noticed, in the case of the rats there is no distinction between what it is they do do and what it is they wish to do. And again, though people don't semaphore perfectly, they mostly do it very well. The philosopher who asks 'What is a philosopher?' is more like someone who has gathered what he can of what people want to do when playing chess or tennis from watching people who don't do it very well. But this, as I said, is not a thing I want to emphasize here. For there is a quite different anxiety in philosophers as comes out in the fact that they ask, 'What is a mathematician?' 'What is one who asserts something about a material thing?' where no question of what it is that these speakers *really* want to do comes in, because mathematicians and train announcers are very successful with language so that what they do when they talk is what they really want to do.

4. *When, then, a philosopher asks, 'What are mathematicians and train announcers?' he must, in a sense, answer his question in asking it.* For he must carefully describe what the class of talkers he wants described actually do if he is to ask his question, 'How are they to be described?'

5. *Now of course this makes his question look nothing in a way in which it is not.* The fact is the philosopher wants *another* description and one of a special sort. And if we remember the answer, 'Talking with his arms', this will give us a hint as to how to describe what it is the philosopher wants. He wants a description which shall remove certain puzzles he feels about how we can claim to know certain things and whether these things amount to this and that which he feels we can claim to know or to something more which he feels we can hardly claim to know. In other words he wants a description of familiar kinds of talkers which shall bring out the epistemological and ontological relations between what they are doing. I am not here concerned to describe more fully what it is he wants.

6. *What I want to do here is to recall with emphasis that when two philosophers are talking about what, e.g. mathematical talkers and train announcers do, they both know perfectly well what they do. So the whole of what the philosophers do is deductive, deductive from the descriptions they both allow. If the deductions were complex, if they were lineally complex, there would be room for deductive anxiety. But they are not.* The steps from the agreed, aseptic, descriptions to the philosophical conclusions or descriptions are childishly short.

7. *And yet Moore, for example, insists on knitting his brows* about what it is that one who says 'I have two hands' or '$326 \times 3 = 988$' is doing. Is the former about a sense-datum to the effect that it is part of a hand? Is the latter a rule, a rule of grammar? Are ethical talkers perhaps not asserting anything which could be true or false?[1]

There is a simple proof that ethical talkers are asserting something which could be true or false. I will make the proof longer than is necessary so as to make it more impressive. A proposition is anything which is asserted, doubted or denied. (Definition. See almost any logic text-book.) One who says 'It was right of Brutus to stab Caesar' asserts something and not merely, if at all, that Brutus did stab Caesar. He is asserting in addition that this action of Brutus' was right. In other words he is also asserting what he would assert if he said 'It was right of Brutus to stab Caesar, if he did'. In other words, he is not only asserting the proposition that Brutus stabbed Caesar but also another proposition. (See definition.) [The proposition is the proposition that Brutus' act was right.] Now every proposition is either true or false. (Law of contradiction.) Therefore that proposition which one who says 'It was right of Brutus to stab Caesar' is asserting in addition to the proposition that Brutus did stab Caesar (assuming that he is asserting the latter) is either true or false. Therefore it is not true that one who asserted that it was right of Brutus to stab Caesar 'would be asserting nothing whatever which could conceivably be true or false, except, perhaps, that Brutus' action occurred'.

Again it isn't true that three hundred and twenty-six multiplied by three comes to nine hundred and eighty-eight. What one who gives a rule says cannot be true or not true. Therefore one who says '326 × 3 = 988' is not giving a rule.

Moore knows these proofs perfectly well of course. We all do. That's what makes them *so* boring.

8. *Take now what Moore says in his Reply about Lazerowitz's paper.*[2] Lazerowitz with great clarity and compactness explains that though taking a hurried glance at philosophers you might think that they were engaged on a scientific inquiry and that the very good ones could tell you what happens when you remember your breakfast, like a doctor can tell you what happens when you digest it, they are not; and that though you might then think that they were engaged on a logical inquiry as to, e.g. whether the admitted features of philosophical discussion entail that it is or is not logical discussion, they are not. In the course of doing this he explains something of how what they are doing differs from these two things which you might think it is. Then searching for a *mnemonic* description, summing up the things he has said, he tries 'Philosophers aren't making statements, factual or not, but are making notational recommendations'.

What does Moore do? He thinks of the most typical case of recommending a notation. It is, as we must all agree, that of a man who (1) points out that though we in ordinary language would not call a so and so a such and such, e.g. a tiger a cat, yet the differences are unimportant or just such as in other cases we don't count; (2) says in so many words 'We ought to call tigers cats' and (3) means by this that we ought to do this as a regular thing. Moore then says that philosophers don't do all that. Undoubtedly he is right.

9. *I call Moore's procedure 'legalistic'.* I don't want to say that a legalistic procedure never does good — especially in the hands of someone so penetrating and utterly first-rate as Moore. On the contrary, without it we could hardly do philosophy. It stops our glibness, it forces us to realize that 'there's more to it than that'. But if we never leave it, it leads to endless worrying, and philosophy becomes hopeless.

Moore's complaints, Moore's refutation, may make Lazerowitz amplify and 'explain' his account of the likeness and unlikeness between philosophical statements and verbal recommendations. But is such 'amendment' wise?[3] I admit I've begun it in my paper in the Moore volume. But I doubt the wisdom of what I did. It only encourages people to think that we are trying to get it right. And the legalists will never be satisfied with what we say until it is reduced to a platitude.[4]

By a legalistic procedure I mean the following: We are trying to describe a newly-discovered but carefully-examined kind of animal. We know all about this animal so there is no question of telling ourselves untruths about it. Even so the legalist won't allow us to stretch or narrow for the occasion the use of old words in order to describe the new animal so as to give us a grasp of its relation to other animals.

10. *We can meet this by describing the animals little point by little point,* by ears and teeth and tails, by food and drink and mates and miles per hour,

by day and night, in winter and in spring. The legalist can do this too. But why should we confine ourselves to this? In other matters, in describing other classes of animals, we adapt language to the occasion. Why not here?

11.*Besides, the detailed description doesn't give us* GRASP. *And wishing for this, the legalist says 'If we looked harder still couldn't we find the correct description in general terms?* He means a description in old general terms without alteration in their use, i.e. keeping them old.

12. *We never shall. For this reason:*

(a) There is already a system of general term descriptions for talkers and in particular for talkers in the indicative. Every classification of facts or propositions generates such a system. Thus we have contingent and necessary facts, and amongst the necessary facts mathematical and non-mathematical ones and so on, and to any class of proposition, π, there corresponds the class of those talkers who in talking are asserting propositions in π.

(b) But all this of course is nothing to the purpose. These indeed are the descriptions which have led to the ontological difficulties, 'Are there then all these different sorts of fact made up of different sorts of entity?', and to the epistemological difficulties, 'How do we know them?' These are the descriptions which so long kept us hanging about those impenetrable coverts where universals lurked, facts preyed upon events, and variables with logical constants frolicked for ever down the rides of infinity.

(c) At last Wittgenstein gave tongue and the quarry went away to the notes of 'Don't ask for the meaning [analysis], ask for the use', and the transformations of the formal mode—transformations such as these: 'X in saying that S is P is asserting a general proposition' means 'X in saying that S is P is using the sentence "S is P" generally'; 'X in saying that S is P is asserting a proposition about mathematical entities' means 'X is using the sentence "S is P" mathematically'; 'X in saying that S is P, e.g. that there's a dagger in the air, is asserting a material thing proposition' means 'X is using the sentence "S is P", e.g. "There's a dagger in the air" materially, i.e. objectively'; 'X in saying S is P, e.g. There's a dagger in the air, is asserting a proposition about a sense-datum merely' means 'X is using "There's a dagger in the air" subjectively'; 'S is P is an ethical proposition' means '"S is P" is an ethical sentence', i.e. 'The sentence "S is P" is used ethically'.

(d) But the benefits of the new formal mode descriptions lie only in this, that they leave us free to begin. They leave us with the old questions though wonderfully transformed. For they leave us with the questions 'What do you mean by "ethically", "subjectively", "generally"?' And if when faced with this question we are obsessed with the subject-matter idea, that is the idea that all sentences in the indicative differ only in the way that sentences about dogs and cats or even wind and water differ, then we shall soon find ourselves back where we started, with unknowable categories of reality for ever seeking to devour each other.

(e) On the other hand *if we permit ourselves to imagine vividly the talkers and the occasions when sentences of the sorts in question are used and then*

describe the talkers by setting down a lot of that about them which makes us say that they are using sentences 'generally', 'ethically', etc., including all their purposes, and therefore purposes other than preparing their hearers for tigers or no cake, and all their ways of supporting their sentences (not tied down by logic-book models) *then we shall have descriptions of all talkers which, though very long and still incomplete, involve nothing but talk, nods, smiles, and surprises.*

(f) Now again it may be asked, 'Is there no system of general descriptions, are there no general words, which would enable us to describe utterances well enough without this endless detail? Does a statistical description in terms of mean, mean deviation, interquartile range, describe well enough the individuals we have examined?' Well enough for what? Well enough for some things but not for others. It all depends. Certainly there is a system of general words for describing utterances—'imperative', 'interrogative', 'indicative', 'indicative used generally', 'necessarily', 'ethically', etc., in fact the system of words already mentioned.

(g) But for removing philosophical puzzles these words won't do until it is too late to save our labours, for they won't do until the point-by-point descriptions have been given. Even then if we go back to the old general words only we shall soon half lose what we have gained. Looking at the detailed pictures of utterances, we saw them all anew and in doing so saw how the old system of descriptions hid so many of their varieties of purpose and of logic; regardless of distortion they were crammed into boxes with labels on—no need to look inside.

(h) It is not because it's bad that the old system won't do, but because it's old. As we all know but won't remember, any classificatory system is a net spread on the blessed manifold of the individual and blinding us not to all but to too many of its varieties and continuities. A new system will do the same but not in just the same ways. So that in accepting *all* the systems their blinding power is broken, their revealing power becomes acceptable; the individual is restored to us, not isolated as before we used language, not in a box as when language mastered us, but in 'creation's chorus'.

NOTES

1. *The Philosophy of G. E. Moore* (ed . by P. A. Schilpp), p. 544.
2. *The Philosophy of G. E. Moore* (ed . by P. A. Schilpp), p. 675.
3. The disastrous effects of qualms in an iconoclast are seen in Mr. Ayer's last book, *The Foundations of Empirical Knowledge*. And people readily mistake mock qualms for real ones.
4. A good example is Stace's note on Whitehead's doctrine that everything is everywhere (*Mind*, January, 1943, p. 61, II. 12-28).

22. Gods

John Wisdom

I. *The existence of God is not an experimental issue in the way it was.* An atheist or agnostic might say to a theist 'You still think there are spirits in the trees, nymphs in the streams, a God of the world.' He might say this because he noticed the theist in time of drought pray for rain and make a sacrifice and in the morning look for rain. But disagreement about whether there are gods is now less of this experimental or betting sort than it used to be. This is due in part, if not wholly, to our better knowledge of why things happen as they do.

It is true that even in these days it is seldom that one who believes in God has no hopes or fears which an atheist has not. Few believers now expect prayer to still the waves, but some think it makes a difference to people and not merely in ways the atheist would admit. Of course with people, as opposed to waves and machines, one never knows what they won't do next, so that expecting prayer to make a difference to them is not so definite a thing as believing in its mechanical efficacy. Still, just as primitive people pray in a business-like way for rain so some people still pray for others with a real feeling of doing something to help. However, in spite of this persistence of an experimental element in some theistic belief, it remains true that Elijah's method on Mount Carmel of settling the matter of what god or gods exist would be far less appropriate to-day than it was then.

2. *Belief in gods is not merely a matter of expectation of a world to come.* Someone may say 'The fact that a theist no more than an atheist expects prayer to being down fire from heaven or cure the sick does not mean that there is no difference between them as to the facts, it does not mean that the theist has no expectations different from the atheist's. For very often those who believe in God believe in another world and believe that God is there and that we shall go to that world when we die.'

This is true, but I do not want to consider here expectations as to what one will see and feel after death nor what sort of reasons these logically unique expectations could have. So I want to consider those theists who do not believe in

338

a future life, or rather, I want to consider the differences between atheists and theists in so far as these differneces are not a matter of belief in a future life.

3. *What are these differences? And is it that theists are superstitious or that atheists are blind?* A child may wish to sit a while with his father and he may, when he has done what his father dislikes, fear punishment and feel distress at causing vexation, and while his father is alive he may feel sure of help when danger threatens and feel that there is sympathy for him when disaster has come. When his father is dead he will no longer expect punishment or help. Maybe for a moment an old fear will come or a cry for help escape him, but he will at once remember that this is no good now. He may feel that his father is no more until perhaps someone says to him that his father is still alive though he lives now in another world and one so far away that there is no hope of seeing him or hearing his voice again. The child may be told that nevertheless his father can see him and hear all he says. When he has been told this the child will still fear no punishment nor expect any sign of his father, but now, even more than he did when his father was alive, he will feel that his father sees him all the time and will dread distressing him and when he has done something wrong he will feel separated from his father until he has felt sorry for what he has done. Maybe when he himself comes to die he will be like a man who expects to find a friend in the strange country where he is going, but even when this is so, it is by no means all of what makes the difference between a child who believes that his father lives still in another world and one who does not.

Likewise one who believes in God may face death differently from one who does not, but there is another difference between them besides this. This other difference may still be described as belief in another world, only this belief is not a matter of expecting one thing rather than another here or hereafter, it is not a matter of a world to come but of a world that now is, though beyond our senses.

We are at once reminded of those unseen worlds which some philosophers 'believe in' and others 'deny', while non-philosophers unconsciously 'accept' them by using them as models with which to 'get the hang of' the patterns in the flux of experience. We recall the timeless entities whose changeless connections we seek to represent in symbols, and the values which stand firm[1] amidst our flickering satisfaction and remorse, and the physical things which, though not beyond the corruption of moth and rust, are yet more permanent than the shadows they throw upon the screen before our minds. We recall, too, our talk of souls and of what lies in their depths and is manifested to us partially and intermittently in our own feelings and the behaviour of others. The hypothesis of mind, of other human minds and of animal minds, is reasonable because it explains for each of us why certain things behave so cunningly all by themselves unlike even the most ingenious machines. Is the hypothesis of minds in flowers and trees reasonable for like reasons? Is the hypothesis of a world mind reasonable for like reasons — someone who adjusts the blossom to the bees, someone whose presence may at times be felt — in a garden in high summer, in the hills when clouds are gathering, but not, perhaps, in a cholera epidemic?

4. *The question 'Is belief in gods reasonable?' has more than one source.* It is clear now that in order to grasp fully the logic of belief in divine minds we need to examine the logic of belief in animal and human minds. But we cannot do that here and so for the purposes of this discussion about divine minds let us acknowledge the reasonableness of our belief in human minds without troubling ourselves about its logic. The question of the reasonableness of belief in divine minds then becomes a matter of whether there are facts in nature which support claims about divine minds in the way facts in nature support our claims about human minds.

In this way we resolve the force behind the problem of the existence of gods into two components, one metaphysical and the same which prompts the question 'Is there *ever any* behaviour which gives reason to believe in *any* sort of mind?' and one which finds expression in 'Are there other mind-patterns in nature beside the human and animal patterns which we can all easily detect, and are these other mind-patterns super-human?'

Such over-determination of a question syndrome is common. Thus, the puzzling questions 'Do dogs think?', 'Do animals feel?' are partly metaphysical puzzles and partly scientific questions. They are not purely metaphysical; for the reports of scientists about the poor performances of cats in cages and old ladies' stories about the remarkable performances of their pets are not irrelevant. But nor are these questions purely scientific; for the stories never settle them and therefore they have other sources. One other source is the metaphysical source we have already noticed, namely, the difficulty about getting behind an animal's behaviour to its mind, whether it is a non-human animal or a human one.

But there's a third component in the force behind these questions, these disputes have a third source, and it is one which is important in the dispute which finds expression in the words 'I believe in God', 'I do not'. This source comes out well if we consider the question 'Do flowers feel?' Like the questions about dogs and animals this question about flowers comes partly from the difficulty we sometimes feel over inference from *any* behaviour to thought or feeling and partly from ignorance as to what behaviour is to be found. But these questions, as opposed to a like question about human beings, come also from hesitation as to whether the behaviour in question is *enough* mind-like, that is, is it enough similar to or superior to human behaviour to be called 'mind-proving'? Likewise, even when we are satisfied that human behaviour shows mind and even when we have learned whatever mind-suggesting things there are in nature which are not explained by human and animal minds, we may still ask 'But are these things sufficiently striking to be called a mind-pattern? Can we fairly call them manifestations of a divine being?'

'The question', someone may say, 'has then become merely a matter of the application of a name. And "What's in a name?"'

5. *But the line between a question of fact and a question or decision as to the application of a name is not so simple as this way of putting things suggests.*

The question 'What's in a name?' is engaging because we are inclined to answer both 'Nothing' and 'very much'. And this 'Very much' has more than one source. We might have tried to comfort Heloise by saying 'It isn't that Abelard no longer loves you, for this man isn't Abelard'; we might have said to poor Mr. Tebrick in Mr. Garnet's *Lady into Fox* 'But this is no longer Silvia'. But if Mr. Tebrick replied 'Ah, but it is!' this might come not at all from observing facts about the fox which we have not observed, but from noticing facts about the fox which we had missed, although we had in a sense observed all that Mr. Tebrick had observed. It is possible to have before one's eyes all the items of a pattern and still to miss the pattern. Consider the following conversation:

'"And I think Kay and I are pretty happy. We've always been happy."

'Bill lifted up his glass and put it down without drinking.

'"Would you mind saying that again?"' he asked.

'"I don't see what's so queer about it. Taken all in all, Kay and I have really been happy."

'"All right," Bill said gently, "Just tell me how you and Kay have been happy."

'Bill had a way of being amused by things which I could not understand.

'"It's a little hard to explain," I said. "It's like taking a lot of numbers that don't look alike and that don't mean anything until you add them all together."

'I stopped, because I hadn't meant to talk to him about Kay and me.

'"Go ahead," Bill said. "What about the numbers." And he began to smile.

'"I don't know why you think it's so funny," I said. "All the things that two people do together, two people like Kay and me, add up to something. There are the kids and the house and the dog and all the people we have known and all the times we've been out to dinner. Of course, Kay and I do quarrel sometimes but when you add it all together, all of it isn't as bad as the parts of it seem. I mean, maybe that's all there is to anybody's life."

'Bill poured himself another drink. He seemed about to say something and checked himself. He kept looking at me.'[2]

Or again, suppose two people are speaking of two characters in a story which both have read[3] or of two friends which both have known, and one says 'Really she hated him', and the other says 'She didn't, she loved him'. Then the first may have noticed what the other has not although he knows no incident in the lives of the people they are talking about which the other doesn't know too, and the second speaker may say 'She didn't, she loved him' because he hasn't noticed what the first noticed, although he can remember every incident the first can remember. But then again he may say 'She didn't, she loved him' not because he hasn't noticed the patterns in time which the first has noticed but because though he has noticed them he doesn't feel he still needs to emphasize them with 'Really she hated him'. The line between using a name because of how we feel and because of what we have noticed isn't sharp. 'A difference as to the facts', 'a discovery', 'a revelation', these phrases cover many things. Discoveries have been made not only by Christopher Columbus and Pasteur, but also by Tolstoy and Dostoievsky and Freud. Things are revealed to us not only by the scientists with microscopes, but also by the poets, the prophets, and the painters. What is so isn't merely a matter of 'the facts'. For sometimes when there is agreement as to the facts there is still argument as to whether defendant did or did not 'exercise reasonable care', was or was not 'negligent'.

And though we shall need to emphasize how much 'There is a God' evinces an attitude to the familiar[4] we shall find in the end that it also evinces some recognition of patterns in time easily missed and that, therefore, difference as to there being any gods is in part a difference as to what is so and therefore as to the facts, though not in the simple ways which first occurred to us.

6. *Let us now approach these same points by a different road.*

6.1. *How it is that an explanatory hypothesis, such as the existence of God, may start by being experimental and gradually become something quite different can be seen from the following story:*

Two people return to their long neglected garden and find among the weeds a few of the old plants surprisingly vigorous. One says to the other 'It must be that a gardener has been coming and doing something about these plants'. Upon inquiry they find that no neighbour has ever seen anyone at work in their garden. The first man says to the other 'He must have worked while people slept'. The other says 'No, someone would have heard him and besides, anybody who cared about the plants would have kept down these weeds'. The first man says 'Look at the way these are arranged. There is purpose and a feeling for beauty here. I believe that someone comes, someone invisible to mortal eyes. I believe that the more carefully we look the more we shall find confirmation of this.' They examine the garden ever so carefully and sometimes they come on new things suggesting that a gardener comes and sometimes they come on new things suggesting the contrary and even that a malicious person has been at work. Besides examining the garden carefully they also study what happens to gardens left without attention. Each learns all the other learns about this and about the garden. Consequently, when after all this, one says 'I still believe a gardener comes' while the other says 'I don't' their different words now reflect no difference as to what they have found in the garden, no difference as to what they would find in the garden if they looked further and no difference about how fast untended gardens fall into disorder. At this stage, in this context, the gardener hypothesis has ceased to be experimental, the difference between one who accepts and one who rejects it is now not a matter of the one expecting something the other does not expect. What is the difference between them? The one says 'A gardener comes unseen and unheard. He is manifested only in his works with which we are all familiar', the other says 'There is no gardener' and with this difference in what they say about the gardener goes a difference in how they feel towards the garden, in spite of the fact that neither expects anything of it which the other does not expect.

But is this the whole difference between them—that the one calls the garden by one name and feels one way towards it, while the other calls it by another name and feels in another way towards it? And if this is what the difference has become then is it any longer appropriate to ask 'Which is right?' or 'Which is reasonable?'

And yet surely such questions *are* appropriate when one person says to another 'You still think the world's a garden and not a wilderness, and that the gardener has not forsaken it' or 'You still think there are nymphs of the streams, a presence in the hills, a spirit of the world'. Perhaps when a man sings 'God's in His heaven' we need not take this as more than an expression of how he feels. But when Bishop Gore or Dr. Joad write about belief in God and young men read them in order to settle their religious doubts the impression is not simply that of persons choosing exclamations with which to face nature and the 'changes and chances of this mortal life'. The disputants speak as if they are concerned with a matter of scientific fact, or of trans-sensual, trans-scientific and metaphysical fact, but still of fact and still a matter about which reasons for and against may be offered, although no scientific reasons in the sense of field surveys for fossils or experiments on delinquents are to the point.

6.2 *Now can an interjection have a logic?* Can the manifestation of an attitude in the utterance of a word, in the application of a name, have a logic? When all the facts are known how can there still be a question of fact? How can there still be a question? Surely as Hume says '. . . after every circumstance, every relation is known, the understanding has no further room to operate'?[5]

6.3. When the madness of these questions leaves us for a moment *we can all easily recollect disputes which though they cannot be settled by experiment are yet disputes in which one party may be right and the other wrong* and in which both parties may offer reasons and the one better reasons than the other. *This may happen in pure and applied mathematics and logic.* Two accountants or two engineers provided with the same data may reach different results and this difference is resolved not by collecting further data but by going over the calculations again. Such differences indeed share with differences as to what will win a race, the honour of being among the most 'settlable' disputes in the language.

6.4 *But it won't do to describe the theistic issue as one settlable by such calculation,* or as one about what can be deduced in this *vertical* fashion from the facts we know. No doubt dispute about God has sometimes, perhaps especially in mediaeval times, been carried on in this fashion. But nowadays it is not and we must look for some other analogy, some other case in which a dispute is settled but not by experiment.

6.5 *In courts of law* it sometimes happens that opposing counsel are agreed as to the facts and are not trying to settle a question of further fact, are not trying to settle whether the man who admittedly had quarrelled with the deceased did or did not murder him, but are concerned with whether Mr. A who admittedly handed his long-trusted clerk signed blank cheques did or did not exercise reasonable care, whether a ledger is or is not a document,[6] whether a certain body was or was not a public authority.

In such cases we notice that the process of argument is not a *chain* of demonstrative reasoning. It is a presenting and representing of those features

of the case which *severally co-operate* in favour of the conclusion, in favour of
saying what the reasoner wishes said, in favour of calling the situation by the
name by which he wishes to call it. The reasons are like the legs of a chair, not
the links of a chain. Consequently although the discussion is *a priori* and the
steps are not a matter of experience, the procedure resembles scientific argument in that the reasoning is not *vertically* extensive but *horizontally* extensive—it is a matter of the cumulative effect of several independent premises,
not of the repeated transformation of one or two. And because the premises are
severally inconclusive the process of deciding the issue becomes a matter of
weighing the cumulative effect of one group of severally inconclusive items
against the cumulative effect of another group of severally inconclusive items,
and thus lends itself to description in terms of conflicting 'probabilities'. This
encourages the feeling that the issue is one of fact—that it is a matter of guessing from the premises at a further fact, at what is to come. But this is a
muddle. *The dispute does not cease to be* a priori *because it is a matter of the
cumulative effect of severally inconclusive premises.* The logic of the dispute is
not that of a chain of deductive reasoning as in a mathematic calculation. But
nor is it a matter of collecting from several inconclusive items of information
an expectation as to something further, as when a doctor from a patient's
symptoms guesses at what is wrong, or a detective from many clues guesses the
criminal. It has its own sort of logic and its own sort of end—the solution of
the question at issue is a decision, a ruling by the judge. But it is not an arbitrary decision though the rational connections are neither quite like those in
vertical deductions nor like those in inductions in which from many signs we
guess at what is to come; and though the decision manifests itself in the application of a name it is no more merely the application of a name than is the
pinning on of a medal merely the pinning on of a bit of metal. Whether a lion
with stripes is a tiger or a lion is, if you like, merely a matter of the application
of a name. Whether Mr. So-and-So of whose conduct we have so complete a
record did or did not exercise reasonable care is not merely a matter of the application of a name or, if we choose to say it is, then we must remember that
with this name a game is lost and won and a game with very heavy stakes. With
the judges' choice of a name for the facts goes an attitude, and the declaration,
the ruling, is an exclamation evincing that attitude. But *it is an exclamation
which not only has a purpose but also has a logic,* a logic surprisingly like that
of 'futile', 'deplorable', 'graceful', 'grand', 'divine'.

6.6 *Suppose two people are looking at a picture or natural scene.* One says
'Excellent' or 'Beautiful' or 'Divine'; the other says 'I don't see it'. He means he
doesn't see the beauty. And this reminds us of how we felt the theist accuse the
atheist of blindness and the atheist accuse the theist of seeing what isn't there.
And yet surely each sees what the other sees. It isn't that one can see part of the
picture which the other can't see. So the difference is in a sense not one as to
the facts. And so it cannot be removed by the one disputant discovering to the
other what so far he hasn't seen. It isn't that the one sees the picture in a different light and so, as we might say, sees a different picture. Consequently the

difference between them cannot be resolved by putting the picture in a different light. And yet surely this is just what can be done in such a case—not by moving the picture but by talk perhaps. To settle a dispute as to whether a piece of music is good or better than another we listen again, with a picture we look again. Someone perhaps points to emphasize certain features and we see it in a different light. Shall we call this 'field work' and 'the last of observation' or shall we call it 'reviewing the premises' and 'the beginning of deduction (horizontal)?'

If in spite of all this we choose to say that a difference as to whether a thing is beautiful is not a factual difference we must be careful to remember that there is a procedure for settling these differences and that this consists not only in reasoning and redescription as in the legal case, but also in a more literal resetting-before with re-looking or re-listening.

6.7 *And if we say as we did at the beginning that when a difference as to the existence of a God is not one as to future happenings then it is not experimental and therefore not as to the facts, we must not forthwith assume that there is no right and wrong about it,* no rationality or irrationality, no appropriateness or inappropriateness, no procedure which tends to settle it, *not even that this procedure is in no sense a discovery of new facts.* After all even in science this is not so. Our two gardeners even when they had reached the stage when neither expected any experimental result which the other did not, might yet have continued the dispute, each presenting and representing the features of the garden favouring his hypothesis, that is, fitting his model for describing the accepted fact; each emphasizing the pattern he wishes to emphasize. True, in science, there is seldom or never a pure instance of this sort of dispute, for nearly always with difference of hypothesis goes some difference of expectation as to the facts. But scientists argue about rival hypotheses with a vigour which is not exactly proportioned to difference in expectations of experimental results.

The difference as to whether a God exists involves our feelings more than most scientific disputes and in this respect is more like a difference as to whether there is beauty in a thing.

7. *The Connecting Technique.* Let us consider again the technique used in revealing or proving beauty, in removing a blindness, in inducing an attitude which is lacking, in reducing a reaction that is inappropriate. Besides running over in a special way the features of the picture, tracing the rhythms, making sure that this and that are not only seen but noticed, and their relation to each other—besides all this—there are other things we can do to justify our attitude and alter that of the man who cannot see. For features of the picture may be brought out by setting beside it other pictures; just as the merits of an argument may be brought out, proved, by setting beside it other arguments, in which striking but irrelevant features of the original are changed and relevant features emphasized; just as the merits and demerits of a line of action may be brought out by setting beside it other actions. To use Susan Stebbing's example: Nathan brought out for David certain features of what David had done in

the matter of Uriah the Hittite by telling him a story about two sheepowners. This is the kind of thing we very often do when someone is 'inconsistent' or 'unreasonable'. This is what we do in referring to other cases in law. The paths we need to trace from other cases to the case in question are often numerous and difficult to detect and the person with whom we are discussing the matter may well draw attention to connections which, while not incompatible with those we have tried to emphasize, are of an opposite inclination. A may have noticed in B subtle and hidden likenesses to an angel and reveal these to C, while C has noticed in B subtle and hidden likenesses to a devil which he reveals to A.

Imagine that a man picks up some flowers that lie half withered on a table and gently puts them in water. Another man says to him 'You believe flowers feel'. He says this although he knows that the man who helps the flowers doesn't expect anything of them which he himself doesn't expect; for he himself expects the flowers to be 'refreshed' and to be easily hurt, injured, I mean, by rough handling, while the man who puts them in water does not expect them to whisper 'Thank you'. The Sceptic says 'You believe flowers feel' because something about the way the other man lifts the flowers and puts them in water suggests an attitude to the flowers which he feels inappropriate although perhaps he would not feel it inappropriate to butterflies. He feels that this attitude to flowers is somewhat crazy *just as it is sometimes felt that a lover's attitude is somewhat crazy even when this is not a matter of his having false hopes about how the person he is in love with will act.* It is often said in such cases that reasoning is useless. But the very person who says this feels that the lover's attitude is crazy, is inappropriate like some dreads and hatreds, such as some horrors of enclosed places. And often one who says 'It is useless to reason proceeds at once to reason with the lover, nor is this reasoning always quite without effect. We may draw the lover's attention to certain things done by her he is in love with and trace for him a path to these from things done by others at other times[7] which have disgusted and infuriated him. And by this means we may weaken his admiration and confidence, make him feel it unjustified and arouse his suspicion and contempt and make him feel our suspicion and contempt reasonable. It is possible, of course, that he has already noticed the analogies, the connections, we point out and that he has accepted them—that is, he has not denied them nor passed them off. He has recognized them and they have altered his attitude, altered his love, but he still loves. We then feel that perhaps it is we who are blind and cannot see what he can see.

8. *Connecting and Disconnecting.* But before we confess ourselves thus inadequate there are other fires his admiration must pass through. For when a man has an attitude which it seems to us he should not have or lacks one which it seems to us he should have then, not only do we suspect that he is not influenced by connections which we feel should influence him and draw his attention to these, but also we suspect he is influenced by connections which should not influence him and draw his attention to these. It may, for a moment, seem strange that we should draw his attention to connections which we

feel should not influence him, and which, since they do influence him, he has in a sense already noticed. But we do—such is our confidence in 'the light of reason'.

Sometimes the power of these connections comes mainly from a man's mismanagement of the language he is using. This is what happens in the Monte Carlo fallacy, where by mismanaging the laws of chance a man passes from noticing that a certain colour or number has not turned up for a long while to an improper confidence that now it soon will turn up. In such cases our showing up of the false connections is a process we call 'explaining a fallacy in reasoning'. To remove fallacies in reasoning we urge a man to call a spade a spade, ask him what he means by 'the State' and having pointed out ambiguities and vaguenesses ask him to reconsider the steps in his argument.

9. *Unspoken Connections. Usually, however, wrongheadedness or wrongheartedness in a situation, blindness to what is there or seeing what is not, does not arise merely from mismanagement of language but is more due to connections which are not mishandled in language, for the reason that they are not put into language at all.* And often these misconnections too, weaken in the light of reason, if only we can guess where they lie and turn it on them. In so far as these connections are not presented in language the process of removing their power is not a process of correcting the mismanagement of language. But it is still akin to such a process; for though it is not a process of setting out fairly what has been set out unfairly, it is a process of setting out fairly what has not been set out at all. And we must remember that the line between connections ill-presented or half-presented in language and connections operative but not presented in language, or only hinted at, is not a sharp one.

Whether or not we call the process of showing up these connections 'reasoning to remove bad unconscious reasoning' or not, it is certain that in order to settle in ourselves what weight we shall attach to someone's confidence or attitude we not only ask him for his reasons but also look for unconscious reasons both good and bad; that is, for reasons which he can't put into words, isn't explicitly aware of, is hardly aware of, isn't aware of at all—perhaps it's long experience which he *doesn't* recall which lets him know a squall is coming, perhaps it's old experience which he *can't* recall which makes the cake in the tea mean so much and makes Odette so fascinating.[8]

I am well aware of the discinction between the question 'What reasons are there for the belief that S is P?' and the question 'What are the sources of beliefs that S is P?' There are cases where investigation of the rationality of a claim which certain persons make is done with very little inquiry into why they say what they do, into the causes of their beliefs. This is so when we have very definite ideas about what is really logically relevant to their claim and what is not. Offered a mathematical theorem we ask for the proof; offered the generalization that parental discord causes crime we ask for the correlation co-efficients. But even in this last case, if we fancy that only the figures are reasons we underestimate the complexity of the logic of our conclusion; and yet it is difficult to describe the other features of the evidence which have weight and there is apt to be disagreement about the weight they should have. In criticizing other conclusions and especially conclusions which are largely the expression of an attitude, we have not only to ascertain what reasons there are for them but also to decide what things are reasons and how much. This latter process of sifting reasons from causes is part of the critical process for every belief, but in some spheres it has been done pretty fully already. In these spheres we don't need to examine the actual processes to belief and distil from them a logic. But in other spheres this remains to be done. Even in science or on the stock exchange or in ordinary life we sometimes hesitate to condemn a belief or a hunch[9] merely because those who believe it cannot offer the sort of reasons we had hoped for. And now suppose Miss Gertrude Stein finds excellent the work of a new artist while we see nothing in it. We nervously recall, perhaps, how pictures by Picasso, which Miss Stein admired and others rejected, later came to be admired by many who gave attention to them, and we wonder whether the case is not a new instance of her perspicacity and our blindness. But if, upon giving all our attention to the work in question, we still do not respond to it, and we notice that the subject matter of the new picture is perhaps birds in wild places and learn that Miss Stein is a birdwatcher, then we begin to trouble ourselves less about her admiration.

It must not be forgotten that our attempt to show up misconnections in Miss Stein may have an opposite result and reveal to us connections we had missed. Thinking to remove the spell exercised upon his patient by the old stories of the Greeks, the psycho-analyst may himself fall under that spell and find in them what his patient has found and, incidentally, what made the Greeks tell those tales.

10. *Now what happens, what should happen, when we inquire in this way into the reasonableness, the propriety of belief in gods?* The answer is: A double and opposite-phrased change. Wordsworth writes:

> '. . . And I have felt
> A presence that disturbs me with the joy
> Of elevated thoughts; a sense sublime
> Of something far more deeply interfused,
> Whose dwelling is the light of setting suns,
> And the round ocean and the living air,
> And the blue sky, and in the mind of man:
> A motion and a spirit, that impels
> All thinking things, all objects of all thought,
> And rolls through all things. . .'[10]

We most of us know this feeling. But is it well placed like the feeling that here is first-rate work, which we sometimes rightly have even before we have fully grasped the picture we are looking at or the book we are reading? Or is it misplaced like the feeling in a house that has long been empty that someone secretly lives there still. Wordsworth's feeling *is* the feeling that the world is haunted, that something watches in the hills and manages the stars. The child feels that the stone tripped him when he stumbled, that the bough struck him when it flew back in his face. He has to learn that the wind isn't buffeting him, that there is not a devil in it, that he was wrong, that his attitude was inappropriate. And as he learns that the wind wasn't hindering him so he also learns it wasn't helping him. But we know how, though he learns, his attitude lingers. It is plain that Wordsworth's feeling is of this family.

Belief in gods, it is true, is often very different from belief that stones are spiteful, the sun kindly. For the gods appear in human form and from the waves and control these things and by so doing reward and punish us. But varied as are the stories of the gods they have a family likeness and we have only to recall them to feel sure of the other main sources which co-operate with animism to produce them.

What are the stories of the gods? What are our feelings when we believe in God? They are feelings of awe before power, dread of the thunderbolts of Zeus, confidence in the everlasting arms, unease beneath the all-seeing eye. They are feelings of guilt and inescapable vengeance, of smothered hate and of a security we can hardly do without. We have only to remind ourselves of these feelings and the stories of the gods and goddesses and heroes in which these feelings find expression, to be reminded of how we felt as children to our parents and the big people of our childhood. Writing of a first telephone call from his grandmother, Proust says:'. . . it was rather that this isolation of the voice was like a symbol, a presentation, a direct consequence of another isolation, that of my grandmother, separated for the first time in my life, from myself. The orders or prohibitions which she addressed to me at every moment in the ordinary course of my life, the tedium of obedience or the fire of rebellion which neutralized the affection that I felt for her were at this moment eliminated. . . "Granny!" I cried to her . . . but I had beside me only that voice, a phantom, as unpalpable as that which would come to revisit me when my grandmother was dead. "Speak to me!" but then it happened that, left more solitary still, I ceased to catch the sound of her voice. My grandmother could no longer hear me . . . I continued to call her, sounding the empty night, in which I felt that her appeals also must be straying. I was shaken by the same anguish which, in the distant past, I had felt once before, one day when, a little child, in a crowd, I had lost her.'

Giorgio de Chirico, writing of Courbet, says: 'The word yesterday envelops us with its yearning echo, just as, on waking, when the sense of time and the logic of things remain a while confused, the memory of a happy hour we spent the day before may sometimes linger reverberating within us. At times we think of Courbet and his work as we do of our own father's youth.'

When a man's father fails him by death or weakness how much he needs another father, one in the heavens with whom is 'no variableness nor shadow of turning'.

We understood Mr. Kenneth Graham when he wrote of the Golden Age we feel we have lived in under the Olympians. Freud says: 'The ordinary man cannot imagine this Providence in any other form but that of a greatly exalted father, for only such a one could understand the needs of the sons of men, or be softened by their prayers and be placated by the signs of their remorse. The whole thing is so patently infantile, so incongruous with reality. . . .' 'So incongruous with reality'! It cannot be denied.

But here a new aspect of the matter may strike us.[11] For the very facts which make us feel that now we can recognize systems of superhuman, sub-human, elusive, beings for what they are—the persistent projections of infantile phantasies—include facts which make these systems less fantastic. What are these facts? They are patterns in human reactions which are well described by saying that we are as if there were hidden within us powers, persons, not ourselves and stronger than ourselves. That this is so may perhaps be said to have been common knowledge yielded by ordinary observation of people,[12] but we did not know the degree in which this is so until recent study of extra-ordinary cases in extraordinary conditions had revealed it. I refer, of course, to the study of multiple personalities and the wider studies of psycho-analysts. Even when the results of this work are reported to us that is not the same as tracing the patterns in the details of the cases on which the results are based; and even that is not the same as taking part in the studies oneself. One thing not sufficiently realized is that some of the things shut within us are not bad but good.

Now the gods, good and evil and mixed, have always been mysterious powers outside us rather than within. But they have also been within. It is not a modern theory but an old saying that in each of us a devil sleeps. Eve said: 'The serpent beguiled me.' Helen says to Menelaus:

> '. . . And yet how strange it is!
> I ask not thee; I ask my own sad thought,
> What was there in my heart, that I forgot
> My home and land and all I loved, to fly
> With a strange man? Surely it was not I,
> But Cypris there!'[13]

Elijah found that God was not in the wind, nor in the thunder, but in a still small voice. The kingdom of Heaven is within us, Christ insisted, though usually about the size of a grain of mustard seed, and he prayed that we should become one with the Father in Heaven.

New knowledge made it necessary either to give up saying 'The sun is sinking' or to give the words a new meaning. In many contexts we preferred to stick to the old words and give them a new meaning which was not entirely new but, on the contrary, *practically* the same as the old. The Greeks did not speak of the dangers of repressing instincts but they did speak of the dangers of thwarting Dionysos, of neglecting Cypris for Diana, of forgetting Poseidon for Athena. We have eaten of the fruit of a garden we can't forget though we were never there, a garden we still look for though we can never find it. Maybe we look for too simple a likeness to what we dreamed. Maybe we are not as free as we fancy from the old idea that Heaven is a happy hunting ground, or a city with streets of gold. Lately Mr. Aldous Huxley has recommended our seeking not somewhere beyond the sky or late in time but a timeless state not made of the stuff of this world, which he rejects, picking it into worthless pieces. But this sounds to me still too much a looking for another place, not indeed one filled with sweets but instead so empty that some of us would rather remain in the Lamb or the Elephant, where, as we know, they stop whimpering with another bitter and so far from sneering at all things, hang pictures of winners at Kempton and stars of the 'nineties. Something good we have for each other is freed there, and in some degree and for a while the miasma of time is rolled back without obliging us to deny the present.

The artists who do most for us don't tell us only of fairylands. Proust, Manet, Breughel, even Botticelli and Vermeer show us reality. And yet they give us for a moment exhilaration without anxiety, peace without boredom. And those who, like Freud, work in a different way against that which too often comes over us and forces us into deadness or despair,[14] also deserve critical, patient and courageous attention. For they, too, work to release us from human bondage into human freedom.

Many have tried to find ways of salvation. The reports they bring back are always incomplete and apt to mislead even when they are not in words but in music or paint. But they are by no means useless; and not the worst of them are those which speak of oneness with God. But in so far as we become one with Him He becomes one with us. St. John says he is in us as we love one another.

This love, I suppose, is not benevolence but something that comes of the oneness with one another of which Christ spoke.[15] Sometimes it momentarily gains strength.[16] Hate and the Devil do too. And what is oneness without otherness?

NOTES

1. In another world, Dr. Joad says in the *New Statesman* recently.

2. *H. M. Pulham, Esq.,* p. 320, by John P. Marquand.

3. e.g. Havelock Ellis's autobiography.

4. 'Persuasive Definitions', *Mind,* July, 1938, by Charles Leslie Stevenson, should be read here. It is very good. [Also in his *Ethics and Language,* Yale, 1945. — EDITOR.]

5. Hume, *An Enquiry concerning the Principles of Morals.* Appendix I.

6. *The Times,* March 2nd, 1945. Also in *The Times* of June 13th, 1945, contrast the case of Hannah v. Peel with that of the cruiser cut in two by a liner. In the latter case there is not agreement as to the facts. See also the excellent articles by Dr. Glanville L. Williams in the *Law Quarterly Review,* 'Language and the Law', January, and April 1945, and 'The Doctrine of Repugnancy', October, 1943, January, 1944, and April, 1944. The author, having set out how arbitrary are many legal decisions, needs now to set out how far from arbitrary they are — if his readers are ready for the next phase in the dialectic process.

7. Thus, like the scientist, the critic is concerned to show up the irrelevance of time and space.

8. Proust: *Swann's Way,* Vol. I, p. 58, Vol. II. Phoenix Edition.

9. Here I think of Mr. Stace's interesting reflections in *Mind,* January, 1945, 'The Problems of Unreasoned Beliefs'.

10. *Tintern Abbey.*

11. I owe to the late Dr. Susan Isaacs the thought of this different aspect of the matter, of this connection between the heavenly Father and 'the good father' spoken of in psychoanalysis.

12. Consider Tolstoy and Dostoievsky—I do not mean, of course, that their observation was ordinary.

13. Euripides: *The Trojan Women,* Gilbert Murray's Translation. Roger Hinks in *Myth and Allegory in Ancient Art* writes (p. 108): 'Personifications made their appearance very early in Greek poetry. . . . It is out of the question to call these terrible beings "abstractions". . . . They are real daemons to be worshipped and propitiated. . . . These beings we observe correspond to states of mind. The experience of man teaches him that from time to time his composure is invaded and overturned by some power from outside, panic, intoxication, sexual desire.'

> 'What use to shoot off guns at unicorns?
> Where one horn's hit another fierce horn grows,
> These beasts are fabulous, and none were born
> Of woman who could lay a fable low.'—

The Glass Tower, Nicholas Moore, p. 100.

14. Matthew Arnold: *Summer Night.*

15. St. John xvi. 21.

16. 'The Harvesters' in *The Golden Age,* Kenneth Graham.

23. Descartes' Myth

Gilbert Ryle

1. The Official Doctrine

There is a doctrine about the nature and place of minds which is so prevalent among theorists and even among laymen that it deserves to be described as the official theory. Most philosophers, psychologists and religious teachers subscribe, with minor reservations, to its main articles and, although they admit certain theoretical difficulties in it, they tend to assume that those can be overcome without serious modifications being made to the architecture of the theory. It will be argued here that the central principles of the doctrine are unsound and conflict with the whole body of what we know about minds when we are not speculating about them.

The official doctrine, which hails chiefly from Descartes, is something like this. With the doubtful exceptions of idiots and infants in arms every human being has both a body and a mind. Some would prefer to say that every human being is both a body and a mind. His body and his mind are ordinarily harnessed together, but after the death of the body his mind may continue to exist and function.

Human bodies are in space and are subject to the mechanical laws which govern all other bodies in space. Bodily processes and states can be inspected by external observers. So a man's bodily life is as much a public affair as are the lives of animals and reptiles and even as the careers of trees, crystals and planets.

But minds are not in space, nor are their operations subject to mechanical laws. The workings of one mind are not witnessable by other observers; its career is private. Only I can take direct cognisance of the states and processes of my own mind. A person therefore lives through two collateral histories, one consisting of what happens in and to his body, the other consisting of what happens in and to his mind. The first is public, the second private. The events in the first history are events in the physical world, those in the second are events in the mental world.

It has been disputed whether a person does or can directly monitor all or only some of the episodes of his own private history; but, according to the official doctrine, of at least some of these episodes he has direct and unchallengeable cognisance. In consciousness, self-consciousness and introspection he is directly and authentically apprised of the present states and operations of his mind. He may have great or small uncertainties about concurrent and adjacent episodes in the physical world, but he can have none about at least part of what is momentarily occupying his mind.

It is customary to express this bifurcation of his two lives and of his two worlds by saying that the things and events which belong to the physical world, including his own body, are external, while the workings of his own mind are internal. This antithesis of outer and inner is of course meant to be construed as a metaphor, since minds, not being in space, could not be described as being spatially inside anything else, or as having things going on spatially inside themselves. But relapses from this good intention are common and theorists are found speculating how stimuli, the physical sources of which are yards or miles outside a person's skin, can generate mental responses inside his skull, or how decisions framed inside his cranium can set going movements of his extremities.

Even when 'inner' and 'outer' are construed as metaphors, the problem how a person's mind and body influence one another is notoriously charged with theoretical difficulties. What the mind wills, the legs, arms and the tongue execute; what affects the ear and the eye has something to do with what the mind perceives; grimaces and smiles betray the mind's moods and bodily castigations lead, it is hoped, to moral improvement. But the actual transactions between the episodes of the private history and those of the public history remain mysterious, since by definition they can belong to neither series. They could not be reported among the happenings described in a person's autobiography of his inner life, but nor could they be reported among those described in some one else's biography of that person's overt career. They can be inspected neither by introspection nor by laboratory experiment. They are theoretical shuttlecocks which are forever being bandied from the physiologist back to the psychologist and from the psychologist back to the physiologist.

Underlying this partly metaphorical representation of the bifurcation of a person's two lives there is a seemingly more profound and philosophical assumption. It is assumed that there are two different kinds of existence or status. What exists or happens may have the status of physical existence, or it may have the status of mental existence. Somewhat as the faces of coins are either heads or tails, or somewhat as living creatures are either male or female, so, it is supposed, some existing is physical existing, other existing is mental existing. It is a necessary feature of what has physical existence that it is in space and time, it is a necessary feature of what has mental existence that it is in time but not in space. What has physical existence is composed of matter, or else is a function of matter; what has mental existence consists of consciousness, or else is a function of consciousness.

There is thus a polar opposition between mind and matter, an opposition which is often brought out as follows. Material objects are situated in a common field, known as 'space', and what happens to one body in one part of space is mechanically connected with what happens to other bodies in other parts of space. But mental happenings occur in insulated fields, known as 'minds', and there is, apart maybe from telepathy, no direct causal connection between what happens in one mind and what happens in another. Only through the medium of the public physical world can the mind of one person make a difference to the mind of another. The mind is its own place and in his inner life each of us lives the life of a ghostly Robinson Crusoe. People can see, hear and jolt one another's bodies, but they are irremediably blind and deaf to the workings of one another's minds and inoperative upon them.

What sort of knowledge can be secured of the workings of a mind? On the one side, according to the official theory, a person has direct knowledge of the best imaginable kind of the workings of his own mind. Mental states and processes are (or are normally) conscious states and processes, and the consciousness which irradiates them can engender no illusions and leaves the door open for no doubts. A person's present thinkings, feelings and willings, his perceivings, rememberings and imaginings are intrinsically 'phosphorescent'; their existence and their nature are inevitably betrayed to their owner. The inner life is a stream of consciousness of such a sort that it would be absurd to suggest that the mind whose life is that stream might be unaware of what is passing down it.

True, the evidence adduced recently by Freud seems to show that there exist channels tributary to this stream, which run hidden from their owner. People are actuated by impulses the existence of which they vigorously disavow; some of their thoughts differ from the thoughts which they acknowledge; and some of the actions which they think they will to perform they do not really will. They are thoroughly gulled by some of their own hypocrisies and they successfully ignore facts about their mental lives which on the official theory ought to be patent to them. Holders of the official theory tend, however, to maintain that anyhow in normal circumstances a person must be directly and authentically seized of the present state and workings of his own mind.

Besides being currently supplied with these alleged immediate data of consciousness, a person is also generally supposed to be able to exercise from time to time a special kind of perception, namely inner perception, or introspection. He can take a (non-optical) 'look' at what is passing in his mind. Not only can he view and scrutinize a flower through his sense of sight and listen to and discriminate the notes of a bell through his sense of hearing; he can also reflectively or introspectively watch, without any bodily organ of sense, the current episodes of his inner life. This self-observation is also commonly supposed to be immune from illusion, confusion or doubt. A mind's reports of its own affairs have a certainty superior to the best that is possessed by its reports of matters in the physical world. Sense-perceptions can, but consciousness and introspection cannot, be mistaken or confused.

On the other side, one person has no direct access of any sort to the events of the inner life of another. He cannot do better than make problematic inferences from the observed behaviour of the other person's body to the states of mind which, by analogy from his own conduct, he supposes to be signalised by that behaviour. Direct access to the workings of a mind is the privilege of that mind itself; in default of such privileged access, the workings of one mind are inevitably occult to everyone else. For the supposed arguments from bodily movements similar to their own to mental workings similar to their own would lack any possibility of observational corroboration. Not unnaturally, therefore, an adherent of the official theory finds it difficult to resist this consequence of his premisses, that he has no good reason to believe that there do exist minds other than his own. Even if he prefers to believe that to other human bodies there are harnessed minds not unlike his own, he cannot claim to be able to discover their individual characteristics, or the particular things that they undergo and do. Absolute solitude is on this showing the ineluctable destiny of the soul. Only our bodies can meet.

As a necessary corollary of this general scheme there is implicitly prescribed a special way of construing our ordinary concepts of mental powers and operations. The verbs, nouns and adjectives, with which in ordinary life we describe the wits, characters and higher-grade performances of the people with whom we have do, are required to be construed as signifying special episodes in their secret histories, or else as signifying tendencies for such episodes to occur. When someone is described as knowing, believing or guessing something, as hoping, dreading, intending or shirking something, as designing this or being amused at that, these verbs are supposed to denote the occurrence of specific modifications in his (to us) occult stream of consciousness. Only his own privileged access to this stream in direct awareness and introspection could provide authentic testimony that these mental-conduct verbs were correctly or incorrectly applied. The onlooker, be he teacher, critic, biographer or friend, can never assure himself that his comments have any vestige of truth. Yet it was just because we do in fact all know how to make such comments, make them with general correctness and correct them when they turn out to be confused or mistaken, that philosophers found it necessary to construct their theories of the nature and place of minds. Finding mental-conduct concepts being regularly and effectively used, they properly sought to fix their logical geography. But the logical geography officially recommended would entail that there could be no regular or effective use of these mental-conduct concepts in our descriptions of, and prescriptions for, other people's minds.

2. The Absurdity of the Official Doctrine

Such in outline is the official theory. I shall often speak of it, with deliberate abusiveness, as 'the dogma of the Ghost in the Machine'. I hope to prove that it is entirely false, and false not in detail but in principle. It is not merely an assemblage of particular mistakes. It is one big mistake and a mistake of a special kind. It is, namely, a category-mistake. It represents the facts of mental life as if they belonged to one logical type or category (or range of types or categories), when they actually belong to another. The dogma is therefore a philosopher's myth. In attempting to explode the myth I shall probably be taken to be denying well-known facts about the mental life of human beings, and my plea that I aim at doing nothing more than rectify the logic of mental-conduct concepts will probably be disallowed as mere subterfuge.

I must first indicate what is meant by the phrase 'Category-mistake'. This I do in a series of illustrations.

A foreigner visiting Oxford or Cambridge for the first time is shown a number of colleges, libraries, playing fields, museums, scientific departments and administrative offices. He then asks 'But where is the University? I have seen where the members of the Colleges live, where the Registrar works, where the scientists experiment and the rest. But I have not yet seen the University in which reside and work the members of your University.' It has then to be explained to him that the University is not another collateral institution, some ulterior counterpart to the colleges, laboratories and offices which he has seen. The University is just the way in which all that he has already seen is organized. When they are seen and when their co-ordination is understood, the University has been seen. His mistake lay in his innocent assumption that it was correct to speak of Christ Church, the Bodleian Library, the Ashmolean Museum *and* the University, to speak, that is, as if 'the University' stood for an extra member of the class of which these other units are members. He was mistakenly allocating the University to the same category as that to which the other institutions belong.

The same mistake would be made by a child witnessing the marchpast of a division, who, having had pointed out to him such and such battalions, batteries, squadrons, etc., asked when the division was going to appear. He would be supposing that a division was a counterpart to the units already seen, partly similar to them and partly unlike them. He would be shown his mistake by being told that in watching the battalions, batteries and squadrons marching past he had been watching the division marching past. The march-past was not a parade of battalions, batteries, squadrons *and* a division; it was a parade of the battalions, batteries and squadrons *of* a division.

One more illustration. A foreigner watching his first game of cricket learns what are the functions of the bowlers, the batsmen, the fielders, the umpires and the scorers. He then says 'But there is no one left on the field to contribute the famous element of team-spirit. I see who does the bowling, the batting and the wicket-keeping; but I do not see whose role it is to exercise *espirit de corps.'* Once more, it would have to be explained that he was looking for the wrong type of thing. Team-spirit is not another cricketing-operation supplementary to all of the other special tasks. It is, roughly, the keenness with which each of the special tasks is performed, and performing a task keenly is not performing two tasks. Certainly exhibiting team-spirit is not the same thing as bowling or catching, but nor is it a third thing such that we can say that the bowler first bowls *and* then exhibits team-spirit or that a fielder is at a given moment *either* catching *or* displaying *espirit de corps*.

These illustrations of category-mistakes have a common feature which must be noticed. The mistakes were made by people who did not know how to wield the concepts *University, division* and *team-spirit*. Their puzzles arose from inability to use certain items in the English vocabulary.

The theoretically interesting category-mistakes are those made by people who are perfectly competent to apply concepts, at least in the situations with which they are familiar, but are still liable in their abstract thinking to allocate those concepts to logical types to which they do not belong. An instance of a mistake of this sort would be the following story. A student of politics has learned the main differences between the British, the French and the American Constitutions, and has learned also the differences and connections between the Cabinet, Parliament, the various Ministries, the Judicature and the Church of England. But he still becomes embarrassed when asked questions about the connections between the Church of England, the Home Office and the British Constitution. For while the Church and the Home Office are institutions, the British Constitution is not another institution in the same sense of that noun. So inter-institutional relations which can be asserted or denied to hold between the Church and the Home Office cannot be asserted or denied to hold between either of them and the British Constitution. 'The British Constitution' is not a term of the same logical type as 'the Home Office' and 'the Church of England'. In a partially similar way, John Doe may be a relative, a friend, an enemy or a stranger to Richard Roe; but he cannot be any of these things to the Average Taxpayer. He knows how to talk sense in certain sorts of discussions about the Average Taxpayer, but he is baffled to say why he could not come across him in the street as he can come across Richard Roe.

It is pertinent to our main subject to notice that, so long as the student of politics continues to think of the British Constitution as a counterpart to the other institutions, he will tend to describe it as a mysteriously occult institution; and so long as John Doe continues to think of the Average Taxpayer as a fellow-citizen, he will tend to think of him as an elusive insubstantial man, a ghost who is everywhere yet nowhere.

My destructive purpose is to show that a family of radical category-mistakes is the source of the double-life theory. The representation of a person as a ghost mysteriously ensconced in a machine derives from this argument. Because, as is true, a person's thinking, feeling and purposive doing cannot be described solely in the idioms of physics, chemistry and physiology, therefore they must be described in counterpart idioms. As the human body is a complex organised unit, so the human mind must be another complex organised unit, though one made of a different sort of stuff and with a different sort of structure. Or, again, as the human body, like any other parcel of matter, is a field of causes and effects, so the mind must be another field of causes and effects, though not (Heaven be praised) mechanical causes and effects.

3. The Origin of the Category-mistake

One of the chief intellectual origins of what I have yet to prove to be the Cartesian category-mistake seems to be this. When Galileo showed that his methods of scientific discovery were competent to provide a mechanical theory which should cover every occupant of space, Descartes found in himself two conflicting motives. As a man of scientific genius he could not but endorse the claims of mechanics, yet as a religious and moral man he could not accept, as Hobbes accepted, the discouraging rider to those claims, namely that human nature differs only in degree of complexity from clockwork. The mental could not be just a variety of the mechanical.

He and subsequent philosophers naturally but erroneously availed themselves of the following escape-route. Since mental-conduct words are not to be construed as signifying the occurrence of non-mechanical processes; since mechanical laws explain movements in space as the effects of other movements in space, other laws must explain some of the non-spatial workings of minds as the effects of other non-spatial workings of minds. The difference betwen the human behaviours which we describe as intelligent and those which we describe as unintelligent must be a difference in their causation; so, while some movements of human tongues and limbs are the effects of mechanical causes, others must be the effects of non-mechanical causes, i.e., some issue from movements of particles of matter, others from workings of the mind.

The differences between the physical and the mental were thus represented as differences inside the common framework of the categories of 'thing', 'stuff', 'attribute', 'state', 'process', 'change', 'cause' and 'effect'. Minds are things, but different sorts of things from bodies; mental processes are causes and effects, but different sorts of causes and effects from bodily movements. And so on. Somewhat as the foreigner expected the University to be an extra edifice, rather like a college but also considerably different, so the repudiators of mechanism represented minds as extra centres of causal processes, rather like machines but also considerably different from them. Their theory was a para-mechanical hypothesis.

That this assumption was at the heart of the doctrine is shown by the fact that there was from the beginning felt to be a major theoretical difficulty in explaining how minds can influence and be influenced by bodies. How can a mental process, such as willing, cause spatial movements like the movements of the tongue? How can a physical change in the optic nerve have among its effects a mind's perception of a flash of light? This notorious crux by itself shows the logical mould into which Descartes pressed his theory of the mind. It was the self-same mould into which he and Galileo set their mechanics. Still unwittingly adhering to the grammar of mechanics, he tried to avert disaster by describing minds in what was merely an obverse vocabulary. The workings of minds had to be described by the mere negatives of the specific descriptions given to bodies; they are not in space, they are not motions, they are not modifications of matter, they are not accessible to public observation. Minds are not bits and the laws it obeys are not those known to ordinary engineers.

As thus represented, minds are not merely ghosts harnessed to machines, they are themselves just spectral machines. Though the human body is an engine, it is not quite an ordinary engine, since some of its workings are governed by another engine inside it – this interior governor-engine being one of a very special sort. It is invisible, inaudible and it has no size or weight. It cannot be taken to bits and the laws it obeys are not those known to ordinary engineers. Nothing is known of how it governs the bodily engine.

A second major crux points the same moral. Since, according to the doctrine, minds belong to the same category as bodies and since bodies are rigidly governed by mechanical laws, it seemed to many theorists to follow that minds must be similarly governed by rigid non-mechanical laws. The physical world is a deterministic system, so the mental world must be a deterministic system. Bodies cannot help the modifications that they undergo, so minds cannot help pursuing the careers fixed for them. *Responsibility, choice, merit* and *demerit* are therefore inapplicable concepts – unless the compromise solution is adopted of saying that the laws governing mental processes, unlike those governing physical processes, have the congenial attribute of being only rather rigid. The problem of the Freedom of the Will was the problem how to reconcile the hypothesis that minds are to be described in terms drawn from the categories of mechanics with the knowledge that higher-grade human conduct is not of a piece with the behaviour of machines.

It is an historical curiosity that it was not noticed that the entire argument was broken-backed. Theorists correctly assumed that any sane man could already recognise the differences between, say, rational and non-rational utterances or between purposive and automatic behaviour. Else there would have been nothing requiring to be salved from mechanism. Yet the explanation given presupposed that one person could in principle never recognise the difference between the rational and the irrational utterances issuing from other human bodies, since he could never get access to the postulated immaterial causes of some of their utterances. Save for the doubtful exception of himself, he could never tell the difference between a man and a Robot. It would have to be conceded, for example, that, for all that we can tell, the inner lives of persons who are classed as idiots or lunatics are as rational as those of anyone else. Perhaps only their overt behaviour is disappointing; That is to say, perhaps 'idiots' are not really idiotic, or 'lunatics' lunatic. Perhaps, too, some of those who are classed as sane are really idiots. According to the theory, external observers could never know how the overt behaviour of others is correlated with their mental powers and processes and so they could never know or even plausibly conjecture whether their applications of mental-conduct concepts to these other people were correct or incorrect. It would then be hazardous or impossible for a man to claim sanity or logical consistency even for himself, since he would be debarred from comparing his own performances with those of others. In short, our characterisations of persons and their performances as intelligent, prudent and virtuous or as stupid, hypocritical and cowardly could never have been made, so the problem of providing a special causal hypothesis to serve as the basis of such diagnoses would never have arisen. The question, 'How do persons differ from machines? arose just because everyone already knew how to apply mental-conduct concepts before the new causal hypothesis was introduced. This causal hypothesis could not therefore be the source of the criteria used in those applications. Nor, of course, has the causal hypothesis in any degree improved our handling of those criteria. We still distinguish good from bad arithmetic, politic from impolitic conduct and fertile from infertile imaginations in the ways in which Descartes himself distinguished them before and after he speculated how the applicability of these criteria was compatible with the principle of mechanical causation.

He had mistaken the logic of his problem. Instead of asking by what criteria intelligent behaviour is actually distinguished from nonintelligent behaviour, he asked 'Given that the principle of mechanical causation does not tell us the difference, what other causal principle will tell it us?' He realised that the problem was not one of mechanics and assumed that it must therefore be one of some counterpart to mechanics. Not unnaturally psychology is often cast for just this role.

When two terms belong to the same category, it is proper to construct conjunctive propositions embodying them. Thus a purchaser may say that he bought a left-hand glove and a right-hand glove, but not that he bought a left-hand glove, a right-hand glove and a pair of gloves. 'She came home in a flood of tears and a sedan-chair' is a well-known joke based on the absurdity of conjoining terms of different types. It would have been equally ridiculous to construct the disjunction 'She came home either in a flood of tears or else in a sedan-chair' Now the dogma of the Ghost in the Machine does just this. It maintains that there exist both bodies and minds; that there occur physical processes and mental processes; that there are mechanical causes of corporeal movements and mental causes of corporeal movements. I shall argue that these and other analogous conjunctions are absurd; but, it must be noticed, the argument will not show that either of the illegitimately conjoined propositions is absurd in itself. I am not, for example, denying that there occur mental processes. Doing long division is a mental process and so is making a joke. But I am saying that the phrase 'there occur mental processes' does not mean the same sort of thing as 'there occur physical processes', and, therefore, that it makes no sense to conjoin or disjoin the two.

If my argument is successful, there will follow some interesting consequences. First, the hallowed contrast between Mind and Matter will be dissipated, but dissipated not by either of the equally hallowed absorptions of Mind by Matter or of Matter by Mind, but in quite a different way. For the seeming contrast of the two will be shown to be as illegitimate as would be the contrast of 'she came home in a flood of tears' and 'she came home in a sedan-chair'. The belief that there is a polar opposition between Mind and Matter is the belief that they are terms of the same logical type.

It will also follow that both Idealism and Materialism are answers to an improper question. The 'reduction' of the material world to mental states and processes, as well as the 'reduction' of mental states and processes to physical states and processes, presuppose the legitimacy of the disjunction 'Either there exist minds or there exist bodies (but not both)'. It would be like saying, 'Either she bought a left-hand and a right-hand glove or she bought a pair of gloves (but not both)'.

It is perfectly proper to say, in one logical tone of voice, that there exist minds and to say, in another logical tone of voice, that there exist bodies. But these expressions do not indicate two different species of existence, for 'existence' is not a generic word like 'coloured' or 'sexed'. They indicate two different senses of 'exist', somewhat as 'rising' has different senses in 'the tide is rising', 'hopes are rising', and 'the average age of death is rising'. A man would be thought to be making a poor joke who said that three things are now rising, namely the tide, hopes and the average age of death. It would be just as good or bad a joke to say that there exist prime numbers and Wednesdays and public opinions and navies; or that there exist both minds and bodies. . . .

4. Historical Note

It would not be true to say that the official theory derives solely from Descartes' theories, or even from a more widespread anxiety about the implications of seventeenth century mechanics. Scholastic and Reformation theology had schooled the intellects of the scientists as well as of the laymen, philosophers and clerics of that age. Stoic-Augustinian theories of the will were embedded in the Calvinist doctrines of sin and grace; Platonic and Aristotelian theories of the intellect shaped the orthodox doctrines of the immortality of the soul. Descartes was reformulating already prevalent theological doctrines of the soul in the new syntax of Galileo. The theologian's privacy of conscience became the philosopher's privacy of consciousness, and what had been the bogy of Predestination reappeared as the bogy of Determinism.

It would also not be true to say that the two-worlds myth did no theoretical good. Myths often do a lot of theoretical good, while they are still new. One benefit bestowed by the para-mechanical myth was that it partly super-annuated the then prevalent para-political myth. Minds and their Faculties had previously been described by analogies with political superiors and political subordinates. The idioms used were those of ruling, obeying, collaborating and rebelling. They survived and still survive in many ethical and some epistemological discussions. As, in physics, the new myth of occult Forces was a scientific improvement on the old myth of Final Causes, so in anthropological and psychological theory, the new myth of hidden operations, impulses and agencies was an improvement on the old myth of dictations, deferences and disobediences.

Study Questions

Ryle: "Systematically Misleading Expressions"

1. What is ("in a sense") the task of philosophy? Why is it a task of philosophy?
2. Show how the following are systematically misleading: (1) quasi-ontological statements; (2) quasi-Platonic statements; (3) quasi-referential 'the'-phrases.

Moore: "Wittgenstein's Lectures in 1930-33"

1. What was Wittgenstein's view with regard to the meaning of words?
2. What was his view with regard to the meaning of propositions?
3. What was his conception of philosophy?

Wisdom: "Philosophical Perplexity"

1. In what sense are philosophical statements verbal? In what sense are they *not* verbal?
2. What is the philosopher's intention?
3. What are pointless doubts? How can they be misleading? How can they be illuminating?
4. How does Wisdom's conception of philosophy differ from Wittgenstein's?

Wisdom: "Philosophy, Anxiety, and Novelty"

1. Why is a philosophical question a request for a description of "a familiar class of animals"?
2. Why is the whole of what philosophers do deductive?
3. What does Wisdom mean by calling Moore's procedure legislistic?

Wisdom: "Gods"

1. Why is the existence of God not an experimental issue?
2. What is the point about the story of the gardner?
3. How can theological debates be settled? In what ways can they not be settled?
4. Explain the connecting technique.
5. What should happen when we ask about the reasonableness or propriety of belief in gods?
6. What is the main thesis of this essay?

Ryle: "Descartes' Myth"

1. What is the official doctrine about minds?
2. Why is it absurd?
3. What is a category-mistake?
4. How does such a mistake occur in connection with talk of minds?
5. What is the origin of the category-mistake?
6. What are the consequences of Ryle's argument?

Selected Bibliography

Fann, K. T. *Wittgenstein's Conception of Philosophy*. Berkeley: University of California Press, 1971. Part 2 [A good book for the beginner.]

Flew, Antony, ed. *Logic and Language,* 1st and 2nd Series. Oxford: Basil Blackwell, 1955. [Contains important and interesting articles by a number of writers.]

Passmore, John. *A Hundred Years of Philosophy*. London: Duckworth, 1957. Ch. 18 [Good discussion of Wittgenstein.]

Ryle, Gilbert. *The Concept of Mind*. London: Hutchinson, 1949. [An important, but often puzzling, work.]

Wisdom, John. *Philosophy and Psycho-analysis*. Oxford: Basil Blackwell, 1957. [Contains some of the selections found in this volume as well as others.]

Wittgenstein, Ludwig. *The Blue and Brown Books*. Oxford: Basil Blackwell, 1960. [These are 'preliminary studies for the *Philosophical Investigations* and in some ways are more readable.]

Wittgenstein, Ludwig. *Philosophical Investigations*. Trans. G. E. M. Anscombe. Oxford: Basil Blackwell, 1953. [Perhaps one of the most influential books in twentieth-century philosophy.]

Logico-Metaphysical Analysis

24. Logical Positivism, Language, and the Reconstruction of Metaphysics

Gustav Bergmann

1. *Introduction.* A philosophical movement is a group of philosophers, active over at least one or two generations, who more or less share a style, or an intellectual origin, and who have learned more from each other than they have from others, though they may, and often do, quite vigorously disagree among themselves. Logical positivism is the current name of what is no doubt a movement. The common source is the writings and teachings of G. E. Moore, Russell, and Wittgenstein during the first quarter of the century. However, two of these founding fathers, Moore and Russell, do not themselves belong to the movement. The logical positivists have also greatly influenced each other; they still do, albeit less so as the disagreements among them become more pronounced. There is indeed vigorous disagreement, even on such fundamentals as the nature of the philosophical enterprise itself. The very name, logical positivist, is by now unwelcome to some, though it is still and quite reasonably applied to all, particularly from the outside. Reasonably, because they unmistakably share a philosophical style. They all accept the linguistic turn Wittgenstein initiated in the *Tractatus*. To be sure, they interpret and develop it in their several ways, hence the disagreements; yet they are all under its spell, hence the common style. Thus, if names in themselves were important, it might be better to choose linguistic philosophy or philosophy of language. In fact, these tags are now coming into use. But they, too, like most labels, are misleading. For one, the concern with language is nothing new in first philosophy or, if you please, epistemology and metaphysics. Certainly all "minute philosophers" have shared it. For another, there is strictly speaking no such thing as the philosophy of language. Language may be studied by philologists, aestheticians, and scientists such as psychologists or sociologists. To bring these studies thoughtfully together is well worth while. Customarily, such synoptic efforts are called philosophy. There is no harm in this provided

they are not mistaken for what they are not, namely, technical philosophy. Rather than being philosophers of language, the positivists, who are all technical philosophers, are therefore philosophers through language; they philosophize by means of it. But then, everybody who speaks uses language as a means or tool. The point is that the positivists, newly conscious of it, use it in a new way.

The novelty is, I believe, radical. Even the greatest innovators never do more, can do no more, than add one or two features to the tradition, perhaps submerge one or two others. The tradition as a whole persists. Features is a vague word. I had better speak of new questions and methods; for they, not the answers we give, matter. The logical positivist neither added nor submerged a single major question. Their characteristic contribution is a method. This may mean radical novelty; it does, I believe, in their case. There is a sense, though, in which the linguistic turn has not even produced startlingly new answers. The answers the positivists give to the old questions, or those which most of them give to most, are in some respects very similar to what has been said before within the empiricist stream of the great tradition. On the other hand, both questions and answers are so reinterpreted that they have changed almost beyond recognition. At least, alas, beyond the recognition of many. Many of the logical positivists themselves, like other innovators before, even thought that they had disposed of the tradition. Some still believe it. I think there is merely a new method, though one that is radically new, of approaching old questions.

This is not a historical paper. I wish to speak as a philosopher. Thus, while I am aware of how much I owe to others, I can only speak for myself. Nor is my intent primarily critical. Yet, such is the dialectical nature of philosophy that we cannot either in thinking or in writing do without that foil the ideas of others provide. This makes us all critics as well as, in a structural sense, historians. Thus, while it is my main purpose, or very nearly so, to explain one kind of logical positivism, I shall, almost of necessity, discuss all others. They fall into two main divisions. The one is made up by the ideal linguists, the other by the analysts of usage, more fully, of correct or ordinary usage. The ideal linguists are either *formalists* or *reconstructionists*. The outstanding for-malist is Carnap. What the reconstructionists hope to reconstruct in the new style is the old metaphysics. Clearly, from what has been said, I am a reconstructionist. There is, third, the *pragmatist* variety. These writers, we shall presently see, are best counted with the ideal linguists. Usage analysis flourishes above all at Oxford and Cambridge. These philosophers are also known as, fourth, the therapeutic positivists or *casuists*. One variant of this view deserves to be distinguished. For want of a better term I shall, with a new meaning, resuscitate an old one, calling this view, fifth, *conventionalist*. This wing is led by Ryle.

The expositor's position determines, as always, his strategy. The argument will center around reconstructionism. But since I believe the method to be neutral in that it may be used by all and any, I shall set it off as clearly as I can from the specific conclusions to which it has led me. Not surprisingly, these conclusions, or answers to the old questions, lie within the empiricist tradition, if it is conceived broadly enough to include the act philosophies of Moore and Brentano. The debt to Hume and the phenomenalists in general is, naturally, tremendous. One clever Englishman recently proposed the equation: Logical Positivism is Hume plus mathematical logic. He has a point, though by far not the whole story. But whatever these specific conclusions may be, I can hardly do more than hint at a few of them. This must be kept in mind throughout. I have, of course, discussed them elsewhere. Here, however, they serve mainly as illustrations, *pour fixer les idées,* for even in philosophy abstractness cannot without disadvantage be pushed beyond certain limits.

2. *The linguistic turn.* What precisely the linguistic turn is or, to stay with the metaphor, how to execute it properly is controversial. That it must be executed, somehow or other, is common doctrine, flowing from the shared belief that the relation between language and philosophy is closer than, as well as essentially different from, that between language and any other discipline. What are the grounds of this belief and how did it arise?

First. There is no experiment on whose outcome the predictions of two physicists would differ solely because the one is a phenomenalist, the other a realist. Generally, no philosophical question worthy of the name is ever settled by experimental or, for that matter, experiential evidence. Things are what they are. In some sense philosophy is, therefore, verbal or linguistic. But this is not necessarily a bad sense. One must not hastily conclude that all philosophers always deal with pseudoproblems. Those who thus stretch a point which is telling enough as far as it goes, are overly impressed with the naïve "empiricism" of the laboratory. Most of them are formalists. Scientism and formalism, we shall see, tend to go together. *Second.* Philosophers maintain in all seriousness such propositions as that time is not real or that there are no physical objects. But they also assure us that we do not in the ordinary sense err when, using language as we ordinarily do, we say, for instance, that some event preceded some other in time or that we are perceiving physical objects such as stones and trees. Outside their studies, philosophers themselves say such things. Thus they use language in two ways, in its ordinary sense and in one that is puzzling to say the least. To decide whether what they say as philosophers is true one must, therefore, first discover what they say, that is, precisely what that peculiar sense is. The inquiry is linguistic. It starts from common sense, for what else is there to start from. These points were pressed by G. E. Moore. His emphasis on ordinary usage and common sense reappears, of course, in the British branches of the movement. The common-sense doctrine also influenced the reconstructionists. It is worth noticing, though, that in the form in which all these positivists have adopted it, the doctrine is not itself a philosophical proposition. Rather, it helps to set their style, assigning to philosophy the task of elucidating common sense, not of either proving or disproving it. In this form the common-sense doctrine also represents at least part of what could be meant by saying, as both Husserl and Wittgenstein do, that philosophy is descriptive. *Third.* This point stands to the second in a relation similar to that between morphology and physiology or, perhaps, pathology. We have seen that philosophers, using language in their peculiar sort of discourse, arrive at such propositions as that there are no physical objects. Taken in their ordinary sense, these propositions are absurd. The man on the street, however, who uses the same language never ends up with this kind of absurdity. We also know that the conclusions one draws depend on the grammatical form of the statements that express the premises. We notice, finally, that sometimes two statements, such as 'Peter is not tall' and 'Cerberus is not real', exemplify the same grammatical form though they say really quite different things. We conclude that philosophers come to grief because they rely on grammatical form. What they should trust instead is the logical form of statements such as, in our illustration, 'Peter is not tall' and 'There is no dog that is three-headed, etc.'. Consistently pursued, the notion of logical form leads to that of an ideal language in which logical and grammatical form coincide completely. Both notions took shape when Russell answered several philosophical questions, some about arithmetic, some about just such entities as Cerberus, by means of a symbolism. There is one more suggestion in all this, namely, that in an ideal language the philosopher's propositions could no longer be stated so that he would find himself left without anything to say at all. 'Peter exists', for instance, has no equivalent in Russell's symbolism, Peter's existence showing itself, as it were, by the occurrence of a proper name for him. Ontology is, perhaps, but an illusion spawned by language. So one may again be led to think that all philosophy is verbal in a bad sense. The suggestion seduced the formalists as well as those who later became usage analysts. It even seduced Wittgenstein. The reconstructionists reject it. According to them, philosophical discourse is peculiar only in that it is ordinary or, if you please, commonsensical discourse about an ideal language.

Ordinary discourse about an ideal language is, indeed, the reconstructionist version of the linguistic turn. But a statement so succinct needs unpacking. Precisely what is an ideal language? I cannot answer without first explaining what syntax is.

3. *Syntax.* Signs or symbols may be artificial, that is, expressly devised, or they may have grown naturally. In either case they do not say anything by themselves. We speak by means of them; we "interpret" them; having been interpreted, they "refer." Syntax deals only with some properties of the signs themselves and of the patterns in which they are arranged. This, and nothing else, is what is meant by calling syntax formal and schemata syntactically constructed formal languages. It would be safer to avoid any term that suggests interpretation, such as 'language', 'sign', or 'symbol'. I shall simply speak of syntactical schemata and their elements. Or one could use a prefix to guard against confusion, calling the elements f-signs, for instance, 'f' standing for 'formal'. In this section, where I discuss only f-notions, I shall suppress the prefix. Later on I shall occasionally take this precaution. In themselves, signs are physical objects or events. Written signs, and we need not for our purpose

consider others, are instances of geometrical shapes. Syntax is thus quite commonsensical business. It is, so to speak, a study in geometrical design. But philosophers are not geometricians. They do not invent and investigate these schemata for their own sake, as mathematical logicians often do, but with an eye upon their suitability for serving, upon interpretation, as the ideal language. Making this claim for any one schema, the geometrician turns philosopher, committing himself to a philosophical position. This is why I insisted that the method as such is neutral. Yet, to introduce neutrally the syntactical notions or categories (f-categories!) which I shall need would be tediously abstract and is, at any rate, quite unnecessary for my purpose. So I shall, instead, introduce them by describing that particular schema which I judge to be, with one later addition, that of the ideal language. Broadly speaking, it is the schema of Russell's *Principia Mathematica*. Very broadly indeed; and I shall have to speak broadly throughout the rest of this section, simplifying so sweepingly that it amounts almost to distortion, though not, of course, as I judge it, to essential distortion.

The construction of the schema proceeds in three steps. First one selects certain shapes and kinds of such as its elements or signs. Then certain sequences of shapes are selected or, if you please, defined as its sentences. Order, as the term sequence implies, enters the definition. Finally a certain subclass of sentences, called analytic, is selected. Turning to some detail, relatively speaking, I shall, in order to fix the ideas, add in parentheses some prospective interpretations from our natural language. *First.* The elements are divided into categories. Though based on shape and nothing else, the divisions are not nominal in that the definitions of sentence and analyticity are stated in their terms. Signs are either logical or descriptive. Descriptive signs are either proper names ('Peter'), or predicates and relations of the first order ('green', 'louder than'), or predicates and relations of higher orders ('color'). Logical signs are of two main kinds. Either they are individually specified signs, connectives ('not', 'and', 'if then') and quantifiers ('all', 'there is something such that'). Or they are variables. To each descriptive category corresponds one of variables, though not necessarily conversely; to proper names so-called individual variables (such phrases as 'a certain particular'), to predicates predicate variables (such phrases as 'a certain property'), and so on. *Second.* Sentences are either atomic or complex. Atomic sentences are sequences of descriptive signs of appropriate categories ('Peter (is) green', 'John (is) taller than James'). Complex sentences contain logical signs ('John (is) tall *and* James (is) short', *'There is something such that* it (is) green'). *Third.* In defining analyticity arithmetical techniques are used; in the sense in which one may be said to use such techniques who, having assigned numbers to people on the basis of their shapes, called a company unlucky (f-unlucky!) if the sum of the numbers of its members is divisible by 13. A sentence is said to follow deductively from another if and only if a third, compounded of the two in a certain manner, is analytic. ('p' implies 'q' if and only if 'if p then q' is analytic.) The definition of analyticity is so designed that when a descriptive sign occurs in an analytic sentence, the sentence obtained by replacing it with another descriptive sign of the same category is also analytic. (In 'Either John is tall or John is not tall', the terms 'John' and 'tall' occur vacuously.) Two such sentences are said to be of the same "logical form"; analyticity itself is said to depend on "form" only, which is but another way of saying that it can be characterized by means of sentences which contain none but logical signs. This feature is import. Because of it, among others, f-analyticity can, as we shall see, be used to explicate or reconstruct the philosophical notion of analyticity which, unfortunately, also goes by the name of formal truth. Unfortunately, because the f-notion of logical form which I just defined needs no explication. The philosophical notion, like all philosophical ones, does. To identify the two inadvertently, as I believe Wittgenstein did, leads therefore to disaster. But of this later.

The shapes originally selected are called the undefined signs of the schema. The reason for setting them apart is that many schemata, including the one I am considering, provide machinery for adding new signs. To each sign added corresponds one special sentence, called its definition, the whole construction being so arranged that this sentence is analytic. This has two consequences. For one, the definitions of the language which, in some sense, the schema becomes upon interpretation, are all nominal. For another, interpretation of the undefined signs automatically interprets all others. Defined signs whose definitions contain undefined descriptive signs are themselves classified as descriptive.

4. *Ideal language and reconstruction.* To interpret a syntactical schema is to pair its undefined signs one by one with words or expressions of our natural language, making them "name" the same things or, if you please, "refer" equally. An interpreted schema is in principle a language. In principle only, because we could not speak it instead of a natural language; it is neither rich nor flexible enough. Its lack of flexibility is obvious; it lacks richness in that we need not specify it beyond, say, stipulating that it contains color predicates, without bothering which or how many. Thus, even an interpreted schema is merely, to use the term in a different sense, the "schema" of a language, an architect's drawing rather than a builder's blueprint. The ideal language is an interpreted syntactical schema. But not every such schema is an ideal language. To qualify it must fulfill two conditions. *First,* it must be complete, that is, it must, no matter how schematically, account for all areas of our experience. For instance, it is not enough that it contains schematically the way in which scientific behaviorists, quite adequately for their purpose, speak about mental contents. It must also reflect the different way in which one speaks about his own experience and, because of it, of that of others; and it must show how these two ways jibe. *Second,* it must permit, by means of ordinary discourse about it, the solution of all philosophical problems. This discourse, the heart of the philosophical enterprise, is the reconstruction of metaphysics. So I must next explain how to state, or restate, the classical questions in this manner and, if they can be so stated, why I insist that this discourse is, nevertheless, quite ordinary or commonsensical though, admittedly, not about the sort of thing

the man on the street talks about. Making the range of his interests the criterion of "common sense" is, for my taste, a bit too John Bullish.

Consider the thesis of classical nominalism that there are no universals. Given the linguistic turn it becomes the assertion that the ideal language contains no undefined descriptive signs except proper names. Again, take classical sensationism. Transformed it asserts that the ideal language contains no undefined descriptive predicates except nonrelational ones of the first order, referring to characters exemplified by sense data which are, some ultrapositivists to the contrary notwithstanding, quite commonsensical things. I reject both nominalism and sensationism. But this is not the point. The point is that the two corresponding assertions, though surely false, are yet not absurd, as so many of the classical theses are, as it is for instance absurd to say, as the sensationists must, that a physical object is a bundle of sense data. Obvious as they are, these two illustrations provide a basis for some comments about the reconstruction in general.

First. I did not, either affirmatively or negatively, state either of the two classical propositions. I merely mentioned them in order to explicate them, that is, to suggest what they could plausibly be taken to assert in terms of the ideal language. For the tact and imagination such explication sometimes requires the method provides no guarantee. No method does. But there is no doubt that this kind of explication, considering as it does languages, is quite ordinary discourse. Yet it does not, by this token alone, lose anything of what it explicates. To say that a picture, to be a picture, must have certain features is, clearly, to say something about what it is a picture of. I know no other way to speak of the world's categorial features without falling into the snares the linguistic turn avoids. These features are as elusive as they are pervasive. Yet they are our only concern; that is why the ideal language need be no more than a "schema." I just used the picture metaphor, quite commonsensically I think, yet deliberately. For it has itself become a snare into which some positivists fell, not surprisingly, since it is after all a metaphor. Of this later. *Second.* A critic may say: "Your vaunted new method either is circular or produces an infinite regress. Did you not yourself, in what you insist is ordinary discourse, use such words as 'naming' and 'referring'? Surely you know that they are eminently philosophical?" I have guarded against the objection by putting quotation marks around these words when I first used them. The point is that I did use them commonsensically, that is, in a way and on an occasion where they do not give trouble. So I can without circularity clarify those uses that do give rise to philosophical problems, either by locating them in the ideal language, or when I encounter them in a philosophical proposition which I merely mention in order to explicate it, or both, as the case may be. But the critic continues: "You admit then, at least, that you do not, to use one of your favorite words, explicate common sense?" I admit nothing of the sort. The explication of common sense is circular only as it is circular to ask, as Moore might put it, how we know what in fact we do know, knowing also that we know it. *Third.* The critic presses on: "Granting that you can without circularity explicate the various philosophical positions, say, realism and phenomenalism, I still fail to see how this reconstruction, as you probably call it, helps you to choose among them." I discover with considerable relief that I need no longer make such choices. With relief, because each of the classical answers to each of the classical questions has a common-sense core. The realist, for instance, grasped some fundamental features of experience or, as he would probably prefer to say, of the world. The phenomenalist grasped some others. Each, anxious not to lose hold of his, was driven to deny or distort the others. From this squirrel cage the linguistic turn happily frees us. Stated in the new manner, the several "cores" are no longer incompatible. This is that surprising turn within the turn which I had in mind when I observed that the old questions, though preserved in one sense, are yet in another changed almost beyond recognition. To insist on this transformation is one thing. To dismiss the classical questions out of hand, as some positivists unfortunately do, is quite another thing. *Fourth.* The method realizes the old ideal of a philosophy without presuppositions. Part of this ideal is an illusion, for we cannot step outside of ourselves or of the world. The part that makes sense is realized by constructing the schema formally, without any reference to its prospective use, strict syntacticism at this stage forcing attention upon what may otherwise go unnoticed. But the critic persists: "Even though you start formally, when you choose a schema as the ideal language you do impose its 'categories' upon the world, thus prejudging the world's form. Are you then not at this point yourself trading on the ambiguity of 'form', as you just said others sometimes do?" One does not, in any intelligible sense, choose the ideal language. One finds or discovers, empirically if you please, within the ordinary limits of human error and dullness, that a schema can be so used. Should there be more than one ideal language, then this fact itself will probably be needed somewhere in the reconstruction; equally likely and equally enlightening, some traits of each would then be as "incidental" as are some of Finnish grammar. More important, all this goes to show that the reconstructionist's philosophy is, as I believe all good philosophy must be, descriptive. But it is time to relieve the abstractness by showing, however sketchily, the method at work.

5. *Three issues.* The common-sense core of *phenomenalism* is wholly recovered by what is known as the principle of acquaintance. (Later on I shall restore the balance by reconstructing what I think is the deepest root of realism. Realism, to be sure, has others, such as the indispensability of the quantifiers, which permit us to speak of what is not in front of our noses. But these roots run closer to the surface.) The word principle is unfortunate; for description knows no favorites. The feature in question is indeed a principle only in that quite a few other explications are found to depend on it. What it asserts is that all undefined descriptive signs of the ideal language refer to entities with which we are directly or, as one also says, phenomenally acquainted. Notice the difference from sensationism. Relational and higher-order undefined predicates are not excluded. The indispensability of at least one of these two categories is beyond reasonable doubt. Nor does the principle exclude undefined

descriptive signs that refer to ingredients of moral and aesthetic experience. If ethical naturalism is explicated as the rejection of such terms, then one sees that a reconstructionist need not be an ethical naturalist. I, for one, am not.

The ideal language contains proper names, the sort of thing to which they refer being exemplified by sense data; 'tree' and 'stone' and 'physical object' itself are, broadly speaking, defined predicates, closer analysis revealing that the "subjects" of these predicates do not refer to individual trees and stones. That this amounts to a partial explication of the substantialist thesis, accepting a small part of it and rejecting the rest, is fairly obvious. Another aspect of the matter raises two questions. Definitions are linguistic constructions, more precisely, constructions within a language. How detailed need they be? What are the criteria for their success? To begin with the second question, consider the generality 'No physical object is at the same time at two different places'. Call it S and the sentence that corresponds to it in the ideal language Ś. Since 'time' and 'place' in S refer to physical time and place, the descriptive signs in Ś are all defined. Their construction is successful if and only if Ś and a few other such truths, equally crucial for the solution of philosophical problems, follow deductively from the definitions proposed for them in conjunction with some other generalities containing only undefined descriptive signs, which we also know to be true, such as, for instance, the sentence of the ideal language expressing the transitivity of being phenomenally later. The construction is thus merely schematic, in the sense in which the ideal language itself is merely a schema. The building stones from which it starts in order to recover the sense in phenomenalism are so minute that anything else is patently beyond our strength. Nor, fortunately, is it needed to solve the philosophical problems. To strive for more is either scientism or psychologism, scientism if one insists on definitions as "complete" as in the axiomatization of a scientific discipline, psychologism if one expects them to reflect all the subtlety and ambiguity of introspective analysis. Formalists tend to scientism; usage analysts to psychologism.

Analyticity is not a common-sense notion. However, the differences that led philosophers to distinguish between analytic and synthetic propositions are clearly felt upon a little reflection. There is, first, a difference in certainty, one of kind as one says, not merely of degree. Or, as it is also put, analytic truth is necessary, synthetic truth contingent. Certainty is a clear notion only if applied to beliefs. Besides, what is sought is a structural or objective difference between two kinds of contents of belief. There is only this connection that, once discovered, such a structural difference will be useful in explicating the philosophical idea of certainty. Second, analytic (tautological) truths are empty in that they say nothing about the world, as 'John is either tall or not tall' says nothing. Third, there is even in natural languages the difference, often though not always clear-cut, between descriptive (not f-descriptive!) words such as 'green' and logical (not f-logical!) ones such as 'or'. Analyticity depends only on the logical words and on grammatical "form." Fourth, descriptive words seem to refer to "content," to name the world's furniture, in a sense in which logical words do not. These, I believe, are the four felt differences which philosophers, including many positivists, express by calling analytical truths necessary, or formal, or syntactical, or linguistic. Without explication the formula courts disaster; its explication has four parts, all equally important. First, our knowledge that all "content" variations of analytic "form" ('George is either tall or not tall', 'James is either blond or not blond', etc.) are true is, in the ordinary sense, very certain. But no claim of a philosophical kind for the certainty of this knowledge can be the basis of our explication; it can only be one of its results. Second, the notions of analyticity and of logical and descriptive words correspond to perfectly clear-cut f-notions of the ideal language. Third, the specific arithmetical definition of f-analyticity in the ideal language (that is, in the simplest cases, the well-known truth tables) shows in what reasonable sense analytical truth is combinatorial, compositional, or linguistic. Fourth, arithmetic, the key to this definition, is itself analytic upon it. Taken together these four features amply justify the philosophers' distinction between what is either factual or possible (synthetic) and what is necessary (analytic), between the world's "form" and its "content." But if they are taken absolutely, that is, independently of this explication, then the phrases remain dangerously obscure. Greatest perhaps is the danger of an absolute notion of form as a verbal bridge to an absolute notion of certainty. Nothing is simpler, for instance, than to set aside syntactically a special class of first-order predicates, subsequently to be interpreted by color adjectives, and so to define f-analyticity that 'Nothing is (at the same time all over) both green and red' becomes analytic. Only, this kind of f-analyticity would no longer explicate the philosophical notion. Ours does. But that it does this is not itself a formal or linguistic truth.

Ontology has long been a favorite target of the positivistic attack. So I shall, for the sake of contrast, reconstruct the philosophical query for what there is. The early attacks were not without grounds. There is, for one, the absurdity of the classical formulations and, for another, the insight, usually associated with the name of Kant, that existence is not a property. In Russell's thought, this seed bore double fruit. On the one hand, when 'Peter' is taken to refer to a particular, 'Peter exists' cannot even be stated in the ideal language; his "existence" merely shows itself by the occurrence of a proper name in the schema. On the other hand, such statements as 'There are no centaurs (centaurs do not exist)' or 'There are coffeehouses in Venice' can be expressed in the ideal language, in a way that does not lead to absurdity, by means of quantifiers, which are logical signs, and of defined predicates, whose definitions do not involve the "existence" of the kinds defined. This is as it should be. Ontological statements are not ordinary statements to be located within the ideal language; they are philosophical propositions to be explicated by our method. Logical signs, we remember, are felt not to refer as descriptive ones do. This reconstructs the classical distinction between existence and subsistence. Ontology proper asks what exists rather than subsists. So the answer to which we are led by our method seems to be a catalogue of all descriptive signs. Literally, there can be no such catalogue; but one would settle for a list of categories, that is, of the kinds of entities to which we refer or might have occasion to refer. But then, every serious philosopher claims that he can in his fashion talk about everything. So one could not hope to reconstruct the various ontological theses by means of a list of all descriptive signs. The equivalent of the classical problem is, rather, the search for the undefined descriptive signs of the ideal language.[1] I used this idea implicitly when I explicated nominalism and phenomenalism. To show that it is reasonable, also historically, consider two more examples. Take first materialism or, as it now styles itself, physicalism or philosophical behaviorism. Interpreted fairly, even this silliest of all philosophies asserts no more than that all mental terms can be defined in a schema whose undefined descriptive predicates refer to characters exemplified by physical objects. Quite so. I, too, am a scientific behaviorist. Only, the materialist's schema is, rather obviously, incomplete and therefore not, as he would have to assert, the ideal language. Russell, on the other hand, when he denied the existence of classes, meant, not at all either obviously or sillily, no more than that class names are defined signs of the ideal language.

*   *   *

NOTE

1. One could argue that this conception of ontology is anticipated in the *Tractatus* (2.01, 2.02, 2.027). But I was not aware of that when I first proposed it.

25. On What There Is

W. V. Quine

A curious thing about the ontological problem is its simplicity. It can be put in three Anglo-Saxon monosyllables: "What is there?" It can be answered, moreover, in a word — "Everything" — and everyone will accept this answer as true. However, this is merely to say that there is what there is. There remains room for disagreement over cases; and so the issue has stayed alive down the centuries.

Suppose now that two philosophers, McX and I, differ over ontology. Suppose McX maintains there is something which I maintain there is not. McX can, quite consistently with his own point of view, describe our difference of opinion by saying that I refuse to recognize certain entities. I should protest of course that he is wrong in his formulation of our disagreement, for I maintain that there are no entities, of the kind which he alleges, *for* me to recognize; but my finding him wrong in his formulation of our disagreement is unimportant, for I am committed to considering him wrong in his ontology anyway.

When *I* try to formulate our difference of opinion, on the other hand, I seem to be in a predicament. I cannot admit that there are some things which McX countenances and I do not, for in admitting that there are such things I should be contradicting my own rejection of them.

It would appear, if this reasoning were sound, that in any ontological dispute the proponent of the negative side suffers the disadvantage of not being able to admit that his opponent disagrees with him.

This is the old Platonic riddle of non-being. Non-being must in some sense be, otherwise what is it that there is not? This tangled doctrine might be nicknamed *Plato's beard;* historically it has proved tough, frequently dulling the edge of Occam's razor.

It is some such line of thought that leads philosophers like McX to impute being where they might otherwise be quite content to recognize that there is nothing. Thus, take Pegasus. If Pegasus *were* not, McX argues, we should not be talking about anything when we use the word; therefore it would be nonsense to say even that Pegasus is not. Thinking to show thus that the denial of Pegasus cannot be coherently maintained, he concludes that Pegasus is.

McX cannot, indeed, quite persuade himself that any region of space-time, near or remote, contains a flying horse of flesh and blood. Pressed for further details on Pegasus, then, he says that Pegasus is an idea in men's minds. Here, however, a confusion begins to be apparent. We may for the sake of argument concede that there is an entity, and even a unique entity (though this is rather implausible), which is the mental Pegasus-idea; but this mental entity is not what people are talking about when they deny Pegasus.

McX never confuses the Parthenon with the Parthenon-idea. The Parthenon is physical; the Parthenon-idea is mental (according any way to McX's version of ideas, and I have no better to offer). We cannot easily imagine two things more unlike, and less liable to confusion, than the Parthenon and the Parthenon-idea. But when we shift from the Parthenon to Pegasus, the confusion sets in — for no other reason than that McX would sooner be deceived by the crudest and most flagrant counterfeit than grant the non-being of Pegasus.

The notion that Pegasus must be, because it would otherwise be nonsense to say even that Pegasus is not, has been seen to lead McX into an elementary confusion. Subtler minds, taking the same precept as their starting point, come out with theories of Pegasus which are less patently misguided than McX's, and correspondingly more difficult to eradicate. One of these subtler minds is named, let us say, Wyman. Pegasus, Wyman maintains, has his being as an unactualized possible. When we say of Pegasus that there is no such thing, we are saying, more precisely, that Pegasus does not have the special attribute of actuality. Saying that Pegasus is not actual is on a par, logically, with saying that the Parthenon is not red; in either case we are saying something about an entity whose being is unquestioned.

Wyman, by the way, is one of those philosophers who have united in ruining the good old word 'exist'. Despite his espousal of unactualized possibles, he limits the word 'existence' to actuality — thus preserving an illusion of ontological agreement between himself and us who repudiate the rest of his bloated universe. We have all been prone to say, in our common-sense usage of 'exist', that Pegasus does not exist, meaning simply that there is no such entity at all. If Pegasus existed he would indeed be in space and time, but only because the word 'Pegasus' has spatio-temporal connotations, and not because 'exists' has spatio-temporal connotations. If spatio-temporal reference is lacking when we affirm the existence of the cube root of 27, this is simply because a cube root is not a spatio-temporal kind of thing, and not because we are being ambiguous in our use of 'exist'. However, Wyman, in an ill-conceived effort to appear agreeable, genially grants us the non-existence of Pegasus and then, contrary to what *we* meant by non-existence of Pegasus, insists that Pegasus *is*. Existence is one thing, he says, and subsistence is another. The only way I know of coping with this obfuscation of issues is to *give* Wyman the word 'exist'. I'll try not to use it again; I still have 'is'. So much for lexicography; let's get back to Wyman's ontology.

Wynam's overpopulated universe is in many ways unlovely. It offends the aesthetic sense of us who have a taste for desert landscapes, but this is not the worst of it. Wyman's slum of possibles is a breeding ground for disorderly elements. Take, for instance, the possible fat man in that doorway; and, again, the possible bald man at that doorway. Are they the same possible man, or two possible men? How do we decide? How many possible men are there in that doorway? Are there more possible thin ones than fat ones? How many of them are alike? Or would their being alike make them one? Are no *two* possible things alike? Is this the same as saying that it is impossible for two things to be alike? Or, finally, is the concept of identity simply inapplicable to unactualized possibles? But what sense can be found in talking of entities which cannot meaningfully be said to be identical with themselves and distinct from one another? These elements are well high incorrigible. By a Fregean therapy of individual concepts, some effort might be made at rehabilitation; but I feel we'd do better simply to clear Wyman's slum and be done with it.

Possibility, along with the other modalities of necessity and impossibility and contingency, raises problems upon which I do not mean to imply that we should turn our backs. But we can at least limit modalities to whole statements. We may impose the abverb 'possibly' upon a statement as a whole, and we may well worry about the semantical analysis of such usage; but little real advance in such analysis is to be hoped for in expanding our universe to include so-called *possible entities.* I suspect that the main motive for this expansion is simply the old notion that Pegasus, e.g., must be because it would otherwise be nonsense to say even that he is not.

Still, all the rank luxuriance of Wyman's universe of possibles would seem to come to naught when we make a slight change in the example and speak not of Pegasus but of the round square cupola on Berkeley College. If, unless Pegasus were, it would be nonsense to say that he is not, then by the same token, unless the round square cupola on Berkeley College were, it would be nonsense to say that it is not. But, unlike Pegasus, the round square cupola on Berkeley College cannot be admitted even as an unactualized *possible.* Can we drive Wyman now to admitting also a realm of unactualizable impossibles? If so, a good many embarrassing questions could be asked about them. We might hope even to trap Wyman in contradictions, by getting him to admit that certain of these entities are at once round and square. But the wily Wyman chooses the other horn of the dilemna and concedes that it is nonsense to say that the round square cupola on Berkeley College is not. He says that the phrase 'round square cupola' is meaningless.

Wyman was not the first to embrace this alternative. The doctrine of the meaninglessness of contradictions runs away back. The tradition survives, moreover, in writers such as Wittgenstein who seem to share none of Wyman's motivations. Still I wonder whether the first temptation to such a doctrine may not have been substantially the motivation which we have observed in Wyman. Certainly the doctrine has no intrinsic appeal; and it has led its devotees to such quixotic extremes as that of challenging the method of proof by *reductio ad absurdum* — a challenge in which I seem to detect a quite striking *reductio ad absurdum eius ipsius.*[1]

Moreover, the doctrine of meaninglessness of contradictions has the severe methodological drawback that it makes it impossible, in principle, ever to devise an effective test of what is meaningful and what is not. It would be forever impossible for us to devise systematic ways of deciding whether a string of signs made sense — even to us individually, let alone other people — or not. For, it follows from a discovery in mathematical logic, due to Church, that there can be no generally applicable test of contradictoriness.

I have spoken disparagingly of Plato's beard, and hinted that it is tangled. I have dwelt at length on the inconveniences of putting up with it. It is time to think about taking steps.

Russell, in his theory of so-called singular descriptions, showed clearly how we might meaningfully use seeming names without supposing that the entities allegedly named be. The names to which Russell's theory directly applies are complex descriptive names such as 'the author of *Waverley*', 'the present King of France', 'the round square cupola on Berkeley College'. Russell analyzes such phrases systematically as fragments of the whole sentences in which they occur. The sentence 'The author of *Waverley* was a poet', e.g., is explained as a whole as meaning 'Someone (better: something) wrote *Waverley* and was a poet, and nothing else wrote *Waverley*'. (The point of this added clause is to affirm the uniqueness which is implicit in the word 'the', in '*the* author of *Waverley*'.) The sentence 'The round square cupola on Berkeley College is pink' is explained as 'Something is round and square and is a cupola on Berkeley College and is pink, and nothing else is round and square and a cupola on Berkeley College'.

The virtue of this analysis is that the seeming name, a descriptive phrase, is paraphrased *in context* as a so-called incomplete symbol. No unified expression is offered as an analysis of the descriptive phrase, but the statement as a whole which was the context of that phrase still gets its full quota of meaning — whether true or false.

The unanalyzed statement 'The author of *Waverley* was a poet' contains a part, 'the author of *Waverley*', which is wrongly supposed by McX and Wyman to demand objective reference in order to be meaningful at all. But in Russell's translation 'Something wrote *Waverley* and was a poet and nothing else wrote *Waverley*', the burden of objective reference which had been put upon the descriptive phrase is now taken over by words of the kind that logicians call bound variables, variables of quantification: namely, words like 'something', 'nothing, 'everything'. These words, far from purporting to be names specifically of the author of *Waverley*, do not purport to be names at all; they refer to entities generally, with a kind of studied ambiguity peculiar to themselves. These quantificational words or bound variables are of course a basic part of language, and their meaningfulness, at least in context, is not to be challenged. But their meaningfulness in no way presupposes there being either the author of *Waverley* or the round square cupola on Berkeley College or any other specifically preassigned objects.

Where descriptions are concerned, there is no longer any difficulty in affirming or denying being. 'There *is* the author of *Waverley'* is explained by Russell as meaning 'Someone (or, more strictly, something) wrote *Waverley* and nothing else wrote *Waverley'*. 'The author of *Waverley* is not' is explained, correspondingly, as the alteration 'Either each thing failed to write *Waverley* or two or more things wrote *Waverley.'* This alteration is false, but meaningful; and it contains no expression purporting to designate the author of *Waverley.'* The statement 'The round square cupola on Berkeley College is not' is analyzed in similar fashion. So the old notion that statements of non-being defeat themselves goes by the board. When a statement of being or non-being is analyzed by Russell's theory of descriptions, it ceases to contain any expression which even purports to name the alleged entity whose being is in question, so that the meaningfulness of the statement no longer can be thought to presuppose that there be such an entity.

Now what of 'Pegasus'? This being a word rather than a descriptive phrase, Russell's argument does not immediately apply to it. However, it can easily be made to apply. We have only to rephrase 'Pegasus' as a description, in any way that seems adequately to single out our idea: say 'the winged horse that was captured by Bellerophon'. Substituting such a phrase for 'Pegasus', we can then proceed to analyze the statement 'Pegasus is', or 'Pegasus is not', precisely on the analogy of Russell's analysis of 'The author of *Waverley* is' and 'The author of *Waverley* is not'.

In order thus to subsume a one-word name or alleged name such as 'Pegasus' under Russell's theory of description, we must of course be able first to translate the word into a description. But this is no real restriction. If the notion of Pegasus had been so obscure or so basic a one that no pat translation into a descriptive phrase had offered itself along familiar lines, we could still have availed ourselves of the following artificial and trivial-seeming device: we could have appealed to the *ex hypothesi* unanalyzable, irreducible attribute of *being Pegasus,* adopting, for its expression, the verb 'is-Pegasus', or 'pegasizes'. The noun 'Pegasus' itself could then be treated as derivative, and identified after all with a description: 'the thing that is-Pegasus', 'the thing that pegasizes'.

If the importing of such a predicate as 'pegasizes' seems to commit us to recognizing that there is a corresponding attribute, pegasizing, in Plato's heaven or in the mind of men, well and good. Neither we nor Wyman nor McX have been contending, thus far, about the being or non-being of universals, but rather about that of Pegasus. If in terms of pegasizing we can interpret the noun 'Pegasus' as a description subject to Russell's theory of descriptions, then we have disposed of the old notion that Pegasus cannot be said not to be without presupposing that in some sense Pegasus is.

Our argument is now quite general. McX and Wyman supposed that we could not meaningfully affirm a statement of the form 'So-and-so is not', with a simple or descriptive singular noun in place of 'so-and-so', unless so-and-so be. This supposition is now seen to be quite generally groundless, since the singular noun in question can always be expanded into a singular description, trivially or otherwise, and then analyzed out à la Russell.

We cannot conclude, however, that man is henceforth free of all ontological commitments. We commit ourselves outright to an ontology containing numbers when we say there are prime numbers between 1000 and 1010; we commit ourselves to an ontology containing centaurs when we say there are centaurs; and we commit ourselves to an ontology containing Pegasus when we say Pegasus is. But we do not commit ourselves to an ontology containing Pegasus or the author of *Waverley* or the round square cupola on Berkeley College when we say that Pegasus or the author of *Waverley* or the cupola in question is *not*. We need no longer labor under the delusion that the meaningfulness of a statement containing a singular term presupposes an entity named by the term. A singular term need not name to be significant.

An inkling of this might have dawned on Wyman and McX even without benefit of Russell if they had only noticed — as so few of us do — that there is a gulf between *meaning* and *naming* even in the case of a singular term which *is* genuinely a name of an object. Frege's example will serve: the phrase 'Evening Star' names a certain large physical object of spherical form, which is hurtling through space some scores of millions of miles from here. The phrase 'Morning Star' names the same thing, as was probably first established by some observant Babylonian. But the two phrases cannot be regarded as having the same meaning; otherwise that Babylonian could have dispensed with his observations and contented himself with reflecting on the meanings of his words. The meanings, then, being different from one another, must be other than the named object, which is one and the same in both cases.

Confusion of meaning with naming not only made McX think he could not meaningfully repudiate Pegasus; a continuing confusion of meaning with naming no doubt helped engender his absurd notion that Pegasus is an idea, a mental entity. The structure of his confusion is as follows. He confused the alleged *named object* Pegasus with the *meaning* of the word 'Pegasus', therefore concluding that Pegasus must be in order that the word have meaning. But what sorts of things are meanings? This is a moot point; however, one might quite plausibly explain meanings as ideas in the mind, supposing we can make clear sense in turn of the idea of ideas in the mind. Therefore Pegasus, initially confused with a meaning, ends up as an idea in the mind. It is the more remarkable that Wyman, subject to the same initial motivation as McX, should have avoided this particular blunder and wound up with unactualized possibles instead.

Now let us turn to the ontological problem of universals: the question whether there are such entities as attributes, relations, classes, numbers, functions. McX, characteristically enough, thinks there are. Speaking of attributes, he says: "There are red houses, red roses, red sunsets; this much is prephilosophical common sense in which we must all agree. These houses, roses, and sunsets, then, have something in common; and this which they have in common is all I mean by the attribute of redness." For McX, thus, there being attributes is even more obvious and trivial than the obvious and trivial fact of there being red houses, roses, and sunsets. This, I think, is characteristic of metaphysics, or at least of that part of metaphysics called ontology: one who regards a statement on this subject as true at all must regard it as trivially true. One's ontology is basic to the conceptual scheme by which he interprets all experiences, even the most commonplace ones. Judged within some particular conceptual scheme — and how else is judgment possible? — an ontological statement goes without saying, standing in need of no separate justification at all. Ontological statements follow immediately from all manner of casual statements of commonplace fact, just as — from the point of view, anyway, of McX's conceptual scheme — 'There is an attribute' follows from 'There are red houses, red roses, red sunsets.'

Judged in another conceptual scheme, an ontological statement which is axiomatic to McX's mind may, with equal immediacy and triviality, be adjudged false. One may admit that there are red houses, roses, and sunsets, but deny, except as a popular and misleading manner of speaking, that they have anything in common. The words 'houses', 'roses', and 'sunsets' denote each of sundry individual entities which are houses and roses and sunsets, and the word 'red' or 'red object' denotes each of sundry individual entities which are red houses, red roses, red sunsets; but there is not, in addition, any entity whatever, individual or otherwise, which is named by the word 'redness', nor, for that matter, by the word 'househood', 'rosehood', 'sunsethood'. That the houses and roses and sunsets are all of them red may be taken as ultimate and irreducible, and it may be held that McX is no better off, in point of real explanatory power, for all the occult entities which he posits under such names as 'redness'.

One means by which McX might naturally have tried to impose his ontology of universals on us was already removed before we turned to the problem of universals. McX cannot argue that predicates such as 'red' or 'is-red', which we all concur in using, must be regarded as names each of a single universal entity in order that they be meaningful at all. For, we have seen that being a name of something is a much more special feature than being meaningful. He cannot even charge us — at least not by *that* argument — with having posited an attribute of pegasizing by our adoption of the predicate 'pegasizes'.

However, McX hits upon a different stratagem. "Let us grant," he says, "this distinction between meaning and naming of which you make so much. Let us even grant that 'is red', 'pegasizes', etc., are not names of attributes. Still, you admit they have meanings. But these *meanings,* whether they are *named* or not, are still universals, and I venture to say that some of them might even be the very things that I call attributes, or something to much the same purpose in the end."

For McX, this is an unusually penetrating speech; and the only way I know to counter it is by refusing to admit meanings. However, I feel no reluctance toward refusing to admit meanings, for I do not thereby deny that words and statements are meaningful. McX and I may agree to the letter in our classification of linguistic forms into the meaningful and the meaningless, even though McX construes meaningfulness as the *having* (in some sense of 'having') of some abstract entity which he calls a meaning, whereas I do not. I remain free to maintain that the fact that a given linguistic utterance is meaningful (or *significant,* as I prefer to say so as not to invite hypostasis of meanings as entities) is an ultimate and irreducible matter of fact; or, I may undertake to analyze it in terms directly of what people do in the presence of the linguistic utterance in question and other utterances similar to it.

The useful ways in which people ordinarily talk or seem to talk about meanings boil down to two: the *having* of meanings, which is significance, and *sameness* of meaning, or synonymy. What is called *giving* the meaning of an utterance is simply the uttering of a synonym, couched, ordinarily, in clearer language than the original. If we are allergic to meanings as such, we can speak directly of utterances as significant or insignificant, and as synonymous or heteronymous one with another. The problem of explaining these adjectives 'significant' and 'synonymous' with some degree of clarity and rigor — preferably, as I see it, in terms of behavior — is as difficult as it is important. But the explanatory value of special and irreducible intermediary entities called meanings is surely illusory.

Up to now I have argued that we can use singular terms significantly in sentences without presupposing that there be the entities which those terms purport to name. I have argued further that we can use general terms, e.g., predicates, without conceding them to be names of abstract entities. I have argued further that we can view utterances as significant, and as synonymous or heteronymous with one another, without countenancing a realm of entities called meanings. At this point McX begins to wonder whether there is any limit at all to our ontological immunity. Does *nothing* we may say commit us to the assumption of universals or other entities which we may find unwelcome?

I have already suggested a negative answer to this question, in speaking of bound variables, or variables of quantification, in connection with Russell's theory of descriptions. We can very easily involve ourselves in ontological commitments, by saying, e.g., that *there is something* (bound variable) which red houses and sunsets have in common; or that *there is something* which is a prime number between 1000 and 1010. But this is, essentially, the *only* way we can involve ourselves in ontological commitments: by our use of bound variables. The use of alleged names is no criterion, for we can repudiate their namehood at the drop of a hat unless the assumption of a corresponding entity can be spotted in the things we affirm in terms of bound variables. Names are in fact altogether immaterial to the ontological issue, for I have shown, in connection with 'Pegasus' and 'pegasize', that names can be converted to descriptions, and Russell has shown that descriptions can be eliminated. Whatever we say with help of names can be said in a language which shuns names altogether. To be is, purely and simply, to be the value of a variable. In terms of the categories of traditional grammar, this amounts roughly to saying that to be is to be in the range of reference of a pronoun. Pronouns are the basic media of reference; nouns might better have been named pro-pronouns. The variables of quantification, 'something', 'nothing', 'everything', range over our whole ontology, whatever it may be; and we are convicted of a particular ontological presupposition if, and only if, the alleged presuppositum has to be reckoned among the entities over which our variables range in order to render one of our affirmations true.

We may say, e.g., that some dogs are white, and not thereby commit ourselves to recognizing either doghood or whiteness as entities. 'Some dogs are white' says that some things that are dogs are white; and, in order that this statement be true, the things over which the bound variable 'something' ranges must include some white dogs, but need not include doghood or whiteness. On the other hand, when we say that some zoölogical species are cross-fertile, we are committing ourselves to recognizing as entities the several species themselves, abstract though they be. We remain so committed at least until we devise some way of so paraphrasing the statement as to show that the seeming reference to species on the part of our bound variable was an avoidable manner of speaking.

If I have been seeming to minimize the degree to which in our philosophical and unphilosophical discourse we involve ourselves in ontological commitments, let me then emphasize that classical mathematics, as the example of primes between 1000 and 1010 clearly illustrates, is up to its neck in commitments to an ontology of abstract entities. Thus it is that the great mediaeval controversy over universals has flared up anew in the modern philosophy of mathematics. The issue is clearer now than of old, because we now have a more explicit standard whereby to decide what ontology a given theory or form of discourse is committed to: a theory is committed to those and only those entities to which the bound variables of the theory must be capable of referring in order that the affirmations made in the theory be true.

Because this standard of ontological presupposition did not emerge clearly in the philosophical tradition, the modern philosophical mathematicians have not on the whole recognized that they were debating the same old problem of universals in a newly clarified form. But the fundamental cleavages among modern points of view on foundations of mathematics do come down pretty explicitly to disagreements as to the range of entities to which the bound variables should be permitted to refer.

The three main mediaeval points of view regarding universals are designated by historians as *realism, conceptualism,* and *nominalism.* Essentially these same three doctrines reappear in twentieth-century surveys of the philosophy of mathematics under the new names *logicism, intuitionism,* and *formalism.*

Realism, as the word is used in connection with the mediaeval controversy over universals, is the Platonic doctrine that universals or abstract entities have being independently of the mind; the mind may discover them but cannot create them. *Logicism,* represented by such latter-day Platonists as Frege, Russell, Whitehead, Church, and Carnap, condones the use of bound variables to refer to abstract entities known and unknown, specifiable and unspecifiable, indiscriminately.

Conceptualism holds that there are universals but they are mind-made. *Intuitionism,* espoused in modern times in one form or another by Poincaré, Brouwer, Weyl, and others, countenances the use of bound variables to refer to abstract entities only when those entities are capable of being cooked up individually from ingredients specified in advance. As Fraenkel has put it, logicism holds that classes are discovered while intuitionism holds that they are invented — a fair statement indeed of the old opposition between realism and conceptualism. This opposition is no mere quibble; it makes an essential difference in the amount of classical mathematics to which one is willing to subscribe. Logicists, or realists, are able on their assumptions to get Cantor's ascending orders of infinity; intuitionists are compelled to stop with the lowest order of infinity, and, as an indirect consequence, to abandon even some of the classical laws of real numbers. The modern controversy between logicism and intuitionism arose, in fact, from disagreements over infinity.

Formalism, associated with the name of Hilbert, echoes intuitionism in deploring the logicist's unbridled recourse to universals. But formalism also finds intuitionism unsatisfactory. This could happen for either of two opposite reasons. The formalist might, like the logicist, object to the crippling of classical mathematics; or he might, like the *nominalists* of old, object to admitting abstract entities at all, even in the restrained sense of mind-made entities. The upshot is the same: the formalist keeps classical mathematics as a play of insignificant notations. This play of notations can still be of utility — whatever utility it has already shown itself to have as a crutch for physicists and technologists. But utility need not imply significance, in any literal linguistic sense. Nor need the marked success of mathematicians in spinning out theorems, and in finding objective bases for agreement with one another's results, imply significance. For, an adequate basis for agreement among mathematicians can be found simply in the rules which govern the manipulation of the notations — these syntactical rules being, unlike the notations themselves, quite significant and intelligible. [2]

I have argued that the sort of ontology we adopt can be consequential — notably in connection with mathematics, although this is only an example. Now how are we to adjudicate among rival ontologies? Certainly the answer is not provided by the semantical formula "To be is to be the value of a variable"; this formula serves rather, conversely, in testing the conformity of a given remark or doctrine to a prior ontological standard. We look to bound variables in connection with ontology not in order to know what there is, but in order to know what a given remark or doctrine, ours or someone else's, *says* there is; and this much is quite properly a problem involving language. But what there is is another question.

In debating over what there is, there are still reasons for operating on a semantical plane. One reason is to escape from the predicament noted at the beginning of the paper: the predicament of my not being able to admit that there are things which McX countenances and I do not. So long as I adhere to my ontology, as opposed to McX's, I cannot allow my bound variables to refer to entities which belong to McX's ontology and not to mine. I can, however, consistently describe our disagreement by characterizing the statements which McX affirms. Provided merely that my ontology countenances linguistic forms, or at least concrete inscriptions and utterances, I can talk about McX's sentences.

Another reason for withdrawing to a semantical plane is to find common ground on which to argue. Disagreement in ontology involves basic disagreement in conceptual schemes; yet McX and I, despite these basic disagreements, find that our conceptual schemes converge sufficiently in their intermediate and upper ramifications to enable us to communicate successfully on such topics as politics, weather, and, in particular, language. In so far as our basic controversy over ontology can be translated upward into a semantical controversy about words and what to do with them, the collapse of the controversy into question-begging may be delayed.

It is no wonder, then, that ontological controversy should tend into controversy over language. But we must not jump to the conclusion that what there is depends on words. Translatability of a question into semantical terms is no indication that the question is linguistic. To see Naples is to bear a name which, when prefixed to the words 'sees Naples', yields a true sentence; still there is nothing linguistic about seeing Naples.

Our acceptance of an ontology is, I think, similar in principle to our acceptance of a scientific theory, say a system of physics: we adopt, at least insofar as we are reasonable, the simplest conceptual scheme into which the disordered fragments of raw experience can be fitted and arranged. Our ontology is determined once we have fixed upon the over-all conceptual scheme which is to accommodate science in the broadest sense; and the considerations which determine a reasonable construction of any part of that conceptual scheme, e.g. the biological or the physical part, are not different in kind from the considerations which determine a reasonable construction of the whole. To whatever extent the adoption of any system of scientific theory may be said to be a matter of language, the same — but no more — may be said of the adoption of an ontology.

But simplicity, as a guiding principle in constructing conceptual schemes, is not a clear and unambiguous idea; and it is quite capable of presenting a double or multiple standard. Imagine, e.g., that we have devised the most economical set of concepts adequate to the play-by-play reporting of immediate experience. The entities under this scheme — the values of bound variables — are, let us suppose, individual subjective events of sensation or reflection. We should still find, no doubt, that a physicalistic conceptual scheme, purporting to talk about external objects, offers great advantages in simplifying our over-all reports. By bringing together scattered sense events and treating them as perceptions of one object, we reduce the complexity of our stream of experience to a manageable conceptual simplicity. The rule of simplicity is indeed our guiding maxim in assigning sense data to objects: we associate an earlier and a later round sensum with the same so-called penny, or with two different so-called pennies, in obedience to the demands of maximum simplicity in our total world-picture.

Here we have two competing conceptual schemes, a phenomenalistic one and a physicalistic one. Which should prevail? Each has its advantages; each has its special simplicity in its own way. Each, I suggest, deserves to be developed. Each may be said, indeed, to be the more fundamental, though in different senses: the one is epistemologically, the other physically, fundamental.

The physical conceptual scheme simplifies our account of experience because of the way myriad scattered sense events come to be associated with single so-called objects; still there is no likelihood that each sentence about physical objects can actually be translated, however deviously and complexly, into the phenomenalistic language. Physical objects are postulated entites which round out and simplify our account of the flux of experience, just as the introduction of irrational numbers simplifies laws of arithmetic. From the point of view of the conceptual scheme of the elementary arithmetic of rational numbers alone, the broader arithmetic of rational and irrational numbers would have the status of a convenient myth, simpler than the literal truth (namely the arithmetic of rationals) and yet containing that literal truth as a scattered part. Similarly, from a phenomenalistic point of view, the conceptual scheme of physical objects is a convenient myth, simpler than the literal truth and yet containing that literal truth as a scattered part.

Now what of classes or attributes of physical objects, in turn? A platonistic ontology of this sort is, from the point of view of a strictly physicalistic conceptual scheme, as much of a myth as that physicalistic conceptual scheme itself was for phenomenalism. This higher myth is a good and useful one, in turn, in so far as it simplifies our account of physics. Since mathematics is an integral part of this higher myth, the utility of this myth for physical science is evident enough. In speaking of it nevertheless as a myth, I echo that philosophy of mathematics to which I alluded earlier under the name of formalism. But my present suggestion is that an attitude of formalism may with equal justice be adopted toward the physical conceptual scheme, in turn, by the pure aesthete or phenomenalist.

The analogy between the myth of mathematics and the myth of physics is, in some additional and perhaps fortuitous ways, strikingly close. Consider, for example, the crisis which was precipitated in the foundations of mathematics, at the turn of the century, by the discovery of Russell's paradox and other antinomies of set theory. These contradictions had to be obviated by unintuitive, *ad hoc* devices; our mathematical myth-making became deliberate and evident to all. But what of physics? An antinomy arose between the undular and the corpuscular accounts of light; and if this was not as out-and-out a contradiction as Russell's paradox, I suspect that the reason is merely that physics is not as out-and-out as mathematics. Again, the second great modern crisis in the foundations of mathematics—precipitated in 1931 by Gödel's proof that there are bound to be undecidable statements in arithmetic—has its companion-piece in physics in Heisenberg's indeterminacy principle.

In earlier pages I undertook to show that some common arguments in favor of certain ontologies are fallacious. Further, I advanced an explicit standard whereby to decide what the ontological commitments of a theory are. But the question what ontology actually to adopt still stands open, and the obvious counsel is tolerance and an experimental spirit. Let us by all means see how much of the physicalistic conceptual scheme can be reduced to a phenomenalistic one; still physics also naturally demands pursuing, irreducible *in toto* though it be. Let us see how, or to what degree, natural science may be rendered independent of platonistic mathematics; but let us also pursue mathematics and delve into its platonistic foundations.

From among the various conceptual schemes best suited to these various pursuits, one—the phenomenalistic—claims epistemological priority. Viewed from within the phenomenalistic conceptual scheme, the ontologies of physical objects and mathematical objects are myths. The quality of myth, however, is relative; relative, in this case, to the epistemological point of view. This point of view is one among various, corresponding to one among our various interests and purposes.

NOTES

1. [I.e., reductio of the doctrine itself.—Ed.]

2. See Goodman and Quine, "Steps toward a constructive nominalism," *Journal of Symbolic Logic,* vol. 12 (1947), pp. 97-122.

26. Two Dogmas of Empiricism

W. V. Quine

Modern empiricism has been conditioned in large part by two dogmas. One is a belief in some fundamental cleavage between truths which are *analytic,* or grounded in meanings independently of matters of fact, and truths which are *synthetic,* or grounded in fact. The other dogma is *reductionism:* the belief that each meaningful statement is equivalent to some logical construct upon terms which refer to immediate experience. Both dogmas, I shall argue, are ill founded. One effect of abandoning them is, as we shall see, a blurring of the supposed boundary between speculative metaphysics and natural science. Another effect is a shift toward pragmatism.

I. Background for Analyticity[1]

Kant's cleavage between analytic and synthetic truths was foreshadowed in Hume's distinction between relations of ideas and matters of fact, and in Leibniz's distinction between truths of reason and truths of fact. Leibniz spoke of the truths of reason as true in all possible worlds. Picturesqueness aside, this is to say that the truths of reason are those which could not possibly be false. In the same vein we hear analytic statements defined as statements whose denials are self-contradictory. But this definition has small explanatory value; for the notion of self-contradictoriness, in the quite broad sense needed for this definition of analyticity, stands in exactly the same need of clarification as does the notion of analyticity itself.[2] The two notions are the two sides of a single dubious coin.

Kant conceived of an analytic statement as one that attributes to its subject no more than is already conceptually contained in the subject. This formulation has two shortcomings: it limits itself to statements of subject-predicate form, and it appeals to a notion of containment which is left at a metaphorical level. But Kant's intent, evident more from the use he makes of the notion of analyticity than from his definition of it, can be restated thus: a statement is analytic when it is true by virtue of meanings and independently of fact. Pursuing this line, let us examine the concept of *meaning* which is presupposed.

We must observe to begin with that meaning is not to be identified with naming, or reference. Consider Frege's example of 'Evening Star' and 'Morning Star'. Understood not merely as a recurrent evening apparition but as a body, the Evening Star is the planet Venus, and the Morning Star is the same. The two singular terms *name* the same thing. But the meanings must be treated as distinct, since the identity 'Evening Star = Morning Star' is a statement of fact established by astronomical observation. If 'Evening Star' and 'Morning Star' were alike in meaning, the identity 'Evening Star = Morning Star' would be analytic.

Again there is Russell's example of 'Scott' and 'the author of *Waverley*'. Analysis of the meanings of words was by no means sufficient to reveal to George IV that the person named by these two singular terms was one and the same.

The distinction between meaning and naming is no less important at the level of abstract terms. The terms '9' and 'the number of planets' name one and the same abstract entity but presumably must be regarded as unlike in meaning; for astronomical observation was needed, and not mere reflection on meanings, to determine the sameness of the entity in question.

Thus far we have been considering singular terms. With general terms, or predicates, the situation is somewhat different but parallel. Whereas a singular term purports to name an entity, abstract or concrete, a general term does not; but a general term is *true of* an entity, or of each of many, or of none. The class of all entities of which a general term is true is called the *extension* of the term. Now paralleling the contrast between the meaning of a singular term and the entity named, we must distinguish equally between the meaning of a general term and its extension. The general terms 'creature with a heart' and 'creature with a kidney', e.g., are perhaps alike in extension but unlike in meaning.

Confusion of meaning with extension, in the case of general terms, is less common than confusion of meaning with naming in the case of singular terms. It is indeed a commonplace in philosophy to oppose intension (or meaning) to extension, or, in a variant vocabulary, connotation to denotation.

The Aristotelian notion of essence was the forerunner, no doubt, of the modern notion of intension or meaning. For Aristotle it was essential in men to be rational, accidental to be two-legged. But there is an important difference between this attitude and the doctrine of meaning. From the latter point of view it may indeed be conceded (if only for the sake of argument) that rationality is involved in the meaning of the word 'man' while two-leggedness is not; but two-leggedness may at the same time be viewed as involved in the meaning of 'biped' while rationality is not. Thus from the point of view of the doctrine of meaning it makes no sense to say of the actual individual, who is at once a man and a biped, that his rationality is essential and his two-leggedness accidental or vice versa. Things had essences, for Aristotle, but only linguistic forms have meanings. Meaning is what essence becomes when it is divorced from the object of reference and wedded to the word.

For the theory of meaning the most conspicuous question is as to the nature of its objects: what sort of things are meanings? They are evidently intended to be ideas, somehow — mental ideas for some semanticists, Platonic ideas for others. Objects of either sort are so elusive, not to say debatable, that there seems little hope of erecting a fruitful science about them. It is not even clear, granted meanings, when we have two and when we have one; it is not clear when linguistic forms should be regarded as *synonymous,* or alike in meaning, and when they should not. If a standard of synonymy should be arrived at, we may reasonably expect that the appeal to meanings as entities will not have played a very useful part in the enterprise.

A felt need for meant entities may derive from an earlier failure to appreciate that meaning and reference are distinct. Once the theory of meaning is sharply separated from the theory of reference, it is a short step to recognizing as the business of the theory of meaning simply the synonymy of linguistic forms and the analyticity of statements; meanings themselves, as obscure intermediary entities, may well be abandoned.

The description of analyticity as truth by virtue of meanings started us off in pursuit of a concept of meaning. But now we have abandoned the thought of any special realm of entities called meanings. So the problem of analyticity confronts us anew.

Statements which are analytic by general philosophical acclaim are not, indeed, far to seek. They fall into two classes. Those of the first class, which may be called *logically true,* are typified by:

(1) No unmarried man is married.

The relevant feature of this example is that it is not merely true as it stands, but remains true under any and all reinterpretations of 'man' and 'married'. If we suppose a prior inventory of *logical* particles, comprising 'no', 'un-', 'not', 'if', 'then', 'and', etc., then in general a logical truth is a statement which is true and remains true under all reinterpretations of its components other than the logical particles.

But there is also a second class of analytic statements, typified by:

(2) No bachelor is married.

The characteristic of such a statement is that it can be turned into a logical truth by putting synonyms for synonyms; thus (2) can be turned into (1) by putting 'unmarried man' for its synonym 'bachelor'. We still lack a proper characterization of this second class of analytic statements, and therewith of analyticity generally, inasmuch as we have had in the above description to lean on a notion of "synonymy" which is no less in need of clarification than analyticity itself.

In recent years Carnap has tended to explain analyticity by appeal to what he calls state-descriptions.[3] A state-description is any exhaustive assignment of truth values to the atomic, or noncompound, statements of the language. All other statements of the language are, Carnap assumes, built up of their component clauses by means of the familiar logical devices, in such a way that the truth value of any complex statement is fixed for each state-description by specifiable logical laws. A statement is then explained as analytic when it comes out true under every state-description. This account is an adaptation of Leibniz's "true in all possible worlds." But note that this version of analyticity serves its purpose only if the atomic statements of the language are, unlike 'John is a bachelor' and 'John is married', mutually independent. Otherwise there would be a state-description which assigned truth to 'John is a bachelor' and falsity to 'John is married', and consequently 'All bachelors are married' would turn out synthetic rather than analytic under the proposed criterion. Thus the criterion of analyticity in terms of state-descriptions serves only for languages devoid of extralogical synonym-pairs, such as 'bachelor' and 'unmarried man': synonym-pairs of the type which give rise to the "second class" of analytic statements. The criterion in terms of state-descriptions is a reconstruction at best of logical truth.

I do not mean to suggest that Carnap is under any illusions on this point. His simplified model language with its state-descriptions is aimed primarily not at the general problem of analyticity but at another purpose, the clarification of probability and induction. Our problem, however, is analyticity; and here the major difficulty lies not in the first class of analytic statements, the logical truths, but rather in the second class, which depends on the notion of synonymy.

II. Definition

There are those who find it soothing to say that the analytic statements of the second class reduce to those of the first class, the logical truths, by *definition;* 'bachelor', e.g., is *defined* as 'unmarried man'. But how do we find that 'bachelor' is defined as 'unmarried man'? Who defined it thus, and when? Are we to appeal to the nearest dictionary, and accept the lexicographer's formulation as law? Clearly this would be to put the cart before the horse. The lexicographer is an empirical scientist, whose business is the recording of antecedent facts; and if he glosses 'bachelor' as 'unmarried man' it is because of his belief that there is a relation of synonymy between these forms, implicit in general or preferred usage prior to his own work. The notion of synonymy presupposed here has still to be clarified, presumably in terms relating to linguistic behavior. Certainly the "definition" which is the lexicographer's report of an observed synonymy cannot be taken as the ground of the synonymy.

Definition is not, indeed, an activity exclusively of philologists. Philosophers and scientists frequently have occasion to "define" a recondite term by paraphrasing it into terms of a more familiar vocabulary. But ordinarily such a definition, like the philologist's, is pure lexicography, affirming a relationship of synonymy antecedent to the exposition in hand.

Just what it means to affirm synonymy, just what the interconnections may be which are necessary and sufficient in order that two linguistic forms be properly describable as synonymous, is far from clear; but, whatever these interconnections may be, ordinarily they are grounded in usage. Definitions reporting selected instances of synonymy come then as reports upon usage.

There is also, however, a variant type of definitional activity which does not limit itself to the reporting of pre-existing synonymies. I have in mind what Carnap calls *explication* — an activity to which philosophers are given, and scientists also in their more philosophical moments. In explication the purpose is not merely to paraphrase the definiendum into an outright synonym, but actually to improve upon the definiendum by refining or supplementing its meaning. But even explication, though not merely reporting a pre-existing synonymy between definiendum and definiens, does rest nevertheless on *other* pre-existing synonymies. The matter may be viewed as follows. Any word worth explicating has some contexts which, as wholes, are clear and precise enough to be useful; and the purpose of explication is to preserve the usage of these favored contexts while sharpening the usage of other contexts. In order that a given definition be suitable for purposes of explication, therefore, what is required is not that the definiendum in its antecedent usage be synonymous with the definiens, but just that each of these favored contexts of the definiendum, taken as a whole in its antecedent usage, be synonymous with the corresponding context of the definiens.

Two alternative definientia may be equally appropriate for the purposes of a given task of explication and yet not be synonymous with each other; for they may serve interchangeably within the favored contexts but diverge elsewhere. By cleaving to one of these definientia rather than the other, a definition of explicative kind generates, by fiat, a relationship of synonymy between definiendum and definiens which did not hold before. But such a definition still owes its explicative function, as seen, to pre-existing synonymies.

There does, however, remain still an extreme sort of definition which does not hark back to prior synonymies at all; viz., the explicitly conventional introduction of novel notations for purposes of sheer abbreviation. Here the definiendum becomes synonymous with the definiens simply because it has been created expressly for the purpose of being synonymous with the definiens. Here we have a really transparent case of synonymy created by definition; would that all species of synonymy were as intelligible. For the rest, definition rests on synonymy rather than explaining it.

The word 'definition' has come to have a dangerously reassuring sound, due no doubt to its frequent occurrence in logical and mathematical writings. We shall do well to digress now into a brief appraisal of the role of definition in formal work.

In logical and mathematical systems either of two mutually antagonistic types of economy may be stiven for, and each has its peculiar practical utility. On the one hand we may seek economy of practical expression: ease and brevity in the statement of multifarious relationships. This sort of economy calls usually for distinctive concise notations for a wealth of concepts. Second, however, and oppositely, we may seek economy in grammar and vocabulary; we may try to find a minimum of basic concepts such that, once a distinctive notation has been appropriated to each of them, it becomes possible to express any desired further concept by mere combination and iteration of our basic notations. This second sort of economy is impractical in one way, since a poverty in basic idioms tends to a necessary lengthening of discourse. But it is practical in another way: it greatly simplifies theoretical discourse *about* the language, through minimizing the terms and the forms of construction wherein the language consists.

Both sorts of economy, though prima facie incompatible, are valuable in their separate ways. The custom has consequently arisen of combining both sorts of economy by forging in effect two languages, the one a part of the other. The inclusive language, though redundant in grammar and vocabulary, is economical in message lengths, while the part, called *primitive notation,* is economical in grammar and vocabulary. Whole and part are correlated by rules of translation whereby each idiom not in primitive notation is equated to some complex built up of primitive notation. These rules of translation are the so-called *definitions* which appear in formalized systems. They are best viewed not as adjuncts to one language but as correlations between two languages, the one a part of the other.

But these correlations are not arbitrary. They are supposed to show how the primitive notations can accomplish all purposes, save brevity and convenience, of the redundant language. Hence the definiendum and its definiens may be expected, in each case, to be related in one or another of the three ways lately noted. The definiens may be a faithful paraphrase of the definiendum into the narrower notation, preserving a direct synonymy as of antecedent usage; or the definiens may, in the spirit of explication, improve upon the antecedent usage of the definiendum; or finally, the definiendum may be a newly created notation, newly endowed with meaning here and now.

In formal and informal work alike, thus, we find that definition — except in the extreme case of the explicitly conventional introduction of new notations — hinges on prior relationships of synonymy. Recognizing then that the notion of definition does not hold the key to synonymy and analyticity, let us look further into synonymy and say no more of definition.

III. Interchangeability

A natural suggestion, deserving close examination, is that the synonymy of two linguistic forms consists simply in their interchangeability in all contexts without change of truth value; interchangeability, in Leibiniz's phrase, *salva veritate.* Note that synonyms so conceived need not even be free from vagueness, as long as the vaguenesses match.

But it is not quite true that the synonyms 'bachelor' and 'unmarried man' are everywhere interchangeable *salva veritate*. Truths which become false under substitution of 'unmarried man' for 'bachelor' are easily constructed with help of 'bachelor of arts' or 'bachelor's buttons'. Also with help of quotation, thus:

'Bachelor' has less than ten letters.

Such counterinstances can, however, perhaps be set aside by treating the phrases 'bachelor of arts' and 'bachelor's buttons' and the quotation "bachelor" each as a single indivisible word and then stipulating that the interchangeability *salva veritate* which is to be the touchstone of synonymy is not supposed to apply to fragmentary occurrences inside of a word. This account of synonymy, supposing it acceptable on other counts, has indeed the drawback of appealing to a prior conception of 'word' which can be counted on to present difficulties of formulation in its turn. Nevertheless some progress might be claimed in having reduced the problem of synonymy to a problem of wordhood. Let us pursue this line a bit, taking 'word' for granted.

The question remains whether interchangeability *salva veritate* (apart from occurrences within words) is a strong enough condition for synonymy, or whether, on the contrary, some nonsynonymous expressions might be thus interchangeable. Now let us be clear that we are not concerned here with synonymy in the sense of complete identity in psychological associations or poetic quality; indeed no two expressions are synonymous in such a sense. We are concerned only with what may be called *cognitive synonymy*. Just what this is cannot be said without successfully finishing the present study; but we know something about it from the need which arose for it in connection with analyticity in Section I. The sort of synonymy needed there was merely such that any analytic statement could be turned into a logical truth by putting synonyms for synonyms. Turning the tables and assuming analyticity, indeed, we could explain cognitive synonymy of terms as follows (keeping to the familiar example): to say that 'bachelor' and 'unmarried man' are cognitively synonymous is to say no more nor less than that the statement:

(3) All and only bachelors are unmarried men
is analytic.[4]

What we need is an account of cognitive synonymy not presupposing analyticity—if we are to explain analyticity conversely with help of cognitive synonymy as undertaken in Section I. And indeed such an independent account of cognitive synonymy is at present up for consideration, viz., interchangeability *salva veritate* everywhere except within words. The question before us, to resume the thread at last, is whether such interchangeability is a sufficient condition for cognitive synonymy. We can quickly assure ourselves that it is, by examples of the following sort. The statement:

(4) Necessarily all and only bachelors are bachelors

is evidently true, even supposing 'necessarily' so narrowly construed as to be truly applicable only to analytic statements. Then, *if* 'bachelor' and 'unmarried man' are interchangeable *salva veritate,* the result

(5) Necessarily, all and only bachelors are unmarried men

of putting 'unmarried man' for an occurrence of 'bachelor' in (4) must, like (4), be true. But to say that (5) is true is to say that (3) is analytic, and hence that 'bachelor' and 'unmarried' men' are cognitively synonymous.

Let us see what there is about the above argument that gives it its air of hocus-pocus. The condition of interchangeability *salva veritate* varies in its force with variations in the richness of the language at hand. The above argument supposes we are working with a language rich enough to contain the adverb 'necessarily', this adverb being so construed as to yield truth when and only when applied to an analytic statement. But can we condone a language which contains such an adverb? Does the adverb really make sense? To suppose that it does is to suppose that we have already made satisfactory sense of 'analytic'. Then what are we so hard at work on right now?

Our argument is not flatly circular, but something like it. It has the form, figuratively speaking, of a closed curve in space.

Interchangeability *salva veritate* is meaningless until relativized to a language whose extent is specified in relevant respects. Suppose now we consider a language containing just the following materials. There is an indefinitely large stock of one- and many-place predicates, mostly having to do with extralogical subject matter. The rest of the language is logical. The atomic sentences consist each of a predicate followed by one or more variables; and the complex sentences are built up of atomic ones by truth functions and quantification. In effect such a language enjoys the benefits also of descriptions and class names and indeed singular terms generally, these being contextually definable in known ways.[5] Such a language can be adequate to classical mathematics and indeed to scientific discourse generally, except in so far as the latter involves debatable devices such as modal adverbs and contrary-to-fact conditionals. Now a language of this type is *extensional,* in this sense: any two predicates which *agree extensionally* (i.e., are true of the same objects) are interchangeable *salva veritate.*

In an extensional language, therefore, interchangeability *salva veritate* is no assurance of cognitive synonymy of the desired type. That 'bachelor' and 'unmarried man' are interchangeable *salva veritate* in an extensional language assures us of no more than that (3) is true. There is no assurance here that the extensional agreement of 'bachelor' and 'unmarried man' rests on meaning rather than merely on accidental matters of fact, as does extensional agreement of 'creature with a heart' and 'creature with a kidney'.

For most purposes extensional agreement is the nearest approximation to synonymy we need care about. But the fact remains that extensional agreement falls far short of cognitive synonymy of the type required for explaining analyticity in the manner of Section I. The type of cognitive synonymy required there is such as to equate the synonymy of 'bachelor' and 'unmarried man' with the analyticity of (3), not merely with the truth of (3).

So we must recognize that interchangeability *salva veritate,* if construed in relation to an extensional language, is not a sufficient condition of cognitive synonymy in the sense needed for deriving analyticity in the manner of Section I. If a language contains an intensional adberb 'necessarily' in the sense lately noted, or other particles to the same effect, then interchangeability *salva veritate* in such a language does afford a sufficient condition of cognitive synonymy; but such a language is intelligible only if the notion of analyticity is already clearly understood in advance.

The effort to explain cognitive synonymy first, for the sake of deriving analyticity from it afterward as in Section I, is perhaps the wrong approach. Instead we might try explaining analyticity somehow without appeal to cognitive synonymy. Afterward we could doubtless derive cognitive synonymy from analyticity satisfactorily enough if desired. We have seen that cognitive synonymy of 'bachelor' and 'unmarried man' can be explained as analyticity of (3). The same explanation works for any pair of one-place predicates, of course, and it can be extended in obvious fashion to many-place predicates. Other syntactical categories can also be accommodated in fairly parallel fashion. Singular terms may be said to be cognitively synonymous when the statement of identity formed by putting ' = ' between them is analytic. Statements may be said simply to be cognitively synonymous when their biconditional (the result of joining them by 'if and only if') is analytic.[6] If we care to lump all categories into a single formulation, at the expense of assuming again the notion of 'word' which was appealed to early in this section, we can describe any two linguistic forms as cognitively synonymous when the two forms are interchangeable (apart from occurrences within "words") *salva* (no longer *veritate* but) *analyticitate.* Certain technical questions arise, indeed, over cases of ambiguity or homonymy; let us not pause for them, however, for we are already disgressing. Let us rather turn our backs on the problem of synonymy and address ourselves anew to that of analyticity.

IV. Semantical Rules

Analyticity at first seemed most naturally definable by appeal to a realm of meanings. On refinement, the appeal to meanings gave way to an appeal to synonymy or definition. But definition turned out to be a will-o'-the-wisp, and synonymy turned out to be best understood only by dint of a prior appeal to analyticity itself. So we are back at the problem of analyticity.

I do not know whether the statement 'Everything green is extended' is analytic. Now does my indecision over this example really betray an incomplete understanding, an incomplete grasp of the "meanings", of 'green' and 'extended'? I think not. The trouble is not with 'green' or 'extended', but with 'analytic'.

It is often hinted that the difficulty in separating analytic statements from synthetic ones in ordinary language is due to the vagueness of ordinary language and that the distinction is clear when we have a precise artificial language with explicit "semantical rules." This, however, as I shall now attempt to show, is a confusion.

The notion of analyticity about which we are worrying is a purported relation between statements and languages: a statement S is said to be *analytic for* a language L, and the problem is to make sense of this relation generally, i.e., for variable 'S' and 'L'. The point that I want to make is that the gravity of this problem is not perceptibly less for artificial languages than for natural ones. The problem of making sense of the idiom 'S is analytic for L', with variable 'S' and 'L', retains its stubbornness even if we limit the range of the variable 'L' to artificial languages. Let me now try to make this point evident.

For artificial languages and semantical rules we look naturally to the writings of Carnap. His semantical rules take various forms, and to make my point I shall have to distinguish certain of the forms. Let us suppose, to begin with, an artificial language L_0 whose semantical rules have the form explicitly of a specification, by recursion or otherwise, of all the analytic statements of L_0. The rules tell us that such and such statements, and only those, are the analytic statements of L_0. Now here the difficulty is simply that the rules contain the word 'analytic', which we do not understand! We understand what expressions the rules attribute analyticity to, but we do not understand what the rules attribute to those expressions. In short, before we can understand a rule which begins "A statement S is analytic for language L_0 if and only if. . .," we must understand the general relative term 'analytic for'; we must understand 'S is analytic for L' where 'S' and 'L' are variables.

Alternatively we may, indeed, view the so-called rule as a conventional definition of a new simple symbol 'analytic-for-L_0', which might better be written untendentiously as 'K' so as not to seem to throw light on the interesting word 'analytic'. Obviously any number of classes K, M, N, etc. of statements of L_0 can be specified for various purposes or for no purpose; what does it mean to say that K, as against M, N, etc., is the class of the "analytic" statements of L_0?

By saying what statements are analytic for L_0 we explain 'analytic-for-L_0' but not 'analytic', not 'analytic for'. We do not begin to explain the idiom 'S is analytic for L' with variable 'S' and 'L', even though we be content to limit the range of 'L' to the realm of artificial languages.

Actually we do know enough about the intended significance of 'analytic' to know that analytic statements are supposed to be true. Let us then turn to a second form of semantical rule, which says not that such and such statements are analytic but simply that such and such statements are included among the truths. Such a rule is not subject to the criticism of containing the un-understood word 'analytic'; and we may grant for the sake of argument that there is no difficulty over the broader term 'true'. A semantical rule of this second type, a rule of truth, is not supposed to specify all the truths of the language; it merely stipulates, recursively or otherwise, a certain multitude of statements which, along with others unspecified, are to count as true. Such a rule may be conceded to be quite clear. Derivatively, afterward, analyticity can be demarcated thus: a statement is analytic if it is (not merely true but) true according to the semantical rule.

Still there is really no progress. Instead of appealing to an unexplained word 'analytic', we are now appealing to an unexplained phrase 'semantical rule'. Not every true statement which says that the statements of some class are true can count as a semantical rule — otherwise *all* truths would be "analytic" in the sense of being true according to semantical rules. Semantical rules are distinguishable, apparently, only by the fact of appearing on a page under the heading 'Semantical Rules'; and this heading is itself then meaningless.

We can say indeed that a statement is *analytic-for-L_0* if and only if it is true according to such and such specifically appended "semantical rules," but then we find ourselves back at essentially the same case which was originally discussed: "*S* is analytic-for-L_0 if and only if. . . ." Once we seek to explain '*S* is analytic for *L*' generally for variable '*L*' (even allowing limitation of '*L*' to artificial languages), the explanation 'true according to the semantical rules of *L*' is unavailing; for the relative term 'semantical rule of' is as much in need of clarification, at least, as 'analytic for'.

It might conceivably be protested that an artificial language *L* (unlike a natural one) is a language in the ordinary sense *plus* a set of explicit semantical rules — the whole constituting, let us say, an ordered pair; and that the semantical rules of *L* then are specifiable simply as the second component of the pair *L*. But, by the same token and more simply, we might construe an artificial language *L* outright as an ordered pair whose second component is the class of its analytic statements; and then the analytic statements of *L* become specifiable simply as the statements in the second component of *L*. Or better still, we might just stop tugging at our bootstraps altogether.

Not all the explanations of analyticity known to Carnap and his readers have been covered explicitly in the above considerations, but the extension to other forms is not hard to see. Just one additional factor should be mentioned which sometimes enters: sometimes the semantical rules are in effect rules of translation into ordinary language, in which case the analytic statements of the artificial language are in effect recognized as such from the analyticity of their specified translations in ordinary language. Here certainly there can be no thought of an illumination of the problem of analyticity from the side of the artificial language.

From the point of view of the problem of analyticity the notion of an artificial language with semantical rules is a *feu follet par excellence*. Semantical rules determining the analytic statements of an artificial language are of interest only in so far as we already understand the notion of analyticity; they are of no help in gaining this understanding.

Appeal to hypothetical languages of an artificially simple kind could conceivably be useful in clarifying analyticity, if the mental or behavioral or cultural factors relevant to analyticity — whatever they may be — were somehow sketched into the simplified model. But a model which takes analyticity merely as an irreducible character is unlikely to throw light on the problem of explicating analyticity.

It is obvious that truth in general depends on both language and extra-linguistic fact. The statement 'Brutus killed Caesar' would be false if the world had been different in certain ways, but it would also be false if the word 'killed' happened rather to have the sense of 'begat'. Hence the temptation to suppose in general that the truth of a statement is somehow analyzable into a linguistic component and a factual component. Given this supposition, it next seems reasonable that in some statements the factual component should be null; and these are the analytic statements. But, for all its a priori reasonableness, a boundary between analytic and synthetic statements simply has not been drawn. That there is such a distinction to be drawn at all is an unempirical dogma of empiricists, a metaphysical article of faith.

V. The Verification Theory and Reductionism

In the course of these somber reflections we have taken a dim view first of the notion of meaning, then of the notion of cognitive synonymy, and finally of the notion of analyticity. But what, it may be asked, of the verification theory of meaning? This phrase has established itself so firmly as a catchword of empiricism that we should be very unscientific indeed not to look beneath it for a possible key to the problem of meaning and the associated problems.

The verification theory of meaning, which has been conspicuous in the literature from Peirce onward, is that the meaning of a statement is the method of empirically confirming or infirming it. An analytic statement is that limiting case which is confirmed no matter what.

As urged in Section I, we can as well pass over the question of meanings as entities and move straight to sameness of meaning, or synonymy. Then what the verification theory says is that statements are synonymous if and only if they are alike in point of method of empirical confirmation or infirmation.

This is an account of cognitive synonymy not of linguistic forms generally, but of statements.[7] However, from the concept of synonymy of statements we could derive the concept of synonymy for other linguistic forms, by considerations somewhat similar to those at the end of Section III. Assuming the notion of "word," indeed, we could explain any two forms as synonymous when the putting of the one form for an occurrence of the other in any statement (apart from occurrences within "words") yields a synonymous statement. Finally, given the concept of synonymy thus for linguistic forms generally, we could define analyticity in terms of synonymy and logical truth as in Section I. For that matter, we could define analyicity more simply in terms of just synonymy of statements together with logical truth; it is not necessary to appeal to synonymy of linguistic forms other than statements. For a statement may be described as analytic simply when it is synonymous with a logically true statement.

So, if the verification theory can be accepted as an adequate account of statement synonymy, the notion of analyticity is saved after all. However, let us reflect. Statement synonymy is said to be likeness of method of empirical confirmation or infirmation. Just what are these methods which are to be compared for likeness? What, in other words, is the nature of the relationship between a statement and the experiences which contribute to or detract from its confirmation?

The most naive view of the relationship is that it is one of direct report. This is *radical reductionism*. Every meaningful statement is held to be translatable into a statement (true or false) about immediate experience. Radical reductionism, in one form or another, well antedates the verification theory of meaning explicitly so-called. Thus Locke and Hume held that every idea must either originate directly in sense experience or else be compounded of ideas thus originating; and taking a hint from Tooke[8] we might rephrase this doctrine in semantical jargon by saying that a term, to be significant at all, must be either a name of a sense datum or a compound of such names or an abbreviation of such a compound. So stated, the doctrine remains ambiguous as between sense data as sensory events and sense data as sensory qualities; and it remains vague as to the admissible ways of compounding. Moreover, the doctrine is unnecessarily and intolerably restrictive in the term-by-term critique which it imposes. More reasonably, and without yet exceeding the limits of what I have called radical reductionism, we may take full statements as our significant units — thus demanding that our statements as wholes be translatable into sense-datum language, but not that they be translatable term by term.

This emendation would unquestionably have been welcome to Locke and Hume and Tooke, but historically it had to await two intermediate developments. One of these developments was the increasing emphasis on verification or confirmation, which came with the explicitly so-called verification theory of meaning. The objects of verification or confirmation being statements, this emphasis gave the statement an ascendency over the word or term as unit of significant discourse. The other development, consequent upon the first, was Russell's discovery of the concept of incomplete symbols defined in use.

Radical reductionism, conceived now with statements as units, sets itself the task of specifying a sense-datum language and showing how to translate the rest of significant discourse, statement by statement, into it. Carnap embarked on this project in the *Aufbau*.[9]

The language which Carnap adopted as his starting point was not a sense-datum language in the narrowest conceivable sense, for it included also the notations of logic, up through higher set theory. In effect it included the whole language of pure mathematics. The ontology implicit in it (i.e., the range of values of its variables) embraced not only sensory events but classes, classes of classes, and so on. Empiricits there are who would boggle at such prodigality. Carnap's starting point is very parsimonious, however, in its extralogical or sensory part. In a series of constructions in which he exploits the resources of modern logic with much ingenuity, he succeeds in defining a wide array of important additional sensory concepts which, but for his constructions, one would not have dreamed were definable on so slender a basis. Carnap was the first empiricist who, not content with asserting the reducibility of science to terms of immediate experience, took serious steps toward carrying out the reduction.

Even supporting Carnap's starting point satisfactory, his constructions were, as he himself stressed, only a fragment of the full program. The construction of even the simplest statements about the physical world was left in a sketchy state. Carnap's suggestions on this subject were, despite their sketchiness, very suggestive. He explained spatio-temporal point-instants as quadruples of real numbers and envisaged assignment of sense qualities to point-instants according to certain canons. Roughly summarized, the plan was that qualities should be assigned to point-instants in such a way as to achieve the laziest world compatible with our experience. The principle of least action was to be our guide in constructing a world from experience.

Carnap did not seem to recognize, however, that his treatment of physical objects fell short of reduction not merely through sketchiness, but in principle. Statements of the form 'Quality q is a point-instant $x; y; z; t$' were, according to his canons, to be apportioned truth values in such a way as to maximize and minimize certain over-all features, and with growth of experience the truth values were to be progressively revised in the same spirit. I think this is a good schematization (deliberately oversimplified, to be sure) of what science really does; but it provides no indication, not even the sketchiest, of how a statement of the form 'Quality q is at $x; y; z; t$' could ever be translated into Carnap's initial language of sense data and logic. The connective 'is at' remains an added undefined connective; the canons counsel us in its use but not in its elimination.

Carnap seems to have appreciated this point afterward; for in his later writings he abandoned all notion of the translatability of statements about the physical world into statements about immediate experience. Reductionism in its radical form has long since ceased to figure in Carnap's philosophy.

But the dogma of reductionism has, in a subtler and more tenuous form, continued to influence the thought of empiricists. The notion lingers that to each statement, or each synthetic statement, there is associated a unique range of possible sensory events such that the occurrence of any of them would add to the likelihood of truth of the statement, and that there is associated also another unique range of possible sensory events whose occurrence would detract from that likelihood. This notion is of course implicit in the verification theory of meaning.

The dogma of reductionism survives in the supposition that each statement, taken in isolation from its fellows, can admit of confirmation or infirmation at all. My countersuggestion, issuing essentially from Carnap's doctrine of the physical world in the *Aufbau,* is that our statements about the external world face the tribunal of sense experience not individually but only as a corporate body.

The dogma of reductionism, even in its attenuated form, is intimately connected with the other dogma: that there is a cleavage between the analytic and the synthetic. We have found ourselves led, indeed, from the latter problem to the former through the verification theory of meaning. More directly, the one dogma clearly supports the other in this way: as long as it is taken to be significant in general to speak of the confirmation and infirmation of a statement, it seems significant to speak also of a limiting kind of statement which is vacuously confirmed, *ipso facto,* come what may; and such a statement is analytic.

The two dogmas are, indeed, at root identical. We lately reflected that in general the truth of statements does obviously depend both upon language and upon extralinguistic fact; and we noted that this obvious circumstance carries in its train, not logically but all too naturally, a feeling that the truth of a statement is somehow analyzable into a linguistic component and a factual component. The factual component must, if we are empiricists, boil down to a range of confirmatory experiences. In the extreme case where the linguistic component is all that matters, a true statement is analytic. But I hope we are now impressed with how stubbornly the distinction between analytic and synthetic has resisted any straightforward drawing. I am impressed also, apart from prefabricated examples of black and white balls in an urn, with how baffling the problem has always been of arriving at any explicit theory of the empirical confirmation of a synthetic statement. My present suggestion is that it is nonsense, and the root of much nonsense, to speak of a linguistic component and a factual component in the truth of any individual statement. Taken collectively, science has its double dependence upon language and experience; but this duality is not significantly traceable into the statements of science taken one by one.

Russell's concept of definition in use was, as remarked, an advance over the impossible term-by-term empiricism of Locke and Hume. The statement, rather than the term, came with Russell to be recognized as the unit accountable to an empiricist critique. But what I am now urging is that even in taking the statement as unit we have drawn our grid too finely. The unit of empirical signifance is the whole of science.

VI. Empiricism Without the Dogmas

The totality of our so-called knowledge or beliefs, from the most casual matters of geography and history to the profoundest laws of atomic physics or even of pure mathematics and logic, is a man-made fabric which impinges on experience only along the edges. Or, to change the figure, total science is like a field of force whose boundary conditions are experience. A conflict with experience at the periphery occasions readjustments in the interior of the field. Truth values have to be redistributed over some of our statements. Re-evaluation of some statements entails re-evaluation of others, because of their logical interconnections — the logical laws being in turn simply certain further statements of the system, certain further elements of the field. Having re-evaluated one statement we must re-evaluate some others, whether they be statements logically connected with the first or whether they be the statements of logical connections themselves. But the total field is so undetermined by its boundary conditions, experience, that there is much latitude of choice as to what statements to re-evaluate in the light of any single contrary experience. No particular experiences are linked with any particular statements in the interior of the field, except indirectly through considerations of equilibrium affecting the field as a whole.

If this view is right, it is misleading to speak of the empirical content of an individual statement — especially if it be a statement at all remote from the experiential periphery of the field. Furthermore it becomes folly to seek a boundary between synthetic statements, which hold contingently on experience, and analytic statements which hold come what may. Any statement can be held true come what may, if we make drastic enough adjustments elsewhere in the system. Even a statement very close to the periphery can be held true in the face of recalcitrant experience by pleading hallucination or by amending certain statements of the kind called logical laws. Conversely, by the same token, no statement is immune to revision. Revision even of the logical law of the excluded middle has been proposed as a means of simplifying quantum mechanics; and what difference is there in principle between such a shift and the shift whereby Kepler superseded Ptolemy, or Einstein Newton, or Darwin Aristotle?

For vividness I have been speaking in terms of varying distances from a sensory periphery. Let me try now to clarify this notion without metaphor. Certain statements, though *about* physical objects and not sense experience, seem peculiarly germane to sense experience — and in a selective way: some statements to some experiences, others to others. Such statements, especially germane to particular experiences, I picture as near the periphery. But in this relation of "germaneness" I envisage nothing more than a loose association reflecting the relative likelihood, in practice, of our choosing one statement rather than another for revision in the event of recalcitrant experience. For example, we can imagine recalcitrant experiences to which we would surely be inclined to accommodate our system by re-evaluating just the statement that there are brick houses on Elm Street, together with related statements on the same topic. We can imagine other recalcitrant experiences to which we would be inclined to accommodate our system by re-evaluating just the statement that there are no centaurs, along with kindred statements. A recalcitrant experience can, I have already urged, be accommodated by any of various alternative re-evaluations in various alternative quarters of the total system; but, in the cases which we are now imagining, our natural tendency to disturb the total system as little as possible would lead us to focus our revisions upon these specific statements concerning brick houses or centaurs. These statements are felt, therefore, to have a sharper empirical reference than highly theoretical statements of physics or logic or ontology. The latter statements may be thought of as relatively centrally located within the total network, meaning merely that little preferential connection with any particular sense data obtrudes itself.

As an empiricist I continue to think of the conceptual scheme of science as a tool, ultimately, for predicting future experience in the light of past experience.

Physical objects are conceptually imported into the situation as convenient intermediaries — not by definition in terms of experience, but simply as irreducible posits comparable, epistemologically, to the gods of Homer. Let me interject that for my part I do, qua lay physicist, believe in physical objects and not in Homer's gods; and I consider it a scientific error to believe otherwise. But in point of epistemological footing the physical objects and the gods differ only in degree and not in kind. Both sorts of entities enter our conception only as cultural posits. The myth of physical objects is epistemologically superior to most in that it has proved more efficacious than other myths as a device for working a manageable structure into the flux of experience.

Imagine, for the sake of analogy, that we are given the rational numbers. We develop an algebraic theory for reasoning about them, but we find it inconveniently complex, because certain functions such as square root lack values for some arguments. Then it is discovered that the rules of our algebra can be much simplified by conceptually augmenting our ontology with some mythical entities, to be called irrational numbers. All we continue to be really interested in, first and last, are rational numbers; but we find that we can commonly get from one law about rational numbers to another much more quickly and simply by pretending that the irrational numbers are there too.

I think this a fair account of the introduction of irrational numbers and other extensions of the number system. The fact that the mythical status of irrational numbers eventually gave way to the Dedekind-Russell version of them as certain infinite classes of ratios is irrelevant to my analogy. That version is impossible anyway as long as reality is limited to the rational numbers and not extended to classes of them.

Now I suggest that experience is analogous to the rational numbers and that the physical objects, in analogy to the irrational numbers, are posits which serve merely to simplify our treatment of experience. The physical objects are no more reducible to experience than the irrational numbers to rational numbers, but their incorporation into the theory enables us to get more easily from one statement about experience to another.

The salient differences between the positing of physical objects and the positing of irrational numbers are, I think, just two. First, the factor of simplification is more overwhelming in the case of physical objects than in the numerical case. Second, the positing of physical objects is far more archaic, being indeed coeval, I expect, with language itself. For language is social and so depends for its development upon intersubjective reference.

Positing does not stop with macroscopic physical objects. Objects at the atomic level and beyond are posited to make the laws of macroscopic objects, and ultimately the laws of experience, simpler and more manageable; and we need not expect or demand full definition of atomic and subatomic entities in terms of macroscopic ones, any more than definition of macroscopic things in terms of sense data. Science is a continuation of common sense, and it continues the common-sense expedient of swelling ontology to simplify theory.

Physical objects, small and large, are not the only posits. Forces are another example; and indeed we are told nowadays that the boundary between energy and matter is obsolete. Moreover, the abstract entities which are the substance of mathematics — ultimately classes and classes of classes and so on up — are another posit in the same spirit. Epistemologically these are myths on the same footing with physical objects and gods, neither better nor worse except for differences in the degree to which they expedite our dealings with sense experiences.

The over-all algebra of rational and irrational numbers is underdetermined by the algebra of rational numbers, but is smoother and more convenient; and it includes the algebra of rational numbers as a jagged or gerrymandered part. Total science, mathematical and natural and human, is similarly but more extremely underdetermined by experience. The edge of the system must be kept squared with experience; the rest, with all its elaborate myths or fictions, has as its objective the simplicity of laws.

Ontological questions, under this view, are on a par with questions of natural science. Consider the question whether to countenance classes as entities. This, as I have argued elsewhere,[10] is the question whether to quantify with respect to variables which take classes as values. Now Carnap has maintained[11] that this is a question not of matters of fact but of choosing a convenient language form, a convenient conceptual scheme or framework for science. With this I agree, but only on the proviso that the same be conceded regarding scientific hypotheses generally. Carnap has recognized [12] that he is able to preserve a double standard for ontological questions and scientific hypotheses only by assuming an absolute distinction between the analytic and the synthetic; and I need not say again that this is a distinction which I reject.

Some issues do, I grant, seem more a question of convenient conceptual scheme and others more a question of brute fact. The issue over there being classes seems more a question of convenient conceptual scheme; the issue over there being centaurs, or brick houses on Elm Street, seems more a question of fact. But I have been urging that this difference is only one of degree, and that it turns upon our vaguely pragmatic inclination to adjust one strand of the fabric of science rather than another in accommodating some particular recalcitrant experience. Conservatism figures in such choices, and so does the quest for simplicity.

Carnap, Lewis, and others take a pragmatic stand on the question of choosing between language forms, scientific frameworks; but their pragmatism leaves off at the imagined boundary between the analytic and the synthetic. In repudiating such a boundary I espouse a more thorough pragmatism. Each man is given a scientific heritage plus a continuing barrage of sensory stimulation; and the considerations which guide him in warping his scientific heritage to fit his continuing sensory promptings are, where rational, pragmatic.

NOTES

1. Much of this paper is devoted to a critique of analyticity which I have been urging orally and in correspondence for years past. My debt to the other participants in those discussions, notably Carnap, Church, Goodman, Tarski, and White, is large and indeterminate. White's excellent essay "The Analytic and the Synthetic: An Untenable Dualism," in *John Dewey: Philosopher of Science and Freedom* (New York, 1950), says much of what needed to be said on the topic; but in the present paper I touch on some further aspects of the problem. I am grateful to Dr. Donald L. Davidson for valuable criticism of the first draft.

2. See White, *op. cit.,* p. 324.

3. R. Carnap, *Meaning and Necessity* (Chicago, 1947), pp. 9ff.; *Logical Foundations of Probability* (Chicago, 1950), pp. 70ff.

4. This is cognitive synonymy in a primary, broad sense. Carnap (*Meaning and Necessity,* pp. 56ff.) and Lewis (*Analysis of Knowledge and Valuation* [La Salle, Ill., 1946], pp. 83ff.) have suggested how, once this notion is at hand, a narrower sense of cognitive synonymy which is preferable for some purposes can in turn be derived. But this special ramification of concept-building lies aside from the present purpoes and must not be confused with the broad sort of cognitive synonymy here concerned.

5. See, e.g., my *Mathematical Logic* (New York, 1940; Cambridge, Mass., 1947), sec. 24, 26, 27; or *Methods of Logic* (New York, 1950), sec. 37ff.

6. The 'if and only if' itself is intended in the truth functional sense. See Carnap, *Meaning and Necessity,* p. 14.

7. The doctrine can indeed be formulated with terms rather than statements as the units. Thus C. I. Lewis describes the meaning of a term as "*a criterion in mind,* by reference to which one is able to apply or refuse to apply the expression in question in the case of presented, or imagined, things or situations" (*op. cit.,* p. 133).

8. John Horne Tooke, *The Diversions of Purley* (London, 1776; Boston, 1806), I, ch. ii.

9. R. Carnap, *Der Logische Aufbau der Welt* (Berlin, 1928).

10. E.g., in "Notes on Existence and Necessity," *Journal of Philosophy,* XL (1943), 113-127.

11. Carnap, "Empiricism, Semantics, and Ontology," *Revue internationale de philosophie,* IV (1950), 20-40.

12. *Op. cit.,* p. 32, footnote.

Study Questions

Bergmann: "Logical Positivism, Language, and the Reconstruction of
Metaphysics"

1. What is reconstructionism?
2. What is meant by the linguistic turn in philosophy?
3. How does this approach differ from traditional philosophy?
4. What does Bergmann hold with regard to (a) phenomenalism, (b) the
   analytic-synthetic distinction, (c) ontology?

Quine: "On What There Is"

1. What are various answers that have been given to the question: "What is it
   that involves us in and indicates ontological commitment?"
2. Why do the first three fail?
3. What does indicate and involve us in ontological commitment? Explain.
4. How do we adjudicate between rival ontologies?

Quine: "Two Dogmas of Empiricism"

1. What are the two dogmas of empiricism? Explain.
2. State Quine's criticism of the first.
3. State his criticism of the second.
4. In what way are ontological questions on a par with science?

Selected Bibliography

Bergmann, Gustav. *Logic and Reality*. Madison: University of Wisconsin
    Press, 1964. [Difficult, but rewarding.]
Bergmann, Gustav, *The Metaphysics of Logical Positivism*. New York: Long-
    mans Green, 1954. [The first seven chapters are especially recommended.]
Munitz, Milton K. *Contemporary Analytic Philosophy*. New York: Mac-
    millian, 1981. [Has a good discussion of Quine.]
Quine, W. V. *From a Logical Point of View*. Cambridge: Harvard University
    Press, 1964. [Presupposes familiarity with logical symbolism.]
Sellars, Wilfrid. *Science, Perception and Reality*. London: Routledge and K.
    Paul, 1963. [Very difficult.]

Linguistic Analysis

27. Performative-Constative

J. L. Austin

Translator's Note: 'Performative-Constative' is a straightforward translation of Austin's paper 'Performatif-Constatif', which he wrote in French and presented at a (predominantly) Anglo-French conference held at Royaumont in March 1958. The case of the discussion which follows it[1] is somewhat more complex. The actual discussion at Royaumont was carried on in both French and English. What appears in the published volume after Austin's text (*Cahiers de Royaumont, Philosophie* No. IV, *La Philosophie Analytique:* Les Éditions de Minuit, 1962, pp. 271-304) is a version of this, based on a transcript but substantially cut and edited, in which the contributions originally made in English were translated into French by M. Béra. It might have been possible, for the present publication, to procure copies at least of those portions of the original transcript that were in English. However, it seemed to me preferable simply to translate into English the entire French text, mainly for the reason that it is this edited version, and this only, that all those taking part are known to have seen and approved for publication.*

G. J. Warnock

One can quite easily get the idea of the performative utterance — though the expression, as I am aware, does not exist in the French language, or anywhere else. This idea was brought in to mark a contrast with that of the declarative utterance, or rather, as I am going to call it, the constative utterance. And there we have straight off what I want to call in question. Ought we to accept this Performative-Constative antithesis?

The constative utterance, under the name, so dear to philosophers, of *statement,*[2] has the property of being true or false. The performance utterance, by contrast, can never be either: it has its own special job, it is used to perform an action. To issue such an utterance[3] *is* to perform the action — an action, perhaps, which one scarcely could perform, at least with so much precision, in any other way. Here are some examples:

> I name this ship *Liberté.*
> I apologize.
> I welcome you.
> I advise you to do it.

Utterances of this kind are common enough: we find them, for instance, everywhere in what are called in English the 'operative' clauses of a legal instrument.[4] Plainly, many of them are not without interest for philosophers: to say 'I promise to . . .'—to issue, as we say, this performative utterance—just *is* the act of making a promise; not, as we see, at all a mysterious act. And it may seem at once quite obvious that an utterance of this kind can't be true or false—notice that I say it can't *be* true or false, because it may very well *imply* that some *other* propositions are true or are false, but that, if I'm not mistaken, is a quite different matter.

However, the performative utterance is not exempt from all criticism: it may very well be criticized, but in a quite different dimension from that of truth and falsity. The performative must be issued in a situation appropriate in all respects for the act in question: if the speaker is not in the conditions required for its performance (and there are many such conditions), then his utterance will be, as we call it in general, 'unhappy'.[5]

First, our performative, like any other ritual or ceremony, may be, as the lawyers say, 'null and void'. If, for example, the speaker is not in a position to perform an act of that kind, or if the object with respect to which he purports to perform it is not suitable for the purpose, then he doesn't manage, simply by issuing his utterance, to carry out the purported act. Thus a bigamist doesn't get married a second time, he only 'goes through the form' of a second marriage; I can't name the ship if I am not the person properly authorized to name it; and I can't quite bring off the baptism of penguins, those creatures being scarcely susceptible of that exploit.

Second, a performative utterance may be, though not void, 'unhappy' in a different way—if, that is, it is issued *insincerely*. If I say 'I promise to . . .' without in the least intending to carry out the promised action, perhaps even not believing that it is in my power to carry it out, the promise is hollow. It is made, certainly; but still, there is an 'unhappiness': I have *abused* the formula.

Let us now suppose that our act has been performed: everything has gone off quite normally, and also, if you like, sincerely. In that case, the performative utterance will characteristically 'take effect'. We do not mean by that that such-and-such a future event is or will be brought about as an effect of this action functioning as a cause. We mean rather that, in consequence of the performance of this act, such-and-such a future event, *if* it happens, will be *in order,* and such-and-such other events, *if* they happen, will not be in order. If I have said 'I promise', I shall not be in order if I break my word; if I have said 'I welcome you', I shall not be in order if I proceed to treat you as an enemy or an intruder. Thus we say that, even when the performative has taken effect, there may always crop up a third kind of unhappiness, which we call 'breach of commitment'.[6] We may note also that commitments can be more or less vague, and can bind us in very different degrees.

There we have, then, three kinds of unhappiness associated with the performative utterance. It is possible to make a complete classification of these unhappinesses; but it must be admitted that, as practically goes without saying, the different kinds may not always be sharply distinguishable and may even coincide.[7] Then we must add that our performative is both an *action* and an *utterance:* so that, poor thing, it can't help being liable to be substandard in all the ways in which actions in general can be, as well as those in which utterances in general can be. For example, the performative may be issued under duress, or by accident; it may suffer from defective grammar, or from misunderstanding it may figure in a context not wholly 'serious', in a play, perhaps, or in a poem. We leave all that on one side—let us simply bear in mind the more specific unhappiness of the performative, that is, nullity, abuse (insincerity), and breach of commitment.

Well, now that we have before us this idea of the performative, it is very natural to hope that we could proceed to find some criterion, whether of grammar or of vocabulary, which would make it possible for us to answer in every case the question whether a particular utterance is performative or not. But this hope is, alas, exaggerated and, in large measure, vain.

It is true that there exist two 'normal forms', so to speak, in which the performative finds expression. At first sight both of them, curiously enough, have a thoroughly constative look. One of these normal forms is that which I have already made use of in producing my examples: the utterance leads off with a verb in the first person singular of the present indicative active, as in 'I promise you that . . .'. The other form, which comes to exactly the same but is more common in utterances issued in writing, employs by contrast a verb in the *passive* voice and in the *second* or *third* person of the present indicative, as in 'Passengers are requested to cross the line by the footbridge only'. If we ask ourselves, as sometimes we may, whether a given utterance of this form is performative or constative, we may settle the question by asking whether it would be possible to insert in it the word 'hereby' or some equivalent—as, in French, the phrase *'par ces mots-ci'*.

By way of putting to the test utterances which one might take to be performative, we make use of a well-known asymmetry, in the case of what we call an 'explicit performative' verb, between the first person singular of the present indicative, and other persons and tenses of the same verb. Thus, 'I promise' is a formula which is used to perform the act of promising; 'I promised', on the other hand, or 'he promises', are expressions which serve simply to describe or report an act of promising, not to perform one.

However, it is not in the least necessary that an utterance, if it is to be performative, should be expressed in one of these so-called normal forms. To say 'Shut the door', plainly enough, is every bit as performative, every bit as much the performance of an act, as to say 'I order you to shut the door'. Even the word 'Dog' by itself can sometimes (at any rate in England, a country more practical than ceremonious) stand in place of an explicit and formal performative; one performs, by this little word, the very same act as by the utterance 'I warn you that the dog is about to attack us', or by 'Strangers are warned that here there is a vicious dog'. To make our utterance performative, and quite unambiguously so, we can make use, in place of the explicit formula, of a whole lot of more primitive devices such as intonation, for instance, or gesture; further, and above all, the very context in which the words are uttered can make it entirely certain how they are to be taken—as a description, for example, or again as a warning. Does this word 'Dog' just give us a bit of detail about the local fauna? In the context—when confronted, that is, with the notice on the gate—we just don't need to ask ourselves that question at all.

All we can really say is that our explicit performative formula ('I promise . . .', 'I order you . . .', etc.) serves to make explicit, and at the same time more precise, what act it is that the speaker purports to perform in issuing his utterance. I say 'to make explicit', and that is not at all the same thing as to *state*.[8] Bending low before you, I remove my hat, or perhaps I say 'Salaam'; then, certainly, I am doing obeisance to you, not just engaging in gymnastics; but the word 'Salaam' does not, any more than does the act of removing my hat, in any way *state* that I am doing obeisance to you. It is in this way that our formula *makes* the issuing of the utterance that action which it is, but does not *state* that it is that action.

The other forms of expression, those that have no explicit performative formula, will be more primitive and less precise, one might almost say more vague. If I say simply 'I will be there', there will be no telling, just by considering the words, whether I am taking on a commitment, or declaring an intention, or making perhaps a fatalistic prediction. One may think of the precise formulae as a relatively recent phenomenon in the evolution of language, and as going together with the evolution of more complex forms of society and science.

We can't, then, expect any purely verbal criterion of the performative. We may hope, all the same, that any utterance which is in fact performative will be reducible (in some sense of that word) to an utterance in one or the other of our normal forms. Then, going on from there, we should be able, with the help of a dictionary, to make a list of all the verbs which can figure in one of our explicit formulae. Thus we will achieve a useful classification of all the varieties of acts that we perform in saying something (in one sense, at least, of that ambiguous phrase).

We have now brought in, then, the ideas of the performative utterance, of its unhappinesses, and of its explicit formulae. But we have been talking all along as if every utterance had to be *either* constative *or* performative, and as if the idea of the constative at any rate was as clear as it is familiar. But it is not.

Let us note in the first place that an utterance which is undoubtedly a statement of fact, therefore constative can fail to get by[9] in more than one way. It can be untrue, to be sure; but it can also be absurd, and that not necessarily in some gross fashion (by being, for instance, ungrammatical). I would like to take a closer look at three rather more subtle ways of being absurd, two of which have only recently come to light.

(1) Someone says 'All John's children are bald, but [or 'and'] John has no children'; or perhaps he says 'All John's children are bald', when, as a matter of fact, John has no children.

(2) Someone says 'the cat is on the mat, but [or 'and'] I don't believe it is'; or perhaps he says 'The cat is on the mat', when, as a matter of fact, he does not believe it is.

(3) Someone says 'All the guests are French, and some of them aren't': or perhaps he says 'All the guests are French', and then afterwards says 'Some of the guests are not French'.

In each of these cases one experiences a feeling of outrage, and it's possible each time for us to try to express it in terms of the same word — 'implication', or perhaps that word that we always find so handy, 'contradiction'. But there are more ways of killing the cat than drowning it in butter, [10] and equally, to do violence to language one does not always need a contradiction.

Let us use the three terms 'presuppose', 'imply', and 'entail' [11] for our three cases respectively. Then:

1. Not only 'John's children are bald', but equally 'John's children are not bald', presupposes that John has children. To talk about those children, or to refer to them, presupposes that they exist. By contrast, 'The cat is not on the mat' does *not,* equally with 'The cat is on the mat', imply that I believe it is; and similarly, 'None of the guests is French' does *not,* equally with 'All the guests are French', entail that it is false that some of the guests are not French.

2. We can quite well say 'It could be the case both that the cat is on the mat and that I do not believe it is'. That is to say, those two propositions are not in the least incompatiable: both can be true together. What is impossible is to state both at the same time: his *stating* that the cat is on the mat is what implies that the speaker believes it is. By contrast, we couldn't say 'It could be the case both that John has no children and that his children are bald'; just as we couldn't say 'It could be the case both that all the guests are French and that some of them are not French'.

3. If 'All the guests are French' entails 'It is not the case that some of the guests are not French', then 'Some of the guests are not French' entails 'It is not the case that all the guests are French'. It's a question here of the compatibility and incompatibility of propositions. By contrast, it isn't like this with presupposition: if 'John's children are bald' presupposes that John has children, it isn't true at all that 'John has no children' presupposes that John's children are not bald. Similarly, if 'The cat is on the mat' implies that I believe it is, it isn't true at all that to say 'I don't believe that the cat is on the mat' implies that the cat is not on the mat (not, at any rate, in the same sense of 'implies'; besides, we have already seen that 'implication', for us, is not a matter of the incompatibility of propositions).

Here then are three ways in which a statement can fail to get by without being untrue, and without being a sheer rigmarole either. I would like to call attention to the fact that these three ways of failing to get by correspond to three of the ways in which a performative utterance may be unhappy. To bring out the comparison, let's first take two performative utterances:

4. 'I bequeath my watch to you, but [or 'and'] I haven't got a watch'; or perhaps someone says 'I bequeath my watch to you' when he hasn't got a watch.

5. 'I promise to be there, but [or 'and'] I have no intention of being there'; or perhaps someone says 'I promise to be there' when he doesn't intend to be there.

We compare case 4 with case 1, the case, that is, of presupposition. For to say either 'I bequeath my watch to you' or 'I don't bequeath my watch to you' presupposes equally that I have a watch; that the watch exists is presupposed by the fact that it is spoken of or referred to, in the performative utterance just as much as in the constative utterance. And just as we can make use here of the term 'presupposition' as employed in the doctrine of the constative, equally we can take over for that doctrine the term 'void' as employed in the doctrine of the unhappinesses of the performative. The statement on the subject of John's children is, we may say, 'void for lack of reference', which is exactly what lawyers would say about the purported bequest of the watch. So here is a first instance in which a trouble that afflicts statements turn out to be identical with one of the unhappinesses typical of the performative utterance.

We compare case 5 with case 2, that is, the case where something is 'implied'. Just as my saying that the cat is on the mat implies that I believe it is, so my saying I promise to be there implies that I intend to be there. The procedure of stating is designed for those who honestly believe what they say, exactly as the procedure of promising is designed for those who have a certain intention, namely, the intention to do whatever it may be that they promise. If we don't hold the belief, or again don't have the intention, appropriate to the content of our utterance, then in each case there is lack of sincerity and abuse of the procedure. If, at the same time as we make the statement or the promise, we announce in the same breath that we don't believe it or we don't intend to, then the utterance is 'self-voiding', as we might call it; and hence our feeling of outrage on hearing it. Another instance, then, where a trouble which afflicts statements is identical with one of the unhappinesses which afflict performative utterances.

Let us look back, next, to case 3, the case of entailment among statements. Can we find, in the case of performatives, some analogue for this as well? When I make the statement, for instance, 'All the guests are French', do I not commit myself in a more or less rigorous fashion to behaving in future in such-and-such a way, in particular with respect to the statements I will make? If, in the sequel, I state things incompatible with my utterance (namely, that all the guests are French), there will be a breach of commitment that one might well compare with that of the case in which I say 'I welcome you', and then proceed to treat you as an enemy or an intruder — and perhaps even better, with that of which one is guilty when one says 'I define the word thus' (a performative utterance) and then proceeds to use the word with a different meaning.

So then, it seems to me that the constative utterance is every bit as liable to unhappinesses as the performative utterance, and indeed to pretty much the same unhappiness. Furthermore, making use of the key provided by our list of unhappinesses noted for the case of performatives, we can ask ourselves whether there are not still more unhappinesses in the case of statements, besides the three we have just mentioned. For example, it often happens that a performative is void because the utterer is not in a state, or not in a position, to perform the act which he purports to perform; thus, it's no good my saying 'I order you' if I have no authority over you: I can't order you, my utterance is void, my act is only purported. Now people have, I know, the impression that where a statement, a constative utterance, is in question, the case is quite different: anybody at all can state anything at all. What if he's ill-informed? Well then, one can be mistaken, that's all. It's a free country, isn't it? To state what isn't true is one of the Rights of Man. However, this impression can lead us into error. In reality nothing is more common than to find that one can state absolutely nothing on some subject, because one is simply not in a position to state whatever it may be—and this may come about, too, for more than one reason. I *cannot* state at this moment how many people there are in the next room: I haven't been to see, I haven't found out the facts. What if I say, nevertheless, 'At this moment there are fifty people in the next room'? You will allow, perhaps, that in saying that I have made a guess,[12] but you will not allow that I have made a statement, not at any rate without adding 'but he had no right whatever to do so'; and in this case my 'I state . . .' is exactly on a par with our 'I order . . .', said, we remember, without any right to give an order. Here's another example. You confide to me 'I'm bored', and I quite cooly reply 'You're not'. You say 'What do you mean, I'm not? What right have you to say how I feel? I say 'But what do *you* mean, what right have I? I'm just stating what your feelings are, that's all. I may be mistaken, certainly, but what of that? I suppose one can always make a simple statement, can't one?' But no, one can't always: usually, I can't state what your feelings are, unless you have disclosed them to me.

So far I have called attention to two things: that there is no purely verbal criterion by which to distinguish the performative from the constative utterance, and that the constative is liable to the same unhappinesses as the performative. Now we must ask ourselves whether issuing a constative utterance is not, after all, the performance of an act, the act, namely, of stating. Is stating an act in the same sense as marrying, apologizing, betting, etc.? I can't plumb this mystery any further at present. But it is already pretty evident that the formula 'I state that . . .'—a formula which, as we put it, serves to make explicit what speech-act[13] it is that we are performing; and also, that one can't issue any utterance whatever without performing some speech-act of this kind.

What we need, perhaps, is a more general theory of these speech-acts, and in this theory our Constative-Performative antithesis will scarcely survive.

Here and now it remains for us to examine, quite briefly, this craze for being either true or false, something which people think is peculiar to statements alone and ought to be set up on a pedestal of its own, above the battle. And this time let's begin with the performative utterance: is it the case that there is nothing here in the least analogous with truth?

To begin with, it is clear that if we establish that a performative utterance is not unhappy, that is, that its author has performed his act happily and in all sincerity, that still does not suffice to set it beyond the reach of all criticism. It may always be criticized in a different dimension.

Let us suppose that I say to you 'I advise you to do it'; and let us allow that all the circumstances are appropriate, the conditions for success are fulfilled. In saying that, I actually do advise you to do it — it is not that I *state,* truly or falsely, *that* I advise you. It is, then, a performative utterance. There does still arise, all the same, a little question: was the advice good or bad? Agreed, I spoke in all sincerity, I believed that to do it would be in your interest; but was I right? Was my belief, in these circumstances, justified? Or again — though perhaps this matters less — was it in fact, or as things turned out, in your interest? There is confrontation of my utterance with the situation in, and the situation with respect to which, it was issued. I was fully justified perhaps, but was I right?

Many other utterances which have an incontestably performative flavour are exposed to this second kind of criticism. Allowing that, in declaring the accused guilty, you have reached your verdict properly and in good faith, it still remains to ask whether the verdict was just, or fair. Allowing that you had the right to reprimand him as you did, and that you have acted without malice, one can still ask whether your reprimand was deserved. Here again we have confrontation with the facts, including the circumstances of the occasion of utterance.

That not all performative utterances without exception are liable to this quasi-objective evaluation — which for that matter must here be left pretty vague and multifarious — may very well be true.

There is one thing that people will be particularly tempted to bring up as an objection against any comparison between this second kind of criticism and the kind appropriate to statements, and that is this: aren't these questions about something's being good, or just, or fair, or deserved entirely distinct from questions of truth and falsehood? That, surely, is a very simple black-and-white business: either the utterance corresponds to the facts or it doesn't, and that's that.

Well, I for my part don't think it is. Even if there exists a well-defined class of statements and we can restrict ourselves to that, this class will always be pretty wide. In this class we shall have the following statements:

> France is hexagonal.
> Lord Raglan won the battle of Alma.
> Oxford is 60 miles from London.

It's quite true that for each of these statements we can raise the question 'true or false'. But it is only in quite favourable cases that we ought to expect an answer yes or no, once and for all. When the question is raised one understands that the utterance is to be confronted in one way or another with the facts. Very well. So let's confront 'France is hexagonal' with France. What are we to say, is it true or not? The question, plainly, oversimplifies things. Oh well, up to a point if you like, I see what you mean, true perhaps for some purposes or in some contexts, that would do for the man in the street but not for geographers. And so on. It's a rough statement, no denying that, but one can't just say straight out that it's false. Then Alma, a soldier's battle if ever there was one; it's true that Lord Raglan was in command of the allied army, and that this army to some extent won a confused sort of victory; yes, that would be a fair judgement, even well deserved, for schoolchildren anyway, though really it's a bit of an exaggeration. And Oxford, well yes, it's true that that city is 60 miles from London, so long as you want only a certain degree of precision.

Under the heading 'truth' what we in fact have is, not a simple quality nor a relation, not indeed *one* anything, but rather a whole dimension of criticism. We can get some idea, perhaps not a very clear one, of this criticism; what *is* clear is that there is a whole lot of things to be considered and weighed up in this dimension alone—the facts, yes, but also the situation of the speaker, his purpose in speaking, his hearer, questions of precision, etc. If we are content to restrict ourselves to statements of an idiotic or ideal simplicity, we shall never succeed in disentangling the true from the just, fair, deserved, precise, exaggerated, etc., the summary and the detail, the full and the concise, and so on.

From this side also, then, from the side of truth and falsehood, we feel ourselves driven to think again about the Performataive-Constative antithesis. What we need, it seems to me, is a new doctrine, both complete and general, of *what one is doing in saying something,* in all the senses of that ambiguous phrase, and of what I call the speech-act, not just in this or that aspect abstracting from all the rest, but taken in its totality.

NOTES

*From *Philosophy and Ordinary Language,* edited by Charles E. Caton (University of Illinois Press, Urbana, 1963), pp. 22-23. Reprinted by permission of Mrs J. Austin, G. J. Warnock and the University of Illinois Press.

1. [Not here reprinted. Ed.]

2. [The French term is '*assertion*'. I am sure that 'statement' is the English term Austin would have used here, and I have so translated '*assertion*' throughout. Trans.]

3. ['*Formuler un tel énoncé*'. The translation is supplied in a footnote by Austin himself. Trans.]

4. The clauses, that is to say, in which the legal act is actually performed, as opposed to those—the 'preamble'—which set out the circumstances of the transaction.

5. ['Unhappy' is a term Austin regularly used in this connection, and he supplies it himself in brackets after the French '*malheureux*'. Trans.]

6. ['*Rupture d'engagement*'. Austin himself supplies the translation. Trans.]

7. ['That is to say, a particular case of unhappiness might arguably, or even quite properly, be classifiable under more than one heading. Trans.]

8. [*'Affirmer'*. I have translated this verb by 'state' throughout. Trans.]

9. [The French phrase is *'peut ne pas jouer'*. Austin himself sometimes used in English the coined term 'non-play' (see, e.g., *How To Do Things with Words,* pp. 18n. and 31), but in a more restricted sense than would be appropriate here. Trans.]

10. English proverb. I am told that this rather refined way of disposing of cats is not found in France.

11. [These three English terms are supplied in a footnote by Austin himself. Trans.]

12. [The French text has *'conjoncture'* here, but this must surely be a misprint for *'conjecture'*. Trans.]

13. [Austin supplies this English term himself. It is in any case the term he regularly used. Trans.]

28. Intention and Convention in Speech Acts

P. F. Strawson

I

In this paper I want to discuss some questions regarding J. L. Austin's notions of the illocutionary force of an utterance and of the illocutionary act which a speaker performs in making an utterance.[1]

There are two preliminary matters I must mention, if only to get them out of the way. Austin contrasts what he calls the 'normal' or 'serious' use of speech with what he calls 'etiolated' or 'parasitical' uses. His doctrine of illocutionary force relates essentially to the normal or serious use of speech and not, or not directly, to etiolated or parasitical uses; and so it will be with my comments on his doctrine. I am not suggesting that the distinction between the normal or serious use of speech and the secondary uses which he calls etiolated or parasitical is so clear as to call for no further examination; but I shall take it that there is such a distinction to be drawn and I shall not here further examine it.

My second preliminary remark concerns another distinction, or pair of distinctions, which Austin draws. Austin distinguishes the illocutionary force of an utterance from what he calls its 'meaning' and distinguishes beween the illocutionary and the locutionary acts performed in issuing the utterance. Doubts may be felt about the second term of each of these distinctions. It may be felt that Austin has not made clear just what abstractions from the total speech act he intends to make by means of his notions of meaning and of locutionary act. Although this is a question on which I have views, it is not what the present paper is about. Whatever doubts may be entertained about Austin's notions of meaning and of locutionary act, it is enough for present purposes to be able to say, as I think we clearly can, the following about their relation to the notion of illocutionary force. The meaning of a (serious) utterance, as conceived by Austin, always embodies some limitation on its possible force, and sometimes—as, for example, in some cases where an explicit performative formula, like 'I apologize', is used—the meaning of an utterance may exhaust its force; that is, there may be no more to the force than there is to the meaning; but very often the meaning, though it limits, does not exhaust, the force, Similarly, there may sometimes be no more to say about the illocutionary force of an utterance than we already know if we know what locutionary act has been performed; but, very often there is more to know about the illocutionary force of an utterance than we know in knowing what locutionary act has been performed.

So much for these two preliminaries. Now I shall proceed to assemble from the text some indications as to what Austin means by the force of an utterance and as to what he means by an illocutionary act. These two notions are not so closely related that to know the force of an utterance is the same thing as to know what illocutionary act was actually performed in issuing it. For if an utterance with the illocutionary force of, say, a warning is not understood in this way (that is, as a warning) by the audience to which it is addressed, then (it is held) the illocutionary act of warning cannot be said to have been actually performed. 'The performance of an illocutionary act involves the securing of uptake'; that is, it involves 'bringing about the understanding of the meaning and of the force of the locution' (pp. 115-16).[2] Perhaps we may express the relation by saying that to know the force of an utterance is the same thing as to know what illocutionary act, *if any,* was actually performed in issuing it. Austin gives many examples and lists of words which help us to form at least a fair intuitive notion of what is meant by 'illocutionary force' and 'illocutionary act'. Besides these, he gives us certain general clues to these ideas, which may be grouped, as follows, under four heads:

1. Given that we know (in Austin's sense) the meaning of an utterance, there may still be a further question as to *how what was said was meant* by the speaker, or as to *how the words spoken were used,* or as to *how the utterance was to be taken* or *ought to have been taken* (pp. 98-9). In order to know the illocutionary force of the utterance, we must know the answer to this further question.

2. A locutionary act is an act *of* saying something; an illocutionary act is an act we perform *in* saying something. It is what we *do, in* saying what we *say.* Austin does not regard this characterization as by any means a satisfactory test for identifying kinds of illocutionary acts since, so regarded, it would admit many kinds of acts which he wishes to exclude from the class (p. 99 and Lecture X).

3. It is a sufficient, though not, I think, a necessary, condition of a verb's being the name of a *kind* of illocutionary act that it can figure, in the first person present indicative, as what Austin calls an explicit performative. (This latter notion I shall assume to be familiar and perspicuous.)

4. The illocutionary act is 'a conventional act; an act done as conforming to a convention' (p. 105). As such, it is to be sharply contrasted with the producing of certain effects, intended or otherwise, by means of an utterance. This producing of effects, though it too can often be ascribed *as an act* to the speaker (his *perlocutionary act*), is in no way a conventional act (pp. 120-1). Austin reverts many times to the 'conventional' nature of the illocutionary act (pp. 103, 105, 108, 115, 120, 121, 127) and speaks also of 'conventions of illocutionary force' (p. 114). Indeed, he remarks (pp. 120-1) that though acts which can properly be called by the same names as illocutionary acts—for example, acts of warning—can be brought off nonverbally, without the use of words, yet, in order to be properly called by these names, such acts must be *conventional* nonverbal acts.

II

I shall assume that we are clear enough about the intended application of Austin's notions of illocutionary force and illocutionary act to be able to criticize, by reference to cases, his general doctrines regarding those notions. It is the general doctrine I listed last above—the doctrine that an utterance's having such and such a force is a matter of convention—that I shall take as the starting point of inquiry. Usually this doctrine is affirmed in a quite unqualified way. But just once there occurs an interestingly qualified statement of it. Austin says, of the use of language with a certain illocutionary force, that 'it may . . . be said to be *conventional* in the sense that at least it could be made explicit by the performative formula' (p. 103). The remark has a certain authority in that it is the first explicit statement of the conventional nature of the illocutionary act. I shall refer to it later.

Meanwhile let us consider the doctrine in its unqualified form. Why does Austin say that the illocutionary act is a conventional act, an act done as conforming to a convention? I must first mention, and neutralize, two possible sources of confusion. (It may seem an excess of precaution to do so. I apologize to those who find it so.) First, we may agree (or not dispute) that any speech act is, as such, at least in part a conventional act. The performance of any *speech* act involves at least the observance or exploitation of some *linguistic* conventions, and every illocutionary act is a speech act. But it is absolutely clear that this is not the point that Austin is making in declaring the illocutionary act to be a conventional act. We must refer, Austin would say, to linguistic conventions to determine what *locutionary* act has been performed in the making of an utterance, to determine what the *meaning* of the utterance is. The doctrine now before us is the further doctrine that where force is *not* exhausted by meaning, the fact that an utterance has the further unexhausted force it has is also a matter of convention; or, where it is exhausted by meaning, the fact *that* it is, is a matter of convention. It is not just as being a speech act that an illocutionary act—for example, of warning—is conventional. A nonverbal act of warning is, Austin maintains, conventionally such in just the same way as an illocutionary — that is, verbal — act of warning is conventionally such.

Second, we must dismiss as irrevelant the fact that it can properly be said to be a matter of convention that an act of, for example, warning is correctly called by this name. For if this were held to be a ground for saying that illocutionary acts were conventional acts, then any describable act whatever would, as correctly described, be a conventional act.

The contention that illocutionary force is a matter of convention is easily seen to be correct in a great number of cases. For very many kinds of human transaction involving speech are governed and in part constituted by what we easily recognize as established conventions of procedure additional to the conventions governing the *meanings* of our utterances. Thus the fact that the word 'guilty' is pronounced by the foreman of the jury in court at the proper moment constitutes his utterance as the act of bringing in a verdict; and that this is so is certainly a matter of the conventional procedures of the law. Similarly, it is a matter of convention that if the appropriate umpire pronounces a batsman 'out', he thereby performs the act of *giving the man out,* which no player or spectator shouting 'Out!' can do. Austin gives other examples, and there are doubtless many more which could be given, where there clearly exist statable conventions, relating to the circumstances of utterance, such that an utterance with a certain meaning, pronounced by the appropriate person in the apropriate circumstances, has the force it has *as* conforming to those conventions. Examples of illocutionary acts of which this is true can be found not only in the sphere of social institutions which have a legal point (like the marriage ceremony and the law courts themselves) or of activities governed by a definite set of rules (like cricket and games generally) but in many other relations of human life. The act of *introducing,* performed by uttering the words 'This is Mr. Smith', may be said to be an act performed as conforming to a convention. The act of surrendering, performed by saying *'Kamerad!'* and throwing up your arms when confronted with a bayonet, may be said to be (to have become) an act performed as conforming to an accepted convention, a conventional act.

But it seems equally clear that, although the circumstances of utterance are always relevant to the determination of the illocutionary force of an utterance, there are many cases in which it is not as conforming to an accepted *convention* of any kind (other than those linguistic conventions which help to fix the meaning of the utterance) that an illocutionary act is performed. It seems clear, that is, that there are many cases in which the illocutionary force of an utterance, though not exhausted by its meaning, is not owed to any *conventions* other than those which help to give it its meaning. Surely there may be cases in which to utter the words 'The ice over there is very thin' to a skater is to issue a warning (is to say something with the *force* of a warning) without its being the case that there is any statable convention at all (other than those which bear on the nature of the *locutionary* act) such that the speaker's act can be said to be an act done as conforming to that convention.

Here is another example. We can readily imagine circumstances in which an utterance of the words 'Don't go' would be correctly described not as a request or an order, but as an entreaty. I do not want to deny that there may be conventional postures or procedures for entreating: one can, for example, kneel down, raise one's arms and *say*, 'I entreat you.' But I do want to deny that an act of entreaty can be performed only as conforming to some such conventions. What makes *X*'s words to *Y* an *entreaty* not to go is something — complex enough, no doubt — relating to *X*'s situation, attitude to *Y*, manner, and current intention. There are questions here which we must discuss later. But to suppose that there is always and necessarily a convention conformed to would be like supposing that there could be no love affairs which did not proceed on lines laid down in the *Roman de la Rose* or that every dispute between men must follow the pattern specified in Touchstone's speech about the countercheck quarrelsome and the lie direct.

Another example. In the course of a philosophical discussion (or, for that matter, a debate on policy) one speaker *raises an objection* to what the previous speaker has just said. *X* says (or proposes) that *p* and *Y objects* that *q*. *Y*'s utterance has the force of an objection to *X*'s assertion (or proposal) that *p*. But where is the *convention* that constitutes it an objection? That *Y*'s utterance has the force of an objection may lie partly in the character of the dispute and of *X*'s contention (or proposal) and it certainly lies partly, in *Y*'s *view* of these things, in the bearing which he takes the proposition that *q* to have on the doctrine (or proposal) that *p*. But although there may be, there does not have to be, any convention involved other than those linguistic conventions which help to fix the meanings of the utterances.

I do not think it necessary to give further examples. It seems perfectly clear that, if at least we take the expressions 'convention' and 'conventional' in the most natural way, the doctrine of the conventional nature of the illocutionary act does not hold generally. Some illocutionary acts are conventional; others are not (except in so far as they are locutionary acts). Why then does Austin repeatedly affirm the contrary? It is unlikely that he has made the simple mistake of generalizing from some cases to all. It is much more likely that he is moved by some further, and fundamental, feature of illocutionary acts, which it must be our business to discover. Even though we may decide that the description 'conventional' is not appropriately used, we may presume it worth our while to look for the reason for using it. Here we may recall that oddly qualified remark that the performance of an illocutionary act, or the use of a sentence with a certain illocutionary force, 'may be said to be conventional in the sense that at least it *could* be made explicit by the performative formula' (p. 103). On this we may first, and with justice, be inclined to comment that there is no such *sense* of 'being conventional', that if this is a *sense* of anything to the purpose, it is a sense of 'being *capable* of being conventional'. But although this is a proper comment on the remark, we should not simply dismiss the remark with this comment. Whatever it is that leads Austin to call illocutionary acts in general 'conventional' must be closely connected with whatever it is about such acts as warning, entreating, apologizing, advising, that accounts for the fact that *they* at least *could* be made explicit by the use of the corresponding first-person performative form. So we must ask what it is about them that accounts for this fact. Obviously it will not do to answer simply that they are acts which can be performed by the use of words. So are many (perlocutionary) acts, like convincing, dissuading, alarming, and amusing, for which, as Austin points out, there is no corresponding first-person *performative* formula. So we need some further explanation.

III

I think a concept we may find helpful at this point is one introduced by H. P. Grice in his valuable article on "Meaning" *(Philosophical Review, LXVII, 1957)*, namely, the concept of someone's *nonnaturally meaning something by an utterance.* The concept does not apply only to speech acts—that is, to cases where that by which someone nonnaturally means something is a *linguistic* utterance. It is of more general application. But it will be convenient to refer to that by which someone, *S,* nonnaturally means something as *S's utterance.* The explanation of the introduced concept is given in terms of the concept of intention. *S* nonnaturally means something by an utterance *x* if *S* intends *(i₁)* to produce by uttering *x* a certain response *(r)* in an audience *A* and intends *(i₂)* that *A* shall recognize *S's* intention *(i₁)* and intends *(i₃)* that this recognition on the part of *A* of *S's* intention *(i₁)* shall function as *A's* reason, or a part of his reason, for his response *r.* (The word 'response', though more convenient in some ways than Grice's 'effect', is not ideal. It is intended to cover cognitive and affective states or attitudes as well as actions.) It is, evidently, an important feature of this definition that the securing of the response *r* is intended to be mediated by the securing of another (and always cognitive) effect in *A*; namely, recognition of *S's* intention to secure response *r.*

Grice's analysis of his concept is fairly complex. But I think a little reflection shows that it is not quite complex enough for his purpose. Grice's analysis is undoubtedly offered as an analysis of a situation in which one person is trying, in a sense of the word 'communicate' fundamental to any theory of meaning, to communicate with another. But it is possible to imagine a situation in which Grice's three conditions would be satisfied by a person *S* and yet, in this important sense of 'communicate', it would not be the case that *S* could be said to be trying to communicate by means of his production of *x* with the person *A* in whom he was trying to produce the response *r.* I proceed to describe such a situation.

S intends by a certain action to induce in *A* the belief that *p;* so he satisfies condition *(i₁)*. He arranges convincing-looking 'evidence' that *p,* in a place where *A* is bound to see it. He does this, knowing that *A* is watching him at work, but *knowing also, that A does not know that S knows that A is watching him at work.* He realizes that *A* will not take the *arranged* 'evidence' as genuine or natural evidence that p, but realizes, and indeed intends, that A will take his arranging of it as grounds for thinking that he, S, intends to induce in A the belief that p. That is, he intends A to recognize his (i_1) intention. So S satisfies condition (i_2). He knows that A has general grounds for thinking that S would not wish to make him, A, think that p unless it were known to S to be the case that p; and hence that A's recognition of his (S's) intention to induce in A the belief that p will in fact seem to A a sufficient reason for believing that p. And he intends that A's recognition of his intention (i_1) should function in just this way. So he satisfies condition (i_3).

S, then, satisfies all Grice's conditions. But this is clearly not a case of attempted *communcation* in the sense which (I think it is fair to assume) Grice is seeking to elucidate. A will indeed take S to be trying to bring it about that A is aware of some fact; but he will not take S as trying, in the colloquial sense, to 'let him know' something (or to 'tell' him something). But unless S at least brings it about that A takes him (S) to be trying to let him (A) know something, he has not succeeded in communicating with A; and if, as in our example, he has not even *tried* to bring this about, then he has not even *tried* to communicate with A. It seems a minimum further condition of his trying to do this that he should not only intend A to recognize his intention to get A to think that p, but that he should also *intend* A *to recognize his intention to get* A *to recognize his intention* to get A to think that p.

We might approximate more closely to the communication situation if we changed the example by supposing it not only clear to both A and S that A was watching S at work, but also clear to them both that it *was* clear to them both. I shall content myself, however, with drawing from the actually considered example the conclusion that we must add to Grice's conditions the further condition that S should have the further intention (i_4) that A should recognize his intention (i_2). It is possible that further argument could be produced to show that even adding this condition is not *sufficient* to constitute the case as one of attempted communication. But I shall rest content for the moment with the fact that this addition at least is necessary.

Now we might have expected in Grice's paper an account of what it is for A to *understand* something by an utterance x, an account complementary to the account of what it is for S to *mean* something by an utterance x. Grice in fact gives no such account, and I shall suggest a way of at least partially supplying this lack. I say 'at least partially' because the uncertainty as to the sufficiency of even the modified conditions for S's nonnaturally *meaning* something by an utterance x is reflected in a corresponding uncertainty in the sufficiency of conditions for A's understanding. But again we may be content for the moment with necessary conditions. I suggest, then, that for A (in the appropriate sense of 'understand') to understand *something* by utterance x, it is necessary (and perhaps sufficient) that there should be *some* complex intention of the (i_2) form, described above, which A takes S to have, and that for A to understand the utterance correctly, it is necessary that A should take S to have *the* complex intention of the (i_2) form which S does have. In other words, if A is to understand the utterance correctly, S's (i_4) intention and hence his (i_2) intention must be fulfilled. Of course it does not follow from the fulfilment of these intentions that his (i_1) intention is fulfilled; nor, consequently, that his (i_3) intention is fulfilled.

It is at this point, it seems, that we may hope to find a possible point of connection with Austin's terminology of 'securing uptake'. If we do find such a point of connection, we also find a possible starting point for an at least partial analysis of the notions of illocutionary force and of the illocutionary act. For to secure uptake is to secure understanding of (meaning and) illocutionary force; and securing understanding of illocutionary force is said by Austin to be an essential element in bringing off the illocutionary act. It is true that this doctrine of Austin's may be objected to.[3] For surely a man may, for example, actually have made such and such a bequest, or gift, even if no one ever reads his will or instrument of gift. We may be tempted to say instead that at least *the aim, if not the achievement,* of securing uptake is an essential element in the performance of the illocutionary act. To this, too, there is an objection. Might not a man really have made a gift, in due form, and take some satisfaction in the thought, even if he had no expectations of the fact ever being known? But this objection at most forces on us an amendment to which we are in any case obliged[4]: namely, that the aim, if not the achievement, of securing uptake is essentially *a standard, if not an invariable,* element in the performance of the illocutionary act. So the analysis of the aim of securing uptake remains an essential element in the analysis of the notion of the illocutionary act.

IV

Let us, then, make a tentative identification — to be subsequently qualified and revised — of Austin's notion of uptake with that at least partially analysed notion of understanding (on the part of an audience) which I introduced just now as complementary to Grice's concept of somebody nonnaturally meaning something by an utterance. Since the notion of audience understanding is introduced by way of a fuller (though partial) analysis than any which Austin gives of the notion of uptake, the identification is equivalent to a tentative (and partial) analysis of the notion of uptake and hence of the notions of illocutionary act and illocutionary force. If the identification were correct, then it would follow that to say something with a certain illocutionary force is at least (in the standard case) to have a certain complex intention of the (i_4) form described in setting out and modifying Grice's doctrine.

Next we test the adequacy and explanatory power of this partial analysis by seeing how far it helps to explain other features of Austin's doctrine regarding illocutionary acts. There are two points at which we shall apply this test. One is the point at which Austin maintains that the production of an utterance with a certain illocutionary force is a conventional act in that unconventional sense of 'conventional' which he glosses in terms of general suitability for being explicit with the help of an explicitly performative formula. The other is the point at which Austin considers the possibility of a general characterization of the illocutionary act as what we *do, in* saying what we say. He remarks on the unsatisfactoriness of this characterization in that it would admit as illocutionary acts what are not such; and we may see whether the suggested analysis helps to explain the exclusion from the class of illocutionary acts of those acts falling under this characterization which Austin wishes to exclude. These points are closely connected with each other.

First, then, we take the point about the general suitability of an illocutionary act for performance with the help of the explicitly performative formula for that act. The explanation of this feature of illocutionary acts has two phases; it consists of, first, a general, and then a special, point about intention. The first point may be roughly expressed by saying that in general a man can speak of his intention in performing an action with a kind of authority which he cannot command in predicting its outcome. What he intends in doing something is up to him in a way in which the results of his doing it are not, or not only, up to him. But we are concerned not with just any intention to produce any kind of effect by acting, but with a very special kind of case. We are concerned with the case in which there is not simply an intention to produce a certain response in an audience, but an intention to produce that response by means of recognition on the part of the audience of the intention to produce that response, this recognition to serve as part of the reason that the audience has for its response, and the intention that this recognition should occur being itself intended to be recognized. The speaker, then, not only has the general authority on the subject of his intention that any agent has; he also has a motive, inseparable from the nature of his act, for making that intention clear. For he will not have secured understanding of the illocutionary force of his utterance, he will not have performed the act of communication he sets out to perform, unless his complex intention is grasped. Now clearly, for the enterprise to be possible at all, there must exist, or he must find, means of making the intention clear. If there exists any conventional linguistic means of doing so, the speaker has both a right to use, and a motive for using, those means. One such means, available sometimes, which comes very close to the employment of the explicit performative form, would be to attach, or subjoin, to the substance of the message what looks like a force-elucidating *comment* on it, which may or may not have the form of a self-ascription. Thus we have phrases like 'This is only a suggestion' or 'I'm only making a suggestion'; or again 'That was a warning' or 'I'm warning you'. For using such phrases, I repeat, the speaker has the *authority* that anyone has to speak on the subject of his intentions and the *motive* that I have tried to show is inseparable from an act of communication.

From such phrases as these—which have, *in appearance,* the character of comments on utterances other than themselves—to the explicit performative formula the step is only a short one. My reason for *qualifying* the remark that such phrases have the character of comments on utterances other than themselves is this. We are considering the case in which the subjoined quasi-comment is addressed to the same audience as the utterance on which it is a quasi-comment. Since it is *part* of the speaker's audience-directed intention to make clear the character of his utterance as, for example, a warning, and since the subjoined quasi-comment directly subserves this intention, it is better to view the case, appearances notwithstanding, *not* as a case in which we have two utterances, one commenting on the other, but as a case of a single unitary speech act. Crudely, the addition of the quasi-comment 'That was a warning' is *part* of the total act of warning. The effect of the short step to the explicitly performative formula is simply to bring appearances into line with reality. When that short step is taken, we no longer have, even in appearance, two utterances, one a comment on the other, but a single utterance in which the first-person performative verb *manifestly* has that peculiar logical character of which Austin rightly made so much, and which we may express in the present context by saying that the verb serves not exactly to *ascribe* an intention to the speaker but rather, in Austin's phrase, to *make explicit* the type of communication intention with which the speaker speaks, the type of force which the utterance has.

The above might be said to be a deduction of the general possibility and utility of the explicitly performative formula for the cases of illocutionary acts not essentially conventional. It may be objected that the deduction fails to show that the intentions rendered explicit by the use of performative formulae *in general* must be of just the complex form described, and hence fails to justify the claim that just this kind of intention lies at the core of all illocutionary acts. And indeed we shall see that this claim would be mistaken. But before discussing why, we shall make a further application of the analysis at the second testing point I mentioned. That is, we shall see what power it has to explain why some of the things we may be *doing, in* saying what we say, are not illocutionary acts and could not be rendered explicit by the use of the performative formula.

Among the things mentioned by Austin which we might be doing in saying things, but which are not illocutionary acts, I shall consider the two examples of (1) showing off and (2) insinuating. Now when we show off, we are certainly trying to produce an effect on the audience: we talk, indeed, for effect; we try to impress, to evoke the response of admiration. But it is no part of the intention to secure the effect *by means of* the recognition of the intention to secure it. It is no part of our total intention to secure recognition of the intention to produce the effect at all. On the contrary: recognition of the intention might militate against securing the effect and promote an opposite effect, for example, disgust.

This leads on to a further general point not explicitly considered by Austin, but satisfactorily explained by the analysis under consideration. In saying to an audience what to say, we very often intend not only to produce the primary response *r* by means of audience recognition of the intention to produce that response, but to produce further effects by means of the production of the primary response *r*. Thus my further purpose in informing you that *p* (that is, aiming to produce in you the primary cognitive response of knowledge or belief that *p*) may be to bring it about thereby that you adopt a certain line of conduct or a certain attitude. In saying what I say, then, part of what I am *doing* is trying to influence your attitudes or conduct in a certain way. Does this part of what I am doing in saying what I say contribute to determining the character of the illocutionary act I perform? And if not, why not? If we take the first question strictly as introduced and posed, the answer to it is 'No'. The reason for the answer follows from the analysis. We have no complex intention (i_4) that there should be recognition of an intention (i_2) that there should be recognition of an intention (i_1) that the further effect should be produced; for it is no part of our intention that the further effect should be produced by way of recognition of our intention that it should be; the production in the audience of belief that *p* is intended to be itself the means whereby his attitude or conduct is to be influenced. We secure uptake, perform the act of communication that we set out to perform, if the audience understands us as *informing* him that *p*. Although it is true that, in saying what we say, we are in fact *trying* to produce the further effect — this is part of what we are doing, whether we succeed in producing the effect or not — yet this does not enter into the characterization of the illocutionary act. With this case we have to contrast the case in which, instead of aiming at a primary response and a further effect, the latter to be secured through the former alone, we aim at a complex primary response. Thus in the case where I do not simply inform, but warn, you that *p*, among the intentions I intend you to recognize (and intend you to recognize as intended to be recognized), are not only the intention to secure your belief that *p*, but the intention to secure that you are on your guard against *p*-perils. The difference (one of the differences) between showing off and warning is that your recognition of my intention to put you on your guard may well contribute to putting you on your guard, whereas your recognition of my intention to impress you is not likely to contribute to my impressing you (or not in the way I intended).[5]

Insinuating fails, for a different reason, to be a type of illocutionary act. An essential feature of the intentions which make up the illocutionary complex is their overtness. They have, one might say, essential avowability. This is, in one respect, a logically embarrassing feature. We have noticed already how we had to meet the threat of a counterexample to Grice's analysis of the communicative act in terms of three type of intention — (i_1), (i_2), and (i_3) — by the addition of a further intention (i_4) that an intention (i_2) should be recognized. We have no proof, however, that the resulting enlarged set of conditions is a complete analysis. Ingenuity might show it was not; and the way seems open to a regressive series of intentions that intentions should be recognized. While I do not think there is anything necessarily objectionable in this, it does suggest that the complete and rounded-off set of conditions aimed at in a conventional analysis is not easily and certainly attainable in these terms. That is why I speak of the feature in question in these terms. That is why I speak of the feature in question as logically embarrassing. At the same time it enables us easily to dispose of insinuating as a candidate for the status of a type of illocutionary act. The whole point of insinuating is that the audience is to *suspect,* but not more than suspect, the intention, for example, to induce or disclose a certain belief. The intention one has in insinuating is essentially nonavowable.

Now let us take stock a little. We tentatively laid it down as a necessary condition of securing understanding of the illocutionary force of an utterance that the speaker should succeed in bringing it about that the audience took him, in issuing his utterance, to have a complex intention of a certain kind, namely the intention that the audience should recognize (and recognize as intended to be recognized) his intention to induce a certain response in the audience. The suggestion has, as we have just seen, certain explanatory merits. Nevertheless we cannot claim general application for it as even a partial analysis of the notions of illocutionary force and illocutionary act. Let us look at some reasons why not.

V

I remarked earlier that the words 'Don't go' may have the force, *inter alia,* either of a request or of an entreaty. In either case the primary intention of the utterance (if we presume the words to be uttered with the *sense* 'Don't go *away'*) is that of inducing the person addressed to stay where he is. His staying where he is is the primary response aimed at. But the only other intentions mentioned in our scheme of partial analysis relate directly or indirectly to recognition of the primary intention. So how, in terms of that scheme, are we to account for the variation in illocutionary force between requests and entreaties?

This question does not appear to raise a major difficulty for the scheme. The scheme, it seems, merely requires supplementing and enriching. *Entreaty,* for example, is a matter of trying to secure the primary response not merely through audience recognition of the intention to secure it, but through audience recognition of a complex attitude of which this primary intention forms an integral part. A wish that someone should stay may be held in different ways: passionately or lightly, confidently or desperately; and it may, for different reasons, be part of a speaker's intention to secure recognition of *how* he holds it. The most obvious reason, in the case of entreaty, is the belief, or hope, that such a revelation is more likely to secure the fulfillment of the primary intention.

But one may not only request and entreat; one may *order* someone to stay where he is. The words 'Don't go' may have the illocutionary force of an order. Can we so simply accommodate in our scheme *this* variation in illocutionary force? Well, we can accommodate it; though not so simply. We can say that a man who issues an order typically intends his utterance to secure a certain response, that he intends this intention to be recognized, and its recognition to be a reason for the response, that he intends the utterance to be recognized as issued in a certain social context such that certain social rules or conventions apply to the issuing of utterances in this context and such that certain consequences may follow in the event of the primary response not being secured, that he intends *this* intention too to be recognized, and finally that he intends the recognition of these last features to function as an element in the reasons for the response on the part of the audience.

Evidently, in this case, unlike the case of entreaty, the scheme has to be extended to make room for explicit reference to social convention. It can, with some strain, be so extended. But as we move further into the region of institutionalized procedures, the strain becomes too much for the scheme to bear. On the one hand, one of its basic features—namely, the reference to an intention to secure a definite response in an audience (over and above the securing of uptake)—has to be dropped. On the other, the reference to social conventions of procedure assumes a very much greater importance. Consider an umpire giving a batsman out, a jury bringing in a verdict of guilty, a judge pronouncing sentence, a player redoubling at bridge, a priest or a civil officer pronouncing a couple man and wife. Can we say that the umpire's primary intention is to secure a certain response (say, retiring to the pavilion) from a certain audience (say, the batsman), the jurymen's to secure a certain response (say, the pronouncing of sentence) from a certain audience (say, the judge), and then build the rest of our account around this, as we did, with some strain, in the case of the order? Not with plausibility. It is not even possible, in other than a formal sense, to isolate, among all the participants in the procedure (trial, marriage, game) to which the utterance belongs, a particular audience to whom the utterance can be said to be addressed.

Does this mean that the approach I suggested to the elucidation of the notion of illocutionary force is entirely mistaken? I do not think so. Rather, we must distinguish types of case; and then see what, if anything, is common to the types we have distinguished. What we initially take from Grice—with modifications—is an at least partially analytical account of an act of communication, an act which might indeed be performed nonverbally and yet exhibit all the essential characteristics of a (nonverbal) equivalent of an illocutionary act. We gain more than this. For the account enables us to understand how such an act may be linguistically conventionalized right up to the point at which illocutionary force is exhausted by meaning (in Austin's sense); and in this understanding the notion of wholly overt or essentially avowable intention plays an essential part. Evidently, in these cases, the illocutionary act itself is not *essentially* a conventional act, an act done as conforming to a convention; it may be that the act is conventional, done as conforming to a convention, only in so far as *the means used to perform it* are conventional. To speak only of those conventional means which are also *linguistic* means, the extent to which the act is one done as conforming to conventions may depend solely on the extent to which conventional linguistic meaning exhausts illocutionary force.

At the other end of the scale—the end, we may say, from which Austin began—we have illocutionary acts which *are* essentially conventional. The examples I mentioned just now will serve—marrying, redoubling, giving out, pronouncing sentence, bringing in a verdict. Such acts could have no existence outside the rule- or convention-governed practices and procedures of which they essentially form parts. Let us take the standard case in which the participants in these procedures know the rules and their roles, and are trying to play the game and not wreck it. Then they are presented with occasions on which they have to, or may, perform an illocutionary act which forms part of, or furthers, the practice or procedure as a whole; and sometimes they have to make a decision within a restricted range of alternatives (for example, to pass or redouble, to pronounce sentence of imprisonment for some period not exceeding a certain limit). Between the case of such acts as these and the case of the illocutionary act not essentially conventional, there is an important likeness and an important difference. The likeness resides in the fact that, in the case of an utterance belonging to a convention-governed practice or procedure, the speaker's utterance is standardly *intended* to further, or affect the course of, the practice in question in some one of the alternative ways open, and intended to be recognized as so intended. I do not mean that such an act could *never* be performed *unintentionally*. A player might let slip the word 'redouble' without *meaning* to redouble; but if the circumstances are appropriate and the play strict, then he *has* redoubled (or he may be *held* to have redoubled). But a player who continually did this sort of thing would not be asked to play again, except by sharpers. Forms can take charge, in the absence of appropriate intention; but when they do, the case is *essentially* deviant or nonstandard. There is present in the standard case, that is to say, the same element of wholly overt and avowable intention as in the case of the act not essentially conventional.

The difference is a more complicated affair. We have, in these cases, an act which is conventional in two connected ways. First, if things go in accordance with the rules of the procedure in question, the act of furthering the practice in the way intended is an act required or permitted by those rules, an act done as falling under the rules. Second, the act is identified as the act it is just because it is performed by the utterance of a form of words conventional for the performance of that act. Hence the speaker's utterance is not only *intended* to further, or affect the course of, the practice in question in a certain conventional way; in the absence of any breach of the conventional conditions for furthering the procedure in this way, it cannot fail to do so.

And here we have the contrast between the two types of case. In the case of an illocutionary act of a kind not essentially conventional, the act of communication is performed if *uptake* is secured, if the utterance is taken to be issued with the complex overt intention with which it is issued. But even though the act of communication is performed, the wholly overt intention which lies at the core of the intention complex may, *without any breach of rules or conventions,* be frustrated. The audience response (belief, action, or attitude) may simply not be forthcoming. It is different with the utterance which forms part of a wholly convention-governed procedure. Granted that uptake is secured, then any frustration of the wholly overt intention of the utterance (the intention to further the procedure in a certain way) must be attributable to a breach of rule or convention. The speaker who abides by the conventions can avowably have the intention to further the procedure in the way to which his current linguistic act is conventionally appropriated *only* if he takes it that the conventional conditions for so furthering it are satisfied and hence takes it *that his utterance will not only reveal his intentions but give them effect*. There is nothing parallel to this in the case of the illocutionary act of a kind not essentially conventional. In both cases, we may say, speakers assume the responsibility for making their intentions overt. In one case (the case of the convention-constituted procedure) the speaker who uses the explicitly performative form also explicitly assumes the responsibility for making his overt intention effective. But in the other case the speaker cannot, in the speech act itself, explicitly assume any such responsibility. For there are no conditions which can conventionally guarantee the effectiveness of his overt intention. Whether it is effective or not is something that rests with his audience. In the one case, therefore, the explicitly performative form *may* be the name of the very act which is performed if and only if the speaker's overt intention is effective; but in the other case it cannot be the name of this act. But of course—and I shall recur to this thought—the sharp contrast I have here drawn between two extreme types of case must not blind us to the existence of intermediate types.

Acts belonging to convention-constituted procedures of the kind I have just referred to form an important part of human communication. But they do not form the whole nor, we may think, the most fundamental part. It would be a mistake to take them as the model for understanding the notion of illocutionary force in general, as Austin perhaps shows some tendency to do when he both insists that the illocutionary act is essentially a conventional act and connects this claim with the possibility of making the act explicit by the use of the performative formula. It would equally be a mistake, as we have seen, to generalize the account of illocutionary force derived from Grice's analysis; for this would involve holding, falsely, that the complex overt intention manifested in any illocutionary act always includes the intention to secure a certain definite response or reaction in an audience over and above that which is necessarily secured if the illocutionary force of the utterance is understood. Nevertheless, we can perhaps extract from our consideration of two contrasting types of case something which is common to them both and to all the other types which lie between them. For the illocutionary force of an utterance is essentially something that is intended to be understood. And the understanding of the force of an utterance in all cases involves recognizing what may be called broadly an audience-directed intention and recognizing it as wholly overt, as intended to be organized. It is perhaps this fact which lies at the base of the general possibility of the explicit performative formula; though, as we have seen, extra factors come importantly into play in the case of convention-constituted procedures.

Once this common element in all illocutionary acts is clear, we can readily acknowledge that the types of audience-directed intention involved may be very various and, also, that different types may be exemplified by one and the same utterance.

I have set in sharp contrast those cases in which the overt intention is simply to forward a definite and convention-governed practice (for example, a game) in a definite way provided for by the conventions or rules of the practice and those cases in which the overt intention includes that of securing a definite response (cognitive or practical) in an audience over and above that which is necessarily secured if uptake is secured. But there is something misleading about the sharpness of this contrast; and it would certainly be wrong to suppose that all cases fall clearly and neatly into one or another of these two classes. A speaker whose job is to do so may offer information, instructions, or even advice, and yet be overtly indifferent as to whether or not his information is accepted as such, his instructions followed, or his advice taken. His wholly overt intention may amount to no more than that of making available— in a 'take it or leave it' spirit—to his audience the information or instructions or opinion in question; though again, in some cases, he may be seen as the mouthpiece, merely, of another agency to which he may be attributed at least general intentions of the kind that can scarcely be attributed, in the particular case, to him. We should not find such complications discouraging; for we can scarcely expect a general account of linguistic communication to yield more than schematic outlines, which may almost be lost to view when every qualification is added which fidelity to the facts requires.

NOTES

1. All references, unless otherwise indicated, are to *How To Do Things with Words* (Oxford, 1962).

2. I refer later to the need for qualification of this doctrine.

3. I owe the objections which follow to Professor Hart.

4. For an illocutionary act *may* be performed *altogether* unintentionally. See the example about redoubling at bridge, p. [434] below.

5. Perhaps trying to impress might sometimes have an illocutionary character. For I might try to impress you with my *effrontery*, intending you to recognize this intention and intending your recognition of it to function as part of your reasons for being impressed, and so forth. But then I am not *merely* trying to impress you; I am *inviting* you to be impressed. I owe this point to Mr. B. F. McGuinness.

29. What Is A Speech Act?

J. R. Searle

I. Introduction

In a typical speech situation involving a speaker, a hearer, and an utterance by the speaker, there are many kinds of acts associated with the speaker's utterance. The speaker will characteristically have moved his jaw and tongue and made noises. In addition, he will characteristically have performed some acts within the class which includes informing or irritating or boring his hearers; he will further characteristically have performed some acts within the class which includes referring to Kennedy or Khruschchev or the North Pole; and he will also have performed acts within the class which includes making statements, asking questions, issuing commands, giving reports, greeting, and warning. The members of this last class are what Austin[1] called illocutionary acts and it is with this class that I shall be concerned in this paper, so the paper might have been called 'What is an Illocutionary Act?' I do not attempt to define the expression 'illocutionary act', although if my analysis of a particular illocutionary act succeeds it may provide the basis for a definition. Some of the English verbs and verb phrases associated with illocutionary acts are: state, assert, describe, warn, remark, comment, command, order, request, criticize, apologize, censure, approve, welcome, promise, express approval, and express regret. Austin claimed that there were over a thousand such expressions in English.

By way of introduction, perhaps I can say why I think it is of interest and importance in the philosophy of language to study speech acts, or, as they are sometimes called, language acts or linguistic acts. I think it is essential to any specimen of linguistic communication that it involve a linguistic act. It is not, as has generally been supposed, the symbol or word or sentence, or even the token of the symbol or word or sentence, which is the unit of linguistic communication, but rather it is the *production* of the token in the performance of the speech act that constitutes the basic unit of linguistic communication.

To put this point more precisely, the production of the sentence token under certain conditions is the illocutionary act, and the illocutionary act is the minimal unit of linguistic communication.

I do not know how to *prove* that linguistic communication essentially involves acts but I can think of arguments with which one might attempt to convince someone who was sceptical. One argument would be to call the sceptic's attention to the fact that when he takes a noise or a mark on paper to be an instance of linguistic communication, as a message, one of the things that is involved in his so taking that noise or mark is that he should regard it as having been produced by a being with certain intentions. He cannot just regard it as a natural phenomenon, like a stone, a waterfall, or a tree. In order to regard it as an instance of linguistic communication one must suppose that its production is what I am calling a speech act. It is a logical presupposition, for example, of current attempts to decipher the Mayan hieroglyphs that we at least hypothesize that the marks we see on the stones were produced by beings more or less like ourselves and produced with certain kinds of intentions. If we were certain the marks were a consequence of, say, water erosion, then the question of deciphering them or even calling them hieroglyphs could not arise. To construe them under the category of linguistic communication necessarily involves construing their production as speech acts.

To perform illocutionary acts is to engage in a rule-governed form of behaviour. I shall argue that such things as asking questions or making statements are rule-governed in ways quite similar to those in which getting a base hit in baseball or moving a knight in chess are rule-governed forms of acts. I intend therefore to explicate the notion of an illocutionary act by stating a set of necessary and sufficient conditions for the performance of a particular kind of illocutionary act, and extracting from it a set of semantical rules for the use of the expression (or syntactic device) which marks the utterance as an illocutionary act of that kind. If I am successful in stating the conditions and the corresponding rules for even one kind of illocutionary act, that will provide us with a pattern for analysing other kinds of acts and consequently for explicating the notion in general. But in order to set the stage for actually stating conditions and extracting rules for performing an illocutionary act I have to discuss three other preliminary notions: *rules, propositions,* and *meaning.* I shall confine my discussion of these notions to those aspects which are essential to my main purposes in this paper, but, even so, what I wish to say concerning each of these notions, if it were to be at all complete, would require a paper for each; however, sometimes it may be worth sacrificing thoroughness for the sake of scope and I shall therefore be very brief.

II. Rules

In recent years there has been in the philosophy of language considerable discussion involving the notion of rules for the use of expressions. Some philosophers have even said that knowing the meaning of the word is simply a matter of knowing the rules for its use or employment. One disquieting feature of such discussions is that no philosopher, to my knowledge at least, has ever given anything like an adequate formulation of the rules for the use of even one expression. If meaning is a matter of rules of use, surely we ought to be able to state the rules for the use of expressions in a way which would explicate the meaning of those expressions. Certain other philosophers, dismayed perhaps by the failure of their colleagues to produce any rules, have denied the fashionable view that meaning is a matter of rules and have asserted that there are no semantical rules of the proposed kind at all. I am inclined to think that this scepticism is premature and stems from a failure to distinguish different sorts of rules, in a way which I shall now attempt to explain.

I distinguish between two sorts of rules: Some regulate antecedently existing forms of behaviour; for example, the rules of etiquette regulate interpersonal relationships, but these relationships exist independently of the rules of etiquette. Some rules on the other hand do not merely regulate but create or define new forms of behaviour. The rules of football, for example, do not merely regulate the game of football but as it were create the possibility of or define that activity. The activity of playing football is constituted by acting in accordance with these rules; football has no existence apart from these rules. I call the latter kind of rules constitutive rules and the former kind regulative rules. Regulative rules regulate a pre-existing activity, an activity whose existence is logically independent of the existence of the rules. Constitutive rules constitute (and also regulate) an activity the existence of which is logically dependent on the rules.[2]

Regulative rules characteristically take the form of or can be paraphrased as imperatives, e.g. 'When cutting food hold the knife in the right hand', or 'Officers are to wear ties at dinner'. Some constitutive rules take quite a different form, e.g. a checkmate is made if the king is attacked in such a way that no move will leave it unattacked; a touchdown is scored when a player crosses the opponents' goal line in possession of the ball while play is in progress. If our paradigms of rules are imperative regulative rules, such non-imperative constitutive rules are likely to strike us as extremely curious and hardly even as rules at all. Notice that they are almost tautological in character, for what the 'rule' seems to offer is a partial definition of 'checkmate' or 'touchdown'. But, of course, this quasi-tautological character is a necessary consequence of their being constitutive rules: the rules concerning touchdowns must define the notion of 'touchdown' in the same way that the rules concerning football define 'football'. That, for example, a touchdown can be scored in such and such ways and counts six points can appear sometimes as a rule, sometimes as an analytic truth; and that it can be construed as a tautology is a clue to the fact that the rule in question is a constitutive one. Regulative rules generally have the form 'Do X' or 'If Y do X'. Some members of the set of constitutive rules have this form but some also have the form 'X counts as Y'.[3]

The failure to perceive this is of some importance in philosophy. Thus, e.g., some philosophers ask 'How can a promise create an obligation? A similar question would be 'How can a touchdown create six points?' And as they stand both questions can only be answered by stating a rule of the form '*X* counts as *Y*'.

I am inclined to think that both the failure of some philosophers to state rules for the use of expressions and the scepticism of other philosophers concerning the existence of any such rules stem at least in part from a failure to recognize the distinctions between constitutive and regulative acts. The model or paradigm of a rule which most philosophers have is that of a regulative rule, and if one looks in semantics for purely regulative rules one is not likely to find anything interesting from the point of view of logical analysis. There are no doubt social rules of the form 'One ought not to utter obscenities at formal gatherings', but that hardly seems a rule of the sort that is crucial in explicating the semantics of a language. The hypothesis that lies behind the present paper is that the semantics of a language can be regarded as a series of systems of constitutive rules and that illocutionary acts are acts performed in accordance with these sets of constitutive rules. One of the aims of this paper is to formulate a set of constitutive rules for a certain kind of speech act. And if what I have said concerning constitutive rules is correct, we should not be surprised if not all these rules take the form of imperative rules. Indeed we shall see that the rules fall into several different categories, none of which is quite like the rules of etiquette. The effort to state the rules for an illocutionary act can also be regarded as a kind of test of the hypothesis that there are constitutive rules underlying speech acts. If we are unable to give any satisfactory rule formulations, our failure could be construed as partially disconfirming evidence against the hypothesis.

III. Propositions

Different illocutionary acts often have features in common with each other. Consider utterances of the following sentences:

(1) Will John leave the room?
(2) John will leave the room.
(3) John, leave the room!
(4) Would that John left the room.
(5) If John will leave the room, I will leave also.

Utterances of each of these on a given occasion would characteristically be performances of different illocutionary acts. The first would, characteristically, be a question, the second an assertion about the future, that is, a prediction, the third a request or order, the fourth an expression of a wish, and the fifth a hypothetical expression of intention. Yet in the performance of each the speaker would characteristically perform some subsidiary acts which are common to all five illocutionary acts, In the utterance of each the speaker *refers* to a particular person John and *predicates* the act of leaving the room of that person. In no case is that all he does, but in every case it is a part of what he does. I shall say, therefore, that in each of these cases, although the illocutionary acts are different, at least some of the non-illocutionary acts of reference and predication are the same.

The reference to some person John and predication of the same thing of him in each of these illocutionary acts inclines me to say that there is a common *content* in each of them. Something expressible by the clause 'that John will leave the room' seems to be a common feature of all. We could, with not too much distortion, write each of these sentences in a way which would isolate this common feature: 'I assert that John will leave the room', 'I ask whether John will leave the room', etc.

For lack of a better word I propose to call this common content a proposition, and I shall describe this feature of these illocutionary acts by saying that in the utterance of each of (1)–(5) the speaker expresses the proposition that John will leave the room. Notice that I do not say that the sentence expresses the proposition; I do not know how sentences could perform acts of that kind. But I shall say that in the utterance of the sentence the speaker expresses a proposition. Notice also that I am distinguishing between a proposition and an assertion or statement of that proposition. The proposition that John will leave the room is expressed in the utterance of all of (1)–(5) but only in (2) is that proposition asserted. An assertion is an illocutionary act, but a proposition is not an act at all, although the act of expressing a proposition is a part of performing certain illocutionary acts.

I might summarize this by saying that I am distinguishing between the illocutionary act and the propositional content of an illocutionary act. Of course, not all illocutionary acts have a propositional content, for example, an utterance of 'Hurrah!' or 'Ouch!' does not. In one version or another this distinction is an old one and has been marked in different ways by authors as diverse as Frege, Sheffer, Lewis, Reichenbach and Hare, to mention only a few.

From a semantical point of view we can distinguish between the propositional indicator in the sentence and the indicator of illocutionary force. That is, for a large class of sentences used to perform illocutionary acts, we can say for the purpose of our analysis that the sentence has two (not necessarily separate) parts, the proposition-indicating element and the function-indicating device.[4] The function-indicating device shows how the proposition is to be taken, or, to put it in another way, what illocutionary force the utterance is to have, that is, what illocutionary act the speaker is performing in the utterance of the sentence. Function-indicating devices in English include word order, stress, intonation contour, punctuation, the mood of the verb, and finally a set of so-called performative verbs: I may indicate the kind of illocutionary act I am performing by beginning the sentence with 'I apologize', 'I warn', 'I state', etc. Often in actual speech situations the context will make it clear what the illocutionary force of the utterance is, without its being necessary to invoke the appropriate function indicating device.

If this semantical distinction is of any real importance, it seems likely that it should have some syntactical analogue, and certain recent developments in transformational grammar tend to support the view that it does. In the underlying phrase marker of a sentence there is a distinction between those elements which correspond to the function-indicating device and those which correspond to the propositional content.

The distinction between the function-indicating device and the proposition-indicating device will prove very useful to us in giving an analysis of an illocutionary act. Since the same proposition can be common to all sorts of illocutionary acts, we can separate our analysis of the proposition from our analysis of kinds of illocutionary acts. I think there are rules for expressing propositions, rules for such things as reference and prediction, but those rules can be discussed independently of the rules for function indicating. In this paper I shall not attempt to discuss propositional rules but shall concentrate on rules for using certain kinds of function-indicating devices.

IV. Meaning

Speech acts are characteristically performed in the utterance of sounds or the making of marks. What is the difference between *just* uttering sounds or making marks and performing a speech act? One difference is that the sounds or marks one makes in the performance of a speech act are characteristically said to *have meaning,* and a second related difference is that one is characteristically said to *mean something* by those sounds or marks. Characteristically when one speaks one means something by what one says, and what one says, the string of morphemes that one emits, is characteristically said to have a meaning. Here, incidentally, is another point at which our analogy between performing speech acts and playing games breaks down. The pieces in a game like chess are not characteristically said to have a meaning, and furthermore when one makes a move one is not characteristically said to mean anything by that move.

But what is it for one to mean something by what one says, and what is it for something to have a meaning? The answer the first of these questions I propose to borrow and revise some ideas of Paul Grice. In an article entitled 'Meaning',[5] Grice gives the following analysis of one sense of the notion of 'meaning'. To say that A meant something by x is to say that 'A intended the utterance of x to produce some effect in an audience by means of the recognition of this intention'. This seems to me a useful start on an analysis of meaning, first because it shows the close relationship between the notion of meaning and the notion of intention, and secondly because it captures something which is, I think, essential to speaking a language: In speaking a language I attempt to communicate things to my hearer by means of getting him to recognize my intention to communicate just those things. For example, characteristically, when I make an assertion, I attempt to communicate to and convince my hearer of the truth of a certain proposition; and the means I employ to do this are to utter certain sounds, which utterance I intend to produce in him the desired effect by means of his recognition of my intention to produce just that effect. I shall illustrate this with an example. I might on the one hand attempt to get you to believe that I am French by speaking French all the time, dressing in the French manner, showing wild enthusiasm for de Gaulle, and cultivating French acquaintances. But I might on the other hand attempt to get you to believe that I am French by simply telling you that I am French. Now, what is the difference between these two ways of my attempting to get you to believe that I am French? One crucial difference is that in the second case I attempt to get you to believe that I am French by getting you to recognize that it is my purported intention to get you to believe just that. That is one of the things involved in telling you that I am French. But of course if I try to get you to believe that I am French by putting on the act I described, then your recognition of my intention to produce in you the belief that I am French is not the means I am employing. Indeed in this case you would, I think, become rather suspicious if you recognized my intention.

However valuable this analysis of meaning is, it seems to me to be in certain respects defective. First of all, it fails to distinguish the different kinds of effects — perlocutionary versus illocutionary — that one may intend to produce in one's hearers, and it further fails to show the way in which these different kinds of effects are related to the notion of meaning. A second defect is that it fails to account for the extent to which meaning is a matter of rules or conventions. That is, this account of meaning does not show the connection between one's meaning something by what one says and what that which one says actually means in the language. In order to illustrate this point I now wish to present a counter-example to this analysis of meaning. The point of the counter-example will be to illustrate the connection between what a speaker means and what the words he utters mean.

Suppose that I am an American soldier in the Second World War and that I am captured by Italian troops. And suppose also that I wish to get these troops to believe that I am a German officer in order to get them to release me. What I would like to do is to tell them in German or Italian that I am a German officer. But let us suppose I don't know enough German or Italian to do that. So I, as it were, attempt to put on a show of telling them that I am a German officer by reciting those few bits of German that I know, trusting that they don't know enough German to see through my plan. Let us suppose I know only one line of German, which I remember from a poem I had to memorize in a high-school German course. Therefore I, a captured American, address my Italian captors with the following sentence: 'Kennst du das Land, wo die Zitronen blühen?' Now, let us describe the situation in Gricean terms. I intend to produce a certain effect in them, namely, the effect of believing that I am a German officer; and I intend to produce this effect by means of their recognition of my intention. I intend that they should think that what I am trying to tell them is that I am a German officer. But does it follow from this account that when I say 'Kennst du das Land . . .' etc., what I mean is, 'I am a German officer'? Not only does it not follow, but in this case it seems plainly false that when I utter the German sentence what I mean is 'I am a German officer', or even 'Ich bin ein deutscher Offizier', because what the words mean is, 'Knowest thou the land where the lemon trees bloom?' Of course, I want my captors to be deceived into thinking that what I mean is 'I am a German officer', but part of what is involved in the deception is getting them to think that that is what the words which I utter mean in German. At one point in the *Philosophical Investigations* Wittgenstein says 'Say "it's cold here" and mean "it's warm here" '.[6] The reason we are unable to do this is that what we can mean is a function of what we are saying. Meaning is more than a matter of intention, it is also a matter of convention.

Grice's account can be amended to deal with counter-examples of this kind. We have here a case where I am trying to produce a certain effect by means of the recognition of my intention to produce that effect, but the device I use to produce this effect is one which is conventionally, by the rules governing the use of that device, used as a means of producing quite different illocutionary effects. We must therefore reformulate the Gricean account of meaning in such a way as to make it clear that one's meaning something when one says something is more than just contingently related to what the sentence means in the language one is speaking. In our analysis of illocutionary acts, we must capture both the intentional and the conventional aspects and especially the relationship between them. In the performance of an illocutionary act the speaker intends to produce a certain effect by means of getting the hearer to recognize his intention to produce that effect, and furthermore, if he is using words literally, he intends this recognition to be achieved in virtue of the fact that the rules for using the expressions he utters associate the expressions with the production of that effect. It is this *combination* of elements which we shall need to express in our analysis of the illocutionary act.

V. How to Promise

I shall now attempt to give an analysis of the illocutionary act of promising. In order to do this I shall ask what conditions are necessary and sufficient for the act of promising to have been performed in the utterance of a given sentence. I shall attempt to answer this question by stating these conditions as a set of propositions such that the conjunction of the members of the set entails the proposition that a speaker made a promise, and the proposition that the speaker made a promise entails this conjunction. Thus each condition will be a necessary condition for the performance of the act of promising and taken collectively the set of conditions will be a sufficient condition for the act to have been performed.

If we get such a set of conditions we can extract from them a set of rules for the use of the function-indicating device. The method here is analogous to discovering the rules of chess by asking oneself what are the necessary and sufficient conditions under which one can be said to have correctly moved a knight or castled or checkmated a player, etc. We are in the position of someone who has learned to play chess without ever having the rules formulated and who wants such a formulation. We learned how to play the game of illocutionary acts, but in general it was done without an explicit formulation of the rules, and the first step in getting such a formulation is to set out the conditions for the performance of a particular illocutionary act. Our inquiry will therefore serve a double philosophical purpose. By stating a set of conditions for the performance of a particular illocutionary act we shall have offered a partial explication of that notion and shall also have paved the way for the second step, the formulation of the rules.

I find the statement of the conditions very difficult to do, and I am not entirely satisfied with the list I am about to present. One reason for the difficulty is that the notion of a promise, like most notions in ordinary language, does not have absolutely strict rules. There are all sorts of odd, deviant, and borderline promises; and counter-examples, more or less bizarre, can be produced against my analysis. I am inclined to think we shall not be able to get a set of knock-down necessary and sufficient conditions that will exactly mirror the ordinary use of the word 'promise'. I am confining my discussion, therefore, to the centre of the concept of promising and ignoring the fringe, borderline, and partially defective cases. I also confine my discussion to full-blown explicit promises and ignore promises made by elliptical turns of phrase, hints, metaphors, etc.

Another difficulty arises from my desire to state the conditions without certain forms of circularity. I want to give a list of conditions for the performance of a certain illocutionary act, which do not themselves mention the performance of any illocutionary acts. I need to satisfy this condition in order to offer an explication of the notion of an illocutionary act in general, otherwise I should simply be showing the relation between different illocutionary acts. However, although there will be no reference to illocutionary *acts,* certain illocutionary *concepts* will appear in the analysans as well as in the analysandum; and I think this form of circularity is unavoidable because of the nature of constitutive rules.

In the presentation of the conditions I shall first consider the case of a sincere promise and then show how to modify the conditions to allow for insincere promises. As our inquiry is semantical rather than syntactical, I shall simply assume the existence of grammatically well-formed sentences.

Given that a speaker S utters a sentence T in the presence of a hearer H, then, in the utterance of T, S sincerely (and non-defectively) promises that p to H if and only if:

(1) *Normal input and output conditions obtain.*

I use the terms 'input' and 'output' to cover the large and indefinite range of conditions under which any kind of serious linguistic communication is possible. 'Output' covers the conditions for intelligible speaking and 'input' covers the conditions for understanding. Together they include such things as that the speaker and hearer both know how to speak the language; both are conscious of what they are doing; the speaker is not acting under duress or threats; they have no physical impediments to communication, such as deafness, aphasia, or laryngitis; they are not acting in a play or telling jokes, etc.

(2) *S expresses that p in the utterance of T.*

This condition isolates the propositional content from the rest of the speech act and enables us to concentrate on the peculiarities of promising in the rest of the analysis.

(3) *In expressing that p, S predicates a future act A of S.*

In the case of promising the function-indicating device is an expression whose scope includes certain features of the proposition. In a promise an act must be predicated of the speaker and it cannot be a past act. I cannot promise to have done something, and I cannot promise that someone else will do something. (Although I can promise to see that he will do it.) The notion of an act, as I am construing it for present purposes, includes refraining from acts, performing series of acts, and may also include states and conditions: I may promise not to do something, I may promise to do something repeatedly, and I may promise to be or remain in a certain state or condition. I call conditions (2) and (3) the *propositional content conditions*.

(4) *H would prefer S's doing A to his not doing A, and S believes H would prefer his doing A to his not doing A.*

One crucial distinction between promises on the one hand and threats on the other is that a promise is a pledge to do something for you, not to you, but a threat is a pledge to do something to you, not for you. A promise is defective if the thing promised is something the promisee does not want done; and it is further defective if the promisor does not believe the promisee wants it done, since a non-defective promise must be intended as a promise and not as a threat or warning. I think both halves of this double condition are necessary in order to avoid fairly obvious counter-examples.

One can, however, think of apparent counter-examples to this condition as stated. Suppose I say to a lazy student 'If you don't hand in your paper on time I promise you I will give you a failing grade in the course'. Is this utterance a promise? I am inclined to think not; we would more naturally describe it as a warning or possibly even a threat. But why then is it possible to use the locution 'I promise' in such a case? I think we use it here because 'I promise' and 'I hereby promise' are among the strongest function-indicating devices for *commitment* provided by the English language. For that reason we often use these expressions in the performance of speech acts which are not strictly speaking promises but in which we wish to emphasize our commitment. To illustrate this, consider another apparent counter-example to the analysis along different lines. Sometimes, more commonly I think in the United States than in England, one hears people say 'I promise' when making an emphatic assertion. Suppose, for example, I accuse you of having stolen the money. I say, 'You stole that money, didn't you?' You reply 'No, I didn't, I promise you I didn't'. Did you make a promise in this case? I find it very unnatural to describe your utterance as a promise. This utterance would be more aptly described as an emphatic denial, and we can explain the occurrence of the function-indicating device 'I promise' as derivative from genuine promises and serving here as an expression adding emphasis to your denial.

In general the point stated in condition (4) is that if a purported promise is to be non-defective the thing promised must be something the hearer wants done, or considers to be in his interest, or would prefer being done to not being done, etc.; and the speaker must be aware of or believe or know, etc., that this is the case. I think a more elegant and exact formulation of this condition would require the introduction of technical terminology.

(5) *It is not obvious to both S and H that S will do A in the normal course of events.*

This condition is an instance of a general condition on many different kinds of illocutionary acts to the effect that the act must have a point. For example, if I make a request to someone to do something which it is obvious that he is already doing or is about to do, then my request is pointless and to that extent defective. In an actual speech situation, listeners, knowing the rules for performing illocutionary acts, will assume that this condition is satisfied. Suppose, for example, that in the course of a public speech I say to a member of my audience 'Look here, Smith, pay attention to what I am saying'. In order to make sense of this utterance the audience will have to assume that Smith has not been paying attention or at any rate that it is not obvious that he has been paying attention, that the question of his paying attention has arisen in some way; because a condition for making a request is that it is not obvious that the hearer is doing or about to do the thing requested.

Similarly with promises. It is out of order for me to promise to do something that it is obvious I am going to do anyhow. If I do seem to be making such a promise, the only way my audience can make sense of my utterance is to assume that I believe that it is not obvious that I am going to do the thing promised. A happily married man who promises his wife he will not desert her in the next week is likely to provide more anxiety than comfort.

Parenthetically I think this condition is an instance of the sort of phenomenon stated in Zipf's law. I think there is operating in our language, as in most forms of human behaviour, a principle of least effort, in this case a principle of maximum illocutionary ends with minimum phonetic effort; and I think condition (5) is an instance of it.

I call conditions such as (4) and (5) *preparatory conditions*. They are *sine quibus non* of happy promising, but they do not yet state the essential feature.

(6) *S intends to do A.*

The most important distinction between sincere and insincere promises is that in the case of the sincere promise the speaker intends to do the act promised, in the case of the insincere promise he does not intend to do the act. Also in sincere promises the speaker believes it is possible for him to do the act (or refrain from doing it), but I think the proposition that he intends to do it entails that he thinks it is possible to do (or refrain from doing) it, so I am not stating that as an extra condition. I call this condition the *sincereity condition*.

(7) *S intends that the utterance of T will place him under an obligation to do A.*

The essential feature of a promise is that it is the undertaking of an obligation to perform a certain act. I think that this condition distinguishes promises (and other members of the same family such as vows) from other kinds of speech acts. Notice that in the statement of the condition we only specify the speaker's intention; further conditions will make clear how that intention is realized. It is clear, however, that having this intention is a necessary condition of making a promise; for if a speaker can demonstrate that he did not have this intention in a given utterance, he can prove that the utterance was not a promise. We know, for example, that Mr. Pickwick did not promise to marry the woman because we know he did not have the appropriate intention.

I call this the *essential condition*.

(8) *S intends that the utterance of T will produce in H a belief that conditions (6) and (7) obtain by means of the recognition of the intention to produce that belief, and he intends this recognition to be achieved by means of the recognition of the sentence as one conventionally used to produce such beliefs.*

This captures our amended Gricean analysis of what it is for the speaker to mean to make a promise. The speaker intends to produce a certain illocutionary effect by means of getting the hearer to recognize his intention to produce that effect, and he also intends this recognition to be achieved in virtue of the fact that the lexical and syntactical character of the item he utters conventionally associates it with producing that effect.

Strictly speaking this condition could be formulated as part of condition (1), but it is of enough philosophical interest to be worth stating separately. I find it troublesome for the following reason. If my original objection to Grice is really valid, then surely, one might say, all these iterated intentions are superfluous; all that is necessary is that the speaker should seriously utter a sentence. The production of all these effects is simply a consequence of the hearer's knowledge of what the sentence means, which in turn is a consequence of his knowledge of the language, which is assumed by the speaker at the outset. I think the correct reply to this objection is that condition (8) explicates what it is for the speaker to 'seriously' utter the sentence, i.e. to utter it and mean it, but I am not completely confident about either the force of the objection or of the reply.

(9) *The semantical rules of the dialect spoken by S and H are such that T is correctly and sincerely uttered if and only if conditions* (1)-(8) *obtain.*

This condition is intended to make clear that the sentence uttered is one which by the semantical rules of the language is used to make a promise. Taken together with condition (8), it eliminates counter-examples like the captured soldier example considered earlier. Exactly what the formulation of the rules is, we shall soon see.

So far we have considered only the case of a sincere promise. But insincere promises are promises none the less, and we now need to show how to modify the conditions to allow for them. In making an insincere promise the speaker does not have all the intentions and beliefs he has when making a sincere promise. However, he purports to have them. Indeed it is because he purports to have intentions and beliefs which he does not have that we describe his act as insincere. So to allow for insincere promises we need only to revise our conditions to state that the speaker takes responsibility for having the beliefs and intentions rather than stating that he actually has them. A clue that the speaker does take such responsibility is the fact that he could not say without absurdity, e.g., 'I promise to do A but I do not intend to do A'. To say 'I promise to do A' is to take responsibility for intending to do A, and this condition holds whether the utterance was sincere or insincere. To allow for the possibility of an insincere promise then we have only to revise condition (6) so that it states not that the speaker intends to do A, but that he takes responsibility for intending to do A, and to avoid the charge of circularity I shall phrase this as follows:

(6*) *S intends that the utterance of T will make him responsible for intending to do A.*

Thus amended (and with 'sincerely' dropped from our analysandum and from condition (9)), our analysis is neutral on the question whether the promise was sincere or insincere.

VI. Rules for the Use of the Function-Indicating Device

Our next task is to extract from our set of conditions a set of rules for the use of the function-indicating device. Obviously not all of our conditions are equally relevant to this task. Condition (1) and conditions of the forms (8) and (9) apply generally to all kinds of normal illocutionary acts and are not peculiar to promising. Rules for the function-indicating device for promising are to be found corresponding to conditions (2)-(7).

The semantical rules for the use of any function-indicating device P for promising are:

Rule 1. P is to be uttered only in the context of a sentence (or larger stretch of discourse) the utterance of which predicates some future act A of the speaker S.
I call this the *propositional-content rule*. It is derived from the propositional-content conditions (2) and (3).
Rule 2. P is to be uttered only if the hearer H would prefer S's doing A to his not doing A, and S believes H would prefer S's doing A to his not doing A.
Rule 3. P is to be uttered only if it is not obvious to both S and H that S will do A in the normal course of events.
I call rules (2) and (3) *preparatory rules*. They are derived from the preparatory conditions (4) and (5).
Rule 4. P is to be uttered only if S intends to do A.
I call this the *sincerity rule*. It is derived from the sincerity condition (6).
Rule 5. The utterance of P counts as the undertaking of an obligation to do A.
I call this the *essential rule*.

These rules are ordered: rules 2-5 apply only if rule 1 is satisfied, and rule 5 applies only if rules 2 and 3 are satisfied as well.

Notice that whereas rules 1-4 take the form of quasi-imperatives, i.e. they are of the form: utter P only if x, rule 5 is of the form: the utterance of P counts as Y. Thus rule 5 is of the kind peculiar to systems of constitutive rules which I discussed in section II.

Notice also that the rather tiresome analogy with games is holding up remarkably well. If we ask ourselves under what conditions a player could be said to move a knight correctly, we would find preparatory conditions, such as that it must be his turn to move, as well as the essential condition stating the actual positions the knight can move to. I think that there is even a sincerity rule for competitive games, the rule that each side tries to win. I suggest that the team which 'throws' the game is behaving in a way closely analogous to the speaker who lies or makes false promises. Of course, there usually are no propositional-content rules for games, because games do not, by and large, represent states of affairs.

If this analysis is of any general interest beyond the case of promising then it would seem that these distinctions should carry over into other types of speech act, and I think a little reflection will show that they do. Consider, e.g., giving an order. The preparatory conditions include that the speaker should be in a position of authority over the hearer, the sincerity condition is that the speaker wants the ordered act done, and the essential condition has to do with the fact that the utterance is an attempt to get the hearer to do it. For assertions, the preparatory conditions include the fact that the hearer must have some basis for supposing the asserted proposition is true, the sincerity condition is that he must believe it to be true, and the essential condition has to do with the fact that the utterance is an attempt to inform the hearer and convince him of its truth. Greetings are a much simpler kind of speech act, but even here some of the distinctions apply. In the utterance of 'Hello' there is no propositional content and no sincerity condition. The preparatory condition is that the speaker must have just encountered the hearer, and the essential rule is that the utterance indicates courteous recognition of the hearer.

A proposal for further research then is to carry out a similar analysis of other types of speech acts. Not only would this give us an analysis of concepts interesting in themselves, but the comparison of different analyses would deepen our understanding of the whole subject and incidentally provide a basis for a more serious taxonomy than any of the usual facile categories such as evaluative versus descriptive, or cognitive versus emotive.

NOTES

1. J. L. Austin, *How To Do Things with Words* (Oxford, 1962).

2. This distinction occurs in J. Rawls, 'Two Concepts of Rules', *Philosophical Review*, 1955, and J. R. Searle, 'How to Derive "Ought" from "Is"', *Philosophical Review*, 1964.

3. The formulation '*X* counts as *Y*' was originally suggested to me by Max Black.

4. In the sentence 'I promise that I will come' the function-indicating device and the propositional element are separate. In the sentence 'I promise to come', which means the same as the first and is derived from it by certain transformations, the two elements are not separate.

5. *Philosophical Review*, 1957.

6. *Philosophical Investigations* (Oxford, 1953), para. 510.

Study Questions

Austin: "Performative-Constative"

1. How does Austin distinguish between constative and performative utterances?
2. What are the kinds of "unhappiness" associated with the performative utterance, and why?
3. Why is the constative utterance liable to the same unhappiness?
4. What is it that we need, and why?
5. What are locutionary and illocutionary acts?

Strawson: "Intention and Convention in Speech Acts"

1. State Strawson's main criticisms of Austin. Be clear as to what Austin's claims are and how Strawson criticizes them.
2. On what issues, if any, is there agreement between Austin and Strawson?

Searle: "What Is A Speech Act?"

1. What is a speech act?
2. What main thesis does Searle advocate in his essay?

Selected Bibliography

Austin, J. L. *How To Do Things With Words.* Oxford: Oxford University Press, 1962. [More accessible than *Philosophical Papers.*]

Austin, J. L. *Philosophical Papers.* Oxford: Oxford University Press, 1961. [Difficult, but important.]

Fodor, J. A. and Katz, J. J., eds. *The Structure of Language.* Englewood Cliffs: Prentice-Hall, 1964. [An excellent anthology; some selections are more technical.]

Searle, J. R. *The Philosophy of Language.* Oxford: Oxford University Press, 1971. [An anthology for the more advanced student.]

General Works on Analytic Philosophy

Munitz, Milton K. *Contemporary Analytic Philosophy*. New York: Macmillan 1981. [More advanced, but an excellent work.]

Passmore, John. *A Hundred Years of Philosophy*. London: Duckworth, 1957. [Thorough discussions of most major figures and movements. Good on pre-analytic traditions too.]

Ryle, Gilbert, et al. *The Revolution in Philosophy*. London: Macmillan & Co., 1957. [A good, elementary introduction to the main figures and forms of analytic philosophy.]

Warnock, G. J. *English Philosophy Since 1900*. London: Oxford University Press, 1958. [Good discussions of Moore, Russell, logical positivism, and Wittgenstein.]

Warnock, Mary. *Ethics Since 1900*. London: Oxford University Press, 1960. [A kind of companion to *English Philosophy Since 1900* by G. J. Warnock.]

Urmson, J. O. *Philosophical Analysis*. Oxford: Oxford University Press, 1956. [Good discussions of logical atomism, logical positivism, and conceptual analysis.]

Sources of More Complete Bibliographies

Ammerman, Robert R. *Classics of Analytic Philosophy*. New York: McGraw-Hill, 1965 pp. 403-410. [Selective but a good bibliography covering most figures and movements.]

Ayer, A. J., ed. *Logical Positivism*. Glencoe: Free Press, 1959 pp. 381-446. [Very thorough on logical positivism.]

Fann, K. T. *Wittgenstein's Conception of Philosophy*. Berkeley: University of California Press, 1971 pp. 113-185. [Exhaustive bibliography covering both the "early " and "late" Wittgenstein.]

Feigl, H. and Sellars, W., ed. *Readings in Philosophical Analysis*. New York: Appleton-Century-Crofts, 1949. (1st edition) pp. 619-626. [Good on logical positivism and related movements.]

Klemke, E. D., ed. *Essays on Bertrand Russell*. Urbana: University of Illinois Press 1970 pp. 447-453. [Selective.]

Klemke, E. D. Rohatyn, Dennis, and Rothschild, M. "G. E. Moore Scholarship, 1903-Present." *Southwestern Journal of Philosophy*, 7, 149-178. [On Moore only.]

Munitz, Milton K. *Contemporary Analytic Philosophy*. New York: Macmillan, 1981 pp. 413-427. [Good general bibliography covering almost all figures and movements in analytic philosophy.]

Quine, W. V. *From a Logical Point of View*. Cambridge: Harvard University Press, 1953 pp. 171-178. [Incomplete, but good on some figures in logico-metaphysical analysis.]

Schilpp, Paul, ed. *The Philosophy of Bertrand Russell*. New York: Harper & Row, 1963. Vol. II, pp. 746-825. [Complete list of works by Russell.]

Searle, J. R., ed. *The Philosophy of Language*. Oxford: Oxford University Press, 1962. [Good on linguistic analysis and the philosophy of language.

Weitz, Morris, ed. *20th Century Philosophy: The Analytic Tradition*. New York: Macmillan, 1966, pp. 380-387. [Selective, covering most forms of analytic philosophy.]

PAPERBACKS AVAILABLE FROM PROMETHEUS BOOKS

SCIENCE AND THE PARANORMAL

____ESP & Parapsychology: A Critical Re-evaluation *C.E.M. Hansel*	$9.95
____Extra-Terrestrial Intelligence *James L. Christian, editor*	7.95
____Flim-Flam! *James Randi*	9.95
____Objections to Astrology *L. Jerome & B. Bok*	4.95
____The Psychology of the Psychic *D. Marks & R. Kammann*	9.95
____Philosophy & Parapsychology *J. Ludwig, editor*	9.95
____Paranormal Borderlands of Science *Kendrick Frazier, editor*	13.95
____The Truth About Uri Geller *James Randi*	8.95

HUMANISM

____Ethics Without God *K. Nielsen*	6.95
____Humanist Alternative *Paul Kurtz, editor*	5.95
____Humanist Ethics *Morris Storer, editor*	9.95
____Humanist Funeral Service *Corliss Lamont*	3.95
____Humanist Manifestos I & II	1.95
____Humanist Wedding Service *Corliss Lamont*	2.95
____Humanistic Psychology *Welch, Tate, Richards, editors*	10.95
____Moral Problems in Contemporary Society *Paul Kurtz, editor*	7.95
____Secular Humanist Declaration	1.95
____Voice in the Wilderness *Corliss Lamont*	5.95
____Rabbi and Minister *Carl Hermann Voss*	7.95

LIBRARY OF LIBERAL RELIGION

____Facing Death and Grief *George N. Marshall*	7.95
____Living Religions of the World *Carl Hermann Voss*	4.95

PHILOSOPHY & ETHICS

____Animal Rights and Human Morality *Bernard Rollin*	9.95
____Art of Deception *Nicholas Capaldi*	6.95
____Beneficent Euthanasia *M. Kohl, editor*	8.95
____Contemporary Analytic and Linguistic Philosophies *E. D. Klemke*	11.95
____Esthetics Contemporary *Richard Kostelanetz, editor*	11.95
____Ethics and the Search for Values *L. Navia and E. Kelly, editors*	13.95
____Exuberance: A Philosophy of Happiness *Paul Kurtz*	3.00
____Freedom, Anarchy, and the Law *Richard Taylor*	8.95
____Freedom of Choice Affirmed *Corliss Lamont*	4.95
____Fullness of Life *Paul Kurtz*	5.95
____Having Love Affairs *Richard Taylor*	8.95
____Humanhood: Essays in Biomedical Ethics *Joseph Fletcher*	8.95
____Infanticide and the Value of Life *Marvin Kohl, editor*	9.95
____Introductory Readings in the Philosophy of Science *Klemke, Hollinger, Kline, editors*	12.95
____Invitation to Philosophy *Capaldi, Kelly, Navia, editors*	13.95
____Journeys Through Philosophy (Revised) *N. Capaldi & L. Navia, editors*	14.95

____Philosophy: An Introduction   *Antony Flew*   6.95

____Problem of God   *Peter A. Angeles*   9.95

____Psychiatry and Ethics   *Rem B. Edwards, editor*   12.95

____Responsibilities to Future Generations   *Ernest Partridge, editor*   9.95

____Reverse Discrimination   *Barry Gross, editor*   9.95

____Thinking Straight   *Antony Flew*   5.95

____Thomas Szasz: Primary Values and Major Contentions   *Vatz & Weinberg, editors*   9.95

____Worlds of the Early Greek Philosophers   *Wilbur & Allen, editors*   8.95

____Worlds of Hume and Kant   *Wilbur & Allen, editors*   7.95

____Worlds of Plato & Aristotle   *Wilbur & Allen, editors*   7.95

SEXOLOGY

____The Frontiers of Sex Research   *Vern Bullough, editor*   8.95

____New Bill of Sexual Rights & Responsibilities   *Lester Kirkendall*   6.95

____New Sexual Revolution   *Lester Kirkendall, editor*   6.95

____Philosophy & Sex   *Robert Baker & Fred Elliston, editors*   8.95

____Sex Without Love: A Philosophical Exploration   *Russell Vannoy*   8.95

THE SKEPTIC'S BOOKSHELF

____Atheism: The Case Against God   *George H. Smith*   7.95

____Atheist Debater's Handbook   *B.C. Johnson*   10.95

____What About Gods? (for children)   *Chris Brockman*   4.95

____Classics of Free Thought   *Paul Blanshard, editor*   6.95

____Critiques of God   *Peter Angeles, editor*   9.95

ADDITIONAL TITLES

____Age of Aging: A Reader in Social Gerontology   *Monk, editor*   9.95

____Avant-Garde Tradition in Literature   *Richard Kostelanetz, editor*   11.95

____Higher Education in American Society   *Altbach & Berdahl, editors*   9.95

____Israel's Defense Line   *I.L. Kenen*   9.95

____Pornography and Censorship   *Copp & Wendell, editors*   9.95

The books listed above can be obtained from your book dealer
or directly from Prometheus Books.
Please check off the appropriate books.
Remittance must accompany all orders from individuals.
Please include $1.50 postage and handling for first book,
.50 for each additional book ($4.00 maximum).
(N.Y. State Residents add 7% sales tax)

Send to _____

(Please type or print clearly)

Address _____

City _____ State_____ Zip_____

Amount Enclosed_____

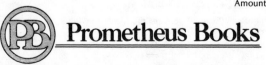

Prometheus Books

700 East Amherst St. Buffalo, New York 14215